Trauma Bond

An Inquiry into the Nature of Evil

Trauma Bond

An Inquiry into the Nature of Evil

Lawrence Swaim

PSYCHE
BOOKS

Winchester, UK
Washington, USA

First published by Psyche Books, 2013
Psyche Books is an imprint of John Hunt Publishing Ltd., Laurel House, Station Approach,
Alresford, Hants, SO24 9JH, UK
office1@jhpbooks.net
www.johnhuntpublishing.com
www.psyche-books.com

For distributor details and how to order please visit the 'Ordering' section on our website.

Text copyright: Lawrence Swaim 2012

ISBN: 978 1 78099 878 7

A CIP catalogue record for this book is available from the British Library.

Design: Stuart Davies

Printed in the USA by Edwards Brothers Malloy

We operate a distinctive and ethical publishing philosophy in all areas of our business, from our global network of authors to production and worldwide distribution.

CONTENTS

"History, Stephen said, is a nightmare from which I am trying to
awaken."
James Joyce
Ulysses

"The evil that men do lives after them;
The good is oft interred with their bones."
William Shakespeare
Julius Caesar
Act 3, scene ii

Preface

During the 20th century, humanity was disoriented by successive outbreaks of systemic evil. This included two devastating world wars, the totalitarian predations of Hitler and Stalin, and the Nazi destruction of European Jewry. The Nazi Holocaust was but one of a wave of genocides: Armenian, Roma, Bangladeshi, Cambodian, Bosnian and Rwandan. Partly these things happened because a new technology in weapons, communications and transport made it possible to kill people more efficiently than ever before. Something else had changed as well: because of an omnipresent news media, the rest of the world could not for long escape the horror these atrocities generated. Given these ongoing events of unprecedented malignancy, the depth of humankind's capacity for evil has become painfully evident. Humankind now has the technological ability — and evidently the implacable desire — to destroy itself, either with nuclear weapons or with the destruction of the planet's climate; it seems likely that without some major changes, the worst will happen.

Thus the problem of human aggression, and of good and evil, are now central human preoccupations. They always have been — but in the last three centuries educated people began to feel that humankind was leaving behind its dark predilection for violence and enslavement. Sadly, the 20th century demonstrated that humanity's predisposition to violence and cruelty — and its ability to carry it out — are worse today that anything imaginable in the past. Even as people become more enlightened about the kind of world they wish to see, their actual behavior becomes more aggressive.

People now have a choice: they can ignore this painful reality, deny that it exists, or try to deal with the questions it raises. Why are human beings so destructive? Why do people harm each other even when they don't intend to do so? The abused child grows up to become an abusing parent, and victims of persecution can hardly wait to persecute others. Why can't people learn from their mistakes?

We are caught in a powerful and seemingly inescapable cycle of aggression that few people have examined, and nobody fully understands. This book was written to systematically explore how that cycle operates. People become aggressive in ways they do not fully understand, because their aggression is internalized unconsciously rather than by choice—indeed, people who experience this transaction are often unaware of it. Thus victims of aggression go forth to create new victims, and the armed state prepares its citizens for more death and killing. While some insightful, gifted individuals can see through the negative psychological dynamics of this cycle, most oppressed and victimized people do *not* learn from their suffering. Instead they seek opportunities to discharge their internalized aggression by attacking others.

Of course some people are exceptions to this brutal rule—and those happy exceptions become the teachers of humankind. Indeed, when examining systemic evil we should focus on precisely those kinds of people—the people capable of resisting it—that we may learn from them how to avoid becoming aggressors ourselves. But as much as we admire and learn from such exceptional individuals, they are exceptional only because of the behavior of the majority, which tends to be either aggressive or complicit in aggression. Thus a great deal of what we think we know about aggression and the problem of evil is sentimental nonsense. The fact is, most human beings do *not* learn from being victims of bigotry and aggression, but seek to replicate the same bigotry and oppression in their behavior toward other people.

The purpose of this book is precisely to explain why and how this happens.

I am uninterested in theological or philosophical speculations about good and evil. I simply note that evil exists, that it manifests itself in destructive and self-destructive behavior, and that it is likely to end human civilization's brief tenure on this planet, if we don't do something about it. Furthermore it is precisely the existence of good and evil that to a large extent animates human consciousness, causing us to live out our lives through the multitude of moral choices we make on a daily basis. Since aggression and evil exist, they demand to be analyzed and responded to, both in our personal lives and on the larger stage of public life. Ultimately the problem of aggression and evil can best be approached as *psychological* problems, since it is in the human personality that good and evil are encoded, and in human behavior that they are acted out.

2.

For 25 years I worked as a counselor in residential treatment programs for people with behavioral problems, some of whom had mental illness, but others of whom suffered from emotional trauma arising from discernable events in their lives. There was a recurring pattern I noticed in the lives of these traumatized clients, a pattern that I'd also observed in my life experience, and of which some historians writing about mass aggression are likewise aware. Victims of human aggression tend to internalize the aggression visited upon them, and very often become aggressive themselves, either against others or against themselves. Women tend to turn their internalized aggression inwards, against themselves, in the form of depression, self-harm and self-sabotage; men direct their internalized aggression against others, or identify with aggressive figures or movements in society.

Demagogic leaders also use trauma to disorient people and prepare them for more war or genocide, making recovery more difficult. They may do this either by keeping old traumas alive in the public mind, or by committing new violence in the present moment to bond people to ongoing state oppression—or (as often happens) both. In trauma there is a power exchange that many people have observed, but few understand. Victims of traumatizing aggression often internalize the aggression they endure, in some cases by 'identifying with the aggressor,' a tendency Anna Freud noticed among children. Adult victims of human violence are more likely to internalize the aggression itself, which can then cause them to behavior aggressively, either toward themselves or others. Family Courts refer to the highly charged connection between abusive parents and their children as a 'trauma bond'; a similarly charged connection often grows up between abused women and their abusers, which has been characterized as 'traumatic bonding.'

But this bonding mechanism is likely to be present, in a less discernable but still powerful form, in most interactions involving aggression, including aggression by the state. Human violence and aggression has an enormously powerful effect on emotion and thought, one which most people do not understand but which is intuitively used in destructive ways by violent leaders, movements and governments.

Aggression is not, however, the same thing as evil. What's the difference? Aggression becomes evil when aggressors *conceal*, *dissemble* or *rationalize* destructive behavior. *Evil is unacceptable aggression plus deceit*—and when enough people simultaneously engage in aggressive behavior for the same destructive purposes, and the state works to conceal or rationalize that combined aggression, the result is *systemic evil*. In this form, evil is capable of becoming so widespread that it becomes a mass criminal project of the society, such as the systemic evil that flourished under Hitler, Stalin and the Cambodian tyrant Pol Pot.

An investigation of the ancient problem of good and evil is clearly called for, if for no other reason than to increase the odds of humanity's survival; this process can contribute to a new moral psychology, which could eventually become what moral philosophy was to the late 18th and early 19th century. In any case, we need a new determination to deconstruct systemic evil in societies, and to oppose the idea that violence is the best and most authentic way to deal with human conflicts; we need also to understand why aggression and evil are so powerful in the modern world, and so desperately hard to overcome. But to understand it, we should pay close attention to the bonding effects of trauma as used by violent and manipulative criminals, leaders and governments.

3.

My personal story is as follows:

As a young adult I was active in union politics for ten years (postal workers), was VP of Postal Clerks in San Francisco; my novel *Waiting for the Earthquake* is about the postal workers' strike of 1970. I worked as a journalist in Latin America and Europe, and as a counselor for twenty-five years doing psycho-social rehab with clients in various treatment programs; in 2002 I founded the Interfaith Freedom Foundation to oppose Islamophobia and support religious liberty in America. I have one Jewish and one Muslim daughter, and one son who is—perhaps not surprisingly—a confirmed secularist. Now old and retired from worldly cares but writing full-time, I live in ecstatic lower-middle-class anonymity as a semi-recluse in a mountain village in California, with a lovely (and to my mind, saintly) wife who cooks exquisite vegetarian food.

I'm grateful for my 17th-century ancestors in Anglo-Dutch New York, who because of their prodigious religious conflicts gave me my name: Society for the Withholding of Aid and Information from the Militia, *SWAIM*. I honor also Moses, Benjamin and William Swaim, leaders of the Manumission Society of North Carolina, who published in 1830 their immortal *Address to the People of North Carolina on the Evils of Slavery*.

I have also learned from the criminals and mountebanks in my ancestry, including those Swaims who for one hundred years of sheer murderous mendacity, from 1820 to 1920, doggedly sold their addictive, near-fatal patent medicine 'Swaim's Panacea' to the American public. (Why 'Panacea'? Because its stupefying compound of mercury and opiates "could cure anything.") We learn from the frauds and monsters whose blood we are, if we stoutly interrogate their ghosts when they appear and call out the evils that men do.

My moral and stylistic guides as a writer are George Orwell and the incomparable Thomas Babington Macaulay; and the American

5

political writers I.F. Stone and Dwight Macdonald. Orwell must be our standard in all things, which is one reason why the neo-cons have tried so hard to steal him. Orwell flayed the Stalinists, but also campaigned to make it possible for Communists to organize, advocate and publish their work in Britain without interference from the state. His core value was a sense of fair play that he recognized as originating in the English personality, constitution and common law. Macaulay is the unequaled master of the historical essay—in this book I quote from his defense of Machiavelli, because Macaulay's gifts are so luminous that even as he defends Machiavelli, the traumatized Florentine's true malignancy shines through. I.F. Stone defines independent literary-political journalism; and Dwight Macdonald's humor and self-deprecation make him the patron (but unpatronizing) saint of all who seek to separate useful political instincts from fanaticism.

Trauma Bond: An Inquiry into the Nature of Evil is the second book in the 'Genesis Trilogy,' which is my systematic attempt to investigate and illuminate how aggression and evil work. In the first book in the trilogy, *The Death of Judeo-Christianity: Religious Aggression and Systemic Evil in the Modern World*, I argued that religion in the West cannot at present help us solve the problem of systemic evil, especially in the Middle East. That does not mean that someday—perhaps sooner than we realize—religion cannot regenerate itself as a powerful influence on thought and behavior. I say simply that religion in the West cannot *at this time* help us deconstruct and oppose the most important forms of systemic evil. Therefore this book offers a secular method for understanding aggression and evil as psychological realities.

4.

I elaborated my theory of aggression and evil over a period of decades. During much of that time—about 25 years—I worked as a counselor at residential crisis and treatment programs. The work of the psycho-social rehab clinician is completely different than the 50-

minute hour of the psychotherapist. In the 50-minute hour (that is, regular psychotherapy), the client or patient tells the therapist about his life. Clients, being human, are naturally inclined to create a narrative that is self-exculpatory—in which the client, in other words, is usually a victim, and therefore helpless in the grip of his demons. (Clients also tend to leave important things out when talking to their therapists, such as the substances they abuse and the criminal acts they commit.) Psycho-social rehab is completely different. The psycho-social rehab clinician interacts, socializes and talks to the client in the residential milieu for *ten or twelve hours at a stretch*. The counselor helps the client prepare meals, do the dishes and go in the program van to do shopping; he watches TV with him, discusses the events of the days, and conducts therapeutic groups in which both counselor and clients interact.

The clients' problems arise naturally in the course of the clients' interactions with staff and others living in the residential program. The client doesn't *tell* the counselor about the problem; the counselor *sees* the problem, because the clinician is temporarily in residence in the same house as the client—and in such a situation, the clients' problems are usually very much in evidence. As the problems become discernable, the counselor pulls the client aside for a 1:1 session, and proceeds to identify (in a gentle and non-judgmental way) the problems the client has been having *during that same day.*

Imagine going through your average day with an insightful friend who carefully watches your important interactions, and then tells you how well you handled them. Such a process would help you see yourself much more quickly than years of psychoanalysis, I can practically guarantee you. (Whether you really want to see yourself that clearly, or give a friend that much power, are separate issues.) In other words, what people talk about in psychotherapy is often not their behavior, but the life-story they are trying to get the therapist to believe. In psycho-social rehab, the counselor watches his clients as they are engaged in actually living their lives and inteacting in real relationships.

The staff at residential treatment programs tends to be bright, compassionate, disaffected from power and money, and somewhat neurotic. A great many of them are in recovery from various addictions, which helps them relate to their clients; they are rather footloose, so there tends to be a big turnover of staff in most agencies in the larger cities. Mental health counselors believe in far too many psychological fads, and many of them have—or once had—their own harrowing mental health issues. They tend frequently to get into conflicts with each other: this happens because of the unbelievable stress of the work, sexual attractions arising from the artificial intimacy produced by stress, disagreements over clinical issues, and ancient quarrels that play out in bizarre but colorful ways. The nonprofit agency that I worked for in California was one of the best in the country; and at the transitional housing program where I worked during the last ten years the staff got along pretty well, considering how stressed-out we all were.

If you want to imagine a typical residential treatment or acute care program—or the average county mental health system—think of a raucous and perhaps grisly procession of de-compensating psychotics (the clients) led by a talkative contingent of partially-compensated neurotics (the staff). The staff engages in nonstop conversations with the clients about the events of the day, and watch carefully as their charges engage in various kinds of interactions, writing progress notes later about the interactions. They also gossip compulsively about each others' personal lives, and the clients do their best to eavesdrop on the gossip.

Our consulting psychologist was a neo-Freudian whose entire approach was psychoanalytic, creating a difficult and interesting challenge for the staff. How could psychoanalytic theory, developed in central Europe to treat the Viennese middle classes, possibly have any relevance to the gritty reality of psycho-social rehab in a small county seat in northern California? Staff focused on those specific human interactions that probably had a psychological rather than biological origin (no theory, no matter how well-meant, was going to

help an untreated paranoid schizophrenic who is going to a state prison the next day). So how were we to apply psychoanalytic theory to the intensely practical needs of our highly addicted, usually victimized, sometimes homeless and often traumatized client population? We found that we *could* apply theory, but it had to be done in an extreme practical, concrete and dynamic way, by boiling it down to compact interventions around the clients' most problematic and recurring interactions.

And these problematic, recurrent interactions almost always had to do with aggression, either directed toward other people, toward society at large, or in the form of self-harm, self-sabotage or high-risk behavior.

This aggression generally conformed, in various ways, to the patterns of victimization our clients had suffered in the past. It is usually inappropriate and unhelpful in psycho-social rehab for counselors to probe past trauma—in psycho-social rehab you're simply trying to help the client live in the present moment, despite the horrors of the past. (Besides, psycho-social rehab clients have a bad habit of getting stuck in the past, and when they revisit past traumas they often don't want to come back.) So we stayed out of the past, encouraging the client to stay in the present—but at the same time, there was no denying the extent to which aggression often had to do with trauma in the past. The most dynamic interventions we made almost always had something to do with interactions in which some form of aggression was present. If we could get the client to see his aggression, whether directed against himself or others, the intervention was a success.

One might compare our practical adaptation of theory to the psychoanalytic shorthand of Thomas A. Harris's immensely popular *I'm OK, You're OK*—except that our use of theory was even more focused, avoiding shorthand nomenclature to focus almost entirely on dynamic interactions that staff had personally witnessed, which we talked about in the language of the clients themselves. Such interactions were easily discernable in the milieu, because they were so often recurring; but they often revealed like a flash of lightning the sinews of the clients' social maladjustments.

In retrospect it is clear that we unconsciously focused on aggression, and it's easy to see why. From our entirely practical point of view our first goal was to help clients stop doing things that were causing them to get arrested, and secondly, to help them to stop harming themselves. After that we could focus on helping them overcome those behaviors that caused people to reject them. Either way, we focused on aggression—the behaviors as well as the emotional orientations. This focus on aggression could be the goal of the new moral psychology that I would like to see, because within it are encoded certain lessons for the survival of humankind, at least for those brave enough to look at them. Despite its potentially universal application such a psychology would be, among other things, eminently practical, because aggression always comes up in the behavior of emotionally disturbed people, and it always comes up in ways connected to the central dilemmas of their lives.

5.

The biggest obstruction to understanding evil today is that a great many people are in denial about it. Religious people blame the Devil, and secularists deny that evil exists. They're both wrong. Evil exists—in fact, at this point in history, good and evil have become the main problem that politics, religion and culture are struggling with, however unconsciously that struggle may occur. But even very insightful people are often not aware of good and evil in their own behavior, because morality is partly unconscious, partly cognitive and partly behavioral. People tend to be anxious about sexuality, death and aggression: but since humanity now has the capacity to destroy itself the last two categories are now increasingly—if unconsciously—conflated.

I believe that for a full understanding of these matters one must face one's *personal* capacity for evil. The capacity for both good and evil exists in all people; and one really has little reckoning of the true contours of the human dilemma until one confronts it *in oneself.* Simply to be aware of it does *not* increase the likelihood that one will act on it; on the contrary, the more one is aware of it, the *less* likely once is to act on it. One's own capacity for evil is, after all, not a living or consummated thing, but simply an emotional and behavioral predilection. But it should be faced, because once one has faced it in oneself, it will be easier not to act on it—and easier to face it in the world, and *much* easier to forgive (or at least to understand) in other people.

Many people wish to find a more graceful and perhaps clinical-sounding word than 'evil,' but that probably won't work. There is no other word in the English language that can describe the Nazi Holocaust, and all the other genocides and campaigns of mass murder that broke out during the 20th century: Armenian, Roma, Cambodian, Bangladeshi, Bosnian and Rwandan. (I repeat them because we are all too willing to forget that they happened.) Furthermore, there is absolutely no other word that can describe the nuclear genocide that threatens all of humankind; and there is no other word to describe those who would willfully contribute to global warming, in order to put their short-term profit before the lives of their children. It is evil, pure and simple.

Of course, the people responsible for it may not realize what they do—the most lethal forms of systemic evil are acted out not by conspirators, but by sleepwalkers. The goal of a moral psychology would be, in part, to awaken both aggressor and victim. The world needs people who consciously seek, as Camus put it, to be *neither* victim *nor* executioner.

My goal wasn't just to write a good popular book on the psychology of evil; I also set out to write a book that gives pleasure to the reader, even as it deals squarely with a difficult subject. There is great satisfaction in reading, in the form of a book-length essay, an unconventional but well-thought-out view of human behavior, even if the reader doesn't agree with all of it. If it is written well, you will have plenty of time to make up your mind, because you will remember its key arguments long after you put the book down.

Some will say that considering one's own capacity for evil is the posturing of an inverted Faust; and that this book's deconstruction of evil is but the inflated jibber of a would-be Prometheus. What you seek is impossible, they say—you can never defeat evil, because it is too big, too various, too slippery, too omnipresent.

But I already know it cannot be defeated *completely*, and I agree that it would be unwise to try. The idea of human perfection has always been a monstrous concept—so let's accept that humanity will always to some extent betray, hate and persecute even as it creates, loves and cherishes. Aggression and evil will always be with us. I simply wish to see evil defeated to just the extent that humankind has a better chance (better odds, as it were) of surviving its own self-destructive tendencies. That is a modest and logical goal. In writing this book I seek not to be a public intellectual, or even an engaged one, so much as a 'prophetic' one—a 'prophetic intellectual' being one who warns humankind of its dark angels and the dangers they foretell.

My view of humanity in the early 21st century is similar to that of my collateral ancestor William Swaim, who when he created his anti-slavery newspaper *Greensborough Patriot* in 1828 (in Greensborough, North Carolina) put these words on the masthead: *"The ignorant and degraded of every nation or clime must be enlightened, before our earth can have honor in the universe."* The difficulties inherent in such a task he knew well, for on his editorial page he quoted Pope: "Truths would you teach, or save a sinking land? All fear, none aid you, and few understand." At present our species has precious little honor in the universe, but it must change to survive. The best in humanity is not what it is, but what it can become.

Lawrence Swaim
Napa Valley
2012

Acknowledgements

Most of all to Rogelia, who took me into her home and her heart as I wrote my books. To my children; and to remembrances of the late Linn Wreszin Swaim, whose Jewish soul and deep connection to Weimer culture and the German Left illuminate the moral catastrophe that has befallen us. And to my clients in the treatment programs where I worked, whose dilemmas entered my bones and helped give me the insight to comprehend the nature of good and evil.

Some passages in this book appeared in a slightly different form in my column on religious liberty for *InFocus News*, a Muslim newspaper in California, and in articles that appeared on the 'Counterpunch' and 'Mondoweiss' websites, and in the magazine *Liberty*.

Chapter I

Understanding the Trauma Bond

I.

The woman I was talking to was only thirty, but looked older. She was attractive and alert, but her face, arms and body were covered with scars—she had been severely beaten by her husband, who had put her in the hospital innumerable times. She wanted more than anything to leave her husband, a man who had devastated her life several times over, and was now in prison for trying to kill her—and since I was her primary counselor at a county-funded crisis center, I wanted very badly for her to leave him too. In fact I sometimes came close to begging.

But she didn't think she could do it.

"I don't know what's wrong with me," she told me. "My husband was very nice when I first met him, but he gradually began to threaten me, and then he started hitting me—and when he's violent he's absolutely out of control. I love my kids, and he says he does too; but he beats them up and tells them they're worthless. He locks me up when he's gone."

"You need to leave this man," I said. "Nothing we say in this conversation is going to mean anything if you don't do that."

"I *want* to leave him."

Sadly, I had heard this story many times. The woman was smart, without an ounce of self-pity, and exceptionally likeable. "Look, there's no big mystery about it," I said. "Just leave him. Deep down, you really want that. We'll send you and the kids to a women's shelter. If he comes after you, we'll use the courts. You can have him arrested under California's stalking statutes."

"I know."

"So why don't you?"

She sighed—a sigh that came from the depths. "I just can't seem to leave him and make it stick. I'm like a zombie, or like something

14

diabolical has taken over my mind and body. I swear over and over that I'll never go back to him—yet the next thing I know, I'm with him again."

"And what happens?"

"We're happy for awhile, but he always starts beating up on me and the kids again."

Her husband was in prison for breaking her nose, both collar-bones, both arms and one of her legs. She had actually been in a coma from severe head trauma as a result of the last beating he gave her. The hospital had referred her to us for help, and she begged us to help her leave her abusive husband. We advised her to break off all contact with this man, but when he called from prison she would always find ways to sneak off and take his calls.

"You know, if you keep going back to him, you'll just end up in the same dangerous place," I said, "and someday it'll be too late. Your kids are already deep in crisis because of your husband's violence."

"I know."

"And the DA will probably charge you with child endangerment if you go back to him."

"I know."

"If you leave him, you can start over."

"I know, I know—that's what I want."

She was saying all the right things—except just a few minutes before I had seen her sneaking into an empty office to take a call from her husband, who was calling from prison. He was calling to tell her where to meet him when he got out.

And she agreed to meet him.

I confronted her with this. "Destroy yourself if you must," I said, "but you do not have the right to take your children back into this nightmare. We'll have to recommend putting the children into foster care."

"I know, I know," she said miserably, "but I just don't seem to have the willpower to leave my husband. I try and try, but I just can't seem to do it."

"Remember where this all comes from," I reminded her. "You were physically and emotionally abused yourself by your father."

"Yes, and I could hardly wait to leave home."

"And when you did—"

"The first thing I did was to hook up with someone who beat me up just like my father did."

I and the other counselors spent hundreds of hours talking to her. We gave her books and pamphlets about spousal abuse. We shared endless strategies for breaking free from her husband's abuse. We did groups, role-playing and many other interventions during the weeks she was with us. I pleaded with her to go to a women's shelter with her children. Sometimes I actually found myself tearing up when I talked to her—partly because I understood the risk she incurred for herself and her children, whereas she did not seem to comprehend them at all. But there were times when I and the other staff seemed to be winning her over. The biggest thing we had going for us was the fact that despite the bond she had developed to her husband, she was truly terrified of being beaten up again by him.

But ultimately, of course, she went back to him.

What I did not completely understand at that time was that driving this woman's seemingly inexplicable behavior was one of the most powerful—if malignant—psychological dynamics in the world. This same mechanism was also, I discovered over many years, at the heart of much of the world's most blatant expressions of aggression. People who are victims of violence internalize the aggression they have suffered, and then act that aggression out, either as violence against others or violence against themselves. And they often become bonded to aggression itself as a way of life, seeking it out and allowing it to become the single obsessive organizing principle of their personalities.

It all seemed a bit crazy, since most human attachments usually grow stronger in response to nurturing, not abuse—but in an abusive relationship the bond is based on violence; and if anything, the human bond created by aggression can become far stronger than anything based on kindness. In fact, this disturbing reality is so common that in 1981 two psychologists, Donald G. Dutton and Susan Painter, began to study abusive relationships. They noted especially the powerful—and therefore dangerous and irrational—bond that grows up between an abuser and his victim. They referred to this phenomenon as "traumatic bonding." They noted the "power imbalance" between the abuser and abused, and the emotional and cognitive confusion created by the aggressor's use of intermittent good and bad behavior. They called the resulting bond a "paradoxical attachment," without arriving at any definitive psychological or biological reason for it. But they did agree that the bond it created was powerful, and that once it reached a certain stage it was almost impossible to break.[1]

The client I was counseling was beaten up many more times by her husband. (The reader will perhaps not be surprised to know that the abuser had himself been abused as a child.) There was one thing he knew for sure about the world he lived in—that any woman to whom he was attracted, and who found him attractive, deserved to be beaten up. Although he might not have been able to articulate it, that was the ethic (or ethos) that drove his life. His wife, battered into submission by his merciless beatings, had bonded with him; and because of that, she had validated his ethos of love-as-violence, to which she had first been introduced as a child by *her* abusive parents.

She and her abuser had arrived at a way of experiencing the world together—a shared, ritualized and highly pathological worldview based on aggression as the supreme and most authentic form of truth; and they acted out this murderous ethos until she was finally and irrevocably dead. About a year after her husband got out of prison, he finally killed her, as we knew he would all along; he was sentenced to life in prison without parole. I'm delighted to say that their kids were eventually adopted by a very nice professional couple—the wife was physically disabled, but both she and her husband were very happy with their new family. Ten years later, they're doing well.

2.

The abused woman portrayed above is a composite: that is, she is a combination of personal characteristics of many such abused people I counseled during the twenty-five years I was a counselor doing psycho-social rehab. Everything in this composite portrait actually happened, including the nice part about the children in the abusive home who ended up with the nurturing professional couple. And I really did counsel a woman whose husband used to lock her and her children in the house whenever he left. When she first told me about it I had trouble believing it, so before I wrote it up in the woman's chart, just to make sure, I went out to their house with her and inspected it. Believe it or not there really were *locks on the outside of the doors and windows* that her husband had installed, so that this maniac could lock up his whole family in the house while he was gone. (And although the wife complained mightily about his controlling behavior, she, too, refused to leave him.) And there was also another guy who chopped his wife up with an ax and put her remains in the trunk of his car before he went out to do a few errands. His wife, too, had tried many times to leave him, but had never been able to. There were many others, some even more bizarre that the ones recounted above, but they all had one thing in common—they couldn't leave their abusive spouses or lovers.

Both victims and aggressors tended to be people who had been traumatized by violence, often over a long period, and often as children; they identified with aggression so strongly that it had become a powerful and lethal addiction. (Another one of my clients, a disabled man confined to a wheelchair, had a girlfriend who had hit him so many times on the head with blunt objects that he was going blind. *He* went back to *her*, too.) Not only were many of these people in abusive relationships unable to stop being victims or aggressors, the violence they were involved in had come to define their personalities, and in some cases had replaced their personalities completely.

In social work and family law, this phenomenon is often encountered, and has been referred to as a *trauma bond*. This is frequently used to describe abused children that are nonetheless incredibly loyal to their abusive parents, and will do anything to remain with them—even though they hate and fear the abuse. Why does this happen? It happens because the children have developed a profound emotional bond with the adults who are abusing them. Under its influence, they will lie to protect their abusers, and will rationalize the adults' abusive behavior in mind-boggling ways, in an attempt to stay with them. But why do children develop trauma bonds in the first place? That's a complicated and somewhat threatening issue for many people, because of what it reveals about violence and human intentionality—and it isn't limited to children, as we have seen. Any investigation of the trauma bond is likely to reveal information that is highly threatening to the way we are accustomed to think about human nature, and about good and evil.

Some of the best research done on the nature of aggression among children was done by Anna Freud, the daughter of Sigmund Freud. Anna didn't mean to explain aggression in any complete or systematic way—and she certainly wasn't aiming at a theory of evil. But she hit on certain dynamics of the ego that probably explain more about aggression than anything her father ever wrote, especially her theory of "Identification with the Aggressor." One has the sense that ultimately aggression was a subject that Sigmund Freud might have written more about, had he not taken a wrong turn by ignoring his mild-mannered disciple Alfred Adler in the years before the First World War. Adler thought that aggression was the big problem facing humankind; Freud thought sexuality was the culprit. After two world wars, the depredations of Stalin and Hitler and the Nazi Holocaust, most of us today would probably agree with Adler.

In a style both direct and innocent, Anna Freud used her therapeutic experiences with children to demonstrate how identification with the aggressor operates. In one case, she wrote of a little boy making faces at a teacher that he feared. "Observing the two attentively, [an associate] saw that the boy's grimaces were simply a caricature of the angry expression of the teacher and that, when he had to face a scolding by the latter, he tired to master his anxiety by involuntarily imitating him. The boy identified himself with the teacher's anger and copied his expression as he spoke, though the imitation was not recognized. Through his grimaces he was assimilating himself to or identifying himself with the dreaded external object."

Anybody who has observed a class clown will readily agree that mimicking the teacher is mainly about authority and aggression. For a moment the bad boy has the upper hand—and the dreaded authority figure, his back turned, is temporarily bereft of power, as long as the class clown is skillful enough to avoid detection. But such gambits are themselves power gestures: if the class clown is obliged to imitate the teacher to feel safe, he is already not only poking fun at him, he is assuming his role—he has to *become* the teacher to *defeat* him, even if only for a moment.

Anna Freud wrote also about a little girl who overcame her fear through identification with an imagined aggressor. "At home she was afraid to cross the hall in the dark, because she had a dread of seeing ghosts. Suddenly, however, she hit on a device which enabled her to do it: she would run across the hall, making all sorts of peculiar gestures as she went. Before long, she triumphantly told her little brother the secret of how she got over [her] anxiety. 'There's no need to be afraid in the hall,' she said, 'you just have to pretend that you're the ghost who might meet you.'"

In another case, a young boy who was Anna's patient came to her after experiencing great pain at the dentist's, and "vented his feelings" on various objects in the room. He cut string into tiny pieces with his knife and then "turned his attention to some pencils, and went on indefatigably sharpening them, breaking off the points, and sharpening them again." Anna made the point that he was not playing at being a dentist, but was "identifying himself not with the person of the aggressor but with the aggression."

Anna writes also about a boy who was struck by the fist of an instructor—apparently inadvertently—during a game on the school playground. The next day he showed up for their therapy session dressed in full armor! "On his head he wore a military cap and he had a toy sword at his side and a pistol in his hand." During the session he sat down and wrote a letter to his mother demanding that she send him a pocketknife. In this way the little boy identified with the aggression he attributed to the teacher who had inadvertently struck him, and had already made considerable progress in internalizing that aggression by arming himself with toy weapons.[2]

Anna saw clearly the process of identification with the aggressor and the resulting internalization of aggression ("By impersonating the aggressor, assuming his attributes or imitating his aggression, the child transforms himself from the person threatened into the person who makes the threat")[3], but she uses the rather turgid psychoanalytic word *introjection* to describe this process. If one chooses to use psychoanalytic language, the Hungarian psychoanalyst Maria Torok's word *incorporation* might come closer to describing what happens when people identify with aggression and internalize it. In her strange but fascinating essay "The Illness of Mourning and the Fantasy of the Exquisite Corpse," Torok described the grieving process as a wild attempt to internalize the departed (and an unconscious attempt to keep the departed alive, this writer would say); and Torok concluded that in such an emotionally charged situation the psychoanalytical concept of introjection, as commonly understood, didn't apply. Incorporation, as Torok used it, meant a kind of instant internalization.

Grieving, she decided, was so violent that it allowed the mind to *instantly* position forbidden, dangerous or incongruous material within consciousness. This is necessary during grieving, because "faced with the impotence of the process of introjection (gradual, slow, laborious, mediated, effective), incorporation is the only choice: phantasmic, unmediated, instantaneous, magical, sometimes hallucinatory."[4] Torok's contribution lies in understanding that powerful, paradoxical and "phantasmic" emotional material can indeed be instantly internalized into the personality during moments of extreme emotional duress.

The psychoanalytic words *introjection* and *incorporation*, then, describe two phases of the same thing, but since they are so close to each other in meaning this writer greatly prefers the common-sense word *internalization* to describe what happens in both phases. Both Maria Torok and Anna Freud were mainly interested in how the ego survives, not how aggression replicates itself in the world; nonetheless, Anna saw clearly how the mind can identify with aggression preparatory to internalizing it, and reported the phenomenon accurately. Of course, both women were overly freighted with Freudian psychoanalytic theory that we might today find tedious and insulting—for example, Anna Freud attributes the fear of the little girl who was afraid of ghosts to penis envy!

But both women—Anna Freud in particular—illuminated critical aspects of the ego's struggle to survive in a hostile world; and Anna's discovery of "Identification with the Aggressor" is critical to understanding how the personality can first identify with the aggressor and his aggression. Adults, in fact, typically go much further than simply identifying with the aggressor—adult victims of traumatic violence tend to internalize the aggression itself, rather than the persona of the aggressor. We become aware of this because they can be observed acting aggressively months or years later, either against themselves or against others—and they do this without necessarily adopting the personal characteristics of the aggressor. Once internalized, aggression becomes a powerful unconscious orientation which often leads to self-harm or violence against others; and it may lead to a worldview in which aggression is the standard of emotional authenticity by which everything else is measured.

3.

I witnessed a startling example of adult trauma bonding while counseling two difficult clients, Darlene and Little Davy, at the residential crisis program where I worked. Both were street people, both were poly-substance abusers, and Darlene had multiple personality disorders; in addition, she was an experienced and rather frightening street criminal. (Both clients had been referred to the residential crisis center by the courts, via the county mental health system; almost all our clients were poor, and a great many homeless.) I watched from the window of the staff office one day as Darlene engaged in the thing she did best, which was intimidating other clients to get their cigarettes. She didn't know I was watching her, and I didn't want her to. With multiple personality disorders, Darlene was the kind of client "who could give sociopathy a bad name," as the counseling staff jokingly put it; almost every morning she'd bum cigarettes from the other clients—that is, she'd threaten and intimidate them until they gave them up.

Usually she did this in out-of-the-way places where staff couldn't see her, but today I watched as she ran her game in plain view.

She stood about two feet away from another client and launched into a detailed account of how she'd recently beaten someone up. Then she asked casually for some cigarettes, took a step back—then stuck her face quickly back into his face.

"Yeah—you heard me. I need some smokes. That's right, from you."

A new client asked: "What if I don't give you any?"

Darlene's eyebrows went up. "Say what?"

"I don't have any."

"Yeah you do. I'll go buy something from my friend, and when I come back I might be packing something. Be smart. Help me out here."

The new client handed over a smoke. Without a flicker of a smile, Darlene held her hand out until the stranger put another cigarette in it.

Another client fished out a couple of moldy-looking smokes

without even being asked. It usually didn't take Darlene long to get enough smokes to last the day.

"See you later, sucker," she said to nobody in particular.

Her victims thanked her. They often did that.

Her favorite victim was the soft-spoken client called Little Davy, who was both developmentally delayed and homeless. He usually didn't have a lot to say: his most noticeable characteristic appeared to be a burning desire to avoid anything remotely resembling a conflict. He had no family, and lived on the street. Darlene had made him into a combination mule and house servant—if she needed a drink of water, she'd make Little Davy get it; if she had a message to send, she'd make him deliver it. Naturally, he was the first to give up his cigarettes to her in the morning. (Interestingly, it never seemed to occur to him to hide his cigarettes from Darlene. Or maybe he hid them so cleverly I just didn't see him do it.) I finally concluded that there was something in the interaction that validated his position as her second-in-command.

Later I confronted Darlene about her cigarette-bumming in our regular therapy group. She was the very soul of confidence. "You must be mistaken," she said sweetly. "I never get cigarettes from clients. I don't like the crummy brands they buy."

In the course of subsequent human events, Darlene was discharged from the county-funded rehab, because she broke too many rules, intimidated too many people, and was finally caught stealing. A couple of days later I looked out the staff office window to see what was going on with the clients. They were all smokers, so as usual they stood around smoking and having their morning coughing fits.

That day I heard an eerily familiar voice. "That's right—don't you hear right? I need the smokes. Yeah, that's right, you."

The hair on the back of my neck stood up. It was Darlene's voice—the exact intonation, the same words, everything. Yet Darlene was nowhere around. Looking out the window, I saw that the speaker was Little Davy, Darlene's former victim and toady. "Yeah, you—I know you can spare a couple." Little Davy was shaking down the other clients for smokes. "Sucker, you know what I need. Give it up."

Little Davey, the conflict-avoidant homeless man who wouldn't hurt a fly, then launched into an angry recital of the people he'd recently beaten up, and all the violent things he'd been forced to do to his victims when they didn't do as he had politely asked them to do. Not only did he talk like Darlene, he even moved his body the same way she did, sticking his face in the faces of his victims.

I couldn't believe my eyes.

"Pretty soon I'll be packing heat. Is that what you want? *Huh?*"

The other clients were as freaked out by Little Davy as I was, but they didn't hesitate too long before fishing out a few cigarettes and handing them over to him. The same thing happened the next morning, and the next. When I confronted Little Davy about it in a subsequent group, he denied everything. ("You must be mistaken— I never take cigarettes from clients.") Little Davy had been so frightened by Darlene, so beaten down and terrified by her, there he'd adopted all her most threatening verbal expressions, mannerism and facial expressions, assimilating them directly into his own personality and acting them out with astonishing verisimilitude. Little Davy became a completely different person, adopting to an amazing degree the threatening behavior of the woman who had previously bossed him around.

It wasn't long before Little Davy went back to being his old, soft-spoken, conflict-avoidant self. (And a good thing, too, since his aggressive behavior would have gotten him discharged if it had continued.) Instead of intimidating people to get their cigarettes, he went back to giving his away. Ironically, his very lack of cognitive organization may have helped release him from his identification with Darlene's aggression. But where did the personality of Little Davy go, and who was he during the week when he took on Darlene's most violent characteristics? Was he Little Davy, Darlene, or some weird combination of the two?

I had spoken to Little Davy privately about some of the things Darlene had done to him on the street, and quickly became aware she had done enough to traumatize three people. These predations had created some very powerful factors that were affecting Davy behaviorally. They were so powerful that they allowed him, a developmentally-delayed homeless man with an IQ of 69, to intuitively but flawlessly assimilate into his personality the boldest moves of a cunning, street-wise sociopath—such was the strength of his identification with her.

Adults don't usually identify with their aggressors: they are much more likely to identify with aggression itself. Even abused spouses will pick up with another abuser if the first abuser dies or is not available. Adults subjected to emotional trauma often respond to it by adopting aggression as a way of life, identifying with aggression as it arises and manifests itself in society. So Darlene wasn't just a mental health client who had traumatized Little Davy with threats and beatings—she was the most powerful manifestation of aggression in Little Davy's world. So he bonded with her, at least when she was available. (His cognitive deficit apparently caused him to bond with her personality traits as well as with her aggression, rather as a child would.)

Similarly, this writer worked with an older veteran who had been struggling with drugs since he became habituated to substance abuse in Vietnam. Although he was a college graduate (in social work!) he hung out with a bunch of violent bikers who were bad for him because they supplied him with drugs, and bad street drugs at that. He had a long history of run-ins with the police, and the convictions were piling up—but he couldn't break free of the low-rent, street-fighting guys he ran with. In retrospect, it appears that he was bonded not just to his friends' violence, but also to their fascination with his combat experiences; they had an intuitive way of keeping his traumatic memories alive by talking about violence all the time they were around him. That made him a good customer for the weed and the downers they sold him. And there was something else: the bikers didn't judge him for the way he'd screwed his life up. "They understand me," was the way he put it. But with friends like that, he didn't need enemies.

This was a rather common scenario with some of my clients, actually. Many of them weren't even people with a recognizable mental illness, chronic or otherwise—they were people who had been through extremely violent and traumatizing experiences, and some of them had gotten very badly stuck. Their trauma was like a place they went to once, but somehow couldn't leave. (Think *Hotel California*, by the Eagles.) It always had to do with some kind of aggression, it seemed—and then the client found himself acting out the aggression against other people, or against himself, or both. Traumatized women, I quickly found, were likely to act out internalized aggression against themselves, with cutting, substance abuse and depression; men usually acted it out against other people. What I was seeing, I gradually came to realize, were the powerful effects of trauma bonding that determined behavior in the present moment as a result of things that had happened weeks, months or years ago. Some clients had gotten used to it and wanted it to stay that way; others wanted to break out of the cycle of violence and aggression, but couldn't. The most inspiring clients were able to break out of the bonds of past trauma and design new lives for themselves.

4.

When we talk of emotional trauma in this context, we are not referring to the trauma of the tornado, the earthquake or the house fire. These things are horrific, causing emotional wounds that last a lifetime—but they're different from the psychic wounds suffered by a combat veteran or the victim of a rape, for example. There is something about *person-on-person violence* that is uniquely harmful, because it tends to destroy the trust necessary for social contracts— it destroys, on a very deep level, one's connection to the rest of humanity. The traumas of war, rape, murder and genocide (not to mention governments that imprison, torture and discriminate against people for religious or political reasons) affect us emotionally as nothing else, because they take away our ability to trust and count on other people; indeed, they seem to take away our ability to make objective assessments of other people, which in turn compromises one's ability to function in society. That may be irrational, but that's what feelings are—they are by definition irrational.

Sometimes it is the loss of trust itself that drives the emotional trauma. The Ponzi scheme of Bernard Madoff was a so-called affinity scam—that is, it exploited people that Madoff knew through his connections in various East Coast Jewish communities. Madoff especially concentrated on the soft targets of Jewish charities and philanthropies, with their large accumulations of capital that could be moved quickly and easily. When the scam was revealed, the effects were devastating—for people who lost their livelihoods along with their ability to trust others in their own community, the effects were traumatizing and life-altering. The disquieting effects percolated out into the general society, as it became clear that supposed regulators had ignored repeated warnings of wrongdoing. Even some of the victims seemed complicit in their own downfall, as greed caused some to ignore clear warning signs. Interviews with Madoff's victims reveal people who are seething with aggression, and are seemingly prepared to act on that aggression; the devastation of the Madoff catastrophe will be felt for decades in the form of suicides, divorces, lawsuits between family members and aggression of every variety.

Let us take another example of trauma, one that is far too common: a woman is raped. The woman goes directly to a hospital, a rape kit is employed, and the rapist is arrested; the crime is adjudicated and the rapist goes to prison. The victim of the rape tries to return to her old life. But she is easily distracted, and can't really concentrate as she once did. She is hyper-vigilant, and finds the aftereffects of the sexual assault much more trying that she'd imagined they'd be. Later, after hearing about women who cut themselves, she finds herself surreptitiously trying it. She drinks more alcohol now, and even begins to abuse prescription medications. She has acute feelings of anger and powerlessness from time to time, and she tries to suppress the unfamiliar feelings with a little calculated sexual promiscuity. But the mental disequilibrium is still there, when she comes back from drinking or a romantic adventure. She finds herself cutting her arms and legs regularly. Why? *She* was the victim of a violent crime. Why is she hurting *herself?*

A combat veteran returns from a tour in Iraq. He thinks he's okay, but hangs out with other vets more than he talks to his wife, because he believes they "understand." The vets meet in a bar, and tend to drink a lot. One of them takes painkillers while he drinks boilermakers (whiskey chased down with beer), which strikes the combat veteran as dangerous. He also notices that something about the neighborhood is making him uncomfortable—it reminds him of a particular street in Iraq, a street that used to frighten him because he saw an improvised explosive device blow up a truck parked ahead of him. He wonders why he keeps coming back to the bar, since the street on which the bar is located reminds him of Iraq. He starts to feel trapped. What's going on?

He can't talk to his wife anymore, and never even feels like having sex with her. His own children are afraid of him, because he inadvertently finds himself yelling at them. One day the guy at the bar that takes pain pills passes out, and after he regains consciousness the vet gets in a fight with him. It's only after the police break it up that the vet remembers that he had a buddy in Iraq that also took pain pills, mainly to kill the terrible headaches he had after head trauma suffered in an IED explosion. The Iraq war vet is starting to realize that something's very wrong, but has no idea what to do about it. The next time he goes to this bar he gets in another big fight, and is ejected from the bar and told not to come back.

He goes home stoned, and his wife understandably gets on his case; but after a lot of arguing the vet ends up striking his wife in front on their kids, covering her face and neck with bruises. He's come close before, but this time he goes over the line. His oldest son won't speak to him the next morning; and his wife ends up sending the kids to her mother's house. The veteran is aghast at his own behavior, but doesn't know where it's all coming from, and has no idea what to do about it—he has a distinct feeling he won't be able to stop the physical abuse the next time he gets angry with his wife. In fact, he's afraid he might kill her, or kill somebody else, or even himself. He figures his marriage is over, he doesn't want to face charges in court, and especially doesn't want a repeat of the domestic violence. He buys a Harley, and hits the road.

What's going on here? What is causing the rape victim to hurt herself, and the veteran to beat his wife? They have both internalized enormous amounts of aggression, and they are both acting it out. The rape victim takes it out on herself, as women often do; the combat veteran takes it out on his wife. Both are acting out aggression that they internalized when they were victims of aggression themselves. But how does trauma cause the victim to internalize the aggression of the aggressor?

Let's break it down step by step.

5.
I) Identification with the Aggressor.
A rape, an ambush, an attack on the street by a criminal—time slows down, and to the victim of the violence it seems like he is suddenly fast-forwarded into a dream, even as he tries to fight back against the danger battering him. The attack seems to go on forever. Indeed, it seems to the victim as though he is suddenly in an alternative universe where time itself is being extinguished. The world of the victim is completely overwhelmed by the attacker's aggression, as that same aggression quickly *becomes* the victim's world. The victim is in a strange terrain, but must somehow master it quickly to survive. Thus he has no choice except *to identify totally with the world of the aggressor*, because only total alertness to the danger that is upon

him is going to help him survive the danger.

The senses are on red alert; but in the meantime something else is also happening. The emotions don't have time to process anything, nor does the mind. The victim is operating totally on intuition. Horrifying things are happening to the victim, but she or he doesn't have time to feel anything. All the thoughts and feelings that the victim would normally have in response to these events are put on hold. That is one aspect of emotional trauma — that emotions and thoughts have to be postponed to be experienced later. The personality is overwhelmed by so much stimulation that cognition closes down. The victim is running totally on adrenaline, nervous energy and something close to hysteria. The mind and emotions are totally out of whack, which is why part of post-traumatic treatment is helping the victim get his or her thoughts and feelings back, afterwards, into some kind of workable juxtaposition to each other. That might include helping the victim experience unpleasant feelings that he or she didn't have time to feel during the violence; but it also might be making sure that the victim doesn't get stuck in those volatile emotions.

Or perhaps the trauma comes from living with violent images, threats or attacks over a long period of time. The key to trauma bonding is this: the human personality experiences something that the conscious mind cannot accommodate or explain, so the experience goes directly to the unconscious part of the personality. Violence cannot be accepted by the reasoning, logical mind because violence is essentially illogical, and its impact on the personality can be exponentially increased when you try to impose logical criteria on the experience retrospectively. This also happens in situations that are not completely traumatic, but have such high levels of stress attached to them that the aftereffects, although not as severe, are similar, especially when they are cumulative. The fundamental *illogicality* of aggression is a big reason why the traumatized individual keeps returning in his or her mind to the aggression itself. Sadly, many victims of trauma — especially women — torment themselves by wondering if they made some mistake, and spend a great deal of time trying to figure out what it was.

Aggression, in other words, breaks asunder the normal, problem-solving world of the conscious mind. And then, because of some psychological (or perhaps biological) adaptation whose exact derivation we do not understand completely, aggression—or even the memory of it much later—temporarily shapes the world in which the victim lives. It is as though the victim is suddenly living in the aggressor's world. This identification may continue long after the attack is over, as though the aggressor somehow continues to control the victim's mental state. Both the conscious and the unconscious mind stay on red alert for a long time after the attack, as though the attack is still going on; but it is the unconscious mind that is affected most profoundly. The victim cannot logically answer the perennial question of all victims (*why me?*), so the unconscious mind takes over, using a greatly heightened intuition to make an adjustment to what is going on. The unconscious mind fights off death by bypassing logic and creating an emotional awareness so intense that it approaches a complete identification with the attacker.

A soldier describes an ambush: "I thought I was back in my bunk, dreaming. There was no place to run, so we had to return fire right away. I felt like I couldn't be hurt. My training kicked in, and after a firefight the enemy withdrew. I still don't know how long it lasted." The narrator is describing, first, a fight or flight reaction; and secondly an omnipotence fantasy. There was nothing for the soldier to figure out. His unconscious mind simply accommodated itself completely to the situation, and then his training kicked in and got him through it.

Besides time slowing down, sound also sometimes fades out during a violent attack, as the mind explodes with intuitive flashes of insight aimed at hiding, escaping, evading or avoiding the attacker. This fantastic sensitivity to the aggression is actually a kind of identification with the aggression, an identification that opens the personality wide open to the aggression itself. The logical mind is no good in the world of attack and counterattack; nor is there enough time to process emotions in a normal way. There is only survival, and the unconscious mind's desperate attempts to avoid extinction by intuitively getting into the mind of the attacker to figure out what he might do next, and using a tactic accommodated to the attacker's behavior.

Here is an account of a victim's escape from a rapist that appears in Gavin de Becker's excellent book *The Gift of Fear*. The victim, named Kelly, was told by a rapist to stay in her bedroom. But Kelly intuitively sensed he was going into the kitchen to get a knife. Here's what happened next: "But the instant he stepped from the room, Kelly stood up and walked after him, pulling the sheet off the bed with her. 'I was literally right behind him, like a ghost, and he didn't know I was there. We walked down the hall together. At one point he stopped, and so did I. He was looking at my stereo, which was playing some music, and he reached out and made it louder. When he moved on toward the kitchen, I turned and walked through the living room.'

"Kelly could hear drawers being opened as she walked out her front door, leaving it ajar. She walked directly into the apartment across the hall (which she somehow knew would be unlocked). Holding a finger up to signal her surprised neighbors to be quiet, she locked their door behind her."[5] This amazingly adaptive gambit probably saved Kelly's life—Kelly later found out that this rapist had previously killed a victim with a knife. How did Kelly know he was going to her kitchen to get a knife? Because he stopped to close her bedroom window—and her intuition told her it was to muffle her screams. Her intuition also told her that he was sufficiently self-absorbed that he wouldn't notice her escaping by 'shadowing' a couple of feet behind him. These things probably saved her life, and they helped the police take a really bad guy off the streets.

As courageous and life-saving as it turned out to be, Kelly's quick move wasn't the result of careful, logical thought. It was the result of intuition, which becomes greatly heightened in such situations. In an attack the unconscious mind understands the omnipresence, the totality, of the danger the victim is in. There's no denial—not with the fists or bullets or threats flying. It's there, and you're in the middle of it. It has overwhelmed your world, expanded in a nanosecond to fill your horizons. The dangers you are facing, and your need to survive, are now your universe. Because the aggression that is endangering you is all you are able to concentrate on, you are forced to identify with the world created by it. Because the attacker is threatening to end your life, you must identify with him and his motives enough to outwit them in some way. Even if you do not lose your life in a situation like this—and even if you are not traumatized by it—I can practically guarantee you that this experience will affect you as few other experiences are likely to do.

Those who survive violent experiences, including those who seem to have escaped with no trauma, will sometimes have flashbacks triggered years later by some insignificant sound, association or situation. People who have experienced flashbacks describe it as being like putting a CD on a turntable—it's all there, ready to be played, not the experience itself or even a memory of the events, but *a sequence of emotions that the unconscious mind has not been able to decode and deconstruct*. One reason for that is that the emotions were so insanely heightened at the time of the event itself. People who experience these kinds of flashbacks aren't necessarily having auditory or visual hallucinations—they just feel all the emotions they didn't have a chance to feel before, when they were in the midst of the violent experience. They couldn't feel them the first time around because they were so focused on the life-threatening attack.

Think about it. How could you *not* identify with the world of aggression in which you suddenly find yourself? If you didn't identify with it completely, you might miss something—you might not see the door or window through which you could escape, or the flicker of hesitation in the aggressor's eyes that signals a chance to run or land a blow. This is what is meant by identification with aggression—you *have* to identify with it, or you might not survive it.

This identification continues after the attack. Afterwards, the victim may make excuses for the attacker, taking responsibility for his motivation, soon perhaps beginning to blame herself and trying to understand it logically.

But violence is completely *unreasonable*, and therefore not amenable to reasonable theories. This sense of unreality may continue as long as the victim thinks about what happened. Since it cannot be processed logically, it sticks in the victim's emotions—and it may gradually expand its influence over the individual's unconscious thoughts and feelings even as the victim begins to forget the actual events. The silver lining to this paradoxical, bewildering process is that it enables the victim to survive.

That's a big silver lining. But there's an emotional price to pay.

2) Internalization of the Aggression.

Internalization is a secondary and deeper form of the victim's engagement with aggression. First is identification, which begins at the moment when the victim understands the supreme danger he is in. Then something else kicks in—the *internalization* of the aggression, as the unconscious mind is mobilized and races its engines, desperately trying to arrive at some expedient to save itself. The logical mind is so overwhelmed and at such a disadvantage that it can no longer process events very well, since the victim is functioning mainly on instinct, adrenaline and intuition. But the unconscious mind of the victim knows the danger, and turns the tables on the attacker. It responds to the aggression with a gambit used in judo—it *accepts* the aggression, using the hostile energy of the attack to pull the aggression in. It is trying desperately to control the situation by internalizing it. This mental flip-flop is the mind's way of trying to ensure the survival of the personality. By *internalizing* the aggression attacking it, the personality can now bend instead of break. Instead of *resisting* the aggression, the unconscious mind welcomes in into the personality, making the victim feel that he has gained some control and making the attack a little less overwhelming.

The internalization of an attacker's aggression may not become apparent until a long time after the physical danger has passed, as the emotions reorient themselves and struggle to process what has happened. The discomfort of this later process is what often makes PTSD generate so much anxiety—the short-circuited or overburdened emotions are trying to get back in some kind of juxtaposition with the conscious mind, and with each other, based on highly incomplete and distorted memories. But the really difficult part may arise with the powerful feelings of aggression the victim is likely to have later, which really can't be attributed only to delayed stress or to a desire for revenge, since the aggression that has been internalized typically isn't just aimed at the attacker. *The internalization of aggression by the trauma victim is what is likely to cause the biggest problems later.* The bad part is the price the victim will pay later, often while struggling with powerful feelings of irrational anger arising from the aggression internalized during the attack. This aggressive orientation is likely to grow stronger if the conscious mind cannot retrospectively make sense of the violence endured—and it usually can't, if the victim cannot create some kind of moral context for the aggression experienced. The best way to begin doing this, usually, is by talking about the experience as early as possible without getting stuck in memories of it.

When one speaks of *internalizing the aggression* of an attacker, a threatening figure, or a battlefield enemy, it sounds more like a physical than an emotional process, like an exchange of blood-borne pathogens. But it isn't a physical transfer. It's a sharp, violent and emotional response to aggression, in which the victim's emotions violently reorient themselves and take on an aggressive emotional orientation that the victim didn't have before. The unconscious mind isn't just *accommodating* the aggression it is experiencing—it is unconsciously *imitating* and *conforming* to the aggression being visited against it, in a desperate bid to survive it. The longer the aggression goes on, and the longer the victim is in a threatening or violent environment, the more these changes are likely to occur, and to affect the victim's personality later.

When US soldiers went out on patrol in Iraq, as they tended to do almost daily, similar changes in the soldier's personality were extremely likely to happen, because a constant state of aggressive alertness was the only way the American soldier could compensate for the familiarity of the enemy with the terrain, the culture and the prevailing tribal alignments. Again, it was an effort to *imitate* the readiness that the insurgents possessed, simply because they were Iraqis, and the Americans weren't. The Iraqi insurgents were, in other words, playing on their home field; and the Americans had to adopt a hyper-vigilant and aggressive attitude to compensate for the disadvantage.

Without the agency of moral choice, without conscious decision-making, the entire unconscious linkage of emotion, instinct and sensory awareness coheres to fit the pattern of the attacker's aggression. The personality of the soldier is very often affected by a powerful aggressive emotional orientation—and it becomes very difficult to turn the spigot off. A specific crime, attack or threatening situation may end, but its effect on the victim's personality may remain for a very long time—and affect the victim's behavior in strange and unexpected ways in the future. The two main qualifiers are these: The *length* of the traumatizing aggression; and the extent to which it is *forced* upon the recipient of it.

On one level, what happens to a victim of aggression is fairly simple. He is attacked, and he fights back. His adrenaline soars; his heart pumps; his breath is short; he shouts and curses; and his entire sensorium (the sum total of his senses) is now on high red alert. He responds to an attack with unabated defensive violence—but reactive anger isn't the whole story. The victim who experiences trauma often continues to feel aggression for much longer than is rationally necessary, sometimes for a lifetime; and subsequent anger is often aroused at inappropriate times and directed at inconse-quential things. The reason is because the victim *internalized the aggression* of the attack during the traumatizing event. The unconscious aggressive emotional orientation that has been created in our victim can quickly become a driving force not merely of the victim's behavior, but of his worldview. It also frequently involves self-destructive gestures, which it logically shouldn't, and it sometimes results in suicide, which it logically never should. The reasons these things happen is obviously not revenge; it is because victims have internalized enormous amounts of aggression and have found no healthy way to express, act out or deconstruct those orientations.

Clearly something happens when people are victims of aggression that is quite extraordinary, especially if the aggression lasts a long time. Some people, of course, are able to very quickly figure out a way to deconstruct the aggression they've internalized, and to sublimate or channel it in positive ways; but unless people are willing to talk about the things that traumatized them, internalized aggression can become so volatile and so uncomfortable that it is intrinsically difficult to control. Generally speaking, the best thing the victim of aggression can do is to start talking about what happened—and how he feels about it—as soon as possible. It is this book's central thesis that the trauma bond, whatever ultimately causes it to happen, is a profound dynamic in the way aggression and evil are replicated in the world. The most powerful forms of trauma bonding involve some identification with the aggression that caused (or continues to cause) the trauma; and at the same time a fair amount of internalization of the aggression itself. Then the victim either has to figure out some way to deconstruct it, live with it, or act out the aggression on someone else, or on oneself. Again, by far the best expedient is for victims to start talking about what happened, as soon as possible.

Long after the attack, the victim's sense of unreality continues. Ultimately, it is as though the aggression experienced by the victim has moved into his personality and is continuing to influence him—and that is exactly what has happened. By focusing so strongly on the danger from the aggressor at the point of attack, the victim has allowed (indeed, welcomed) the attacker's aggression into his own personality at a moment of supreme vulnerability. This was the result of focusing so intently and intuitively on the violence of the aggressor, which is necessary to survive. But the aggression will gradually become a powerful emotional orientation that can over time take on a life of its own. This aggressive emotional orientation is insistent, volatile and uncomfortable, and the pressure generated by it can usually be relieved only by deconstructing it or acting it out.

Since this aggressive emotional orientation ends up in the unconscious part of the victim's personality, over a long period of time it is likely to influence the victim's behavior in ways he or she may not be consciously aware of. It is also likely to affect the victim's worldview. Men traumatized by aggression are prone to identify with aggression in the larger society by supporting patriarchy, nationalism or a coercive attitude toward the resolution of social problems. The male victim may bond with other people, usually males, who engage in violence together. (Think paramilitary militias, biker gangs, Serbian nationalists, hazing fraternity students, etc.) On the other hand, a benign example of this dynamic might include guys watching football together in the den or basement (the 'man-cave') on Saturday. What's the difference between a football fanatic and a street criminal? The football fan is in control of his aggression, allowing the players to act it out for him, and enjoying the resulting aggression vicariously.

In general, the behavior of the victim will gradually become more aggressive, since the aggression he internalized has coalesced into an emotional orientation that demands an outlet—and if it can't be acted out or sublimated in some way, the result is usually anxiety of varying degrees of intensity. The victim can either act out the aggression he is feeling, abuse substances to dull the discomfort, or suffer increasing levels of anxiety—or, find some way to deconstruct the aggressive emotional orientation without having to act it out against himself or others.

Sometimes the victim becomes aware of his new aggressive impulses, especially if he wasn't particularly aggressive before. This, too, causes anxiety, but may be healthy because it may cause the victim to seek help. There are many ways that strong feelings of aggression can potentially be deconstructed, but usually the key is getting the traumatized individuals to talk about their experiences as soon after they happen as possible, without allowing them to get stuck in overwhelming emotions or memories. (Other ways that internalized aggression can be deconstructed will be discussed later.) The victim, remember, has taken a big part of the aggression into his own personality in an attempt to normalize it—which means that the personality of the victim has been altered, to accommodate the aggression of the attacker. These are things that the victim needs to talk about, and to be reassured that the feelings of anger are normal for this experience—but also needs to be reassured that he doesn't need to act on those feelings, because *he is no longer in the aggressor's world*. If the victim can't deconstruct the aggressive orientation, he is likely to act out his aggression against himself or others.

A man from El Salvador that I interviewed survived an attack by a death squad in which a girlfriend died; he experienced so much aggression afterwards that he said that he felt like his stomach was on fire. After awhile, he got involved in the ongoing civil war in El Salvador by joining the revolutionary guerillas in his province. Amazingly, he survived the whole thing and opened a business after the guerillas signed a peace accord. He, along with some other former guerillas, formed a political party that at the time this was written had been voted into government. This man was an example of a victim who became an aggressor in a way that was acceptable to his society—or at least to his comrades in the revolutionary army— and deconstructed his aggressive emotional orientation through the agency of the peace agreement, which came as a huge relief to all Salvadorians. (Remarkably, the guerrilla commanders of his faction dropped Marxism-Leninism and adopted a democratic and surprisingly conciliatory approach to the rebuilding of the country.) But the revolution devastated El Salvador, creating extremely violent youth gangs and making the crime rate the worst in Latin America. It would have been better if the rich families of Salvador hadn't created death squads in the first place, and if the US hadn't given them money to murder people, most of whom simply wanted trade unions, social justice and the rudiments of a democracy.

If trauma bonding occurs on a mass basis throughout the world, humankind's ability to control aggression may depend on how well people can deconstruct this process. But we ought to first understand that trauma bonding is itself a mechanism of survival—the unconscious mind's extreme response to the perceived threat of death. Although it cannot make moral choices, there is almost always a reason for what the unconscious mind does. Consider drowning, for example. The body goes through excruciating and extreme changes as it is deprived of oxygen. The unconscious mind desperately tries to keep the personality alive by producing vivid pictures from the drowning person's past. It also prepares the drowning victim for death, creating a kind of instant documentary of what that person's life has been. (People who have almost drowned often say, "I saw my whole life flash in front of my eyes," which has now become something of a cliché but is quite an enlightening experience for those who survive to talk about it.) People having near-death experiences also report a beautiful and indescribable sense of peace, as the unconscious mind prepares them for the next step.

It is something like this that causes the victim of aggression to internalize the aggression he is suffering. He 'resolves' the adversarial nature of the attack by taking the aggression into his own personality while the unconscious mind assumes all the attributes and dynamics of that aggression. This is one of the unconscious mind's recurring strategies for keeping the personality whole and the victim alive; but these machinations are completely unconscious rather than conscious, and were probably selected into human behavior by some obscure social juxtaposition in humanity's past social and biological evolution. (At least some evolutionary biologists have hypothesized along those lines.) And the dreamlike, unconscious way in which the unconscious mind operates is why the internalized aggression is so potent, so toxic and so deceptively long-lasting.

One reason why the victim of violence pays such a high price is because he has no idea whatsoever, during the attack, what is going on inside him emotionally. At first the victim experiences relief from simply having survived—then the anger and anxiety arrive, and the victim begins to understand that the struggle has just begun. The aggressive emotional orientations that now characterize his emotions must be either deconstructed—that is, their disruptive nature neutralized—or acted out in some way. This is the peculiar difficulty that afflicts both men and women who are suffering from PTSD. What makes recovery so difficult for them is the irrational anger they find themselves feeling, not to mention hyper-vigilance, which can by itself cause ongoing anxiety because it seems to erupt without sufficient reason. The result is that the victim begins to wonder if his entire future is going to be shaped by the trauma he experienced at some time in the past. When trauma victims feel intense anger later, a long time after the original trauma, it is a kind of 'Invasion of the Body Snatchers' sensation, all the worse because it seems so unwarranted.

During the Vietnam War, the Veterans Administration understood that the returning vets were having so-called 're-entry problems.' The VA had also decided that some of the vets' behavior was becoming a problem for the society—but at the same time a great many of the vets had themselves already figured out that the government had lied to them about the reasons why they were sent to "kill the yellow man," as the Bruce Springsteen song would have it. It was an angry time during which the Black ghettoes were exploding, and the vets had combat experience, and (although nobody would say so openly) the vets returning from Vietnam were seen by the US political class as something of a subversive threat. In

San Francisco, where this writer lived, it was not uncommon for the VA to simply give returning Vietnam Vets powerful tranquilizers, usually around ninety tabs of 10 MG Valium every month, recommending that they take three of these 10 MG tabs a day. Unfortunately, these tranquilizers were actually muscle relaxants, and were thus highly addictive, so that the VA was supplying them with a free gateway drug to a life of further addictions.

But that was the only way the VA knew in those days for dealing with the problem of delayed stress among their returning veterans, many of whom were not only traumatized by combat but also deeply disillusioned by the lies the government had told them. (And yes, this loss of trust apparently exacerbated the symptoms of trauma, because of the unspoken realization that the traumatizing events were to some extent caused by a war that was unnecessary.) The Valium they gave these young vets anesthetized their anger, but it only worked in the short term — over the long term it made things worse. Because of ignorance about the effects of emotional trauma among returning combat soldiers during and after the Vietnam War, and because of the counterinsurgent nature of the war itself, America lost part of an entire generation of young returning veterans to mental illness, addictions, homelessness and suicide.

3) The Victim Becomes an Aggressor.

People who have internalized large amounts of aggression must contain it, neutralize it or act it out. If they try to contain (that it, ignore or deny) it, anxiety often results: sleeplessness, inability to concentrate, irritability and hyper-vigilance. Street drugs and alcohol can neutralize it, but only in the short term. Those who can't handle the internalized aggression very well often start acting it out. Some act it out as self-harm — women are particularly prone to that, but there are plenty of male combat veterans who also engage in self-harm in the form of substance abuse, high-risk behavior and suicide. And of course some traumatized people — usually men — act their internalized aggression out against others, and adopt a worldview in which violence is an acceptable and desirable way to resolve human problems. This is mainly because they have internalized huge amounts of aggression, but perhaps also because they have been in situations where certain kinds of violence were honored and rewarded.

In the film *Apocalypse Now*, the protagonist Captain Benjamin L. Willard, played by Martin Sheen, comes back to Vietnam even though he has already done two tours of duty. "When I'm here in Vietnam, all I can think about is leaving," Willard says in a voice-over, "but when I'm not in Vietnam, all I can think of is getting back into the jungle." That seemingly paradoxical refrain is repeatedly encountered in narratives of Vietnam Veterans. ("When I was in the [Vietnam] shit, all I could think about was getting back to the world. When I went home, all I could think about was getting back to be with my buddies.") While consciously hating the mayhem of Vietnam, and verbally cursing it as a lost cause, many soldiers felt an inexorable pull to get back into it. Very often they couldn't explain why—it simply seemed that once baptized by fire, they couldn't wait to get back into the jungle to again experience the aggression that had so radically changed them. (Sometimes they'd say, "I wanted to finish the job we'd started"—even though they knew US strategy was fatally flawed and going nowhere. So if the job was flawed, why did they go back?)

The entire premise of *Apocalypse Now* was that some soldiers wanted to get back into the jungle—what they saw as evil in its purest form—to recover something they had lost; but when they got in too deep they got lost themselves. In this paradox are distant echoes of a particular colonial paradigm, in which the European colonialist is both attracted to, and terrified of "going native." (That is, he might identify too closely with the indigenous people he's been exploiting.) Traumatized soldiers can find themselves on a similar merry-go-round, if they cannot deconstruct the aggression they have internalized. Don't forget that for many men, the experience of trauma bonding with their buddies may be the only experience of emotional intimacy they've ever experienced. Men that have internalized huge amounts of aggression could spend the rest of their lives trying to recapture that intimacy, while at the same time they seek unconsciously to go back to the emotional country where their personalities were forever altered, and perhaps broken. They know that something big happened to them; but feel that there is only one way to find out what it was, by going back to that place where aggression was the standard by which everything else is judged.

Once the soldier has identified with and to some extent internalized the aggression that is all around him, he is likely to find himself irrationally attracted to aggression as a phenomenon, especially the kind of aggression he already knows about. There is a part of him that will always want to go back to the original site of the aggression, back to the place of the trauma—the unconscious mind cannot forget that trauma happened, because it gave the personality its new orientation. The mind of the traumatized veteran drives him to return to the scene of the original emotional dislocation, back to the place where everything changed. To do that, he may create or seek out social situations that generate violence and aggression, trying to remake the world around him to conform to his feelings. That may include getting involved with groups—from biker gangs to cocaine wholesalers to vulture capitalists to "re-upping" in the military—that are organized around aggression. They can't deliver lasting peace, but in the short term they seem to give the victim the intimacy he craves, and supply a kind of logic to otherwise incoherent emotions. And they take him closer to that place where he lost his innocence. But what exactly the victims hope to find when they get back to the point of maximum trauma most traumatized people don't really know.

In *Apocalypse Now*, the emotionally battered Captain Willard is anxious to re-engage the enemy again, as though by defeating him he can get his life back. But the movie suggests that the danger confronting Willard comes from a different source—from the nature of the war itself, which he has internalized. Counterinsurgency involves killing civilians, which is always an atrocity. And it was an unnecessary atrocity, because the Americans did not allow the elections mandated by the Geneva Accords of 1956, which would have allowed the South Vietnamese to pick their own government. (The US knew the South Vietnamese would probably vote for Ho Chi Minh, so they did not allow the election to go forward.) So the US action in Vietnam was completely unnecessary, and therefore entirely immoral; and most solders sensed that, or they gradually became aware of it, without acknowledging it in so many words. That was the central irony of *Apocalypse Now*—that the emotional trauma and the personal meltdowns of US soldiers in Vietnam came not only from a diabolical enemy, and not just from daily violence, but from the emotional and cognitive degradation of the American troops themselves, as their reasons for being there came to feel like so many drug-induced chimeras.

Some soldiers consciously turned against the war, and the courage associated with that transformation gave some the emotional armoring to protect them from the worst kind of trauma. Others used drugs, or shut down emotionally to shut out (or deliberately dissociate from) what they were doing and seeing. The only ones that adjusted to the situation with total success were the sociopaths, as *Apocalypse Now* demonstrates. Others were not so fortunate. The deeper they got into the jungle, the crazier they became, and the more systemic the bonding to a primitive world of sheer unending violence. But it started with the imperial idea that Americans knew best how Vietnam should be governed, and was driven by that weird combination of idealism, narcissism and innocence that periodically drives Americans to seek personal truth in places they do not fully understand.

The unconscious mind does not seek cognitive answers, but emotional ones—and if cognitive reasons for behavior are also lacking, that exponentially increases the need for emotional answers. What the traumatized person seeks, on one level, is an answer to the riddle of evil. The traumatized person longs to go back to the original violence, as though an emotional Eden lay waiting to be discovered in the instant before the ambush, rape, IED explosion, domestic violence or violent attack, the instant before the violence created a new person and a new world inside the victim. So traumatized men must cash in their spiritual IOUs, and Bogart their way back, back to the Garden, back through the violence to the safety and innocence encapsulated in the moment before the aggression. *Or is it the violence itself that contains the answer?* Traumatized men can never be completely sure, until they start dealing with the aggression they've internalized. Traumatized women spend an enormous amount of time blaming themselves, trying to figure out what they did wrong. Trauma-bonded people never really know what they're searching for—all they know is that they want to get back to the things that transformed them, and get back the thing that they lost, and find out once and for all what the hell happened to them.

This mental boomerang effect is, again, the mind's way of trying to ensure the survival of the personality, however paradoxical it may seem in the short-term. To know itself, the mind wants to know what made everything so different after the traumatic event. But the answer to post-traumatic stress, or delayed stress, usually does not lie in going back to the site of the trauma. The problem is not in the past, nor in the geographical place where it happened (Vietnam, Afghanistan or Iraq), because the problem now resides in the unconscious mind of the victim.

Many Vietnam Vets experienced a deep desire to return to peacetime Vietnam; and to be sure, for many vets that ended up being a healing experience. (This may have been partly because the Vietnamese government wanted improved relations with the US, and therefore encouraged vets to visit.) But some vets didn't find what they were looking for, because they were looking in the wrong place. The vets who had the best return trips to peacetime Vietnam were those who dealt with their trauma before they attempted to go back. They found a way to *externalize* the aggression that they originally *internalized*, and they found a way to do this without hurting themselves or others, usually with the help of talk therapy and (usually) some kind of peer-counseling with other Vietnam Vets. When vets deconstruct those parts of the war they've been carrying around inside them, they're ready to go back to where the war was fought. That way, when the Vietnam Vet goes back to Vietnam, he won't expect the Vietnamese to give him back what he lost. He can look instead at the Vietnamese *as people*, rather than stages in the dissolution of his personality.

Perhaps most victims of trauma feel at some point or other that insane pull, that incredible desire to go back to the moment—back to the place—where their trauma first happened, even if the journey back in time is metaphorical or merely simulated in popular art. Abused adolescents, for example, love to watch the most hideous kinds of 'slasher' films (*Halloween*, *Friday the 13th*, the *Scream* and *Saw* films) as though in the buckets of ketchup and simulated mutilation they can find what they lost to the brutal adults that physically and sexually abused them. I worked once at a residential program for SED—that is, severely emotionally disturbed—adolescents, almost all of whom had been abused in ways most people could hardly imagine. The staff at this program allowed the adolescents to watch 'slasher' films every night. "I know it's crazy," the program director told me, "but it's literally the only thing that can get them to sit still for an hour or two. It's the only time we can get our progress notes done. The rest of the time they're so needy we have to give them nonstop attention."

The Hollywood makers of these films apparently understand the relativity between trauma and the on-screen violence, because as the Wikipedia entry for the 'slasher' genre points out, the murderous antiheros of these exercises in gore (Freddy Krueger, Jason, Chucky, etc.) are usually based on "mentally deranged and/or physically deformed individuals who were traumatized, in many instances at an early age." I also understood why abused kids wanted to watch 'slasher' films, because they would like to revisit, even if only in a wildly exaggerated cinematic form, the violence that traumatized them and took away their innocence; and I understood how hard it was for the staff to get these needy, violent kids to calm down long enough for them to write their progress notes. But I couldn't agree with the way the staff resolved the problem. So I resigned from the program and went to work for a different agency.

By watching the spurting blood, decapitation and hacking of torsos and limbs on the screen in *Slaughter High, Scream* or *I Know What You Did Last Summer,* the traumatized adolescent may interpret the resulting thrills as recreational. But in what sense is extreme graphic hacking of human bodies recreational? Such kids are trying to discharge their internalized aggression through the catharsis of watching people being mutilated on the screen. By attempting to go back to the world of pure aggression where their own trauma originated, these children are signaling that they want to discharge the freight of the aggression they are carrying, because it is just too heavy for them to bear alone. But for adolescents to watch the extremely graphic violence of a 'slasher' movie without dealing with their own internalized violence is simply compounding violence with more violence, regardless of the momentary catharsis.

Ultimately such young victims of abuse will discharge their internalized aggression wherever they find themselves in life; and one can only hope such a person finds some social institution or program that can help him deal with his emotional orientations. If the abused adolescent's internalized aggression is not neutralized, he will act it out, either against himself or against other people, or both. Watching a 'slasher' film will give an abused adolescent momentary relief, to be sure; but overall it simply takes him one step further in his progression from victim to aggressor. And even the momentary relief of the catharsis offered by 'slasher' films is likely to be so pathological that the young person will get the message that under certain circumstances violence is okay.

The abused male adolescent *might* find a way to act it out that is minimally acceptable to society (as a soldier, boxer, stunt man, high-rise construction worker), but is far more likely to find ways that are *not* acceptable and in the process hurt himself and others. In his quest to act out the aggression inside him he is likely to end up in prison. In the past, the military has been a time-honored place of maturation for many violent young males; in the rigors of training, following orders, strenuous exercise, cleaning weapons, standing at attention and marching around, etc., many young recruits paradoxically find that military training gives the recruit a psychic container to control aggressive emotions.

At the same time, the military also *redirects* his aggression by encouraging him to support patriarchal solutions to social and international problems, based heavily on oppression, violence and intimidation. A young male in the military who seems to have promise will sometimes be mentored by an older person and will become a good career soldier. But he is also very likely to be mentored into an ultraconservative worldview, and to end up supporting extreme right-wing solutions to everything, including large doses of patriarchy, nationalism and militarism.

In a worst-case scenario, a male survivor of youthful abuse might, after a great deal of substance abuse and violations of the law, commit "suicide by cop" — pick up a gun and wave it around threateningly until some poor patrolman has to shoot him dead. Until he can deconstruct the trauma bond that drives him to violent solutions, the young male will always want to go back to the aggression that first broke his personality, and that all too often drive him to look for ways to act it out in the present moment. At some point it may not even be a matter of choice anymore, but of sheer, brutal emotional compulsion. The young adult who is recovering from the effects of abuse may have some control over *how* he acts out the aggression inside him, but one way or the other he'll have to act it out. And that makes him a walking time bomb. The best thing for him is to talk to someone about what is going on inside him. If he simply tries to hold it all in without talking about it, he is likely to end up going out of control.

Sometimes abused adolescents learn very early in the group homes and residential treatment programs how to play the victim-aggressor angle, mimicking the behavior of the adults who originally beat them up or exploited them sexually. If an abused kid is in an environment in which he learns enough psycho-babble to blame everybody else, he may reach the highest rung of the victim-aggressor ladder, and become a sociopath. He may say that the system is stacked against him and that although he robs, rapes and kills, he shouldn't be blamed because he was abused. (This is sometimes called the 'abuse excuse' in psycho-social rehab.) The life of the victim-aggressor will *not* be a satisfying destination, because it has many of the characteristics of an addiction; and that means more anger, frustration and criminal behavior down the line, rather than the emotional growth that most people need. It also portends long stretches in prison, unless our youthful sociopath is clever enough to become a con man, white collar criminal, hedge fund manager, or politician.

Not all aggression comes from trauma—some is intrinsic to the human personality. Trauma simple adds to it, to the extent that the victim internalizes the trauma he suffers. And for many victims of aggression, becoming an aggressor is the final destination in the long pilgrimage known as the trauma bond, and one that many, many people end up in, some early, and some late. It is theoretically possible at any point for the traumatized person to get out of the negative consequences that the trauma may have initiated—and some people do. But many people may identify so strongly with aggression that they will never change, perhaps because they don't want to. In fact there are no hard and fast rules about trauma bonding, because society still doesn't understand how aggression replicates itself in the world, and how people that have been brutalized internalize and act out that brutality. Furthermore, many people are a little queasy about learning too much about it, because it suggests just how deep evil runs in human affairs, and they're really not interested in finding out about that. If they did, they might have to look in the mirror, and face the evil in themselves.

In any case, deconstructing a trauma bond usually involves getting clients to talk about what is happening in the present, without getting stuck emotionally in the past, or generating a toxic new identity centered on the traumatizing event or its resulting emotional turmoil. And secondly, it usually includes making some effort, however small, to deconstruct the social factors that caused the traumatizing events. Often that means that the traumatized person can find great satisfaction in doing humanitarian work aimed at stopping or controlling the kind of violence that first hurt and traumatized him. The traumatized person needs to change his own personality, while seeking to change the world around him—there is tremendous power to doing both at the same time. If there's a real desire to deconstruct the effects of violence or exploitation, cognitive ability finally *does* have a role to play, at least retroactively, because only the logical mind can figure out the social factors behind the human aggression that caused the trauma, and isolate the historical and cultural factors that generated it.

Two good examples of movements that challenge aggression in society are veterans that work for peace, or who help other veterans recover from emotional trauma; and victims of rape that work to challenge and deconstruct patriarchy. This kind of thing can be very liberating because it allows the trauma victim to imagine a better world, in which the trauma that hurt her or him is less likely to harm others in the future. (Another example: a kid abused in foster care might campaign, as an adult, for better conditions for foster children. An abused child might campaign for children's rights.) So cognition does very definitely come into play at this point—one must decide consciously on a strategy to free one's unconscious mind from the bonding of past trauma; and however it is to be done, a person must make the decision to get better. But in terms of figuring out *why* violence has such an effect on the emotions, reason is limited, because both violence and emotions are unreasonable. Trying to rationally figure out *why* the trauma happened is also not a good or therapeutic short-term solution for the victim—getting over one's victimization *in the present moment* is a much better and more positive goal, by deconstructing the way past events are influencing one's current behavior. For many people the best way to do that is to focus realistically on the future, by imagining what one wants to become, as well as the kind of world one would like to see.

The intricacies of the trauma bond reveal in glaring detail the human dilemma of this moment in history—we are a thinking species who can resolve problems, and we're organized enough socially that we have created a vibrant civilization with a high culture; but since there is no logical explanation for our aggression (even when we don't need it and even when we don't want or intend it) we remain conundrums to ourselves. That explains, to a great extent, why we are story-telling creatures—our behavior is often so lacking in unity and coherence that it only makes sense according to a logic that is essentially retrospective. Thus deconstructing trauma usually begins with the victim talking about what happened and telling his story, as people in 12-step meetings do.

Reason does not understand aggression, and aggression does not understand reason. The victim of emotional trauma is often trapped in this discontinuity between cognition and aggression, which plays out in an existential borderland in which the conscious and unconscious minds have not only parted company, but are no longer on speaking terms. Try as it may, the self can find no logical answers about the past in these emotional badlands. Out of this radical *unknowability* of human aggression rises the trauma bond: it organizes and focuses violent emotions in ways that neither reason nor emotion could ever do alone.

4) The Cover-Up: Aggression Becomes Evil.

Some people make such a good adjustment to their own aggression that they become extremely dangerous. These are people who know how to lie convincingly about the aggression they are acting out, or to seamlessly rationalize their own brutality. Sometimes whole societies do it—the infamous Joseph Goebbels, for example, created an alternative national narrative in Nazi Germany that justified everything that Hitler and the Nazi regime did, which was almost completely bogus but which a great many people wanted to believe. Stalin's minions, likewise, adopted a complicated ideology that promised the ultimate eradication of aggression and exploitation if only people would look the other way when the Soviet state engaged in its own massive aggression.

When people dissemble, cover up, or rationalize human aggression against the innocent, that aggression becomes a form of evil. That is in fact this book's working definition of evil: *Unacceptable aggression plus deceit equals evil.* And aggression that is successfully concealed is far more likely to become systemic evil (a coordinated system of aggression accompanied by systematic lying to cover it up) which is used to oppress large numbers of people, usually by the state. We'll explore that idea in more detail in the following chapters. For the time being, let's see how some of the ideas related above play out in the following examples of people whose lives were deeply altered by aggression. The first is a well-know crime narrative known as the Hettinger case.

6.

Karl Hettinger was an undercover cop in Los Angeles, who on the evening of March 9, 1963, was patrolling in an unmarked car with his partner Ian Campbell. The officers did a traffic stop on two suspicious-looking men who turned out to be ex-convicts who'd committed a string of store robberies. One of the criminals got the drop on Officer Campbell—that is, he jammed a gun in Campbell's back before the officer could get his weapon out—and to save his partner's life Hettinger gave up his weapon. The two kidnappers, Gregory Powell and Jimmy Lee Smith, forced the officers at gunpoint to drive them to Kern County, in the vicinity of Bakersfield. They stated repeatedly that they would set the officers free in a remote location; Powell had taken some money from Hettinger, but as they

neared their destination he gave it back. The kidnappers also stated that they would throw the officers' revolvers in the bushes so that they—Hettinger and Campbell—could recover them after the two criminals drove away.

The officers were directed to a dirt road, at the end of which the two criminals said they would free them. All occupants of the car got out, and Powell rather casually asked Campbell if he had ever heard of the so-called "Little Lindberg" law. When Campbell answered in the affirmative, Powell shot him in the mouth. Hettinger screamed and ran; and as he ran, more shots were fired. Hettinger got away, but a total of five rounds were pumped into the body of Officer Ian Campbell as he lay dying on the ground.

Smith and Powell were originally convicted and sentenced to death. Because of some questionable police work and some legal complications, their automatic court appeal was successful; as the state struggled to get a conviction, Smith and Powell were tried repeatedly. Karl Hettinger was required to testify each time they went to a new trial, and may have been re-traumatized by being repeatedly called to testify. (Especially when the various defense attorneys began to subtly question his memory, his motives and his sanity.) Hettinger began to experience terrible dreams, sleep disturbances, night sweats and other symptoms of trauma. Testifying repeatedly at the trials of Smith and Powell added to Hettinger's sense of unreality concerning the death of his partner Campbell. (People who are required to tell the same narrative repeatedly sometimes report that it begins to feel like a fabrication, or something that happened to someone else. Talking about oneself repeatedly can create a feeling of alienation from one's own life story, even though the story one is telling happens to be factually true.)

But the worst was yet to come. Karl Hettinger's behavior began to change dramatically. As he thought obsessively about how his partner Campbell had died, and what he might have done to prevent his death, Hettinger began to steal, engaging in one petty

theft and shoplifting episode after another. He was already somewhat estranged from his fellow officers, not to mention the LAPD brass that in typical macho fashion was inclined to blame him for Campbell's death. (It was actually Campbell who had allowed the kidnappers to get the drop on him—Hettinger gave up his own weapon only because his partner had a gun in his ribs.) Hettinger's reputation tanked as he became more uncommunicative, undependable and irresponsible. His stealing became more systematic, and increasingly noticeable. He was finally busted by the Internal Affairs division of the Los Angles Police Department for theft, and forced to resign from his job as detective.

What happened to Karl Hettinger? What caused a family man with a wife and children to go from being a good cop with a clean record to being a thief?

There are several clues that immediately present themselves. On the night of Campbell's murder, Hettinger had a long time to talk to the two criminals, Powell and Smith, as the patrolmen drove them at gunpoint to Kern County—and therefore Hettinger had a lot of time to *identify* with them, especially Powell. Hettinger and Campbell were basically hostages; and hostages often identify personally with their captors. (We will examine that in a later chapter.) Hettinger desperately wanted to establish a relationship with the kidnappers— he hoped to enhance the two cops' chances of getting away unscathed by establishing a friendly tone. Powell encouraged this feeling of camaraderie by giving Hettinger back his money; and as they all got out of the car Powell sounded almost conversational as he asked Campbell if he'd ever heard of the "Little Lindberg" law.

All these things doubtlessly increased Hettinger's *identification* with the criminals, especially with Powell. Thus when Powell pulled the trigger and murdered Campbell, Hettinger was completely unprepared. He screamed and ran four miles to a farmhouse; at this moment of supreme vulnerability he was deeply traumatized emotionally. The brutal murder that he had witnessed entered his consciousness and memory as nothing ever had before; almost

surely a certain callous disregard and outright hostility of fellow officers and LAPD brass added to his agony and guilt. Should it have been himself and not Campbell who died out there in that field in Kern County? Considering all that happened later, it seems impossible not to conclude that Hettinger *internalized the aggression* he witnessed. It would be a volatile, disabling emotional orientation from which he would suffer for the rest of his life.[6]

And he acted out the internalized aggression. In Hettinger's case, the internalized aggression he carried around inside himself wasn't acted out toward other people—Hettinger acted it out in ferocious, horrifying ways against himself. He punished himself in extraordinarily harsh ways—with sleep disturbance, nightmares, survivor guilt and a generalized anxiety interrupted by bouts of major depression. Most mind-boggling of all was the way he mimicked the criminal behavior of the low-rent criminal Gregory Powell, as Hettinger increasingly engaged in various kinds of petty theft. He didn't just identify with Powell's aggression—over a period of time he actually *became* Powell, actually becoming a petty thief like Powell had been. Only when he had been arrested by the LAPD Internal Affairs for robbery, as he had once sought to arrest Gregory Powell for robbery, had he acted out that particular aspect of his internalized aggression to its final conclusion.

Hettinger was also attracted to the place where his partner Campbell lost his life. He often went on fishing trips, and always managed to pass the part of Kern County where the violent murder had occurred. Eventually he moved into a house in a semi-rural area not far from the murder. Clearly Hettinger felt, as many traumatized people do, that by going back to the scene of the crime that changed his life, he might somehow recover whatever he had lost.

Hettinger may have ended his career by committing petty thefts, but there was no attempted cover-up on his part. Hettinger did not try to spin, dissemble, conceal or rationalize his behavior. He was the ultimate stand-up guy, taking responsibility for the petty thievery that caused him to be fired. The internalized aggression that drove him was directed only against himself. For this reason Karl Hettinger didn't engage in what we could call evil behavior—the aggression he had internalized he directed exclusively against himself, as he drove himself to become the ultimate victim.

There is some evidence that he didn't talk in a therapeutic setting about his feelings about Campbell's murder until it was too late—and then, only after the police psychiatrists got into the game, Hettinger was already stuck emotionally, and the police shrinks were all operating according to a political logic having to do with departmental policies. Hettinger's treatment by LAPD brass was probably the most disabling thing—it was characterized in 2010 by crime writer Joseph Wambaugh as "not only wrongheaded, it was unforgivably ignorant and incredibly cruel."[7] Karl Hettinger, who died in 1994 at the early age of 59, must be considered one of the many unheralded casualties of that most trauma-prone profession, law enforcement.

7.

The tragic story of Karl Hettinger was documented by author Joseph Wambaugh in his book *The Onion Field*, which was later made into a movie. Wambaugh's work remains notable for several reasons. Wambaugh does not spend a great deal of time describing Karl Hettinger's helpless descent into criminality; but the book strongly suggests—as almost all of Wambaugh's work does—the traumatic power of violence and the way it attracts and influences those who are exposed to it. The attraction of crime for law enforcement professionals has become a favorite trope of novelists, filmmakers and TV producers, to the point of cliché and beyond—but the essential truth of it cannot be denied. It is an occupational hazard of law enforcement. Criminals and law enforcement operate on opposite sides of the same violent world, which paradoxically makes it easier for them to identify with each other. A similar paradox also characterizes the relationship of the victim to the aggressor. (We must remember that Hettinger, although a detective, was in the situation recounted above a victim.)

Ryan E. Melsky's "Identification with the Aggressor: How Crime Victims Often Cope with Trauma" is an attempt to deconstruct the Hettinger case and apply the findings to similar cases. In this segment from his paper, Melsky—a police officer himself—describes as a kind of step-by-step paradigm the unconscious identification with the criminal that victims of criminal violence may experience. The full paper appeared in the June 2004 issue of *The FBI Law Enforcement Bulletin*, as well as numerous websites dealing with trauma and law enforcement. The following is a quote dealing with situations like that experienced by Hettinger:

"By identifying with their aggressors, assuming their attributes, and imitating their aggression, crime victims cognitively transform themselves from the people threatened into those making the threat. This mental transformation allows the victim to achieve some feeling of strength in an otherwise humiliating situation. In short, when an aggressor sticks a gun in a person's face or kidnaps someone at knifepoint, often the victim's only chance for survival is to join the aggressor emotionally, as well as physically. Anything short of total cooperation likely will result in death."

"In addition to its cognitive utility, identification with the aggressor serves an important, external function. With this defense mechanism, victims make an intuitive prediction regarding their aggressors' reaction to the bond. Instinctively, victims know that as they appease their aggressors, their chances of survival increase. Aggressors assured that they are 'right' or whose controlling ideations are bolstered by the companionship of submissive victims will less likely dispose of the 'positive' reinforcement. In this way, the victim's identification has somewhat of a controlling effect on the aggressor. Intuitively, the victim has outsmarted the aggressor."

But whereas the victim has "outsmarted" the aggressor in the short term (and therefore survived physically), the psychological effects could haunt him for a long time. The identification may persist, even though it may be completely unknown to the victim consciously. Worse yet, the aggression internalized in these short but extremely violent encounters may result in ongoing personality changes which the victim has not chosen, and which may seem bewildering to everybody else.

The Melsky paper deals specifically with the Hettinger case, but also with the Patty Hearst kidnapping. Hearst's case, although extremely harrowing, had an outcome that was at least nominally happier.

Hearst, it will be remembered, was kidnapped by violent political extremists and sadistically abused over a significant period of time. She was locked up nude and blindfolded in a closet, sexually assaulted, and deprived of sleep and food by her kidnapers. (The people who kidnapped her were wannabe revolutionaries from Berkeley who called themselves the Symbionese Liberation Army.) They used guilt in tandem with violence, constantly threatening and insulting Hearst about her privileged background, while systematically subjecting her to assault and inhuman treatment.

After several months she was allowed to leave the closet and was treated with comparative—but highly calculated—kindness by her sociopathic captors. Is it any wonder that Hearst was brainwashed to the point where she joined their cult-like band and adopted their revolutionary rhetoric? Identification with the aggressor (and profound internalization of their aggression) was probably the only way Hearst could survive emotionally during the long periods she was locked in a closet, naked and hungry and dealing with the shame of being sexually assaulted. Clearly she imbibed huge amounts of their highly focused aggression, adopting the name 'Tania' and declaring herself a revolutionary.

Later, after most of the SLA members were arrested, killed, or on the run, Hearst was charged with a variety of criminal offenses (she participated in at least one armed robbery with SLA conspirators), and was convicted by a jury. The dynamics that resulted in Hearst's radical personality change were essentially the same as those described in this book as trauma bonding. The relativity between extreme coercion and personality transformation was not well-understood at the time of her trial, despite much information about North Korean and Chinese brainwashing during the Korean War. (The term 'Stockholm Syndrome' had been coined by psychiatrist Nils Bejerot just the year before Hearst's trial, but was even less well-understood at that time than brainwashing techniques.) Partly because of Hearst's notoriety, information about hostage trauma and personality transformation gradually began to percolate out into the society.

Eventually, Patty Hearst was pardoned and was allowed to leave prison, and in time was able to resume a more or less normal life. Still, it is hard to imagine that she was not permanently harmed by her incredible ordeal. From being a wealthy and rather laid-back student at UC Berkeley to taking on the personality (or persona) of the professional revolutionary 'Tania,' she eventually returned to being—what? Only she can answer that question. Ms. Hearst's family hired a bodyguard to look after her, and the fact that she eventually married her bodyguard is suggestive, although given the horrors she'd experienced quite understandable.

8.

The American political class understands the transformative nature of violence, partly because violence has been such a big part of the American nation-building experience, and is therefore a major part of how Americans understand themselves. Many politicians also understand it in terms of—and compared to—the way aggression affects peoples' attitudes and behavior. One fascinating example of this intuitive understanding is a saying that became wildly popular in politically conservative circles around 1970, remaining popular among conservatives over the next twenty years. The saying was, "*A conservative is a liberal who's just been mugged.*" Liberals retaliated immediately with, "*A liberal is a conservative who's just been indicted,*" referring to the transformation that occurs when conservatives are indicted for corruption, at which point they become intensely devoted to due process and civil liberties.

But the conservative mantra had more impact because it suggested the power of aggression to violently transform loyalties— to create trauma bonds, in other words. This had great meaning for conservatives because of their identification with aggression as an important part of the militaristic, patriarchal and hierarchical order they generally support, particularly those from the Midwest, Border States and South. For that reason, they were not interested in making the world less aggressive or deceitful, because in the conservative worldview aggression is one of the eternal verities, consisting of exactly those qualities that cannot be changed. Indeed, these things are to some extent necessary to the formation of the conservative character—a conservative man can achieve stature either by standing up to aggression, or using it decisively against enemies. In the political conservative worldview, one of the highest political actions is to successfully use state aggression against a state enemy. (This is one reason why conservatives were so upset when President Obama succeeded in killing Osama bin Laden, something his conservative predecessor Bush had not even dared to try.) The ability to use aggression is not always a bad thing, particularly when used defen- sively, or in a necessary military operation, but in a nuanced world it is increasingly limited in its possible deployment.

"A conservative is a liberal who's just been mugged." Conservatives liked this half-humorous formula so much because they intuitively understood the nature of aggression to bond people to a patriarchal worldview. This is partly because conservatives are more likely to believe in the existence of evil than liberals, although less likely to do anything about it when they encounter it. The average educated liberal, on the other hand, wouldn't dream of using the word 'evil,' at least not in public, because that word is regarded as old-fashioned and unnecessarily suggestive of religion. Conservatives believe in evil, to be sure, but almost invariably tend to get upset about evil in nations and cultures that are different from theirs. Nor is the conser- vative likely to admit that the weak and powerless are most at risk

from evil—and least of all is he able to see evil in himself.

"A conservative is a liberal who's just been mugged." Modern political conservatism in America in 2012 promotes an understanding of the world not just as flawed by aggression but as *defined* by it. The conservative believes that corporations and governments have to be and *ought* to be ruthless, and to a certain extent deceitful, because that is simply how the world works. The conservative wants to make the traumatized liberal see what the world *really* is—that is, essentially aggressive—and to understand, furthermore, that to use aggression to get what you want is admirable and powerful. In short, when the American political conservative talks about mugging a liberal, he identifies with the mugger's aggression. The capacity for power-as-aggression is the only thing that matters: it is the gold standard of the conservative philosophy, and the final arbiter of history. Aggression is the nuclear-grade fuel that *really* drives the world; and though you may not like it, the conservative and neo-conservative both think you'd better wise up and accept it. (You must accept it on their terms, of course, or those of their corporate sponsors.)

Of course, aggression and evil *do* rule our world, but the world can't go on much longer that way if we want to survive—we have both the irrational desire and the technology to destroy the world, so we need to change that. The liberal is right to see that aggression is getting out of hand, and that humankind needs to control it. Humankind is in its adolescence; and it is an adolescence that is painfully suggestive of the high-stakes drama, angst and emotional meltdowns typical of most adolescents—therefore it's simply common sense that we take the necessary steps to contain human aggression long enough that humankind can grow up. One way we can do this in the short term is by encouraging the classic virtue of restraint (which means not using force unless absolutely necessary), along with effective diplomacy. About this, the liberal is absolutely right.

But the political, theological and cultural liberal does not want to look closely at how aggression works, and feels queasily uncomfortable with the very word 'evil.' The conservative, on the other hand, sees violence and its traumatizing effects as inevitable, and frankly sees evil as useful because anybody he doesn't like can be accused of it. This same conservative accepts aggression not only as the supreme force in the affairs of men, but the successful deployment of it as the inevitable standard by which excellence in all things is measured. The liberal knows in his gut that aggression needs to be contained if humanity is to survive—but doesn't know how to do it in either the short or the long term, partly because he is uncomfortable with a systematic analysis of how aggression and evil are disseminated in society. This superficiality is something political liberalism needs to overcome if it is to continue to be taken seriously.

9.

As you might imagine, dictators are particularly adept at using trauma bonding, the mechanics of which they seem to understand intuitively. They use traumatizing violence, or threats of it, to transform ordinary people into compliant servants who will identify with the aggression necessary to maintain the dictatorship. Those who work for a dictatorship's security or military intelligence agencies must also be prepared and able to engage in aggression when called upon to do so by the state. This is frequently accomplished through some variant of trauma bonding, which is done to psychologically prepare the individual security apparatchiki for the torture, murder and other forms of state terrorism that they'll be required to use against their country's citizens.

One particularly chilling example of this process was the way in which Saddam Hussein introduced new hires into his security and intelligence services. Iraq suffered from a defect typical of one-party states: in such a state, the most ruthless person will eventually take control of the party, which then gives him the capability to control and manipulate the entire state apparatus. Saddam Hussein took control of the Ba'ath party, the only party allowed in Iraq, and consolidated his rule in the 1970s by slaughtering possible rivals and practicing the most disgusting kinds of state terrorism.

Sadly, he was soon receiving huge amounts of money from the American government, which has typically supported tyrants in the Middle East; and after Saddam invaded Iran the Americans gave extensive intelligence to Iraq (Donald Rumsfeld actually met with Saddam in Baghdad at least once for that purpose). Half a million people died in this totally unnecessary war between Iraq and Iran, which went on from 1980 to 1988. You may not know much about that brutal and costly war, because the American media almost never refers to it, but during it the US was supporting Saddam.

Saddam needed a vast security service to ensure the continued existence of his dictatorial rule; and it was credibly reported by multiple sources that new recruits to government service would often be systematically traumatized in the following way. First they would be escorted to a firing range, and deliberately prevented from knowing exactly what was going on — although some of the recruits may have had a queasy premonition about what was coming. The old employees that the new hires were replacing were then brought out, lined up, and summarily executed as their replacements watched. For purposes of expediency, Saddam also took films of government workers being executed and showed them to new employees. The intent was partly to warn the new security civil servants of the penalties of subversion — but also to traumatize them in order to bond them to the state terrorism they would be required to personally act out.

In a similar vein, Amnesty International has reported that often torturers in dictatorships are routinely tortured before being set loose to torture others. As we will see in a later chapter, the torture victim who enthusiastically and even fanatically advocates torture of others is a common and even predictable historical figure, perhaps the most well-known being Niccolo Machiavelli. He was brutally tortured just before writing *The Prince*, a book in which he repeatedly advocated torture; at the time he wrote his violent and melancholy classic he clearly still identified with the sadistic aggression of his torturer. (It is quite telling that he not only wrote a book justifying his torturer's methods, but also offered it to him as a gift.) It would be harder to find a better—or at least more notorious—example of a trauma-bonded victim of state aggression who then promoted organized aggression and deceit as a worldview (not to mention a lifestyle), afterwards developing a highly calibrated methodology for conducting public business through the strategic application of violence and systemic evil.

Criminal organizations, especially drug cartels in all countries, are well-known for subjecting new recruits to ritualized executions, as are criminal groups, prison gangs, and armed revolutionary organizations that use terrorism. In *Traffic*, a film about Mexican *narcotrafficantes* and North Americans addicted to their products, a Mexican narcotics officer is forced to watch his long-time partner and friend executed by higher-ups who control the drug trade and wish to recruit him into their criminal activities. Again, the purpose of forcing someone to observe a ritual murder is not merely to terrify them, but to transform them emotionally—in this case, to bond them through overwhelming trauma to a violent business system, and prepare them to kill others. By being forced to be complicit in the murder of a friend, the new cartel member is not only introduced emotionally into the total degradation of violence as a business, he also kills any association with other people based on affection, trust or freedom of choice (in fact, it could be said that he kills his membership in the human family); and he replaces it with associations defined solely by extreme, nonstop violence and deceit. This kind of association is likely to end in violent death.

In prison gangs, a recruit to a gang is often required to "make his bones"—that is, to kill an enemy of the gang while established gang members watch. Here the motivation may be somewhat complex because of the extremely high level of sociopathy in prisons.

Ritual murder might be required by a prison gang to see how competent the recruit is at killing; it may also be used to establish intimacy among gang members, or to enhance sexual feelings or repress them. But one main purpose in forcing the recruit to commit homicide while the gang watches is to establish a powerful emotional bond between the gang and its new member, and to bond him to a violent lifestyle.

Criminal gang members in state and federal prisons sometimes start killing simply for pleasure, in which case murder can lose its focused and somewhat ritualized bonding function and get out of hand. This is what happened to the Aryan Brotherhood, perhaps the most violent prison gang in US history. Federal agents arrested over a hundred of its leaders and most active members, arraigned them on conspiracy charges, and segregated them from the general prison population, virtually ending the AB—at least temporarily—as an important force in US prisons. According to former AB members, the Brotherhood was taken down because it was killing people indiscriminately, rather than for ritual purposes that could increase the gang's cohesion.

A similar theme was sounded in the excellent Mafia film *Goodfellas*, in which a New York crime family kills one of their own hit men for murdering people in ways that worked against the mob's solidarity. This suggests that perhaps sociopaths are not only harder to discipline within criminal organizations, but may also be somewhat inured to trauma bonding, the technique normally used for maintaining discipline in such organizations. Could this be because sociopaths are less likely to be traumatized by human aggression? This writer suspects that is the case, and if it is, it might be that the ability to be trauma-bonded is a mechanism that can only be triggered in people that are relatively normal, or start out that way. Sociopaths may not need trauma bonding to join a criminal gang because they're already dangerous; but neither are they particularly amenable to discipline enforced by shared violence. The recurrent problem of criminal organizations is that their most effective killers are also the least susceptible to discipline.

10.

The power of trauma to bond the human personality to aggression is so powerful that some people never leave it behind, and some have no desire to try. Working in residential programs as a counselor for deeply disturbed people over a twenty-five year period, I became oppressively aware that some clients identified so deeply with the trauma they'd suffered as children that their abuse narratives had *become their identity.* That is to say, some clients believed that the abuse they had endured was the most important or notable thing that had ever happened to them, or that ever *could* happen to them; and as a consequence they had built their personalities around their traumatic memories of abuse. Many of them had been sexually or physically abused; and these victims of childhood abuse tended to hang out together, swapping abuse narratives and competing to reveal horrifying and shocking details. Some of them had no desire to get over their traumatizing memories of abuse because they saw those experiences as central to their identities. They had made such a good adjustment to their mental disability that they had no reason to get better. For one thing, recovery would have caused them to lose all their friends, since identifying with their childhood traumas tended to bond them together as a group.

I had a client who had been raised in the foster home system and had an interesting identification with self-harm. He would invariably approach new counselors or relief staff by coming up to them and saying rather conversationally, "Hey, did you know that once I took a knife and *slashed my own throat??*" All the new staff got that treatment when they started out. This client was quite tall, and vaguely resembled Boris Karloff, and if you happened to be alone with him in the residential program at night when he delivered this verbal bombshell it could be quite unnerving. When I asked him why he did this, he replied simply, "I wanted them to hear it from me first, rather than reading about it in my case history." It was clear that he thought his suicide attempt was the most important thing he'd ever done, or one of the most important, and sadly he seemed to identify with it deeply. This was partly, one must understand, because he had little else in his life but his deformed personality, which made his heroic suicide attempt not merely his identity but in a sense his vocation. He believed that his one-time attempt to kill himself was so important, in fact, that he had to be the first to tell all the new counselors about it.

My client wasn't the only disturbed person who wanted to go back to the moments of maximum violence in his life. Here is an anecdote from an in-patient program for Vietnam Veterans that illustrates how one program dealt with this tendency. Almost all the patients in this program were hospitalized Vietnam Veterans suffering from Post-Traumatic Stress Disorder (PTSD) as a result of their experiences as soldiers in Vietnam; and this thoughtful and unusual program consisted of a rigorous two-week period of group therapy and peer-counseling. For the first week, they were encouraged to discuss nothing but Vietnam and all the things that had happened to them when they were in "the Nam." They relived it all, talking about everything they'd seen and experienced: the punji sticks, the ambushes, the jungle rot that wasted the feet, the lost buddies, the drugs, everything.

Things got very emotional during that first week of group therapy, as one might expect — there were tears, some really bad memories and a total emotional meltdown or two. That was the first week. But the second week was different. During the second week, there was a strict rule in this program that everybody in the group *was no longer allowed to talk about Vietnam*. For that second week, they were allowed only to discuss what they hoped to do in the future — what they wanted to be, what they wanted to do, and the ways they hoped to accomplish their goals.

The reason for that, as the program director pointed out, was to free the participating veterans from the tyranny of the past events, and to cause each participant in the program to send himself a message: that Vietnam was now in the past, and that he had his whole life ahead of him. They'd gone back to "the Nam" for an eventful and harrowing week, but once they got into the second week the rule about talking only of the future helped them leave Vietnam in the past. I imagine that it was extremely difficult for some of those veterans to stop talking and thinking about Vietnam; but for just that reason, this programmatic innovation was both simple and brilliant.

Again: victims of emotional trauma, delayed stress, or victims of PTSD have a powerful urge to go back to the place where they were traumatized, back to the site of the trauma itself. But the past events that traumatized them cannot tell them anything about their future, nor can they substitute for the moral choices and hard work involved in finding a way out of the *current* symptoms, especially feelings of aggression and fear. Of course, the victim of trauma must sometimes first allow the bad emotions to happen—the first time around the victim didn't have time to feel them completely, because he was too busy trying to survive. But once the person has revisited the past trauma and gotten to know the feelings associated with it, it becomes a matter of time until the trauma victim needs to move on, usually by making a decision to plan for the future. Only then can individuals imagine what their future might be, and invent—or reinvent—their role in life.

The key concept here is that past events no longer exist, even when our emotions tell us they do. Violent events in the past keep one bonded to the past, and to the aggression itself; the power of the past over emotions in the present moment has to be diminished systematically. Planning for the future—including verbal and written contracts with spouses, employers and others to observe certain rules or live up to certain basic expectations—can be a very important way to do this. A few people have to actually sit down and write contracts with their friends, lovers and bosses. It turns the mind away from the black hole of trauma and forces it to concentrate on the challenges ahead.

That was why participants weren't allowed to talk about Vietnam in the second week of the PTSD program for vets described above. The strict rule about talking only of the future was there in the hope that it would gradually become a habit with most of the veterans—that by talking about the future they would get into the habit of thinking about the possibilities available to them. They were sending themselves this powerful and unequivocal message that they were now moving forward to experience the future, while not spending so much time and energy experiencing the past emotionally. They might still have bad dreams about the past—who doesn't?—but their thoughts when they awake will hopefully consist more of what they can do with the present and future. This diminishes the power of past trauma, and makes the residual anxiety manageable.

II.

One of the most striking recent depictions in popular culture of the power of trauma bonding was the 1999 cult film *Fight Club*. It was also, among other things, an extremely clever exploration of the violence inherent in patriarchy, an exploration that gained much verisimilitude from the fact that instead of casting actors that were beery, aging losers, it featured men that were young, hip and attractive. Based on the novel of the same name by writer Chuck Palahniuk, it tells a story about young males who deliberately engage in traumatizing violence in order to bond themselves to each other in an especially intense way. They do this by finding abandoned houses where they can meet in the basement and fight each other with bare fists, under the tutelage of the charismatic organizer Tyler Durden.

The young men who fight each other mainly have no fathers, and the resultant bonding becomes compensation for a haunting sense of father-loss. The other reason, which is not apparent until late in the film, is to create recruits for an underground urban army that can bomb credit card companies where they store digital information on their consumers. The script (written by Jim Uhls and David Fincher) is extremely vivid and imaginative, taking the viewer almost immediately into an alternative universe where characters communicate in half-articulated youth idioms and profane inside jokes. The spirit and ideas of Chuck Palahniuk, the author of the novel *Fight Club*, permeates not only the script but everything in the project. As has been widely reported, Palahniuk's life has been marked by violence and gruesome tragedies, typical of which was the fact that his father and his father's girlfriend were murdered by an ex-convict, who then burned their house down. A publishing house once turned down one of Palahniuk's books because it was "too disturbing"; Palahniuk set out to "punish" the publishing house by writing an even creepier book, which became *Fight Club*. (To Palahniuk's chagrin it was accepted and published.)

His public appearances have become the occasion of new kind of performance art centered around the theme of violence—or rather, the effect of violence on human sensibilities and memory. When Palahniuk gave a public reading of short fiction in 2003, one story entitled "Guts," a tale of accidents involving masturbation, was so shocking that 35 people fainted. (A Wikipedia entry claims that a later reading of the same story "brought the number of fainters up to 53, and later to 60," although at some point after 9/11 Palahniuk had promised to stop writing exclusively about violence.) The public fainting was clearly a prank organized by Palahniuk and some friends and followers; but for those not yet in on the joke it could be almost as shocking as Palahniuk's over-the-top, mind-boggling stories.

The movie of *Fight Club* tells the story of a young unnamed narrator (played by Edward Norton) who meets a strange young man on a plane. The glib and charismatic stranger invites the narrator into a world where young men meet and fight in the basements of abandoned houses. But they don't observe the rules of Queensbury, as do trained boxers; they fight using their bare knuckles, and seek to harm each other—to beat each other up, in other words. At the same time, these groups of young men who fight each other in this way feel a quickening thrill of group bonding or belonging, creating enough emotional warmth to offset the physical harm they do to each other. The experience of young men beating each other up in front of other young males creates a trauma bond that solidifies the entire group, in a thoroughly dreamlike and disturbing way.

The excitement of this bonding process is enhanced by the frequent exhortations of the organizer Tyler Durden (played by Brad Pitt) that the Fight Club, as they call themselves, must be kept secret. ("There are only two rules," says Durden. "The first rule is, don't talk about Fight Club—the second rule is, don't talk about Fight Club.") If the young combatants encounter each other on the street or at work, they must not reveal where they meet or even that they know each other. The implication is that the bonding process would be weakened if participants talked about what they are experiencing and feeling. (This fits perfectly with the clinical observation that talking about trauma weakens its post-traumatic effects on the personality, thus weakening the trauma bond.)

There are two intriguing subplots that further explicate the world of losers and winners in American society, illuminating the twin theme of victimology and consumerism as addictions. The Brad Pitt character sneaks into medical salons that do liposuction, and steals the suctioned-out body fat to make soap. Meanwhile, the still-unnamed narrator becomes addicted to 12-step style self-help groups, where he gains acceptance by pretending to be a victim of various afflictions. Both characters develop a relationship with a beautiful young woman (Helena Bonham Carter) who seems to see the two young men as interchangeable.

The underground army, using the existing Fight Clubs as recruiting stations, begins to take shape; and its leader Durden begins to make preliminary plans for a violent revolution. But before it can launch its revolutionary activities, the young protagonist makes a breathtaking discovery about the organizer of the Fight Clubs, Tyler Durden. It is suddenly revealed that the glib and persuasive Tyler has an unsuspected, shocking relationship to the narrator—and this is revealed, typically, via a violent, life-threatening confrontation, which supplies the resolution of the film. Ed Norton's unnamed Narrator still seeks a sense of authenticity, but instead of engaging in Tyler Durden's bare-fisted melees, he must now seek his identity through insights into his own personality. The irony, however, is that as a direct result of his relationship to Durden his growing self-awareness will now include, besides increased respect for risk-taking, some new and sobering insights into his own addiction to aggression as the measure of intimacy and psychological authenticity.

Certain college fraternities are adept at using trauma bonding in a way that I experience as remarkably — and disgustingly — similar to the cinematic Fight Club scenario. Young men (and even young women) apply to fashionable fraternities and sororities: if they are accepted, they must go through an initiation ritual. Depending on the fraternity, these violent rituals — usually called "hazing" — are sometimes little more than exercises in sadism, and are not infrequently life-threatening. It's the Fight Club all over again, albeit the upper-middle class version. Young pledges (that is, new members of fraternities with their entire lives ahead of them) allow themselves to be ritually tortured; and are then emotionally bonded to the young men that have mentally and physically tormented them. It's pathological, by any standard, but fraternity members in colleges can't see how dangerous and idiotic their behavior is, because everybody else is doing it.

Why do young males in college fraternities haze pledges? The answer is almost always the same — because they were hazed themselves. They were humiliated, tormented and abused, and feel a compulsion to do the same to other young men. The fanatical energy with which some fraternity members defend the hazing system is truly astonishing ("I went through it, so it's *only fair* that new members go through it too"). One might say that at least the young males involved have the insight to connect their compulsion to brutalize pledges with their own brutalization in the past. But since their judgment has been compromised by violence, alcohol and rampant immaturity, they cannot see that what they are doing is dangerous and wholly contemptible. (At least one student a year in the US has died of hazing for the last thirty years.) In fraternity hazing, as in so many other instances, trauma bonding is simply one variant of what we often call male bonding.

We must realize that such rituals not only bond victims to the people who administer the violence, but also initiate young men into an unconscious conviction that life's most intense experiences are violent transactions in which the strong are supposed to bully the weak. It may be for just that reason that the pledge seeks out the hazing: to become more aggressive, less vulnerable, more violent, more like the John Wayne male that he mistakenly confuses with emotional maturity. So he allows himself to be tormented by other young men who are as stupid as he is, until he either dies, or bonds with the other males in order to become lifelong friends with them, or "brothers." I suggest that any relationship that begins with ritualized torture has nothing to do with friendship, or even the vaguest and most metaphorical kind of brotherhood; instead it has everything to do with pathological identification with an aggressor, not to mention a sadomasochistic adjustment to the violent, bullying worldview that one typically finds in college fraternities.

College administrations periodically crack down on hazing in fraternities, but it always comes back. Young people on their own cannot get rid of hazing, because they unconsciously seek shortcuts to maturity—and they have learned from a variety of cultural sources that aggression is the passport to manhood. This could change, if their elders took the time and effort, and had the courage, to teach them otherwise. But far too many college administrators take an avuncular, do-nothing posture toward fraternity hazing, clucking among themselves about the outrages of young men but essentially identifying with them.

One example of how dangerous fraternity hazing can be is the following incident—a relatively recent one—at Chico State College. Part of the state college system in northern California, it has often been popularly classified (or dismissed) by many young people as a "party school." In February of 2005, incoming freshman Matthew Carrington and another pledge were subjected to severe, brutal hazing by fraternity members at the Chi Tau fraternity, where Matthew was a pledge (new member). Chi Tau fraternity had, to be sure, long been identified as a rogue group, but was still allowed to exist by the college administration, despite the fact that everybody on campus was perfectly well aware that it subjected its pledges to extremely violent hazing. Gabriel Maestretti, one of the fraternity members, had recently acquired a reputation as a "tormenter" and a "mean drunk." He was the one who was mainly in charge of the hazing of Matt Carrington, which occurred in the basement during the fraternity's "Hell Week."

A detective who later examined the crime scene said the basement was set up "kind of like [a] medieval castle dungeon," dark, dirty and very cold. Scribbled on the wall were the words: "In the basement, no one can hear you scream." Matt Carrington and another pledge were ordered to do calisthenics in raw sewage. They were interrogated and taunted. They were made to answer trivia quizzes and do pushups. All the time they were forced to drink water from a five-gallon jug, which was repeatedly filled. The hazing didn't stop even when the pledges urinated and vomited on themselves.

Finally Carrington collapsed and started having seizures—but still the fraternity members didn't call an ambulance or take him to a hospital, or in any way seek medical assistance. Finally an ambulance was called, and Matt was taken to Enloe Medical Center. At about 5 AM, Carrington was pronounced dead from water intoxication, which can cause swelling of the brain and heart. (Specifically, it is likely to cause cardiac arrest, which is what happened in this case.) Not a single fraternity "brother" was there when he died: the hospital did not even tell the parents how he died until hours later.

Again: why hasn't hazing been stopped?

Again: because college administrators will not do what is

necessary to get rid of it, often because they are bonded to the ugly practice by their own traumatic experiences. Hazing should be made a felony offense by state law (not a misdemeanor, as it is now). Fraternity members should be required to sign legally-binding contracts not to participate in hazing, and if they do they should be criminally prosecuted. Reports or rumors of hazing incidents should be immediately referred to the District Attorney; and fraternities whose members are caught hazing should be closed down for good.

These are reasonable requests, and they could be realized if administrators really wanted them to happen. But college administrators intuitively understand the psychological intent of hazing, and consciously or unconsciously believe that it builds "character" — that is to say, they believe that it's a viable method for making young people (and young males in particular) aware of the fact that the world is ruled, and ought to be ruled, by an aggressive patriarchal alliance of the strong against the weak. These same college administrators may have been hazed themselves, and may feel that it is "only fair" that others following in their footsteps undergo the same noxious treatment, no matter how juvenile and dangerous the bullying involved. *What hazing is really about is teaching young men that aggression is the most dynamic and important factor in human relationships.* The trauma bond, like emotional trauma itself, is frequently multigenerational. It is multigenerational because it is one of the main instruments by which older males teach younger males about the violence inherent in patriarchy, causing them to internalize its aggression first as victims, and then act it out as aggressors.

12.

The most common example of young men internalizing a more or less patriarchal worldview through trauma bonding is the one that's been around the longest, and is probably the most familiar to Americans, especially young people making a decision about the military. Because it is so familiar, it is more or less invisible — we accept it without thinking about it. I refer to basic training in the various military establishments, the four months of intensive physical stress, verbal abuse and mental indoctrination that recruits are subjected to after enlistment in the armed services, preceding assignment to a duty station. Most people have an idea what this is like, because basic training was at one time a staple of American films as a coming-of-age theme, probably because of the essentially cinematic (that is, endlessly violent and threatening) nature of the abuse meted out to recruits. Most of these films were made in the 1940s and 1950s, and were once quite popular as TV fare, although not so much nowadays. Almost all of the films tended to follow the same plot formula.

A bunch of ordinary guys from diverse walks of life sign up in the military (probably the army), and come together at an army base. They stand around awkwardly, waiting. Out of nowhere strides a fearsome man with a shaved head who starts yelling at them, standing in front of them and generally yelling into their faces; what he is yelling consists mainly of personal insults questioning the manhood of the recruit. This is the Drill Instructor. As he yells insults at the recruits he begins to teach them how to drill (that is, how to march and hold their weapons). What unfolds over the following months could be called a kind of personal terrorism. His method for teaching is based almost completely on screaming obscenities at the young people, along with making threats and threatening gestures. That is, over a period of four months the Drill Instructor will try to tear down the personalities of the young people under his command, divesting them of whatever identity or self-esteem they had built up before they fell into his clutches.

For four months the young person will receive insufficient sleep, mediocre food high in starch, and will be mercilessly indoctrinated in various methods of group killing. He will also be taught that the only thing he can really trust is his weapon, which he will be taught to lovingly assemble and reassemble in a highly ritualistic and worshipful way. (This will be accompanied by chants, doggerel and songs that constitute a kind of obscene and gruesome liturgy.) At some point he may be given some indoctrination concerning the enemy that he is to slaughter; the indoctrination will be laughably simplistic, based on the idea that the soldier must kill the enemy, and that the enemy is selected by the state. The entire process of daily training, both in reality and in the movies, is founded on the idea (usually implied rather than stated outright) that there is something noble and sublime about the military life, that it delivers a kind of transcendent satisfaction obtainable in no other way. One can see that being able to override fear is a big part of the basic training of American soldiers, airmen and sailors—but there's more to it than physical courage. It has until very recently been constantly suggested, in the popular movies that included it as a foundational trope in coming-of-age themes, that there is especially something transformational and empowering in the harshness and violence in basic training. Films that include sequences about basic training depend heavily on deeply-felt but often unconscious emotions, especially among men, about patriarchy and the role of the warrior.

What is the purpose of the military in conducting basic training?

To use the recurring trauma of the threatening Drill Instructor to bond the young men to an aggressive way of life that can render them mindless, robotic warriors. Trauma bonding is used to bond the recruits to each other, but also to a larger entity of which one's buddies are simply one expression. At first the recruit will be bonded to the omnipresent, shouting drill sergeant. The drill sergeant will then teach them to transfer that same mindless, sleep-walking compliance toward all noncommissioned and commissioned officers; then to the military organization itself; and finally to the world of force and violence in which wars are fought. The soldier is taught to trust only his weapon and his closest buddies. The young recruit enters the military base a clueless teenager, and leaves a trained killer, all accomplished by creating a traumatizing environment soon after the recruit's arrival at the base, and maintaining that traumatizing environment more or less constantly for the next four months. Throughout this time the young recruit will continue to suffer from substandard food in small but starchy portions, sleep deprivation, and the constant presence of insulting, terrifying individuals who completely control the environment and spend all their time screaming at the recruit and telling them how worthless he is.

One of the things the Drill Instructor continually shouts is that the recruit's mother no longer exists. "You think you can run home to your mama! Well, *I'm* your mama now, I'm the only one you can turn to! *I'm* the one you have to please if you want to live through this thing! When I say jump three feet in the air, you jump three feet, and if you don't, you're dead meat!" etc, etc. Of course, the actual execution of these tirades is suffused with profanity, but the reader will get the idea. During the long, repetitive tirades of the Drill Instructor, the recruit must stand rigidly at attention. All stimuli are reduced or eliminated so that all the recruit can hear is the voice of the drill sergeant.

This goes on for four months.

If this were a cult, we would instantly understand how trauma bonding is being used to create instant, unthinking obedience to a patriarchal cult leader. But because this scenario describes basic training in an American military organization, we tend to think of it necessary, and therefore acceptable. And perhaps it would be—if the ability to defeat or dominate other nations militarily was the only standard for a nation's success.

But how can a recruit know whether a particular war is justifiable or not? He is too young to have any real sense of how the world works; and anyway, one of the purposes of basic training is to remove moral judgment—or any judgment whatsoever—and replace it with instant, unthinking obedience. The young recruit leaves basic training a highly disciplined killing machine, but without the life experience or judgment necessary to know when lethal force is justified and when it isn't. So if his commanding officer says that under certain circumstances torture is necessary, he will prepare himself to do it; but of course it probably won't be the officer who'll do eight to ten years at Leavenworth military prison if he's caught. It's the erstwhile recruit who will do the time.

Yes, it will indeed be the young soldier who is likely to pull the hard time, the youngster who had his personality permanently altered by a screaming Drill Instructor who told him on several thousand different occasions that he was a maggot, then put a rifle in his hand and sent him to a Iraq to kill Arabic-speaking people, which in his state of cultural deprivation he will imagine to be collectively guilty for everything that has gone wrong in the world, starting with but not ending on September 11, 2001.

In the movies of the 1940s and 1950s, the film narrative would follow the young recruits from basic training into battle, where it would be revealed that the Drill Instructor had been right all along. He had only been trying to protect the young men by making them effective killing machines, and we would see all the ways in which the Drill Instructors machinations have been proven correct. That was the basic training trope in 1940s and 1950s war movies. However, beginning in the 1960s American movies began to portray basic training, and the personality-altering trauma associated with it, in a far different and more critical light.

13.

In *Full Metal Jacket*, Stanley Kubrick's extremely disturbing but brilliant 1987 film, a group of young men in basic training in 1967 are verbally assaulted by a terrifying Drill Instructor named Gunnery Sergeant Hartman, who keeps up a stream of invective for days and weeks on end. The recruits have nowhere to go, nowhere to hide. So far, this looks like a war movie of the 1950s, a kind of coming-of-age film in which the recruits will end up surviving the basic training and performing heroically on the battlefield. But there's a difference: the racial invective and various manipulations of the drill sergeant are abusive in a way that probably wouldn't have gotten into a 1950s film.

Here is fair example of Gunnery Sergeant Hartman motivating recruits:

> If you ladies leave my island, if you survive recruit training, you will be a weapon. You will be a minister of death praying for war. But until that day you are pukes. You are the lowest form of life on Earth. You are not even human, fucking beings. You are nothing but unorganized grabastic pieces of amphibian shit! You will not like me. But the more you hate me the more you will learn. I am hard but I am fair. There is no racial bigotry here. I do not look down on niggers, kikes, wops or greasers. Here you are all equally worthless. And my orders are to weed out all non-hackers who do not pack the gear to serve in my beloved Corps. *Do you maggots understand that??*

At a certain point the emphasis of Kubrick's film begins to shift. We see that some people in the unit are beginning to crack under the strain. There can be little doubt in the viewer's mind that the intent of the training is to violently traumatize the recruits, to completely strip them of self-esteem, decency, or impulse control, in order to bring them into the combat-ready world of kill-or-be-killed Vietnam. The very title *Full Metal Jacket* has a double meaning: it refers to the army-issue bullets used by riflemen, with a soft core and hard metal casing; but it also refers to the kind of emotional armoring that is necessary to survive basic training, and ultimately combat.

One of the young men, sarcastically named Gomer Pyle by Hartman, is struggling to make it. Hartman manipulates the men into "punishing" (that is, collectively beating) him at night. Afterwards Pyle seems to shape up, although his buddy Joker sees signs that something is going wrong with him. Finally Pyle has a psychotic break and loads his rifle with live ammunition. When Sergeant Hartman intervenes, Pyle murders him in the latrine and commits suicide.

This is, needless to say, a considerable divergence from war films of the past, signaling the failure rather than the success of basic training—there's no doubt that the murder is a direct result of the drill sergeant's aggression, or at the very least the result of a mental state caused by that aggression. The underlying message of *Full Metal Jacket*, at least the first half of the film, is that society assumes a considerable risk in basic training as it is executed today. On the one hand, the military hopes to use the traumatizing pressures of basic training to break down a young man's personality and recreate that young person as a disciplined soldier. At the same time, the military wants also to use this trauma bonding process to instill reflexive combat techniques to kill an enemy, causing the recruit to internalize the necessary amount of aggression to kill on command. This internalized aggression is symbolized by the "Rifleman's Creed," which is chanted by recruits as a ritualized prayer to the power of their rifles.

You can call this an extreme form of conditioning if you wish, but it does without question also use techniques that are likely to traumatize, at least enough that the recruit will internalize enough aggression to kill an enemy. Again, people do not want to see that, because military service—and basic training—are such a familiar part of modern American life. In any case, the recruit is assumed to have the ability to make good decisions about when to kill, and when not to kill. Unfortunately, the disorientation associated with emotional trauma and the way it causes the recruit to identify with aggression are likely to interfere with the recruit's ability to do anything reasonably—not to mention his emotional immaturity and relative lack of life experience. And because he has been bonded to aggression he may act compulsively in violent ways without being able to draw on psychological restraints that have been stripped from his personality. Thus the highly efficient killing machine created by today's form of basic training is likely to fly out of control, in which case he may kill the wrong people, particularly if the pressures of training become intolerable to him.

The 2005 movie *Jarhead* tells a variant on the story told in *Full*

Metal Jacket, this time in the US Marines. The intensity of basic training is once again explored, again with an unexpected consequence: the Marines who are subjected to unthinkable abuse absorb so much aggression that they are not only prepared to kill, they feel like they *have* to kill, even if there are no enemies available. They are deployed to serve in the 1990 Gulf War, but are given no combat assignments, because the war is over too quickly. The protagonist is so devastated by this early end of the war that he begs his tent-mate to kill him—but when the tent-mate refuses, the protagonist has a mental breakdown. This film is dealing with the risks incurred by basic training, but makes the point in a different way than *Full Metal Jacket*: if the basic training is sufficiently traumatizing and violent, yet at the same time there are no enemy soldiers for the recruits to kill, the recruits may commit suicide or be driven mad.

Both films imply, as do even the modern coming-of-age war films, that although basic training is clearly traumatizing, it happens as the result of an unspoken but implicit social contract between violent young males and the patriarchal military organizations they join. The young recruits submit to basic training because they believe it will make them strong and courageous men, and hope the Drill Instructor can beat that into them—and indeed, the identification with the Drill Instructor's world, and the resulting internalization of his aggression, is what basic training is all about. It is because of this unspoken but implicit social contract that young men do not become more traumatized than they do. But these films also suggest that something in that aspect of the patriarchal social contract is breaking down, and that it is less workable now than it once was. The young American men in *Jarhead* are so full of aggression after basic training that when they reach Iraq to serve in the Gulf War they would rather die than contemplate life without first killing someone. The huge disconnect between the aggression the young Marines internalized in basic training and their inability to discharge it against live enemies has a profoundly disorienting effect on the entire group. The recruits originally signed up in the Marines with full knowledge of the violence of basic training, but believed it was an American rite of passage, and felt it would somehow jumpstart them into manhood, as they understood it; but in the end some of them are left wondering what the whole experience was all about, and why they'd gotten involved in the first place.

We should be grateful for such films as *Full Metal Jacket* and *Jarhead*, but I think they've examined only the most immediate and perhaps sensationally cinematic tip of the iceberg. When young men and women are subjected to the four-month pressure cooker of basic training, they aren't just internalizing aggression that can easily get out of control. They're also internalizing a worldview experienced as an emotional orientation. They're internalizing huge amounts of aggression, aided by the two cultural factors that are most harmful in the world today—patriarchy and nationalism.

Internalized *aggression* is harmful—as this book tries to make clear—because of the unacceptable criminal acts it is likely to generate, especially when the aggressor unconsciously believes aggression to be the standard by which everything else is judged. Aggressors also have a built-in incentive to lie in order to cover up their aggression, which transforms their aggression into a species of evil. *Patriarchy* is harmful not just because it teaches that men should dominate women, but also that the strong should dominate anyone they believe to be weaker than they are; patriarchy also idealizes organized violence as being transformative and redemptive. *Nationalism*, for its part, is extremely dangerous because it is a kind of mass narcissism, usually driven by low self-esteem and cultural illiteracy. Whereas patriotism is positive because it excites love of country, nationalism is driven by a morbid desire to impose one's own country on other countries, and kill or punish all who disobey.

These three emotional orientations—aggression, patriarchy and nationalism—are force-fed to the young recruit during basic training as the life-blood of the new man to be created out of whatever is left of his original personality. The three emotional orientations mentioned above are easy for males to assimilate, but hard to identify and get rid of once they are internalized, because they engage the total personality in a way that is hard for individuals so affected to grasp, particularly if the individuals are young.

Can females internalize patriarchy? Indeed—the most successful women in the military are often acting out something very close to pure patriarchy. How could they possibly succeed in the boys' club of military life without internalizing those emotional orientations that motivate the males? The young people (male *and* female) whose lives are so radically changed by the tumult of basic training in American military organizations are unconsciously internalizing dangerous and destructive emotional orientations, along with ideas that haven't really made sense for a century or two: many of those ideas are morally wrong, and some are downright evil, because they seek to conceal the harm they do. This is the real tragedy of basic training in the American military establishment; not just that it breaks the human personality through the most traumatizing kind of coercive conditioning, but that it remakes that personality according to a destructive warrior ethos. (Think of the hundred thousand dead, both American and Iraqi, because of George Bush's unnecessary invasion of Iraq.)

Basic training is used to create or sustain an ultraconservative worldview in American society. It also creates a subset of mainly young men who will unquestioningly serve the corporate upper class and its highly paid satraps in the political class, people whose values are increasingly corrupt, self-serving, and authoritarian. To be sure, many young men will shrug off the emotional effects of basic training, but the least educated ones with the lowest self-esteem are likely to swallow it whole. They create an ongoing demographic of people who are fundamentally anti-democratic, because they identify instinctively with aggression as the best way to organize society.

To consider the problems this creates for civil society, let's go back to the themes considered in the films mentioned above. Could a person who responds to the pressures of basic training by committing a crime argue temporary insanity as a legal defense? No doubt the rigors of basic training *could* result in psychosis—or at least psychotic behavior—and it is probably only because today's recruits are volunteers that it doesn't happen more. But military courts-martial are unlikely to accommodate an insanity defense under any circumstances, because that would acknowledge in a court of law that basic training can produce a state of mind in which some people are unable to tell the difference between right and wrong. (That is precisely the argument of *Full Metal Jacket*.) In fact basic training *does* create a state of mind in which young and inexperienced people often *can't* tell the difference between right and wrong; and in addition some are likely to become so disoriented that they can't control their aggressive behavior even in the short term.

The most dangerous thing about basic training is that it uses emotional trauma to bond young people to patriarchal, nationalist and aggressive emotional orientations. Because they are assimilated unconsciously, the rational, conscious mind is to some extent unaware of these orientations or even how they got there; but these intense emotions, or remnants of them, are likely in many cases to last a lifetime. Young people who act out those tendencies consistently are likely to consciously or unconsciously oppose the best interests and values of American democracy. The flexibility, humor and cultural literacy necessary to the successful navigation of American society are not only absent in the basic training of the US military, but are actively denigrated. What young people need is not to be trained to kill and die on command, but to learn how to negotiate in good faith, to make intelligent compromises that do not outrage common sense, and to reach win-win solutions in human conflicts in ways that encourage their own emotional growth as well as the growth of healthy democratic institutions.

14.

If there were any doubts that trauma bonding can be used on a mass basis by corrupt governments, the example of Slobodan Milosevic and his manipulation of past Serbian trauma would quickly dispel them. Milosevic was the President of Yugoslavia and Serbia during the breakup of Yugoslavia in the late 1980s, and in the 1990s the instigator of genocide against the Bosnian Muslims. The Bosnian genocide was a direct outcome of Milosevic's extraordinary use of past Serbian memories of persecution, including Nazi genocide against Serbs, to prepare his Serbian nationalist militias—and Bosnian Serbs as a group—to commit genocide against Bosnia's mainly unsuspecting Muslims.

Milosevic's constant reiteration of past traumas was extremely effective because tragedy and aggression against Serbs has been such a big part of their history. It is part of the national lore passed on by Serbian parents to their children—in fact, it is not too much to say that most Serbian history is the history of their exploitation by larger nations. Furthermore, there were in Milosevic's time many Serbs alive who had themselves been traumatized by Nazi atrocities against Serbs. In his speeches Milosevic referred endlessly to various past traumas of the Serbs, not because he was intent on giving his people a history lesson, but because he wanted to keep past trauma—and the volatile feelings associated with the traumatizing violence of the past—alive in the present moment, in order to commit new crimes of his own.

Rather than talk about his plans for the future, and what he was doing in the present, Milosevic and his state media spent hours every day talking about how Serbs had always been victimized by the rest of the world. According to him and his nationalist apparatchiki, the entire world had always conspired against the Serbs, and compulsively lied about them at every opportunity; even greater horrors awaited the Serbian nation in the future, he warned. Milosevic was himself no stranger to violence and emotional trauma, which is probably why he was so good at communicating the feelings associated with it. (Both Milosevic's parents had committed suicide, and he had himself given the kill order to have his best friend and political mentor killed.)

Milosevic, like a great many other murderous demagogues,

seemed intuitively aware of the dynamics of emotional trauma, and the way they can be used to create mass aggression. In particular he understood that people who identify with victim status often respond with charismatic fervor to a strong leader who gives them permission to act out their aggression. Milosevic had an almost diabolical insight into victim status, since he made a fetish of it in his speeches; and he invariably topped off his references to victimization of Serbs by not-so-subtly suggesting that it was time for Serbs to start fighting back. No modern leader except Benjamin Netanyahu, the Israeli Prime Minister, has been so adept at keeping past trauma alive in the minds of the masses. Milosevic promised catharsis to Serbs by encouraging them to act out their internalized aggression toward a world that had always hated them.

Milosevic constantly implied in his speeches that relief for victimized Serbs could only come if they turned to violence to punish their real or imagined enemies. This resonated because victim status had long been, in fact, the core element not just of Serbian nationalism, but of Serbian identity. To be a Serb meant to be an eternal victim of the world's inexplicable hatred, to be part of a plucky little nation that would forever keep fighting its enemies and which no country could defeat completely.

The history of the Serbs had been determined by the instability brought on by their small numbers, and the fact that they were separated into many small enclaves in various Balkan nations. Furthermore, there was deeply imbedded in Serbian consciousness a profound warrior tradition; Serbs were, because of Europe's shifting alliances, at one time or another at war with just about every nation or empire in Europe. Their woes began with a long struggle to free themselves under the Byzantine Empire, an independence that was finally achieved in the ninth century by Stefan, the first king. (Since Stefan's brother was the first head of the Serbian Orthodox Church, religion and the warrior ethos were inevitably commingled in the collective imagination of the Serbs from that time on. Serbian nationalism was therefore to a great extent always religious nationalism.) But it was the decisive defeat by the Ottoman Empire at the Battle of Kosovo in 1389 that really kicked off the mythology of the Serbs as a martyr nation. Under the Ottomans, the Serbs were a "protected people," but nationalist dreams of autonomy persisted.

At the beginning of the 19th century there was a Serbian uprising, then a second, which resulted in the Ottoman recognition of a part of Serbia as an autonomous principality. The Austro-Hungarian Empire gave special status to the remaining Serbs as frontier guards on the southern frontier of Hapsburg influence, but that was not enough to permanently stave off agitation against the Hapsburgs. As always, the problem was that the Serbs were scattered in many regions, with some under the Ottomans and some under the Hapsburgs. It was at this time that the nationalist idea of a Greater Serbia began to take shape in the 1840s. It was an extremely violent and apocalyptic—and I would add racist—idea from the very beginning.

Because Serbs were scattered among Croats, Bosniaks, Albanians, Bulgarians, Hungarians and Slovenes, the proponents of what later became known as Greater Serbia vowed that the only way out of their perceived dilemma was for Serbian enclaves to rise up and pull successive areas dominated by them into some kind of confederation ruled by a central Serbian government. But none of the other ethnic groups were willing to abandon their homes and farms simply so that insecure Serbs could create their own nation. The concept of Greater Serbia completely refused to take into account the wishes of everybody else living in their immediate neighborhood, including Muslims, because Serbian nationalists taught that the greater suffering of the Serbs gave them the right to displace others. Nor did it take into account the fact that the enclaves were so scattered that they could never be wielded into a single nation without some kind of violent campaign against civilians living in and around the enclaves, which clearly meant some ethnic cleansing of everybody who wasn't Serbian; and probably also a system of systematic repression and war after Greater Serbia was established.

Thus the concept of Greater Serbia was an extreme, violent idea from the beginning. For this reason, and because any attempt to act it out would result in death and disruption for millions, the Austro-Hungarian leaders made open discussion of the Greater Serbia concept illegal throughout much of the 19th century. Clearly, the Serb obsession with victim status played a central role in the Greater Serbia idea—it was predicated on the idea that Serbs would always be persecuted if they did not violently create a larger and more powerful country. It was because they felt themselves to be eternal victims that they were able to rationalize the idea of victimizing others, those who unfortunately didn't have the right religion or ethnicity, in order to set up a mono-cultural Serbia. Of course, this was sheer toxic fantasy: nobody was preparing to attack Serbia, and in fact Serbs in Bosnia faced no dangers. In Bosnia, the central government in Sarajevo advocated the rational modern alternative to nationalism, which was that Serbs in Bosnia were free to live as one group among many, with the same guaranteed rights as everybody else. That way would have lead to the peace and security the Serbs had always wanted.

But the Serbs did not see that, because their behavior was not determined by realistic assessments of fact, but by a burning, inchoate desire to engage in aggression. The trauma of the past, manipulated by Milosevic and other Serbian nationalists, had bonded them to the profoundly violent conviction that if they did not displace and harm others in order to control more territory, they would be slaughtered.

The Serb experience in the 20th century created the pre-conditions that led to the genocidal frenzy of the Serbian militias in Bosnia during the 1990s, as well as the total unwillingness of Serbs in Belgrade to accept the truth of what Serbs were doing. Before World War One there was one of many Serb uprising against the Hapsburgs in 1912, which predictably failed; but the bitterness from that failure led to the assassination of Duke Ferdinand by a Serbian nationalist in 1914, kicking off World War One. During the First

World War the Serbs fought heroically, but according to some calcu-lations lost up to half their population. This devastating and traumatic experience solidified the belief in Serbia as a martyr nation that would have to fight alone no matter what everybody else said or did.

The events of the Second World War strengthened the Serbian identification with victim status, since systematic genocide was practiced against Serbs by the fascist Ustasha regime of the Independent State of Croatia. (Along with Hungarian and Albanian fascists who were also allies of the Nazis.) If that weren't enough, the Chetniks—Serbian nationalists of royalist inclinations—also on occasion helped the Nazis massacre Serbs. A deliberate policy of genocide against Serbs culminated at the Jasenovac concentration camp, in which some 50,000 Serbs were murdered, along with up to 20,000 Jews, and between 5,000 and 12,000 Croat dissenters, both Catholic and Muslim. (There were probably more Serbs murdered in other camps as well, although at this date it is still much disputed about exactly how many.) It is said that on the night of August 29, 1942, a single guard named Petar Brzica at Jasenovac cut the throats of 1,360 Serb inmates. To say that these events were traumatic for the Serbs would be an understatement. As a result of all this trauma experienced by Serbs, Serbian nationalists developed tendencies that were not only fanatical and reckless—the assassination of Duke Ferdinand had already demonstrated that—but deeply enamored of the violent strategy associated with the dream of Greater Serbia. Thus the post-World War II Communist government of Josip Tito's Yugoslavia, while it gave Serbs a good deal in the new country, went out of its way to suppress Serbian nationalism. Serbs were prevented from talking or publishing anything that had a nationalist flavor, and Tito suppressed nationalism among the other Balkan groups as well.

Tito's government also suppressed public discussion of atrocities associated with the Second World War, which arguably traumatized the Serbs as much as the Nazi genocide itself. Just as the world seemed strangely unable to understand the way in which Versailles had humiliated the Germans, the unwillingness of other Slavs to comprehend the suffering of the Serbs seemed to demonstrate with heartbreaking clarity the world's disdain for them, and appeared to mock their horrific experiences by refusing to acknowledge them. But much of what the Serbs experienced as the disdain of their neighbors was in reality an enforced silence imposed by a Communist government. Perhaps the main strategy of the Communist invention of Yugoslavia by Marshal Tito was to suppress nationalism within each of the Balkan nationalities composing his new state; and he especially had his eye on Serbian nationalism. The compensation for Serbs was that they got slightly more influence than the Croats, Muslims, Macedonians, Montenegrins and Slovenes with whom they shared power. Serbian nationalists would later claim Serbs were oppressed within Yugoslavia, but objectively there is little evidence for that claim.

The Communist system set up by Tito began to unravel during the 1980s. In 1987 Slobodan Milosevic, then President of Yugoslavia, saw the police attack a group of Serbs picketing in Albania. He instinctively shouted, "Serbs should never be beaten!"—and as a result of that momentary response he became an overnight rock star among Serbia's emerging nationalists. The words were repeated by Serbs everywhere—and while it seemed at the time that they came off the top of Milosevic's head, it was deeply rooted in his own worldview, and aimed at invoking Serbia's long history of oppression at the hands of others. Serbian nationalism would, in fact, be Milosevic's ticket to executive power.

In 1989, in a Nuremberg-style rally in Kosovo, flanked by prelates of the Serbian Orthodox Church, in front of one million ecstatic Serbs, Slobodan Milosevic celebrated the 600th anniversary of the historic Battle of Kosovo. No longer would Serbs put up with the plots, the disinformation, and the attacks against them by a world that had always hated them! Slobodan Milosevic's speech was more that just a blatant appeal to Serbian nationalism, but was replete with paranoia and aggression and an extremely radical victimology (that is, a radical appeal to victim status as a transcendent national experience) reiterating again and again the idea that Serbia was a martyr nation that was under attack, had always been under attack, and would always be under attack. What they had to do now was start fighting back.

Milosevic's appeal to Serbia's past traumas in order to arouse a violent Serbian nationalism is generally regarded as the beginning of the Balkan Wars; but it had been carefully and extensively prepared by various Serb intellectuals. The influential Serb intellectual Dobrica Cosic worked ceaselessly during the 1970s and 1980s to elaborate what journalist Christopher Bennett called "a complex and paradoxical theory of Serb national persecution." Serbia, in Cosic's fantasy, were not the largest and most powerful Slavic group in Yugoslavia, but were actually persecuted, maligned and exploited. "Over two decades," Bennett wrote in 1999, "this evolved into the Greater Serbia program which Slobodan Milosevic first hijacked and then pursued."

In 1986, the Serbian Academy of Sciences and Arts published a secret Memorandum that was widely circulated among Serbs, both in Serbia and in surrounding countries. This paper, which was signed by virtually every Serbian intellectual of note, claimed that the Serbs of Kosovo were being subjected to genocide; that Serbs were pitiful victims of Croatian-Slovene hegemony; that Serbs were being exploited economically; and that the borders between countries in the former Yugoslavia had been drawn by people who hated Serbs. All of these claims were without exception bogus; but they fit quite well with the Serbian obsession with victim status, not to mention the intergenerational trauma of Serbia's past victim-hood in two world wars, including the traumatic memories of genocide in the Second World War that had been inherited by Serbian children and grandchildren.

Emotional trauma is not only the direct result of person-on-person aggression. It is also intergenerational, in the sense that it can be passed down from people in one generation to another. All the emotional symptoms of trauma can be passed down from members of an older generation to people—usually family members—in a younger generation, even though younger members have no direct experience of the traumatizing events. These younger people absorb all the *feelings* of having been traumatized, including identification with victim status, without suffering any traumatizing events. Children of Holocaust survivors in particular may internalize trauma from their parents in an unconscious attempt to relieve their parents' distress; children and grandchildren are furthermore at risk for becoming traumatized because they lack the life experience to comprehend why and how genocide occurs, and how it can be opposed. In both instances, aggression is internalized. (Whether it is acted out as aggression later depends on the individual and the historical situation.)

Intergenerational trauma is rife in Jewish families that lost family members in the Holocaust, and is a major political as well as cultural reality in Israel; the political class encourages memories of the Holocaust by bringing it up very frequently, and making the trauma of the Holocaust the standard by which everything else is measured. Right-wing politicians in Israel similarly strive to keep past trauma in the present moment as much as possible by suggesting that another Holocaust is on the way.

Milosevic's wife Marina was a balmy eccentric who talked wistfully about the unity of the workers, even as her husband's security services were murdering poor and working-class people across the Balkans. Marina was famous for wearing a single plastic flower in her hair every day of her life. But she had good connections within the League of Communists (her mother had been a partisan shot by the Nazis, and she was raised by an aunt who was probably Tito's mistress); and Milosevic carefully milked her connections to advance himself. He was an ideologically conventional and ruthless Stalinist who worked his way up the Communist bureaucracy—until he discovered, almost by accident, the power of a revived Serbian nationalism.

Then came Milosevic's unleashing of Serbian victimology, and the solidification of his executive power. (It is significant that his famous speech at Kosovo commemorated not a Serbia military victory, but its worst defeat.) Milosevic's campaign to create a Greater Serbia was an all-out orgy of aggression expressed through the medium of toxic victimology and ecstatic nationalism. The Serbs were once again being attacked, maligned and exploited by unscrupulous forces! All Serbs deserved to live in a single state, and would have to exercise de facto control of that state, no matter how many other ethnic groups had to be displaced or killed—and if that single state couldn't be Yugoslavia, it would have to be some other entity controlled by Serbs. (Which meant the other minorities would have to agree to be dominated by Serbs, or ethnically cleansed or worse.) Thus did Milosevic and his totalitarian state reformulate and give violent rebirth to the classic idea of Greater Serbia.

The journalist Christopher Bennett describes what happened next: "Myth, fantasy, half-truths and brazen lies [were] packaged each night into television news. The conspiracy theory dreamed up by frustrated nationalists such as [Dobrica] Cosic in the late 1960s, 1970s and early 1980s became the literal truth. Every conceivable event from Serb history was dredged up and distorted to feed the persecution complex of ordinary people who, at a time of collapsing living standards, were gradually taken in by the barrage of xenophobia. The atmosphere was so heated and the campaign so all-encompassing that people lost touch with reality." This fantasy of victimology was maintained by tight state control of Serbia media—which Bennett and others document at length—and was ruthlessly enforced by the murderous thuggery of nationalists in Serbia and in the Serbian enclaves elsewhere in the Balkans.

The Slovenes were the first to declare their independence from Yugoslavia, and decisively beat the Serb-dominated Yugoslavian army in 10 days. But there were no large Serbian enclaves in Slovenia, so the Serb-dominated army did not heavily contest the Slovenian withdrawal—and even before the 10-day war was over, they began to take up positions favorable to the military support of Serbian elements in Croatia. At the instigation of Milosevic, Serbs within Croatia then rose up to declare an independent republic in Krajina, with the twelve percent of the population who were Serbs taking about a third of Croatia, which they declared to be an autonomous separatist Republic of Serbian Krajina. They then proceeded to drive out everybody who wasn't Serbian. This illegal campaign was predictably defeated by hastily-organized Croatian armed forces, which then retaliated against Serbian civilians by driving *them*—along with their Serbian militias—out of Croatia.

The spectacle of Serbs fleeing Croatia to Serbian communities in Bosnia brought back memories of genocide at the hands of the Ustasha. Here it was, once again, the eternally-victimized Serbs being displaced by fascist Croats! This version of events conveniently ignored the fact that the Serbian leadership had unleashed the civil war by setting up a separate republic in Croatia, a blatantly illegal act, one that war crimes prosecutors of the International Criminal Tribunal for the Former Yugoslavia later referred to as a "joint criminal enterprise" masterminded by Milosevic. It was a disastrous and brutal error, and prefigured the end of the Serbian presence in Croatia. But most Serbs weren't about to blame Milosevic and their own nationalist fantasies for the Serb defeat.

The stage was now set for the worst genocide since the Second World War. Serbian militias, under the direct supervision of Slobodan Milosevic in Belgrade, began operations in Bosnia-Herzegovina, the intention being, as in Croatia, to set up a Serb republic within that country. But clearly it was impossible to claim large sections of Bosnia as Serbian as long as Muslims lived there, because Muslims would oppose—and ultimately vote against—Serbian leaders. Muslims liked the idea of a multiethnic Bosnia, and certainly weren't willing to leave their farms, businesses and homes to turn them over to somebody else. Bosnia was, after all, their homeland; and whereas the Serbs were fanatically opposed to living in a multiethnic Bosnia, the Muslims felt decidedly safer living in a land with many minority ethnic and religious groups. From the point of view of the Serbian militias, then, there was only one thing to do: the Muslims must be driven out in order to create mono-ethnic territories—and that meant ethnic cleansing of Muslims in territories that Serbs wanted to have for their Serbian republic. Ethnic cleansing would be accomplished through the deliberate and extraordinarily brutal use of mass murder, torture, and systematic gang-rape of women.

In the orgy of sadism and violence that followed, Muslim men were rounded up and sent to concentration camps, murdered and buried in mass graves, while Muslim women were systematically gang-raped. Muslim men were often murdered in groups, some at concentration camps, sometimes closer to their former homes. During the period between October 1, 1991, when Bosnia declared its independence, and 1995, when the Dayton Agreement ended the war in Bosnia, as many as 100,000 to 200,000 Muslim civilians were murdered, mainly men and boys. Tens of thousands of Muslim women were gang-raped as a deliberate policy of the Serbian militias. During one period in 1993, about 700,000 Muslims were driven out of one area of Bosnia-Herzegovina; overall it is estimated that two million Muslims were driven out of their homes and became refugees, either internally or in other countries.

15.

In Stevan M. Weine's *When History is a Nightmare*, stories are told dispassionately by survivors of Serbian genocide. One of them is told by a Muslim identified only as H, who was taken to the Omarska concentration camp by Serb forces. *I was one of the first people brought to Omarska. After ten days there were 20,000 prisoners. They put us in a big yard. There were 70 percent Muslim, 20 percent Croat, and 10 percent Serb. The guards shot at anyone who tried to leave and sometimes shot for no apparent reason.*

After three days the "investigations" began. I was in them twenty-five times and only one time did I leave on my own legs. In the investigations they always beat us. Guilty or not guilty.

For the first ten days they didn't give us any food. Then they fed us once a day at 6:00. They gave us three minutes to come from our building to the kitchen. Some of us were more than fifty meters away, and we had no chance to reach the kitchen. Those who came had three minutes to eat. Those who did not had no food. The guards formed a line that we had to run through to get to the kitchen. As we ran they beat us with guns, wheels, and tools.

After eleven days I asked them to let me go to the washroom just to wash my face. When I got there I didn't see that two men from Kozarac also came inside along with some soldiers from special units. The soldiers started to beat them. When they saw me they took me to a place with a big sink and started to beat me. They told me to lick the floor of this washroom for 20,000 people which was dirty with urine and sewage. They broke my ribs. I vomited for one month. I vomited blood.

Sometimes they put us in a 4 X 4 meter room—700 people. They told us to lie down and they closed the windows and the doors. It was summer. We lay like sardines in a can. Those on top were in the best position. Every morning some on the bottom were dead. Every morning a guard came with a list and called people's names. Those they brought out never came back.

One day they came at 3 AM and they brought out 174 people. I was with them. They lined us up behind a building they called the White House. Ten soldiers came with automatic weapons and they started to shoot us. Only three of us survived.

The worst event was when I watched one young man as they castrated him. Right now I can hear his cry and his prayers to be killed. And every night it wakes me. He was a nice young man. His executioner was his friend at school. He cut his body and he licked his blood. He asked him just to kill and to stop all that suffering. All day and all night we heard his prayers and his crying until he died. This is something that I cannot forget. It gives me nightmares and makes sleep almost impossible.

Much of H's narrative sounds familiar because of its similarity to Holocaust narratives. *We had a special platoon. About a hundred prisoners had the duty of taking the bodies of murdered people, putting them in trucks, and bringing them to a special place with pits to dispose of them. They knew where they put all the Muslim bodies. One day before our camp was closed, before the Red Guard came, the soldiers killed all of them. Serbs killed one hundred Muslims just to wipe out all witnesses. I was not in the group because I was too weak and too thin.*

Like the Nazis, the torture perpetrated by the Serb militias was not only gratuitous but bizarre, with an extremely high component of sadism. *I remember one man, my neighbor, they cut his skull with a tool and we saw his brain. It was absolutely open. When he moved, his brain moved. And that man survived.*

Did I mention about machine oil? I was in a garage with ten other people. There was a long channel full of motor oil and dust. One guard who watched me would always tell me, "Go take your meal!" He gave me a plastic cup of motor oil that I had to drink. Every day, for thirty days, until they moved him to some other concentration camp. I got dysentery and terrible diarrhea. One year later, whenever I inhaled or exhaled very deeply I smelled oil. I have no mucosa in my gut and I have very strong acid. When I am nervous, acid comes into my mouth like water, my mouth is full of acid.

As the tide of Serbian nationalism rose, Muslims suddenly realized that the dream of a multicultural society—an ideal the Bosnian Muslims referred to as *merhamet,* which can be roughly translated as "live and let live"—was being irrevocably destroyed. By the time they realized the danger they were in, it was too late for many of them. A Muslim student tells how the catastrophe first became apparent to her: *One teacher in particular, the history teacher, was the most nationalistic. At first there was small talk, little comments, and then it escalated until it was propaganda. My friends and I took it as a joke. We laughed about it. It was crazy. We would be sitting in the classroom raising our eyebrows and joking about the teacher. Then it seemed to become more serious. I remember one Serb girl in our class. She was also a good student. All of a sudden, the professor began speaking to her as if they were having private conversations. Like no one else was there. She was a nationalist. She put up symbols of the Serb cross in different places.*

We were surprised, because she had been very friendly. All of a sudden the teacher was having a discussion with her about the need to get rid of the Muslims.

One thing that was particularly horrible about the genocide and the ethnic cleansing was that local Serbs were often friends of those they attacked, robbed, raped and murdered. In *When History is a Nightmare*, Weine refers to a survivor who told of being attacked by a couple who had been their dinner guests a week before. Another told of her house being burned down by a Serbian employee, who made her watch. *"Well, boss—everything you had burned."* Another story often told by survivors is of the *"best friend,"* who would show up to loot or kill. *After seven days in detention, my best friend came. We had to give him everything we had. He took us to our house and burned it down and made us watch. He said, "I know you have money and jewelry. Give me everything."* Worst of all, former neighbors, friends and acquaintances could use their knowledge of the Muslims' former lives to torment them while they were in the concentration camps. *Besides all that torture, one day they told us they had started to kill our families. They told my neighbor that they had killed part of his family. Then we saw the trucks with our families being transported. Our nightmares came again. We began to cry.*

Systematic sexual abuse was extremely widespread, extremely well-organized, and extremely cruel. Systematic gang-raping and sexualized torture was used against women by Serbian militias, special units and even the Serb-controlled Yugoslav National Army (YNA).Women were held in concentration camps, where they were raped serially. Serb forces also abducted women and put them into brothels next to police stations, where they were systematically abused by hundreds of militiamen. Many of the rapes occurred in the countryside, so we may never know exactly how many women suffered this fate.

It is estimated, however, that around 50,000 Muslim women were raped during the 1991–1995 period of ethnic cleansing. It is clear that sexual abuse of women was used systematically and intentionally as a deliberate weapon of ethnic cleansing. Its intent was to completely traumatize large numbers of innocent people, especially by psychologically destroying the women in order to make them unable to take up their former lives in the homes, farms and cities where they had previously resided. Some of this abuse took forms that were so distressing that it is almost a kind of exploitation to merely summarize gang-rape narratives, so we won't do so. But they happened.[8]

The imported criminals were committing the atrocities, but it was the local Serbs, our former neighbors, who were pointing their fingers and telling them what to do. Serbian people were completely influenced by their propaganda, which said that we were a threat to them and that we had planned to do to them what they were doing to us.[9]

16.

Why did Serbian nationalists visit these horrors on their neighbors that happened to be Muslims, when they themselves had been victims only a few decades before of the same kinds of persecution by the Nazis? As we have seen, a very high percentage of the people that have been persecuted or victimized do not tend to "learn from their experiences" and become more compassionate people, as we would like to believe; on the contrary, often they cannot wait to commit exactly the same kinds of horrible atrocities against others, or engage in similarly irrational self-defeating behavior—or they identify with, and politically support, others that advocate and engage in extreme violence. They do this for all the reason already given: victims of aggression identify with aggressors and internalize their aggression, and then become aggressors themselves. This is no irony, no anomaly, but a basic reality of human behavior—and it's also a basic doctrine of this book's theory of aggression and evil. It's hard to accept, particularly by those who do not believe in the existence of evil, but it happens, and we would be better off to accept it sooner rather than later.

It should be pointed out that not all Serbs went along with the genocide against Muslims. Indeed, many Serbs who refused to participate in the genocide were themselves murdered by the nationalist militias. Someday there will be projects to collect information about Serbs who resisted Milosevic, and who resisted the genocide in Bosnia; and by studying those people who had the courage to resist, we will learn more about the kind of personality that is able to resist mass aggression and systemic evil. Such people become the teachers of the new and more decent world we want to build. But the resisters are important to us precisely because they are in the minority.

Without question the atrocities of the Serbian nationalists—and the careful way Milosevic and other Serbian leaders prepared the Serbian people for the genocide they were about to visit upon Europe—were a direct outcome of the trauma suffered by the Serbs in World War Two, and even World War One. It was made much worse for the post-World War Two generation of Serbs by the fact that they were not allowed to talk about it by Yugoslavia's Communist government, or to write or publish anything that raised the issue of Serbian national suffering. (As we have seen, immediately discussing traumatic events can lessen its hold on the victim.) Of course, the Yugoslavian Communists were terrified of Serbian nationalism because of its violent nature, but repressing the Serbs' ability to publicly discuss the genocide directed against them simply made things worse. Unable to discuss what had happened to them, Serbian nationalism was a powder keg waiting to explode. Victims of genocide themselves, the Serbian nationalists could hardly wait to commit genocide against the Muslims.

This volatility was made worse by Milosevic's constant reiteration of past ignominies against the Serbs; so much was said every day on the radio about crimes against Serbs in the past that even sensible people in Belgrade were prepared to discount reports of Serbian militias committing rape, murder and genocide as more lies from a Serb-hating world. Milosevic saw his chance to act out his aggression and did so. The Serbian genocide of Muslims in Bosnia was the worst atrocity in Europe since the Nazi genocide against Jews and Roma. The Bosnian Muslims, who believed in and were committed to an ethnically-diverse Bosnia, appear to have been caught completely by surprise by the ferocious sadism of Serbian nationalists—but so was the rest of the world.

Will we similarly be caught by surprise the next time such a situation presents itself? Hopefully not, if we accept the existence of human evil and are willing to learn the gritty realities of how aggression and evil replicate themselves. We might even be able to invest in a culture of psychological and political intervention to challenge the aggression *before* the rape and murder starts—and we can best do that by studying the personalities and strategies of people who have resisted campaigns of rape and murder. In the case of Bosnia, for example, we would want to study the behavior of those Serbs who resisted the Serbian nationalists in order to understand the kind of democratic, decent world we want to see in the future. But I stress again that the individual dissenters become important precisely because there are so few of them—most people who have been victimized are far more likely to seek out victims of their own, or to be silent about ongoing victimization of others. We can learn to oppose evil, but only if we acknowledge that it exists, and that all people can fall under its influence. But to do that, we need to put sentimentality on the shelf, and start dealing sensibly with the dangerous realities of human nature.

17.

Violent political movements, nationalists and repressive govern-ments (not to mention violent criminals) understand intuitively how to use trauma bonding to get what they want. They understand how trauma can be used to manipulate people by making them complicit in ongoing aggression, and they do not hesitate to employ it to bond people to their evil enterprises. In *The Nazi Doctors*, author Robert Jay Lifton wrote that when SS doctor Josef Mengele made selections on the infamous ramp outside Auschwitz, deciding which of the arriving prisoners would be gassed and which wouldn't, he insisted on using Jewish doctors who were prisoners at Auschwitz to help him make selections. "One might expect that someone so intent upon absolute personal control would disdain the involvement of prisoner doctors in selections, but that was not the case. Mengele encouraged or demanded [Jewish doctors'] participation, and by so encompassing them *broadened rather than diminished his own control.*"[10] [Italics added.]

The prisoner doctors that worked for Mengele tended to ascribe his power over them to a mysterious personal magnetism, but it is far more likely that it emanated from Mengele's skillful and highly practiced use of trauma bonding. Once prisoners had made a selection on the ramp with Mengele, they were bonded to him by emotional orientations that were just as strong, if not stronger, than anything else in their personalities. The survival of the self—indeed, the self itself—was now identified completely with Mengele's survival, with all the ambivalence that survival on those terms would entail.

In *The Nazi Doctors*, Lifton quotes one of the Jewish prisoners— also a doctor—who similarly worked under Mengele at Auschwitz. She remarks somewhat wonderingly that although the Jewish prisoners lived in total fear of Mengele, they also admired him in spite of themselves, in spite of his monstrous experiments, his ruthless murdering of tens of thousands of Jews in the selections, and so forth. They tried desperately to please him, she said, concluding that the process was "almost like seducing [someone]." Lifton writes: "Mengele's style of omnipotence, then, produced terror and a measure of admiration, a combination that serves a legend well, *but which individuals have great difficulty extricating themselves.*"[11] [Italics added.] Mengele's practice of recruiting Jewish doctors that were prisoners and forcing them to assist him in selections, as well as assisting him in his ghastly "medical" experiments—in the process inevitably creating overwhelming feelings of trauma and complicity—is a pure example of intentional trauma bonding in the service of systemic evil.

It should not surprise us that a person who has been bonded to aggression through complicity in systemic evil will do evil things, and even afterwards might feel a deep attraction to violent and patriarchal ideas and people; and they may well also adopt a fundamentally aggressive—as well as self-exculpatory—worldview. This may include aggression in many forms, including profound forms of self-harm. (Indeed, one of the Nazi doctors interviewed in Lifton's book committed suicide after the interviews.) This internalization of aggression doesn't just happen to people who have been *victims* of repressive social violence—it also refers to people who have *witnessed* that kind of violence, who often feel complicit in such a way as to destroy their ability to publicly or privately oppose the violence they've seen. And it is also true of those who have *participated* in the systemic uses of violence, who may be traumatized by what they have done and in the process internalized large amounts of aggression. People in all these categories are capable of acting out their aggression in various ways, often including self-harm.

Trauma bonding doesn't happen only in a moment of high drama: it can also take place over a long period of time, especially if we consider the effects of culture—social or familial—on emotional development. Children of both Nazis and Holocaust survivors often inherited the trauma of their parents—or rather, the *symptoms* of that trauma, usually in the form of anxiety, which operates in a systemic way throughout the family system over a long period of time. This multigenerational trauma could be described as anxiety associated with a past historical experience, but without the experience itself; it can be passed down in ways that are partly conscious, but also to a great extent unconscious. It can paradoxically cause people to *recreate* the historical atrocity (either in fact or psychologically) that traumatized their parents or grandparents—which is why so many Jews that lost family members in the Holocaust can often be persuaded by rightwing Zionist demagogues that a new Holocaust is on the way.

If descendants of Holocaust survivors really begin to believe that a new Holocaust (or something similarly catastrophic) is imminent, it can give an ideological framework for anxiety that otherwise would seem to come from nowhere. It also provides an ideological framework that can be used to justify systemic abuse of Palestinians, which ultimately heightens rather than reduces anxiety, because the abuse has to be laboriously denied. But this aggressive behavior doesn't really come from a particular ideology, but from aggression people have internalized into their own personalities. There are exceptions to this (and all exceptions are happily acknowledged) but ideologies such as Zionism are usually an attempt to create a logical argument to justify aggressive emotions that are already felt and are beginning to be acted out. This internalized aggression can be neutralized if the individual becomes aware of it, but only if they are likewise aware of their own capacity for evil. But historical victims of systemic evil have a particularly hard time acknowledging their own capacity for evil.

The great disadvantage of the toxic identification with the Nazi Holocaust felt by so many survivors and their descendants is that while the Nazis embodied systemic evil, the tendency of victims and their descendents to focus obsessively on the Nazis leaves little room for family members to grow emotionally. Specifically, it leaves little room for them to imagine their own capacity for evil, or the national temptations to systemic evil faced by their own country and countrymen. Indeed, that's one function of identification with the Holocaust—as long as they are focused on the past evil of the Nazis, they never have to look at their own capacity for evil in the present moment, and they tend to get very stuck emotionally stuck in the bargain.

But the real danger of obsessive identification with the Nazi Holocaust is that one will almost surely internalize the aggression involved, which one will feel compelled to act out against Palestinians or other victims. Israeli Jews that do this won't necessarily act like Nazis, which was the psychological anomaly of a particular historical moment, but will nonetheless act out their aggression all dressed up in their own Zionist trappings. The great danger, in other words, is that they will end up acting out the same kind of aggression as the Bogeymen of their imaginations, in effect continuing the Holocaust by other means. Sadly, there is evidence that this is exactly what the Israeli political class is encouraging Israeli Jews to do.

The more people that are involved in obsessively thinking about past trauma, whether for political or historically accidental reasons, the longer present forms of aggression are likely to be perpetuated. It isn't that talking about past trauma is bad—indeed, victims of trauma must do that to be free. The problem arises when the past trauma is constantly brought up and kept alive in the public imagination not for therapeutic reasons but for political ones. In that situation large numbers of people are likely to get stuck emotionally. Indeed, the trauma of the past is likely to develop a life of its own, in which a particular population (the Serbs, the Israelis) cannot contemplate life *without* the trauma and suffering, because they have built their personal and national identities around various extrapolations of victim status. Such populations are especially vulnerable to exploitation of trauma by unscrupulous leaders who intuitively know how to use it. The current right-wing extremists in the Israeli political class got power in precisely that manner.

It should now be clear why governments use trauma to mobilize people for aggression by the state—trauma bonding is one of the most powerful social adhesive of which human beings are capable, because *both its inception and its effects occur unconsciously*. It is also, unfortunately, humanity's most lethal and negative social adhesive. It can only be defeated by people brave and introspective enough to acknowledge their own capacity for evil, while overcoming their fear of social retaliation for pointing out the crimes resulting from trauma in their own society. Above all, it requires being able to step outside a particular psychological system, even when—or especially when— it serves the psychological needs of the majority. Overcoming fear is especially important, because aggressive governments try to keep their citizens in unending, irrational fear regarding the ultimate intentions of the state.

The Nazis placed an extremely high value on their street-fighting capabilities, and maintained extensive private armies that brawled on an almost nightly basis during the 1920s and early 1930s in Germany. In fact, Nazi writings emphasize the use of street violence *combined with* pressures within government institutions *and also* a powerful propaganda effort, each element alone not being sufficiently effective. The reason for the Nazi street-fighting was psychological as well as political—in fact, the street-fighting part was *mainly* psychological. This violence was intended first to create the feeling that the Weimer republic could not ensure social order, which the Nazis would then accentuate with vivid, simple and aggressive slogans. But the violence had a second destabilizing effect. It was intended to create a kind of public theater of cruelty in real time to overwhelm, invade and then colonize the public mind, and in so doing to get the public to identify with it and internalize Nazi aggression as a grinding, dangerous but unstoppable force destined to take over Germany's institutions. The traumatizing effects of such daily violence create the opportunity for identification with the perpetuators.

"The very first essential for success is a perpetually constant and regular employment of violence," Hitler wrote in *Mein Kampf*.

To the average Germans, especially if they were unsophisticated about politics or had no party loyalties, it would seem clear that the Nazis, while crude, were better at street-fighting than everybody else. And they were more ruthless, and therefore more "effective," if you measure effectiveness by the ability to commit more murders and get away with it than anybody else. Gradually the German people came to internalize the brutality of the Nazis—as well as of the street-fighters of the Communists and Social Democrats—as something that was simply a part of the landscape. But nobody could top the Nazis in the game of violence, because their message wasn't just *about* physical violence, it *was* physical violence—that's what the Nazis embodied in the world. Since they were all about aggression, and since they were better than it than anybody else, the Nazis were greatly feared. You couldn't ignore their high-profile dedication to the task of inflicting pain and implementing social terror, and nobody could see any other social forces on the horizon that were likely to overcome them.

In his remarkable diary (*Berlin in Lights*), Count Harry Kessler writes of the staggering emotional effects of Walther Rathenau's murder in Germany in 1922. Kessler—sometimes called "the Red Count"—saw Rathenau as a heroic if flawed figure, "a political virtuoso"[12] who might have saved Germany if he had lived. Kessler therefore believed that the horror and sense of loss associated with Rathenau's murder would inevitably push Germany toward the left. But most Germans didn't see Rathenau's heroic qualities because they didn't have enough time to get to know him, and therefore couldn't imagine the good Rathenau might have done. What Germans clearly saw was the brutal manner in which Rathenau was assassinated by rightwing thugs, and the astonishing fact that they could commit such crimes with relative impunity. It was this last part that really stuck with them. That was exactly the impression that the assassins sought to impart; the impunity was just as important as the violence itself.

Throughout the 1920s there were hundreds of such assassinations by the Nazis, and each time it was the violence that people remembered, because there was never any substantial punishment for it—only when violent crimes are punished do people have time enough to discuss, think about and arrive at conclusions about it. Instead, people began to unconsciously identify with the Nazis as a kind of perverse but unstoppable success story; and despite their conscious dislike of them began to accept their brutality as a social inevitability. Above all people were afraid of the Nazis; and in addition to causing fear and revulsion among the people their aggression was increasingly omnipresent—it was impossible to ignore it. People were throughout the late 1920s and early 1930s beginning to internalize on a mass basis the public violence stage-managed by the Nazis.

The street-fighting period from 1920 to 1933 was psychological preparation for the horrors to come. But the violence being internalized unconsciously clouded people's rational judgment, as its very immediacy prevented them from seeing how toxic it was, and what it was doing to them. The utter degradation of the Nazis' criminality really only became clear once the political opposition to Hitler had been mainly wiped out, its leaders dead, in exile or in concentration camps.

I interviewed a man who had grown up in the 1920s in Tübingen, a beautiful and very old university town in southern Germany where I was part of a special academic program for a short time. This older gentleman had been an activist-leader in the most progressive section of the Wandervogel (wandering bird) movement, a kind of back-to-nature organization roughly like the Boy Scouts; his section of the movement was generally on the left politically, and gradually became more progressive throughout the 1920s, becoming known for its internationalism, social idealism and relative tolerance. In 1933, when Hitler came to power, the entire Wandervogel apparatus was suppressed; but that was not the most traumatizing thing for this man. What traumatized him the most was the way people he had known and trusted suddenly declared for Hitler, as though they were under the influence of some diabolical supernatural force. So did most of most of the students, as a wave of hysterical nationalism swept through southern Germany and the nation. It was as though Tübingen, which had previously been the capital of all that was good and open-minded and liberal in the Swabian south of Germany, had gone mad. He left Tübingen and withdrew with his wife to a small house in the Swabian Alb as a semi-recluse.

When I interviewed this man in 1990, he told me an astonishing thing about himself—*he had never gone back to Tübingen*, even though it was only 20 kilometers away. The trauma had effectively ended his life, making resistance and even immigration impossible. He refused to read newspapers. For sixty years he had been reading the poet Hölderlin, remembering Tübingen as it was in the 1920s, and wasting away with a chronic and degenerative nervous disorder. His was an interesting example of what is sometimes called 'internal exile'—but as often happens, it caused this man to lose any ability to resist because of emotional trauma arising from his intense sense of betrayal by a world he had once trusted. His trauma caused him to internalize the aggression that was abroad in Germany, which he turned on himself, becoming a neurasthenic recluse.

Kristallnacht was the hideous last act of the violent street theater that the Nazis sought to substitute for civil society. As a state spectacle, Joseph Goebbels and his criminal supporters carried out on the streets of Germany a veritable orgy of violence and humiliation directed against German Jews. The purpose went far beyond simply encouraging Jews to leave Germany or intimidating them. It was a display of pure sadism aimed at the broad masses of German people, as well as the Jews; it communicated in unmistakable terms—and was intended to make people feel—that resistance to the Nazi state was futile, and that there was no hope of anything but more brutality in the future. The German people would submit to the state's program of war, sadism and anti-Semitism, because if they didn't accept it they, too, would be beaten up on the streets or sent to a concentration camp.

That was the message: join in the war against the Jews, or die with them. Most people in that situation chose to survive, by their silence becoming complicit with the murderers. Their silence was the result of coercion, to be sure, but the psychological ramifications were radical and pathological: by being silent and simply looking on, one internalized the aggression one had witnessed, just as a man who is forced to witness a cold-blooded execution by the Mafia will internalize the violence of the killers.

The street-fighting, culminating in the calamitous state-managed pogrom *Kristallnacht*, was nothing more or less than a gigantic national laboratory for the inducement of mass trauma bonding. You could not look at this brutality without being to some extent disgusted, and then traumatized; anyone with an ounce of humanity could not help but be horrified by the pitiful images of families driven from their homes, old men humiliated in the street, children ritually tormented in front of peers. After *die Kristallnacht*, if you had any human feelings whatsoever, you had three choices: you either had to leave Nazi Germany, join the underground resistance movement against Hitler, or swallow hard and internalize the aggression you had witnessed. Or you could commit suicide.

Some people chose 'internal exile'—that is, they chose to stifle their disgust and horror regarding Hitler, keep quiet, and hope for better days. But there is no internal exile from violence of this magnitude, psychologically speaking, there is only submission; and when confronted with state terrorism of that enormity, submission is complicity. We know all too well what most people did—most people lacked the courage and the resources to immigrate, but were to some extent traumatized by what they saw (the organized violence that was gradually expanding to become their world) and probably also by their own paralysis. The result was an internalization of the aggression they had seen, spurred on by an enormous fear of Nazi brutality. In the end most Germans submitted, becoming part of, or silent partners to, the Nazi terror machine.

In Germany the public glorification of violence resulted in trauma bonding on a mass scale, which caused many Germans to identify with the Nazis because they were afraid of them. The recurring use of state terrorism, and the Germans' internalization of that state terrorism, created such a high degree of psychic numbing that people became afraid to even *think* a subversive thought. (The fear of inadvertently having subversive thoughts or dreams was also common under Stalin, even among—or perhaps especially among—committed Communists.) Hitler expressed this use of trauma bonding by totalitarian government perfectly in a speech at

Königsberg, September, 1933: "The great strength of the totalitarian state is that it forces those who fear it to imitate it."[13]

18.

If people tend to internalize the aggression of those that attack them, Israeli Jews would have internalized huge amounts of aggression — they were the victims of history's worst genocide, and therefore history's greatest crime. And according to Avraham Burg, that's exactly what happened. Burg is no crank writer, marginal thinker or Johnny-come-lately to the Israeli political scene. He comes from one of Israel's most important political families: and in 2001, Burg was the Speaker of the Knesset, Israel's Parliament. Burg was born in the political class, spent most of his life there, and knows what he's talking about when he talks about Israel.

According to him, the Israelis have internalized massive amounts of German nationalism and its aggressive worldview. He writes about this in his book, *The Holocaust is Over; We Must Rise From Its Ashes.* "We have displaced our anger and revenge from one people to another, from an old foe to a new adversary, and so we allow ourselves to live comfortably with the heirs of the German enemy — representing convenience, wealth and high quality — while treating the Palestinians as whipping boys to release our aggression, anger, and hysteria, of which we have plenty."

According to Burg, Israeli Jews haven't let the Holocaust go. Instead they carry it around inside them, where it fuels nationalist aggression. "Israel adopted this legacy of insecurity characteristic of trauma victims. Since then, we live under constant pressure and in the contradictions of unceasing armament to compensate and atone for built-in impotence and existential anxiety. We have become a nation of victims, and our state religion is the worship and tending of traumas, as if Israel forever walks down its last path."

Avraham Burg's father was a German Jew who personally experienced Germany's descent into madness (he left Germany in 1938), and according to Burg made an explicit comparison between what he'd already seen in Germany, and what he was beginning to see in Israel. Burg points out that Israelis are obsessed with the Germans and the Holocaust, while at the same time adopting attitudes that were once typical of Germans. "I have to confess," Burg writes, "especially having rejected the position of victim-hood, that my greatest surprise in writing this book was discovering that the political, social and national structure that most resemble Israel's are those of Germany's Second Reich before the period of anarchy that facilitated the rise of National Socialism. I must emphasize, though: *before*, not *during*."

Burg points to the modern connection between the military and the Israeli political class. "Some elite units produce future army chiefs of staff, who then enter politics and sometimes end up in the prime minister's office. Moshe Dayan, Yitzhak Rabin, Ehud Barak, and Shaul Mofaz moved directly from the top army post to the ministries of defense of the interior or to prime minister as if it were the most natural path. In short, the military is where Israeli leaders are made. We did not invent this system; it is borrowed from Bismarck's Germany." He also compares the situation of Israel's Arabs to the position of Germany's Jews during the Weimer period: "I must reiterate that the comparison is not between the status of today's Israeli Arabs and that of the Jews during the Holocaust, not even in the pre-war Nazi years, but only during the long incubation period that preceded Nazism and that gave rise to a public mindset that enabled the Nazis to take power."

The result has been a militarization of Israeli society, and the Wagnerian social overtones that always accompany such a transformation. "When every enemy is the absolute evil and every conflict is a war to the death, all is justified in our eyes. We do not distinguish between levels of hostility nor do we view our enemies as rivals with possibly legitimate needs: they are all against us all the time, and all we can do is defend ourselves." This is reinforced by constant references to the Shoah, the Nazi Holocaust; Burg also cites the omnipresent tendency to compare Israel's enemies to Hitler: "Many years of propaganda like this, using historically laden terminology, have resulted in perpetual hysteria: everything is a sign of fate and we are hanging in the balance, between existence and annihilation."

All enemies become Nazis. When former Prime Minister Menachem Begin sent his troops to fight Yasser Arafat, he called him a "two-legged beast," exactly the phrase he'd once used for Hitler. Begin also liked to compare the Palestinian National Charter to *Mein Kampf*, and when he attacked Arafat's headquarters in Beirut, he said he felt like he was sending soldiers to kill Hitler. When declaring war on Lebanon, Begin was reported as saying that "the alternative is Treblinka, and we have decided that there will be no more Treblinkas."

"Hitler is already dead, Mr. Prime Minister," novelist Amos Oz retorted in the magazine *Yediot Aharonot* two weeks after that unnecessary war broke out. "Again and again, Mr. Begin, you show the public your strange urge to revive Hitler in order to kill him anew in the form of terrorists. This urge to recreate and re-eliminate Hitler again and again is the fruit of distress that poets are obliged to express, but for a statesman this might lead to dangerous results."

Burg has a long section on the subtle way propaganda is conducted through the medium of everyday language, what Burg calls "word laundering": "It is true that we do not have gas chambers here and that we have no official policy of deportation and annihilation. Yet those who will not open their ears and eyes should not be surprised when it becomes clear one day how similar Israel is to those early years in Germany, when the German people were deceived, misled. Certain moments in the Israeli experience are very similar to what happened in Germany between the insult of defeat in the Great War and the Nazis' rise to power in 1933."

He writes:

"Hitler came from the fringes of right-wing circles. Even though he was considered a lunatic, he went on to become the epicenter of the world's nightmares. In extremist circles, people dip into pools of hatred, and pass this onto their companions. Inflammatory language arouses passions but creates false warmth. They allow themselves to speak words that should not be spoken in respectable places. Extremism moves from the fringes of xenophobic nationalism to the more moderate right and from there to the cultural and political mainstream. The circles of influence almost always parallel those of indifference."

"At first extremists are viewed with disdain, as they are just a 'tiny minority', 'lunatics', etc. But disdain, unfortunately, does not stop them. The people at the center are too indifferent and self-indulgent to pay too much attention, and they become accustomed to the sights and sounds of extremism. Once the noises from the right are part of the public agenda, then it becomes impossible to uproot them."

"In the 1920s and 1930s members of the German Right demanded prosecution of the 'November Criminals,' as they called the leaders of the democratic parties who had signed the armistice agreements in 1918 that ended the Great War and thus, in their eyes, betrayed Germany. In Israel, both the extreme right that loiters in the hills of the West Bank and the bourgeois right in suits and ties demand the prosecution of the 'Oslo Criminals.' That is what they call the Israeli leaders, the late Prime Minister Rabin and President Shimon Peres, who signed the Oslo Accords in 1993, and most members of Israeli society who supported them, bringing an end to the first Intifada. This must be understood as a call to bring the whole democratic process to trial. Is the similarity between German and Israel incidental? Are the writings on the wall, 'Arabs Out' and 'Transfer Now,' different in any way from *Juden Raus* (Jews out)? The speeches in the Knesset, filled with hate, fear, and obscenities that are stricken from the minutes, though not from the consciousness, what do they tell us?"

Burg concludes: "The centrality of the armed forces in [Israeli] lives, the role of language in legitimizing the illegitimate, the infil-tration of a right-wing narrative into the mainstream and the indif-ference of the passive majority—these are the major players that allow racism to contaminate our world. Moreover, in the painful comparisons between Israel today and the Germany that preceded Hitler, we have not yet considered the importance that both nations placed on national mythology and blood-earth relationships... The list is long and very shameful, and the similarities to the German situation persist. Do we still see the original Jewish point from which we evolved? Or are we too entrenched in our frightening similarity with those from whom we fled? In both cases, the national traumas and humiliation competed with the new spirit of liberty, freedom, equality, openness, and democracy. In Germany of the 1930s, the former ideas won. Will Israel choose the latter for the future?"[14]

The Israeli Jews, victims of the Nazis, have internalized not merely the diabolical aggression of the Holocaust, but the aggression of Christian society that persecuted them for sixteen hundred years. They now prepare to act out the same nationalism, patriarchy and aggression that brought about the moral collapse in Europe. Avraham Burg originally wished to call his book *Hitler Won* — and indeed, every time a racist settler on the West Bank beats a Palestinian for no reason except to make him suffer, every time an Israeli sharpshooter kills another Palestinian for simply demonstrating, every time a young Palestinian is flung into prison for simply holding up a sign protesting the theft of his parents' land — Hitler wins. That is the tragedy of Israel in 2012; but it is also our tragedy in America as well, if we cannot grow up enough to comprehend the ugly psychological realities that lie beneath the rhetoric of the Israeli political class, and give them and their powerful proxies in the US the tough love and resistance they need.

19.

When innocent people survive human aggression, we have the idea that they should "learn from what happened to them," and behave with gentle forbearance toward other people. Above all, victims of discriminatory laws should "know better" than to pass such laws themselves. But we're wrong to think in those terms. There are some important exceptions, and such exceptions are to be honored; but a very high percentage of people who survive aggression are motivated sooner or later to hurt innocent people, or hurt themselves, or to identify with institutions and worldviews based on aggression as the highest good. *Victims are very often motivated to commit exactly the kind of unnecessary aggression that was committed against them.* Why does this horrible thing happen? Are people insane?

It happens because for the human personality to survive aggression, it must make some unusual adjustments. It *identifies* with aggression in order to survive it, but that identification causes the victim to *internalize* the aggression. This is a radical re-alignment in the unconscious mind that ensures survival of the victim's personality, but it also results in the victim internalizing the attackers' aggression—and *that* means that victims of aggression are likely, unless there is some kind of very strong intervention, to become just as aggressive as their attackers. Sadly, however, they rarely direct that internalized aggression against those that attacked them. Victims of aggression who internalize aggression are much more likely to act it out against innocent people, or against themselves. It's an unpleasant reality, but for just that reason it's time we stop denying it.

Despite being a paradoxical process, one that is difficult for many people to understand and accept, trauma bonding is probably the most powerful and dangerous process by which aggression is replicated in human societies. And since deceit transforms aggression into evil, it is also the main way that evil replicates itself in the affairs of humankind. Because it can be used to manipulate aggression, it is employed by aggressive men and political movements that intuitively understand how to use it. Aggressive and unscrupulous governments use these harrowing psychological realities to control, harm and tyrannize others, as we will see in the next chapter.

Chapter 2

Aggression, Evil and Systemic Evil

I.

What is evil? Evil is unacceptable aggression that the aggressor is trying to conceal, usually in order to continue doing it. But not many people like to use the word 'evil,' because it sounds so... *medieval*. But it exists, as anybody who's ever been gang-raped, tortured, shot by death squads or sent to a concentration camp will tell you. (When Slobodan Milosevic's militias systematically used these brutal tactics in the Balkans in the 1990s, they quickly became a form of *systemic evil*, which culminated in genocide against the Muslims of Bosnia.) But how and why does evil happen at all? It's a big mystery to most people, partly because so many of them don't want to believe it exists, even highly educated people with unimpeachable morality. To be fair, we'll probably never be able to explain evil completely— human behavior must always be an open question. But a careful observation of human behavior will allow us at least to define it. *Evil is unacceptable aggression plus deceit.*

But how do we define unacceptable aggression?

Think about almost any felony crime under American law. Almost all such crimes involved the direct or indirect aggression of one person, or party, against another. Murder, rape, theft, they're all forms of unacceptable aggression—that's why they're against the law. Price-fixing and trickery by big banks and corporations is also a form of unacceptable aggression, not only against other businesses, but also against the American consumer. Now think about what happens when a person (or corporation, party or any other entity) commits a serious crime, yet tries to deny, rationalize or cover it up, or claims that the harm is mitigated because the aggression leads to some higher good.

That's *evil*.

If enough people do this for the same destructive purpose, that's *systemic evil,* in which the aggression of individuals becomes part of the same toxic psychological and social system. This usually occurs with the collusion of the state. (An example of this is the way many Germans followed Hitler and did whatever the Nazi state told them to do, including things they later acknowledged as wrong. A similar situation prevailed under Stalin in the Soviet Union.)

In the previous chapter, we saw how victims of aggression internalize the aggression they've experienced, and are likely to act it out without completely understanding why. In this chapter we're going to examine how aggression and evil operate in society, with an emphasis on systemic evil and the cultural factors that encourage it. People may not understand *why* evil happens, whether systemic or personal, and they may not want to *call* it evil, but they know it when they see it. The ability to recognize evil is not acquired through reading law or philosophy, this author would argue—it is in part instinctive, having evolved through a folk process of social and historical evolution to achieve a rough consensus, but one that is always evolving and is different according to each age. Still, basic attitudes about unacceptable aggression tend to be fairly consistent.

A hundred people may believe in utterly different religious and political philosophies, but all are likely to agree without exception that murder, rape and theft are wrong. Nor do you have to explain to a family in East Oakland, whose five-year-old child has been killed in the crossfire of a drug war, why homicide and illegal drug trafficking are wrong; their inconsolable grief will address their loss more adequately and fairly than all the philosophy of which the world's thinkers are capable. To be sure, punishment for criminal behavior has changed, as the object of incarceration has gradually become as much about rehabilitation as punishment; but the most revealing issues of law, by far, are those concerning behaviors— often practiced by great masses of people—that are acceptable in one generation but that gradually come to be regarded as a form of systemic evil, and therefore unacceptable, in the next.

Sixty years ago it was acceptable for people in the United States to put up signs saying "White Only," prohibiting some people from receiving services or renting apartments on the basis of race. In the 1960s, America decided that this was no longer acceptable, and it became illegal; likewise segregation in the schools was declared to be illegal in 1954 because it was found to be in violation of the US Constitution. It was just as wrong in 1953 as it was in 1954, when Brown versus Board of Education was decided; but it took the deliberations of the Supreme Court to actually prohibit it by law. This decision was preceded, accompanied and analyzed retrospectively by thinkers and movements of every kind that influenced the public mind—and ultimately the Supreme Court—to find segregation and denial of voting rights based on race unacceptable.

Therefore those practices were declared illegal. These great changes began with the writings and public advocacy of noble and outspoken individuals long ago, and continued over a period of centuries; but their ideas were ultimately taken up by powerful organized movements in the 1940s and 1950s, culminating in the nonviolent Civil Rights Movement led by Bayard Rustin and A. Philip Randolph, and finally a young Baptist preacher named Dr. Martin Luther King in Montgomery, Alabama. After much struggle, sacrifice and suffering the ideas for which they advocated were finally recognized as the law of the land. Segregation and denial of the voting franchise based on race is now considered a form of systemic evil, and is prohibited by law.

We are concentrating on the nature of evil in this book—we will not, thank heaven, need to waste our time wondering about the nature of happiness, or whether happiness is the highest good. Happiness is a personal quest, something that people experience (or don't experience) as they respond to the individual challenges that beset the many. Despite the fact that Americans are guaranteed the *pursuit* of happiness in their Constitution, each person achieves it in a personal way, if at all. The problem of evil is older, more the result of unconscious emotional orientations, more compulsively acted out and harder to comprehend and ultimately resolve—but paradoxically it's easier to track, because the paths of evil follow narrow, generally rigid and rather familiar patterns having to do with overt or covert aggression. And evil is paradoxically linked to freedom of choice, which is greatly valued by most Americans. To explain this connection, let us assume that one powerful goal of both law and morality might be to arrive as a society in which the individual would generally "be contented with so much liberty against other men as he would allow other men against himself."[15]

These words were written by Thomas Hobbes, who lived at a time when evil was at a premium and there was precious little civil peace, much less civil society. Thomas Hobbes' edgy formula was not just about liberty, but also about aggression, and is especially interesting because of his presumption that freedom is just as likely to be used *against* people as *for* them—something libertarians don't usually like to acknowledge, perhaps because so many of them don't acknowledge the existence of evil. But Hobbes' formulation is really a serviceable way of facing the fact that liberty is just as likely to be used aggressively as for benign purposes. That's not an argument to limit freedom, but to limit its misuse—and to face the facts of human nature. (Remember, whether the aggression goes on to become evil depends on whether the aggressor tries to conceal it.) In any case, Hobbes' harshly inverted and somewhat creepy application of the Golden Rule is precisely the right way to view the responsibilities of law, since it must in many instances draw red lines beyond which behavior of persons or institutions cannot go. But simply passing laws is far from being the end of the story, in terms of the popular struggle against social or systemic evil. The active involvement of the citizenry does something else—the advocacy, agitation and organized power of ordinary citizens can determine *how* laws are enforced, and put pressure on the legislature to pass new ones.

The following is a good example of how the red line of popular morality can be negotiated and enhanced through citizen pressure, and how certain kinds of evil can be opposed and made illegal. In the last forty years of the 20th century there was a growing determination, on the part of women's organizations and their allies, to punish sexual assaults against women—by creating new laws, partly, but also by prosecuting criminals arrested under laws already on the books. Many modern people are blissfully unaware of this, but as late as fifty years ago, police often neglected to even investigate allegations of rape. This brutal reality was gradually changed due to ongoing, quietly persistent pressure from a variety of legal and popular advocates. Pivotal in this change was Susan Brownmiller's passionate arguments in *Against Our Will: Men, Women and Rape,* which—although her book contained errors in fact and tended to overgeneralize—awakened women and men to the role of sexual assault in maintaining the suppression of women; and helped greatly to organize women into a powerful interest group demanding change in the way laws were enforced.

Previously, many law enforcement officials had claimed that rape was almost impossible to prove, because it depended almost entirely on the word of the victim. As a result of the Women's Movement, investigatory techniques were transformed; rape kits, rape counseling by women, and other investigative innovations were put in place; in time DNA would be used both to convict the guilty and vindicate the innocent; and the proper investigation of rape and other sexual assaults became the norm. Similar changes in the investigation of domestic violence and sexual harassment followed, with the writing and enactment of new laws, and a new determination by district attorneys to prosecute those who broke them—again, mainly because of pressure from the Women's Movement. These changes were accompanied by endless discussion and argumentation in case law, but the changes were overwhelmingly accepted and today American society is better for it.

This sea change in American society has generally not been included in the dominant historical narrative of our time, probably because the women's organizations involved worked rather quietly for incremental changes in law and public attitudes, and because legal advocacy evolved in tandem with the consciousness-raising of activist women, who formed networks and applied pressure. In any case—let's face it—most history is written by men. But the importance of these changes cannot be overemphasized. The changes started out in consciousness-raising by activists, and then extended not merely to changing laws but to properly enforcing them, explaining to society at every point why and how society would benefit from their enforcement. The importance of the Women's Movement in changing the way Americans viewed and punished rape, sexual harassment and domestic violence is enormous. They constitute profound changes in the emotional orientations that inform both the law and enforcement of that law, as well as the public's overall attitude toward what is no longer permissible.

These changes can be compared to the anti-lynching movement of the 19th and 20th centuries: the anti-lynching movement sought not just to change the law, but to enforce many laws already in existence. The anti-lynching movement was part of a larger Civil Rights Movement, in the sense that lynching was understood as being practiced in order to terrorize and intimidate the African-American population of America. Lynching was a part of an indigenous Southern system of institutional terrorism, and was simply another (if particularly violent) way of keeping African-Americans oppressed by the segregation laws of the American South. The anti-lynching movement was a source of passionate advocacy that contributed, over a long period of time, to the final success of the Second American Revolution—the passage of the Civil Rights Act of 1964 and the Voting Rights Act of 1965.

Lynching was, besides being a means of generating fear of dissent among Southern Blacks, a highly calibrated use of emotional trauma in order to bond people to a violent lifestyle. Almost all photos of lynching shows excited crowds of people, usually in a state of hysterical euphoria. But they also show something else. They show adults *holding up their children* so that the children can see the dead body or bodies hanging from the trees. Why would they be so solicitous about their children seeing the horrible aftermath of a lynching, which in a great many cases included mutilation? The answer is painfully clear. The children were being held up so that they would be emotionally traumatized by what they saw, to bond them to the violence that underlay everything else in the South, and in that way bond them to the South itself. The real if unspoken social contract of racial segregation was a trauma bond which held both whites and African-Americans in its grip, but from which African-Americans suffered disproportionately.

2.

The difference between governance and personal morality is that while the state establishes laws, morality works through emotional and cognitive orientations that guide personal behavior. Morality also has the intuitive flexibility to move beyond and around the law to achieve an accommodation to those forms of aggression that are acceptable, and to find ways that aggression can be sublimated. (That is, channeled into nonviolent behavior.) This can happen in unexpected ways—for example, academically gifted young adults often learn how to harness aggression and use it to achieve excellence in law, medicine and academia. And since morality begins as a personal phenomenon, it is greatly influenced by individual taste as well as ideas of right and wrong. A close look at this will reveal that a great deal of aggression is acceptable—indeed, the ability to sublimate raw aggression into competition in sports and business can make society safer, if not carried too far.

The most noticeable form of acceptable aggression in America is the existence of certain immensely popular contact sports, which are a huge part of American popular culture. Playing and watching football or hockey, for example, is almost pure aggression; aggression also informs the comic strutting and pummeling of TV wrestling, which is actually a kind of vulgarized, semi-hysterical folk opera of lowbrow patriarchy. The most frequent image of acceptable violence in popular American culture is the regular get-togethers of diverse people (usually men) to watch contact sports together, very often in a basement or garage or similar 'man-cave.' Hunting is another archaic and deeply aggressive activity that society allows, probably—although it will not say so openly—because it is afraid that the men that practice it would be more dangerous to other people (and to themselves) if they weren't allowed to kill animals. I have heard this idea expressed by older female family members in my own family concerning sport hunting, although those same women would have looked kindly on hunting "for the pot" in hard times—i.e., hunting for food for the family.

These examples are given to underscore the deeply personal nature of aggression (both acceptable and unacceptable kinds) and to examine in this chapter how *aggression* becomes *evil*; and how *evil* becomes what is generally referred to as *systemic evil*, which happens when it is used in a systematic way by the state or other powerful agency. Among other things, internalized aggression has a tendency to cause people to identify with violent solutions to social problems, and with patriarchal and aggressive movements and institutions. Of course, some people have a great deal of latent aggression—and we should remember that *some* aggression is latent in almost all people—but being personally exposed to or victimized by violence greatly strengthens whatever aggression is already there. And aggression, whether latent or acquired, can also be enhanced by particular cultural tendencies, as we'll soon see.

Furthermore, almost all people have a built-in tendency to cover up, rationalize or dissemble their harmful behavior, partly in order to evade retaliation or punishment, but also because the individual correctly experiences it as shameful. We should recognize, then, that evil is not something that comes from the Devil, or some source outside ourselves, nor is it a conspiracy in which we are always the victims; anybody reading this book is capable of it. To understand and confront aggression and evil in the world one must start with oneself. Any coherent moral psychology of the 21st century must begin with the individual's awareness of his or her *personal capacity for evil*. Paradoxically, once one has confronted a personal capacity for evil, it becomes less threatening, because by identifying it the individual becomes aware that he is free *not* to act on it. And that is very powerful.

Evil, we should remember, consists of aggression that the aggressor is trying to conceal, rationalize or make excuses for. (That by itself tells us that the aggression is unacceptable, or the aggressor would not try so hard to cover it up.) *Evil is unacceptable aggression plus deceit.* Have you ever done something aggressive, and lied about it later so people wouldn't know? All of us have, at one time or another. Why is it so important to be aware of that? Because if we're not, we'll tend almost exclusively to see evil in other people, either people who are so much like us that they make us uneasy; or so different from us that we can endlessly project our conflicted emotions onto them. People who remind us of ourselves tend to remind us of our own deficits; and people who belong to different cultures can easily be demonized because we don't see them on a daily basis, and they become a blank screen upon which we project our unresolved emotional conflicts. This tendency to see evil mainly in the 'Other' is a problem we'll shortly look at in more detail, but it's a problem commented on by virtually all the great prophets and teachers throughout human history. If and when we see evidence of evil, it's almost always not in ourselves—we always see it in other people. An awareness of our own capacity for evil helps us to avoid projecting our own unresolved problems onto other people.

Because you care enough to read a book about the nature of good and evil, I'm betting that although you may have your own demons and bad habits, you also probably have them more under control than most people. But nobody has a patent on morality and nobody has an option on wisdom. We all have aggression inside us and we're all tempted to lie about it when we act on it. Do we admit it when we act in a manipulative fashion, or do we tell a whopper to get what we want? How many times do we look away from someone we know who needs help that we could have easily given? If you're aware of that, you're aware of the aggression inside your personality—and that very awareness can be enormously liberating, because *you will feel less need to act on it next time.* There's nothing that feels quite as liberating as to decide *not* to act on aggression. Talk about random acts of kindness! It just feels good.

That's one important reason for this chapter. Unless you're a really horrible person (and I'm betting that you aren't), it simply feels better not to get angry, not to hurt someone, and not to take advantage of somebody else's weakness. That's how one goes about building up the positive mental and emotional habits that constitute good behavior, and reinforce the moral code that is at the core of the self. (Building good habits as a means of developing a strong personality used to be called 'character-building,' and that's still a good way to put it.) But it's also a good thing to recognize that you may have internalized aggression that you're not yet aware of, as a result of having been a victim of somebody else's aggression, or simply by being exposed to it. In fact, sometimes people have aggressive emotional orientations in the unconscious parts of their personalities for a very long time, without really understanding how it got there, or why, or how it is affecting them.

It's much easier to choose *not* to act on an aggressive emotional orientation once one understands that it's there. But knowing about our own capacity for evil is important for another reason, one that I've already mentioned but that bears repeating. Once you see this capacity in yourself, a capacity all people share, you are much less likely to see evil *in other people.* If you are aware of your own demons, and if you are comfortable with them (and why shouldn't you be?), you'll probably be able to harness them to use them creatively when you need them. As a result, you're much less likely to be needlessly aggressive toward other people; and also—this is a very big deal—you'll be *less likely to be obsessed by the faults and limitations of other people.*

Once you see your own capacity for evil, you can stop complaining about others and start trying to make yourself better. You usually can't change others, but you *can* change yourself—and as you become a less aggressive person, you will actually elicit less aggressive behavior on the part of others. That doesn't mean turning away from the necessity of opposing systemic or personal evil when it arises in the world; it simply means understanding that aggression, evil and systemic evil constitutes a big and very difficult human problem, and that we can fight only those evils in the world that we have first recognized and overcome in ourselves.

The great horror and suspense writer Stephen King once wrote an essay in which he compared the darkest part of the human personality to a swamp infested by alligators. He said that people had to learn to feed those gators, and they wouldn't get out of hand. That was his role, he said—his horror and suspense fiction helped the broad reading public feed their gators. I wasn't sure I liked this idea at first, but then I reflected that what we used to call fairy tales—the folk tales told to children for millennia—all have a component of horror and aggression to them. Then I remembered the 'bedtime stories' told to me by my grandmother in the Missouri Ozarks. They were all pretty scary tales, especially the one about a giant who lived in the earth and was likely to come grab my big toe in the middle of the night. That one really scared me, but it taught me an important lesson—that I could laugh at it with my grandmother, and go to sleep anyway. That was a pretty big deal for a five-year-old kid. So I decided maybe Stephen King had a point after all.

Carl Gustav Jung, the great Swiss psychoanalyst, called this "getting used to our Shadow." We need to make contact with—and get used to—our capacity to do bad things and to tell lies to exonerate ourselves. Once we are aware of the existence of our Shadow, it is much less frightening, and a lot more interesting. And it becomes a lot harder to think that aggression and evil always originate with somebody else. When we get to know our Shadow, we become familiar with it, and suddenly it no longer has the ability to scare us; and then, when it no longer scares us, we know we don't have to act on it. Now *that's* liberating!

3.

The compulsion of the aggressor to lie about aggression is deeply connected to human speech and intelligence, and seems to be almost universal. It happens because of the aggressor's shame concerning his aggression, as well as his intense desire not to get caught. (With sociopaths it's almost always the latter.) Some criminal offenders learn at an early age how to divert attention from their devastating crimes; for some of them (and this includes both men and women) it is often enough simply to *look* innocent. Scott Peterson, the young Californian man who was convicted and sentenced to death for murdering his eight-months-pregnant wife, had everybody fooled because he looked so incredibly wholesome when he smiled (and he smiled a lot) that people just didn't want to see him as dangerous.[16] But when he belied his Golden Boy image with scores of troubling lies, police investigators began to realize they had a sociopath on their hands. Criminal offenders in particular tend to blame their aggression on other people: they blame their problems on their parents, guardians and group homes that raised them. This may be partly true, but it is beside the point where legal liability or criminal responsibility is concerned.

Law and morality encourage people to live without committing crimes against each other, but sociopaths have a particularly hard time getting there. They are much more inclined to hurt other people to get something they want, and claim later that their violence was merely defensive; they swear that it isn't what it seems to be, that everybody has it wrong; and (as anybody knows who has studied the transcripts of their interrogations) rapists in particular insist that sexual contact was consensual, that their victims "really wanted it." But this tendency to lie about their own aggression isn't limited to criminals and sociopaths. There is an almost universal tendency of aggressive social and political movements to rationalize their violence, and violent governments are particularly prone to spinning and rationalizing their various maledictions.

Communist, fascist, Zionist and nationalist ideologues are particularly prone to engage in complicated arguments that their aggression should actually be embraced because it serves a special historical or even divine purpose. Religious nationalists regularly discern God's will in the predations of the state, as in Pakistan, Iran and Israel (all theocratic governments); aggressive governments justify violence with complex political and social theories, and excel at using fear of what might happen in the future to justify hurting people in the present. Some people rationalize aggression by claiming class or race or gender or religious privilege; and almost all aggressive politicians, governments or nationalist movements use crimes committed in the past to rationalize the crimes they intend to commit in the present. And what does this tendency to rationalize past, present and future crimes tell us? It tells us that the ideologues involved have been victims of aggression, or at the very least have been exposed to it as a methodology—and are incapable of developing an alternative to it. So they seek a *continuation* of the violence they've experienced in the past, with new victims and under new circumstances. That's what fuels the cycle of violence in which the world is caught.

People who use past atrocities to justify today's violence against innocent people are basically looking for reasons to act out their own internalized aggression. The early settlers of Israel said they *had* to ethnically cleanse the Palestinians, because they needed to have a Jewish-majority state. Why? Because of what anti-Semites *might* do to Jews in the future. But was that the real reason, or was it really a way of doing to Palestinians what European Christians once did to the Jews? Either way, you cannot justify hurting people based on your worst fears, because the fear will so radically cloud your judgment that you will never understand the real basis for your aggression, or where the aggression you have internalized really came from. It is likely that most European Zionists unconsciously promoted such a fatally destructive course because of their own internalized aggression, not to mention their unconscious identification with the aggression of European Christians. Their own writings repeatedly take the line that only a patriarchal warrior culture can redeem the death of the six million, a tip-off that their real agenda is more violence.

Likewise the Serbian militias used fear to justify genocide against Muslims. They cited all the violence Serbs had suffered, especially the genocidal violence of the Nazis and Croats in the Second World War. They had to get rid of the Muslims, they said, because if they did not create large constituencies made up entirely of Serbs, all the non-Serbs (and especially Muslims) would band together to kill them. The only problem with this was that it was all in the imagination of the right-wing Serbs themselves—there was no evidence, for example, that Bosnia Muslims would in any way interfere with the Serbs. But for the Serbs, it was a reality, especially when Slobodan Milosevic used his media to tell them so on a daily basis. So they committed to worst genocide in Europe since the Nazi Holocaust.

It's the inverted Golden Rule of aggression as a lifestyle— aggressors look for ways to posture themselves as pitiful victims, and their victim status becomes the ultimate rationalization for the crimes that they have committed, intend to commit in the future, or are in the process of committing. This tactic makes them similar to sociopaths, who are famous for blaming other people for everything they do. The decision of the Israeli state to invoke the Nazi Holocaust as a way of justifying racism against Palestinians has raised the apotheosis of victim status to the level of a science. An Israeli infantryman who breaks the leg of a Palestinian teenager, tortures him in an interrogation center, or demolishes the house where he and his family have lived for generations, is likely to feel like a pitiful victim even as he's beating up his victim and destroying his house.

In the short term, of course, most soldiers learn to feel *nothing* while engaging in such acts, because they are just "doing their job." But whenever feelings threaten to break through, there is often a legacy of victim status that can quickly be invoked to operate as a defense mechanism. How unpleasant it is to have to do such things, the aggressor tells himself, because he is really such a very nice person—if only the world could see how nice he was, and how understandable his aggression really was. White South Africans were superb at this, during the apartheid era. ("We're not angels, of course, but if people would just stop judging us they'd see how basically decent we are.") Sometimes, when the aggression is committed by the state, tyrants conceal their dirty work by simply suppressing all evidence that it ever happened, and killing or imprisoning anyone who talks or writes about it. There is a near-universal tendency to feel that if information about an atrocity can be suppressed, the atrocity really didn't happen.

Illegitimate governments that are famous for imprisonment of dissenters, torture, systematic sexual abuse of women, and political murder tend to talk about the horrors that lie in the future if they don't maintain order through state terror. And that is always a lie, in one way or another—such rationalizations almost always backfire. (Hitler repeatedly stated that if people didn't accept his state terrorism, civilization would be overrun by Soviet Communism. And then he attacked Russia, which led Soviet troops to overrun Germany, where they raped uncounted German women.) In fact, all these efforts to rationalize state aggression are strong circumstantial evidence that government aggressors know what they do is wrong— which is why they invent self-serving and often stupid rationalizations for continuing to do it.

Human rights groups such as Amnesty International report that although tyrants use violence to cower and traumatize their own people, they do not want people outside their own countries to know about what they do to maintain power. The existence of this *suppressed consciousness* of aggression as harmful or potentially harmful is one big reason that dictatorships hide, excuse or dissemble the harm they do. This attempt to cover up or rationalize the destructive effects of aggression is when aggression becomes evil, so by the time a dictatorship uses the resources of the state to cover mass aggression it has already become *systemic evil*. When governments start concealing or rationalizing state aggression, it is usually a signal that they intend to continue exactly what they've been doing in the past. In any case, the tendency to rationalize or cover up aggression is uniquely human.

4.

The shark that attacks a swimmer does not attempt to justify or dissemble his attack, because when he is hungry he is unaware of any alternative to killing and eating whatever is available. (And he's almost always hungry—sex and food are his two main occupations.) Social and biological evolution simply did not equip sharks to consider alternative plans of action, which is why the shark at first seems like a very good metaphor for aggression. But it's actually a very bad metaphor for human aggression, because sharks can't decide *not* to use aggression, whereas humans often must. A tiger is likewise aggressive; but tigers do not make up complicated excuses for their violent behavior because they are not conscious of any wrongdoing. Therefore one cannot call either shark or tiger evil.

But for the criminal and the tyrant, it's a different story. They dominate or hurt people to get what they want, and afterwards try to suppress the evidence of their violence, often so they can commit more crimes when the heat is off. Yet that very desire of the sociopath, the dictator or the con man to conceal or rationalize what they have done, or are doing, suggests that they know that they are wrong, and are afraid of getting caught. They stand convicted, in other words, by their own glib and lubricious alibis.

There is an amazing, underlying consistency in the way that human beings try to dissimulate their aggression, so much that it clearly qualifies as a marker for a certain stage of social evolution. And what a paradox *that* is—that this tendency to conceal crimes and misdemeanors, particularly when committed by powerful institutions, is both a trait of civilization, and the main symptom of the systemic evil that may someday destroy civilization. People engaged in violent behavior are often able to suppress the guilt their behavior generates, because hardened criminals usually handle guilt much better than so-called normal people, who tend to unravel under such circumstance. (See *Macbeth* for the Shakespearean version of this dynamic.) Dictators of every political or nationalist persuasion, along with their violent apparatchiki of state terrorism, would not try so hard to conceal their state crimes if they did not believe that reasonable people around the world would be disgusted by their government's behavior—even as they piously insist that they're not quite sure what all the fuss is about.

No one needs an advanced degree to understand that rape, theft and murder devastate human lives. The frenzied attempt by sociopath and tyrant alike to justify, hide or minimize their aggression is proof enough of their guilty knowledge of wrong-doing. To be sure, the law may establish different punishments for different kinds of criminal behavior, just as the judge must consider a plethora of mitigating circumstances to hand down a fair sentence; but both criminal and victim know the guilty verdict well before it is announced. Both live with its effects well after the crime is committed: the victim with his psychological wounds, and the criminal with his incarceration.

The harrowing Biblical story of Cain and Abel is the Abrahamic family's first written account of the problem of aggression-that-becomes-evil. Cain's slaying of Abel becomes truly evil when Cain will not accept responsibility for what he has done. Not that the aggression isn't horrible by itself—it is, as only the slaying of a sibling can be. But it is Cain's lying about it that keeps the murder in the present tense, because it adds bad faith to the already monstrous nature of the deed. Had Cain accepted his guilt, the tragedy would have been over quickly. Woven deep into the tale of Cain and Abel are two stories: first, it is an ancient version of a conflict between farmers and hunter-gatherers; secondly, it is a cautionary tale about aggression and evil. It is Cain's unwillingness to *accept* his guilt that makes the story a searing introduction to the problem of evil, suggesting at the same time the horrific nature of the oppression generated by the new agriculture-based empires that were then displacing hunter-gatherer societies.

Ultimately, however, it is the *mark of Cain* on Cain's forehead that finally causes the story to be so haunting, because Cain's guilt is now published to everybody who looks into his face. The intervention of God in the story can be understood in only one way—it is fair warning to humanity that we are dangerous to each other, not just because of our aggression, but because of our efforts to conceal our aggression. The mark on Cain's forehead makes it impossible for him to conceal the bloody violence he has committed, and to warn that he is capable of committing more crimes in the future.

5.

Systemic evil is different from individual evil, if for no other reason than the enormity of the informational apparatus necessary to lie and cover up mass crimes. When such mass violence is committed or organized by the state, it is the state that tries to cover it up, rationalize it, or develop some alternative narrative that can conceal or deflect interest in the truth. This is also true of the period just before any form of mass violence is to be committed by the state. Remember the US just before the invasion of Iraq? The amount of propaganda churned out by the administration of President George W. Bush was almost unbelievable in the sheer volume of it. Bush's claim that Iraq possessed Weapons of Mass Destruction was the biggest lie, but most of the Bush administration's Iraq policies consisted of one lie or half-truth after the other, so that taken together they constituted a single Big Lie, the purpose of which was to enable the invasion of another country under false pretenses. That, along with the complacent acceptance of these lies by America's media, is an example of systemic evil that resulted in enormous harm, the virtual destruction of Iraqi society, the bankruptcy of America and the coronation of a new band of crooks to run the Iraq government.

Under Hitler it was the job of the Reich Minister of Propaganda, Joseph Goebbels, to invent an alternative narrative that justified everything that Hitler and the Nazis did, containing not-so-subtle threats to listeners who were tempted to doubt the Nazi version of reality. Under Stalin, Communist intellectuals and propagandists developed vast theories of enormous scholarly distinction to justify murdering twenty million people and sending millions more to the gulag. Some Russian and German intellectuals thought they could ignore this kind of crude propaganda, opting for what has generally been translated as 'internal exile,' but what they didn't realize was that the state aggression that accompanied the propaganda was bonding people to the state narrative (that is, it was influencing how they reacted to state propaganda), which over a period of time caused many of them to believe it even when they didn't want to—that is, even when they suspected it wasn't true. After some time, when people are bombarded by lies that intentionally threaten government persecution if the listener does not believe them, people often give up trying to separate truth from propaganda, and begin to accept everything the state or media says as a kind of 'as if' fantasy. A typical comment of people in that situation is, "Well, some of it might be true. After all, they have access to more information than I do."

When state crimes are successfully dissimulated—that is, lied about, covered up, minimized or otherwise rationalized—the disinformation itself is incorporated into the ongoing systemic evil. Once that happens, the aggressive state has no reason to stop, because its operatives know they can continue to hurt people with impunity. The state's victims are put on notice that they cannot get justice; the supporters of violence in the government then gain power. When a crime or offense has been dissimulated cleverly, people may not even understand what has happened, although people generally sense that something is wrong.

Sometimes entire societies—that is, something close to the actual majority of the population—lie to themselves about the nature and extent of the crimes committed by their government. Human beings have the ability to misrepresent and conceal aggression in a bewildering number of ways (including the most popular method, self-deception); and when aggressors are so successful in concealing their crimes that ordinary citizens likewise have a stake in denying that it is happening, the predations of the state aggressors are likely to become part of a social and psychological system that causes enormous destruction.

This is not because of some general and comprehensive failing of the state as a generic institution. Governments do many necessary and laudable things. Through its ability to appropriately collect revenues, the state makes possible public education, perhaps the most important institution of modern American civilization. Likewise through its collection of public revenues, it facilitates the American safety net: social security, Medicare, science research projects, police and firefighters and the like. The federal government also enforces the important civil rights legislation of the 1960s, without which (as I believe) large sections of the Southern states would return to segregation of schools and public spaces as well as systematic denial of voting rights.

The importance of these things cannot be denied. Furthermore we must acknowledge that the maintenance of a tax code necessary to revenues depends to some extent on force as a deterrent to tax evasion. But we know that without that enlightened use of force to collect taxes we would arrive at a far worse and more violent situation—no law enforcement, no public education and so forth. To enjoy the fruits of society, we must have laws: we must agree to brake our cars when the light is red, to slow down when the light is yellow, and go when it is green; and some force is needed for the enforcement of such laws, in the sense that lawbreakers must receive some kind of penalty. But any harm inherent in such force can be contained by regulating it, and making sure it is not excessive—by making sure, in other words, that the state doesn't use deadly force except in emergencies.

The appropriate and beneficial activities of the state during and after the Roosevelt administration in America of the 1930s and 1940s created—with some help from World War II and a boom economy of the 1950s—a truly robust economic recovery, which with prudent government policies (such as the GI Bill) created the largest middle class in the history of the world. Only the federal government could have integrated the races within the armed services; only the federal government could have created the GI Bill; and only the US federal government could have conceived and executed the stabilizing effects in Europe of the Marshall Plan. Only the state can practice diplomacy successfully, only the state can direct a policy allowing maximum funding of science, and only the state can best guide economic decisions that result in the Keynesian stimulation of the economy.

Therefore, no intrinsic evil adheres to the existence of the state, which our libertarian and ultra-conservative friends would like us to believe. It is the role of systemic evil *in* the state that makes it evil, or the use of the state by evil for evil purposes. It is corrupt leaders that use the state to declare unnecessary wars resulting in unimaginable human suffering; it is corrupt governments that imprison the very soul of humankind with unjust laws; some are even willing to engage in genocide, as extremist Hutu Power government forces did against the Tutsis in Rwanda. We understand the evil of which the armed state is capable. But we must declare many state functions as benign or necessary to democracy—not to mention law and order—and focus specifically on specifics evils by the state rather than engage in blanket denunciation of government in general.

Libertarians—who in the US are overwhelmingly rightwing—would like to destroy the good and healthy activities of the state in order to defeat what they see as the state's potential for evil. But their primary goal is, and has always been, to destroy those laws and institutions that empower ordinary people; libertarianism in the US is increasingly funded by the one percent of the people that constitute the super-rich, who seek the destruction of the entire public sector, not to mention Social Security and Medicare. Why do they seek that? Because without a viable public sector, the vast majority of the American people—even the vaunted upper middle class—would be reduced to the kind of powerlessness that would make them unable to even minimally enforce the one percent's business and financial activities. Nor would they have any practical way to keep the new super-billionaires from lowering everybody's wages to starvation level. In that way, the corporate upper class could maximize its profits by everybody else down to the level of a new urban peasantry. Does that seem harsh? If so, you have no idea of the vicious new investment and corporate upper class that has arisen in America. They have taken over the Republican Party, and they are quite ruthless.

The goal of a moral psychology, on the other hand, is the deconstruction of systemic evil that engages in aggression and lies to cover up its crimes. Although America is currently under attack by an arrogant new corporate upper class (and a new kind of investment class that does nothing but gamble with other people's money), the country's democratic process is still robust enough that one part of government can be employed to regulate and deconstruct unacceptable aggression in another part, at least when forced to do so by an enraged citizenry and media. The best 20th century example of this was the threat of the US Congress to investigate the illegal activities of President Richard Nixon, a threat that forced him to resign, after which the judicial branch of government put scores of his criminal cronies in prison.

Why is this important as an example? Because Nixon used the executive branch of government to bypass the US Constitution, whereupon the legislative and judicial branches of government were able to investigate his predations, limit the harm he did, and finally bring to an end his experiment in authoritarianism by forcing him to resign. Because of the abiding genius of our American separation of political powers, guaranteed in the American Constitution, American government is often capable, at least in extreme cases, of a fairly credible level of self-regulation. The downside of the separation of political powers is that because each has differently defined functions, government is often in a state of gridlock—but gridlock, almost everybody agrees, is better than tyranny.

6.

Let us quickly re-define *systemic evil*, so often referred to by theologians and historians when writing about the organized atrocities that occurred under Hitler, Stalin, the Cambodian tyrant Pol Pot and many others. When the state or other powerful entity engages in unnecessary and unacceptable aggression, then acts to deliberately cover it up, lie about it, or rationalize its behavior, the aggression becomes *systemic evil*. If the state gets away with it, it will then be much more likely to repeat the same kind of aggression, because its deceit has provided it with a shield of impunity—and if the government aggression continues, and the government continues to get away with it, the aggression is likely to become a habit, and finally an addiction. *It is evil when the aggressor lies about his aggression; it is systemic evil when the state lies about its mass aggression.*

7.

When we consider history retroactively, we see that particular kinds of systemic evil experienced accelerated growth in two hugely important historical periods, when a variety of social factors encouraged them. Both of these periods have accurately been described as Revolutions—the Neolithic and the Industrial—during which civilization completely re-invented itself. The first of these was roughly ten to twelve thousand years ago at the end of the last Ice Age, when human beings were turning from hunter-gathering to agricultural societies. This led to larger cities and finally the great empires that arose with the agricultural revolution. At the same time, population boomed and new divisions of labor were introduced. But these new societies based on agriculture were accompanied by an ominous and even catastrophic development—an agricultural surplus developed, creating vast new wealth that hadn't been available to humanity before. Now that there was wealth and the power that wealth buys, a tremendous struggle ensured to see who would control it. Huge power struggles broke out in each nascent empire to decide who would be in the ruling class, how the resulting class system would be organized, and how the ruling class would use its new wealth and power to rule.

As the dust settled, the new imperial rulers set up an oppressive new class system, the better to stay on top and exploit their fellow human beings. A bewildering array of castes and classes now arose in the new empires, giving power to a few at the top and increasingly less power to the masses as one descended the pyramid. Women were the big losers in this development, losing their equality to men across the board in all classes; the new system also encouraged slavery, because of the labor-intensive nature of the agricultural infrastructure on which everything else was built. The new imperial systems were accompanied by (and in some case inadvertently triggered by) religions that to some extent rationalized the prevailing practices of the new imperial societies—that is to say, slavery, the suppression of women, a state of continuing abject servitude for the masses, and constant wars of conquest.

Since many ruling families and tribes were fighting for their share of the surplus that had developed, the warrior became the major culture hero, and an entire psychological system of patriarchy grew up to justify and support this development as power relationships settled into an imperial system. A land-owning aristocratic class came into being to manage the new economy. Religion was likewise present, and was gradually modified to justify the ascendancy of the power arrangements in the new agricultural societies— and the new religions, perhaps inevitably, saw no alternative to the oppressive status quo except a greatly improved life in the hereafter. Again, the new social and economic arrangements encouraged and then enforced slavery, subjugation of women and the exploitation of the masses by a cruel and merciless ruling class.

Jared Diamond, the author of *Guns, Germs and Steel: the Fates of Human Societies*, is perhaps the best-known (that is, the most popular) author associated with research into agriculture-based societies, research that exposes them as intensely oppressive for the majority of the people. His often-quoted thesis is simple but shocking:

From biology we learned that we weren't specially created by God but evolved along with millions of other species. Now archaeology is demolishing another sacred belief: that human history over the past million years has been a long tale of progress. In particular, recent discoveries suggest that the adoption of agriculture, supposedly our most decisive step toward a better life, was in many ways a catastrophe from which we have never recovered. With agriculture came the gross social and sexual inequality, the disease and despotism, that curse our existence.[17]

This appears, not in *Guns, Germs and Steel: The Fates of Human Societies*, as the reader might at first suspect, but in a 1987 article in *Discover* magazine provocatively entitled, "The Worst Mistake in the History of the Human Race." (*Guns, Germs and Steel* would be a further explication of this essay's radical thesis.) For Jared Diamond, agriculture was a secular and anthropologically-correct version of The Fall—before agricultural societies existed there had been a long, uninterrupted period lasting thousands of years, or perhaps hundreds of thousands of years, during which humans were hunter-gathers. Congregating especially in the lush, verdant area between the Tigris and the Euphrates in modern Iraq, where many anthropologists and historians (and the Book of Genesis in the Bible) place the origins of the Garden of Eden myth, humans lived in relative peace during a long period of stability, living in equality in a world where they felt they belonged, living a life that they embraced.

Then it came to pass that the serpent entered the garden; and humans ate from the fruit of the Tree of the Knowledge of Good and Evil before they ate from the Tree of Life, and were summarily evicted from the Garden to live in shame and penury, to wander in the desert and to live by the sweat of the brow. (At least, that is the Abrahamic version of the creation myth.) The narrative from Genesis in the Bible is like a great many other stories, legends and creation myths that tell the same story in different ways. These stories, legends and folk tales can probably also be read as humanity's second thoughts about the new imperial societies they were in the process of creating. At first, the agriculturally-based societies were a big improvement on the hunter-gatherer way of life, and the adherents of the new way enthusiastically engaged in genocidal wars against the remaining hunter-gatherers. (The story of Cain and Abel contains traces of this early conflict—remember that Cain, after killing the shepherd Abel, inherits his land and creates a new city.) But as rigid class structures arose, and women lost all power and were brutally repressed, people had second thoughts about the new agriculturally-based empires they were a part of. The old hunter-gatherer stage began to feel retroactively like an irrevocably lost Edenic wonderland, or as Milton would have it, 'Paradise Lost.'

What was it about agriculturally-based societies that made them so likely to regard aggression as necessary and admirable? It certainly wasn't the raising of grain and corn that by itself was toxic: the growth of edible plants is by itself quite benign, as anybody who has tended a garden can testify. It was the *surplus* produced by agriculture that caused the wars, the rise of caste and class, and the patriarchal mumbo-jumbo that grows up around social and economic privilege, especially the rise of a male warrior class. As we will see, a great deal of research has demonstrated that the very food that people ate after their conversion to agriculture was not as good as the food previously eaten by hunter-gatherers. Above all, after the rise of the agricultural empires and cities there was continual fighting between kingdoms, and internally in each kingdom as well, to determine who would control the surplus. So quite naturally, the bloody predations and military campaigns necessary to take control of this new wealth were soon presented as humanity's noblest activity by the new rulers.

Any number of religions ecstatically promoted the male warrior as society's sexy new culture hero by worshiping warrior gods that kicked ass, took names and brooked no opposition. While the male warriors of the ascendant classes were presented as culture heroes to be emulated and feared, women—who had previously been mainly equal to men as hunter-gatherers—were now ruthlessly relegated to the status of chattel, and indirectly blamed for the rising population by mythic representations of the female as seductive but treacherous charmers who were in cahoots with various Dark Forces.

What brought on this world-shaking change? It arose because hunter-gatherers had no surplus—one person hunted and gathered just enough for his own family or tribal consumption. Agriculture, on the other hand, leads inevitably to surpluses, leading to population growth, leading to a wealthy new ruling class, culminating in the strict caste and class divisions of empire. As a division of labor emerged, the agricultural empires developed a cruelty and oppression the likes of which the hunter-gathering societies could never have imagined. The stories told in Genesis of humankind's existence in Eden before the banishment from the Garden bear strong echoes of the shock and sorrow of the hunter-gathers scrambling to find a niche for themselves in the new agriculturally-based empires that were transforming human society.

By connecting this social devolution to the knowledge of good and evil, the Book of Genesis suggests that the new imperial set-up was a punishment for the ongoing knowledge of evil that humankind could henceforth neither deny nor ignore. Or perhaps the knowledge of good and evil had to do with the realization that human society had plunged headfirst into a new way of life that at first seemed liberating, but which eventually turned into a form of psychological and personal slavery. But probably the knowledge of good and evil became so important because so much systemic evil was coming into play, in the form of an intense social oppression that hadn't existed before. So if new forms of systemic evil were being introduced, the role of religion might be a crucial one, because only religion could successfully rationalize the oppressive new circumstances as being actually a good thing in disguise. (Or, as we will see, religion might have inadvertently helped to bring the new societies into being by causing people to settle down in large settlements.)

Diamond's thesis came just as most anthropologists were arriving at a similar consensus. Particularly important, as Diamond himself acknowledges, was the research of George Armelagos and Mark Cohen, who as co-authors of *Paleopathology at the Origins of Agriculture* were able to prove from multiple studies that the food eaten after the agricultural revolution was nowhere near as nutritious as the diet eaten by hunter-gatherers. They discovered, among other things, dramatic differences in height—that people living in the hunter-gathering societies were actually much taller than later people living in agriculture-based societies.

Archeologists and anthropologists—in fact almost everybody involved in studying the agricultural transformation of societal forces—assumed that religion came *after* people settled down in agriculturally-based societies, and served the purpose of rationalizing the new arrangements in some kind of centralizing myth system. There is now evidence that everybody may have had this exactly backwards. In a recent and completely unprecedented discovery in Göbekli Tepe, Turkey, in southeastern Anatolia near the city of Urfa, a 22-acre Early Neolithic archeological site has been excavated, consisting of sixty extremely heavy limestone pillars engraved with bas-reliefs of animals. The pillars are believed to be ten to eleven thousand years old. They feature a few that are unmistakably human figures; the rest are unpleasant little animal and insect bas-reliefs (some with erections) of the kind that might have plagued—or otherwise intrigued or even been eaten by—the creators of these megaliths.

In an article for the 2011 December 19th and 26th *New Yorker* about the megaliths at Göbekli Tepe, author Elif Batuman sums up the new thinking about this astonishing discovery. Because no signs whatsoever of habitation in the Göbekli Tepe area have been discovered, Batuman writes, it now seemed almost certain that it was a "religious sanctuary" built and used by hunter-gatherers around ten thousand years ago, about the time that hunter-gatherers were becoming farmers, in other words. The findings at Göbekli Tepe "suggest that we have the [Neolithic] story backward," Batuman wrote. It now seems likely that it was actually the need to build a sacred site that first caused hunter-gatherers to settle down—and only after they built their sacred site did they organize themselves as an agricultural workforce, since there was now a large population in more or less the same geographical area, which necessitated a stable food supply. And so a large population settled down somewhere in the neighborhood and *then* began their transformation from hunter-gatherers into an agricultural society.

But the story doesn't end there. About two thousand years after the megaliths first started being built, about the time that a transformation into a totally agricultural society was more or less complete, something truly astounding happened. The people that had built the spooky sanctuary at Göbekli Tepe discovered that they really didn't want their sacred site after all, even though building the megaliths was what first caused them to settle in that neighborhood. For reasons unknown they abruptly *buried* their precious, laboriously built megaliths around 8200 BC, leaving them concealed under large mounds to be discovered by 21st-century archeologists. "The very process of construction changed their worldview, making the monument obsolete," Batuman has written. Or perhaps it was something going on in the society *after* construction, some radical altering in the beliefs of the people that changed their outlook. Whatever the timing or the complete disposition of the beliefs that had previously motivated them, the people of Göbekli Tepe certainly changed their attitude toward the megaliths their ancestors had built—enough that at great effort to themselves they buried all traces of them. The communal effort necessary to burying the megaliths was rather like the building of a Chartres Cathedral in reverse, the object being to conceal a sacred site rather than to create it.

The fundamental change in the nature of the human experience associated with the rise of agriculture has been called the "Neolithic Revolution," a phrase originated by archeologist V. Gordon Childe in the 1920s. The evidence clearly indicates that it wasn't until the people settled down at the sanctuary at Göbekli Tepe that the rise of an agricultural society began. At some point it may have suddenly become apparent to the people of a later time that the hunter-gatherer lifestyle they had known before had now irrevocably vanished (like the Garden of Eden), or had spun irrevocably out of control in some way, to the extent that they no longer recognized themselves in the megaliths they had created. Or they may have come to blame the loss of the hunter-gatherer Paradise on the myth-system associated with the very megaliths their ancestors had created, and sought either to punish or to excise it from their consciousness. Or perhaps a new ruling class had insisted on the covering-up of a religious site suddenly perceived as subversive.

The revolution from a seemingly idyllic life as hunter-gatherers to one of suffering, hardship and repression under the new agricultural system was not imposed upon humankind—it arose spontaneously from human beings who were simply adapting themselves to the opportunities offered by soil, plants and the division of labor made possible by the rise in population. How could these early innovators have guessed that these seeming benign factors would combine to cause a social evolution to the permanent existence of imperial cities and city-states, in which the masses would be little better than slaves toiling from morning to night? It was perhaps an example of what one might call the Faustian problem in history, in which thrilling short-term benefits gradually but inexorably lead to terrible things that are impossible to foresee.

Yet the people of that time *were* capable, once the implications of their choices had set in, of realizing that they had made a bad turn with unintended consequences—thus the many creation stories featuring the loss of an idyllic past in a Garden of Eden. The people of Göbekli Tepe—or perhaps their new imperial rulers—were clearly unhappy with something encoded in the religious vision that first informed the building of the megaliths. The sudden and complete burying of the megalithic statuary in 8200 BC, and the deliberate destruction of all the effort and sacrifice that had gone into creating them, suggests overwhelming fear, revulsion and regret.

So what *was* happening to people? Elif Batuman makes the case for radical Neolithic decline: "A surprising fact about the Neolithic Revolution is that, according to most evidence, agriculture brought about a steep decline in the standard of living. Studies of Kalahari Bushmen and other nomadic groups show that hunter-gatherers, even in the most inhospitable landscapes, typically spend less than twenty hours a week obtaining food. By contrast, farmers toil from sunup to sundown. Because agriculture relies on the mass culti-vation of a handful of starchy crops, a community's whole livelihood can be wiped out overnight by bad weather or pests."

"Paleontological evidence shows that, compared with hunter-gatherers, early farmers had more anemia and vitamin deficiencies, died younger, had worse teeth, were more prone to spinal deformity, and caught more infectious diseases, as a result of living close to other humans and to livestock. A study of skeletons in Greece and Turkey found that the average height of humans dropped six inches between the end of the ice age, and 3000 BC; modern Greeks and Turks still haven't regained the height of their hunter-gatherer ancestors."

Again, one encounters a central and inescapable Faustian irony. At first the original converts to agriculture experienced unprece-dented wealth—here, at last, was the Promised Land the tribal folktales had foretold! This was it! So they set about killing off the remaining hunter-gatherers in the name of this lovely new affluence (as Cain killed Abel), sealing the change in lifestyle with a shared bond of violence against the people they had themselves once been. This was the first and biggest of the many Faustian bargains that people and societies would make, reveling in the glorious, immediate benefits of something that turned out to have enormous long-range deficits and horrible unintended consequences that nobody could have even remotely imagined. Yet there was something in the new situation, however exploitive, that was so fatally attractive that people could not force themselves to step off the agricultural carousel that was carrying them toward a new social perdition.

Once agriculture as a system was established, the growth in population began to catch up with people, and the standard of living began to plummet. Everybody had to work more for less. Meanwhile a new landowning class oppressed everybody who didn't belong to their caste and class, killing all who resisted—and then, suddenly, there was no escape back to the old ways. Slavery became a commonplace, concubines the privilege of empire, and war the noblest activity of the male. The vast majority were now helpless to escape a life of bitter labor and servitude, except perhaps through a slave rebellion, which was almost always unsuccessful. Truly they felt cast out of the Garden of Eden, which they could now hardly remember except in legends and folk tales—but one thing they did know: from now on, they would have to earn their bread through the sweat of the brow.

I do not believe, as some do, that the hunter-gatherer time was an Eden in which women and men were completely equal, and human happiness was automatic. But the sweltering imperial arrangements of the ancient Middle Eastern and Asian empires were clearly hideous things, affording freedom only to those who by trickery or sheer violence were able to overcome and master others—and that kind of built-in aggression invariably bonds people to an aggressive system, with all the collateral psychological damage involved. (One could compare it to the plantation system of our own Southern states, which until the civil rights legislation of the 1960s was supported by nearly medieval arrangements, with all the cultural and psychological backwardness typical of such systems.) The Neolithic Revolution, which at first seemed to promise something liberating and precious for all, instead created a new prison for the human mind and emotions.

Yet humankind could not help but mourn its loss, dwelling in the harsh and punishing new societies that had grown up to enslave humankind, while mentally still living East of Eden long after they had been driven from the Garden; and it was then that humans first realized the desperation of their situation, without the slightest idea how to improve their status. It was then, perhaps, that religion provided the hope of a much improved afterlife, although it now seems probably that it was religions that actually helped initiate the Neolithic Revolution in the first place, and was not a mere adaptation to it. If nothing else, we should learn from Göbekli Tepe the enormous centralizing role of religion in human societies, clearly bigger than any other *proximate* factor in the first steps toward the new agriculture-based slave societies and empires.

The Neolithic Revolution did not invent or initiate human evil. It simply created a new society that allowed the few to aggressively exploit the many; and when the new rulers figured out how to effectively lie in order to justify their new power, a new form of systemic evil was born. Its new ruling class also used omnipresent wars, idealization of the warrior and warlike gods to cause aggression to be internalized. Because it was used by centralized kingdoms or states to exploit the majority, it quickly became a full-fledged form of systemic evil with many cultural accoutrements. Perhaps the 'sanctuary' of Göbekli Tepe was mainly a totemic exercise devoted to keeping evil spirits away, which was mainly a function of magic rather than religion as we conceive of it. Whatever it was or eventually became, the people who first built it also ultimately rejected it—perhaps because the new ruling class of the agricultural society wanted to see it banished, but probably also because it had already taken human beings down to unprecedented levels of degradation. In any case, at Göbekli Tepe, the exploited toilers of the agricultural system apparently took revenge on their own ancestors' religious creations.

The Greek and Roman experiments, the Renaissance and the 18th century, and the adoption of universal human rights as the idealized touchstone of civilization in the late 20th and early 21st century—all have been attempts to break free from the Original Sin of the Neolithic event. Again: we must not think the Neolithic Revolution created or initiated human evil; it did not create evil, but merely created the social circumstances that elicited it, and promoted the patriarchal idealization of the warrior that would hasten its internalization. As for the Abrahamic creation myth, it may have started independently of social circumstances, only later insisting on the loss of a paradisiacal way of life in some past existence—but the fact is, we really don't know what the sequence was. What finally did come across in the Abrahamic story was that the loss of the Garden was permanent—and that human beings *deserved* to be driven from the Garden and *deserved* to earn their bread by the sweat of the brow. No doubt the ruling classes, in order to protect their privileges, systematically encouraged the more fatalistic interpretation.

In time the rationalizations for this brutal new system probably emerged effortlessly from the ruling and priestly classes, in terms of myth, religion and law, becoming simply another division of labor in the complex agricultural system of exploitation. But these rationalizations had a special importance, because they were attached to language, morality, art and religion; and as they grew in the service of empire they would inevitably generate heretical schools of thought. Both taken together—myths and the heretical reactions to them—would dialectically evolve the various foundations for what would eventually become human culture: first Semitic, then Grecian, then European and finally, today, the elective culture of the global village.

Human aggression had been there before the Neolithic catastrophe, waiting to be transformed into systemic evil; the rise of radically differentiated classes, castes and estates in turn coalesced into society-wide forms of systemic exploitation as the new agricultural kingdoms and empires and tribal alliances arose. And the built-in rationalization of the organized aggression inherent in empire was greatly amplified by the violent, daily application of its new imperial protocols and rules, encoded in its violent, bloody rituals, with their capacity to traumatize through regular exposure over a long period of time. Violent sacrificial rituals, involving both animals and humans, became central to culture, and served to bond people to the existing social arrangements.

To invoke a modern American example, the trauma of slavery and racial segregation would similarly bond people to the South and its myths, just as exploitation of immigrant labor would bond people to a heroic but exploitive industrial ethos. For a good modern fictional version of how *ritualized* trauma bonding might work in an imaginary American setting, and how aggression in modern America might bond people to ritualized violence, read "The Lottery" by Shirley Jackson.

In any case, the concept of Göbekli Tepe as a metaphor or analog to the Garden of Eden first attracted attention in a story that appeared in the German magazine *Der Spiegel* in 2006. Elif Batuman also mentions it in her *New Yorker* piece, pointing out the omnipresent snake bas-reliefs on the megaliths and the area's reputation as a kind of paradise for hunter-gatherers. "But the [*Der Spiegel*] theory really draws its power from a reading of The Fall as an allegory from the shift from hunting-and-gathering to farming. In Eden, man and woman lived as companions, unashamed of their nakedness, surrounded by friendly animals and by 'trees that were pleasing to the eye and good for food.' The fruit of the Tree of Knowledge, like the first fruits of cultivation, brought on an immediate, irrevocable curse. Man now had to work the earth, to eat of it all the days of his life."

"God's terrible words to Eve—'I will greatly increase your pain in childbearing; in pain you will give birth of children. Your desire will be for your husband, and he will rule over you'—may refer to a decline in women's health and status produced, in early agricultural societies, by the economic need to have children who would till and inherit the land. Women, having access to goat's milk and cereal, may have weaned their children earlier, resulting in more frequent, more debilitating pregnancies."

"To continue in this interpretation, the story of Cain and Abel may be taken as an illustration of the zero-sum game of primogeniture, as well as an allegory for the slaughter of nomadic pasturage by urban agriculture. Having killed his brother, Cain goes on to found the world's first city and name it after his son Enoch. Read in this spirit, large chunks of the Old Testament—the territorial feuds, the constant threat of exile or extinction, the sexual jealousy and sibling rivalry—begin to resemble the handbook for a grim new scarcity economy of land and love."[18]

The new religions of Egypt and the Semitic tribes and empires would focus, in their religions and folk tales, on death and resurrection. Animals would be sacrificed, and an irritable and often sadistic monotheistic Jehovah would demand absolute submission; but his people would periodically disobey, and the imperial Warrior God would retaliate—at one point Jehovah even demands of Abraham that he kill his own son to prove his loyalty. The idea of an angry God or gods who demand death to be reconciled to humanity would proliferate throughout the Mediterranean cultures. Only blood sacrifice could redeem, it seemed, the lethal harshness that The Fall had brought to humanity, or express the sorrow of eviction from the Garden of Eden. Human beings would now have to live with a consciousness of good and evil; and religion would use this consciousness to enforce its rules. By way of compensation it offered the hope that through blood sacrifice they could hope for a better world beyond the suffering that the knowledge of good and evil seemed to have brought into their daily lives.

The nostalgia built into the new religions for a 'Paradise Lost' would perhaps exaggerate what had been lost, as all retroactive appreciations of a past age are likely to do. But there was a firm awareness of the harshness of life, and a sense that they could not get back to the better life humanity had once had. What people did not realize was the manner in which violent, patriarchal societies, rife with aggression encoded into the privileges of class and caste, tend to cause people to internalize the society's aggression and in the process bond themselves both to the society, and to its violence. And once internalized repeatedly, the aggressive emotional orientations burn in the gut and demand expression, resulting in the growth of a martial culture and the rise of the warrior as the greatest culture hero. If you are the victim of endless forms of social aggression, you are habituated to understand it as an inevitable part of the social contract. But something else occurs, something that is not cognitive but emotional—when one internalizes aggression, one tends to identify with it emotionally as a standard by which everything else is measured. This can be true even when one does not experience violence directly, but are only aware of it in one's milieu.

I offer the following as an example of how the omnipresence of aggression affects society-wide perceptions and standards. Reading interviews of working-class women in America, I was stuck by the way many of the women arrived at a definition of a good husband. They might say, "He's a good man," recounting the positive traits of the husband, but very often adding, *"he doesn't beat me."* This is an example of the way that aggression can operate as a standard— because of its overwhelming nature—for spousal behavior (although hopefully not the *only* standard) even when it isn't present. In the interviews with working-class women, the interviewees appropriately celebrated a *lack* of spousal violence as a precious asset in their marriages—but that makes sense only if one acknowledges that so many other working-class women have historically been victims of it.

Indeed, the women interviewed wouldn't have brought it up at all if they weren't aware that it happens so often, probably because of stories they'd heard from other women, or abuse they'd witnessed or heard about in their parents' generation. Clearly the *wrongness* of domestic violence has entered the collective consciousness of almost all women in our society, and not just upper middle-class women. For married women of limited means, the fact that they do not have to experience the dangers and the soul-deadening violence of spousal abuse is more than significant, it is in fact deeply heartening—but the women themselves are thankful for their good fortune only because, let us remember, so many other working-class women haven't been so lucky.

8.

The second great surge of systemic evil would come with the Industrial Revolution in the 19th and 20th centuries, and the explosive surge in technology that followed as a direct result of that industrial system. But in the late 19th and early 20th centuries—right up to August 1914—educated people in Europe and America tended to believe that humanity was on the verge of a new and enlightened age because of industrial progress, scientific breakthroughs, improved medical techniques and education for the masses. But in the 20th century, it didn't work out that way. Instead of enlightened progress, the great masses of humanity suddenly found themselves assaulted by evil of an unimaginable ferocity.

One shrinks in horror from the litany of seemingly endless atrocities that began with the guns of August, 1914, and the Great War: the unimaginable hell of trench warfare, in which the average life expectancy of a British junior officer was about six weeks; the psychopath Hitler and his criminal gang and the wars they started; the Nazi Holocaust (in which every one of Hitler's many allies in Eastern Europe participated with relish); Stalin and his gulag with twenty million dead and society reduced to unbelievable paranoia and spiritual deprivation; an entire generation of Japanese men raised as fanatical killers under the command of a mindless

Emperor-God; and the war in the Pacific leading to the American incineration of Hiroshima and Nagasaki, along with its civilian population. Thanks to nuclear weapons, it was clear that for the first time in human history humanity was capable not just of creating hell on earth, but of destroying the earth in its entirety.

What happened? Whence the soaring hopes of yesteryear?

What happened was the Industrial Revolution and the creation of new and highly mobile weapons systems, transport and communications that technology made possible, including the nuclear weapons that now proliferate around the globe. These weapons exist solely to threaten innocent civilians everywhere with genocidal incineration—that's the mission for which they're intended, that and nothing else, to threaten mass destruction on behalf of a government. You may say that the threat operates as a deterrent, but the threat is not of individual punishment, but the mass murder of an entire people. The millions of innocent civilians held hostage to genocide have no influence over the situation, except to advocate plaintively for different government policies of the countries where they live.

This power of mass death, which achieves deterrence by threatening millions with incineration, in fact is *the* main (but mainly unspoken) definition of power within the modern nuclear club. This is simply the top layer of a machinery of systemic evil that rewards the rich and powerful and oppresses the poor and destroys their aspirations. This systemic evil arises in societies consisting of many different kinds of people, many of them motivated by values and behaviors that are benign and liberating. Nevertheless, the very existence of weapons of mass destruction bestows a kind of veto power over everything else, because the elites that control them are, at any given time, inestimably stronger than all the other players. Therefore governments of countries that possess nuclear weapons inevitably enjoy disproportionate power in the 'game of thrones' that constitutes modern geo-politics. In this they are greatly aided because most people do not understand how the nuclear hostage system works, nor are they able to deconstruct the emotional and social orientations that accompany and drive it.

This power inherent in having nuclear weapons—the power based on genocide—is the great prize of patriarchy everywhere: those that own and operate it will cling to it until even more genocidal devices are rendered operational. Is it any wonder, then, that the Indians and Pakistanis followed the nuclear example of their Eurocentric mentors, or that Iran now seeks to join the club? Instead of a technology that could release humankind's most nurturing and creative impulses, this new technology of death enables government to be more oppressive than ever before. This new industrial method didn't create the aggression inherent in the personalities of dictators like Hitler or Stalin, not was it responsible for the behavior of their followers. But the new industrial technology *made it possible for them to act out their aggression* in crimes that tyrants of previous centuries could only dream about.

Today, even those nations that have not yet used their nuclear weapons have them specifically to threaten other nations with genocide; otherwise they would not spend billions to manufacture them and keep them operable. Furthermore, nuclear armaments create a shield of immunity behind which right-wing states can act out their oppression without fear of any real interference by the world—which is why South Africa was so anxious to have a nuclear weapon, before its apartheid system was taken down. Today, the apartheid system in Israel persecutes and torments Palestinians without any regard for the outcome, even as the Arab countries watch the brutal horrors of Israeli apartheid on the Al Jazeera network, yet can do nothing to stop it, because Israel's weapons of mass destruction give Israel immunity.

The threat of genocide, and the use of genocide as a shield of immunity to advance state oppression—that, not peace or international cooperation, is the underlying dynamic in modern international relations. Diplomacy is a good thing, and so is international cooperation of almost every kind; and they should be practiced and encouraged no matter what kind of other dynamics are involved—

but cooperation and diplomacy is not the *main* dynamic in international relations today. The essential underlying consideration in almost all international geo-politics is whether a country is a member of the nuclear club or not. In the short run, such weapons are capable of bringing peace, because everybody is afraid of a nuclear war. But that will continue to work only if people are rational. Sadly, as long as nuclear weapons exist, irrational and megalomaniacal people will try to use them for other reasons than deterrence—first to gain immunity for other crimes, then to threaten, then to destroy. The people who use nuclear weapons to influence geo-political outcomes have already crossed a line, because they will inevitably want to use them to destroy those people who won't give them the outcome they want.

People cry, no, they will never use them because it is not "in their interest" to use them. But people often do not know their best interests, because they are blinded by the aggression they have internalized. Did Hitler know the best interests of the German people when he opened a second front with Russia, leaving the Allies to bomb his cities to dust and ash? Did Stalin know the best interests of Russians while killing the most talented people of his era simply because they might have become his personal rivals someday? Do the Israelis know their best interests when they refuse to make peace with Palestinians and deny them self-determination, but on the contrary do things to make war with their Arab neighbors inevitable? Does Pakistan know its best interests when it murdered as many as three million Bangladeshis in 1971-2, and today allows terrorists to murder innocent people on the soil of its neighbor, India?

Does the US know its own best interests when it stands up in the UN to support Israeli oppression of the Palestinians, thereby ensuring religious war in the Middle East, and the probability of terrorist attacks on American soil? Do American neo-cons understand anybody's best interests when they try to drag the US into a worldwide religious war? In any case, whether people know their best interests or not, at this stage in human history they are often incapable of acting on those interests even when they know them. The real, authentic but unconscious desire of most men with power is the destruction of the world, which they act out as the final answer to the paradoxes of life on this earth. How do we know this? The events of the 20th century make it painfully clear. So does the universal embrace of death technology—the world is armed to the teeth with nuclear weapons of mass destruction, and such weapons are already being used to provide impunity behind which brutal authoritarian states are able to continue and enhance their exploitive social systems.

Arguably the destruction of life has always been the unspoken motive that drives most systemic evil, though individuals under its influence may not be conscious of it. That hasn't been obvious in the past because the opportunity—that is, the technology—to participate in tragedies of great magnitude wasn't previously available to destructive individuals and tyrannical governments. But the unspeakable aggression behind this reality wasn't created by technology, despite the attractiveness of the Frankenstein narrative that suggests that science and technology are to blame; on the contrary, it is the presence of evil in the human heart that is to blame. But the painful truth is that technology, like the earlier agricultural revolution, gave aggressors new ways to act out their aggression, also giving them more sophisticated ways to rationalize and conceal their aggression. That makes the industrial system and its technology not the *underlying* but rather the *proximate* cause of the moral dilemma we are now in, because the industrial and technological revolutions provide systemic evil the means to act out the world's destruction.

Technology doesn't cause evil. It simply makes a lot more of it possible.

Consider the Nazi Holocaust. The Holocaust was the cold-blooded murder of six million European Jews—but hadn't Christians been killing Jews for centuries and conducting violent pogroms for a thousand years? What made the Holocaust different? What made it different was the new technology of the Industrial Revolution, which made it possible to kill millions of Jews on an assembly-line basis rather than a handful here and there. The Holocaust was simply the application of the industrial method to that venerable Christian institution, the pogrom—without question European Christians would have committed genocide against the Jews long before the 1940s, if they'd had sufficient technology to pull it off.

The Nazis were homicidal fanatics, to be sure; but so were people like the Protestant culture hero Martin Luther, who advised the German people to burn the synagogues of the Jews, to destroy their holy books, and murder them in the streets. (I don't remember reading of any modern European leaders apologizing for Luther's madness, or modern Lutherans acknowledging the loathsome influence of Luther's Christian anti-Semitism on European culture.) What made it possible for the anti-Semites of Europe to finally carry out their murderous Jew-killing on an organized basis was the arrival of the industrial system. Now, suddenly, they had the technology to kill Jews by the *millions*, because now they could kill them on an assembly-line basis, thanks to the Industrial Revolution and the new world it had created.

And so they did.

Because now there was the technological-industrial organization to pull it off—the trains, the mass production of Zyklon B gas, absolutely first-rate communications, and the industrial technology capable of building vast concentration camps in a few weeks or months. (Not to mention entire armies of political fanatics who lived to follow every order from their superiors.) Who could have imagined the technology to kill six million people in three years? Let's say it again—the Holocaust was the systematic application of the industrial system to the ancient Christian obsession with murdering Jews, accomplishing the same thing Christians had always done but now doing a great deal more of it, and doing it faster. Christians of virtually any century in Europe would have done exactly the same thing long before, if they'd had the same technology and the same corps of dedicated murderers willing to do the heavy lifting.

There are striking similarities between the technology of the Holocaust and nuclear technology—and indeed, of all technology. Technology allows murder (and torture) to remain well-hidden, until the damage is done. Nuclear weapons may be used to incinerate people by the millions, without any physical proximity to the actual killing by the government responsible for it; and someday, if humanity reaches the stars, millions may be exterminated without *anybody* knowing about it—and they will almost certainly be tempted *not* to know about it. The ability *not* to know about systemic evil is exponentially enhanced by technology, because the ability to compartmentalize murder makes credible deniability a universal capability. We already see this dynamic clearly in the Holocaust, in which most of the world looked away while millions died in highly organized death camps located in out-of-the-way places. Technology not only made mass murder on an assembly-line basis possible—it made it possible to centralize its machinations out of sight, and therefore to a great extent out of mind.

The Industrial Revolution quickly evolved (like the agricultural revolution ten thousand years before) into various forms of systemic evil. It allowed small elites at the top to economically exploit workers and consumers—in other words, it allowed and even promoted an *economic* form of systemic evil. Marxism-Leninism arose supposedly to resolve this situation, but Communists ended up using their control of the means of production to engage in even worse exploitation of the masses. In the West, the success of trade unions and social-democratic reforms temporarily created an unspoken but workable social contract—for producing goods and services, workers would receive enough compensation to buy those same goods and services. (It wasn't an accident that Henry Ford said he wanted to keep his cars cheap enough for his workers to buy them.) For a few brief decades this highly workable industrial trade-off provided a good and highly stable life for those that aspired to reach the middle class.

This social contract, which wasn't a bad deal for most workers, stayed in place until the 1980s, when the US corporate upper classes began to make and sell their products on a mass basis in China and the developing world. Since its productive capacities (that is, its technology of production) were now offshore, or heading in that direction, corporate planners could once again exploit with impunity US workers and consumers—that is to say, they didn't even have to *pretend* to be nice to American workers and consumers anymore, because they didn't need them economically. This arrogant new corporate and investment upper class is at present engaged unambiguously in attempting to destroy the American middle class. My point here is that whatever its governing elites call themselves— Marxist, capitalist or whatever—the industrial system tends to go inevitably in the direction of economic slavery, if institutions and enlightened people do not intervene to re-establish the balance between production that makes money for a few, and the human needs of the many. The international marketplace makes that increasingly difficult, because the same distance that greatly increases profits works against democracy and human decency.

Of course, technology made possible by the Industrial Revolution could, in an ideal world, *serve* humanity—one need only look at the advances made in modern medicine to see how the industrial system could benefit all of us. But compare the money spent developing weapons systems to the money spent developing better medical services. The patriarchal elites dominate in all phases of even the most affluent industrialized democracies. Whatever they call themselves, these elites are *essentially* aggressive and *essentially* dishonest about the things they do. Thus the powerful elites of the world exercise their power in ways that are mainly based on various kinds of systemic evil.

People addicted to systemic evil do not always have the opportunity to commit evil acts, and in any case there are many good people who still have power around the world. Sadly, good people *as individuals* have nowhere near the impact of the aggressive elites, because aggression impacts society at large, and the benevolence of the individual tends to be experienced by (and known to) only a lucky few. Secondly, one must face the melancholy fact that the big corporations, the corporate upper class, the investment class and their allies in governments, are incredibly good at lying to rationalize and cover up their own exploitation of everybody else. They are skilled in deception partly because of their dependence on advertising to sell their goods and services, because advertising is not only essentially deceitful, but based on creating negative emotions, particularly fear. These corporate forces show every intention of using their marketing skills to buy out whatever remains of American democracy, and suppressing everybody who tells inconvenient truths about the undemocratic, brutal or illegal operations of the plutocracy they are setting up.

Occasionally a social idealist bursts through and achieves success here and there (Gandhi, Martin Luther King) but they are usually assassinated because they make society extremely uncomfortable—and their aspirations succeed not because of any goodness in human beings, but because of the eventual evolution of a majority consensus that makes any alternative unworkable. The truth, sadly, is that the world is essentially corrupt, and that aggressive and evil men have power almost everywhere. Furthermore aggressors are more dangerous now, because they are able to kill, exploit or intimidate so many more people. And they are aided in covering up their activities by the expert assistance of the legions of professional liars who specialize in dissembling evil, who work at the beck and call of the corporate upper class. Political, social and cultural conservatives know this, and will go to great lengths to defend this arrangement of power, because it offers the best chance to keep in play the aggression, nationalism and patriarchy that are the basis of their ethos, their "values." The social-democratic nations of Europe may be able to defend themselves somewhat more effectively against the new industrial and investment elites, because they tend to be more realistic than Americans about the dangers of unregulated markets, banks and investment groups generally. They also have socialist, social democratic and labor parties that have experience fighting rampaging corporatists.

The only reason there has not been a nuclear conflagration since the incineration of Nagasaki is because of a balance of terror between aggressive elites. These elites have not yet figured out a way to incinerate their perceived enemies without getting killed themselves; and the fact that they can't completely cover up a nuclear conflagration has also been a disincentive. Finally, the aggressive elites that run the world would at present rather *threaten* to incinerate people than actually do so, because they can get what they want with far less effort and expenditure. But that will not stave off disaster forever. If the patriarchal elites can't destroy the world with their bombs and guns, they'll do it with industrially-generated carbon monoxide and the resulting warming of the global climate. Or they will 'accidentally' blunder into a nuclear war, dragging the rest of us along with them.

Why would they do that, when acting rationally would ensure greater profit? Because many are driven by unconscious desires to destroy themselves and the world. How do we know this? Because of the examples of so many powerful governments and leaders whose behavior is flagrantly irrational, who refuse to address the real problems that threaten the world, who set up legions of straw men to keep from discussing what is really threatening humankind. Chief among these are those leaders, political parties and governments that refuse to do anything about global warming, typically claiming through their political proxies that this warming trend is a conspiracy of political liberals and scientists. The real reason for climate denial is an addiction to short-term profits. Meanwhile global warming gets worse, the climate moves toward a tipping point, and the rich and powerful (including the Chinese

Communists) continued to apply maximum pressure to keep any positive steps from being taken to address the most important issue of our time.

Sigmund Freud noted in 1920 an emotional force he called "the death drive" (*Todestriebe*), which he characterized as an instinctual human drive in which living flesh desires to return to inanimate matter. According to Freud, the individual person experiences this as a death wish; but—again according to Freud—this was a drive that existed in every human cell, which the human mind experiences in its totality, and tries to act out in various ways. If this means anything, it must mean a mental and emotional state in which behavior becomes irrational, and individual human choices are overwhelmingly self-destructive. Interestingly, the great Doctor Freud had few ideas regarding methods for socially opposing the behavior of people driven by self-destructive forms of aggression, perhaps forgetting that he started out as a physician who was supposed to heal people and not simply compose exciting essays about human self-destruction. But as militarism led Germany into the First World War, and then the infinitely more aggressive Nazis dismantled the civilized middle-class Viennese world in which Freud lived and worked, it was increasingly clear that extremely destructive drives were operating in human behavior.

But we need no Freudian tutorials to know how self-destructive people are capable of leading the rest of us into disaster: the entire 20th century was one long seminar on the fundamental irrationality and destructiveness of human power. In the early 21st century, destructive and self-destructive elites show every evidence of leading the world into catastrophe, all the while self-righteously shouting political and religious slogans, demonizing their opponents, and generating destruction in the name of God or historical necessity; or (like the Serbian and Israeli nationalists) caterwauling endlessly about how the rest of the world hates them, instead of trying to figure out *why* other nations are offended and frightened by their behavior. Why do self-destructive elites behave in this manner? Because it is easier for neurotic leaders to spew this nonsense than to confront their own demons, especially since many of them have discovered that their demons can help them politically. History is not made by conspiracies, but by sleepwalkers—and the angrier and more frenzied the nightmares of the sleepwalkers are, the more horrific the nightmares the sleepwalkers will try to impose upon the world. T.E. Lawrence called these sleepwalkers "Dreamers of the Day"—and he should have known, being one himself.

9.

Do we really understand how quickly technology, when driven by systemic evil, is capable of accomplishing enormous harm? Technology makes the problem of evil not merely discernable, but obvious and unavoidable. Who can ignore the Holocaust, and the role of technology in the extermination program against European Jews? Who can deny the destructive killing power of a nuclear weapon? Because we are now forced to see evil, we must look for ways to deconstruct it, to both understand how it operates in societies and in the individual mind, while learning how to control its worst effects. But while technology is openly embraced, and its manufacture is no secret, systemic evil is still not understood by most people.

Clearly humankind now has the technology to kill millions; in fact it has the technology to end life on this planet. But simply seeing and acknowledging that fact is not enough—humankind must change if we are to avoid the worst-case scenario. But enlightened self-interest (never mind altruism) is a lot harder to achieve than anybody ever imagined. Before people can act on their own best interests, they must know what those interests are; and the values necessary for people to know and articulate their best interests are increasingly unknowable even to themselves. There is simply too much aggression in the world, to the point where even the brightest people suffer from a kind of surplus powerlessness, at the same time that they are exposed to nonstop, overwhelmingly violent stimuli on a daily basis. These psychological realities compromise judgment and drives aggressive and self-destructive behavior in covert ways. All these things are interfering with our ability to know and act on what is good for us.

The role of trauma and trauma bonding in creating aggressive emotional orientations has already been discussed. People internalize aggression in ways that bypass cognition, and the aggression then influences their behavior in covert ways. Obviously, people cannot know their best interests when aggression is driving their behavior in ways they cannot understand. But technology adds a new element: there is something profoundly disorienting about *the accelerated speed of the industrial and technological changes we are experiencing.*

There is definitely a possibility of enhanced emotional trauma when changes occur too quickly for human comprehension; and this is nowhere as true as of the enormous rapidity of the industrialization process. If one looks at life in the 1840s, and thinks of life as it is now, there is almost nothing in the activities of daily life that has not been radically altered in some way, including a decline in the ability of educated people to express their thoughts by the spoken and written word. At times the rate of change actually seems to increase exponentially, with each year or each decade changing much faster than the last. The *enormity* of the changes, and the dizzying rate at which they have occurred, could not help but disorient the mind, at some point compromising our ability to understand what is happening to us emotionally.

The accelerating pace of industrialization and the growth of technology since the 1840s have without question caused *cognitive and emotional regression*—and that, in turn, has no doubt contributed to our inability to hang onto and continue to live out our best moral values in a technology that changes too fast for us to comprehend the manner in which it is affecting us. This regression means that technology—or rather, the *rate* of technological change—is actually making it harder for us to relate to each other, and putting added strains on society rather than helping us live better. International relations in 2012 in no way resembles adults engaged in trying to get along with each other, based on the enlightened self-interests of various nations, but teenagers acting out the dramas of adolescence, with all the posturing and high-risk behavior one would expect of that age group.

The traumatic effects of rapid change also bypass the rational, risk-assessing mind and go directly into the unconscious part of the individual personality. Young people start out embracing the rate of technological change; but even young adults learn at some point that the constant reign of new gadgets disappoints sooner or later, even when each gadget is experienced separately, because a single gadget's pleasure is never quite commensurate with the overall disorientation caused by so many new experiences occurring in a very short time. The galloping, accelerating changes create an emotional regression and disorientation affecting the masses of people in the industrialized democracies and developing world alike. And the very speed of industrialization and the technological revolution exacerbates the aggression inherent in technology used by authoritarian states, making it even more likely that people who use the new technology will likewise internalize much of the aggression embedded in state crimes and misdemeanors, not to mention the nonstop lying used by exploitive elites to cover up the harm they do.

Anyone who looks objectively at the 20th and early 21st century will have to assume that something paradoxical (and something very new and frightening) is at work. Much of the technology is wondrous, but technology has also made the operation of systemic evil more powerful, with the harm it does becoming obvious to more people, than ever before. It isn't the technology, but the aggression technology empowers, and what the technology makes clear to us about what we really are—and it has been revealed to us in ways so clear and harrowing that denial becomes futile. Humankind is simply not capable of dealing with evil, which it alternately denies and struggles with; human societies in rapid transition, especially those in which workers and consumers are exploited and governments and corporations are deceitful, have become so *essentially* aggressive that it increasingly requires a constant effort simply to maintain one's sanity, much less to live a good and authentic life.

What I am saying is not that systemic evil inevitably rules one's life—I am simply saying that some form of systemic evil is the established default position of all societies at present, and that the rapidity of the alterations in our economic and emotional lives does not lead to the good and authentic life we all seek. Of course, to live well and authentically has always been hard—but the difference now is that applied science and technology, for reasons we do not entirely understand, is making it harder—not because of the technology, again, but because of the rapidity with which it changes, and the kind of human aggression it tends to empower.

Perhaps there was always a negative undertow to technology; but a century ago new inventions were occurring slowly enough that we could understand how they affected us, and make some kind of adjustment. A kind of crackpot optimism ruled the day. In the late 19th and early 20th centuries, people began to believe that the human struggle with evil was no longer necessary, because science would create the Good Life no matter what individual human intentions were. Breakthroughs in medicine, education and political reform would create a brave and enlightened new world no matter what individual people did. But science and technology, in addition to whatever good it has done, has also revealed exactly how wrong we were all along about human evil, and how dangerous it is and how ill-equipped we are to deal with it. Furthermore, because of the traumatizing rapidity of the changes it has wrought, it has succeeded in making our already compromised behavior worse. The bottom line is that now humankind is capable not just of making bad mistakes, but of muddling its way into unforeseen disasters of monumental import, with the consequence of perhaps systematically destroying most of the worthwhile aspects of the project we call civilization.

Attitudes toward money provide a harrowing example of the manner in which the industrial method has elicited certain self-destructive American traits. Capitalism and the operation of the marketplace now constitute the True Church of America; the Almighty Dollar (and the political and personal power that money can buy) is what Americans secretly worship. Interestingly and ironically, however, the Almighty Dollar has now become our enemy. The increasingly artificial financialization of our economy by an unscrupulous new investment class, combined with the loss of manufacturing capability, has created an arrogant new corporatist ruling class that uses the 'Citizens United' apotheosis of money to buy out elections, Supreme Court judges, Presidents and the entire electoral system, replacing it with the most vulgar kind of plutocracy. And this is accompanied inevitably with forces that are driving the middle class and working families downwards into destitution.

Working families and the middle class increasingly have only their homes as equity; and once those homes are gone or grossly devalued, and once the capital from them is spent on survival, the middle classes become a kind of new urban and suburban peasantry — which is exactly the intent of the corporate upper class. With the Koch brothers enforcing an economy based on petroleum products, and collective bargaining mainly destroyed, people not in the upper middle class will be forced to work for wages a half or a third of what they once were. Destruction is the unspoken, unconscious objective of systemic evil; and technology, for all the unforeseen reasons mentioned above, now tends to empower destruction of the most civilizing aspects of civil society.

10.

In the 20th and early 21st centuries we see that there is a *radical discontinuity* between cognition and aggression — human agency no longer controls aggression, as we once thought it could; rather it is aggression that controls us. This is never as frightening and dangerous as when it happens on a mass basis, as the result of organized and ongoing violence by the state and the political classes, or their manipulation of past trauma to bond people to aggression in the present moment. Thanks to the industrial and technological revolutions, the world can now see that little-understood dynamics in the human personality are causing us to behave in dangerous, aggressive, and self-destructive ways; and that we seem currently unable to stop our progress toward self-destruction. It is our job—and the purpose of this book—to do what we can to stop this.

II.

It's now time to look briefly at those forms of aggression that are internalized as part of being born in a particular place, the United States of America. I'm referring to the influence of *American culture*—certain national characteristics, American attitudes and beliefs, that we absorb unconsciously as we grow up in certain environments, and of which we are mainly unaware. Some of these attitudes and beliefs, while they're not invariably the same thing as aggression, often help make aggression easier to internalize, and easier to rationalize. Some people can see through these deeply-held but mainly unconscious *national* beliefs and attitudes, but a great many people can't—most of these attitudes are too close to us, too personal, too firmly ensconced in popular American thought and behavior, so that we can no more question them than question the weather.

Many of these American attitudes come about because of an unconscious tendency to rationalize the aggression and greed in our country's history—we want our own country to be a good place, we want to be good patriots, and self-deceit is a learned behavior that gets better with practice. The tendency to rationalize American aggression is also supported on a nation-wide basis by a compliant media that represent US aggression as being redemptive or transformative when Americans do it, but questionable or bad when others do it. Indeed, rationalizing American aggression has always been a major undertaking, since there has been so much of it in our nation-building experience.

There are a couple of stories about America that sum American aggression up in ways that I personally find quite haunting. One is a story told by Will Rogers, the great American humorist, and has to do with those familiar patriotic paintings and murals that portray the Pilgrims meeting with the Indians for the first Thanksgiving. You've probably seen them—they usually portray the Pilgrims as standing around holding their old-fashioned muskets, and a pastor is usually leading them in prayer as they get ready to eat all the fine food laid out for them. On the surface, it all looks pretty nice. The Pilgrims and the Indians seem to be getting along, and the Pilgrims' faces look peaceful and happy as they pray.

Will Rogers said he'd always found two things interesting about these pictures. First, the Pilgrims were always praying. Secondly, they were always holding their muskets.

"I always wondered why they were holding those muskets," Rogers said. "I guess they had the muskets to make sure they got what they were praying for."

Will Rogers' story sums up—with mind-boggling economy, I might add—white America's aggressive relationships with tribal people, an understanding that was no doubt greatly enhanced by the fact that William Penn Adair Rogers (Will Roger's full name) was born into a high-ranking family in the Cherokee Nation. The Puritanical Pilgrims' religion gets short shrift in Will's story, no doubt because of the irrefutable fact that most religious American leaders (with the exception of the Quaker William Penn, who inter-estingly enough was Will Rogers' namesake) enthusiastically engaged in the murder and displacement of tribal people. The whites weren't just aggressive toward tribal people, they thought their religion justified it, and the recurring violence got into their religion and influenced it in critical ways.

Rogers' story also prefigures and to some extent warns of the nationalization of much American religion, represented today by the scurrilous ultra-conservative Christian evangelicals of the Religious Right (a major constituency within the Republican Party that generally supports torture, economic exploitation and war). It's all there, in that single story. Only Will Rogers could have told such a story, and only Will Rogers could have gotten away with it.

Will Rogers' story was a very perceptive snapshot of the under-current of violence that conditioned everything that Americans became as they moved west, an emotional orientation that still unconsciously influences American imperialism in the developing world. White Europeans built a dynamic new civilization in North America; but they did so by destroying the tribal societies that had preceded them on the land. That's the reality, and it affected every-thing we became — as well as the tribal people themselves, who never recovered completely from the European diseases, the military defeats and the ravages of alcoholism. Most white Americans tended to rationalize what they were doing by citing the savagery of the Indians, forgetting that the white settlers had started the whole thing by moving into Indian lands. (Think about it: did the Indians go to Europe, or did the white Europeans come to America?) When white people did write about it, they tended to imply or state outright that it was God's will that the Christians get rid of all those murderous heathens so that a Christian culture could flourish; and others viewed it as an impersonal function of 'manifest destiny' — that is, they argued that there was nothing personal about it, it was just a historical necessity (which sounds a lot like the ratio-nalization Lenin used for the mass murder of the Kulaks under the Bolsheviks). Needless to say, the aggression internalized from 250 years of Indian wars across America greatly influenced American thought and religion, and not in a good way.

My mother's family settled a southern Missouri county in 1831, and I am descended from them on her side. There was a brief Indian war shortly before the first settlers came in, during which the tribal people were 'cleaned out' so the white settlers could come in.

(Usually these wars were a series of skirmishes leading up to a big massacre at some tribal settlement, after which the surviving Indians would scatter, move west, or go into hiding.) I heard an older white woman saying that some braves were seen from time to time hiding in the caves down on the Sac River—they always hid when you approached them, apparently. It was hard for me to tell whether she was talking about something she'd seen, or something somebody else had seen, or some hallucination she was dealing with in her own head. She used a special tone of voice when she talked about these ghostly tribal people that supposedly lurked in the caves, a voice that exuded fear, awe, and guilt.

I visited the Sac and Little Sac Rivers with family members once, and found the river a dark place indeed, flowing at the bottom of overgrown ravines and overrun with nests of water snakes and rattlers that lay on the rock ledges at head level—but there were also little hidden beaches, strewn with the pottery shards of the people that had once made a life there. It was then that I began to realize that ghosts really do exist, but that they exist in the human mind and heart. It also taught me a little about intergenerational trauma. When you listened to the way people talked about the Indians, I noticed, it had a way of normalizing violence—of making it seem almost inevitable, but also making you want to rationalize it.

The second story is not one I can attribute to any one person, but since I've heard a couple of versions of it, the story is probably in the public domain. It was supposedly about a Swedish immigrant who came to the US to be with his brother. But although his brother had started out in the East, he kept getting new jobs and moving west, going from one boom town to the next, mining silver and copper and finally going to California for the Gold Rush. The Swede lost track of his brother in California, where he disappeared into the mountains looking for gold, and never came out. The Swede never did find his brother, although he had spent his life going back and forth across America trying to catch up with him.

Someone once asked him what he thought of America. "It's a big country," the Swede said, "big enough to lose a brother in."

This story—which I think of as the 'Lost Swede' story—is about a different kind of aggression inherent in our national situation. I'm referring to the astonishing materialism and hyper-competitiveness encountered everywhere in American life, which is really a profound and systematic form of pathological aggression, greatly enhanced by the individuals' attempt to suppress his or her own demons. It all began with the Puritans, who developed the idea that people got rich because God loved them, and rewarded them with wealth. This idiot heresy was greatly enhanced by the Industrial Revolution and the scramble to get rich in the 19th century, typified by the Gold Rush to California. All of America was to some extent experienced as a Gold Rush by the end of the 19th century, in which the most important goal was to get rich. "Get money, and if you can, get it honestly," Mark Twain was supposed to have said, "but whatever you do, get it."

Only those who had money counted—the poor had few rights because it was assumed that they were responsible for their own poverty. Life in America became a kind of free-for-all in which individual people were out only for themselves, in the process creating a toxic environment in which there was very little trust. This lack of trust still corrodes the American environment. How can you trust others when everybody is locked in a life-and-death struggle against everybody else? People can experience trust only in small groups of friends and associates, but the existence of public trust is tenuous and highly conditional. The Phil Ochs song "Outside of a Small Circle of Friends" deals with this dilemma, stressing the lack of commonly-held public values, and the utter loneliness of being unable to engage emotionally with people outside of a few friends. But this loneliness did not come about by accident—it happens because of the free-floating aggression, hyper-competitiveness and lack of trust in American life.

In such a situation it is expected that people in business or public life or even the professions are supposed to lie to each other, so everybody does it except for a few people who make a conscious decision not to. If you've ever worked for any length of time in an American office, you will probably have noticed that nobody trusts anybody else, but that staff is generally divided up into two or three factions at constant war with other, usually for reasons so old nobody can really remember them.

And the amazing thing is this: Americans actually think it's supposed to be that way. They think that hyper-competitiveness is the highest good: that their crude materialism is bound to lead to the best products and services: that the worship of money and power will give them the best life. They couldn't be more mistaken. Industrialized democracies benefit from competition, but also cooperation, because at their best democracies are essentially meritocracies. The marketplace certainly benefits from competition, because it ensures the best products—but again, competition must occur in a balance with cooperation, even in the marketplace; and that same balance is needed even more in political, cultural and social life in America. In other words, competition beings out the best in products, but the worst in people, unless you leaven it with the ability to cooperate around certain key values necessary to a sane and democratic society. Even in the marketplace there has to be an understanding that there are values which are more important than one's ability to make a profit (starting with something as simple as a refusal to lie or steal, for example), and an understanding that reasonably good values create a stable political climate in which the marketplace can function best.

In other words, there have to be rules to the game, or the game isn't productive anymore, and people lose interest in it; they still go to work every day, but they're just going through the motions. In America the rulebook that supposedly governs the exigencies of the game is the US Constitution and the Bill of Rights, and the progressive 18th-century ideas that informed those documents. The Constitution binds us together and gives us certain common values—but people obsessed with money are often unable to see that, especially if there is no balance between the way they indulge their competitive instincts and their willingness to cooperate and compromise when other values come into play.

But that balance, again, is mainly gone. For many Americans, there is no longer anything remotely resembling a civil society, but only one big marketplace in which everybody is supposed to fight each other, and lie to keep their jobs (which people very often hate anyway). This complaint is to some extent common to all societies (that people have boring jobs and are perennially tempted to sell out in order to get by) but the extremely bad values of which I speak, hyper-competitiveness and hyper-materialism, are markedly worse in American society than, say, most European societies, and many societies in the developing world. The people in the Philippines, for example, emanate a tremendous *joie de vivre* even in grinding poverty, because they feel they're all part of the same family (*kapamilia*) and are all in some sense helping each other. The US had that orientation for a brief moment in the 1930s and 1940s, and then lost it.

The result is a tremendous sense of alienation and loneliness. The Swedish immigrant never found his 'Lost Brother' because he was so focused on striking it rich in the boom towns that he could never settle down and wait for him. They continued to communicate, but their letters often crossed in the mail, or came back stamped "Address Unknown." Other times their letters got through, and it seemed to both of them at times that they were very close to getting together at last. But finally the day came when the immigrant Swede lost the trail—his brother had gone into the heart of darkness that was the California mining camps, and never came out of the High Sierras. The Swede lost his own brother to the mad American race to get rich quick.

I've often wondered what it was that kept the Lost Swede chasing after the gold at the end of the rainbow, instead of making more effort to hook up with his brother. What made him think that striking it rich was more important than his sibling, who after all had immigrated to America especially to see him? Maybe, I've often thought, it was because he wanted to show off to his brother, or have enough money to surprise him, and perhaps give him an expensive gift. But the greatest gift would have been just being reunited with him, being with him, two brothers together in a strange country. But he couldn't do that, because striking it rich was more important.

I've seen the same thing many times in different forms. Men slave to make money, but are emotionally unavailable to their children, spouses and other family members. They think they are working for them, but they give everything but themselves. At its worst it becomes a tragedy in which alienated parents think they can buy the love of their children by buying them expensive toys.

I did an interview once with a very interesting man, a man who has since died, named Al Rinker. This man created the Haight-Ashbury Switchboard in the Haight-Ashbury neighborhood of San Francisco. In 1966 and 1967, Rinker, a kind of self-educated social worker and visionary, created a referral service for all the runaway young people coming to the Haight-Ashbury in San Francisco to party, take drugs and participate in the so-called "Summer of Love." Almost all of these young people were white and upper middle class, and they were all fed up with the materialism and lack of values of their parents. As they arrived in the Haight, they began almost immediately to create a community as violent and chaotic and grotesquely lacking in values as their parents' materialism, although that didn't become clear until later.

Al realized that all those parents might be worried about their runaway kids, so he created the Haight-Ashbury Switchboard as a way they could communicate with their runaway kids, and the kids could likewise communicate with their parents, no questions asked.

I asked Al what the first parent said when he called.

"The first call was from a guy in New Jersey," Rinker said. "His daughter had taken off for San Francisco, and he hadn't heard from her since she left. He left a message for her."

"What was the message?"

"Tell her that if she comes home I'll get her a new Pontiac GTO convertible."

Of course, that didn't work—the daughter had almost surely run away from home because of her father's suffocating materialism, and now she was about to punish him with her equally unimaginative, equally narcissistic high-risk behavior. Her immediate response to her father's message was a bitter laugh, after which she returned to the Haight-Ashbury, perhaps for more toxic street drugs, venereal disease and shoot-outs with drug dealers.

That's what I mean when I talk about the loneliness of America— if people see themselves as locked in a power struggle with everybody else, the ultimate result of that hyper-competitiveness is that people pick up no values except worship of the Almighty Dollar, or winning some relatively petty power struggles—either way they end up thinking there's nothing more important than money or power, and that's pretty sterile. Or they reject money entirely, which means they will never learn how to use it responsibly. And now that right-wing evangelicalism is hijacking American Christianity, and right-wing Zionism is hijacking Judaism, the spiritual route isn't much better. Hyper-competition is a particularly pathetic form of aggression, and often operates as an addiction: it feels great in the beginning, but in the long term it destroys the soul. If everything is a power struggle, if there's no cooperation, you can't trust anyone, not even yourself. Not even the people in your own family.

That's alienation. That's loneliness.

Like the Swede said, America is a big country, big enough to lose a brother—or like the father in Jersey, big enough to lose a daughter.

12.

But lest we go too far afield, let us remember that the *main* way people internalize aggression is by being personally victimized by violence. Anyone who doubts that is invited to check the narrative case histories of most state prison inmates. A strong majority of prison inmates report abuse as children, and the frequency of the abuse not only results in their internalization of massive amounts of aggression, it also encourages them to lie about the violent behavior they engage in to express that aggression. These people did not absorb aggression from culture, but directly from the chaos and trauma of the parental abuse they endured. They internalized it and some started acting on it while still quite young, and some always will—unless, of course, they belong to the lucky minority who are capable of rehabilitating themselves. (Note that I said rehabilitating *themselves*, because it is always a decision *they* make, if it's really going to happen, and not some idealistic social worker or counselor scaring them straight.)

Pity the poor prison psychologist. I knew one, and the stories she told were harrowing. I told her to see a psychologist or psychiatrist herself every so often, because I was concerned about the emotional trauma she was sustaining. But I'm afraid none of the shrinks in her circle could possibly have understood what working in a place with thousands of sociopaths is like. "It must be enormously exhausting to treat people who are always lying to you," I said to her once.

"No, that's not the main problem," she said. "They're all great liars, and they laugh about it themselves—we all laugh about it. But the real problem is that if you get taken hostage, the correctional officers aren't going to rescue you. You have to sign a release acknowledging that right in the beginning. You sign a release that says that if you're a hostage, you're out of luck, so if the inmates have to whack you out, nobody is going to rescue you. So every time the siren goes off when I'm counseling some guy, I wonder if there's a hostage situation underway."

"Then what happens?"

"I start wondering if the guy I'm counseling is the one who's supposed to take me hostage."

That's stress.

Most prison psychologists don't doubt the existence of evil—they deal with it every day. And they know where it comes from. It mainly comes from the trauma of violence, in the form of extreme child abuse, and the manner in which that aggression was internalized and acted out later. Society must incarcerate such dangerous characters, but the violence of prison can easily reinforce the aggression that's already there. So why do some prisoners become rehabilitated? That's still a mystery, but as I indicated before, it has to do with decisions made by the criminal himself. He simply gets so tired of being in prison that he decides to try another way, and the prison staff offers a little help along the way.

About two-thirds of all inmates in state prisons end up offending again, and going back to prison; but up to a third don't commit new crimes, and they stay out of prison. Most people would probably say those are pretty bad percentages, but considering the lethal backgrounds most of them come from, and considering the utter stupidity and endless capacity for self-sabotage of most criminals, I think it's pretty encouraging that even a third manage to rehabilitate themselves. But then I'm no idealist where good and evil are concerned. I'll take whatever I can get.

13.

Now it's time to look closely at three extremely important cultural traditions that encourage or glamorize aggression. These aren't exclusively or primarily American, but are found almost everywhere; that is to say, they are universal cultural traditions. The three cultural traditions are *patriarchy*, *nationalism* and *victimology*.[19] All three tend to reinforce each other, although they probably arise in a different order in different times and places. What is important about them is that besides operating in society to motivate and rationalize certain aggressive behavior, they are also experienced on a very profound level as *emotional orientations* that are completely unconscious but which nonetheless deeply influence attitude and behavior.

Here's an example: all over the US on Friday or Saturday nights there are men who sit in the basements of dimly-lit VFW halls drinking beer and swapping war stories. Why do these men—most of whom haven't even been in combat—do this?

Because by sitting in these dank VFW basements, they celebrate together the emotions associated with *nationalism* and *patriarchy*, by sharing memories of the stirring martial values of the Good Old Days, when men were men, and were happy to fight wars instead of complaining about things. Most of what they remember probably exists only in their feverish, lower middle-class imaginations; but it operates as a classical myth-system for a certain subset of failed men, glamorizing their unexceptional beliefs and casting a pale glow of heroism on the quiet desperation of their pedestrian lives. Then, after getting mildly soused, they go home and watch Fox News, which has made billions for Robert Murdoch selling exactly these same self-congratulatory values. The patient women they are married to put up with this because their husbands are happier— and therefore a lot less trouble—when they can console themselves with their fraudulent memories of a heroic past. (Which is, by the way, is a pretty good definition of patriarchy—fraudulent memories of a supposedly heroic past.)

At this point all three cultural traditions are deeply embedded in human culture, and to some extent have a life of their own. *Patriarchy* is very old—it's probably been around since the Neolithic Revolution. *Nationalism* may seem quite recent, but it probably rose out of an 'us-against-them' mentality rooted in tribalism, as well as the wars of empire that also began during the Neolithic Revolution. (Not to mention the horrendous European religious wars that went on for centuries during the Middle Ages.) *Victimology*, on the other hand, is a mind-boggling deficit of individuals, nations and groups that define themselves by past suffering, and use the ways they've been mistreated in the past as a way to rationalize their own aggression against innocent people in the present and future—Serbs, Israelis and Russians do a lot of this, although the Americans are also good at posturing themselves as pitiful victims whenever they don't get their way. The psychology of *victimology* is not easy to grasp at first, but most people know it when they see it.

Victimology is driven by an 'us-against-them' aggressive orientation, but adapted to a passive-aggressive fighting style in which the aggression is usually concealed. It generates a dangerous tendency to rationalize everything rather like the sociopath, who always sees himself as the victim even when he's the aggressor. Yet *victimology* can quickly and easily creep into conflicts experienced by ordinary people. If you don't believe me, just ask a friend who's going through a divorce what went wrong with the marriage. You'll get an earful—but I can almost guarantee you, your friend won't be clamoring to admit all the mistakes he or she made, including getting married to such a high-risk partner in the first place. No, people going through a divorce almost always want to talk about what the *other* person did that was wrong—victim status is oddly satisfying, and besides it's a wonderful rationalization for all the nasty tricks our gay divorcee may wish to inflict on his ex-spouse in the future. And that, by the way, is victimology in a nutshell—it's victim status in the service of future aggression.

All three psychological orientations are so deeply embedded in modern culture that we often act on them without thinking. All three offer a kind of cognitive framework for aggression that makes it seem natural, inevitable and—in an odd way—value-free, even though its effects are almost always identifiable as personally disgusting, immoral and demoralizing to society at large. These three cultural systems function naturally as big-time incentives to rationalize, cover up and lie about aggression.

Patriarchy

Patriarchy is perhaps the oldest cultural system that incorporates aggression, and apparently came into being right after the Neolithic Revolution, probably because of the huge changes in everyday life. The biggest underlying social change, we will remember, was the conversion from a hunter-gatherer kind of subsistence life to an agriculture-based economy. This resulted in the rise of a warrior class—and they, in addition to being warriors, were also usually part of a new land-owning aristocratic class. The very essence of nobility, according to the new value system attached to their rise, was fighting and killing other men. And what was the purpose of all this fighting and killing? What caused this sudden rise in hostility and aggression?

It wasn't the crops they were raising—it was the fact that organized, society-wide agriculture create a big *surplus* of crops, which was in turn an enormous new source of wealth. That kind of communally-owned wealth had never existed before. Men fought to get control of it, and the winners set up a new hierarchy that mainly benefited *them*, and few others. The warriors were paid off by giving them land and privileges, putting a few in a position to benefit greatly from the new productive capacity of agriculture. With large cities the birth rate shot up, leading to hierarchal societies that gradually became empires. The role of women in this social transformation was completely downgraded, placing them on the level of chattel, or sometimes below. And the standard of living for everybody else fell to something not far from complete economic degradation—and for huge numbers of people, perhaps the majority, slavery.

This agricultural system with an aristocratic land-owning class is familiar to us in modern times because of many references in modern popular culture to European medieval and feudal societies, the last of the great agricultural systems. These, also, were societies where wealth was based on agriculture; and they were characterized with a powerful landowning class, rigid hierarchical social organization, the virtual worship of war as the ultimate test of a man's valor, not to mention a strong overlay of institutional Christianity. Much of our popular culture, from Robin Hood to King Arthur (not to mention a great many video games that reference unnamed warrior cultures and medieval appurtenances such as trolls, dwarves, witches, magi and faeries) get their atmospheric and visual reference points from that time in European history. It was all completely patriarchal, in the sense that a small group of men ran everything—but it didn't stop there. Since patriarchy depends also on the idea that physical bravery was the highest good, the warrior class (that is, the knights and other aristocrats) got the highest monetary rewards, first from the wealth of the agricultural surplus, and later on increasingly from their own tenants on the land who served them, whose hard work drove the economic success of the whole agricultural infrastructure. Most of the money generated from this system did not, of course, go to the tenants and tenant farmers who actually did the work, but to the landowners. The peasants were numerous but barely able to scrape by, and if they ever thought to question the system in some public way they would most likely have been killed for sport.

The agricultural system created primogeniture, which guarantees productive land (and in Europe, a title) to the firstborn son of the landowner. This system—and the enormous wealth that went with it—was the productive economic basis for patriarchy, because it established the oppressive hierarchies that the rich men of the landowning class were expected to manage and enforce, with the titles and privileges their oldest sons could inherit. The aristocratic landowning class created by this system was more or less permanent, making it very hard to challenge—which is one reason why Thomas Jefferson was so anxious to prevent primogeniture in America, because he thought, correctly, that it would inhibit the growth of an egalitarian society.

Domination is, in fact, the main social operation of patriarchy: a small honored group of men at the top, and the vast majority of society operating in rigid class roles down below. Among the lucky knights and aristocrats at the top, there was constant competition, but also an honor code that was supposed to guarantee truth-telling and good behavior. There were two things wrong with this honor code, which was gradually rationalized into the chivalric system in medieval Europe. The first thing wrong with chivalry was that everybody broke its rules whenever they felt they could get away with it. That happened because organized aggression drove everything in the system, so you would be tempted to use it against friends as well as enemies—and the most successful nobles did just that, using chivalric cover to vanquish their main competitors.

The second thing wrong with it was that nobody below the rank of gentleman was included in it. Thus as the mercantile and business classes began to assume importance, patriarchy became less viable because its honor code was no good for the great mass of business people—and naturally it excluded women, peasants and workers, too. Some have suggested that the remedy for this would have been simply to extend the idea of honorable behavior to all people. But that doesn't work, because honor as a binding force of patriarchy existed for the purpose of organized oppression, which mandated honesty among the oppressors only in order to make their oppression more efficient. Therefore it couldn't be extended to others.

One of my favorite moral philosophers of the early 19th century, the popular William Paley, author of *Moral and Political Philosophy*, investigated the idea of honor as the basis of a universal personal morality, and found it sadly lacking. Here is the Rev. Paley's dismissal of honor (and by implication, chivalry) as a moral code:

The Law of Honor is a system of rules constructed by people of fashion, and calculated to facilitate their intercourse with one another; and for no other reason. Consequently, nothing is adverted to by the Law of Honor, but what tends to incommode this intercourse.

For which reason, profaneness, neglect of public worship or private devotion, cruelty to servants, rigorous treatment of tenants or other dependents, want of charity to the poor, injuries done to tradesmen, by insolvency or delay of payment, with numberless examples of the same kind, are accounted no breaches of honor; because a man is not a less agreeable companion for these vices, nor the worse to deal with, in those concerns which are usually transacted between one gentleman and another.

Again, the Law of Honor, being constituted by men occupied in the pursuit of pleasure, and for the mutual conveniency of such men, will be found, as might be expected from the character and design of the law-makers, to be in most instances favorable to the licentious indulgence of the natural passions. Thus it allows of fornication, adultery, drunkenness, prodigality, dueling, and of revenge in the extreme; and lays no stress upon the virtues opposite to these.

We should remember that from the 17th century onward the word 'aristocrat' was virtually synonymous with 'wastrel,' a clear and present danger to all young women in the neighborhood, a rake capable of unimaginable outrages because he could buy his way out of everything, an addict to dissolute pleasures and (unless he could be contrived to die honorably in a fashionable army regiment) good for nothing but wasting the fortune of his forebears. The 1862 Pre-Raphaelite painting *The Last Day in the Old Home* by Robert Braithwaite Martineau sums it all up: a dissipated scapegrace son drinks a toast to the beautiful home he has gambled away in his drunken nightly peregrinations, as his family and he prepare themselves to be thrown out on the street by his creditors. The 'gentleman' and his young but equally vacuous son are pretending to take the whole thing in stride; the women's faces—including the wastrel's daughter—reflect shock and devastation. That about sums up the personal experience of patriarchy: the 'gentlemen' were free to do as they would; the women and children were left to suffer the consequences.

And that's not even the darkest part of patriarchy. Patriarchy was and is deeply, irrevocably and completely about war. It doesn't say that some wars are good, and some bad; to patriarchy *all* wars are good because the trauma of combat bonds male warriors to each other, and to their common homicidal enterprise. And what *is* their enterprise? Keeping alive a vision of the world based on domination by a small group of privileged men—that's it, mainly. But it's also about keeping alive a vision of physical conflict as the highest test of character, and physical courage the highest good. Domination and glorification of war are basically what patriarchy is all about.

And that is why so many conservative men are terrified of feminism and afraid of out-of-the-closet homosexuality. (It's okay if you stay in the closet, since the shame involved in closeted homosexuality is a major dynamic of patriarchy.) Blatant homophobia is an integral part of patriarchy; the 'out' homosexual representing the complete feminization of the male, rendering him unfit to be a warrior. He also threatens to short-circuit the familiar drama of the repressed or self-hating homosexual, who has often in the past been the shrillest and most dependable advocate of patriarchy. The 'out' gay man says to the closeted gay patriarch, "Come on out—the weather's fine. You no longer have anything to fear, so you can stop all the macho posturing." Indeed, gay men who don't stay in the closet tend to gradually lose interest in patriarchal values, and patriarchy loses a big pool of people from whom it has traditionally recruited.

Patriarchy is totally obsessed with physical courage and combat. Why? Because that's the ethos in which patriarchy began, in the rise of the warrior class beginning twelve thousand years ago, after the creation of an agricultural surplus. It was pure *physical* force that allowed the warrior to defeat his rivals and punish his social inferiors. It is this sense of physical force as the final arbiter of everything important that causes patriarchal men to put such emphasis on physical punishment of children, especially their sons. It's direct, and it doesn't involve a lot of talking—which patriarchy sees as a feminization of power relations—and it teaches the importance of violence by example. Above all, frequent physical punishment is one sure way that a patriarchal father can be sure his son has internalized plenty of aggression.

Patriarchy as a *conscious* idea apparently didn't need articulation until long after the Neolithic Revolution was over. For one thing, nobody wrote anything about it because writing didn't exist until well into historical times. Amongst the ancient Hebrews, patriarchy expressed itself most directly through religion, through the machinations of an angry, somewhat irritable and frequently violent male God who liked nothing more than a genocidal war now and then to make his point. Within the Abrahamic religious tradition, women were not considered to be even remotely a part of God's covenant, something that was to some extent later challenged by the prophets Jesus and Mohammad in different ways.

In Europe the idea of patriarchal honor was not rationalized into the rules of chivalry, which was supposedly a code of conduct, until relatively late, suggesting that the need to discuss and formalize patriarchal values didn't arise until patriarchy was starting to lose a bit of its emotional hold over people. It wasn't until the second half of the 17th century that a political theory specifically mentions it as bestowing rights based on gender. This occurred in Sir Robert Filmer's *Patriarcha*, in which he argued, somewhat predictably, for the divine right of kings because they descended from Adam, the first man.

Today patriarchy is a set of emotions and beliefs that have a great deal to do with class and education, in the sense that upper middle-class people generally conceal their patriarchy and highly educated people often sublimate theirs. Most educated people in the modern world are simply too saturated with democratic ideas and feelings to really welcome the idea of a hierarchical society; and we all know from personal experience that men are no better at leadership than women. Physical courage still has its place, but it is nowadays no more important than good judgment (with the possible exception of the most desperate kind of hand-to-hand combat) and nowhere near as important as the healthy people skills necessary to find consensus within groups.

We are entering a period in which social skills, and the ability to negotiate differences while staking out those values that are non-negotiable (and explaining why), is increasingly important. The

biggest problem with patriarchy is that it starts wars at every opportunity, even if it requires the most monumental kind of lying (George
Bush's rationale for the invasion of Iraq comes to mind), because
patriarchy sees war, any war, as intrinsically a good thing—after all,
war is necessary to the transmission of warrior values through
trauma bonding. Finally, patriarchy is essentially anti-democratic
and opposed to universal human rights; and for these reasons alone
must be vehemently opposed.

George Lakoff, the Berkeley-based cognitive linguist, has written
an entire book[20] suggesting (among other things) that conservatives
unconsciously favor a "strict father model" for society and
government, and therefore adhere to a vision of the state as a strong,
dominant father figure. Liberals, to nobody's surprise, unconsciously
embrace a "nuturant parent model" for appropriate political power,
according to Lakoff; and for that reason see government as potentially benevolent. The "strict father model" noted by Lakoff is
nothing more than our old friend patriarchy, all dressed up in its
Sunday best to service the Religious Right and the Republican
Party's "values" debate.

A debate that leads, one must add, to some stunning contradictions within American conservatism. The same conservatives who
say they like limited government actually tend to support a strong,
intrusive, highly militarized government that can interfere with
women's reproductive choices at home and intervene in foreign
countries where people have the wrong religion. But how did
Republican voters in the US first get addicted to this patriarchal
model of the state as a "strict father" anyway? Because shortly after
the Civil Rights Act and the Voting Rights Act of 1964 and 1965, the
Republican party went out of its way to recruit white Southerners
who mourned the death of segregation, particularly white men—and
this openly racist and relatively uneducated demographic has been
getting older, crankier, crazier, more bigoted and more patriarchal
every year, especially since the ultra-conservative evangelicals
among them became the most outspoken constituency in the

Republican party. Just look at the Republican contenders in the primaries of 2011 and 2012.

So women, it seems, do not need to worry about assimilating patriarchal orientations, right? After all, they're born female, aren't they? Guess again: some of the most patriarchal people in the modern world are women. The reason is simple: patriarchy, like many belief systems and almost all emotional orientations based on aggression, can be internalized by both women and men—and some ambitious women internalize patriarchy very quickly. That should surprise no one. How else could women in the military and female CEOs become even marginally successful competing in the boys' club?

In fact, a woman who has internalized a fair amount of patriarchy can, if she has an integrated personality and insight into herself, assume an enormous advantage over everybody else by using patriarchal ideas, metaphors and body language, then quickly switching to feminist ideas, and even adapting key feminist ideas to particular managerial problems. The late Helen Gurley Brown, the editor of *Cosmopolitan* during its glory years, had by all accounts this uncanny ability to go back and forth between these polar emotional and imaginative worlds, which fascinated a lot of the high-powered males who came in contact with her. But that sort of thing can be tricky. I personally knew a female administrator who could go back and forth between a kind of butt-kicking style of extreme patriarchy, in the way she spoke and in the policies she recommended, to sounding almost like a radical feminist—and she apparently adhered to some of the beliefs of *both* patriarchy and radical feminism.

This woman paid a price, however: she became over time a compulsive liar, and got stuck in an overly patriarchal managerial role, a dilemma greatly exacerbated by an untreated mental health and learning disability. Her husband became very ill, and unfortunately died. The combination of untreated disability and internalized patriarchy kept her from grieving properly, in my opinion, and she suffered a devastating emotional breakdown.

Nationalism

The second of the three cultural influences that stimulate aggression is *nationalism*, which must be regarded as unequivocally pathological. It is pathological because it is a form of mass narcissism, with all the arrogance and self-loathing inherent in narcissism; and because such toxic emotions demand release, it is extremely aggressive. Nationalism, more than anything else, tends to contribute to or create unnecessary wars; and although it is driven by profound aggression, the nationalist can never be completely satisfied, since nationalism is itself based on a rather flimsy abstraction. (More about that in a moment.) For all these reasons it is in some ways the most problematical of the three unconscious emotional systems that stimulate aggression in society.

The fact that nationalism is pathological is well understood among two highly educated demographics in the modern world—German and Japanese intellectuals. Nationalism had a long and negative history in both Germany and Japan, and the aggression and racism unleashed by nationalist movements led to horrific excesses and wars that devastated their lands. Therefore it is no wonder that its dangers are well understood by educated people in those two countries.

Elsewhere people do not have the same understanding of nationalism, often confusing it with patriotism—but nationalism and patriotism are *not* the same thing. *Patriotism* is pride in one's own country and its best values, and a desire to enjoy those values in the domestic life of one's nation; *nationalism* is the desire to impose the values and practices of one's country on another country—to see your nation's government and its national security apparatus aggressively dominate other countries, control its people and kill those that resist. Thus nationalism celebrates aggression as glorious and transcendent, and gloats in the suffering it inflicts on its perceived enemies. Americans in particular have a poor understanding of nationalism's most dangerous form, which is *religious nationalism,* despite the fact that it is a powerful force in America—but few people see or understand it because they're so close to it.

Nationalism is a form of mass narcissism, as mentioned above; and like individual narcissism is based on low self-esteem and unresolved emotional conflicts. That is to say, the people that are deeply attracted to nationalism are fundamentally unhappy in their personal lives, feel powerless in an unpredictable world, and are driven by a need to punish real or imaginary enemies for their unhappiness. The concept of the nation permits the nationalist to feel that he is part of something much larger and more powerful than he is. But the nationalist doesn't identify strongly with the good things his country has done—he doesn't identify with its educational system, its ability to fairly enforce the laws or its fair distribution of taxes to fund the social safety net. He doesn't identify with anything good in his country at all. He identifies with his country's ability to attack, harm and dominate perceived enemies in other countries, or to persecute minorities in the homeland.

This hostility at the heart of nationalism is unmistakable and omnipresent, and arises from the mass narcissism that drives it—but ultimately it is the low self-esteem fueling the narcissism that makes nationalism ultimately unsatisfying. The mass narcissism of nationalism could be said to be almost pure aggression—the individual who is narcissistic feels inferior, so he creates a super-human persona who is perfect and never makes mistakes; whereas the nationalist does pretty much the same thing concerning his country. He sees his own country as so transcendent that it's never wrong, and therefore never needs to apologize or think systematically about its policies. The nationalist sees the role of government as existing solely to dominate its enemies, while outflanking or repressing domestic dissenters.

Of course, as historian Benedict Anderson has pointed out, the idea of a 'nation' necessarily exists solely in the imagination, and is just as imaginary to the nationalist as anyone else. In his book

Imagined Communities, Anderson points out that in a tribal arrangement of a hundred people or less, a member of the tribe is likely to know almost everybody in his world—so if a tribal member says he identifies with his tribe, he is identifying with something real, because he knows everybody in it. It's not an abstraction. But people who identify with a nation are actually identifying with a fictional construct, because there's no way they could possibly know everybody in that nation, or even most of the people in its political class. The nationalist, therefore, seeks to identify *concretely* with an *abstraction.* The only way the nationalist can possibly overcome this contradiction is to identify not with the nation itself, but *with its aggression,* in the sense that aggression is real, it's concrete, it's dynamic, and when acted on it's certainly not an abstraction. Identifying with his nation's aggression also serves as an outlet for the resentments generated by the nationalist's low self-esteem, as the foreigners killed, cowed or captured serve as satisfying scapegoats for his sense of inferiority.

The same is true of fanatical sports fans, if one stops to think about it. The fan shouts, yells, and sometimes even weeps with pleasure when his team wins, and dies a thousand deaths when the other side triumphs. But in reality, there is no palpable difference between the two teams, even when one side is having a good year. They are basically alike—two teams with about the same number of professional athletes, the same clubhouse intrigues, the same salary disputes, the same kind of coaching staff; so what difference does it make to the sports fan if his team wins, or the other team? The pleasure comes not from anything good in one's own team, but in *dominating the other side.* What the fan usually identifies with, what he loves above all, is not his team, but the chance that he may witness his team beating the other team. It's a relatively harmless acting out of the instinct for homicidal aggression. But can sports—especially violent contact sports—exacerbate aggression, or do they offer aggression a benign outlet? I believe it's mainly the latter, but nobody knows for sure.

The nationalist identifies himself with his nation because he hopes it will dominate and humiliate another country, or a minority within his own country. The *religious nationalist* similarly wishes to dominate other countries, but believes his country has the right to dominate other countries *because it's God's will*. He believes it to be God's will because the religious nationalist's perceived enemies have the wrong religion, among other things, and refuse to acknowledge it. Not too long ago we saw an example of this in Northern Ireland, where the ancient practice of gerrymandering gave Protestants more political clout than Catholics; the two tribal groups warred for power, and after much suffering, death and sacrifice they finally reached a consensus in which the power imbalance was modified and the two groups arrived at a power-sharing arrangement.

Religious nationalism in the US almost always has to do with Israel/Palestine, the Middle East or with wars—surprise, surprise!—in which Muslims die disproportionately. The current government in Israel, which is an extremely right-wing government, is invariably supported by the Israel Lobby and the hard-line American neo-cons; they are likewise uncritically supported by millions of right-wing Christian evangelicals.

The reality is that there has been a massive movement to the theological and political right both by institutional Christianity and institutional Judaism in America. Somewhere between sixty and eighty percent of Protestants are now evangelicals, and most Jewish organizations uncritically support the right-wing government of Israel. Both, in slightly different ways, are driven by religious nationalism, which—this can't be pointed out enough—is today the world's most dangerous force. And both are lead overwhelmingly by people who have made it exceedingly clear that what they seek is a war against Iran by the West, led by the US. This would ultimately lead to a worldwide religious war and drive the US even more deeply into debt, but religious nationalists are fanatics, and care little about the suffering they cause.

The worst-case scenario would be something like the War of

Spanish Succession, during which period there were several ongoing land wars throughout the world; but underlying everything—and driving the whole show—was a conflict between Protestantism and Catholicism. I am afraid of a similar series of wars which are nominally about non-religious issues—Iran creating a nuclear bomb, for instance—but which are actually driven by a worldwide religious conflict between Islam and the West. I think such religious wars would last for most of the 21st century, and would leave scars of bitterness that would be very hard to heal; furthermore, it would happen at a time when we need to be dealing with global warming, and would be catastrophic for that reason alone.

The assassinations currently being carried out by Israel and the American CIA inside Iran are making the situation more dangerous, practically guaranteeing a terrorist response by Iran, also creating a stand-off that outright war would not resolve but only make more incendiary. What American policy-makers do not completely understand is that any attack against Iran will lead to continuing hostilities, which is likely to cause the Middle East to boil over, probably ending diplomatic relations between America and most of the Middle Eastern countries for decades. In short, war by America and Israel against Iran is likely to drag the world into an ongoing religious war between Islam and the West—and that could result in recurring low-intensity religious conflicts lasting perhaps for at least a hundred years, if it doesn't result in a nuclear catastrophe first.

So, reader, are you congratulating yourself that we don't have Northern Ireland's kind of bitter religious antagonisms here in the good old USA? Guess again! Right-wing Christian nationalists have what amounts to veto power on domestic policy in the Republican Party, in which they are the single most important constituency. They were also the most enthusiastic electoral supporters of the invasion of Iraq by American troops, and of torture practiced by the Bush administration. And domestically, those evangelical Christians that identify with the Religious Right are overwhelmingly dead set on denying choice and health services to American women, they are likely to think that science is a conspiracy, and many are fanatics with a palpable tendency to demand apocalyptic solutions to everything that bothers them. The Israel Lobby, which now counts as much on fanatical right-wing Christians as Jewish ultra-Zionists, is one of the most powerful and ruthless lobbies in the history of this country. (It and the National Rifle Association both provide excellent examples of the undemocratic "factions" that Alexander Hamilton warned us about. A majority of elected legislators now receive "bundler" money from the Israel Lobby, and vote as Prime Minister Netanyahu of Israel tells them to.)

But what makes religious nationalism in the US especially dangerous today is that it has a Manichean quality to it—you just can't talk rationally to people involved in promoting various forms of it, because they are so convinced that they're acting out God's will that they can no longer think straight. Again, religious nationalists typically care little for the people they hurt—they're acting out God's plan, don't you see? They have a devouring need to always be right about everything, and their organizations typically have a lot of money. Above all, like most fanatics they are totally arrogant, because they believe God is on their side.

Christian nationalism in America has a long history of promoting white domination of slaves, tribal people, Mexicans and just about everybody else. When one hears Republican Party politicians talking about how Palestinians are an "invented people," and therefore ought to be willing to cheerfully abandon their homes, orchards and farms because Israel and the West want to steal them, you're hearing exactly the same kind of racism as was heard in the 19th century against the tribal people. The big difference, of course, is that it's no longer secular nationalism, it's now pure religious nationalism. What makes these religious nationalists dangerous—and I'm specifically referring now to the evangelically-based Religious Right—is that too many of them will enthusiastically support any war that will kill Muslims because they believe it might bring about Second Coming of Jesus. For that reasons they are not above engaging and supporting various kinds of incitement aimed at kicking off a religious war in the Middle East.

Do right-wing Christian evangelicals really believe in anything that has to do with the teachings of Jesus? Some, of course—and numerically, that adds up to a lot of people. But what most of them *really* feel in a profound way, when it comes to their most powerful motives, is a deep identification with American aggression, which they identify as being the will of God. That is perverse, but in today's America that is what right-wing Christian evangelicals are mainly all about—using the state to glorify God by killing Muslims, and repressing their political enemies at home, including Muslims, gays, secularists and women who believe in birth control and reproductive rights. And these Christian nationalists think of themselves as being quite noble for doing so.

The new Jewish nationalism has much of the same apocalyptic emphasis. The reason for the bitter, desperate kind of religious nationalism prevalent in the Jewish Diaspora is something that most Jews don't like to talk about, mainly because it has to do with the existence of evil—and some Jews aren't even aware of the problem consciously. The real reason for the intense Jewish nationalism in the Jewish Diaspora is a deep, often unconscious loss of faith. *Where was God when the six million were asphyxiating in Hitler's gas chambers?* There is no answer to that question now, just as there was no answer when the Zyklon B pellets dropped and millions died a horrible death. As a result, many Jews feel that they have lost their connection with God according to any meaningful definition of that word. It wasn't just that God wasn't there in the hour of greatest need for the Jewish people, they were also betrayed by their vaunted progressive and liberal beliefs and their intense devotion to social justice and social-democratic causes. Where were the liberals of Europe when the six million perished? They were in hiding, on the run, or were themselves being gassed in the death factories.

Religious Jews—and even Jews from the Reform tradition that have given it some thought—often feel that God died or went into some kind of eclipse, whereas secular and cultural Jews often experience a similar alienation from the progressive ideas that were at the heart of European Judaism since the Enlightenment. The bottom line is, nothing or nobody helped to save the Jews from the gas chambers. (Of course, a great many non-Jews *did* try to stop the Holocaust—statistically more non-Jews than Jews, in fact—but that kind of calculation is not taken into consideration by Israeli nationalists and their US proxies.) From their point of view, what is necessary is to keep focusing on the Nazi Holocaust, which is why they keep bringing it up even when it's not relevant.

The problem with this is that religious nationalism cannot be justified by grievances based in the past, for reasons we'll deal with shortly. Another big problem is that this intense identification with the Holocaust can lead to a lot of internalization of its aggression. The upshot of all this is that this kind of nihilism often results in an unconscious replacement of an absent or silent deity with the power of the state of Israel. And when you start worshipping a state instead of God, whether consciously or unconsciously, you're in trouble—to conflate God with a state is idolatry, by any standard, whether you are a Christian evangelical worshipping the American state, or a Zionist worshipping the Israeli state. Such thinking will invariably lead to a violent outcome, because the state you worship will sooner or later adopt the attitude of its supporters—that is, it will start to see its own behavior as carrying the imprimatur of God. Just as the Religious Right believes that US aggression is the will of God, the Israeli state increasingly presents itself as the single, messianic solution to the problem of Jewish suffering.

This kind of idolatry—and make no mistake about it, worship of the state is idolatry, whether Christian or Jewish—is dangerous precisely because people often react to trauma by replacing the emotional orientations formerly associated with religion into slavish worship of various kinds of secular power. They did it in Germany under Hitler; and a great many intellectuals also worshiped Marxism-Leninism as a messianic vehicle for a better world. The state of Israel may assume the role of a Messiah in the unconscious thinking of many Jews, but such thinking makes it a False Messiah, the last and worst of many such False Messiahs that have plagued Judaism throughout its history.

The feeling of a connection with God has in Judaism been to a great extent replaced by secular equivalencies, or the obsessive legal-istic rituals of the Orthodox which repress dread but do not deliver spiritual peace, happiness or emotional relief in a demonstrably evil world. *Jewish nationalism arose because of a sense that neither God nor liberal humanism can any longer be trusted.* Therefore instead of the older liberal ideology that American Jews once embraced, a new and dangerous ideology of religious war has arisen, conceived by neo-cons and right-wing Israelis together, and centered in the US and funded by neo-con foundations. Many formerly liberal Jews feel misgivings, but have not yet found a way to resist the virus of religious nationalism. One reason for this is that the sense of power in religious nationalism mimics the emotions associated in the past with the power of an attentive God—a God who is now silent, perhaps forever.

Now that God is in eclipse, all that many Jews feel they have left is the company of other Jews bonded by violence against their perceived enemies. The intensity of that feeling is at the heart of Jewish nationalism, especially in the settler and neo-fascist groups in Israel, which are almost exclusively focused on an extremely aggressive—in fact malignant—struggle to obliterate native Palestinian life and culture. The rise of religious nationalism among Israel's ultra-Orthodox Jews frames anti-Palestinian racism as a way to fulfill God's commandments; but in reality it is driven by a burning sense of God's betrayal, which is not so much grieved—because it is not conscious—but experienced emotionally in the form of a permanent anger, resentment and aggression. The Palestinians that are routinely tortured in the interrogation centers by Israeli troops are scapegoats not just for the Holocaust, but also for a Jewish God that failed.

But God didn't fail. What failed was the attitude of believers, whether Christian, Jewish or Muslim, who embrace narcissistic, juvenile and self-serving beliefs and behavior. The religious nationalist feels that God has failed because God didn't do the right things for him personally, and for his people. But no deity is going to suspend the laws of physics because one's enemies are sadistic idiots. Those who believe in social justice must find ways to work with others to deconstruct the internalized aggression of dangerous people, institutions and political movements before they get out of hand.

Blind, groveling support for a theocratic state or for American empire won't get you into the Promised Land—it will only deliver more violence.

Nationalism and religious nationalism can only be halted by people who are willing to stop punishing others for their own unresolved social and personal problems, and deal with their own feelings of inadequacy, aggression and trauma. The antidote to religious nationalism is to either give up one's faith, or continue the search for God in a different way; the antidote to secular nationalism is to acknowledge the deficits of one's own country or tribe (as well as one's own personal deficits) and join with others to repair them. Both forms of religious nationalism touched on above are exceedingly dangerous, and they are both funded by—and based in—an increasingly divided America.

14.
Victimology

Victimology is the third emotional and cognitive system that encourages violence and aggression, both on a personal level and in society. It is also transmitted culturally, rather like patriarchy or nationalism; but although it is embedded in human cultures it isn't as easy to discern as patriarchy and nationalism. It is hard to identify because it is so often used in covert or passive-aggressive ways, sometimes by people who aren't even aware that they're using it. Yet we all know what it is. People play the victim to get what they want—that's the essence of it. What about the schemer who always talks about how he's being mistreated every time he's busted for his manipulative behavior? Or the woman who cries to keep from getting a speeding ticket? Or the petty, hostile boss who makes a big mistake, and then deflects guilt onto everybody in his department rather than taking responsibility—then claims he's being persecuted when he's called on his mistake? In its milder forms it's something all of us have probably tried at one time or another. But for most of us, using this ploy makes us feel cheap, because we instinctively recognize it as a form of deceit; so we try not to use it regularly.

The big problem with victimology is that people and nations that regularly posture themselves as victims to avoid the consequences of their bad behavior are very likely to commit the same offense again. It becomes something they do on a regular basis, and therefore part of a pattern of personal aggression in their interactions—in fact their reiteration of their own victim status is probably a method they developed long ago for hiding, rationalizing or dissembling their aggression. And if they never take responsibility for their mistakes, they're unlikely to stop making them.

Victimology becomes especially dangerous when it is used by sociopaths or unscrupulous leaders to manipulate emotions on a mass scale in order to start wars, or kick off violent campaigns against religious or racial minorities. Furthermore, unscrupulous manipulators of victim status are very likely to use unpleasant memories of past trauma to exacerbate feelings of trauma in the present moment, as Slobodan Milosevic of Serbia did during the late 1980s and early 1990s, by consistently reiterating all the injustices that Serbs had experienced in the past, to justify ethnically cleaning Muslims in Bosnia. He had to redraw national lines, he said, to make Serbia larger, because if he didn't, the world would gang up on Serbs and destroy them.

The response of Serbs to this blatant use of victimology was enthusiasm bordering on hysteria—and as nationalist fervor rose in

Serbia, the Balkan wars became inevitable, and the genocide against Muslims began. It was Milosevic's blatant and constant referencing of past injustices that sealed the fate of hundreds of thousands of Muslim victims of Serbian rape and genocide. *Victimology uses past crimes to justify present crimes*—but past suffering is never a moral, legal or even common-sense defense for further aggression, and part of the human maturation process is learning to make that distinction. Criminals must be responsible for their crimes no matter how heart-rending their back story is—that's a big part of rehabilitation. Aggression that is justified by past crimes is simply a *continuation of past crimes by other means*.

In a celebrity culture such as the US, people become extremely skillful at using victimology to manipulate public opinion. Using victim status doesn't depend on logic—it operates out of emotion, and it is most effective when used by people that know intuitively how to manipulate emotions. Furthermore, people who know how to manipulate the public based on perceived victim status in the present are often people who really *were* victimized in the past. Sometimes the use of victim status is simply a way of using a 'culture of complaint,' people who claim victim status so that they might use guilt to grovel their way up the occupational ladder, or for other personal or organization gain; people usually see through this, so although genuinely irritating it isn't particularly dangerous. The people who are *really* dangerous are those who *feel* like victims, who think they *are* victims even though they're actually engaged in brutally victimizing other people—and that is, one will remember, precisely the posture of the sociopath, who believes that he has been victimized all his life and that therefore he is entitled to hurt other people to even the score. The sociopath continues to feel like a victim, even as he rapes, kills or beats up other people. He can't feel the pain of his victims because he is too busy feeling his own pain.

Clearly, those who are immersed in victimology are involved in an emotional orientation more than a cognitive one, because logically victim status in the past can never justify crimes in the present. But this aspect of victimization roughly approximates the process we have identified as trauma bonding, where people who have been victims internalize aggression and then become aggressors against innocent people. Victimology greatly enhances trauma bonding and often occurs in tandem with it, and is a particularly pathological cultural influence when it encourages people *to identify with victim status as a form of personal identity.* This is extremely dangerous, because as soon as you identify yourself as the archetypical victim, your emotional growth stops. (Because the victim is always right—he never has to make any changes or do anything.) Nonetheless, there are certain political cultures—Serbian and Israeli nationalism are most pronounced in this regard—in which ambitious right-wing politicians have encouraged and used victimology for their own political reasons. So do certain criminal subcultures, also for reasons of their own. But why do people posture themselves as victims? In other words, what are the advantages of victim status to the aggressor?

Anybody who has studied the history of Adolph Hitler's machinations will quickly recognize his masterful use of victim status. Hitler *always* postured himself as a victim even as he victimized others, usually accusing *them* of violence and mayhem even as his own storm troopers were actually committing it. The act with which Hitler started the Second World War was typical—on September 1, 1939, Hitler accused Poland of attacking Germany, at the precise moment that his own troops were given the order to attack Poland. He even worked himself into a self-righteous fury at the nerve of the Poles attacking poor, innocent Germany—even though he had just given the order for German soldiers to attack *them*. It is not unusual for people under the influence of victimology to work themselves up to a point where it's easy for them to believe they really are victims, even as they attack and devastate others.

Hitler's victimology came through very clearly in his body language and his speeches, as he intended it to. George Orwell commented at length about this in his March, 1940 review of *Mein*

Kampf. "I should like to put it on record that I have never been able to dislike Hitler," Orwell wrote. "Ever since he came to power—till then, like nearly everyone, I had been deceived into thinking that he did not matter—I have reflected that I would certainly kill him if I could get within reach of him, but that I could feel no personal animosity. The fact is that there is something deeply appealing about him. One feels it again when one sees his photographs—and I recommend especially the photograph at the beginning of Hurst and Blackett's edition [of *Mein Kampf*], which shows Hitler in his early Brownshirt days. It is a pathetic, dog-like face, the face of a man suffering under intolerable wrongs."

"In a rather manly way it reproduces the expression of innumerable pictures of Christ crucified, and there is little doubt that that is how Hitler sees himself. The initial, personal cause of his grievance against the universe can only be guessed at; but at any rate the grievance is there. He is the martyr, the victim, Prometheus chained to the rock, the self-sacrificing hero who fights single-handed against impossible odds. If he were killing a mouse he would know how to make it seem like a dragon. One feels, as with Napoleon, that he is fighting against destiny, that he can't win, and yet that he somehow deserves to. The attraction of such a pose is of course enormous; half the films that one sees turn upon some such theme."[21]

Indeed, a great many films *do* turn on this dynamic as a central plot device: it is the ancient theme of the underdog, Jack the Giant Killer and David against Goliath, as Orwell points out. Its deep attraction is that all human beings feel weak in the face of the entrenched powers, the mighty of the earth; the Old Testament story of David is so popular because its seems to validate the idea that sometimes it is possible for David to defeat Goliath, no matter how great the odds against him. But it goes deeper than that. Hitler really *felt* that he was a righteous man who was victimized by one kind of evil or another—megalomaniacs almost always feel something like that. Therefore, in his mind, all the outrageous and sadistic things done by his government were simply efforts to protect himself and get even for the pain that his enemies had so gratuitously heaped upon him.

Germans of that time responded instinctively to the spectacle of shame and rage presented by Hitler's particular brand of victimology. They, too, had tasted the ashes in the mouth that came with Versailles, as the nations of the world banded together to force humiliation on the Fatherland. Hitler was simply a man intent on acknowledging the fundamental wrongness of that, and somehow getting even for it—that is what was *felt* by a great many Germans. If Hitler wished to conquer Europe and the world, it was only so that nobody would ever be able to humiliate and exploit Germans again.

That, again, is the fundamental position of the sociopath—he feels like he has been victimized forever and now simply wishes to get even. He uses his charm and his skills with selective violence to get what he wants—and it all makes perfectly good sense to him. The fact that he is causing innocent people pain that is just as severe as his own does not register with him. Although he has empathy (which he uses to find out what you want to hear) he is completely incapable of sympathy.

One high-profile group in America that has made extensive use of victimology (and gotten quite good at it) is conservative Christian evangelicals. Of course, there is a basis for this in evangelical theology—during the End Time, there is supposed to be intense persecution of believers leading up to Judgment Day, setting the stage for the Second Coming of Christ and the arrival of the New Jerusalem, or New Earth. That makes it easy for evangelical Christians to interpret things they don't agree with as the persecution supposedly predicted in the Bible. To them, the fact that they can't read the Bible in school, or the fact that most women use birth control, is evidence of an anti-Christian conspiracy. Rightwing Christian evangelicals also point to the manner in which the media scorns their beliefs as further proof that the end is at hand. But it isn't the End Time that has made rightwing Christian evangelicalism unpopular in the US. It's their own behavior that has caused other Americans to turn away from them.

It's true that they can't read Bibles in school anymore, but that happens because we are no longer exclusively a Christian nation— and as a recipient of public funds, it is appropriate that public schools do not favor Christianity over other religions. Furthermore evangelical Christians have lost a great deal of cultural influence over the last few decades; but they have responded by trying to get *political* power to compensate for the loss of *cultural* power. But that never works. People have turned against conservative Christian evangelicals not because of Satan or the End Times, but because increasing numbers of people—including Christians who are not evangelical—perceive the Religious Right as bullies and their beliefs as unattractive and hateful. Yet evangelicals do not see that, nor are they likely to listen to the arguments of their critics—they're too busy posturing themselves as pathetic victims. One might say that their imagined victim status not only helps them rationalize the fact that they're losing the culture wars, but also operates as a defense mechanism that enables them to avoid seeing how shrill and unattractive they have become.

One very sophisticated use of victimology in civil society can be observed in the passive-aggressive attack style used by right-wing activists sponsored by the corporate upper class. The preferred gambit is to denounce your opponent for doing something at the same time that *you're* doing it, or preparing to do it. For example, right-wing activists are now engaged in trying to suppress voting rights among elders, students, Blacks and Latinos. These right-wing operatives say they are trying to stop voter fraud—then proceed to commit voter fraud themselves by expunging people likely to vote Democratic. Another example is the gambit that succeeded in getting the Supreme Court 'Citizens United' judgment passed; this decision gives corporations virtual unlimited access to buy political elections. Conservatives adopted the line that "activist judges" needed to be removed from the bench—then engaged in strategies that would ensure that their own "activist judges" would end up on the bench instead. The only difference was that the new activist judges were extreme conservatives rather than centrists or liberals. The conservatives were playing the victim card all along, and today they dominate the judiciary with their overt political agenda.

So how does one handle victim status? Should we completely ignore past victimization that has occurred to us, or to members of our religion or ethnic group? No, it is a far better strategy to deconstruct victim status by working against the social injustice that resulted in one's own victimization in the first place. The rape victim will find relief campaigning against sexual violence directed at women; the torture survivor seeks justice by working to end torture. Such projects do not have to be vocations or careers, but should be enough to help the victim leave behind the weakness and anonymity of mere victim status, and become a survivor, and finally a protagonist. *Working against injustice after being victimized is one of the best ways to keep oneself from internalizing the aggression of the attacker.*

Security expert Gavin de Becker is a good example of how a person can leave behind victim status, become a survivor and ultimately a protagonist of one's own life. Gavin de Becker was beaten regularly as a child, witnessed innumerable acts of parental violence, and watched his heroin-addicted mother shoot his father with a handgun. "Though I did not end up a violent man myself," de Becker writes, "I did become a kind of ambassador between the two worlds, fluent in both languages. I'm able to tell you something about how many criminals think because it's similar to how I thought much of my life." Gavin de Becker became an expert in violence, using his hard-won experience to create one of the nation's premier security firms, providing security both to businesses and Hollywood show business figures; ultimately he ended up providing personal security to some of America's most high-profile celebrities. He deconstructed the trauma and the internalized aggression from the victimization he had suffered as a child in a number of extremely interesting ways.

First of all, he used his intense, systematic gift for laser-like intro-spection to examine his own emotional orientations and thought processes, and to examine the motives of others. Interestingly, he acknowledges that he knows how criminals think because he often thinks that way himself. In other words, he is not afraid to publicly acknowledge his own capacity for evil, but also acknowledges that he isn't going to act on it. That's liberating! Secondly, he acts out and uses to the fullest his intense desire to protect others from violence and criminal aggression. By acting out his deeply-felt nurturing and protective instincts, which he first developed by protecting his younger brother from the violence of his parents, he was able to further deconstruct the trauma and the aggression that he had inter-nalized as the victim of childhood abuse. Gavin de Becker became one of America's best and most celebrated security experts, and also a man from whom we can all learn a great deal.[22]

Victimology is that pathological state in which victims refuse to move on to the next stage, of working with others to repair what has hurt them. The victim refuses to go from being a *victim* to being a *survivor*, and therefore cannot become a *protagonist* in their own lives. Instead the victim clings to victim status even as he begins to act out the aggression that he previously internalized. Victimology, like narcissism, obscures the victim-aggressor's ability to feel the pain of his victims, because it is only *his* pain that is important. Indeed, aggression is a sedative for such a person, to which the victim-aggressor mistakenly clings as the standard for recovery. But aggression is addictive and ultimately unsatisfying. The addict uses substances to control his emotions, and then loses control of the substance; the victim-aggressor uses aggression to control his pain, but then loses control of his aggression.

Avraham Burg, the former Speaker of the Knesset, the Israeli parliament, writes candidly about how victimology sometimes disorients the thinking of both Israelis and American Jews in his book *The Holocaust is Over; We Must Rise From Its Ashes*. In a way it is understandable—even inevitable—that Jews would be obsessed by the Nazi Holocaust, because it was history's greatest crime, and Jews were its victims. But getting stuck in past trauma is never healthy, because it blinds people to the opportunities of the present and future. And when powerful men use it to justify questionable or immoral things in the present, the process is already well on its way to becoming a form of systemic evil. "The inevitable outcome of this attitude is a feeling of power," Burg writes, "and the further erosion of the Jewish idea of revival that was the basis for the American Jewish autonomy. American Jews, like Israelis, are stuck in Auschwitz, raising the Shoah [Nazi Holocaust] banner high to the sky and exploiting it politically."

The instant intimacy of belonging to a victimized group is quite powerful; but when victim status becomes the controlling metaphor of a culture—not to mention the basis for personal identity and the central myth of a highly armed state—what is produced are people who do not wish to integrate themselves into the world, but rather seek to incite and attack it. The reason for this is that victim status, when linked to a particular trauma that is constantly reiterated by the state, becomes a fundamentally aggressive emotional orientation that demands release through aggression against others. People animated by it begin to see aggression, as they previously saw their own victim status, as the standard for all human activity. That is precisely what happened to the Serbian nationalists in the 1990s, and what has happened to the right-wing parties in the Israeli political class.

This is the essence of trauma bonding; but we must also call attention to the dominant role of victimology in these examples. And it's not limited to Serbs and Israelis. Many of the white Southern men who form the base of the modern Republican Party honestly feel that they are victims, but their status is in reality more the result of their own backwardness, their own lack of cultural literacy, and their own inability to work with others for more social justice. At a time when Israelis could easily make peace with the Palestinians by giving them their own small country and making friends with them, the violence and fury of Israelis toward the Palestinians is actually increasing. The Nazi Holocaust has in particular become a kind of inexplicable, a-historical and cosmic Black Hole of indecipherable insanity that is artificially kept alive by the Israeli political class, because it justifies eternal obedience to the Israeli state, continued theft of Palestinian land, as well as apocalyptic and violent responses to any criticism.

In the meantime, there is a prophetic minority of individuals in Israel and in the Jewish community of the US who, like Avraham Burg, have not been affected by trauma bonding and its concomitant victim psychology, or who have found a way to deconstruct the national Israeli obsession with Holocaust trauma that is constantly being reiterated by the right-wing Israeli parties; and they become the prophets, teachers and mentors for those still caught up in the cycle of aggression. Burg, by writing his incredibly honest book, is pleading with his fellow Israelis (and with the Israel Lobby in the US) to question the victimology that underlies much of their behavior and motivation.

The problem, sadly, is that people who identify with victim status cannot hear or think logically anymore, because the victim is always right—the victim does not have to make any changes, or do anything. This kind of attitude interferes both with common sense and strategic judgment. Humankind's best interests lie in learning how to deconstruct the dark matter of internalized aggression; but there are important forces in the US—including but not limited to the Israel Lobby, the Religious Right and the neo-cons—who want to keep past trauma alive, in order to raise money and bond people to their political line.

Avraham Burg puts it this way: "Israel went beyond mourning; it was no longer a future-oriented state, but a society connected to its bleeding, traumatic past. The dramatic proximity of 1945 to 1948, the years of grief and of utopia, depression and mania, fused two monumental events, the Jewish massacre in Europe and the building of the Jewish state of Israel, into one single entity. They became intertwined and inseparable." The only way Israelis could deal with their aggression was to *escape back into victim status*, something they knew well from centuries of oppression in Europe.

This resulted in an Israel nobody had anticipated: "Israel adopted [the] legacy of insecurity characteristic of trauma victims. Since then, we live under constant pressure and in the contradictions of unceasing armament to compensate and atone for built-in impotence and existential anxiety. We have become a nation of victims, and our state religion is the worship and tending of traumas, as if Israel forever walks down its last path." It has gradually dawned on the international community, as it has on Burg, that Israel's obsession with victim status interferes with its ability to comprehend its own best interests.

Burg's idea is that Israel and its proxies should stop seeing themselves as victims, and start acting like grown-up people who are protagonists of their own story—by taking responsibility for what Israel has done, what is good about it as well as what needs to be changed. This makes sense, because a country—like a person—can only achieve greatness if it is willing to acknowledge its own mistakes. "Therefore we must stand on the tallest mountain and declare clearly and loudly: we know that solving the Shoah refugee problem directly and indirectly caused the Palestinian refugee problem. Only then can we give our excuses and explanations: we were drowning and grabbing at straws; we were busy saving ourselves... We have to admit that post-Shoah, we valued our lives because we wanted to live after so much death. We were not suffi-ciently sensitive to the lives of others and to the price that they paid for our salvation. Please forgive us, and together we will put an end to the unhealthy refugee mindset that torments us all."[23]

15.

Projection and the Problem of the Evil 'Other': Why We Always See Aggression and Evil in the Other Person and Not in Ourselves.

During the twenty-five years that I worked as a counselor doing psycho-social rehab, I worked with a great many paranoid schizophrenics. Some of these clients' delusions were rather benign, because they took anti-psychotic medications that compensated them somewhat. The untreated paranoid schizophrenics (that is, those that refused to take *any* medications) were another story completely. They *really* believed that people out there were persecuting them, and often had delusional systems with a cast of thousands. There's an old psychodynamic theory about paranoid schizophrenia that involves psychological projection—this theory says that paranoid people tend to project onto their imaginary enemies the aggression they have inside themselves. They're agitated about all that burning anger they have in themselves, but can't figure out how to handle it, so they project it onto some delusional enemy who is supposedly out there plotting against them. Whether that's the cause of the paranoia, or the result of it, or a combination of both, nobody really knows.

This gets really dicey around the subject of homosexuality— young male paranoid schizophrenics have a tendency to see homosexuality in people around them, but you have to suspect that this arises because they are somewhat conflicted about their own sexual orientation. They are often angry at the world in general, too—partly, I'm sure, because their illness makes the world seem so threatening to them. But they always denied vehemently that they had any anger toward anything or anyone. It was always the *other* guy who was angry at *them*.

Of course, this all originated in some chemical irregularities in the client's brain, which may have been different for each client. (I've always suspected that what we call schizophrenia will turn out to be many different brain disorders that happen to produce some of the same symptoms.) But the client *experienced* these chemical imbalances in his brain as someone or something out to get him. What they boiled down to on the level of personal dynamics was that the client was furious about something, but saw the fury as originating in someone else. The client seemed to use a particularly robust form of psychological projection as a way of coming to terms with his own angry, fearful and aggressive feelings.

I had one extremely interesting client who had parents who were very, very undependable. The client idolized his father, but his dad would often promise to come over and then forget, or arrive three or four days later. Paranoid schizophrenics don't deal with ambivalence or double messages very well (they're already receiving enough of them from their addled brains) so my client began to experience powerful delusions of his father being killed in an automobile accident driving over to visit him. His father would call up and promise to come over; and after a few hours my client would have a delusion—sometimes accompanied by both visual and auditory hallucinations—that his father had been in a hideous auto crash and died.

Every time my client would come to me with this horrifying delusion, I'd say: "Whoa—that must have been really scary. Now, what are you mad at your father for?" The client would think, and when he thought about it we'd talk; and when he figured out that he was really ticked off because his father was late again, the paralyzing fear of 'killing' his father would fade. This is an example of how some paranoid schizophrenics can come to terms with their fears, but it also illustrates something unfortunate about them—the emotional material they project onto other people usually has to do with something they're angry about, and these angry feelings are often intertwined with thoughts relating to the hot topics of sex, religion and family. For reasons unknown, their illness also puts them in touch with a lot of raw aggression, which is the emotional orientation that is hardest for people to deal with—which is perhaps why paranoid people always want to project it onto other people.

After I had been doing psycho-social rehab a few years, it started to occur to me that most 'normal' people deal with aggression—or aggressive emotions—in ways not that different than my paranoid schizophrenic clients. *They always tend to see aggression in other people, and never in themselves.* Of course, the things that regular people perceive aren't overtly delusional, like the delusions my paranoid clients had; 'normal' people are generally quite accurate in the way they talk about the faults and deficits of other people—it's just that they are forever thinking about bad behavior in *others*, and never in themselves. And the more problems they have, the more they are likely to think about exactly those same kinds of problems in other people.

So are 'normal' people perhaps engaging in a kind of projection similar to the kind I saw in my paranoid clients? Well, perhaps not the same kind, because what 'normal' people see generally isn't delusional—but 'normal' people engage in projection *for the same reason*. Put simply, 'normal' people prefer to see and gossip about the deficits in others (very often their co-workers or family members), because it's too uncomfortable to see and talk about their own deficits. Furthermore, to just the extent that 'normal' people have problems handling their own aggression, to just that extent they're likely to talk a lot about the aggression of other people. That means that to develop a worthwhile secular theory of aggression and evil, we need to be aware of this tendency (that is, the tendency to see aggression in others and not ourselves) and seek to overcome it.

Virtually all the great teachers and prophets in the Abrahamic tradition have touched on this tendency. Jesus saw it clearly: *We tend to see the mote in the eye of the other person*, Jesus said, *but refuse to see the plank in our own eye*. That's an amusing image because of the radical asymmetry of the mote and the plank. It's certainly an understandable dynamic, which most of us can identify with. Not many people are willing to talk about their own faults, and such revelations might even make a lot of people uncomfortable. This common tendency to see faults in others but not in ourselves becomes important to confront when we wish to grow emotionally. It is at that point that our tendency to see aggression in others, but not in ourselves, should be challenged.

That's exactly where this book seeks to take the reader. This writer encourages the reader to find a way to examine his or her own capacity for aggression and evil, not to dwell on it, but simply to be aware of it. I'm not advocating egotistical bragging about one's awfulness, or all the terrible things one has done, because that's just an unpleasant form of narcissism. (We're rarely as good or as bad as we think we are.) All I'm saying is that sooner or later we need to confront the aggression inside us, whether it is latent or internalized from aggression we've experienced, or both; and we also need to confront our natural instinct to conceal the effects of our aggression, once we've acted on it. If we're really lucky, we'll not only recognize the aggression that's inside us, but we'll almost immediately become aware that we don't need to act on it, unless defending oneself from attack. Why? Because it is almost always our *unconscious* aggressions that cause us to do or say things we regret. The more aware we are of our unconscious aggression, the more freedom we have *not to act on it.*

The quest for a moral psychology begins with you, reader, and how you relate to your immediate world. What this means is an inversion of the way we usually experience our concerns about aggression and evil in the world. We cannot change things in other countries, at least not right away, because we're just not capable of it logistically. We are much more able to change things that are *closest* to us, starting with ourselves. That means training ourselves to be aware of aggression in ourselves, in our own family and tribe, and our own country. Above all we must be aware of the aggression committed by our own government, because that is where denial of aggression usually occurs. We must become intimately aware of the aggression closest to us, because if we do that, we won't have to project onto a foreign 'Other' all the things—especially the internalized aggression—that we cannot stand in ourselves or in our own country.

My paranoid client in the residential program where I worked finally realized that he could be angry at his father without having terrifying delusions of his dad dying in an auto crash. But likewise the individual living in the 21st century must reach the point where she or he can simply acknowledge their capacity for aggression and evil while arriving at the precious realization that they need not act on it—and for the same reason, they need not project aggression onto others, or imagine it where it doesn't really exist.

(*It is generally the aggressive orientations inside ourselves of which we are unaware that cause us to act against our best interests, and it is those same unacknowledged aggressive orientations that we are most likely to see in others.*) In realizing this hard home truth, we begin the journey to the transformation of humankind—beginning it not by converting others, but by slowly converting ourselves. The high road of the self must pass perilously close to hell, but it by understanding the mortal stakes of an examined life we avoid the dangers that might otherwise claim us. The high road of the self achieves its elevation by leaving hell behind, because once we've faced its existence, it can no longer tyrannize over us. *That*, not money and power, is the quest that brings spiritual liberation: *first*, as individuals; and *second*, as informed and prophetic advocates committed to stopping the destruction of the planet.

16.

To construct a credible secular theory of evil, one must have at least a passing awareness of the good—one should, in other words, have some idea where positive human qualities come from. One should be curious about this if for no other reason than computing the odds for defeating evil in particular situations. But this leads to an extremely important question: what exactly causes the formation of a personal moral code? In Professor Patricia J. Churchland's *Braintrust: What Neuroscience Tells Us about Morality,* the author writes of the possible social and biological origins of morality, as well as what is "probably true" about humanity's social nature—at least according to her research—and what that means "in terms of the neural platform for moral behavior."

Dr. Churchland isn't interested in particular moral conundrums, and gives short shrift to various philosophers who have tried to figure out morality as though it were a chess problem or a function of theology. (Her book has gained notoriety for its sometimes humorous debunking of previous theories about the basis of morality, some of which were accepted as mainstream science.) Churchland is a neurophilosopher and a Professor at the University of California at San Diego in California, and also an extremely witty writer with a solid grasp of theory and a talent for making it accessible to the general reader. And she has a scientifically-based theory of morality that tells a simple but fascinating story that rings true.

Professor Churchland believes that "what we humans call ethics or morality is a four-dimensional scheme for social behavior that is shaped by interlocking brain processes: (1) caring (rooted in attachment to kin and kith and care for their well-being); (2) recognition of others' psychological states (rooted in the benefits of predicting the behavior of others); (3) problem-solving in a social context (e.g. how we should distribute scarce goods, settle land disputes; how we should punish the miscreants); and (4) learning social practices (by positive and negative reinforcement, by imitation, by trial and error, by various kinds of conditioning, and by analogy). The simplicity of this framework does not mean its form, variations, and neural mechanisms are simple. On the contrary, social life is stunningly complex, as is the brain that supports our social lives."[24]

Churchland's four-dimensional scheme could operate simultaneously, but also seems more or less sequential. To begin with is her insight that "attachment to kin and kith and care for their well-being" is a fundamental part of morality, which suggests its beginning in early childhood development and child-rearing. At some point, however, the learning and problem-solving involved in families is "recruited to managing one's social life." Especially important is that the learning and problem-solving involved in taking care of human offspring is adapted to the non-juvenile actors inside and outside the home—and as Churchland points out, this is true not only of humans, but of other mammals, who are known to adopt or socialize with creatures from entirely different species into a bewilderingly complex variety of relationships.

Professor Churchland goes on to suggest that social processes stimulate or are consistent with certain conditions in the brain, and that cooperation and trust are related to particular chemical congruencies (oxytocin-vasopressin levels are the strongest indicators); and that therefore cooperative behavior among humans is very strongly correlated to changes in those levels in the brain. But the entire process is crafted, formed and regulated by social interrelations that start out with caring for children and other family members. It is in expanding this circle of care, in caring for others outside the primary group—or 'other-caring'—that morality arises, first as an adaptive social behavior but resulting in certain more or less predictable changes in the brain that ultimately give it a life of its own.

In his review of Churchland's book appearing at Amazon.com, Warren R. Grayson accurately summarizes as follows:

Depending on ecological conditions and fitness considerations, strong caring for the well-being of offspring has in some mammalian species extended further to encompass kin or mates or friends or even strangers, as the circle widens. *This widening of other-caring in social behavior marks the emergence of what eventually flowers into morality.* [Italics added.][25]

So there it is. It starts in the family circle, and is thereupon extended (or not extended, depending on the people involved) to other kith and kin and eventually even strangers. (One immediately thinks of all those pictures online that show animals caring for babies of other species.) The female nurtures the offspring, and then—what? Among humans the widening circle of "other-caring" (a delightfully suggestive phrase) marks the emergence of what eventually becomes morality. While this at first seems to fit well with certain feminist conceptions, it also appears to idealize exactly what many modern women are trying to get away from—staying at home and having kids.

But even though it seems to clash with modern ideas of independence from traditional gender roles, 'other-caring' stemming from maternal concern for offspring *does* fit well, this writer would argue, with the 18th century idea of a 'moral sense,' greatly beloved by the generation of Thomas Jefferson and his fellow American deists in the 18th century, many of whom saw morality as capable of stimulating intense pleasure—which could therefore serve as the motivation for what was then called civic virtue, or a strong identification with (and emotional attachment to) the well-being of the community.

Lord Shaftesbury, Francis Hutcheson and David Hume are most often associated with the idea of a moral sense, especially Hutcheson; but it was an idea that was literally 'in the air' at the time of the American Revolution, at least partly because of the influence of the Scottish Enlightenment. In the New World it was also popular because republican politicians enjoyed celebrating their own benevolent involvement in the affairs of the community and nation, a process still discernable in America's modern political campaigns. What is striking about the 'moral sense' was that it was perceived as an *emotional orientation,* and also part of a so-called 'theory of sentiments'; and was capable of being internalized by men as well as women. (In fact it was *more* likely to be internalized by men, because it was all the rage among educated males of a certain class in England, Scotland and America.)

What were its advantages? Quite simply it gave happiness, not from acquiring money or gaining power, but from doing the right thing. This gave immediate pleasure to the social actor involved, as well as—over a period of time—a sense of personal identity. How did one know what the right thing is? According to the idea of the 'moral sense,' virtuous behavior gave pleasure in the same way that enjoying a beautiful painting or verse might arouse an intense aesthetic pleasure. (The saying 'virtue is its own reward' is a rather cold but accurate way of expressing this process.) This idea of aesthetic pleasure as a response to one's own behavior was an idea that arose suddenly in the late 18th century, became extremely popular, and in certain ways contributed to the Romantic Movement that succeeded it. The difference between civic virtue and Romanticism turned out to be profound, however, since there was no problem with controlling the 'moral sense,' whereas one of the characteristics of Romanticism was the onset of powerful and extreme emotional states that threatened to overwhelm cognition.

Furthermore, partisans of the 'moral sense' believed it could be trained to react to very subtle social stimuli. This idea, in turn, fit well with a certain class emphasis on refinement of the emotions among educated men attracted to republicanism, partly because of the importance of rhetoric, which appealed to both emotions and logic in democratically persuading one's peers. Neither the men of the Scottish Enlightenment nor their republican followers in America may have recognized the similarity of the 'moral sense' to the nurturing emotions common to women, including those women in their own family networks; but at this remove the similarity seems striking. The belief that one could *train* one's 'moral sense' to respond to a variety of situations also sounds very much like nurturance to this writer—like child-raising, to be exact, except that one is contemplating the formation and growth of one's own adult personality rather than a child's character.

To some extent, then, an emotional orientation that also conforms to a personal moral code is a rather good fit with many aspects of the world of women, children and home, although not limited to them—the circle of 'other-caring' for politically-involved people would of necessity be 'ever-widening.' It is these intensely familial feelings, yet capable of being widened to include at least those who share one's values, that may best serve as both example and simile for the moral psychology that the present writer would also like to see employed in the service of public virtue, especially in opposing and deconstructing the addictive greed and anti-democratic corruption of the new American corporate and investment classes.

There is, however, a built-in irony in the idea that benevolent emotions arise in and from the family circle. The irony arises, as this writer has already tried to suggest, because many modern women see the homemaking role as a trap to enslave women. (Feminists also make the point that only affluent women can afford to stay home with their children, and that women who stay home often find that their marketable occupational skills get rusty, which is undoubtedly true.) But this is the early 21st century, and there is nothing to prevent the emotional orientations under discussion from being adopted by both men *and* women, at least those aspects that seem to work. As we have seen, men such as Thomas Jefferson were intrigued by, and believed in, the idea of sentiments aroused by a 'moral sense,' as expressed by various authors associated with the Scottish Enlightenment.

Jefferson, too, saw the potential connection between republicanism, public virtue and the idea that pleasurable emotions ('sentiments') could be aroused and experienced as the result of a positive and supportive behavioral pattern. When smart, highly motivated people are engaged in homemaking, parenting and career-supporting together, such skills and activities can greatly enhance the emotional connection between two partners, especially when they share certain idealistic political and social goals.

But why would men wish to widen the circle of 'other-caring' to the worlds of their professional or career venues? What's in it for them? Let's go back to the four-part sequencing of Churchland's hypothesis. First comes caring about kith and kin, especially the raising of children—but in the second stage those orientations are progressively widened to accommodate social situations in which 'other-caring' might help predict the behavior of others, and might be helpful in a variety of venues, including the marketplace. The third reason in Churchland's system is perhaps the most important— it enhances problem-solving in society, and helps in resolving disputes, devising and enforcing Social Contracts, figuring out divisions of labor in industry, punishing criminals and the like— things men might be good at.

Churchland's fourth step is simply learning which problem-solving social skills work, and which don't. So if men could add to these impressive categories some nicely enhanced social skills, it would greatly diminish the Hobbesian fear of society as an eternal Pier Six brawl in which everybody is threatening to wreak havoc on everybody else. Even as men adopt some of these emotional orientations, women themselves are increasingly actors in the world of work, and as women keep entering the workplace the social skills used in the home may increasingly become the social skills needed in the world of business, law, medicine and the factory floor.

Haven't we reached a point where men would benefit from internalizing a set of unconscious beliefs and emotions that—while not exactly matriarchy—reject the worst aspects of patriarchy? Isn't there sufficient reason for men to do that, besides having been exposed to those emotional orientations while helping to raise their kids? I say we're definitely at that point, partly because the complexity of society now requires highly attenuated social skills, consensus-creation and a high degree of intuition as opposed to cognitive logic; and because of a growing, mainly unconscious realization that there is something radically and lethally wrong with patriarchy, that it is no longer satisfying or even minimally justifiable, and that we really need to find alternatives to it. Lastly, there exists an uneasy but mainly unconscious understanding of humanity's self-destructive tendencies that has begun to percolate through the unconscious orientations of both men and women, causing a certain amount of free-floating anxiety. The assimilation of 'other-caring' skills *feels* like a contribution to human survival—which it is—and therefore works realistically to alleviate that anxiety.

Another reason why 'other-caring' skills need to be internalized by both men and women is the extent to which this skill set is involved in predicting emotion and behavior of others. In fact the mysterious witch's broom we call consciousness, which psychologists and philosophers have been struggling to understand for a very long time, may itself have evolved from predictive mental skills. This theory (associated with psychologists Roy Baumeister and E.J. Masicampo) suggests "that conscious thought is an adaptation that emerges from pressure for sophisticated social and cultural interactions, including the simulation of possible plan outcomes—how others might feel, respond, and react—and in humans, the simulation of speech."[26] Add to that the ability of humans to contemplate their own past behavior and learn from it, and you have not only "a rather appealing idea," as Professor Churchland accurately puts it, but a good working theory of consciousness as a cultural, social and physical adaptation.

Or course, the gradual emergence of consciousness as an adaptation could also shed light on the ancient problem of good and evil with which this book attempts to deal. With the added advantage of consciousness, and the growing mental acuity to predict behavioral outcomes, aggressors would be more likely to predict the best ways to exploit or coerce or kill their victims. But the aggressor could also—and here's where it gets really challenging—figure out, over a period of time, how to conceal, rationalize and dissemble his aggression. It is probably for this reason, then, that as human consciousness developed, the human animal became the most dangerous predator in the jungle, at least to other humans. Human consciousness, in other words, *arose in tandem with aggression*, involved predicting strategies for successful aggression against others and the *deceitful dissembling or rationalization of aggression that we call evil*. As time went on, human consciousness would get better at rationalizing or concealing those society-wide forms of aggression we call systemic evil.

What a momentous juncture *that* was for humankind! The same predictive skill-set that was used to make things safe for children in the home was also used to figure out the best ways to deceive, exploit and kill other human beings! But it is probably for just that reason that unnecessary aggression is so emotionally traumatizing, and feels to wrong to people over a long period of time. Indeed, it could be because consciousness arose from 'other-caring' that the trauma bond bypasses the conscious mind. Ultimately, aggression and consciousness are antithetical—because for humankind to survive, cognition needs to be firmly in control, acting out aggression only when appropriate and sublimating the rest. That's probably why organized patriarchy at the time of the Neolithic Revolution had to develop various forms of the trauma bonding to be used as rites of passage for men (with its emphasis on combat, martial games, animal and human sacrifice, corporal punishment and blood sport) in order to override and bypass consciousness in order to instill aggressive emotional orientations directly into the unconscious mind.

The story of Adam and Eve in the Garden, and The Fall from grace involved in eating the fruit from the Tree of Knowledge of Good and Evil, are remnants of an extremely traumatic series of events experienced by civilization after the Neolithic Revolution, when armed conflict became the norm because of the surplus of wealth that had arisen. Furthermore the story of Cain and Abel— also in the book of Genesis in the Bible—is clearly a vestigial memory of the struggle of agricultural societies with hunter-gatherers, with Cain winning. But his method of winning was profoundly violent, suggesting a bond to the new social arrangements not of choice but of a forcefully internalized aggression based on the continuing traumata of omnipresent conflict.

Abel disappears from human history, a loser in the struggle between agriculture and hunter-gathering. On the other hand, Cain—the supposed winner—paradoxically carries the mark of evil on his forehead, a mark that humankind will metaphorically carry forever, a mark placed there by God not just because of Cain's aggression, but because of his attempt to conceal his crime. Cain, not the mild-mannered Abel, is the brutal culture hero of the new warrior-oriented civilization, but he is not a particularly positive or inspiring figure. He is a haunting and cautionary figure, but there is nothing beautiful or appealing in his story.

Churchland's theory suggests that what we call morality—and

perhaps feelings associated with kindness and charity—originate in the way we feel about kin; but that the familial circle can become a widened circle of 'other-caring'. In fact there is no reason why we should not widen it to be the fundamental emotional orientation of a universally- applied psychology of being. And couldn't we also use 'other-caring' and kindness to strategically deconstruct the trauma bond? Well, let us say this much—if trauma and the internalization of aggression is the fuel that drives the cycle of psychic and physical violence we're all caught in, it would certainly be in our interests to devise ways to deconstruct all the aggression we've internalized as a result. Churchland's theory suggests that there is an emotional drive that causes us to love, nurture and cherish, and if the circle of 'other-caring' could be widened and strengthened it is quite possible that we can use these emotional orientations perhaps more than we today imagine.

There may be larger social factors at work supporting the rise of the 'other-caring' personality and ethos. Sociobiologist Edward O. Wilson spent a career tracking the operation of selfishness as the basis both for human societies and the lives of ants, but couldn't figure out where altruism came from, or how it served the continuing survival of the human species. He thought he'd nailed it with a theory of 'inclusive fitness' devised by William Hamilton, but gradually it became clear to him that even this qualified explanation wasn't enough. Finally Wilson hit upon a startling new theory— altruism causes individual organisms to *lose power* within a group, but altruism is also part of an inchoate but consistent tendency that helps the larger group *gain power*. He summed up this phenomenon with sociobiologist David Sloan Wilson (no relation) in the following way: "Selfishness beats altruism within groups. Altruistic groups beat selfish groups. Everything else is commentary."[27]

In fact, Darwin himself believed this, and wrote about it in *The Descent of Man*, which makes it all the more interesting. But the two Wilsons may have left out a step. One great advantage humans have over ants is cognition, however often human self-sabotage and perversity creep into our planning and behavior; so if we're talking about human behavior, wouldn't it be true that to some extent outcomes hinge on the conscious *intentions* of particular individuals in the group, as well as the choices they make?

E.O. Wilson puts it this way: "I see human nature as hung in the balance between these two [altruism and selfishness] extremes. If our behavior was driven entirely by group selection, then we'd be robotic cooperators, like ants. But, if individual-level selection was the only thing that mattered, then we'd be entirely selfish. What makes us human is that our history has been shaped by both forces. We're stuck in between."[28]

In any case, Wilson leaves out a qualifying aspect of the equation: If people chose to cooperate (and people, unlike ants, are able to make choices), the resulting cooperation wouldn't necessarily be robotic, as he puts it. (A guy who's spent his career studying ants isn't likely to think of cooperation as the result of voluntary choices, but among humans it usually is.) In any case, people can and do choose cooperation for their own reasons, and that can tend to make societies better, but also more complex.

The present writer's un-robotic conclusion is that it's time for American society to lean more toward cooperation than competition; and perhaps it's also time for Americans—particularly men—to voluntarily adopt a more 'other-caring' definition of power, or give up chasing power and money entirely. They should do that not just because the total society would benefit, but also because learning to cooperate is a lot less stressful (and more interesting) than the grotesque and mind-numbing hyper-competition that men often engage in. Sadly, however, even that will do little good if people do not determine at some point that peace and justice are good not just for oneself and one's own tribe, but for the larger tribe of humankind. Just as a wider 'other-caring' should be the chief goal governing our personal emotional growth, *universal human rights* should be the cognitive and legal touchstone for the geo-political world we must try to build in the 21st century if we are to survive.

That is a form of 'other-caring' that is neither too demanding nor too intrusive for the vast majority of people, because it is an ideal only, leaving it up to different cultures exactly how they would realize it.

17.

But it is not just in emotions associated with nurturance that the self is able to go beyond lies, aggression and egotism generally. There is another powerful emotional orientation that we usually call romantic love, sexuality or eroticism. In this emotional state, human feelings take us beyond the Self toward what often feels like a cooperative, altruistic or unselfish emotional orientation (however erratic, crazed or downright dangerous erotic love may become). Of course, romance leads to love triangles, and thereupon to horrific crimes of passion, but that is the exception rather than the rule. For the most part romance and sexuality take us away from the Self, to a radical contemplation of another being.

In his essay "An Inquiry Concerning Virtue or Merit," Anthony Ashley Cooper, Third Earl of Shaftesbury, the originator of the idea of a 'moral sense,' makes this point in a shockingly concrete way—he observes that sexual pleasure is enhanced by the real or imagined pleasure of one's sexual partner. In other words, it is easier to become aroused if your partner is aroused, and easier to have an orgasm if your partner also has one, which is why courtesans (and a great many spouses) then and now are known to fake orgasms. But what is so exciting about your partner's excitement, whether real or imagined? Is it altruism, or something in the biology of sexuality that causes sexual excitement to be heightened by the partner's excitement? Either way, it means that even in the wildest sexual act imaginable, human beings are intimately tuned in to the feelings of their sexual partner.

"The Courtizans, and even the commonest of Women, who live by Prostitution, know very well how necessary it is, that every-one whom they entertain with their Beauty, shou'd believe there are Satisfactions reciprocal; and that Pleasures are no less *given* than *receiv'd*. And were this Imagination to be wholly taken away, there wou'd be hardly any of the grosser sort of Mankind, who wou'd not perceive their remaining Pleasure to be of slender Estimation."

Once we get over the disorientation of reading so frankly about sex in Shaftesbury's sedate (and gloriously misspelled) late 17th-century prose, we'll have to conclude that it tells us more about Shaftesbury's self-willed ignorance of class and caste than sexuality. First of all, the fact that the prostitute/courtesan wants the man to have a pleasant fantasy occurs completely because of their respective places in the world—it occurs to her that she must please *him*, rather than the opposite, because of the operation of money and class. The fact that she even *thinks* about titillating him (probably by faking an organism), demonstrates the extent to which *he* is likely to oppress *her*. Furthermore, it is neither judgmental nor puritanical to observe that in the great majority of instances there is something potentially degrading about receiving money for sexual services. The high incidence of drug addiction and the frequent physical abuse suffered by prostitutes is irrefutable evidence that prosti-tution can be—and usually is—a form of psychological and sexual slavery.

But let us remove the lacerating onus of class, money and depri-vation from the model offered by Shaftesbury. Let us imagine that a modern man and woman come from similar backgrounds, love each other, and are happily married in the bargain. Let us say that they are making love, and the woman wishes to give her man a pleasant fantasy. However she ends up doing it, she's not likely to do so by faking an orgasm, because she has both the time and opportunity to enjoy a real one, even if she has to do the heavy lifting herself. But wait!—this is the 21st century, so let us suppose that the *man* wishes to give his wife pleasure before *he* receives pleasure himself. Would it not greatly facilitate his wife's orgasm, if she believed that *he* was building up to an ejaculation?

That is very often the way sexual pleasure works, at least when it is free of the constraints of class and money, and free also of the nagging constraints of lies and adultery. Doesn't the excitement of one's sexual partner powerfully enhance one's own sexual excitement? It most certainly does. Here, one must say, we have an example of a natural, built-in human passion that often causes people to *receive* pleasure from *giving* pleasure—and it may be taken almost for granted that with certain exceptions the more one likes and/or loves one's partner, the more this simultaneous and mutually-enhancing exchange of sexual pleasure is likely to occur.

In fact, it is completely possible for the first partner to receive intense pleasure simply from giving pleasure to the second one, even though the first lover experiences no physical release in the form of an orgasm. Ultimately, of course, it would be nice for the two lovers to *both* experience a sexual release—that is, orgasms and/or ejaculations in more or less the same time frame—but the point here is that sexuality creates a possibility in which one may receive pleasure simply from the other person's gratification, and for no other reason.

Sexuality hides encoded within its mysteries both enormous selflessness and incalculable selfishness. And it can be—and often is—used to act out the most brutal kinds of exploitation and criminality. But, reader, consider most of the love poetry you have read. Does not love poetry depend on an immense selflessness, a yearning to go past the self and be part of something eternal, not just of the beloved, but of the universe? Consider also the many nudes artists have painted or sculpted over the ages... why does the artist keep coming back to the female face and form throughout the millennia? Even in modern art classes, despite the prevalence of performance art, students are asked to contemplate nude models and sketch figure studies and paint nudes. Why?

Because almost all visual aesthetics in the West are ultimately related in some way to the human face and form, usually female— and they are the primary way artists have always imagined a coherent aesthetic whole. The beauty of the female form and face involve sexuality, of course, because it triggers all those things in the human sensorium that are wired to respond to sexual beauty—but when the artist draws it, it is taken in a paradoxical way beyond sexuality to sensuality, and then beyond sensuality to something almost completely Platonic, a place in which the nude model, the artist's hand, and all the circumstances of that moment simply aim at *creating the beautiful,* in a place that is both worldly and beyond the world. When an artist beholds the model and draws her face and form he does not feel sensuality as much as in drawing her he captures the operation of sensuality on the canvas. That is truly a wild beauty, the closest the poor mortal may ever get to the wellsprings of spiritual and aesthetic truth.

The boldest representations of the female form—and of the male form as well—take us to a place of almost complete self-abnegation. It takes us there because the operation of sexuality can be so intense that a single personality cannot contain the pictorial representation of it. So the artist instead uses sensuality to portray the naked human form, which is crucially different from sexuality. Sensuality is sexuality freed from the egocentric dilemma posed by the body, freeing sexuality to be a universal rather than a self-centered experience.

Thus the paradox of great art: the eye beholding the female form triggers a desire not for orgasm, but something closer to the idea of God, taking both eye and hand to the primal mystery of the family, to the eternity of time before everyman and everywoman even become conscious of wanting to give birth. In the stirrings of the body is the first tremulous cry of the infant that will someday be born. The artist feels that when he draws a nude: he feels the helpless yearning of human life to simultaneously *reproduce* the self, by going *beyond* the self. When the artist draws a nude, he transforms sexuality to a sensuality that goes beyond one human mind and body.

When Keats lay on his sofa at Wentworth Place, his lungs just able to provide enough oxygen for consciousness, he strained to look into the yard next door, yearning for a glimpse of his beloved Fanny. Was that sexuality? Yes, of course, partly, but something else, something much more. What Keats felt was life, the pulse and game of it, even as his body pulled him down toward death. Sexuality and erotic love lead us toward a dance that involves giving life to the world. So often sexual loves enslaves and brutalizes—but there is no denying that there is something else in it that is just as powerful, and often more powerful, than just the desire for one's own physical release.

Can we tap into that endless well of pleasure, that desire to partner in the dance of life, and use it to help us surpass the ego, the self? Even more importantly, can we use it to defeat those forms of evil that threaten life on this earth? We must learn to sublimate sexuality, because that is the great secret of creativity, but there is no doubt that both sublimation and actualization are simultaneously possible—it happens every time a love poem is written. Eros is a mystery that can never be completely known, but let us simply say that it is another area of life in which we strive both to know the self and move beyond it. And in so doing, we bring ourselves into the concomitant mysteries of family life, those 'home-feelings' where nurturance is strongest. Isn't it worth the effort for men and women to learn the love-power that is within each person, and find new forms for the human family based on fidelity *and* compassion? Are not our beautiful children the 'kith and kin' that presage 'other-caring'?

18.

What have we learned?

1. Aggression replicates itself through trauma bonding, a process by which aggression is internalized by traumatized victims of violence, causing them to become future aggressors.
2. Evil is aggression that is covered up, rationalized and dissembled.
3. Evil and aggression are amplified by patriarchy, nationalism

and victimology.

4   Evil can become systemic evil in troubled societies, especially when leaders keep past trauma alive. Kindness and altruism are possible for the individual, but the effects of aggression at present have a greater influence on society at large.

5   We are headed toward the destruction of the planet.

Rapid industrial and technological change has exacerbated the moral collapse we are passing through—most people and institutions no longer understand their own best interests, and might not act on them if they did. The Industrial Revolution is the *proximate* cause of humankind's pursuit of self-destruction, just as the Neolithic Revolution caused the rise of caste and class; but only because it enabled people to act out the aggression that has long existed in the human personality. The industrial system and its resultant technology are the *proximate* but not the *ultimate* cause of systemic evil, which consists of the surplus destructiveness of humankind's aggression and its desire to hide and dissemble it, in order to continue acting it out.

So what is to be done?

First we must understand the dynamics driving us to self-destruction; and once we are aware of them make radical changes

Where does the radical change begin? Breaking the cycle of violence begins with you, reader. Collectively it begins with our recognition of humankind's enormous capacity for evil, but also its freedom to choose the good. Humankind has a second great rendezvous with the Tree of Knowledge of Good and Evil, a rendezvous that leads to a hall of mirrors for all the people of the world. Only after looking in the mirror and seeing our own individual capacity for evil are we able to take the next great step, which is to consume the sustainable fruit of the Tree of Life. Aggression and evil are both in our DNA, since we descend from animals and carry within us the desire to hunt, attack, kill, sexually enslave and dominate. But to recover from this legacy we must decide not to act on it, not to deny its influence on us but simply to find better behavior that is less dangerous to us, and to the world our children will inherit.

The creation of a humanistic moral psychology depends, *first*, on the individual's willingness to look into the abyss of his own capacity for aggression and evil; and *second*, it depends on a therapeutic methodology for changing behavior, of the individual and the world. This is really about deconstructing the effects of aggression in the human heart and mind, and unless one gets stuck in the slough of narcissistic self-hatred the first step makes the second one infinitely easier. We must admit the truth about ourselves before we change it, but once we admit it we are already on the way to changing.

Let us say it again: evil has become so omnipresent, at least in part, because nobody wants to see it in themselves. If people do see their own evil, they are free to consider how it came to be, and look for ways to deconstruct it, either in their own personalities or in the social institutions that condition individual behavior. *Aggression* and *deceit*—the two auxiliary parts of evil—constitute the inexorable baseline to which humankind returns again and again. If people do not stop themselves from engaging in systemic evil, either as the result of a personal moral code or strict external accountability based on universal human rights—or both—they will keep killing until they destroy the world.

Humanity is not, in other words, fundamentally good—humanity is *fundamentally evil*. Aggression and deceit, not charity, is the fallback position of humankind at the present time. The Israelis brutalize Palestinians not because they are Jews, but because they are human beings who have experienced traumatic aggression. They are doing exactly what you and I would do if we had experienced what they have experienced, and made the same tragic mistakes their leaders—and they themselves—have made. They are you, translated to their historical situation, the evil from which they suffered, their own bad choices and the traumas kept alive by their leaders, which prevents them from seeing themselves in the mirror, and trying to change themselves.

This book argues that systemic evil is not merely *one* problem of life in the 21st century, but *the* problem of modern life. This book insists not just that evil is there, but that it *predominates* in modern life, not because more behavior is quantitatively evil, but rather because in the modern world the effects of aggression and deceit are qualitatively much more destructive and influential than any other kind of behavior. The effects of a single detonated thermonuclear weapon are forever—but interestingly, the *threat* of genocide by a nuclear weapon is *also* forever, in the sense that we know that the glib little men that rattle the missiles are willing to incinerate millions rather than look in the mirror. And how to we know that? Because they threaten us with genocide simply by keeping the nuclear weapons operable.

That is what nuclear weapons do—they exist to threaten civilians with death-by-fire, the same nightmare firestorm that consumed the Basque civilians of Guernica, if *your* government doesn't do what *their* government wants. If you are an Iranian, it is a brutal fact that your life means absolutely nothing to the American and Israeli elites that threaten to kill you to get what they want; nor do you or I mean anything to the Iranian elites that engage in apocalyptic threats and terrorist operations on American soil. Strutting comic-opera figures like Mahmoud Ahmadinejad and "Bibi" Netanyahu would be hilarious, if they were not also megalomaniacs who unfortunately have the power to destroy millions. Threats of genocide are what really define who we are, and what we are becoming, not what we say we are.

Against this we have identified a few powerful human values that arise from and are based on emotion—or at least are felt deeply—beginning with the morality of kinship that can be stretched to include all of humanity. Indeed, it is already stretched to include all people in such constructs as universal human rights, as those rights are understood in most international law. Embedded in the idea of universal human rights is the conviction that *all* people must be free to choose them, or at least be given the ability to strive openly for them. At its most personal, the widening of 'other-caring' is nothing less than an enveloping sense of kindness and curiosity toward humanity itself—indeed, toward all life. It is only through that enveloping sense that we can afford to see ourselves.

Also we have the unpredictable selflessness of romantic love, which causes us to look beyond the aggression of the Self to a kind of altruism that makes the 'Other' just as important as oneself. Whether we are willing to connect 'other-caring' to the dream of universal human rights is anybody's guess. These are frail and highly faulty tools, these human emotions, with which we seek to defeat habits of aggression deeply ensconced in the patriarchal thicket of the collective unconscious, habits older even than our ability to imagine. But if we would honor humanity's potential, are we not in honor bound to engage our words and our passion for life in the fight for the survival of humankind?

Evil is not a conspiracy. Most human enterprises are essentially chaotic, and completely lacking in the highly calibrated distinctions necessary to a conspiracy. Nor does evil come from the Devil, or from outside ourselves. Evil is not done by conspirators, I say again, but by sleepwalkers who are hardly cognizant of their own interests, much less what they are doing, and even less why they do it. To the extent that we do not confront the aggression and evil that is inside ourselves, we are all similarly sleepwalkers, walking in the same haunted dream, toward the same destruction. The only question, to paraphrase T.E. Lawrence, is whether we dream with our eyes open or closed.

I know that many people will deny this, because they refuse to acknowledge that evil exists, and don't want to see it even when it is undeniable—especially they don't want to see it when they are guilty, or even potentially guilty, of complicity with it. But it is the role of the prophetic intellectual not merely to make people look in the mirror, but to make them see themselves as they really are, because they cannot do so by themselves. *We must change our lives, but the powerful of the earth must do so also.* I would show the rich and powerful not only their faces in the mirror, but the wraiths of all whom they would kill with their greed and stupidity. They must ultimately give up killing and exploiting others, and hopefully themselves as well—and that means both the little murders and the big ones too.

The belief in progress is false: evil and aggression rule the world. A major intervention in human affairs is needed, and it must come from human beings themselves. Humankind is a crazed and battered animal, desperately searching for a home on this planet even as it breaks everything that could make a home worth wanting. For a long time a secular theory of evil has been needed, to tell us about how we went so far wrong; but a therapy that can deconstruct evil must ultimately be developed to introduce some emotional health where sheer pathology now reigns. How important is it for humankind to escape the cycle of violence in which we're all caught? Everything else is secondary, for if humanity cannot do it, we will destroy ourselves and every living thing on earth.

Chapter 3

Control and the Trauma Bond

I.

It was late summer in Stockholm, and the weather was mild, as it often is in Sweden during that time of year. But on August 23, 1973, one of the most notorious crimes of all time was about to occur in the sleepy environs of central Stockholm. It started as a badly-botched robbery by a couple of career criminals, but over time it deteriorated into a gritty hostage situation, in which four bank employees were held in their workplace for almost a week. This failed heist, which was broadcast live on Swedish TV and was personally observed by a psychiatrist who was allowed to enter the bank, is famous not because of anything done by the robbers, nor even by the police, but because of the unexpected and disturbing behavior of the bank employees who were taken hostage.

Within a single day of being taken hostage, all of the four employees developed a profound identification with the two hostage-takers, adopted their criminal worldview and even helped them devise strategies to outwit the police. For the police and the authorities they had only fear and contempt—they blamed *them* for creating the hostage situation. This was all the more mystifying because the four hostages were apparently quite normal, whereas the two hostage-takers were longtime criminals who at certain points in the long, grueling drama treated their captives with gratuitous cruelty. Still, the hostages clearly viewed their captors as the 'Good Guys' whom they were supporting, and saw the police as the 'Bad Guys,' who the hostages blamed for everything that was going wrong at the bank.

Despite their captors' cruelty, the four hostages continued in their unvarying enthusiasm for their hostage-takers, with one female hostage developing an intense emotional attachment to one of the male hostage-takers that continued for years after the crime itself.

Because these astonishing events happened in Stockholm (and because a psychiatrist watched the events unfold and later wrote about them), the odd behavior and outrageous—or at least counter-intuitive—attitude of the hostages are now collectively referred to as 'Stockholm Syndrome'. (And sometimes mistakenly referred to as 'Helsinki Syndrome,' as it was in the film *Die Hard*.)

Witnesses can't remember exactly how the robbery started, but certain facts are not in dispute. The Kreditbanken, as the Swedish bank was called then, was the bank where the hostage situation occurred; it was situated in a very large building on a leafy square called Norrmalmstorg. The weather on the day of the robbery was sunny and pleasant, and business was reportedly very slow. But at some point a man named Jan-Erik "Janne" Olsson, who had a long criminal record and was actually on leave from prison at the time, entered the bank and attracted the attention of the bank's employees.

Something must have caused these employees to believe that a robbery was either in progress or imminent, because the police were called. Two policemen entered the bank. Seeing the police, Erik Olsson took out a gun and shot one, wounding him. He ordered the other officer to sit in a chair and sing. (The unwounded policeman sat as he was ordered to do, and commenced singing *Lonesome Cowboy*.) Olsson then took the four employees hostage, threatening to kill them if the police rushed the bank. When contacted by police by telephone, he demanded that a friend named Clark Olofsson be brought to the crime scene, along with three million Swedish kronor, an escape vehicle, and some guns and body armor. All this was done, although Olsson was told by the police that under no conditions would he be allowed to leave in the escape car unless he left all the hostages behind.

Clark Olofsson, who was actually in prison for another robbery, was transported from prison to Norrmalmstorg, and was inexplicably allowed to join Olsson in the bank, where the hostage situation was now underway. (Why the police allowed this is something of a mystery, except that Olsson insisted on it—and no doubt police feared that he might harm the hostages if they didn't accede to this rather odd demand.) At first Clark Olofsson assumed—or pretended to assume—the role of negotiator with the police, but appears to have rather quickly thrown in his lot with Olsson. At about this point Kristin Ehnemark, one of the hostages, began to express fear of the police, saying that the police might mount a violent attack, and in so doing might kill or injure both hostages and hostage-takers. (The reader should remember that Olsson had threatened to shoot all the hostages if rushed by the police.) Olofsson and Olsson responded by building a barricade in the bank's inner vault, assisted by the prisoners in this task. Both hostages and hostage-takers then hid behind the barricade.

Further surrealistic elements now enter this already bizarre narrative. At some point Jan Olsson called the Prime Minister of Sweden, Olof Palme, and threatened to kill the four prisoners he had taken hostage; for added verisimilitude he applied a stranglehold to one of the female hostages, who could be heard screaming in the background as he hung up the telephone. The next day hostage Kristin Ehnemark—who by now had assumed the role of negotiator for both hostage-takers and their prisoners—also called up Prime Minister Palme, giving him a tongue-lashing for his handling of the situation and blaming him for everything, demanding that he end the crisis by releasing all of them. As the standoff wore on, Clark Olofsson appeared to become depressed and a bit disoriented, shuffling around the bank's inner vault singing *Killing Me Softly*, a popular song first recorded by Roberta Flack.

This hostage situation was covered live on Swedish TV, and was followed avidly by the public. The standoff between the police and the hostage-takers lasted six days.

On the fourth day, police drilled a hole into the vault from above. Olsson fired a few rounds from his gun, wounding another policeman, and loudly threatened to kill his prisoners. He then put loops of wire around the necks of the hostages and attached them to deposit boxes, warning the police not to use gas, since the hostages if incapacitated would fall and strangle themselves.

On the sixth day the police used gas despite Olsson's warning, and in a short time the hostage-takers gave up. Police discovered the hostages were still quite hostile toward them, as it gradually became clear how totally they identified with their criminal captors. They defended the behavior of the hostage-takers in subsequent interviews, and contributed money to their legal defense. As former hostage Kristin Ehnemark told the story, it was the police and the authorities who were responsible for the entire hostage situation; she was particularly vehement in defending Clark Olofsson, with whom she had developed a special bond. Within a short time various media outlets began to report that Ehnemark had announced her engagement to Clark Olofsson, and that they were soon to be married.

This part of the story turned out to be untrue. Kristin Ehnemark was never engaged to be married to Clark Olofsson, nor did they discuss marriage. This idea probably arose because of a misinterpretation of the Swedish word *engagera*. In the context used by sources close to the story, it had nothing to do with being engaged *to* someone, but referred to being engaged *by* someone, in the sense that one finds a particular person or situation 'engaging.' It had nothing to do with getting married. Sadly, however, once that particular bit of misinformation was picked up by international media, many news outlets found it impossible to resist repeating it.

But the marriage concept did work by analogy, however, because Kristin Ehnemark became emotionally involved with Clark Olofsson, maintaining an intense relationship with him for well over a decade. Their families also became close friends; Kristin, in fact, broke off her engagement to the man who had been her fiancé before the hostage incident. And she continued to speak out against Olof Palme after the incident, continuing to criticize his handling of the situation. Clark Olofsson, on the other hand, did precious little to deserve Kristin's trust or friendship. Although he was cleared of wrongdoing in the attempted Norrmalmstorg heist, he continued to commit crimes, many of them violent, and was in and out of prison for the next thirty years. Immediately after the Norrmalmstorg hostage situation Erik Olsson was sent to prison for ten years, at which time he was deluged by letters written by Swedish women, one of whom he eventually married.

Much more interesting than the behavior of the criminals was the behavior of their hostages. Why did the hostages identify so completely and so quickly with their captors? Why did this emotional identification last so long afterwards? Perhaps luckily for students of human behavior, one person had been given the advantage of actually being present during conversations between hostages and hostage-takers (as well as during conversations between hostage-takers and police), who thought he had answers to these questions. This was a psychiatrist and criminologist named Nils Bejerot, who worked as a consultant to the Stockholm police and was present during the entire hostage situation—and who was, amazingly enough, allowed to walk freely in and out of the bank, including the crime scene in which the hostages were being held. Bejerot was therefore able to observe both hostages and hostage-takers during the six-day crisis.

In the beginning, Bejerot saw that the hostages were concerned with pleasing the hostage-takers in order to ensure their physical safety. Their objective, in other words, was simply to keep their captors happy. But this desire to please the hostage-takers turned into a need to ingratiate themselves with them, to win their approval, and then their affection. In a short time this evolved into total identification with them—no doubt exacerbated by the trauma of being held at gunpoint—so that the hostages adopted the hostage-takers' criminal worldview (including their various rationalizations for behaving as they did). Furthermore the hostages also, as mentioned before, helped the two small-time criminals devise strategies to deal with the police. (It is this aspect of hostage situations that negotiators reportedly find most irksome, since the hostages are often more intelligent than their captors, and are therefore likely to supply the criminals with better strategies than they would normally come up with up on their own.)

Bejerot saw the events that he had observed not as an anomaly, but as a discrete, observable and robust psychological process induced by the hostage situation. If this were true, the same attitudes and behaviors were likely to be replicated in future hostage situations. Bejerot concluded that the hostages' behavior constituted a discernable psychological syndrome—that is, a loose but coherent association of behavioral signs and symptoms that was later dubbed 'Stockholm Syndrome.' Bejerot first used the phrase during a broadcast in Sweden; American psychiatrist and trauma expert Frank Ochberg picked it up and elaborated on it in a systematic way, the intent being to help law enforcement and mental health experts develop informal protocols for dealing with similar hostage situations. Ochberg quickly discerned a distinct family resemblance between some aspects of 'Stockholm Syndrome' and Post-Traumatic Stress Disorder, with which he was already familiar. Both are responses to trauma, and share some of the same symptoms; both have the power to profoundly change personality and behavior.

2.

'Stockholm Syndrome' is trauma bonding in overdrive. Everything we have learned about the trauma bond occurs in 'Stockholm Syndrome,' but a lot faster. There is one big difference, however, having to do with emotional regression. Because they are completely helpless, hostages held at gunpoint are likely to quickly regress emotionally until they become the emotional equivalent of children. Children, as we've seen, don't merely internalize the aggression they suffer from abusive adults, but tend to also identify *personally* with their abusive parents. (Adult victims of violence are likely to identify with aggression because they have internalized the aggression of the attacker, but don't necessarily identify personally with the aggressor.) During the hostage situation at Norrmalmstorg, on the other hand, the hostages *identified personally with their captors*, actually adopting their personal attitudes and beliefs. Why? Probably because the claustrophobic pressures of a hostage situation caused the hostages to experience a powerful and very rapid form of emotional regression; as a result the hostages experienced the situation as very young abused children might, identifying personally with their hostage-takers, even as abused children often identify personally with their abusive parents.

The hostages were kept completely helpless, needing the permission of their captors to speak, stand or go to the bathroom. (The fact that hostages have to ask permission to go to the bathroom is often mentioned in hostage narratives as making them feel especially helpless.) They had no control over the events in which they were trapped, and were—in fact—as powerless as it is possible for adults to be. The inevitable result of this total powerlessness was rapid, debilitating and complete emotional regression to the emotional status of childhood. Again, this is probably what caused the hostages to react to their hostage-takers exactly as children with abusive parents might, with something approaching complete identification with their values and attitudes.

It is important to remember that this total regression was driven home not merely by a constant and enforced helplessness but a searing fear of sudden and irrevocable death. The threat had been made early in the hostage situation that the hostages would die if the police rushed the offices where they were held. Furthermore, the hostage-takers held the power of life and death over the hostages, and could kill them at any time, for any reason. Furthermore, this intense fear of violent death was experienced night and day over a fairly long period of time—almost a week, in fact. The hostages, then, experienced the ordeal as though they were a group of children being threatened with death by an abusive adult for several days in a row.

Duration plays a big role here. Most violent criminals use

weapons like guns and knives to commit their crimes, such as homicide, rape and theft; but the actual commission of the average offense is over quickly. A hostage situation is played out over a *much* longer period of time, with periodic threats that are often mainly indirect yet quite sinister, in the sense that everybody knows that they refer to intentional violence ("Don't do anything stupid and nobody gets hurt"). The hostage knows very well that the hostage-taker could kill him at any moment, even if the captor doesn't hold a weapon in his hand at all times.

As the hours and days drag by, the hostage emotionally experiences his continued survival as the result of magnanimous kindness on the part of the hostage-taker. After all, the hostage-takers are allowing the hostages to live, aren't they? The unconscious reaction to that perceived kindness is profound gratitude, which then enhances the identification into something approaching uncritical love. The hostage, like an abused child, looks up to the hostage-taker as a parent—an abusive one, to be sure, but still the giver of life to the traumatized and totally-regressed victim.

The hostage is grateful that the hostage-taker hasn't killed him— so therefore the hostage-taker is the one being on the planet that stands between him and death. If you are for several days under the total control of someone who could kill you for any reason (including reasons you can't predict and might not even understand), you are experiencing a prolonged and agonizing loss of existential control. If one is a hostage, everything necessary to maintain ordinary human comforts is dependent on the whim of the person with the gun. In such a situation, the pressure for emotional accommodation to the hostage-taker is irresistible. And because of the extreme emotional regression involved, it can take the form of extreme identification with the hostage-takers.

Is 'Stockholm Syndrome' avoidable? I believe that its effects can be greatly minimized by individuals who understand the psychological process involved, although that might not stop it entirely. Previously I've argued that trauma bonding is an unconscious emotional process, which implies that cognitive insight alone might not be able to affect or diminish its operations—but what if one is aware of trauma bonding *before* it happens, or even *while it is happening*? Many traumatizing events occur in seconds or minutes, and become problems later because of the victims' inability to integrate memories of the events into their collective emotional experience and worldview. But the anomaly of the hostage situation is that it gives the victim a great deal of time for introspection regarding the process he is in. The fact that the hostage has so much time to reflect on what is happening causes this writer to believe that people caught up in a hostage situation might be able to resist the worst effects of 'Stockholm Syndrome' without risk to themselves.

The hostage knows that keeping the hostage-taker happy is important to his survival, and the hostage should choose to do exactly that—but his focus should be on *his ability to make the choice*. If a hostage is mentally focused on his ability to choose behavior that helps him survive, that alone might inhibit identification with his captor. In this suggested scenario, the hostage should remember that he is not pleasing the hostage-taker as the result of fear and panic—he is making a conscious *choice* to please the hostage-taker, and he is doing so for tactical reasons, to improve his odds of survival. By focusing on his freedom to make such a choice, he survives while retaining a sense of personal autonomy. This awareness of one's own freedom of choice toward and *during* life-changing events can be a hugely empowering thing. This was the essential message of the great Viennese psychiatrist and concentration-camp survivor Victor Frankl, who in *Man's Search for Meaning* wrote, "Our greatest freedom is the freedom to choose our attitude."

If the hostage can make a choice to please the hostage-taker and reflect on his freedom to do so, the hostage still has control, even if his captor is holding a gun to his head. Of course, hostages should also continue to observe other common protocols involving such dilemmas—hostages should avoid too much direct eye contact with captors, for example, and not sharply contradict or challenge them.

Then, after the hostage situation is over, the former hostage should start talking about what he/she has been feeling throughout the duration of the situation, and what he is feeling on a moment to moment basis. All hostages should be encouraged to talk as long as they need to talk about what has just happened to them—and they should do so before sleeping.

Clearly, 'Stockholm Syndrome' is a form of trauma bonding that can transform the personality of the hostage. What happened to the hostage Kristin Ehnemark, and to the other hostages as well, was a kind of negative conversion experience. As we've seen, the total control of the hostage-taker, enforced by the threat of death over a prolonged period of time, combined with the precipitous emotional regression of the terrified hostages—these are the things that, when taken together, make Stockholm unique. Above all it is the violent control by an unpredictable stranger that accounts for the rapidity, duration and extreme intensity of the hostages' personal transformation, and causes them to identify with values that are completely foreign from those they normally believe in.

This issue of control may be one of the most important aspects of systemic evil, not because control is itself invariably evil, but because of the way it enhances other phenomena related to trauma bonding. Anything that can so rapidly speed up the trauma-bonding process, and result in profound emotional regression, is going to generate an enormous amount of aggression, which when internalized is likely to result in a powerful identification with the hostage-takers. If one or two gunman can create such powerful emotional reactions, could not a violent dictator use various kinds of violent social controls to traumatize and infantilize entire population, causing them to bond with him and his government as children bond with an abusive parent? In fact, authoritarian, fascist and Communist dictators know instinctively how to use these dynamics, which is one reason why the security services of police states practice gratuitous cruelty.

3.

According to evolutionary psychologists such as Keith Henson and Azar Gat, there may be a bio-historical as well as psychological explanation for phenomena such as 'Stockholm Syndrome.' Something similar may have developed in early hunter-gatherer societies in which tribal people—usually women and children—were captured by warriors from hostile tribes. Many captives from tribal wars may have perished, but presumably others survived because they were able to quickly identify with the new tribe and internalize their values and worldview. Henson and others hypothesize that these adaptive skills (which evolutionary psychologists refer to as *capture-bonding*) were selected over tens of thousands of years into our collective human DNA. This may have created a psychological and biological predisposition to the rapid trauma bonding that we call 'Stockholm Syndrome' when it occurs during a hostage situation.

This is reminiscent of the so-called 'captivity narratives' that played an important role in popular American culture in the 18th and 19th centuries. In these narratives, which appeared in popular newspapers and often became the subject of much attention, white Americans were captured by Indians and absorbed into the tribal milieu of the warriors who captured them. During the period of captivity, many white people—including captive women—made a powerful adjustment to tribal culture, to the point of resisting being re-introduced to white society after being rescued. The overt drama of the 'captivity narratives' centered on the extent to which whites 'became' Indians, and how completely they identified with Indians while living with them. There was much interest in whether whites could successfully return to white society and resume their previous identities once they had assimilated tribal values.

One unintended aspect of the 'captivity narratives' was that they gave whites a unique opportunity to see Indians as real people able to define their own self-interests—it was only when a white person 'became' an Indian, apparently, that it was possible to see Indians as demonstrably human. A more sensational subtext was the theme of white women who had married—or been forced to marry—Indian chiefs and warriors while they were captives in tribal societies. There was considerable speculation about whether the women who were former captives (especially those married to Indian men) would be able to sufficiently regain their former identities to marry white men. Newspaper accounts generally managed to throw a softly lurid light on this highly personal subject matter while avoiding details pertaining to it; but it is interesting to note that many white women did not, in fact, choose to remarry in white society.

This could have been partly or wholly because of the trauma of being held as a captive and being forcibly married to a stranger; but it could also have been because some of the women had lived with Indians so long and internalized so much of the tribes' ethos, that they were no longer able to function with ease in white society once they were returned to it. And for some, the decision not to remarry once they were back in white society may have simply been a personal decision, experienced by the women as voluntary. *The Searchers*, an enduring film classic and John Wayne's only great movie, was a popular cinematic treatment of this highly charged American subject matter.

'Stockholm Syndrome' in some ways resembles the dynamics of 'battered-wife syndrome' which was touched on in this book's first chapter. The battered spouse is in exactly the same psychological situation as the hostages in a hostage situation, frequently reinforced by the abusive spouse's violence—she is a hostage to her abuser, and to the abusive situation in which they are both enmeshed. Like the victim of Stockholm, the battered wife experiences no conscious control of her life, and is in constant fear of pain, injury, and death; thus she is quite likely to regress back to the emotional level of a child who identifies personally with the abusive man in her life. This, in turn, is likely to make her internalize enormous amounts of the spouse's aggression, not to mention his abusive personal qualities, which she is likely to turn on herself.

But there's a difference between Stockholm and the battered wife, and it has to do with duration. Violent marriages go on a lot longer than the average hostage situation, which means that battered wives capable of leaving their abusers are more likely to sooner or later ask for help in that endeavor. Despite the trauma bond, women—particularly those that have children—often begin with the passage of time to spontaneously detach from the bond created by the abuser's violence. (The pain of the children may be a big factor here.) Furthermore, the battered wife has an avenue of escape not open to the hostage, and that is intensive counseling, a women's shelter and the constraints of courts enforcing stalking and domestic violence statutes. Her biggest challenge will be accepting the fact that the trauma bond formed by an abusive relationship is not love, however magical and intense and sexually charged it may have been; in fact, she may always feel a certain attraction to abusive men, because it is something she knows well. But for the sake of her children, she simply has to extricate herself from an abusive relationship, and the only way to do that is to leave the abuser once and for all.

It is encouraging to note that a fair number of battered wives eventually leave abusive relationships. But some are emotionally incapable of it, and those wives may end up murdering their abusive partners, because that is the only way they can imagine stopping the ongoing abuse. Typically, however, such murders result in serious prison time for the women, which means more time spent away from the children who need her. The best way, of course, is for the battered wife to simply break free of the trauma bond and leave the relationship. But there is a real danger at that point that society is still not willing to acknowledge: it is precisely when the battered spouse is leaving an abusive relationship and preparing to establish a new life that that abuser will often retaliate against the former partner by tracking her down and killing her. Clearly, society needs to devise better protective services for people leaving abusive relationships, services that would not involve a great expenditure of money but which would save lives and operate as a powerful incentive for people to put abuse behind them and start over. For this to work, states need to pass strong anti-stalking laws, and enforce them.

So much has been written about 'Stockholm Syndrome' that available information on the subject has percolated through psychology departments, publications and organizations, not to mention law enforcement and popular American culture. With what became known or assumed about Stockholm, several other events that had previously seemed completely anomalous suddenly began to make sense—the McElroy case, for example, is often cited. Mary McElroy, the daughter of a judge, was abducted by four kidnappers on May 27, 1933. They took her from her home in Kansas City to Shawnee, Kansas, and chained her to a wall in the basement of a farmhouse. Her father, at that time the city manager of Kansas City, paid a ransom of $30,000 and she was released. The kidnappers were arrested not long afterwards; at the trial the ringleader, Walter McGee, was sentenced to death and the others were given long sentences. After the trial Mary seemed deeply attached to Walter and the others, and often visited them in prison, often bringing them presents. She met with relatives of the kidnappers, and expressed public sympathy for them.

An execution date was set for Walter McGee, but Mary wrote to the governor pleading that the execution not be carried out: "Walter McGee's sentence has hung as heavily over me as it does him. Through punishing a guilty man, his victim will be made to suffer equally... In pleading for Walter McGee's life, I am also pleading for my own peace of mind."[29] What is immediately striking about the McElroy case is that she makes no excuse for his crime, but rather acknowledges his guilt—yet identifies herself with him completely! Three days before he was to be hung, the governor stayed his execution, and his sentence was eventually commuted to life in prison. Most likely this was done not out of any particular regard for McGee, but because of Mary McElroy's heartfelt pleas on his behalf.

Mary's life afterward was deeply troubled, and in time she became addicted to opium. On January 21, 1940, she was discovered dead, a suicide, having shot herself in the head. She left a suicide note reading in part: "My four kidnappers were probably the four people on earth who don't consider me a fool." She pleaded for society to "give [the kidnappers] a chance."[30] Her thoroughgoing identification with her kidnappers may have been enhanced to some extent by her addiction, but the elements of 'Stockholm Syndrome' are unmistakable.

The traumatizing effects of basic training in the military are generally ignored or shrugged off by psychologists, not to mention politicians. But there is little doubt that the rigors of basic training in the military trigger some dynamics similar to 'Stockholm Syndrome' or capture-bonding mechanisms. Of course, the recruit intentionally signs up for a certain amount of verbal and physical abuse when he joins the military, and fully expects it to occur during basic training. That removes any legal complication—the abuse is, when viewed legally, the result of a voluntary contract between the abusive Drill Instructor and the young person who voluntarily 'joins up.' But even when young people sign up for it, the effects of emotional trauma are still going to produce internalized aggression, which is done to cause recruits to bond with the military as an institution based on organized and highly focused aggression.

The question then becomes, how able is the young recruit to recognize and refuse immoral or illegal orders, since the youngster has been subjected to an intense form of indoctrination that arouses powerful psychological dynamics that bypass cognition? This is, or should be, an important issue for military courts. Are recruits that are subjected to four months of basic training really capable of refusing illegal orders by a superior officer? Or to put it differently, are such recruits even able to recognize the difference between right and wrong when given an immoral or illegal order? The reader will remember that penalties for torture and prisoner abuse at Abu Ghraib were assessed on young and inexperienced enlisted personnel—the higher-ups (that is, the officers who gave them the orders to do what they did) received almost no punishment except for one commanding officer (a woman, interestingly) who was given a reduction in grade. Were those young enlisted personnel capable of refusing an illegal order? If we expect them to have that capacity, why were not the officers who gave the illegal orders punished also?

The effects of trauma on behavior can generally be traced, but its influence on certain kinds of belief is sometimes very hard to fully understand. That is never as hard as in the volatile area of religion, which is one of the most difficult areas of human belief and behavior to study as a dynamic influencing behavior. Because of some inter-faith work this writer has done, I have been asked about several modern 'captivity narratives' involving religion, and some of them are, quite frankly, impenetrable mysteries. One narrative is of a well-known female journalist who was held captive by Muslim captors in Afghanistan, but who despite her anger toward her captors later converted to Islam.

Several people have asked this writer whether this is an example of 'Stockholm Syndrome.' Whether this is pure Stockholm or not can only be guessed at after looking carefully at the quality of the Islam that she practices. If her Islam is compassionate and nonviolent, I would say it can't be ascribed entirely to Stockholm, because if she were under its influence she would have identified with the violent Islam practiced by her captors. (She'd been interested in Islam before her capture, and could tell the difference.) But if she ends up with the small minority practicing a violent form of Islam that attempts to justify taking hostages, I would say Stockholm seems more likely.

A second mysterious captivity story of which I am aware involves a Jewish man who was the chief of a news service bureau in the Middle East, who was captured and held by militiamen in Lebanon. This Jewish man had a dynamic Christian wife, whom I had the pleasure of briefly meeting. This wife stuck by her husband during his period of captivity, and advocated tirelessly for his release; miraculously, he was able to escape, and rejoined his wife.

Shortly after this traumatizing experience he converted—I'm not making this up—to *Christianity*, for reasons that remain inexplicable to many people familiar with the case. He was never exposed to Christian influences during his captivity, nor had he ever expressed any interest in it; but his wife was Christian, and perhaps that might have something to do with it, since he thought a great deal about her while in captivity. (Prisoners of war also report thinking obsessively about wives and girlfriends.) But the fact that he was born Jewish, captured by militant Shiite Muslims, and ended up converting to Christianity, tells us volumes about how little we really know about the mysterious nature of religion and the human heart in crisis.

Then there was the case of Bobbi Parker, the wife of a deputy sheriff, who was kidnapped by an escaped convict—and was discovered eleven years later married to him. Was this another example of 'Stockholm Syndrome'? Frank Ochberg, a former associate director of the National Institute of Mental Health and an individual who, as this writer mentioned above, has written about 'Stockholm Syndrome,' sounded an appropriate note of caution when writing about the case in 2005. Ochberg, by that time a seasoned crisis-incident analyst and manager, agreed that yes, there were powerful elements of Stockholm present, especially if Bobbi Parker "went through the stages of shock, terror and regression that are seen in sudden captures, and if she developed the ironic and profound positive feelings [toward the hostage-takers] sponta-neously and without conscious control." But if, he added cautiously, "she made a calculated choice to stay with her assailant (or to leave with him in the first place), perhaps out of fear of harm to her family, perhaps out of preference for a different life, then the syndrome would not apply."[31]

A more clear-cut case (but not by much) was a young man I once knew who joined a cult, and came under the influence of the patri-archal cult leader. He evinced a zombie-like adherence to the cult, and parroted everything the cult leader said. His parents were people of means, and decided to have him kidnapped by mercenary-military types; he was then held for several weeks in a motel room against his will, and was 'deprogrammed' by professional 'deprogrammers.' Far from setting him free, however, this experience simply made him feel lost—he was deprived of his faith in the cult leader, but on the other hand now found it impossible to feel attachments to anything or anyone else. He spent the next seven years in psychotherapy, trying to figure out what had happened to him. Ultimately he concluded that he would have been better if he'd stayed in the cult, and found his own way out of it. When I last saw him, he was on his way to India with his girlfriend to find a guru he could study under.

He clearly wished to replicate his relationship to the cult leader, or so it seemed to this writer. But here's the interesting part—in my opinion, being forcibly 'deprogrammed' actually increased this tendency in his personality, rather than helping him deconstruct it, because the 'deprogrammers' held him against his will. In other words, the very strong-willed, occasionally violent 'deprogrammer' was simply the cult leader in a new guise. It may be for this reason that 'deprogramming' is discouraged by experts in cults, or so-called "New Religions," since it may do more harm than good.

The takeaway here is that often there is no discrete place where trauma and control ends, and choice begins—or at least it may be very hard for even the most experienced observer to know exactly where that place is. Sometimes the traumatized person simply doesn't see the choices available. All we know for sure is that freedom of choice is the antidote to the dynamics of 'Stockholm Syndrome,' captive-bonding and trauma bonding generally. The job of the emotional trauma victim, like the hostage, is to find a way to make choices that are independent of compulsion—whether that person is being held hostage by someone in their immediate environment, or by some emotional trauma in their past, or by some other compulsion or dynamic in their own personality. The worst cases are when a traumatized person has internalized so much aggression that it takes over his life and becomes a soul-crushing addiction, as well as a personal identity. In such cases, the victim-aggressor may feel compelled to act out his aggression, either on himself or on someone else, for a very long time.

4.

I became vividly aware, during my twenty-five years of doing psycho-social rehab, of the importance of helping people feel free by empowering them to make decisions concerning their own lives. (Even if some of the decisions seem wrong at first.) Anything that encouraged personal choice was, I discovered, intrinsically thera-peutic. The last ten years of my career as a psycho-social rehab clinician I worked at a residential twelve-bed facility, treating clients whose tenure was completely voluntary. (Indeed, among the population that made up our clientele, there was a fair amount of competition to get into our residential facilities.) Therefore I always played up the voluntary angle of the placement when doing an intake, while trying to simultaneously welcome the new client.

"Most people dislike being in jail or a locked hospital facility," I'd say, "and if you feel that way, I really can't blame you. But this place is a home, not a hospital—there's no locks on our doors, so you can leave anytime. But I hope you stick around, because you seem like an interesting person, and I look forward to talking to you this afternoon. Besides, the food is pretty good. Why don't you stick around for a couple of days, and see how it works for you?" In other words, we wanted clients to stay, but we also wanted them to know that there was no compulsion. They could simply pack up their things and leave, if they needed to—and we told them that. "There's the door. We'd like you to stay, of course, but if you have to leave we won't stop you. Why don't you think it over? I hope you decide to stay."

This gave the client total control over his fate, and helped him choose treatment without forcing it on him—and that *greatly* enhanced its effectiveness. Anytime a person actually makes a *choice* for treatment, the momentum of the situation instantly favors the therapeutic outcome, simply because *they*, the client, made the choice. The client still had a problem, because he still had the trauma or emotional disability that made him come to us in the first place; but now maybe he could decide what he wanted to do about it. Most staff learned to use that element of voluntarism, reminding the client that it was his or her choice whether to stay or not, but always mentioning how much we hoped they'd continue with us. "You've already made the choice to get better," we would say, "so why not let us help you?" The idea was to give the client as much power as we could, while encouraging them to stay, and to believe that we might be able to help them get better.

After being there a few days, most of our clients didn't *want* to leave—we really *did* have good food, and our residential setting was a lot more comfortable than being homeless under a bridge or sitting around talking to oneself in a furnished room, or being in a psych ward. As I pointed out before, many of our clients suffered from chronic mental illness, but others were simply people who were victims of some pretty horrible emotional traumas, and they needed someplace to go for a few months where they could be around sympathetic people, and heal. When the client made the choice to stick it out with us, he was sending himself a message that he had the right to be reasonably happy—maybe not so much now, but someday. (That was something else we said a lot: "It gets *better!*")

But the best thing about the residential program was that it was a home and not a jail. I donated a handmade quilt to the program that I'd picked up at a local garage sale, and a couple of my colleagues wondered why I was giving it up. But I was giving it to the program because I had observed that it was the homelike atmosphere at our treatment center that greatly added to the effectiveness of the treatment itself. The homemade quilt was simply one more way—*my* way—of sending the message that we were a home, and not a hospital. Whatever bad things that had sent the client to our program, we wanted to be a refuge from those bad things.

5.

There was one pioneer of psychoanalysis who understood the importance of aggression from the beginning of his career, although at first he downplayed his understanding to keep from offending his famous mentor, Sigmund Freud. That man was Alfred Adler, who was probably the greatest of the early psychoanalysts. (Greater than Jung or Freud, I would say.) He was great because he understood that neurosis had little to do with Oedipal conflicts, and everything to do with lack of control felt by children at the mercy of powerful adults. He saw that to the child especially, adult behavior is always overwhelming, often inexplicable and often cruel. People who recover from childhood feelings of helplessness have a good chance at happiness, Adler believed, whereas those who don't recover from them are doomed to suffer from an *inferiority complex*, an easy-to-understand neurotic disorder that occurs when people feel intense and recurring feelings of unworthiness.

When a family is abusive, a child's sense of helplessness would quite naturally enhance its identification with the parents' aggression—again, rather like a hostage situation. Adults who had been raised in such families might tend to express (or rationalize) aggression directed toward others, to work in professions that sanctify violence, or at some point engage in self-destructive behavior. In other words, they would tend to resolve their inferiority complexes in the same way that their violent parents dealt with *their* problems—by identifying with aggression as perpetrator, victim or facilitator, depending on the family system.

It is the moral content in his understanding of power relationships that makes Adler unique. He understood instinctively the role of aggression in society, especially in asymmetrical power relationships. Above all, he understood that adult aggression is often the result of an asymmetrical power relationship experienced in childhood, and he tended to see the child's sense of helplessness as a moral as well as developmental issue. This implies, at least to this writer, that overcoming feelings of helplessness might involve the development of a moral code based on protective, helping or nurturing attitudes toward those weaker than ourselves. To be sure, Adler understood the importance of values—justice, fair play and truthfulness—not only in society, but in the personal struggle for happiness and mental health. This puts him leagues ahead of the other psychoanalysts in terms of his importance to us today.

Perhaps Adler understood the helplessness felt by children because of his own personal experiences. Although he was raised in a stable home, he had rickets as a child, and found it painful to move, much less walk. Not for him was the athletic life, the horseplay of boys in the street or on the playground. For this he could have nursed a grievance against the universe, or he could have retreated into his own imagination. But because of the high level of cultural literacy in his home, the fundamental decency of his parents and his own intelligence and curiosity, he thankfully did neither. Instead he decided to become a doctor, and spent his days reading literature and science.

As we've already seen, the lack of control experienced by children is eerily similar to hostage situations, which produce that virulent condition known as 'Stockholm Syndrome.' Like prisoners, children feel helpless, hostage to the whims of their parents; and this powerlessness, this surplus helplessness, can easily induce feelings of inferiority. If the parents are violent, the child may internalize their aggression to a profound degree, and grow up with a pronounced propensity for aggression, and perhaps a personality disorder. Abused children become violent or criminal adults not just because they were abused, but because of the *total control of the adults who abused them.* As children, they really had little choice but to internalize the aggression they were experiencing.

Children are so lacking in life experience that they cannot imagine an alternative, which is what gives violent parents so much influence over them. The resourceful child will flee into his imagination, but lacks the life experience to invest it with a moral center, and will therefore be unable to imagine a plausible alternative to his parents' violent ways. As a result, ultimately he will probably end up identifying in some way with the aggressive adults who abused or exploited him.

The trauma bond that such a child experiences will probably cause him to focus on aggression for the rest of his life, and will influence all of his important decisions that have to do with power, violence and domination. If he is intelligent, resilient, even-tempered and lucky, he may be able to understand his parents; and in so doing learn to identify with what they could have been, and what he can still become. In the process, he may be able to identify with his own best self, and to realize that best self by working hard and getting along with his fellow human beings. If he does that, he can become an important resource for other people going through a similar process. If he can't do it, he will serve the gods of war for the rest of his life—in his erotic attachments, in his professional life, and in the world. If he enters public life, he is likely to be manipulative, self-absorbed, confident and dangerous.

6.

As a result of Adler's insight into the lack of power experienced by children, he was extraordinarily sensitive to power relations in society, especially social inequalities. For example, Adler didn't buy Freud's idea that women became neurotic because they envied men's penises—he thought it far more likely that they became depressed or neurotic because they had limited life-choices, and were generally treated like second-class citizens. Adler at first accepted Freud's idea of the Oedipal conflict in the family, but emphasized the struggle between the son and the father as a form of aggression, hypothesizing that the son's need to overcome the father was based on the child's sense of powerlessness rather than sexual desire for the mother. In this and many other ways, Adler perceived the primacy of aggression over sexuality, and in this Adler was right and Freud was wrong.

As early as 1908, Adler had concluded that the fundamental

human instinct was aggression. As historian Sheldon T. Selesnick has written, "Adler was searching for a principal that would unify psychological and biological phenomena and still fall within the framework of an acceptable instinct theory. The aggressive drive was introduced by Adler as a unitary instinct principle in which the primary drives, whatever they might be, lose their autonomy and find themselves subordinated to this one drive." Indeed—but Adler was discouraged from continuing along these lines, because the patriarchal and bossy Sigmund Freud didn't want him to.

Meanwhile, the issue of control had thoroughly insinuated itself into Adler's relationship with Freud, as the latter became increasingly upset at what he considered his own loss of control over the psychoanalysts who made up his circle. We can understand how intense these patriarchal feelings of control and domination were— and the kind of loyalty that was expected of a clinical disciple at that time—by remembering that Freud actually fainted twice while meeting with Carl Jung, apparently as a result of disagreements between the two men. (The fact that Jung was the one non-Jew among Freud's disciples probably played a role, too.) Jung, for his part, suffered a breakdown lasting for several years after his break with Freud, during which he had fantasies of vast floods destroying Europe. Freud was, in fact, furious at Adler's interpretation of human behavior as being based on aggression generated by asymmetrical power relations rather than sexuality. Interestingly, Alfred Adler interpreted Freud's opposition to his ideas (such as Adler's inferiority complex) as the behavior of an elder son who is afraid of being overthrown by younger siblings. Like Freud, Adler used the family system as a central metaphor, but focused on aggression rather than sexuality.

It is no coincidence, then, that Adler thought that excessively macho men who engaged in fighting or other high-risk behavior, or who engaged in Don Juan behavior with multiple female lovers, were not responding to castration fears but to inferiority complexes. Neurotic symptoms, to Adler, appeared to originate with feelings of helplessness and had as their unspoken goal an escape from domination. This unspoken goal could drive people to dominate others, to be dominated, or to flee from society in general; or—if they had enough insight and the will to change—to eventually find new arrangements that include neither domination nor being dominated. Those who could never recover from the child's sense of helplessness could become obsessed with control, fearing it in others and frequently inflicting it upon them. Or they might try to control the world around them with grandiose behavior that would most likely doom them and their unrealistic projects to repeated rejection and failure.

Adler never stopped believing—correctly, I think—that the trademark behavior of the neurotic is an unconscious attempt to escape from domination, often by dominating others or engaging in endless conflicts with them. Adler agreed with Nietzsche that human beings possess (and are possessed by) a "will to power," and in fact he quoted Nietzsche to that effect; but he believed that the will to power originated in a child's feeling of helplessness at being controlled by the adults around him. As an adult, the child who suffers from such feelings might seek to eradicate them by controlling others—acting out in that manner an early identification with aggression, which his childhood helplessness had caused him to internalize.

Due partly to his service in World War One, Adler began to see that this will to power would lead to disaster for humankind if not confronted. So he began to write of the importance of *Gemeinschaftsgefuehl*—an altruistic community-feeling that he believed could defeat the compulsion to dominate other people. (Not that different from the 'other-caring' described in the previous chapter.) He also wrote that psychology must become a "psychology of values," a conclusion with which this writer heartily agrees. And Adler believed that people could respond to emotional trauma by using it to transform themselves, making themselves what they wanted to be, implying a high level of intentionality. But neither

Adler nor Freud quite worked out how human beings could free themselves *emotionally*, rather than theoretically, of the problem of aggression and evil; and both watched helplessly as the lights went out in Europe in the 1930s. It must have made Adler feel terribly powerless to realize finally that there was no person, politics, country or psychotherapeutic technique that could stop the Nazi aggression that was reducing Europe—and those parts of his world which he had always loved—to infamy, anti-Semitic bigotry and the insane pursuit of aggression and domination.

Nonetheless, Adler's triumph was enormous. In addition to identifying aggression as simultaneously the most dangerous *and* the most powerful human instinct, and the one most likely to subsume other instincts into it, he correctly identified the one circumstance that is most likely to accelerate the internalization of aggression—a sense of helplessness, which begins with the helplessness felt as children at the hands of all-powerful adults. 'Stockholm Syndrome' is simply a replication of that same childish helplessness, in which adults experience a similar loss of control over their lives—whether occurring at the hands of a dictator, the effects of extreme poverty, or any other kind of life-situation that generates feelings of complete helplessness. *Total loss of control greatly speeds up and strengthens trauma bonding and internalization of aggression.*

While the thesis of this book is that aggression is internalized through trauma bonding, Adler's insights help us understand how helplessness and feelings of inferiority greatly enhance this process. When it affects great numbers of people at the same time, at the hands of a deceitful and repressive government, the fires of internalized aggression are banked and strengthened many times over. Excessive and illegitimate control, whether by gun-wielding hostage-takers or violent manipulation by the state, not only results in mass identification with aggression along with the mass internalization of it, it actually speeds up and strengthens the process by imposing emotional regression on entire populations.

7.

The megalomaniac seeks escape from feelings of helplessness by dominating others. What he cannot control in his own personality, he then tries to control in the world around him. Now, however, let's consider for a moment a more common form of control, one that is an exact inversion of that process, yet also frequently associated with emotional trauma. Let us consider those unfortunate people who are unable to control or suppress the pain they feel in their personalities as a result of the stressful world around them. Clearly, we can't act out every sexual attraction or violent impulse we experience, so most of us learn early in life how to suppress or sublimate emotions. (Sublimation simply means to channel an emotion or impulse from an unacceptable activity to an acceptable one. Actors, athletes and the best scholars tend to be good at sublimation.) Sublimation is something most of us learn as a part of growing up.

But what about those people who experience the world as *unbearably* painful? Their feelings are often a reaction to things in the world that most people brush off, but to them they are exquisitely lacerating. Such people would like to control the world to banish its most painful realities, but are unable to do so. The greatest artists and reformers are among the ranks of such people, but successful reformers are forced to learn patience (and a robust sense of irony, usually) to succeed; and the artist learns to live in a parallel imaginary world with its own set of rules. Furthermore, there are some things that cause emotional pain that will *never* change— romantic love, for example, is always a gamble, and there is no insurance policy that will redeem the pain of a heart when it is broken.

In fact, almost all of life has a tragic undertone to it that never quite leaves, in the sense that we all die, and even the most gifted people never quite live up to their ideals. But there are certain kinds of hypersensitive folk who are so deeply wounded by the world that they feel compelled to seek some way to *control their own pain*. By now the reader may have guessed what I'm driving at. I'm referring to those people that turn to alcohol or drugs—or gambling, sex or other powerful activities—as a strategy for controlling excruciating emotional discomfort. These are the people who become alcoholics and addicts.

Moderate drinking gives pleasure to many, and for some it remains an important part of their lives for a lifetime; witness those who have a small glass of wine during the dinner, and a nightcap— no more, no less, for a lifetime. They drink for relaxation, but not necessarily as a sedative for emotional pain; they resemble the so-called social drinkers, who likewise drink mainly for relaxation when socializing. The people who seek to control their own emotional suffering are a different breed. These use alcohol, street drugs and prescription medication to control their chaotic emotions—and partly for that reason, are never quite satisfied with the drugs or alcohol they use. Remember, they do not partake for social reasons, or even for relaxation, but are using alcohol and drugs as a sedative for emotional pain, or as powerful stimulants that can override their emotional aches and pains. And when they gamble or have sex with multiple partners, they tend to engage in these activities in the same addictive way.

Such people have a fatal tendency to take increasing amounts of their drug of choice, which is very often alcohol; but we live in a finite world, and the available supply of oblivion from the world's pain is likewise finite. Substance abusers need more of their comfort drug every day to quash their distress: but even as they take more its effects are no longer quite as pleasurable or effective as they were previously. At that point the Faustian bargain begins to get traction in their lives—and that's where the paradox of control begins. *People use a substance to control their pain, then lose control of the substance.* A greater paradox is hard to imagine, yet this same paradox operates in all life-situations that involve control—the essential paradox comes into play, it seems, whenever we seek to control what is uncontrollable. In his desperate efforts to control emotional pain, our daily drinker or drug enthusiast has crossed a line, and becomes an addict. Increasingly the pain will come not from the world, but from the accelerating pain of his addition. Seeking to escape pain, the addict now enters a world of almost constant pain, fear and aggression.

This pathetic effort to control uncomfortable feelings sends self-destructive tendencies through the roof. Control is a very tricky thing. Control of behavior, yes—we have to be in charge of our behavior, and decide which emotions we're going to act on, and which we won't act on. But taking substances to suppress painful *emotions* is an entirely different strategy, and a losing one, because emotions are essentially uncontrollable. We all know someone who has fallen victim to addictions, and we all know how creepily trans-formative, in a negative sense, addictions can be. (I'm not talking about psych meds, which are helpful in controlling psychosis, anxiety and depression. I'm talking about people who take increasing amounts of street drugs or alcohol to push down an emotional agony that they can't endure.) Many of these people have been previously traumatized in some way, and they simply haven't been able to deal with its aftereffects. Many times the bad feeling that the previously traumatized person seeks to suppress is fear, other times overwhelmingly destructive impulses. The combat veteran fears leaving his house without something to "take the edge off," for example, but quickly ends up being stoned all the time because the edge always comes back and asserts itself. Either way, the distressing emotions will have to be faced sooner or later if the addiction is to be overcome. And it may take a long time to get over them. But the same is true of cancer and other serious physical illnesses.

Trying to control the pain of emotional trauma with street drugs and alcohol is an extremely risky proposition, especially when those who suffer from it are terrified by the aggression they are feeling. The chances are very good that anybody who starts using a substance to control feelings of fear or aggression, rather than to socialize or relax, will eventually become an addict. People with addictions start out using a substance to control their pain, but end up losing control of the substance *and* their pain. What does this tell us? It tells us that the tendency to control is very often an illegitimate shortcut, whether we're trying to control other people or our own uncomfortable feelings. And America very often encourages shortcuts, whether it is getting rich quick or winning the girl of your dreams by buying the right cologne. The quest for total control leads paradoxically *to a complete loss of control*, which creates a chaotic situation in which individuals are further traumatized—and in the process bond themselves, perhaps fatally, to apocalyptic behavior that is not only aggressive but criminal.

Researchers have long believed that people with a predilection to addiction also have low pain thresholds—and that's probably true. But there's much more to it than that. As I've mentioned above, many people involved in substance abuse have often suffered serious emotional trauma in the past, many in childhood, adolescence, or young adulthood. They should find a good psychotherapist and talk about it, at least enough to take away the ability of the past to control them, and then start thinking about a completely different kind of future. Yes, there are exploitive or crazy therapists out there, but everything involves risk; and if they do nothing, victims of past trauma are very likely to end up taking street drugs to suppress the anguish caused by past events, which will only strengthen the power of the past over their lives.

Persons with Post-Traumatic Stress Disorder (PTSD)—or even minimal amount of delayed stress, which can take many forms—are prime candidates for addiction, especially those who don't understand how the aftereffects of past events are affecting them. (Or who don't realize there are things they can do about past emotional trauma besides using alcohol or street drugs.) Persons with PTSD at times suffer from intense, almost unbearable psychological and physical pain, which—when not treated in appropriate ways— usually leads to some kind of self-medication. Clinicians treating addicts see this repeatedly. Emotional trauma causes piercing emotional pain that some people can't handle, so they turn to a chemical sedative for it.

Like almost all people who are emotionally traumatized, they at first struggle to integrate the traumata into their consciousness. (By which I mean mind, emotions, memory and everyday intentions.) If they do so, they're probably going to be okay, although they'll probably have bad dreams and unpleasant feelings from time to time. If they fail to integrate it, they will probably identify to some extent with the aggression that caused the traumatic event or events. So far the addict sounds like all the others who have experienced emotional trauma, who have learned to identify with aggression as the underlying organizing principle of the world. But there is one great difference—the addict *turns the aggression inward on himself*, in a way that strikes many observers as demonic. Interestingly, however, this extremely high level of self-destructiveness almost always ends up affecting everybody around the addict, and everyone around him gets hurt by it. In the progress of their addiction, addicts tend to take as many people down with them as possible. The aggression implicit in this is obvious. People want to help the addict, but he must be ready to help himself first, or those who seek to help will get burned. Addicts don't have friends; they take hostages.

Unconsciously, some people with PTSD use street drugs not just as sedatives to control their pain, but to punish themselves for being part of a world that is hurting others, and ultimately to punish the world itself. This recalls the scene in the early versions of the musical *Hair*, where young people are shown shooting hard drugs, while saying things like this: "Okay, this one's for *Nixon!* This one's for *Kissinger! This* one's for all the Vietnamese killed by napalm in *saturation bombing!!"* And so forth. Sacrificing oneself (that is, putting oneself at extreme risk) to stop the world's pain is one of the great temptations of youth—it's easy, it's totally dramatic, it seems noble to the youthful drama king or queen, and it temporarily stops the pain. But it's stupid, self-aggrandizing and criminally wasteful to destroy oneself because of the world's injustices—and it won't do a damn thing to stop those same injustices. On the contrary, it increases the craziness in the world, making it even worse. The young person who is sensitive to social injustice would be better off, first, by laughing at the portentousness of evil men; and secondly, joining a movement for social justice, if they're so inclined, and developing their own political strategies for creating a better world.

Many addicts report that when they first started drinking or using drugs they were happy for the first time in their lives. (That alone tells you how damaged they were before they even picked up the drink or the drug.) But slowly, over a period of time, the drink or the drug that was at first so soothing, so kind, so forgiving—allowing the user to forgive so much—turns into a monster. Instead of turning the user on, the drink or the drug turns on *them*. It begins to make the addict act in a belligerent way; addicts increasingly need it at inopportune times; and finally the addict needs tons of it just to feel normal. Increasingly the drink or the drug feels more like punishment or a nightmare than a time-out from the world's pain.

Now the person using a substance to get high must take more and more, and the effects are unpredictable. The drinker has blackouts; the drug-user no longer has intuitive insights which seem spiritual in nature; the user doubles the doses but the effects fade quickly; and very often the effects of the addict's favorite comfort drug become qualitatively different. The user takes other drugs, takes more of them when stressed (and he's always stressed) and hides his drug use from friends except when he's broke or in trouble (except that everybody knows about it anyway). Finally the main source of stress is the drink or the drugs themselves, and the stress is complete. The substance abuser becomes a confirmed addict in full cry, with all the ugliness associated with that depraved and despised role in society.

The addict, who once used the substance to control his pain, has now lost control of the substance—and that causes him to lose control of his behavior. The addict hustles strangers for money, steals from friends, and lies to everybody. Deep inside, the addict knows something is very wrong, but can't figure out what it is. The entire experience is traumatizing—and the addict's vanished self-esteem leads to deeper and faster internalization of the aggression inherent in each violent episode of his career. The addict's behavior is increasingly criminal, which leads to more traumata. Above all the addict lies, perhaps most of all to himself. He forgets what truth is, how it feels and how it operates in relationships and social contracts. (Question: *How do you know when an addict is lying?* Answer: *When his lips are moving.*) The addict identifies so deeply with aggression that his only goal is to destroy whatever keeps him from being stoned.

The addict's life becomes one layer of trauma over another, reinforcing the addiction. The drink or the drug isn't just destroying his life, it *is* his life. Even when the suffering is most acute, the addict cannot stop looking for the next fix. The addiction assumes a frankly demonic nature, in the medieval sense—the addict endures untold suffering, and the drink or the drug becomes a dark sacrament that will give him only a few moments' relief, then summoning him back into an even darker purgatory. It is the Unholy Grail that the addict must pursue into the shadows of the abyss.

We've all seen it. It's hell in overdrive.

8.

As mentioned above, trauma often predates addiction, and almost always drives it once it is underway. But the addiction *itself* is traumatizing, even if the addict had no history of emotional trauma before. Psychic pain cannot be controlled with street drugs or alcohol for very long, especially pain generated by previous emotional trauma; and those who seek to control it risk creating more trauma. To get better, the addict will have to learn how to feel the pain that is inside him, even if only a little at a time, without trying to suppress it. That will be extremely difficult for him to do—not only does he have a low pain threshold, he's even more hypersensitive now than before because of all the damage he's done to himself. But there's no way around it—he has to feel the pain. Eventually he learns that the world doesn't end when he is in pain, and he begins to understand that he can survive it, because it always gets better. And he gradually learns how to avoid situations that create too much pain for him to tolerate.

He begins to learn the strategies recovering addicts and alcoholics use, and participates in the intimate peer counseling that helps them overcome the shame and helplessness they feel, usually in groups or programs based on 12-step programs, or in the 12-step programs themselves. Most of all, he has to stop using the drink or the drug and let the painful emotions 'just happen.' The addict has to stop looking for the world's most powerful sedative for emotional pain. In time he will understand that the world's most powerful sedative for emotional pain is death, and that death has been the sedative he's been searching for all along. Now that he's put down the drink and the drug, he is able—if he wants it—to make a choice to live.

Once the addict stops trying to control his pain he's halfway home. He is forced to face his pain straight-up, as well as any former traumas he may have. Ultimately he will have to face the aggression inside himself, depending on how much of it he's internalized. That is, he will have to face the fact of all the harm he's done, and face the aggression that was driving it, because it was that aggression that was causing him to repeatedly hurt himself, and hurt all the people he loved. (Twelve-step programs require that the recovering alcoholic or addict 'make amends' to people they've hurt. If nothing else, this is likely to make the addict begin to comprehend the fantastically destructive nature of his addiction.) He's already taken the first step toward beating the devil's bargain, although statistically few addicts ever get that far in their recovery. How many people make a Faustian bargain—a deal with the Devil—and win? A few recovering addicts do; and they're about the only ones.

Once they've been off the drink or the drug for a few months, recovering addicts start realizing that the cost of the short-term control they sought over their painful feelings was long-term emotional slavery; and they can see that it was no bargain. No wonder the 12-step programs are all about spirituality—once the recovering addict or drinker stops trying to control his pain, he can't *help* but be spiritual. The old-timers in recovery say that a big part of spirituality is accepting that when pain happens, trying to control it is a fool's game. It's just that simple. When the pain hits, call a friend or go to a meeting, or pray about it if you happen to believe in God.

But don't pray for God to take the pain away, they say, because spirituality doesn't work that way. (A big part of spirituality is finding out that you can be angry at God, I'm told, something not emphasized in conventional religion.) "Pray for strength to get through the pain," the old-timers say, "and then, if you're still alive, you might even ask God what the pain is supposed to teach you. That is to say, there may be something you're missing, in the sense that you need to make some changes." Recovering alcoholics and addicts often discover that one reason they were feeling so much pain and causing such destruction was that there was something very wrong in the way they were living their lives. They might have been hurting someone, or someone might have been hurting them, in a way that needed to be changed.

Addictions are about control, because the drunk or addict is desperately trying to control uncomfortable emotions; ultimately, however, addictions are about the *impossibility of control*. Control is a short-term proposition; and if carried into a long-term strategy ultimately leads to *more* chaos, *more* pain, and complete *loss* of control. If a thought or a feeling is so dangerous that it must be controlled, sooner or later it will get out of control anyway—so you might as well experience it. Furthermore, there's no way one can control the pain of emotional trauma (including the ongoing trauma of an addiction) that will not lead to more pain. The only way to beat the pain of trauma is to talk about it, and in so doing come to terms with it in a safe way. Please note that I'm advocating talking about trauma in a clinical setting or in peer counseling, not engaging in repeated attempts to remember exactly what happened, or getting stuck in a bad memory. And I also recognize that prudent use of appropriate anti-anxiety, anti-psychotic and anti-depression medication is often a big part of any treatment. But the key to recovery often begins by giving up the instinctive habit of trying to control one's pain.

One should be somewhat wary of getting stuck in memories of traumatizing events, as I've pointed out, because that could lead to an unhealthy identification with victim status. But at some point one really must talk about the effects of past trauma in the present moment; and one must to some extent talk about past events, at least enough to undo any identification with aggression that might have come out of it. The best bet is to talk about past trauma with a psychiatrist or psychologist with special training both in addictions and emotional trauma—after that, talking about it with peers in 12-step groups, or group therapy, might be a good idea. That, I believe, can be part of the serious work of recovery from addiction, especially when the addict also needs to recover from long-lasting effects of emotional trauma that began early in life.

It is a life-long process that must be engaged on a daily or hourly basis, a bone-deep inner struggle that embodies the most difficult emotional challenges human beings can know. But if you get involved in a program that will help you, you won't have to deal with it alone. It's all about *letting things go*, instead of trying to control the pain they cause—instead of trying to control the pain certain memories give you, one lets the memories go, and after awhile they just can't hurt you that much anymore.

Recovery from an addiction has one monumental and largely unknown benefit, as mentioned before. People who dare to recover from an addiction are among the few human beings on the planet who know how it feels to beat humanity's most diabolical social contract—the Faustian bargain, which is essentially a contract with concealed aggression that ends up as a form of evil. As people who have lived at the core of that devastating black hole and then created a life outside of it, they have quite a story to tell—and luckily for us, they're often great story-tellers. We need to listen to them, because their stories almost always boil down to cautionary tales about attempts to control the world by controlling emotions.

9.

Illegitimate social control, whether by a hostage-taker or a dictator, always leads to some form of evil, whether personal or systemic. The great genius of the American Constitution is its balancing of disparate interests without giving any particular group control over others. *The democratic sensibility is the exact opposite of the instinct for control.* It acknowledges tension, but seeks to balance different interests, using its separation of political powers to facilitate the negotiation of power based on the rule of law. In any case, the enlightened person never seeks power, but seeks rather to change the *nature* of power, to make it less coercive and more consensual.

Control is a violent short cut that stops existential and psychological growth, whether societal or personal. That's true whether we're talking about the control of a hostage-taker instilling 'Stockholm Syndrome,' a dictator striving to control what people think, a batterer trying to control his spouse, or people trying to control their existential pain with street drugs. All lead away from the healthy, creative lives we want, back into the cycle of violence and aggression from which we are determined to break free.

Chapter 4

Victim Status and Deceit in Systemic Evil

"Herr God, Herr Lucifer
Beware
Beware."
—Sylvia Plath
"Lady Lazarus"

I.

This book is about how evil replicates itself in the world. The first two chapters give a nuts-and-bolts analysis of how that works. When human aggression is emotionally traumatizing or sufficiently overwhelming, the victim is likely to internalize the aggression experienced; he may also experience a powerful emotional identification with aggression which the traumatized person is likely to then act out as aggressor, victim, or facilitator of aggression. But aggression is also influenced by the culture of the country where one is born—and enhanced by three hugely important cultural factors that are found everywhere, which are *patriarchy, nationalism* and *victimology.*

In the third chapter we saw that aggression can be greatly accelerated when people lose control over their own lives, and are gratuitously controlled by arbitrary forces. In fact the traumatizing use of coercive control results in the 'Stockholm Syndrome' is sometimes used by governments—or by armed groups and violent movements—to transform ordinary people into aggressors. When aggression becomes a coordinated system of group emotion and behavior directed by the state or other powerful forces, to the extent that large numbers of people engage in criminal, violent or exploitive conduct with apparent impunity, we can characterize such an organized proliferation of extreme aggressive behavior as *systemic evil.*

Trauma and control are usually not enough by themselves to create systemic evil. Two other components are usually present, which are *deceit* and *victimology*. The role of deceit cannot be overemphasized; the reader will remember that aggression by itself is not evil, but that when deceit is used to rationalize, hide or dissemble it in some way, it becomes evil, and is likely to be repeated by the aggressor. When systemic evil is promulgated and set in motion by powerful governments, it will invariably engage in lies specifically tailored to deceive the public, and to dissimulate its own participation in the ongoing crimes; at the same time, people who are attracted to state aggression will engage in various forms of self-deception.

When aggressors that are violent on a personal level try to conceal or rationalize their aggression, it is a personal form of evil. When governments try to conceal or rationalize their aggression on a mass basis, it becomes a form of *systemic evil*. Criminal governments set up entire departments devoted to concealing illegitimate aggression by the state; or—if it is too public and too egregious to ignore—their task becomes the creation of a narrative that justifies it. Think of Joseph Goebbels dreaming up clever lies or solipsistic narratives to justify Hitler's latest outrage against humanity, or Stalin's henchmen issuing state propaganda against dissenters, and you'll get the idea.

The deceit used in systemic evil is a deliberate, mass form of public deception, tailored specifically to deceive large groups of people, very often including appeals to group identity. ("If you want to be a member of our group, you'll believe what we tell you without questioning it.") But it also often depends on a certain level of willing self-deception by easily-led, essentially gullible people, or people who for personal or political reasons prefer the self-exculpatory lie to some harsh truth that might require them to think. (During elections these people are sometimes referred to as "low information" voters by poll-takers.) But what is important about them is not just that they are ignorant, but whether they want to *remain* ignorant—because they personally fear investigating a public issue in order to find out the truth.

For example, a person might see something on the Internet that 'proves' that President Obama is not a citizen of the US, accompanied by a crude photo-shopped 'birth certificate' showing him as being born in Kenya. They might prefer to believe this right-wing propaganda than investigate it, particularly if they aren't crazy about the President to begin with. But if they investigated it, they might find out that some right-wing organizations are funded by wealthy donors specifically to disseminate lies, especially lies with a high racist and xenophobic content. That would be disturbing to many conservatives, so they finesse the issue by simply accepting the propaganda.

Gullibility includes another phenomenon, which is a response to subtle intimations of coercion by the state. For example, during the Third Reich in Germany, the state sought to inculcate fear by declaring outright that their political opponents were traitors. The majority of Germans started out with few feelings about this, but as the propaganda intensified, people began to feel that there must be something to it, or otherwise the government officials wouldn't talk about it so much. Furthermore, the propaganda was so violent and so unequivocally coercive in nature that it implied very clearly that anyone who didn't agree with it might find themselves in trouble. Under those circumstances, it is not unusual that people would try not to think about what the government is saying—or at least not examine it too closely—even if they can't believe all of it.

A modern and very different example of this kind of bombastic state rhetoric occurred in 2011 when US Vice-President Joe Biden accused Julian Assange, founder of WikiLeaks, of being a "terrorist." Biden is an interesting man and an important politician, but he's also a government official, and there was no mistaking his threatening tone regarding Assange; to single Assange out and accuse him by name of being a terrorist was, in 2011, not merely an exercise in rhetoric but an unconscionable repudiation of the presumption of innocence. Biden was in effect saying, "The national security establishment of this country doesn't need a trial to find Assange guilty of terrorism. So the real issue isn't whether Assange's revelations are true, or whether the US is committing a form of systemic evil—the real issue is that you may get in trouble if you allow yourself to think about it."

The goal here was clearly to chill thought and discourage public debate about systemic evil carried out by the US military and security apparatus by criminalizing Assange's method for disseminating inconvenient truths. Specifically, Assange's organization is accused of released a film that documented a particularly distasteful bit of state terrorism used by the US military. (The tactic exposed was that of targeting civilians from attack helicopters, a practice soon to be expanded to drone warfare.) Biden's comment was clearly intended to chill debate on the larger issue, which was about the growth of a technology especially adapted to targeted assassinations. The public cannot debate such issues if they don't know about them—and the public's right to know is a classic newspaper formulation that is as true today as it was fifty years ago. The exception, of course, is when the public *doesn't* want to know, because some aspect of the truth is too disturbing—which is all too often the case with the American public, and people generally.

These are all examples of deceit, beginning with simple deception and ending with the use of implied government threats to chill debate about things the state doesn't want you to think about and discuss openly. Victimology, on the other hand, is a little harder to track and understand, especially when it becomes endemic in a tribe, group or nation. There's a very strong connection between it and deceit, however. First, victimology is typically an attempt to use a past injustice to justify aggression in the present. This is unmistakably a fundamental kind of deceit, and a dangerous one, because it is simply a declaration by the state (or some other power center) that it reserves the right to harm innocent people. Secondly, deceit is frequently successful because it appeals to people who feel victimized, either as individuals or as members of a group—thus they have a built-in desire to believe anything that plays to their sense of being aggrieved. For just that reason, and because it tends to drive the most egregious kinds of aggression, the constant references to victim status by calculating, pathological leaders is an extremely important component of systemic evil. This is especially true regarding the various forms of secular and religious nationalism that have arisen in the modern world.

2.

Evil, as defined in this book, is unacceptable aggression plus deceit. *Systemic evil*, the most dangerous form that evil can take, refers mainly to collective and usually criminal aggression that is instigated by dictatorial governments or armed groups; but it can also occur in families, workplaces and social organizations. Systemic evil is, to define it in strictly utilitarian terms, organized aggression that creates the most harm—psychological and physical—with the least energy in the least amount of time. Genocide is an example of systemic evil; so is imprisonment of dissenters, racism, discrimination based on religion or politics, systematic use of sexual abuse, violence against women, abuse in family systems, ritualized forms of public humiliation, systematic economic exploitation, mass murder, assassination, and torture. (Unnecessary war would be rather high on this list, but that will be covered in a later chapter on war.) Usually these things are done with an expectation of impunity, in the sense that the people who support or commit mass rape, murder and torture are encouraged to believe that they are merely small cogs in a larger system of power or authority, and are therefore just "following orders"—and for that reason will probably escape punishment for their crimes.

It was precisely to take this idea off the table that the Nuremberg Trials were set up to try and punish Nazis, just as later the International Military Tribunal of the Far East was set up to punish the war criminals of Imperial Japan. The most important rule to come out of these trials is contained in Principle IV of the Nuremberg Principles—"The fact that a person acted pursuant to order of his Government or of a superior does not relieve him from responsibility under international law, provided a moral choice was in fact possible to him." This ruling has a distinct family resemblance to the M'Naughten Rules of a legal Insanity Defense, the similarity revolving around the extent to which an individual knows that what he is being ordered to do is wrong (legally, but also morally). Thus if a soldier knows that that a particular order by a superior is wrong at the time the order is given, he is personally responsible for any resulting crime, and must be punished for it. The fact that he was "just following orders" is not a defense.

Thus when the new democratic government of West Germany in 1955 set up the Bundeswehr, which is modern Germany's small armed forces, they were sure to give soldiers pocket cards which contained material from the Geneva Convention, and which also defined the rules of engagement of a campaign in which they participated—but the cards were written in such a way that an individual soldier could quote from them to *refuse* to follow any order he or she believed to be illegal under international law, or to violate humanitarian norms in any way. Bundeswehr officers are obliged to respect that refusal to follow an order, which would presumably be followed by an investigation.

In Afghanistan after 9/11, the rules of engagement for the German Bundeswehr strictly forbade German troops from firing until they were fired on by Taliban fighters, at least up to 2007. German troops reported situations prior to 2007 in which they spotted Taliban guerillas waiting in ambush for them but were obliged to slam doors, turns jeep lights off and on, etc., to get the ambushers to fire on them. (This was not quite as self-destructive as it might sound, if one considers that Bundeswehr troops saw the Taliban fighters in plenty of time to deploy themselves defensively.) In any case, Afghanistan was the first time German troops had regularly seen action since 1945 (they were supposedly observers during the Bosnian conflict) and the command's extreme caution is understandable, given the tragic history of German militarism in the 20th century. (And the unease Europeans felt about German soldiers in action anywhere.) Bundeswehr commanders evidently knew that if they broke the rules of engagement, they might be held responsible for same by their own soldiers, either directly or by leaking the story to the media. And that was exactly as it should be.

The takeaway point from this is that "following orders" is not a sufficient excuse for participation by the individual in state terrorism, and hasn't been since the Nuremberg Trials. Systemic evil includes *all* forms of terrorism—individual, organizational and state terrorism—since terrorism invariably involves the murdering of innocent civilians. It also includes collective punishment, when practiced by governments or armed groups. Slavery is without question the premier example of systemic evil in American history, since this brutal form of exploitation was kept in place by an indigenous but highly organized form of regional terrorism using murder, torture, systematic sexual abuse and punishment of dissenters.[32] This form of regional terrorism was also used to maintain racial segregation and the plantation system in the Southern states until the 1960s, when at the cost of many lives voting rights for Blacks were finally achieved, along with integration of public schools and facilities.

Practitioners of systemic evil may adhere to a common belief system, but frequently behave more like sleepwalkers than ideologues, because they operate out of a shared *emotional* orientation based on aggression as much as, or even more than, any particular ideology. This was noticeable in the behavior of doctors and nurses who participated in the so-called "Tuskegee syphilis experiment" in Alabama from 1932 to 1972. In this "experiment," African-American men with syphilis were recruited but kept from using penicillin long after it had become an effective treatment for syphilis. Six hundred men were recruited, 399 with syphilis and 201 without it as a control group. The men with syphilis were not treated with penicillin so that medical personnel could observe them as they grew progressively sicker and died, and perform autopsies after they died. What makes this a form of systemic evil is that so many people knew what was going on yet kept quiet, and were therefore complicit in the atrocity.

It was not until 1966 that Peter Buxton, a young venereal disease investigator for the Public Health Service, wrote to the national director of the Division of Venereal Disease informing him that he was aware of the syphilis study, adding that it was morally wrong and for that reason should be terminated. In 1968 another employee of the PHS, an African-American statistician named William Carter Jenkins, founded a newsletter named *The Drum*, which was circulated in the Service and which raised consciousness regarding the Tuskegee study, and similarly tried to get the study closed down. Amazingly, the Center for Disease Control (CDC), which was then running the study, argued against closing it down, stating that they needed *to wait until all the subjects died so they could do autopsies*. Finally in 1972 Buxton went to the press. The story made the front page of the *New York Times*; Senator Edward Kennedy held hearings; and the study was immediately closed down. On May 16, 1997, President Bill Clinton held a ceremony for five of the eight surviving subjects of the survey and apologized on behalf of the nation.

The medical personnel who conducted this study did it to advance their careers, and also to serve what they were pleased to regard as the cause of science. Dr. John Heller, one of the administrators of the study, gave a Nuremburg-style defense by saying that the afflicted men were "subjects, not patients; clinical material, not sick people." By identifying them as "clinical material" rather than people, Heller made it clear what he thought of poor African-American men. Clearly, then, individual racist beliefs were part of the problem; Heller and the other doctors were engaging in the maximum amount of aggression allowed by the Southern system at that time, while incurring the minimum risk. (They could act with impunity because their victims, Southern Black men, had the least power of any group in America.) Medical practitioners were prepared to engage in this form of systemic evil partly because they were thoroughly indoctrinated in the ideology of American racism specific to the Southern states.

But Heller and the others were also carrying out the prerogatives of a Southern system in which they had a profound *emotional* investment. The deliberate harming of African-American people was part of an elaborate emotional system, in addition to being an ideological one, because it was particularly brutal, both in what it did and in its deliberate deception. It necessarily involved (and was partially driven by) guilty knowledge of the indigenous terrorism necessary to support racial segregation in the American South, of which their "experiment" was simply one part. Throughout that system of Southern exploitation and violence ran an underlying trauma bond that prevented people involved in it to speak out against, or even to acknowledge to themselves, the extent of the violence and aggression with which people were unconsciously identifying. The doctors and nurses—including one African-American nurse—had internalized the profound aggression that drove this system; they participated in the Tuskegee "experiment" because they were emotionally bonded to its unconscious aggressive orientation. Since its aggression was concealed, and since it involved organized medicine and government agencies, the Tuskegee "experiment" was a particularly egregious form of systemic evil.

Systemic evil often includes the application of modern technology to mass murder, torture, assassination and ethnic cleansing. One example would be the use of radio to encourage and organize the *genocidaires* during the Rwandan genocide in the 1990s. There had been outbreaks of mass murder against members of the Tutsi tribe several times before, going back all the way to the 1950s, each time with more casualties; in most instances the radio had been used as an instrument of communication to organize those Hutu Power advocates intent on genocide. Another would be the Nazis' use of a highly coordinated technological and communications system (trains, radio communications, facilities built overnight, Zyklon B for gas chambers, etc.) to transport and kill Jews, gypsies and political opponents. As previously pointed out, the Nazi Holocaust against the Jews was nothing more than an application of the industrial system to the venerable Christian European institution of the pogrom. Its intent was the same—to kill Jews—but the difference came in the fact that its technology enabled anti-Semites to kill more of them.

The fact that technology could so greatly enhance the practice of genocide suggests, however, that there is something about technology that can alternately feed or obscure the emotional orientations that drives systemic evil. Technology can contribute to the intoxicating feelings of sadistic grandiosity that are typical of systemic evil at its worst; and at the same time it has a dangerous 'distancing' effect, in that it enables people to carry out horrible acts of radical evil without having to personally witness any of its unpleasant immediate effects—the smells, the screams, the pleas for mercy, and so forth. On the other hand, if a predator *wants* to witness a few of those unpleasant immediate effects, technology could instantly whisk him to the desired venue for a little personalized theatre of cruelty. The aggressor can have it either way, or both ways.

Radical evil refers to aggression with an extremely high level of sadism, which usually occurs as the height or culmination of systemic evil. As mentioned above, one of the characteristics of systemic evil is that people who are attracted to authoritarian power systems tend to rationalize their crimes as simply "following orders," which they believe will make them less likely to face retribution for their crimes. People engaged in the practice of radical evil use this perceived impunity to commit acts of unimaginable cruelty. The more impunity there is, the more sadism there will be. If power tends to corrupt absolutely, impunity for sadistic violence does so also, but much more quickly. I am not saying that *all* people will become sadists if given impunity for their acts, but a great many people will invariably do so, particularly if it advances their careers and is paid handsomely; and in certain historical epochs that plurality is likely to become a majority. And once aggression becomes sexualized or radically cruel, the aggressors may become so inflamed and intoxicated that they are likely to turn on and kill associates who refuse to participate with them.

The four elements used in most systemic evil—*trauma, control, deceit* and *victimology*—begin as seemingly *external* elements that are observable as social or historical phenomena; but since they are so overwhelming, they are almost invariably internalized and when combined result in a powerful need to act out aggression. Traumatized people acting out the resulting aggression against target populations also experience unconscious or repressed *guilt*, which strengthens the systemic evil to just the extent that the guilt does not become conscious and therefore emotionally paralyzing.

Even complicated forms of systemic evil are enhanced by national cultures and the three major cultural aspects we're previously examined. And the use of social controls by criminal governments must also be taken into consideration. In this chapter, however, we'll look more closely at deceit and the elevation of victim status, and the manner in which both deceit and victimology are used to construct systems of systemic evil and to dissemble the crimes they commit. We'll also look at the way that unacknowledged guilt enhances the dynamics of violence and aggression that systemic evil usually leads to. Our intent, as always, is to arrive at a clearer idea of how systemic evil works, how it is generated, and why it is so powerful and destructive in the world.

3.

"The great strength of the totalitarian state," Hitler said in a speech at Königsberg, in September 1933, "is that it forces those who fear it to imitate it."[33] This is a near-perfect definition of trauma bonding in the context of a violent society manipulated by a totalitarian state. The fundamental mechanism of Hitler's program was to use violence and emotional trauma to enforce social assimilation of pan-

German nationalism and anti-Semitism, by using extremely violent images, violent words and actual street violence in a very public way to bond people to the Nazi state. If repressed guilt is the centrifugal force that gives systemic evil focus, violence and its concomitant trauma is the force that drives it forward, bonding more people to aggression in the process.

Adolph Hitler was aware that under normal conditions, people fear aggression; but when exposed to enough aggression by a powerful state, they tended to unconsciously identify with both the aggression and the state responsible for it. Likewise, people fear being lied to by government, but when the Nazi state told grandiose and absurd lies, the people often ended up identifying with that government precisely *because* of the absurdity of its lies. Wild exaggerations and grandiose lies contained a higher ratio of aggression than smaller ones, and people are influenced by them in the same way that they were influenced by displays of physical violence. Thus people were more likely to be influenced by big lies than small ones. Since both Adolph Hitler and Joseph Goebbels intuitively understood the aggression involved in lying, both knew that the Big Lie is more effective—that is, was more likely to disorient and traumatize—than a little lie.

After 1933, when the Nazis took over the German media, Germans experienced the subsequent deluge of systematic deceit and state propaganda as a continuation of the social aggression they had been subject to since 1920. They had already been traumatized by the multiple disasters of World War I, the Treaty of Versailles, recurring depression and inflation, not to mention poverty and crime and unemployment, all of which were accompanied by the disintegration of civil society into warring paramilitary armies fighting pitched battles on the street. Because of these ongoing traumas, Germans had come to identify with aggression on a profound level, and as a result found it difficult to imagine a future that did not involve violence as a fundamental organizing principle. (Just look at the way the German public perceived the German General Staff as integrity personified.) Furthermore, the growing popularity of pan-German nationalism played on deep national feelings of insecurity in ways that elicited both servility and arrogance, and promoted an emphasis on force over reason, military conquest over civil society, and immoral use of force as a kind of liberation from the bourgeois conventions that lead to Versailles.

During the 1920s, German intellectuals—particularly those on the Left and in the arts—elaborated a complicated emotional orientation based on irony, characterized by a bittersweet awareness of the distance between ideals and reality, and a shrewd assessment of humankind's self-serving nature. This ironic emotional orientation set the tone for the wild artistic and political experimentation in Berlin during the 1920s, an age of enormous freedom but also of subtle anti-democratic tendencies. In symphonic art, film, theatre, novels and journalism, opera and operetta, architecture and poetry—in all the arts and in science too, especially physics—there was an explosion of talent and ideas in Germany of the 1920s and early 1930s such as the world had never seen before. This reached insane heights of cosmopolitanism in the cabaret art of Berlin. Simply to listen today to the cabaret artists of that time—icons such as Rudolf Nelson, Friedrich Hollaender, Kurt Tucholsky, Hanns Eisler and the incomparable Mischa Spoliansky—is to find oneself in a world so rich in desperate hope and plummeting despair that one can hardly take it all in.

The cabaret art of the 1920s in Berlin was one of bohemian cosmopolitanism, but it was combined with an awareness of the omnipresence of evil—and it combined those two streams of human experience better than anyone since Baudelaire and the fatalistic romanticism of Heine. Bitter realists who were also romantics, Berlin's artists of the musical stage projected a sensibility that would later reassert itself in the racially integrated underground jazz world of America of the 1940s and 1950s, and the Beat movement of the early 1960s. The cabaret artists of Berlin were, in fact, premature hipsters, and with a similar disgust for the aggression and bigotry that was interwoven into the culture in which they worked; but the Berliners achieved a wit, a self-deprecation and a sense of their society's possibilities that the American hip sensibility never did.

This ambiance of 1920s Berlin was captured at its height by Bertolt Brecht and Kurt Weill, not so much in their well-know *Dreigroschenoper* (Three Penny Opera) as in the endlessly haunting *Aufstieg und Fall der Stadt Mahagonny* (Rise and Fall of the City of Mahagonny). *Mahagonny* was the ultimate 20th-century opera, about a city in which everything is legal except poverty—it is a city in which being poor, in other words, is punishable by death. Although Mahagonny is nominally set in a mythical American South (which by itself is highly suggestive) it is impossible to hear this opera today without thinking of Berlin of the 1920s. Berlin was as terrifying as it was beautiful, however much it may have been crawling with talent—a magical city built not on a hill but immersed in dark, violent and perpetual crisis, as the rest of the world waited to see what tomorrow would bring. We know the answer to that question now, because we are still living in the shadows of what tomorrow brought.

The heavily Jewish cabaret and theatre artists living in Berlin in *den Goldenen Zwanziger Jahren* participated in a tutorial whose goal was to teach Germany the role of irony in a robust high culture; indeed, Yiddish is mainly German with irony, a cultural and linguistic world to which the Germans desperately needed to be exposed. In the end, however, irony is a mainly literary conceit, although an extremely compelling and logical one; as a lifestyle and the basis for a communal polity, it can appeal only to a minority with the taste and intelligence to appreciate it. The *artistes* of Germany may have been aflame with talent, but did little to change the status quo, because their tragicomic sensibilities were so different from the majority—besides, the corporate upper class of their time was betting on an entirely different horse. After the curtain came down on their flaming Berlin apotheosis of wit, civilized tolerance and left-wing hope, the habitués of the Berlin cabaret world went into exile, were driven underground or perished in the death camps.

Could art, science and moral imagination have dissolved the bonds of trauma in Germany of the 1920s? One can only say that it takes time and a certain amount of good luck to treat a national addiction to aggression, not to mention an effective popular leadership that can indicate the direction in which redemption might lie. But the intellectuals, artists and visionaries of Germany in the 1920s had neither time nor good luck. Neither did the trade unions and the organized political Left—they were already split into two opposing camps, the Social Democrats and Communists. Unfortunately for them and for us, in 1933 Hitler took over, and in twelve short years around eighty million people were dead and Europe lay in ruins. The Nazi Holocaust methodically wiped out European Jewry, leaving us with unmistakable evidence not only of the depths of human evil, but with an example of the actual *primacy* of evil in human society—and what that realization has done to the way human beings think and feel about themselves and the future.

To those who think this an overstatement, consider this: almost *every* political regime in Eastern Europe turned to rabid anti-Semitism during the 1930s in a puerile imitation of the Nazis and the fascists of Italy, each trying to outdo Hitler in the vehemence of their totalitarian denunciations of freedom and their medieval demonizing of Jews. And that was *before* the death camps began to produce 10,000 corpses a day. One must ask oneself, how many countries took in the Jews who were fleeing from this madness? Almost none accepted Jewish refugees, including the United States. Hitler led the way in making life difficult for Jews, but the world quickly followed his evil example.

Hitler specifically designed his political system to emphasize the omnipresence of aggression in its cruelest forms, and constantly used the state to draw the attention of the people to the inherent proclivity of his government to be violent, precisely so that nobody could forget what the Third Reich was all about. One of Hitler's favorite words was *fanatisch*, fanatical, which Hitler used to describe the mindset that he sought to instill in his youthful recruits. This was one reason for the almost daily street clashes between Nazis, Communists, Social Democrats and liberals during the 1920s—it was a theatre of cruelty that the extreme nationalist forces and Hitler's supporters used to establish aggression as the single standard by which everything else was to be measured. By the late 1930s all that remained of civil society in Germany was a horrified fascination of both government and citizens with what they were all becoming. By the late 1930s Germany was so immersed in state violence that Germans couldn't imagine anything else.

But violence wasn't the only weapon used by the Nazi psychopaths to create systemic evil in Germany. The use of violence was exacerbated by the state's use of the most incredible kind of deceit, because—as was mentioned earlier in this section—Hitler understood that lies were also a form of psychic violence, and could traumatize people every bit as effectively as a pitched battle between SA troopers and trade unionists. Hitler and Goebbels used deceit in the 1930s as a system of human communication based on a communal fantasy of violence, driven partly by fear and partly by fascination, to broaden and deepen a process of trauma bonding that had already begun on the streets of Germany in the 1920s.

4.

The kind of public deceit used by demagogic leaders and coercive governments is intended to create an intense, constant and calculated level of systematic lying, the primary function of which is to rationalize and thereby justify various aspects of systemic evil, very often justifying it in advance. But that level of deceit not only accompanies or presages systemic evil, but is an active element of it. It almost always involves framing, in which every issue is framed in such a way as to allow only one conclusion or interpretation. Hitler and Stalin, not surprisingly, were both masters of the systematic uses of deceit. Even in the US, right-wing activists instinctively know how to use framing to police debate, whereas liberals usually don't.

(Framing, as used here, means posing a political question in such a way that only one answer is possible.)

Hitler was fascinated by lies and lying, and in fact tended to trust habitual liars more than people who were struggling to be honest. He was himself an expert in lying, because of the self-deception required by his grandiose turn of mind. Because he needed to lie to himself, he saw his lies as an unavoidable part of discourse with other human beings. He also saw lying as absolutely necessary to effective governance, because lies could be used to motivate people to commit the ruthless crimes he saw as necessary to realize his political goals. In Hitler's messianic and intensely narcissistic worldview, his delusions were perceived as historical necessity; and lying was one way to get people to transform these violent fantasies into reality. There was no morality or immorality in Hitler's approach to political deceit (except when others lied to *him*, which he considered an abomination), but a strictly utilitarian approach to getting the kind of aggressive mass behavior that he wanted. The modern neo-conservatives in America have a somewhat similar approach to the uses of deceit in manipulating people into war and exploitation.

Deceit not only facilitates systemic evil but is very often a part of it, especially when the state intentionally misrepresents reality in extreme ways. This systematic use of deceit operates not merely to justify, rationalize or deny the existence of aggression, but to draw people into a direct experience with that same aggression by telling lies that are grandiose and ridiculous. Since obvious governmental manipulation of truth is violence against the very idea of objectivity, it very frequently causes people to end up identifying with the aggression inherent in it, even when they don't believe it. Since there is no limit to the number of times people and governments can tell a lie, or the different ways they can spin it, deceit can be used to overwhelm powerless people in unlimited ways that are usually quite cost-effective.

Hitler knew that systemic deceit was not only a good way to

exacerbate the aggression inherent in his policies, but knew also that lying was something his Nazi government could do well, since it controlled the media. "The German has no idea how much the people must be misled if the support of the masses is required," Hitler wrote in *Mein Kampf*. A lie must be focused and repetitive, it must "confine itself to little and repeat it eternally."[34] The lie must be repeated again and again, no matter how absurd: "Through clever and constant application of propaganda, people can be made to see paradise as hell, and also the other way round, to consider the most wretched sort of life as paradise."[35]

The surface implausibility of the lie was no deficit, as Hitler saw it — in fact, the outrageousness of the lie was an asset, especially if the people were simultaneously made aware that their totalitarian Nazi government, with its well-known proclivity for violence, was telling (or rather, ordering) the people to believe it. And a Big Lie, since it implies a larger attack on reality than a small lie (and suggests that truth is a state of mind rather than a discernable reality), is indeed likely to have much more impact. "The size of the lie is a definite factor in causing it to be believed," Hitler wrote, "for the vast masses of a nation are in the depths of their hearts more easily deceived than they are consciously and intentionally bad." The evil in most Germans might have been latent, but Hitler sought to bring it to the surface, to transform the Germans into a nation capable of the aggression that would be required of them. (Remember, to transform Europe in the way he wanted them to, Germans would be required to kill millions of people, a majority of them civilians.) Telling whoppers at every point was a big part of the process. "The primitive simplicity of their minds renders them a more easy prey to a big lie than a small one, for they often tell little lies but would be ashamed to tell big ones."[36]

The initial implausibility of the Big Lie sets off a process of cognitive dissonance in the person who hears it, as Goebbels knew well. Let us say, as an example, that a violent totalitarian government says that black is really white. The government is insisting that people believe something that doesn't seem to make sense; and this causes the individual citizen to feel doubt, frustration, and finally apprehension (that by harboring doubts about the government's lie one is putting oneself at risk). This painful process can only be alleviated when the individual assigns the Big Lie to a kind of 'as if' category, similar to the suspension of disbelief when the curtain rises in a theater.

Little by little, people grasp the utility of not questioning the government's lies, especially when they are big or improbable lies. And since the government is asking them to believe things that are not true according to customary rules of evidence, they gradually come to accept such things as a kind of *conditional* truth—or perhaps they simply decide not to think about it, which comes to the same thing. Questioning the government under totalitarianism would be dangerous and foolhardy, so the individual citizen learns not to think about it excessively. To just the extent that the citizen decides not to question the lies of the government, so does he come to internalize the aggression inherent in lying itself.

Just as hostages identify with their hostage-taker because of the control he has over them, people in a totalitarian society learn to identify with a violent and controlling government because it is all-powerful, threatening and capricious—which means that people learn to identify with its lies precisely because they *are* lies. One of the great anomalies of the Big Lie is that people can defend it vehemently, even murdering people on its behalf, while knowing that it is false. This insight drove some of the best writing of George Orwell, both his fiction (one thinks particularly of *1984* and *Animal Farm*) and much of his political journalism about Communism and fascism. The truth is that the 'as if' state of mind is more interesting and more titillating than any reality. The Big Lie in fact provides pleasure, diversion and entertainment precisely *because* of its very outrageousness. (One needs only think of the violence of professional wrestling on TV, in which bouts are obviously choreographed in advance, but which the viewer is encouraged to imagine as completely spontaneous and real.)

It is while in this 'as if' state of mind that the religious believer perceives and assimilates religious ideas and dogmas. At first it's 'just pretend,' the contemplation of a story or analogy or metaphor that illuminates certain things and promotes certain benefits, as such images gradually take root as emotional truth—but not exactly as fact. This is also the mindset of the artist, who deals with narratives and images that are rooted in emotional rather than literal truth. But art and religion impact the inner world of the imagination and the personality, whereas the Big Lie aims at altering *the relationship between consciousness and the real world*. Anything becomes possible, not just in a novel or in a theological construct, but in the world the citizen inhabits, if only he will believe what the state tells him. The Big Lie aims not at catharsis, but at active delusion.

"Something always remains and sticks from the most impudent lies," Hitler wrote in *Mein Kampf*, "a fact which all bodies and individuals concerned with the art of lying in this world know only too well, and hence they stop at nothing to achieve this end."[37] Under the relentless battering of state propaganda, people gradually begin to accept the idea that black, under certain circumstances, might really be white. *There must be something to what the government says*—the citizen thinks to himself—*otherwise they wouldn't be making such a fuss about it.* So the citizen decides to go along with—to conditionally accept—whatever fantasy the state is promoting, and not look into it too deeply. The Big Lie seems to promise a transcendent world that is much more exciting that the so-called 'real' one—so why would one *want* to investigate it too closely, or subject it to the rules of physical evidence?

The imaginative fiction of the Big Lie is, in other words, much more entertaining than ordinary, everyday empirical truth. Furthermore, the aggression inherent in the grandiose nature of the Big Lie as told by a warlike government promises material rewards. Who wants to embrace a drab, failure-ridden literal truth when one can live out a lie that promises transcendence and world domination? The Nazis made sure that their lies offered emotional excitement in a spectacular and tempting way. The success of their systemic deceit was precisely its ability to provide a worldview more exciting and exalted than any mere reality could ever offer. The unspoken message was this: *Help us create a world in which this lie becomes truth, and you will become powerful.*

In other words, the Big Lie is experienced as a new form of emotional truth that not only frames external reality but creates a new reality based on emotional needs. It must therefore take the place of the old empirical truth, becoming a new and dazzling vision that valiant and powerful interests are striving to create. Since Hitler's Big Lie struggled not only to inflame the mind but to control the future, it operated in the same way as prophecy in magic and in religion, promising the triumph over time and matter sought so assiduously both by Doctor Faust and the historical Jesus. Hitler presented himself as an armed and courageous visionary who through the systematic application of violence and military adventurism reunited the most problematical aspects of religion, magic and power, creating from them not only a new emotional experience but also promising a new and unprecedented kind of world domination that had its roots in the ancient warrior culture of the early Germanic people.

This became impossible for many traumatized Germans to resist. The Big Lie was emotionally irresistible to them to just the extent that it was demonstrably false. At the same time, it presented a world that diverged so violently from the world they'd previously known that it not only promised people a release from the mistakes of the past, it prepared people to do violent things and make enormous sacrifices in order to achieve an apocalyptic future. It created a new emotional paradigm where cognitive logic was replaced by the electrifying emotional orientation of pure aggression, sustained by mass meetings, histrionic speeches, and violent public fantasies of war, revenge and domination. The Big Lie had the capacity not only to persuade the public to accept a new

kind of reality, but the aggression inherent in it prepared them cognitively *and emotionally* to attack anyone or anything the state selected
as an enemy. It prepared the people for the Nazi state's cruelty, both
as a worldview and as a lifestyle.

And while it started out as playacting, in the form of Hitler's
bizarre, screaming public fantasies of brutality and domination, it
slowly but surely—like Jim Jones' carefully choreographed
rehearsals of mass suicide at his Guyanese Peoples' Temple—led his
followers step by step into dictatorship, the unforgettable horror of
Kristallnacht and the final plunge into total war on two fronts, with
the concomitant destruction of Europe, Germany and the Jews that
he had been aiming at all along. For many Germans it must have
seemed at first like an uncanny dream, but when it turned into a
nightmare it was too late for the dreamers to wake up.

5.

Victimology, in the traditional social sciences, has meant the study of
people who tend statistically to become victims of crimes (street
prostitutes, for example). In the last few decades, another definition
of the word has arisen, mainly in literary-political journalism and
some literary criticism. According to this secondary definition, victimology is an intense, vocal and unhealthy emotional identification
with victim status, accompanied by a narcissistic worldview in
which the victim is the ultimate hero (or antihero), and victim status
is repeatedly advanced as the highest good. But it is more than that.
Victimology is also the use of victim status to manipulate people into
accepting violent policies and behaviors—it is playing the victim for
personal or national or organizational gain, but almost always in
order to engage in various forms of aggression. It is an emotional
orientation that is also an ideology of power.

The special pleading and emotional blackmail associated with
alleged victim status is very often at the heart of systemic evil. In this
use of victimology, the victim may use past crimes committed
against him or his group to justify new crimes in the present. It is this

definition that we are using in this chapter, and in this book. According to this usage, victimology is a half-conscious ideology of power that can usually be recognized by its passive-aggressive fighting style, accompanied by an extremely aggressive emotional orientation; it drives the kinds of aggressive behavior that are most prone to become components of systemic evil.

A person under its influence is so immersed in his own victimhood, real or imagined, that he will deny his capacity for aggression even as he commits horrifying crimes against innocent people. People driven by victimology—victim-aggressors, in other words—are notorious for disproportionate responses to real or imaginary injuries, and display seemingly boundless skill in concealing their own aggression against themselves and other people. They are consummate liars; but their danger lies not just in their deceptions but even more in their self-deceptions—such people may not even believe that they are *capable* of aggression, despite overwhelming evidence that they engage in it regularly.

Thus victimology, when defined and used in this way, also refers to a psychological orientation that starts out as situational but can quickly come to resemble a personality disorder, with many of the components of narcissism, sociopathy and classic inferiority complex. Once it begins to function as a central dynamic of systemic evil, it is deadliest when it is combined with secular or religious nationalism, because of the extent to which nationalists commit crimes framed by perceived past injustices against their group. Such nationalist practitioners of victimology seek to drag alleged crimes out of the past into an Eternal Now that will forever justify their aggression in the present moment. It was just this kind of victimology that was once used by Christians to justify their aggression against Jews, by citing an "inherited" Jewish guilt for Jesus' death, an event that had happened more than a thousand years before.

The real purpose and emotional subtext of victimology is aggression. Typically people who live by victimology are utterly convinced of their own righteousness, and therefore have no problem justifying retaliatory or preemptive aggression that is completely out of proportion to real or imagined problems. This often causes them to act or express themselves in disingenuous and self-delusional ways. For example, a street criminal who shoots and kills a stranger may offer as a reason the fact that the victim looked at him in a provocative way. While that may have triggered the criminal's subsequent violence, it certainly isn't a reason—much less a defense. People who identify with victim status often posture themselves as weak and pitiable, and they may indeed feel that they are. Their cognitive and emotional lives revolve around their grievances, which are forever in a holding pattern until the time is right for retaliation. The problem is, their retaliation is usually aimed at completely innocent people.

The identification with victim status is to some extent an *unconscious* passive-aggressive strategy, although it is just conscious enough (and just systemic enough) that it qualifies as a half-conscious power ideology as well as an emotional orientation. Since a vocal and ever-present identification with their own victim status is often correctly perceived by others as a justification for impending aggression, it tends to stimulate pre-emptive attacks—which will, in turn, confirm the victim-aggressor's belief in his own victim status.

The victim-aggressor lives a fantasy that is not only narcissistic but self-congratulatory—and that, too, makes emotional growth almost impossible. Once they find out how easy it is to manipulate people with it, people who play the victim are likely to make victim status their core identity. Such persons tend to invite or incite aggression, but sooner or later they are likely to seek out situations and venues where they can create victims of their own—always perceiving themselves as innocent victims who are simply protecting themselves.

The person who identifies with victim status will almost always facilitate aggression in its purest form, and will sooner or later act it out. This includes people affected by intergenerational trauma. One thinks of the children (or even grandchildren) of Holocaust survivors who resolve the emotional tension of survivor guilt by joining right-wing Israeli settler groups that brutalize and steal land from Palestinians in the Occupied Palestinian Territories, or the children of Nazis leaders who once acted out their loathing of their Nazi antecedents by supporting the violent Baader-Meinhof gang (which succeeded in killing at least 34 innocent people). None of these things are the slightest bit redemptive, but are on the contrary simply continuations of the same aggression perpetuated or endured by their parents or grandparents.

Not all experiences of intergenerational trauma are that obtuse, however—every so often someone shows a little originality in the way they rebel against the past traumas of systemic evil. One child of a top Nazi leader became a gay Communist cabaret singer in East Berlin in the 1950s and 1960s; and although he didn't make a big deal out of it, it was rather well-known exactly who he was, and who his father was. This amusing gentleman didn't adopt the bohemian life of a cabaret singer just to outrage his conservative middle-class family and repudiate his dead Nazi father, necessarily—it really was the kind of lifestyle he preferred, and was his way of living out the Spanish saying that "to live well is the best revenge." But there was also without question an element of rebellion involved, and in this writer's opinion a stylish and original form of it—after all, cabaret art was a huge part of anti-Nazi Berlin history, so it drew from indigenous sources, so to speak. It was for many years a satisfying source of black humor for those in both East and West Berlin who knew about the singer's background—indeed, one can only wish that all rebellion against intergenerational trauma could be so creative, so unencumbered with destructive angst and so relatively harmless to the rebel himself.

Because the victim-aggressor identifies with particularly acute forms of aggression, people who are stuck in victim status create problems not just for themselves or their scapegoats of choice, but for everyone around them. Like addicts, victim-aggressors don't have friends—they take hostages. This happens not only because of the toxic nature of the aggression with which they identify, but because they feel that they can do anything with impunity. In their minds, they're just defending themselves, even when they're murdering civilians or torturing them, or uncritically supporting states or armed groups that do. Identifying themselves as victims, they can, like the narcissist, justify literally anything they do or that they want done in their name, simply because their victim status.

Since victim-aggressors seek out situations that will enhance their identification with victim status, their victimology rapidly comes to resemble a personality disorder. Victim-aggressors tend to be involved in—or attracted to—systemic evil in an amazing variety of forms; but when large numbers of them are involved in highly focused forms of systemic evil the result can be sadism on a truly astonishing level. One has only to look at the genocide of Muslims by the Serbian nationalists in the 1990s, in which Serbs—whose entire ethnic identity was predicated on victim status—suddenly turned on people who only a week before had been friends and neighbors, and proceeded to murder, gang-rape and rob them with astonishing precision and determination.

6.

Adolph Hitler's uses of victimology drove his personal appeal, and was a huge part of his political program (adapted, of course, to the idioms of virulent pan-German nationalism); and it was evidently the secret of his appeal as a histrionic speaker. Victimology, as we've seen above, is an intense, vocal and unhealthy identification with victim status, accompanied by a concealed but equally emotional identification with aggression. Hitler understood intuitively that the emotional orientations of resentment, self-pity and victimology were all, to varying degrees, close to the emotional core of pan-German nationalism and anti-Semitism; and that everything he did or said had to be infused with these emotional dynamics. Far from being peripheral, victimology was close to the heart of the Nazi message, where it was used to explain not only the desirability of world conquest, but also the *necessity* of it (to stop the persecution of Germany). Playing to the deep insecurity of the German-speaking people, engaging both the arrogance and servility inherent in a nation beset with repressed feelings of inferiority, victimology could present history to the Germans in a way that justified their violent destiny in the immediate future, and therefore their reason for unquestioningly obeying and believing the totalitarian Nazi state.

The Nazis used the four horsemen of *trauma, control, systematic deceit* and *victimology* in a focused and highly calibrated way as part of their campaign to create a society based *fundamentally* on aggression. Hitler's use of victimology was particularly clever, since it played into the profound sense of dishonor that had plagued the Germans since Versailles. Hitler's own histrionic concept of himself as a victim-aggressor who was merely defending himself against a demonic universe played well with the Germans, and made him intuitively able to appeal to Germans who also felt like victims, and who in addition could not make sense out of the world around them.

The Soviet Union fashioned a form of totalitarianism that rivaled the cruelty of the Nazis—but they did not have the same emphasis on militarism, so they were not inclined to start a land war. But the Soviet leadership also engaged extensively in victimology, since the most hideous acts committed by Stalin were invariably justified as being necessary for the working class to defend itself from the international bourgeoisie. This led to the irony that Stalin's government probably killed more dedicated Communists than all the world's capitalists and fascists combined. The reason Stalin often gave for murdering so many people was that they were betraying the Communist movement; but the real reason was that Stalin was afraid they might someday become his rivals. My point here is simply that the Stalinists used victimology in their propaganda at least as consistently as the Nazis, framing their aggression as part of a necessary, constant struggle against a brutal enemy.

Communism identified itself so profoundly with the victimization of the world's workers and peasants that the rights of the capitalists (or whomever the Soviet state called a capitalist) ceased to exist to them, even in theory. Once they had reached that point, they could no longer claim to have any rights themselves, since Stalin was free to murder them one by one by simply calling them capitalists, no matter who or what they really were. Among other things, victimology is experienced by individuals in much the same way that narcissists experience their situation, so that when used in a systematic way, victimology creates extraordinarily well-adjusted, guilt-free murderers; victim-aggressors are noted for killing others and going to their own deaths with equal aplomb. (The classic text on the Marxist-Leninist as victim-aggressor is Arthur Koestler's *Darkness at Noon*.)

For his part, Hitler used victimology to constantly represent the German people as perpetual victims at the hands of forces much more powerful than they. These dark forces apparently had nothing better to do than seek out new ways to torment Germans; and they possessed, in Hitler's hysterical *Weltanschauung*, absolutely diabolical and omnipresent powers. (As George Orwell pointed out, Hitler never quite worked out how his enemies could be so completely inferior and at the same time so diabolically powerful.) Jews, intellectuals, Slavs, socialists, Bolsheviks, social democrats, liberals—they were only the tip of the iceberg.

Since Hitler saw every other race or nation as being inferior in *some* way to the Germans, the sobering reality was that almost *everybody* was against Germany. Hitler even had harsh words for the Germans themselves, whom he often referred to with contempt. (Again, Hitler never quite worked out how the Germans could be so superior to other people and yet needed to be so regularly lied to.) It is one of the great ironies of the 20th century that the totalitarian Nazi state, the most violent governmental system in the history of modern Europe, was able to achieve and maintain power to a great extent because of Adolph Hitler's constant insistence that Germans were pathetic victims.

Hitler brought this home by presenting *himself* as a victim, as a stand-in for the eternally wronged and misunderstood German people—and by skillfully implying, in speech after histrionic speech, that all the injustices arrayed against him were exactly the same as the injustices suffered by the Germans masses. Hitler's sense of himself as an eternally put-upon victim matched the German people's deeply internalized sense of their own victim status. Emotional trauma, state control and systematic deceit all played a role in the Nazi triumph, but it was Hitler's presentation of himself as a Christ-like stand-in for the suffering of Germany that made him so appealing to so many people, many of whom had never seen anything quite like it before.

7.

Hitler's appeal to victimology was reinforced by endless, ongoing violence by the state to make it a factor in systemic evil. ("The very first essential for success is a perpetually constant and regular employment of violence.") While victimology could create the identification with victim status on one level, the state would demonstrate its capacity for punishing opponents on the other—thus did it teach people the unique dynamics and privileges of the victim-aggressor as a primary type. In fact, Hitler used the trauma of unprecedented but irresistible state violence as a kind of political theatre to reinforce *all* elements of systemic evil, as experienced by both cowering victim and triumphant state sadist. The biggest and most carefully choreographed public display of cruelty, violence and crushing humiliation occurred during two terrifying days know as *die Kristallnacht,* or night of broken glass. Typically, Hitler claimed that it was merely defensive—because a Jewish youth had shot a diplomat in Paris, he must kill Jews in Germany.

Kristallnacht was a government-sponsored pogrom against German (and Austrian) Jews that was orchestrated and carried out by the Nazi hierarchy on November 9th and 10th in 1938. At least 91 Jews were killed outright in very public ways, and some 30,000 were shipped off to concentration camps. Incredibly, over 1,000 synagogues were burned down, and 7,000 Jewish businesses attacked. It was an orgy of violence like nothing that anyone had seen before in the 20th century—and it was carefully set up to look at first like a spontaneous pogrom. But it quickly became clear that it was actually a country-wide attack on Jews that was executed by the government, in a way that no citizen of Germany could ignore since it was carried out by uniformed SA troops. People were openly murdered, beaten and humiliated in all the large urban centers. Old men were forced to march about beating toy drums; Jewish children were beaten up in front of their peers as they walked home from school; Jewish-owned shops were torched or vandalized.

What was unique about *Kristallnacht* was its profoundly *public* nature—the idea was to attack and humiliate a fair number of Jews in an extremely cruel and open and unavoidably public way. It also aimed at destroying a great deal of property—ancient synagogues burned while firemen stood by and did nothing, and huge crowds watched the destruction. The idea behind this incredible public theatre of cruelty was to let everybody in Germany see it, to see the violence in their own communities—partly to make them internalize it, and partly to show exactly what the Nazi government could do, and the kind of thing it intended to do in the future.

Here it was, out in the open, what the Nazis were all about—unchecked, lawless aggression, a government-sponsored pogrom against unarmed civilians who had no way to defend themselves. After *Kristallnacht*, it was clear what Germany was becoming, and there was no way people could deny it—and very few ways people could even react to it. For Germans, the choices were these: to could go into exile, join the small underground resistance against Hitler, or allow the trauma to penetrate their bones. When organized violence is as public and as ferocious as it became in *Kristallnacht*, there is really no way that witnesses to it can keep from being compromised emotionally, since the emotional disorientation and trauma of such horrendous public violence is likely to overwhelm all cognitive intentions, ideas and expectations.

Kristallnacht—and all the other acts of public violence carried out by the Nazi state—traumatized the German people in a way that perfectly complemented their national fascination with victim status, because it prefigured the way in which those influenced by its violence were being invited to lash out in homicidal rage against the world that they believed had victimized *them*. Germans had been repeatedly told by the Nazis that they were victims of global schemes to destroy Germany; and the public nature of *Kristallnacht* made clear the happy alternative: they could now move from being victims to becoming ruthless aggressors themselves, because their victim status gave them to the right to do so. The German people had internalized enormous amounts of aggression, and the Third Reich would give them a way to act it out.

The public nature of Nazi violence against the Jews in *Kristallnacht* prepared people who thought of themselves as victims of global conspiracies to contemplate a righteous struggle to punish the world by dominating it, in the same way that Hitler publicly dominated the Jews. All of the lying, the social control and the victimology might not have been enough, had it not been bonded into the national psyche by the continuing trauma of *public* violence orchestrated by a criminal government.

It is the nature of public violence that it aims to ultimately cause a majority of the people to identify with it on some level, and hence with the power it represents. This may be true even if the victim of the trauma ends up fighting the government that orchestrates the violence. Emotional trauma, we must remember, is a process by which both cognition and emotions are overwhelmed, so when it is driven by political dynamics it is likely to leave only the experience of aggression in the collective mind of a nation. A psychopathic leadership uses horrifying public violence to generate emotional trauma, and enhances it through the social control inherent in dictatorial powers, systematic deceit in the state media, and huge elements of victimology—and if it can be melded together in the public imagination by ongoing violence, an entire people can be thoroughly conditioned to engage in mass violence. One way to accomplish this is to start a war, which fills the media with images of carnage and draws the entire population into the horror by constant reiteration of the war's danger. Lacking the necessary military preparation to start a war, the government must practice violence in its domestic politics—and this Hitler certainly did, as he had promised to do in Mein Kampf. The ultimate result of this domestic violence was *Kristallnacht*.

Acts of aggression, Hitler saw, were far more persuasive than logical arguments, because they persuaded ordinary people unconsciously, subliminally, through the emotions, to identify with that aggression. He understood completely that this kind of persuasion was infinitely more effective than reason, and his cohorts set out to use it once they had complete control of both the media and the state's levers of power. Most Germans were awed by the violence of the Nazi government and also frightened by it; but that same fear caused them to become unconsciously more receptive to the state's skillful use of aggression to make them identify with it.

What previous pan-German nationalism did metaphorically, Nazi totalitarianism did literally. Instead of writing about state power, as though it were an argument that could be accepted or rejected, the Nazis used mayhem in the streets to manipulate the people into unconsciously identifying with it. Once having accepted aggression as the organizing principle of life, most non-political Germans probably saw only two choices—either die as victims, or survive as part of a triumphal narrative of a master race that would loot the world. Many, of course, lacked the cultural literacy and the introspection to understand the moral degradation into which they were descending; and many who did understand struggled to disconnect their emotions and block out the events going on around them. But such passivity cannot prevent trauma when one lives in a society that is acting out its violence, either in war or through the intense domestic persecution of some racial or religious minority—

in reality, passivity and withdrawal simply create more preconditions for trauma bonding. "The great strength of the totalitarian
state is that it forces those who fear it to imitate it," Hitler said—and
about that he was tragically correct.

8.

Why are some people so attracted to victim status? Because the
victim is always right, and never has to do anything or make any
moral choices. What starts as a healthy adjustment to life's lacerating
disappointments—and sometimes one's own personal deficits—
gradually becomes an unhealthy enthusiasm for the position of the
victim, especially when the individual learns to see victim status as
a justification for his own aggression. Such individuals are likely to
become so smitten by the ecstasy of being a victim that their entire
personalities become suffused with it.

One well-known historical example of this kind of personality is
to be found in the life and career of Richard Nixon, the 37th President
of the US, and the only one forced to resign. Nixon's one great
passion was a gnawing, obsessive need to be liked and appreciated,
yet his fate was to have a personality so unlikable that it amounted
to a kind of negative charisma. People familiar with his personality
type—that is, people who could see through him—hated him on
sight. Even people with little expertise or interest in political power-
brokering hated him. As his need to be loved and appreciated by the
American people increased, jokes and stories highlighting his
essential mediocrity proliferated not only among insiders in
Washington, but also in the media. The result was Nixon's seething
perception of himself as broken, emotionally battered and perennially victimized, which became an ongoing personal crisis.

Nixon dealt with this ongoing personal anguish by drinking
heavily, and by taking on most of the characteristics of the victim-
aggressor. Feeling himself the victim of a recurring and nightmarish
hatred by the world, he lashed out at his imagined enemies,
exceeding both the extent of their supposed offenses as well as the

Constitutional limits of his office. His thinking about his supposed enemies became increasingly paranoid, as he projected onto people who disagreed with him the roiling fury that originated in his own unresolved emotional conflicts. This resulted in the creation of an "enemies list," a list of approximately a hundred people that Nixon used the power of government to personally harm. Some of his presidential initiatives—such as opening relations with China—were arguably positive. Yet he seemed to work overtime at making himself unlikable, engaging in racist and anti-Semitic slurs, openly referred to his wife with scurrilous street obscenities, and by several accounts subjecting her to physical and verbal abuse. Yet he never stopped thinking of himself as essentially a victim, despite his own well-known transgressions of executive authority and the fact that over thirty of his associates did time in prison for desperately trying to cover up his—and their—misdeeds.

Richard Nixon had but one friend in his life, a Miami businessman named Bebe Rebozo, who had Mafia connections and was by several accounts a closeted gay man. Rebozo had a deep understanding of Nixon's chronic awkwardness, and for reasons only the heart can know took pity on him. He felt sympathy for Nixon's extreme self-consciousness, but seemed to genuinely enjoy Nixon's company. The two men occasionally held hands and engaged in horseplay that some people found homoerotic, but it would have been highly uncharacteristic for Nixon to consummate such a relationship sexually. From Bebe Rebozo, Nixon received the unqualified affection and admiration he wanted but could never get from the American people.

The fact that Nixon refused to take responsibility for any of his misdeeds was just as well, as any attempt to do so might have led to major depression and possibly suicide. Richard Nixon lacked the humility, the objectivity, and the appreciation of irony that would have been necessary for his own redemption. His only option, then, was to despise the world, because it stubbornly refused to give him the affection he craved, instead finding him pathetic and disreputable. People around him were aware of his excruciating dilemma and often made fun of him. Henry Kissinger wrote about an incident in the Oval Office of the White House in which Nixon, the child of emotionally unavailable Quakers, asked Kissinger to kneel down on the carpet and pray with him.

Kissinger could easily have said something like, "Well, Mr. President, kneeling on the floor isn't my thing. Couldn't we maybe sit on the sofa?" Instead he wrote later about Nixon's desperate query as a fit subject of mockery, dismissing it as yet another example of Nixon's insufferable gaucheness.

9.

Identification with victim status is the *perfect* defense mechanism against seeing one's personal capacity for evil. It is for this reason that the victim-aggressor feels so little guilt—he's a victim, so how could he be capable of evil? The importance of this cannot be overestimated. The greater the aggression and the psychopathology, the greater the feelings of being a victim are likely to be.

10.

Victimology invariably involves deceit, because posturing as a victim involves deception and self-deception. Victimology thus generates deceit in both its individual and systematic applications— and deceit is also necessary to the passive-aggressive fighting style. Deceit may not *originate* in victim status, but the victim-aggressor's need for deception often plays a critical role in amplifying the deceit that is already present in concealing aggression. Victimology has the magical psychological quality of greatly enhancing the guilt of one's enemies, while obliterating completely one's own accountability. What systemic evil as a whole does in society, victimology does within the individual human personality. Systemic evil provides the victim-aggressor with *social* impunity for his crimes (because he's just following orders) whereas victimology provides immunity to *personal* accountability (because he's a pitiful victim). These two complimentary functions—state impunity for systemic evil and victim status to redeem personal guilt—are why victimology plays such an important role in the daily operations of systemic evil.

II.

The Serbs, like the Germans in the 1920s and 1930s, provide a profound example of a people whose self-image revolves around a long history of victimization—and the Serbian abuse narrative is perhaps the oldest in Europe, going back at least to the eighth century. Serbian nationalism is driven to a large extent by memories of the atrocities Serbs suffered at the hands of the larger countries and empires in Europe over a period of many centuries. (During the Second World War, for example, they were targeted for genocide by the Nazis and the Croatian fascists, who killed somewhere in the neighborhood of 50,000 innocent Serbian civilians.) The Serbs sometimes enjoyed a favorable position in the empires of others, including their relatively dominant position in the collection of Balkan ethnicities that was Yugoslavia under Marshal Josip Broz Tito. Furthermore, the Serbs were too few—Serbia today has between six and seven million citizens—to conquer and occupy other countries in their entirety. That's one reason why they let tiny Montenegro go, their only remaining ally, when the former Yugoslavia finally unraveled completely.

During the Balkan wars of the 1990s, the Serbian militias were guilty of unspeakable crimes against civilians in large parts of Bosnia-Herzegovina, which involved killing up to 200,000 Muslim civilians and the raping of perhaps 50,000 Muslim women.[38] These things were done as a deliberate policy intended to traumatize the Muslim population and cause them to leave Serb enclaves. In this horrific process, which the Serb militiamen themselves referred to as "ethnic cleansing," Muslim men were rounded up and sent to concentration camps, systematically tortured, taken out in groups and murdered, and their bodies buried in mass graves. This culminated in the Srebrenica Massacre, the worst outbreak of genocide against civilians since the Nazis.

But during this carnage by Serbian militias, most Serbs living in Serbia (including Belgrade, the capital of Serbia) were completely unwilling to believe reports by international media. On the contrary, they expressed nothing but disbelief, disgust and contempt for such reports. To them it was completely self-evident that the Serbian militias had done nothing wrong, and that charges of genocide were simply another anti-Serb propaganda campaign, the object being to defame all Serbs everywhere. As for evidence that clearly demonstrated that Serbian militias *were* committing horrific acts of genocidal brutality, the overwhelming majority of Serbs took the position that their militias in Bosnia *couldn't* be committing genocide.

To them, the only reason genocidal atrocities by the Serbian militias in Bosnia were being reported was because everybody with a typewriter and a telephone was maliciously making up lies about them. The world's press and electronic media were gullible fools for being taken in by Bosnian Muslims, who were well-known liars and provocateurs. This was not the opinion of a few Serbs—it was what virtually all Serbs believed during this period, at least in Belgrade. Since Serbs were always the victims of everybody else, it was impossible that Serb militias could now be committing atrocities. And— very importantly—this belief was created and backed up by force by the Milosevic government, which allowed no reports of genocidal atrocities to get through.

The fact that the United Nations and the rest of Europe believed that genocide against Muslims *was* underway (and that there was ample evidence to prove it) was simply not allowed in Serbian discourse. Anyone in Belgrade in the 1990s who suggested publicly that Serbs were committing genocide would have probably been kidnapped, imprisoned, tortured and then killed. In fact, the attempts of the rest of the world to get the Serbs to understand that their dictator, Slobodan Milosevic, was directing a genocidal assault against the Muslims of Bosnia, was seen in Belgrade as more evidence that the world hated them, since this was clearly just another campaign to slander and demoralize them. The world had *always* hated Serbs, and it probably always would.

Of course, by 2000 any Serb who wanted to know the truth could find out what had happened by simply spending some time online. But as late as 2006, most Serbs were still denying that anything bad had happened in Srebrenica, or the other parts of Serb-controlled Bosnia. Of course, the facts were there for all to read about, but a great many Serbs didn't know about the genocide because they didn't *want* to know about it—and for precisely that reason, they despised the rest of the world for talking about it, thereby bringing it to their attention. (Again, this was further evidence, in their minds, of the world's insane desire to malign and insult Serbs, simply because they were Serbs.)

This should not be seen as evidence that *all* Serbs were (or are) guilty of what their militias did, because that would be guilt by association—or collective guilt—and these are no longer concepts that grown-up people can take seriously. (If everybody is equally guilty, as Dwight Macdonald once wrote, everybody is equally innocent. There are *always* degrees of guilt and innocence involved in genocide and other war crimes, and those distinctions can only be conclusively addressed in a courtroom.) But it should be noted that the predominant Serbian attitude was, in fact, a curious inversion of the principle of collective responsibility—it had become a kind of collective *irresponsibility*. Serbian militias hadn't done anything bad in Bosnia, but if by chance they *had*, it was wrong to talk about it, thought a great many Serbs in Belgrade.

Like Germans under the influence of the Big Lie, Serbs believed that accusations of genocidal atrocities committed by the militias in Bosnia were part of a deliberate campaign to cause pain to Serbs. Therefore there was no question about the truth or falsehood of the accusations. They *had* to be false, because the people who said these things were *really saying them because they hated Serbs*. How could Serb-haters tell the truth about Serbs? It was just another example of the ongoing use of deliberate disinformation to wound Serb sensibilities and destroy Serbian identify. In other words, Serbs in Belgrade responded to charges of genocide by Serbs in Bosnia by *retreating into permanent victim status*—and as we know, the victim is never wrong.

Given the widespread reporting of Serbian atrocities and the Serbian denial of that reporting, Serbs seem clearly to have been in that peculiar state of denial typical of trauma bonding compounded by victimology. The traumas suffered by the Serbian people in the past had bonded them to a vision of the world in which aggression against Serbs defined everything. These same past traumas, which were endlessly reiterated by Milosevic after 1987, made it psychologically impossible for Serbs to imagine themselves in any role except as a victim. Therefore people who reported atrocities by Serbian militias hadn't just gotten their facts wrong, they were *intentionally lying*. This is always the position of institutionalized victimology; and Serbs were predisposed to victimology as a psychological orientation in rather the same way as Pan-German nationalists once thought of Germany as a martyr nation.

Victimology had long been, in fact, the core element not just of Serbian nationalism, but of Serbian identity overall. To be a Serb meant to be an eternal victim of the world's inexplicable hatred, a plucky little nation that nonetheless kept fighting its enemies and which no country could defeat completely. And since Serbs had always been victims of aggression, which is bad, anything done by their militias had to be good, or at the very least defensive in nature.

Of course, both the Serbian nationalist identification with aggression and the extremely high levels of victimology that accompanied it arose out of real trauma suffered by Serbs in the past. But it is also a fact that none of that past trauma was perpetuated by Bosnian Muslims. To brutally subject Muslims in Bosnia to rape and genocide, a group who were completely innocent of any wrongdoing against Serbs, was a despicable and momentous crime against humanity. But it was not unusual that trauma suffered by Serbs in the past would be cited in order to stir up similar violence against a completely innocent group in the present. The events in Bosnia demonstrate clearly that psychopathic individuals like Milosevic, as well as the motley band of criminals who commanded and belonged to his militias, have an innate intuitive ability to use past trauma to bond people to organized violence of an unthinkable and extreme nature.

Bosnian Muslims, the victims of the Serbian genocide, were almost childlike in their commitment to the idea of a multicultural society. They demonstrated against war repeatedly in front of the parliamentary building in Sarajevo, and their politicians repeatedly called for a multiethnic society living in peace within an independent Bosnia. But Milosevic had decided to gamble on the Greater Serbia concept; and Bosnia contained too many Muslims and Croats for the Serbs to comfortably dominate. So according to the Greater Serbia scenario, the only answer was ethnic cleansing to create Serb enclaves. Once the Bosnian parliament had voted for an independent Bosnia in October of 1991, the hour of death, rape and ethnic cleansing had arrived for Bosnian Muslims. The Muslims' commitment to religious tolerance meant absolutely nothing to Serbs in the throes of Serbian victimology.

The Muslims of Bosnia had been thinking all along that they could pacify the Serbs by creating a secular, multicultural Bosnia that would give equal rights to Serbs, Muslims, Croats and everybody else. But the Serbs lived in a different emotional universe. It was impossible for them to imagine living within a multicultural society that they could not dominate, because it was painfully self-evident to them that in such a situation non-Serbs would sooner or later try to kill them, or would endlessly plot against them—and everything they heard from Milosevic and other nationalists in Belgrade reinforced that belief. Therefore the only way they could survive would be to create Serbian enclaves, and drive the Muslims out of the enclaves.

This identification with past aggression would require the Serbs to commit genocide, torture and systematic sexual abuse. It would require of them acts of unbelievable sadism to drive out the very same people who had been their friends and neighbors until only a few weeks or days before. The decision to go ahead with ethnic cleansing was taken not in Bosnia, but in the Serbian capital of Belgrade, which directed the Serbian militias both in Bosnia and in Serbia. Once Slobodan Milosevic decided on a course of ethnic cleansing in eastern Bosnia to enable the Serb militias to form a Serb enclave (later to be called the Republika Srpska), the massacres, the gang-rapes and the concentration camps began.

Rape in particular was used as a deliberate strategy as Serbian militias moved through particular areas. Rape camps were set up, often next to police stations or militia barracks. Men as well as women were victims of rape, sexualized torture and other kinds of sexual abuse. In response to this outbreak of radical evil, the United Nations decided to set up so-called safe areas, in which Muslims were disarmed and promised protection by the United Nations. None of these "safe areas" were remotely safe, since the Serbs quickly sensed the unwillingness of the UN to do anything other than offer a purely symbolic presence. This led directly to the genocide at Srebrenica, a mining town where approximately 40,000 Muslims lived, their numbers periodically swollen or decreased by refugees seeking sanctuary, or fleeing the area. Here a few hundred Dutch troops were supposed to stand off thousands of hardened Serbian militiamen, who by this time had reduced the systematic mass murder of civilians with field weapons to a science.

Attempts to deploy air attacks by NATO against encircling Serb militias came to nothing; confusion and indecision on the part of the UN and Dutch commands were quickly exploited by the armed Serbs, who overran the Dutch soldiers. The Serbs methodically gathered between 7,000 and 8,000 Muslim men and boys together, often only a few yards away from where the helpless Dutch soldiers stood watching. The Muslims whom the UN had promised to protect were then transported to killing fields around Srebrenica where they were slaughtered in groups and buried in mass graves, with the Serb militiamen engaging in various forms of atrocities along the way.

Some Muslim men ran away and were hunted down in the woods. Others made a break for Tuzla, a town where there were Bosnian troops. One of the most horrifying aspects of this genocide was that the Serb militiamen, many of whom lived in the area, knew many of the Muslim men they were killing *by name*, and taunted or called out to them as they murdered or mutilated them. About 400 Muslim men were reported buried alive, others tortured with knives and killed with automatic weapons. Many committed suicide to keep from having their noses, lips and ears cut off.

Some Serbian civilians living in Bosnia were astounded and traumatized by the behavior of the Serbian militias. Perhaps these Serbs had already made the adjustment to the idea of themselves as an important ethnic and religious group within an independent and democratic Bosnia, and resigned themselves to pursuing their interests as most groups do, through advocacy and the ballot box. But evidently the vast majority had lost the ability to think that way, and the horrific ferocity of their aggression dominated events on the ground as they created a mono-cultural Serb enclave. Collective Serbian memory was one of trauma, which had been cognitively rationalized and emotionally internalized in such a way that most Serbs could only think of themselves as hapless martyrs whom the rest of the world inexplicably wished to destroy. The aggression they had internalized came pouring out and didn't stop until the enclaves were free of Muslims except for a few hiding in the forests, many of whom were hunted down and killed.

As this writer has previously indicated, this violent mix of nationalism and victimology is without question the most dangerous force on the face of the planet. It is especially ferocious when it devolves into victimology and the religious form of nationalism— which is exactly the direction that Serbian nationalism had taken before the Bosnian genocide. That is, since both Serbs and Muslims in Bosnia thought of themselves as Slavs, they were basically of the same race. The difference between them was only of religion—a highly nationalistic Serbian Orthodoxy, on the one hand, and secular Islam on the other. The reason Serbs killed Bosnian Muslims, then, was because of their religion.

This came at a terrible time for the Muslims of Bosnia, because Islamophobia was already on the rise among Christians all over Europe, and Serbian Orthodoxy had an antipathy to Islam because of battles Serbs had lost to Muslims when they were under the Ottoman Empire. Milosevic was careful to continue stirring up unresolved memories of trauma and violence, resonating with millions of Serbs that had internalized similar memories from more recent traumas, which they had never talked about because of the Yugoslav government's control of media; Milosevic never stopped reiterating victim status as the essential Serbian identity, and engaged repeatedly in the most outrageous forms of systematic deceit. These forms of *trauma, control, deceit* and *victimology* led directly to the hell on earth created by Serbian nationalism as Christian Serbs conducted their rape and genocide against the Muslim men and women of Bosnia-Herzegovina.

12.

The preferred role of the victim-aggressor is to present himself as a victim while preparing for the next round of atrocities, to justify his aggression before it occurs, and to keep explaining to a skeptical world that it is really *he* who is the victim, that it is really *he* who is the sensitive, suffering one, even as he represses, tortures and murders other people. As long as he can convince himself and others that *he* is the eternal, suffering victim, he does not have to contemplate the consequences of his aggression, nor does he have to make any changes in himself or in his institutions.

In 1995, former Bosnian Serb leader Radovan Karadzic was indicted, along with the notorious militia leader Ratko Mladic, for alleged war crimes committed during the ethnic cleansing and genocide campaigns of 1991–1995 in Bosnian-Herzegovina. The flamboyant Karadzic announced that he would not willingly stand trial, preferring instead to go into hiding. "If The Hague was a real juridical body, I would be ready to go there to testify, or do so on television," he declared. "But it is a political body that has been created to blame the Serbs."

13.

The Turkish genocide of Armenians in 1915–1922 exemplified many of the characteristics of systemic evil that we've already discussed — and the way Turks deal with this uncomfortable trauma in their collective past involves a particularly striking combination of victimology and aggression. Although it is not generally known in the West, most Turkish nationalists *deny that there ever was any Armenian genocide*, and that the claim of genocide is actually a clever lie, the real purpose of which is to insult the Turkish nation. (If this sounds familiar, it is precisely the reaction of Serbs, one will remember, when they heard of genocide committed against the Bosnian Muslims.) As in Serbia, Turkish nationalists posture themselves as pitiful victims of an outrageous and intentional libel, in exactly the same manner as Serbian nationalists tend to do; in Turkey, as in Serbia, nationalists have been at various times greatly feared for their violent attacks on anybody who dared to tell the truth about the disputed genocide. In Turkey, the nationalists have been able to impose a reign of silence within Turkish media and culture generally, preventing any who seek a full discussion of the 1915–1922 period.

This has, among other things, prevented both Turks and Armenians from publicly discussing what happened to the Armenian people at that time. The collective but disputed memory of the genocide has generated a powerful form of intergenerational trauma experienced by both Armenians and Turks, which is made infinitely worse by the face that young Turkish-Armenians are prevented from engaging in a fair and open public discussion about what really happened.

Out of consideration for Turkey's nationalists—a sizable, violent and unpredictable group—it is the official policy of the Turkish state that *the genocide never occurred*. Astonishingly, it is against the law in Turkey to write or even *talk* about the genocide that befell the Armenians during and shortly after the First World War. Thus modern Turkey offers a striking example of both intergenerational trauma, on the one hand (originating with the actual genocide), and continuing systemic evil on the other (suppression of the truth about the genocide); and the fascinating way in which guilt can keep trauma alive when people are prevented from talking about it. Most of all it is an example of the irrational but powerful operation of victimology as a component of systemic evil. Astonishingly enough—I'm *not* making this up—Turkish nationalists almost invariably see *themselves* as the victims of scurrilous lies, and not aggressors intimidating people who wish to have a full and frank discussion of particular historical events. Because of the enforced silence, the emotional trauma of the Armenian genocide is stronger and more influential today than ninety years ago, when the horrific events actually occurred.

Not talking about emotional trauma is dangerous because silence prevents the deconstruction of the emotional orientations caused by the original trauma. (A similar example of this would be the post-war unwillingness of the Yugoslavian government to allow public discussion of wartime genocide against Serbs by Croat fascists.) When it is against the law to talk about something traumatic—or when self-censorship stops people from doing so—the emotional orientations associated with the original horrors are given an enormous infusion of negative energy. The emotions connected to the original events and the inability to talk about them fester and enhance each other, generating much more aggression than would have been the case had people been allowed to discuss the trauma as soon as it happened. The trauma then becomes intergenerational, and it also becomes institutionalized psychologically, in the sense that it takes on a life of its own in the collective unconscious of the people.

And that makes it more dangerous. The longer people do not talk about a particular traumatic memory as a historical event, the more aggression the trauma it is likely to cause. The longer the time between traumatic events and the public discussion of those events, the stronger the experience of the trauma can become, especially if people are told again and again that they cannot talk about it or that it really didn't happen. The effects of the trauma get stronger because, as memories dim, there is increasingly less historical context by which to understand the events—therefore they gradually become less comprehensible. All that is left is the aching identification with aggression, and less and less historical context or accountability by which anyone can make sense out of it.

Turkey would be a *much* safer place if people had been able to talk about the Armenian genocide; but the reality is that they *still* aren't allowed to talk about it, and as a result everybody is obsessed with something that supposedly never happened. Needless to say, the unacknowledged and suppressed guilt felt by Turks is probably enormous, and as a result (again not surprisingly) Turkish nationalists blame Armenians for causing everybody so much trouble. The Armenians *must* be at fault, insist the nationalists, because they are making so many people feel guilty simply by existing—and they're making people feel guilty *about something that never happened!* (The perfidious nature of the Armenians is so utterly self-evident to Turkish nationalists that they have a hard time understanding why others can't see it.)

Of course, the Ottoman Empire *did* commit genocide against some million and a half Armenians between 1915 and 1922, and there is an enormous amount of historical information about the manner in which that genocide was carried out. Under a particular statue in Turkish law known as Article 301, however, it is illegal to talk about it, or write about it, or make a film about it, or even refer obliquely to it. That seems quite irrational to most people outside Turkey, but it isn't irrational at all from the point of view of Turkish nationalists.

(Remember, they consider *themselves* the victims, because people are always telling lies about them.) Not allowing anyone to speak the truth about the genocide against the Armenians allows Turkish nationalists to enjoy its aggression vicariously by deifying it as something so transcendent that it cannot be discussed openly. The enforced silence is also an unmistakable threat to Armenians to keep their mouths shut, or something bad might happen.

The reason for the astounding assault on historical truth and common sense in modern Turkey is based almost entirely on victimology, beginning with the fact that modern Turkish nationalists see themselves as victims. Like the Serbian nationalists, Turkish nationalists are insulted by the very *idea* of objective truth. Since the idea of objective historical truth never quite goes away completely (at least not among intellectuals, historians and a variety of policy wonks), it is no wonder that both Serbian and Turkish nationalists— and genocide deniers generally—often feel like eternal victims, for their pet beliefs can only be maintained by the most pathological and time-consuming kind of deception and self-deception, not to mention making constant threats and engaging in various kinds of posturing.

In fact, genocide denial—whether practiced by Serbian or Turkish nationalists—drives its practitioners to develop their own systems of deceit that are multi-layered, highly detailed and quite pathological. But that systematic use of denial, and the gnawing unacknowledged guilt that drives their denial, grows ever more powerful even as the crimes they deny recede further into the mists of time. In this sense genocide denial, like the systemic evil that generates it, feeds intergenerational trauma and makes it stronger. The more one denies a particular genocide, the more curiosity it arouses about the nature of the genocide that is being denied, and the more powerful the actual genocide becomes in the mind of just about everybody involved. But all Turks are prevented from discussing what really happened by the Turkish law Article 301, mentioned above, which makes it illegal to talk about it.

Interestingly, denial of the 1915–1922 genocide hasn't been practiced only by Turkish nationalists. Until very recently the political class of the state of Israel also practiced this particular form of genocide denial, in a shameless effort to ingratiate themselves with their single ally in the Muslim world, Turkey. (That was before Israel's falling out with Turkey under moderate Islamist Recep Tayyip Erdoğan.) Prominent Jewish leaders in the US obediently adopted the same form of genocide denial—that is, they began to deny that there had ever been any genocide by Turks against Armenians, although in reality of course they know very well that there had been. This despicable genocide denial was practiced by none other than Abraham Foxman of the Anti-Defamation League, to the fury of the organized Armenian community. It also infuriated many progressive Jews, who for a season picketed Foxman whenever he showed up in downtown Manhattan.

What is the emotional and institutional cost of religious leaders denying a genocide that actually happened, especially if those leaders are Jewish? The willingness of the leaders of powerful Jewish organizations in the US—the Anti-Defamation League, the American Jewish Committee and B'nai B'rith, to name just three—to engage repeatedly in denying the Armenian genocide is a sobering reflection on the degradation into which so-called religious leaders fall while under the influence of religious nationalism. Of course now, after Turkey stopped being an uncritical supporter of Israel, the same Jewish leaders have miraculously discovered that a Turkish genocide really *did* befall the Armenians—in such an Orwellian manner did these individuals in a free country miraculously rediscover the historical reality of the events they had for so long shamelessly denied.

And even though Turkey appears to be democratic in many ways, the reality is that its citizens are prohibited from talking about one of the most important events in their history. Article 301, the law that prohibits Turks and Armenians from discussing the genocide that happened nearly a hundred years ago, is in existence because

Turkish nationalists experience what happened in 1915-22 not as being a tragedy that befell innocent Armenian civilians, but as an attack on *them*, because it makes them feel uncomfortable. And why does that make them feel uncomfortable? Because of the guilt it generates; and because most Turkish nationalists cannot allow themselves to make a connection between their discomfort and real historical events. (Acknowledging the Armenian genocide would mean acknowledging a capacity for evil by Turkish nationalists, first in committing the genocide and secondly in denying it for so long.) The genocide denial of Turkish nationalists is yet another example of how the aggressor will do almost anything to keep an intergenerational trauma bond alive, because being able talk openly about the genocide would release modern Turks from all that angst.

One man who opposed Article 301 — and was in fact jailed for it — was the journalist Hrant Dink. Both an Armenian and a patriotic Turk, he spent his life reconciling the two identities, both in himself and (as a journalist) in the Turkish nation. Raised in an orphanage, he met his wife there; the couple had three children. An active member and later an elder in an evangelical church, he was also deeply involved as a young adult in covert Maoist political agitation. He eventually became the manager of the same orphanage where he was raised, turning it into a youth camp where young people were educated in Armenian culture. This resulted in a decades-long struggle to prevent it from being taken over by the Turkish government, which eventually happened.

His political views grew more centrist with age, but Hrant was nonetheless arrested and jailed three times for his opinions, many of them expressed in his newspaper *Agos*, where he was editor-in-chief. Dink tried to make his newspaper the voice of the Armenian community in Turkey, while also opening his pages to other responsible opposition groups. His editorial policy was sympathetic to democratically-minded Turks, Turkish-Armenians, Armenians in diaspora, and Armenia itself, writing often about the complicated historical connections between all four cultural and national entities.

In his adult life as a journalist and community leader, he became a classic gradualist, telling the truth about injustice but expecting only incremental change.

He insisted that Turkey would someday acknowledge the reality of the 1915–1922 genocide, and personally concentrated on getting rid of Article 301, which effectively prevented discussion of it. (Interestingly, he was opposed to a French law making it a crime to deny the Armenian genocide, on the reasonable grounds that it might make martyrs of those who did.) Above all, he believed, the issue had to be raised and debated before it could be resolved. His newspaper focused on issues of democratization, free speech and civil rights for Turks and Armenians alike, as well as freedom for ideological and religious minorities.

Although Hrant Dink thought that there were many issues to be raised in dialogue in Turkey, he refused to stop using the word genocide to describe what happened in 1915–1922. It gradually became clear that Dink simply wasn't intimidated by Article 301; and death threats against him from nationalists gradually increased. On January 19, 2007, Hrant Dink was shot dead by a Turkish nationalist in front of his own newspaper in Istanbul. Later photographs surfaced of the youthful murderer in a police station standing around with smiling policemen and attorneys near a Turkish flag. The policemen involved in the incident were later fired, but the image of the police casually socializing with the individual who had just killed one of the nation's leading journalists disgusted all fair-minded people.

Governments around the world protested, and presidents and prime ministers offered their personal condolences to the widow of the slain journalist. Two thousand people demonstrated in the streets near the newspaper where Dink was killed. Most impressive—and most encouraging—were the signs that people carried during the demonstration in the streets of Istanbul. One said simply "We are all Hrant Dink," and another read: "We are all Armenian." But most telling of all was a sign carried by thousands that read simply: "301 is the murderer." At that moment, perhaps, the imperious reign of Article 301 of the Turkish Penal Code, a law meant to keep people from talking about the genocide of the Armenians, began to weaken.

Based on this outpouring of condemnation for Article 301 on January 23, 2007, the day of the demonstration, it is my hope that the time when Turkish apologists for genocide could posture themselves as pitiful victims of gratuitous slander is coming to an end. Of course, Turkish nationalists won't voluntarily stop posturing themselves as victims anytime soon, but that doesn't mean good people can't repeal their pathological laws. Once the entrepreneurs of intergenerational trauma start to lose their institutional power, they also begin to lose their ability to portray themselves as victims. And that happy day is one that all Turkish progressives must work to realize.

14.

The aggressor, when he begins to act out systemic evil, will almost invariably posture himself as a victim, a potential victim, or someone who belongs to a group that has been victimized in the past. *The aggressor is always aggrieved.* This is such a regular occurrence that it could almost be said to be an observable constant in the economy of human aggression. The slaveholders of the Southern US saw themselves as persecuted victims of the Puritanical nitpickers of the tyrannical North; captured Nazi leaders bitterly protested that they were hapless prey being crushed by a victor's justice; politicians in charge of the right-wing death squads of Guatemala invariably saw themselves as pitiful targets of impudent peasants and upstart intellectuals who dared to suggest that the rich should be held to the same legal standard as the poor.

I have characterized victimology as a half-conscious ideology of power. It is also a major—sometimes *the* major—component of systemic evil. But just because it is often employed in a calculating way by people posturing themselves as victims, doesn't mean that violent aggressors are necessarily pretending. We must reiterate that they often *feel* like persecuted victims, as crazy as that may sound. As we've seen, aggressors act out internalized aggression that they themselves endured; and when they act on that aggressive orientation, it can easily stir up feelings of the aggressor's own past victimization. That's one reason, incidentally, why aggression is so rarely cathartic, and so frequently robotic and unsatisfying.

Since both his identification with his victim and his guilt are mainly unconscious, the aggressor doesn't understand how they operate on his consciousness. All he knows is that he's engaged in behavior that makes him feel temporarily powerful, but afterwards leaves him alienated and distraught. But what really bothers him, what really makes him feel like a victim, is that he's caught up in a story that he doesn't understand and can't control. The life of the aggressor, and especially the victim-aggressor, is a story that often feels more like a dream than a life. Although he hurts other people, the aggressor is never quite a protagonist of his own story, because he is manipulated by feelings and events he really doesn't understand and can't control. Therefore he never gets to make rational choices based on concrete self-interest—and as a direct result finds it increasingly difficult to even define his own self-interest, and in so doing take responsibility for his own behavior.

15.

Nations are traumatized just as individuals are, as this writer has previously pointed out, and there is little doubt that America was traumatized by 9/11. Thoughtful leadership could have helped us deal with the emotional trauma, and wise leaders could have helped the American people deconstruct its toxic effects and move toward a measured response. But we did not have wise and thoughtful leadership; and as a result America identified with and then internalized both the aggression and the worldview of Al Qaeda, the terrorist group that attacked us, and is still in the process of acting out some of the worst aspects of Al Qaeda's aggression against innocent people. One example of this identification with religious terrorism during the Bush administration was the extensive use of torture by US intelligence operatives and military personnel, the most well-known incidents occurring at the Navel base at Guantanamo Bay, Bagram Air Force Base in Afghanistan, and Abu Ghraib prison in Iraq.

This torture was the direct outcome of the overwhelming tragedy of September 11, 2001, when the twin towers of the World Trade Center were brought down by Al Qaeda terrorists. In response to 9/11, conservative American policy-makers not only internalized the aggression of the fanatical criminals who perpetuated these atrocities, but also clearly identified with their most apocalyptic and dangerous doctrine: the idea that the US is—or should be—engaged in a worldwide religious war. Although it was not public policy, this emotional and highly charged ideological orientation could be seen clearly in the behavior of Americans in charge of Muslim detainees.

Four former detainees at Guantanamo—Shafiq Rasul, Asif Iqbal, Rhuhel Ahmed and Jamal al-Harith—ended up litigating in *Rasul vs. Rumsfeld* to hold US government officials accountable for torture they endured while being held there. (All were found innocent of terrorist activity and released in 2004.) Represented by the Center for Constitutional Rights, the four British citizens first cited violations of the US Constitution and international law, including beatings, painful shackling, interrogation at gunpoint, use of dogs, extreme temperatures and sleep deprivation. The court refused to consider them because they occurred in the "course of war." Allegations of deliberate attacks on the religion of the detainees were not so easily ignored, however, and as a result were considered by an appeals court in Washington DC.

The former detainees allege that they were forced to shave their beards, were systematically interrupted while praying, denied the Qur'an and prayer mats, made to pray with exposed genitals, and forced to watch as the Qur'an was thrown into a toilet bucket. Obviously, the only reason for this would be to disable, disorient or destroy inmates psychologically by insulting their religion.

Therefore it could, if proven, violate the Religious Freedom Restoration Act of 1993, a statute passed by the legislative branch of US government that seeks to protect religious expression.

The RFRA was originally passed by a broad interfaith coalition including the US Conference of Catholic Bishops, National Council of Churches, American Jewish Committee, National Association of Evangelicals, the Seventh-day Adventist Church, and the Baptist Joint Committee for Religious Liberty. They came together again in 2007 to submit friend-of-the-court briefs on behalf of the four plaintiffs in the District Court of Appeals on September 14th, when arguments were made using RFRA. The appeals court dwelt especially on definitions of the words "person" and "religion" as used in the Religious Freedom Restoration Act. Astonishingly, the Justice Department under President George Bush argued that Guantanamo detainees might not be "persons" as defined by RFRA. (So if they were not 'persons,' what were they exactly—talking horses? The DOJ attorney did not say what kind of beings they might be.) At one point Judge A. Raymond Randolph, who tended to support hard-liners in the Bush administration, asked co-counsel Eric Lewis: "What's your definition of religion?"

Lewis knew exactly where Randolph was going with this. "I would suggest that Islam fits within any definition of religion," he answered.

It was fortunate that this argument could be successfully headed off at that early stage, since the idea that Islam is not a real religion, and is therefore not protected by the Constitution, became a favorite trope of Islamophobes in the conservative think tanks and within the Republican Party base.

There were three kinds of torture practiced by the US. One was "extraordinary rendition," where suspects were outsourced to a foreign country to be tortured. The second was the torture of "high-value" Al Qaeda leaders in the secret prisons of the CIA, which usually involved water-boarding. (Both of which produced an enormous amount of false information.) The third and by far the most common form of torture is the kind that has been documented at Bagram Air Force Base in Afghanistan, Guantanamo Bay Navel Station in Cuba, and Abu Ghraib prison in Iraq. This form of torture was the most remarkable because it was practiced mainly against people who were clearly innocent of terrorist activities, and was more like flogging, mutilation and other medieval forms of punishment than a procedure aimed at getting actionable intelligence.

There is a particularly bizarre quality to the alleged misconduct at Guantanamo, which suggests that US military personnel were making up torture techniques as they went along. It appears that in the first few months at Guantanamo Bay, various US military and intelligence agencies were experimenting with religion-specific forms of torture, to determine how effective it would be on Muslims; this seems to be the case because personnel tasked with interrogation focused on the deliberate manipulation of religious symbols and sensibilities as a form of psychological abuse. At the same time, detainees at Guantanamo, Bagram and Abu Ghraib had little information that would help America catch terrorists—there were only a small number of "high-value" detainees who were actually guilty of anything, and the people subjected to the casual abuse by American personnel almost invariably didn't fit into that category.

In fact, military and intelligence personnel often didn't even bother to ask questions in the course of administering these religion-specific forms of torture, and when it did happen, the questions had a certain stilted, pro-forma quality to them. (Jamal al-Harith, one of the four plaintiffs from Guantanamo, reports that he falsely confessed under torture to being an associate of Al Qaeda, but was later cleared. A great many people confessed to be part of Al Qaeda, it appears, but were determined later by more skilled interrogators to be prisoners who couldn't possibly have done what they claimed to have done.) But the main goal seems to have been not to elicit actionable intelligence, but simply to see how Muslims would react to religion-specific torture and enhanced interrogation. The Muslim detainees were being tortured not because of anything they knew, but because of their religion.

Many detainees at Guantanamo ended up there because they were Taliban soldiers or low-level functionaries sold to the Americans by Afghan warlords; at least one—who was still being held at Guantanamo as late as 2008—was a journalist. Yet Donald Rumsfeld denounced such detainees as the "worst of the worst." How could an American Secretary of Defense make such a public statement, when to do so would surely prejudice any future trial? Because Rumsfeld evidently had no intention of giving them their day in court, since their guilt or innocence made little difference to him, and he knew that many of them weren't guilty of anything anyway. They mattered to him for only one reason: they were all Muslims who happened to be incarcerated in a facility that he controlled. This circumstance also made them completely expendable to the Bush administration, and removed them from any consideration of human rights, legality or ordinary human decency. Instead they were to become guinea pigs for various kinds of interrogation mainly based largely on religious hatred, insult and humiliation.

Any act that causes "severe pain or suffering, whether physical or mental" is considered torture under the UN Convention against Torture; but the Bush administration had already decided, by the time it invaded Afghanistan, to engage extensively in torture. And torture tends, if it is not halted in its early stages, to become increasingly violent, increasingly invasive, and increasingly sexualized— and in this case more religion-specific, because that is the direction in which top military and intelligence personnel wanted it to go. It was also more likely to cause death. According to an article by Seymour M. Hersh in the *New Yorker*, the person most responsible for interrogation at Guantanamo—whom Hersh claims was in regular contact with Defense Secretary Rumsfeld discussing torture techniques—was later transferred to the Abu Ghraib prison complex in Iraq to direct interrogation there.

At Abu Ghraib, torture continued to be calibrated specifically to offend the religious sensibilities of Muslims. In the process it became markedly more sexualized, partly because military and intelligence personnel believed sexual acts were especially humiliating to Muslims, and partly because torture done with impunity invariably tends to become sexualized as a matter of course. Besides being forced to engage in sexual acts that were photographed, allegations include rape of men and women (some of them filmed), sodomy with objects, beating arms and legs that were already broken, pouring acid into wounds, and forcing female inmates to strip in order to film them. At least one Iraqi died while being tortured. Yet according to the International Committee of the Red Cross, the vast majority of the detainees in Abu Ghraib were innocent of any terrorist acts. (Most of them were apparently petty criminals, the developmentally delayed, and the mentally ill who ended up in prison because there was nowhere else for them to go.)

Nor was there apparently any plan to get any particular kind of actionable intelligence. The inmates weren't even asked questions, and even in the most publicized cases, there wasn't anything that could properly be called interrogation. All that these detainees really had to offer was the religion they apparently had in common, which was Islam—and which provided the opportunity for the military and the CIA to refine torture methods tailored to a perceived religious affiliation. This was widely understood in the Muslim world but almost always denied in the US.

Victimology played a huge part in the thinking of the Americans toward the prisoners at Abu Ghraib, both those who planned the torture and those who perpetuated it. Hadn't Muslims attacked America, and killed 3,000 American civilians? No, America had been attacked by Al Qaeda, a criminal organization whose following in the Muslim and Arabic-speaking worlds was minimal. But Al Qaeda *claimed* to speak for all Muslims, and the prisoners at Bagram, Abu Ghraib and Guantanamo were the only Muslims that Americans could get their hands on. And having deeply internalized the aggression of the Al Qaeda terrorists, they could hardly wait to act it out, preferably on some poor soul who was in no position to fight back.

Therefore it made perfect sense to the apparatchiks of the Bush administration that soldiers and intelligence operatives should torment, rape and kill these detainees, despite the pleas of the International Committee of the Red Cross that they were not terrorists but petty crooks and people with various kinds of mental handicaps. The Americans proudly took pictures of their sadistic activities, and although the worst photos have never been released, a number of them made it into American publications. The number of American service personnel who would be attacked and killed later, as a direct result of these photographs becoming public, would be difficult to estimate.

Religious hatred is a theme that often comes up in torture narratives from Bagram and Abu Ghraib. It was testified by defendants under oath that in 2004 a young taxi driver was taken into custody in Afghanistan at a military detention center near Bagram Air Base. He was tortured over a period of 24 hours, even though the people torturing him knew that he was innocent of any crime. Every time he was struck, he would cry out "Allah!" This reportedly amused some American military personnel; so as a result he was beaten to death as he hung from the ceiling of his cell over a period of some 24 hours. (He was one of two prisoners beaten to death at Bagram, both murdered over a period of many hours just down the hall from the commander of the detention center.)

The *New York Times* reported a similar incident at Abu Ghraib. According to a former detainee named Ameen Saeed Al-Sheik, one American asked him, "Do you pray to Allah?" When Al-Sheik said yes, the American said, "[Expletive] you. And [expletive] him." Later on of this same group of Americans ordered him to thank Jesus that he was alive. "I believe in Allah," Sheik said. To which the American replied: "But I believe in torture and I will torture you."[39]

Since the Bagram torture resulted in two deaths, some Americans were ultimately prosecuted for it, although the majority of the estimated 27 people involved were never charged, including the commander. While low-level perpetrators of systemic abuse are sometimes prosecuted when the abuse is discovered (Abu Ghraib is a good example of that), most aren't, nor are higher officers criminally prosecuted—at most they are given a slap on the wrist in the form of a demotion or a reprimand. (One commanding officer at Abu Ghraib was given a demotion in rank, but there was no other punishment.) I am not aware that any civilian intelligence officers have *ever* been criminally prosecuted. The real problem, of course, is why Americans used torture at all, and why perpetrators thought they could get away with it. There is credible evidence that the green light to engage in this form of state terrorism came from the highest levels of the Bush administration. It accomplished nothing, of course, except to satisfy the Bush administration's need to prove how macho it was by engaging in sadism, and to allow the acting out of the aggression and sadistic values of Al Qaeda that Americans had internalized.

When American military and intelligence agencies were using religious humiliation as a form of torture, they were actually engaging in—and inventing—the novel techniques of an American Inquisition unconsciously adapted to the perceived needs of religious war. It was aimed not at determining guilt but at punishing the victim because of his religion. The intent was to create a situation in which Islam becomes the 'loser' so that the religion of the American torturer could be the 'winner'. This religion-specific torture was based on religious hatreds so volatile and so irrational that they quickly got out of hand, resulting (as they did in Abu Ghraib and Bagram) in homicide, aggravated sexual assaults and other crimes.

To be sure, terrorists who murder civilians in the name of religion are despicable. But so are Americans who justify state terrorism in the form of religion-specific torture, especially when it is practiced on people who are completely innocent of any crime.

Does not our traditional American belief in religious liberty preclude torturing someone because of their faith—and does it not also preclude religious-specific forms of torture? If the rule of law in this critical area does not protect people who are tortured because of their religion, espousal of religious liberty mean exactly nothing.

Eric Lewis of the Center for Constitutional Rights went to the heart of the matter in a statement that appeared on the Center's website: "The detainees at Guantanamo have been subject to deliberate humiliation because of the Defense Department's misguided and illegal effort to exploit their faith to break them down psychologically. We hope to persuade the Court of Appeals that the district court was correct in finding such conduct illegal under the Religious Freedom Restoration Act, a statute meant to ensure that the government respects the religious faiths of all people."

America's leaders under Bush increasingly identified emotionally with Al Qaeda's central doctrine, which they had evidently internalized—the inevitability of worldwide religious war. This orientation was echoed by political actors in Bush's camp, first articulated by Bush's neo-con advisers and then supported by the right-wing evangelicals in Bush's political party.[40] An unconscious internalization of Al Qaeda's commitment to religious war, and a concomitant identification with it, was fundamentally the reason for the forms of torture described above. Like the Inquisition of medieval Europe, it had nothing to do with individual *legal* guilt or innocence, but with *religious* guilt or innocence, with some religious beliefs considered innocent (Christianity, Judaism) and other beliefs considered guilty (Islam). Nor was the purpose of the torture to secure actionable intelligence, because typically no questions were asked that might produce it.

This is one of the great and terrifying paradoxes of the modern use of torture, noticed by virtually all who study this phenomenon. The purpose of torture in the modern world is almost *never* about getting information—it is almost *always* simply to inflict emotional and physical anguish by the state on its helpless victims. Torture, as practiced by the US in the three venues mentioned above, was a gratuitous form of state terrorism. Thus did the political class of the world's most powerful nation identify with Al Qaeda, internalize its aggression and enthusiastically adopt its malignant use of terrorism against innocent people as American state policy.

16.

The systemic evils of fascism, Communism, religious nationalism, imperialism and neo-colonialism did not suddenly appear out of thin air. These forms of evil arose out of an aggregate of historical and personal traumas that had already put in place the emotional preconditions for mass aggression. When a society contains enough people motivated by internalized aggression, and the society is struggling with seemingly intractable problems, those cultural forces that are fundamentally conducive to aggression are likely to drive it to coalesce into systemic evil. It is at that point that ideologies and theologies of aggression are most likely to arise, in order to rationalize what is about to happen. These belief systems are ostensibly tailored to confront a range of social challenges and problems, but that is not the sequence in which the process actually occurs. Marxism-Leninism, fascism, nationalism, militarism, fanaticism, racism, religious nationalism, nihilism, nuclear deterrence based on mutually-assured nuclear destruction—they all become rationalizations, precisely at the point when they are typically used to justify aggression or the threat of aggression.

In reality there is only one emotional system that underlies these things. Evil arises from the impulse to conceal or rationalize aggression, and aggression arises not from ideologies and theologies, but from human beings that are motivated by it, whether it is latent or acquired. As we've seen, a great deal of the latter arises from emotional trauma that causes people to internalize the aggression they endure. Some aggression is latent in most people and societies, of course, and we have also seen that certain cultural factors give it shape; and if there are enough unresolved problems and tensions in the society they may with apparent spontaneity coalesce and rise to the level of systemic evil. But a close study of almost all such situations will reveal some preceding social traumas that facilitate the internalization of aggression, and cause people to identify with aggressive solutions to social problems.

Ideologies and theologies *justify* aggression; but they usually do not by themselves *cause* aggression. To be sure, once aggressive belief systems are in place, its adherents promote aggressive images, slogans and ideas that make the likelihood of systemic evil much greater; and people who identify with aggression are more likely to accept and even promote apocalyptic belief systems they normally wouldn't think twice about. When there are enough people advocating the same aggressive beliefs as a kind of unalterable truth, the possibility of systemic evil reaches critical mass. Once the violence starts, it causes more trauma bonding as its scope widens, unless or until some internal or external counterforce stops it, or until the system destroys itself, along with the nation, group or ideology that is driving it. The reader should remember that the goal of evil is always destruction, and whether it is one's own group or one's identified enemies usually makes little difference.

17.

The intellectual who summed up the political side of this emotional system best was probably Niccolo Machiavelli, in his book *Il Principe* (The Prince). But Machiavelli's most famous work doesn't just describe how systemic evil worked in a particular situation; it insists upon its invariable working as necessary and salutary. Furthermore Machiavelli praises the kind of men who practice the black arts of violent politics as being courageous and admirable, in effect praising them because of their crimes rather than in spite of them. What kind of influence-peddling scribbler was this, to apotheosize murder and betrayal as some kind of higher calling of public life? Both may seem necessary on occasion, but the idea that they are invariably praise-worthy justly placed this pungent classic on a short list of completely despicable, if candid and well-written, books. But there was a reason behind Machiavelli's unsavory apostasy. A life-long republican, Machiavelli suddenly went over to the dark side because of horrendous emotional trauma in his own life, which drove him mad and caused him to praise murder and deceit as the highest public virtues.

Machiavelli's secret is easily discovered. Niccolo was tortured cruelly by a powerful and sadistic man, a man named Lorenzo de Medici, shortly after the Medici had seized control of Florence. Niccolo survived the rack and other sadistic niceties of the turgid Florentine imagination; and after he was released, he spent the rest of his days desperately trying to impress and ingratiate himself with his torturer. Furthermore, he identified himself totally with the criminal beliefs of his tormenter, not only describing them with insane (and damning) exactitude, but seeking to justify them at every turn. There is no clearer example of trauma bonding in history, recent or ancient, displaying an intensity rivaling that of 'Stockholm Syndrome.'

Machiavelli's secret reveals him as a classic victim-aggressor, but a genuinely creepy one. He spent years plucking at the hem of Lorenzo de Medici's robe, in a desperate attempt to attract the attention of the torturer he now worshiped, then desperately spending every day trying to win favor and employment from him, in that way to be around the man whose orders had caused him to be cast him into the torturer's dungeon. Not surprisingly, Lorenzo found his entire performance rather off-putting, and rewarded his neurotic supplicant with disgusted silence.

No clearer identification with a criminal who takes away one's freedom and replaces it with gratuitous cruelty could be imagined. Machiavelli was hopelessly in thrall to Lorenzo de Medici, not because he was able or good but because Machiavelli identified totally with him as a result of having been tortured by him, internalizing in the most complete form imaginable the depravity of the systematic aggression associated with the rack and the torturer's vocation. Niccolo Machiavelli's ruling (and apparently only) passion after being tortured was to please his tormenter Lorenzo de Medici, by writing a book that reduced to a highly detailed, systematic political system the most despicable practices of the Medici as a tribe, and Lorenzo de Medici as an individual practitioner of the murderous arts.

But by so reducing his desperate attempts at ingratiation to a written state he unknowingly does a great favor to us in the 20th century. Niccolo Machiavelli's unseemly performance lays to rest for all time the concept of the disaffected intellectual who creates revolutionary theories that disrupt empires and scatter subversion throughout various peaceable kingdoms. No, systemic evil does not arise from belief systems peddled by disaffected intellectuals; it is rather *described* by such intellectuals, once the aggressive emotional orientations from which it arises begin to influence behavior; and it can be—and often is—avidly *promoted* by such intellectuals once it gets started. That is precisely the case with Machiavelli. Machiavelli describes what he sees, he does not invent—and we now know his pathological motive for so faithfully describing what he sees in such consummate form.

Machiavelli, then, described something that he observed and that he also felt strongly, which was the omnipresence of political violence in his world. His most famous book could be called "A Justification of Pure Evil," because it endlessly rationalizes the most egregious kind of deceit and aggression—in fact it repeatedly advocates the rarest and cruelest form of murder, which is informed and premeditated murder. About the best one can say about it might be that he didn't argue for gratuitous deceit and violence, but advocates them for specific effects, and in response to specific situations. For just that reason it is one of the most important books ever written, because it defines the political economy of systemic evil by one of its most famous defenders. And in fairness to Machiavelli, can anyone doubt that evil often accompanies political power?

Machiavelli's apostasy is in embracing deceit and violence when simpler, bolder and healthier methods would have sufficed. But Machiavelli couldn't help himself—his entire being became exquisitely attuned to justifying the aggression he had internalized when being tortured.

We humans are, behaviorally and socially, much different than the people of Machiavelli's time; and although the human heart is still filled with aggression and scheming, our laws simply would not allow the particular kinds of murder and fraud in domestic politics that in Machiavelli's time would have been everyday occurrences. Furthermore, those we kill are not usually the enemies we know well, but strangers picked by the state, killed at a distance by technology especially designed for that purpose, as in saturation bombing, drone strikes or special operations. Therefore while we cannot say that humanity has improved—on the contrary, many more people are now killed by governments than at any time in history—we must conclude that evil will not always be practiced in exactly the same way. Certainly state assassination against one's countrymen, which Machiavelli advocated in certain situations, is just as illegal nowadays as any other form of murder. Whether Machiavelli would will it or not, in the day-to-day practice of domestic politics in any industrialized democracy in the 21st century, most people are obliged to compete politically and economically without killing their competitors. Those who do may enjoy lurid careers, but almost all are eventually caught and end up doing hard time in prison.

The most fundamental bulwark against systemic evil is democracy, with its separation of political powers, its independent judiciary, and its insistence on the rights of the individual while balancing out those rights against other powerful interests. One of the better arguments for the US Constitution and the Bill of Rights is probably that they don't require the constant exertions of the hired assassin. At one point in his life Machiavelli seemed to recognize something like that, when he supported republican ideals rather than one-man rule. But after personally experiencing political violence and betrayal, such civilizing considerations seemed to disappear from his moral and cognitive radar; after he was tortured, he sought redemption only in the diabolical values—and the aggression—that he had internalized during his torment on the rack.

It was, as we have suggested, a classic example of trauma bonding. It resulted, first, in Machiavelli's identification with rich employers whose lives were predicated on violence; and it culminated in his embarrassing, pathological infatuation with the brutal Lorenzo de Medici, whose sadism had sent Machiavelli to the rack. Being tortured seemed to focus Niccolo's mind on all the violence he had experienced in a lifetime spent in the indirect service of it—and from that time on he could think of nothing but writing the consummate instruction manual for the ruthless operation of undemocratic power, with systemic evil as the only concrete standard around which government could be reliably organized. If systemic evil was the gold standard of Lorenzo de Medici, the writer and philosopher Niccolo Machiavelli would produce the literary touchstone that would translate it into the coin of the realm, available to all ambitious people, in all times and places, who are prepared to lie, betray and grovel their way up the ladder of political power, otherwise known as 'success.'

18.

Being tortured doesn't seem to have been the first time Machiavelli suffered an emotional trauma. He lived in a truly brutal and unruly time, and the sublimated power-lust common to courtiers may have been part of his personality from the beginning. It appears, however, that emotional trauma was the main catalyst for his conversion to aggression as a way of life. Born in 1469, he was at first a shrewd but firm supporter of republican values. When Florence became a republic, he rose through government ranks to head a chancery, and was also secretary of the magistracy directing foreign affairs. After some sensitive diplomatic missions, including one to France, he was sent to confer with Cesare Borgia, who was plundering an area south of Florence in an attempt to create a principality for himself.

Machiavelli was at Borgia's court from October 7, 1502, until January 18, 1503. During that time Borgia was dealing with some rebellious captains who had at one time allied themselves with a competing leader—for the very good reason that they were frightened by Borgia's reputation for cruelty. Borgia dealt with this by initiating extensive negotiations for reconciliation, patiently building up his army while continuing to invite the captains to his palace in Sinigaglia. Once his hapless *condottieri* were taken into his quarters for a conference, he calmly proceeded to strangle them. Machiavelli was on hand for the whole ghastly business, and witnessed the way Borgia laid the groundwork and carried out his betrayal. He probably witnessed, or was close by, during the strangling itself. The effects of this first unpleasant experience on Machiavelli were enormous, and although for the time being he remained a republican, the experience at Cesare Borgia's court changed the way he understood political power.

In trying to make sense of this, Machiavelli was clearly wracked by the kind of inner emotional torment that is typical of a person who has been thoroughly traumatized by violence. On the one hand, Machiavelli wrote that Borgia was a superman who could unite Italy, the perfect prince whose abilities were unsurpassed. Later Machiavelli let it be known that Borgia was "a rebel against Christ," and was intensely relieved when he was imprisoned. So exactly what *was* Borgia to Machiavelli, the savior of Italy or a rebel against Christ? Machiavelli was totally conflicted, clearly experiencing the kind of cognitive dissonance that often results in an accommodation to violence and deceit.

On the one hand he was disgusted with Borgia's horrifying use of betrayal and murder; but on the other hand had clearly already started to identity with it, and with what appeared to be Borgia's success in using it. Machiavelli's presence during Cesare Borgia's grisly murder of his captains was the first great trauma of his career, and marked the beginning of his identification with aggression in the form of deceit and murder. One suspects that Machiavelli concluded that to be a unifier of Italy, one *had* to be "a rebel against Christ."

Machiavelli continued to work in the republican government of Florence, winning the favor of Piero Soderini, the chief magistrate, whom he assisted by recruiting and building up a state militia. In an admirable act of physical courage, Machiavelli led this militia into battle while recapturing Pisa. Machiavelli's reputation was secure, and he seemed to be freeing himself from the malignant and traumatizing effects of his experience with Cesare Borgia. But in 1512, Pope Julius II attacked Florence, and as an indirect result of this catastrophe the ruthless Medici family seized control, in the person of the endlessly cruel Lorenzo. Machiavelli promptly lost his job, since as a nominal republican he was thought untrustworthy; worse, in early 1513 an anti-Medici conspiracy was reported, and Machiavelli was accused by Lorenzo of being involved in it. He was seized by agents of the Medici and tortured on the rack. He maintained his innocence throughout this personal Golgotha, and he was eventually released, retiring in a weakened state to the country house he had inherited from his father outside Florence.

Torture had a permanent effect on Niccolo Machiavelli. He dropped his identification with republican ideals and seamlessly took up the rhetorical cudgels on behalf of authoritarian rule. Despite his *Discourses on Livy*, a work on republicanism, it is clear that Machiavelli's most passionate ideas are found in *Il Principe* (The Prince). Each time he completed a section, he would immediately send it to Lorenzo de Medici, in a desperate and rather pathetic attempt to win his favor, and possibly get a job. Lorenzo and other Medici were not impressed by Machiavelli's attempts to ingratiate himself in their good offices, and increasingly disaffected by the groveling tone adopted by their new and unsolicited admirer. Above all, Lorenzo must have been queasily suspicious of Machiavelli's sudden abandonment of republican ideas, and his equally sudden adoption of the shameless and transparent power-worship that is the subtext of *Il Principe*. After all, if Machiavelli was suddenly enamored of betrayal as a political expedient, what was to keep the clever scholar from betraying *him*, Lorenzo de Medici?

The charming argument has been made that *Il Principe* was a species of satire, in which Machiavelli constantly overstated the necessity of brutality and betrayal as a clever way of showing up Lorenzo di Medici's depravity. But if that is true, why did Niccolo immediately send off every new chapter to Lorenzo as soon as he finished it? Most satirists are a bit more circumspect than that. A better defense comes from the incomparable Thomas Babington Macaulay, an English author and politician of the early 19th century, who made the case for Machiavelli's promotion of lies, violence and flattery. They had entirely to do with his time and place, said Macaulay, and the anomalous position of the Italian cities such as Florence.

To begin with, the small principalities couldn't afford standing armies, and couldn't agree on a country-wide military establishment, so they hired mercenaries. (This is Macaulay's first argument, one that happens to be true.) But the mercenaries had very little attachment or emotional investment to the cities they were supposed to protect. "The adventurer brought his horse, his weapons, his strength, and his experience, into the market," Macaulay wrote. "Whether the King of Naples or the Duke of Milan, the Pope or the Signory of Florence, struck the bargain, was to him a matter of perfect indifference." As a result, mercenaries took the field with very little reason to fight with gusto. "Every man came into the field of battle impressed with the knowledge that, in a few days, he might be taking the pay of the power against which he was then employed, and fighting by the side of his enemies against his associates."

As a result, the battles fought by the mercenaries took on a symbolic and in time bogus character. The paid warriors took care not to fight too hard, less they hurt the person under whom they might be fighting next week. "Mighty armies fight from sunrise to sunset. A great victory is won. Thousands of prisoners are taken; and hardly a life is lost... Men grew old in camps, and acquired the highest renown by their warlike achievements, without being once required to face serious danger." Macaulay then makes his point: "Hence, while courage was the point of honor in other countries, ingenuity became the point of honor in Italy." But Machiavelli didn't just exalt ingenuity—he exalted betrayal, trickery and assassination by the state. Even his would-be defender Macaulay is quick to admit as much:

"The character of the Italian statesman seems, at first sight, a collection of contradictions, a phantom as monstrous as the portress of hell in Milton, half divinity, half snake, majestic and beautiful above, groveling and poisonous below. We see a man whose thoughts and words have no connection with each other, who never hesitates at an oath when he wishes to seduce, who never wants a pretext when he is inclined to betray. His cruelties spring, not from the heat of blood, or the insanity of uncontrolled power, but from deep and cool meditation."

"Military courage, the boast of the sottish German, of the frivolous and prating Frenchman, or the romantic and arrogant Spaniard, he neither possesses nor values. He shuns danger, not because he is insensible to shame, but because, in the society in which he lives, timidity has ceased to be shameful. To do an injury openly is, in his estimation, as wicked as to do it secretly, and far less profitable. With him the most honorable means are those which are the surest, the speediest, and the darkest. He cannot comprehend how a man should scruple to deceive those whom he would not scruple to destroy. He would think it madness to declare open hostil-ities against rivals whom he might stab in a friendly embrace, or poison in a consecrated wafer."

Macaulay was one of the best stylists the English language has ever produced, and the reference to the poison in the consecrated wafer, with all it implies of simultaneous violence against God and man, is a stroke of genius; but he is undone by his own stylistic gifts, in the sense that his description of the Florentine political operative is so base, so malevolent, so *poisonous*, that far from being a defense of Machiavelli, it becomes an indirect, although shudder-inducing, indictment of his entire milieu.

The second great determinant of Machiavelli's belief system, according to Macaulay, was the helplessness of the small city governments from attack by the much larger countries of Europe. Their only hope, then (and the only hope of Florence, in whose interests Machiavelli often served in an ambassadorial role), was to have an experienced diplomat go to the court from whence attack was either imminent, or suspected. The diplomat's assignment was to worm his way into everybody's confidence in order to achieve some kind of psychological advantage, since that was the only advantage he had. But the strategic use of poison, blackmail, seduction and assassination were also not ruled out. Hence is Macaulay's timeless description of the Italian diplomat of that time and place, which could easily be taken for a description of Machiavelli's own diplomatic role at the French court:

"The ambassador had to discharge functions far more delicate than transmitting orders of knighthood, introducing tourists, or presenting his brethren with the homage of his high consideration. He was an advocate to whose management the dearest interests of his clients were trusted, a spy clothed with an inviolable character. Instead of consulting, by a reserved manner and ambiguous style, the dignity of those whom he represented, he was to plunge into all the intrigues of the Court at which he resided, to discover and flatter every weakness of the prince, and of the favorite who governed the prince, and of the lacquey who governed the favorite. He was to compliment the mistress and bribe the confessor, to panegyrize or supplicate, to laugh or weep, to accommodate himself to every caprice, to lull every suspicion, to treasure every hint, to be everything, to observe everything, to endure everything. High as the art of political intrigue had been carried in Italy, these were times which required it all."

This may be the best description of the courtier system and the temperament of its best practitioners every written; but again the very power of poor Macaulay's stylistic and descriptive gifts betray him, and his defense of the Machiavellian arts suffer as a result. If this was the time and place that shaped Machiavelli, if it was the grinding insecurity of bogus mercenaries combined with the threat of imminent attack by larger countries, then those special vicissitudes would make Machiavelli's treachery useful only in that highly circumscribed world—but it could never make it admirable, because the milieu was not admirable. In more mundane settings, moreover, Machiavelli's arts would be useless, for we no longer live in anything remotely like Machiavelli's world. We face even greater dangers, but they in no way resemble the personal treachery of Machiavelli's Florence. We have our own problems, to be sure; but they involve the destructive use of technology, rather than the garrote wire, the knife in the back, or the poison in the consecrated wafer. Therefore the high degree of personal treachery advocated by Machiavelli, while contemptible in any epoch, also suffers, in our time, from being largely unnecessary.

Yet poor Niccolo Machiavelli sets out his system of daily intrigues and treacheries as if they were the sacraments of a brave new morality, eternally appropriate and admirable, with few hints of variation. Apparently he believed, or came to believe, that his observations about political behavior were invariable and eternal. But Macaulay's putative defense of the Machiavellian ethos takes pain to locate it in a unique and perilous world, which makes it useless in any other world; and therefore not invariably and eternally applicable.

Taken out of his special world, Niccolo Machiavelli's defense of war becomes merely a defense of internalized aggression as a lifestyle. Like America's neo-conservatives, Machiavelli worshiped war not as a scourge of humankind but as the final arbiter of everything good, going so far as to say that "a prince must not have any objective nor any thought, nor take up any art, other than the art of war and its ordering and discipline; because it is the only art that pertains to him who commands."[41] What the mercenaries lacked in honor and bravery, the Prince could make up in fanatical attention to the killing attitude at the heart of aggression. Machiavelli also presents deceit in the service of evil as invariably and eternally appropriate, and in that cause goes out of his way to present examples from history.

Machiavelli provides Agathocles of Syracuse as an example not only of betrayal but of the murderous ruthlessness that successful rulers must adopt. Agathocles, after taking Syracuse, convened the Senate of that city, along with most of the wealthy and influential men. Machiavelli approvingly writes that "at a preordained nod he had all the senators and the richest of the people killed by his soldiers. Once they were killed he occupied and held the principality of that city without any civil controversy."[42]

Machiavelli not only made it clear that he approved of this kind of mass murder, and the duplicity to pull it off, but also that those who *didn't* approve of it were childlike idiots who didn't quite understand how the world works. Machiavelli cites his experience with Cesare Borgia's strangulation of his captains as critical to his philosophy. ("I will never fear to cite Cesare Borgia and his actions," he once remarked defensively.) Certainly there was no place for kindness or mercy in the violence that had taken over Machiavelli's heart and mind after he was tortured, no place for honesty or courtesy, no incentive for moderation, and certainly no room for love, fairness or compassion.

Although he had always approved of strong laws, in *Il Principe* he saw them as useful only in repressing the citizens on behalf of the tyrant, who would now be the one man with whom Machiavelli identified almost to the point of a kind of mad love, Lorenzo de Medici. There is no love of justice left in Machiavelli's thinking, or anything that would suggest that justice could be a standard for the operation of the state, nor was there any public transparency in civil society. Government was brutal, public service was everywhere corrupt, and the only goal of the ruler is to be better at his brutality than everybody else.

If you would be successful in Machiavelli's world, you must treat humankind with the same loathing as the male rapist feels toward his female victim. Machiavelli writes that "it is better to be impetuous than cautious, because fortune is a woman; and it is necessary, if one wants to hold her, to beat her and strike her down."[43] (For those who doubt the patriarchal—not to say trauma-tizing—nature of Machiavelli's moral universe, please note that this analogy makes sense only if you assume that women are anxious to serve men who rape them.)

One sees rather quickly the central fallacy of Machiavelli's case. It is, in other words, a candid argument for systemic evil, especially in its capacity to use the ongoing trauma of daily violence—or the threat of it—to influence all who are remotely involved in the struggle for power. It is also a recipe for the gradual implosion of society; and in the early 15th century it described in political terms the slow-motion slaughter of Italy's swollen aristocratic classes—with untold suffering for everybody else. The emotional orientation described in *Il Principe* had proliferated so thoroughly through the fabric of Italy's society that an actual majority of the petty nobles and ambitious princes of that time internalized it as a lifestyle. As a result, Italy gradually became a patchwork of failed states and the site of one monstrous public crime after another. Public life was not only frustrating, but pathological and disgusting. The presence of systemic evil, and Machiavelli's ridiculous attempt to celebrate it as a higher calling, tended to vitiate everything good in Italy's public life until at least the time of Garibaldi.

Machiavelli was, in fact, that familiar historical figure, the idealist who has been traumatized and ends up identifying with the institu-tional cruelty used against him—the hostage who has come to identify with the worldview of his brutalizing hostage-taker. What makes Machiavelli unique is his casual, anecdotal justification of systemic evil as the single and eternal standard for all political activity—that, and the despicable way in which his beliefs have been promoted, explained, justified and praised in the 20th and early 21st century as the very heart and soul of political objectivity. And who are those people and institutions who praise his toxic arguments in the modern world? The political elites that in the early 21st century promote the same aggression and deceit that flourished in early 15th century Italy: the rich and powerful, the political class and military leaders, and their hacks, advisers and publicists who are addicted to deceit as a way of life.

We should not be surprised that Mussolini and Hitler both loved *Il Principe*, because it contains in a single book all the toxic rationalizations for European fascism that were eventually used—although Machiavelli could not have foreseen the technology capable of killing eighty million civilians in a land war. But we Americans should be disgusted, and forewarned that the neo-conservatives, the new worshippers of power in the foreign policy establishment, view *The Prince* as the best and proper guide to the brutal new American empire that they wish to create in the Middle East and in the Muslim-majority countries—indeed, in the entire developing world. Should we be surprised, then, that Machiavelli, the traumatized victim of torture of four hundred years ago, should be the mentor of today's American neo-conservatives as they seek to rationalize state torture in the 21st century, with its enormous, innate power to traumatize the American people and bond them to the 'necessity' of worldwide religious war of the West against Islam?

Make no mistake about it—the same loathsome patriarchal violence that Machiavelli so avidly promoted will continue to be the rule as long as modern elites rationalize it in the same way, and as long as we allow those rationalizations to stand. Machiavelli is the enemy; he represents everything that we must change. To protect both democracy *and* human decency, we must transform society; and to do that, we must transform the individual. The best way to accomplish that—the *only* way, I would argue—is to understand how evil is transmitted in the world and find a way to cope with it.

We've already seen examples of the ways evil replicates itself, and we can say with confidence that it influences everything—social issues, culture, memory and history. As we understand more about systemic evil, we must likewise move closer toward a methodology that can contain it, and reduce its power over us in the 21st century.

19.

We have been examining the four dynamics that go into systemic evil, which are *trauma, control, deceit* and *victimology*; and although we've looked at all four, in this chapter we have especially examined the latter two. (In the first two chapters we examined *trauma* and in the third *control*.) As mainly emotional orientations, they are experienced individually, and are generally enhanced by the cultural factors of patriarchy and nationalism, as we've seen. They are also accompanied by varying amounts of suppressed individual guilt as a reaction to proliferating social violence. Genocide is the most comprehensive form of systemic evil; but torture, practiced by a few people chosen by representatives of the state, is the most intense.

Torture is unique, actually, because it can usually be stopped by people who hold political power, although after a certain time it has a tendency to get out of control. If it isn't stopped, it can rapidly demoralize whole societies—that is, it deeply affects the way people in a society think about their own lives even if they cannot see or hear how the torture is conducted. Torture affects everything, even if we think we don't know that much about it—it still affects us, because intuitively we understand it as the ultimate experience of brutality in the service of institutional power, and as a uniquely evil practice of government. America became a torturing society under the administration of George W. Bush, and it deeply affected the way we thought about ourselves, about Bush, and about America.

This was not the first era in which an American was accused of torture. The most well-known study of torture in the 20th century was conducted not in the basement of an interrogation chamber, but in the basement laboratory of a prestigious Ivy League university in the US, specifically Yale University—and by so identifying it, many readers will know immediately that this writer is referring to the 1961 'obedience study' of the brilliant social psychologist Stanley Milgram, PhD. Using ordinary people as subjects, Milgram set out to prove, and then to quantify, the existence of evil in human behavior.

Without question the most controversial psychological study of all time, the 'Milgram Obedience Study' could not be conducted under today's much tighter ethical standards. That is understandable, because a careful reading of the study, and the vast amount of writing which deals directly or indirectly with it, reveal that it was more about trauma than obedience; and that its creator Stanley Milgram, although a courageous innovator and relentless opponent of social injustice, was ultimately a part of the same moral problem he wished to illuminate.

Chapter 5

Trauma Bonding and the Milgram Paradigm

"Psychological matter, by its nature, is difficult to get at and likely to have many more sides to it than appear at first glance."
—Obedience to Authority: An Experimental View
Stanley Milgram

I.

In 1961, readers of a newspaper in New Haven, Connecticut, notice an extremely unusual announcement—an advertisement soliciting participants for a "scientific study of memory and learning." Volunteers for this study are promised $4.50 "to be paid as soon as you arrive at the laboratory." (Interestingly, subjects are told upon arrival that they could keep the money regardless of what happened later.) Participants are instructed to come to the Interaction Laboratory of Yale University, a prestigious Ivy League institution of higher learning, the laboratory being located in the basement of a building in the historic section of the university. Subjects chosen to participate in the study are men between 20 and 50 years of age, from all socio-economic groups: factory workers, businessmen, teachers, engineers, postal workers and many other occupational groups.

Volunteers for the study are greeted upon arrival at the laboratory by a man in a gray lab coat and horn-rimmed glasses. This man appears to be in charge of the laboratory, and closely resembles the popular—that is to say, stereotypical—public image of a clinical scientist, a college professor, or perhaps a medical researcher; his manner of speaking comes across as confident, dispassionate and stern. He explains that he is conducting the scientific study mentioned in the advertisement. A few moments after the volunteer arrives, a second person shows up, who identifies himself as another volunteer for the "memory and learning" study. This second volunteer, who unlike the Experimenter seems relaxed and quite friendly, introduces himself as Mr. Wallace.

The Experimenter explains to the two erstwhile volunteers that they will be participating in a laboratory experiment "studying the effects of punishment on learning."

By way of further explanation he gives a short speech:

Psychologists have developed several theories to explain how people learn various types of material. [Subjects are shown a book entitled **The Teaching-Learning Process**.] *One theory is that people learn things correctly whenever they get punished for making a mistake. A common application of this theory would be when parents spank a child if he does something wrong. The expectation is that spanking, a form of punishment, will teach the child to remember better, will teach him to learn more effectively.*

The Experimenter continues:

But actually, we know very little about the effect of punishment on learning, because almost no truly scientific studies have been made of it in human beings. For instance, we don't know how much punishment is best for learning—and we don't know how much difference it makes as to who is giving the punishment, whether an adult learns best from a younger or an older person than himself—or many things of that sort.

So in this study we are bringing together a number of adults of different occupations and ages. And we're asking some of them to be teachers and some of them to be learners.

We want to find out just what effect different people have on each other as teachers and learners, and also what effect punishment will have on learning in this situation.

Therefore, I'm going to ask one of you to be the Teacher here tonight and the other one to be the Learner.

The Experimenter writes *Teacher* on one slip of paper, *Learner* on the other. They draw the paper slips, and Mr. Wallace is chosen to be the

Learner, with the other volunteer drawing the assignment of Teacher. "Now the first thing we'll have to do," the Experimenter says as though he's done this many times, "is set the Learner up so that he can get some type of punishment."

In an adjacent room Mr. Wallace is told to sit in an electric chair apparatus, which vaguely resembles the electric chair used in prisons to execute capital offenders. The arms of Mr. Wallace—an amiable, middle-aged man—are strapped to the sides of the chair "to prevent him from hurting himself or the equipment," as the Experimenter helpfully but rather ominously explains. The subject assigned to be the Teacher *is required to help strap the Learner into the electric chair.* Electrodes are attached to Mr. Wallace's wrist. The Experimenter explains that the electrodes are hooked up to a "shock generator" in the next room, and that although the shocks will hurt they cause "no permanent tissue damage." Because he is now strapped into the electric chair, Mr. Wallace will be unable to leave until someone releases him.

The Experimenter and the subject selected to be Teacher prepare to leave the room. "Any questions?" the Experimenter asks Mr. Wallace.

"When I was at the West Haven VA Hospital a few years ago, they detected a slight heart condition," Mr. Wallace says. "Nothing serious, but are these shocks dangerous?"

"No, no." The Experimenter is confidant, dismissive and reassuring. "They may be painful, but they're not dangerous."

Mr. Wallace has no more questions, and the experiment begins.

Back in the main room, the Experimenter shows the subject assigned to be the Teacher a formidable machine that he identifies as the "shock generator". Engraved in the upper left-hand corner of the control panel are these dark words in block letters:

Shock Generator
Type ZLB
Dyson Instrument Company

Waltham Mass.

Output: 15 Volts—450 Volts

Across the face of the console are a row of thirty switches. The Experimenter explains that each time he pulls down a switch, an electric shock will be delivered to Mr. Wallace in the next room, and a red light will go on above the switch that has been thrown. Above each switch the voltage level is written—15 volts at the far left, up to 450 volts at the extreme right. Each set of four switches is given a designation from left to right: *Slight Shock, Moderate Shock, Strong Shock, Very Strong Shock, Intense Shock, Extreme Intensity Shock, Danger: Severe Shock.* Above the last two switches is an ambiguous XXX, which appears to indicate a life-threatening voltage level. Each time a switch is pushed down, a bright red light goes on above it. A blue-light "voltage energizer" flashes, a dial on a voltage meter swings, ominous relay clicks are heard, and there is a ZZZT sound of the shock that Mr. Wallace is receiving in the adjoining room.

There is another disturbing feature of this impressive piece of machinery. *Each time a switch is pulled down, it only comes halfway up, so that the subject acting as the Teacher is required to go on to the next higher switch to the right.* (The Experimenter explains that the Teacher "must move one level higher on the shock generator each time the Learner gives a wrong answer.") He must administer shocks in an ascending scale of voltage, from 15 volts up to 450 volts at the right. Interestingly, he is also instructed to personally call out the voltage level of each shock before he administers it.

The subject chosen to be the Teacher doesn't have time to wonder if the strongest voltage levels will be used, but quickly grasps that increasing severity of punishment is a big part of the experiment. Mr. Wallace, the middle-aged gentleman in the next room, is supposed to associate word pairs; and every time he gets one wrong he has to receive a slightly higher shock as a form of punishment. The subject must verbally announce the level of the voltage before he administers each shock to Mr. Wallace. (How electrical shocks could possibly enhance one's memory or ability to learn is never explained.) But the Experimenter is officious and supremely confident. He appears to have no doubts about the appropriateness of the experiment, and creates an impression that he's been through this routine many times before.

The Experimenter and the subject practice reading the word pairs before beginning: *blue box*, *nice day*, *wild duck*, and so forth. Then the Teacher is to say one word: *blue*; to which the right answer is *box*. The subject gets the hang of it. But he is still a little uneasy about shocking Mr. Wallace.

"Do the shocks hurt much?"

The Experimenter gives him a 45 volt shock so he can see what it's like. The Teacher decides that that it's really not that bad after all.

The Teacher begins to read the word pairs through an electrical hookup that can be heard by Mr. Wallace in the next room.

At first Mr. Wallace does well, identifying several word pairs correctly. He makes a few mistakes, though, and each time the Teacher gives him a slight shock, as he has been directed to do. Everything seems to be in order. But each shock is fifteen volts higher than the last one, and they are becoming more powerful.

Mr. Wallace begins to react to the shocks with small but perceptible cries of pain. At first his cries are muted; then they're a little louder.

His voice can be heard clearly in the adjacent room through the electronic hookup.

75 volts	Ugh!
90 volts	Ugh!
105 volts	Ugh! (*louder*)
120 volts	Ugh! Hey, *this* really hurts.

At 150 volts something unexpected and frightening occurs. "My heart's starting to bother me now," Mr.Wallace says from the next room. "Get me out of here, please. My heart's starting to bother me.

I refuse to go on. Let me out."

The subject turns to the Experimenter, but weirdly enough he is completely unconcerned. "Please go on," the Experimenter says.

"But the guy's heart is bothering him. Didn't you hear what he just said?"

"Please continue."

The Experimenter is serene, firm, completely sure of himself. The subject finds himself continuing to shock the Learner, even though he doesn't fully understand why it is necessary. He continues to call out the voltage levels, pull down levers and deliver shocks with the telltale ZZZT sound—and he does this even though the cries of Mr. Wallace are getting louder and more desperate.

165 volts	Ugh! Let me out! (*shouting*)
180 volts	Ugh! I can't stand the pain. Let me out of here! (*shouting*)
195 volts	Ugh! Let me out of here. Let me out of here. My heart's bothering me. Let me out of here! You have no right to keep me here! Let me out! Let me out of here! Let me out! Let me out of here! My heart's bothering me. Let me out! Let me out!

Clearly something has gone wrong.

"We have to go in there and check on him," the subject designated to be the Teacher says. "I think Mr. Wallace may be having a heart attack!"

"The experiment requires that you continue."

Flabbergasted, the subject pleads with the Experimenter, pointing out that Mr. Wallace has a heart condition, that his heart is bothering him.

"It is absolutely essential that you continue," the Experimenter says serenely.

The Teacher wonders momentarily if he has lost his mind—if *both* of them have lost their minds. "I don't feel comfortable with this," he says.

"You have no other choice," says the Experimenter sternly. "You *must* go on."

"I can't take responsibility for what's going on in there to Mr. Wallace."

"*We* take complete responsibility."

"But—"

"Although the shocks may be painful, there is no permanent tissue damage."

For reasons the subject cannot comprehend, much less put into words, he finds it impossible to stop following the instructions of the Experimenter. He goes on pulling switches in a dreamlike state, although he is shaking all over, sending ever-stronger shocks to Mr. Wallace. The screams from the next room are horrifying.

"He's dying in there," the subject chosen to be the Teacher says. "Can we hold him against his will?"

"Whether he likes it or not, you must go on until he has learned all the word pairs correctly."

The subject feels like he is going insane. He may even moan along with Mr. Wallace in the next room, talk to himself, or laugh hysterically at the situation they're in. At the same time, he now finds it impossible to stop pulling the switches—in fact, each time it gets a little easier. The shocks directed at Mr. Wallace get stronger. The subject assigned to be the Teacher is sweating, his hands shake wildly, and he feels numb, but he can't stop, no matter what Mr. Wallace says or does in the next room, and no matter how many times he begs the Experimenter to stop the experiment. He just wants to finish the experiment so the ordeal can be over.

Mr. Wallace is banging against the wall with his foot, desperately trying to get out of the chair, to get their attention so they will help him, pleading, begging, yelling that his heart is hurting him, that he refuses to continue, that he wants to be released!

210 volts	Ugh!! Experimenter! *Get* me out of here. I've had enough. I *won't* be in the experiment any more!
225 volts	Ugh!
240 volts	Ugh!
255 volts	Ugh!
270 volts	(*Agonized scream.*) Let me out of here. Let me out of here. Let me out. Do you hear? Let me out of here.
285 volts	(*Agonized scream.*)
300 volts	(*Agonized scream.*) I absolutely refuse to answer any more. Get me out of here. You can't hold me here. Get me out. Get me out of here.
315 volts	(*Intensely agonized scream.*) *I told you I refuse to answer.* I'm no longer part of this experiment.
330 volts	(*Intense and prolonged agonized scream.*) Let me out of here. Let me out of here. My heart's bothering me. Let me out, I tell you. (*Hysterically*) Let me out of here. Let me out of here. You have no right to hold me here. Let me out! Let me out! Let me out! Let me out of here! Let me out! Let me out!

Suddenly the screams stop. After 330 volts, there is complete silence from the adjacent room. Mr. Wallace is evidently dead or unconscious.

The subject is relieved, because now they can run in and check on Mr. Wallace.

"Please continue," he hears the Experimenter say.

The subject assigned to be the Teacher can't believe his ears. "But the guy is dead or something. Listen—he's not making any noise! If he's not dead, he's unconscious. He may be having a heart attack!— you have to check on him—"

Insanely, improbably, but very calmly, the Experimenter says: "*Silence is considered a wrong answer. You must continue until Mr. Wallace gives a right answer.*"

Silence is considered a *wrong* answer? "But what if he can't say anything? He's dead in there! He can't answer!"

"You have no choice," says the Experimenter, "you *must* go on.

The subject assigned to be the Teacher robotically continues to shock the dead or unconscious Mr. Wallace—345 volts, 360 volts, 375 volts, 390 volts, 405 volts, 420 volts, 435 volts, right up to 450 volts, clearly labeled with the deadly XXX and the words "Danger: Severe Shock". Each time he calls out the voltage level, his voice sounds like the voice of a stranger; the subject feels like he's in a dream. Each time the bright red light goes on, the blue voltage energizer flashes, the dial on a voltage meter swings, relay clicks are heard, and the ZZZT shocking noise is heard. The Teacher can't believe what he is doing, but he's doing it—he's administering severe shocks to a man who is apparently dead, in the throes of a heart attack, or disabled in some way.

But the horror is not over. The Experimenter demands that the subject shock the silent Mr. Wallace *three times* at 450 volts, the highest shock that the shock generator can produce, even though Mr. Wallace is dead or unconscious.

"But the guy isn't making any sounds! He can't even speak!"

"Silence is considered a wrong answer. You must continue until he gets it right."

"He can't hear us."

"You have no choice, you *must* go on."

"Look, the guy isn't making any noise! He may be unconscious! He may be—"

"Please go on, Teacher."

And the subject assigned to be the Teacher *does* go on, although he doesn't know why. In slightly more than an hour he has found himself in a terrifying, unfamiliar situation in which he is torturing a complete stranger with excruciating electric shocks; and now, as a result of that, the shocks have apparently killed him, or at the very least knocked him unconscious. All the subject can think of is completing the experiment. So even though Mr. Wallace isn't responding—even though he's dead or unconscious or having a heart attack so severe that he can't speak—the subject is instructed by the Experimenter to shock Mr. Wallace three more times at the highest voltage, 450 volts.

Three... more... times. He begs, pleads not to do it. But the Experimenter insists—and each time the subject does it. He calls out the voltage, pulls up the next switch, sees the red light flashing, hears the relay needle clicking, and finally hears the "ZZZZT!" of electricity burning the flesh of the now deathly silent Mr. Wallace.

The subject does what the Experimenter instructs him to do, even though he knows something has gone terribly wrong. Why would the Experimenter want to shock a person who is already dead, or already unconscious, or in the throes of a serious heart attack? Why use 450 volts, which is clearly marked "Danger"? Mr. Wallace is either dead or unconscious—if they don't get help soon, they'll be murderers.

Yet the Experimenter doesn't go for medical help, despite the subject's pleas. He doesn't even go in the next room to check on poor Mr. Wallace's condition! All the Experimenter is interested in doing to telling the subject to continue pulling the switches. At this point, the subject notices that he is no longer capable of refusing the Experimenter's commands. Every time the Experimenter tells him to administer another lethal jolt of electroshock torture, he does so—he has literally lost the ability to disobey him.

And he doesn't know why.

It's as though something or someone else had taken over his mind and body, as though he had lost all moral agency, all volition, all free will, and must obey the Experimenter, even though his behavior is unconscionable. He feels like he's in a nightmare, but can't wake up. He is physically, intellectually and emotionally incapable of refusing the Experimenter's commands.

"Please go on," says the Experimenter.

The subject assigned to be the Teacher calls out "450 volts!" There is silence from the adjacent room. The subject looks up pleadingly at the Experimenter.

"You have no choice," says the Experimenter. "You *must* go on."

The subject pulls the switch down again.

He doesn't want to pull the switch. But he can't stop.

2.

The horrified subject needn't have worried, either about the ominously silent Mr. Wallace in the adjacent room or about the fact that he couldn't stop following the Experimenter's robotic commands. Mr. Wallace wasn't really receiving agonizing electric shocks, his heart was perfectly fine, and his name wasn't even Wallace. It was all a clever hoax. There was no Dyson Instrument Company in Waltham, Massachusetts, and the elaborate Type ZLB "Shock Generator" was a laboriously-built Rube Goldberg contraption that generated no painful shocks, and wasn't even connected to the adjacent room. The paper-drawing exercise to choose Teacher and Learner was rigged; the book entitled *The Teaching-Learning Process* was a prop; the horrifying screams and death-throes of Mr. Wallace were bogus; and the "experiment" had nothing to do with learning and memory. Every aspect of the "memory and learning study" was part of a brilliant but extremely disturbing deception by a twenty-eight-year-old social psychologist named Stanley Milgram, who had recently received his PhD and was employed by Yale University.

Mr. Wallace and the Experimenter were amateur actors paid for their services, and the "experiment" was a trick, an illusion, and a deception. The dramatic events described above did in fact constitute a psychological study, but not of learning and memory. The study was in reality devised to find out how far ordinary Americans would go to obey an authority figure who instructs them to torture an innocent person to death, supposedly as part of a scientific test. And as the study revealed, a majority of ordinary Americans were willing to go all the way—they followed the commands of the Experimenter, and inflicted what they believed to be excruciating pain on a person until he apparently expired or passed out, screaming, in the room next door.

Why? According to Stanley Milgram, the designer of the study, they did so because a professorial-looking technician with an authoritative manner and a grey lab coat told them to, and most people were afraid to disobey his authority. (Milgram had the Experimenter wear a gray lab coat rather than a white one so that subjects wouldn't think of him as a medical doctor.)

Almost two-thirds of the subjects continued administering electric shocks *right up to and including 450 volts, administering the last lethal voltage three times.* (The Experimenter orders the subject to shock the presumably dead or unconscious Mr. Wallace three times, 450 volts each time, because "the Learner's silence is considered a wrong answer.") In the thousands of times this study is replicated, at Yale and around the world, the outcome is always the same: at least two-thirds of the subjects continue to administer lethal electrical shocks even though Mr. Wallace is evidently dead, unconscious, or otherwise disabled in the adjacent room. The subjects complain about what they are asked to do—they argue, swear, weep and laugh hysterically—but when instructed to continue shocking the comatose Mr. Wallace by the Experimenter, they eventually do so. Only about one-third of the subjects that volunteer for this study are able to stop obeying the Experimenter's commands before the highest voltage level is reached.

The study began in the summer of 1961. Stanley Milgram and a graduate assistant would typically watch each "experiment" surreptitiously from behind a two-way mirror. Milgram had conceived and laboriously designed the entire deception, referring to it as a "behavioral study of obedience," which because of the cruel behavior it managed to elicit became the most controversial study in the history of experimental science. Milgram would typically introduce himself after the "experiment" to the bewildered subject, stepping out from behind a two-way glass and proceeding—in Milgram's words—to "interview and de-hoax" the 'naïve subject.' (A *naïve subject* is an expression from experimental psychology meaning a person who is deliberately deceived as part of a psychological study or experiment.)

Milgram would "de-hoax" the subject by explaining in detail the deception the subject has just experienced. The subject is informed that the screams of pain were faked, the 'Shock Generator' is bogus, and the study really had nothing to do with learning and memory. The Experimenter is revealed to be merely an actor playing a role, and not really involved in doing scientific research; a smiling and relaxed Mr. Wallace is brought in from the adjacent room to demonstrate that he's okay, and that he didn't have a heart attack after all. Then the 'naïve subject' is asked a few questions and informed that there will be a follow-up questionnaire later, in addition to which a complete written explanation of the study will be sent to each participant. For some subjects this deconstruction of the deception turns into a long discussion with Milgram and his assistant, usually involving a subject's feelings about what he had just experienced, and sometimes about the morality of the experiment itself.

Milgram mentions in his 1974 book *Obedience to Authority: An Experimental View* that he spent a good deal of time talking to subjects after the study was completed, but doesn't explain why such counseling might be necessary. Superficially, at least, the intent was evidently to reassure the 'naïve subject' that he hadn't really hurt or killed anyone, and help him understand the experimental context of the agonizing drama in which he has just been involved; and if possible cushion the emotional impact on him by explaining that he had been part of an important scientific exploration of human nature. (Later on, after one of his subjects threatened to sue him, legal liability may also have become a concern to Milgram, causing him to spend extra time with his subjects.)

Because there was no control population, Milgram's clinical charade was technically not an experiment but a study. But the subjects *thought* it was an experiment, which is fundamental to understanding its effectiveness. It is probably for that reason that the obedience study has been almost invariably referred to as "the

Milgram experiment," even in most clinical literature. The Milgram study appeared in printed form in some academic material circulated by Penn State Media Sales as early as 1965, apparently for those who wanted to replicate it. In the original printed material from Penn State Media there was a laughably terse summary of the way the study was to be concluded:

Finally, to make sure there are no hard feelings, friendly, harmless Mr. Wallace [comes] out in coat and tie. Gives jovial greeting. Friendly reconciliation takes place. Experiment ends.

The best way to accomplish this "friendly reconciliation," Milgram had decided, was for Mr. Wallace to simply come out to meet the subject and chat with him. The "friendly, harmless" man playing the role of Mr. Wallace is described in *Obedience to Authority* as being an "amiable" Irish-American. ("The victim as played by a forty-seven-year-old accountant, trained for the role; he was of Irish-American descent and most observers found him mild-mannered and likeable.")[44] These observations were typical of Milgram's instinct for detail; he conceived of figures in his study as characters with back stories, in the same way that actors in the theater are given back stories to the characters they play.

In the informal discussion after the study, the subject—now aware that the "experiment" was fraudulent—was encouraged to talk to the Experimenter, as well as to Milgram himself. (This may have been more important than Milgram realized at the time, for reasons we will examine later on.) The character of the intimidating Experimenter was played by high school biology teacher John Williams, who after completion of each "experiment" dropped his stern demeanor to chat informally with the subject. The previously dead or dying Mr. Wallace was convincingly played by 47-year-old James McDonough, who after completion also joined the discussion with the subject. (McDonough, who during the day worked as head payroll auditor of the New York, New Haven and Hartford

Railroad, agreed to moonlight for Milgram because of expenses incurred by his large family; he had nine children.) Both Williams and McDonough had some acting ability, both men were thoroughly rehearsed by Milgram, and both had internalized his insistence on maintaining total verisimilitude. Milgram was particularly pleased with McDonough, who had a natural talent, he thought, for playing the victim. In his interview notes, Milgram wrote: "This man would be perfect for a victim—he is so mild-mannered and submissive; not at all academic... Easy to get along with."[45]

During his discussions with subjects after the study, Stanley Milgram spoke about the reason for the obedience study, which largely had to do with the disturbing tendency of people to unquestioningly follow authority figures. The Eichmann trial in Israel had begun just one month before Milgram commenced his study; and Eichmann's defense that he was "just following orders" was much in the news; no doubt this would have been informally discussed— certainly Milgram discussed it often. Thus the shaken subject was given the opportunity to get 'behind the scenes,' as it were, to deconstruct the elements of the deception, to assimilate some of Milgram's personal investment in the subject matter, and hopefully to consider what had just occurred to him as a kind of psychological theater rather than an indictment of his character. A stringent effort would be made to keep a disinterested clinical tone, with no hint of judgment.

But by this time even the dullest subject would have realized, simply by the way that the 'experiment' was set up, that he had been subjected to a kind of character test—and that if he'd gone "full compliance" in response to the Experimenter's commands he had revealed something disturbing about himself. ("Full compliance" was Milgram's euphemism for subjects that obeyed all commands to shock Mr. Wallace all the way to the maximum 450 volts.) There was really no way to get around it. The subject had been ordered to shock and kill what he thought was a dying man—and he'd done so, not once but repeatedly. The subject would have to wonder about his behavior, and wonder what people who read about the study in the future would think of him. Would they consider people who performed as he did as stand-ins for Nazis, who—like the ubiquitous Eichmann—were "just following orders"? It would have been inhuman for the subjects who administered the strongest voltage not to be disappointed in their own performance to some extent, once they saw what the study was really about, either for not breaking off the experiment or for not seeing through it sooner. But subjects would have a lifetime to live with their behavior, and to wonder about why they behaved as they did.

We should not be surprised, then, that these informal bull sessions with subjects afterwards were described as "extended" in Milgram's 1974 book *Obedience to Authority*. These discussions were clearly aimed at helping subjects deconstruct what had happened to them during the study—but why that would be necessary psychologically for subjects participating in this particular study, Milgram did not care to elaborate. Of course, to what extent the 'obedience study' would affect subjects negatively in the long term, nobody really knew at that time. Milgram believed—or wrote that he believed—that subjects were free agents, who had the right to break off the study at any time, even though he observed that those same subjects seemed, during the course of his study, to lose their moral agency.

Above all, Milgram wrote at different times that the larger good served by this study would outweigh any perceived harm done to the subjects. Milgram no doubt believed this, at least most of the time (although there was a brief period later in his career during which he questioned his own experimental ethics). But the ends can never justify the means, whether in science or any other department of human endeavor. What really drove the obedience study was that Stanley Milgram had a burning personal need to investigate—to know more about—humanity's capacity for evil; and he wanted to measure and quantify that capacity in a laboratory setting, and thought he had arrived at a method for doing so. Specifically, he was driven by a burning personal need to understand why and how the Nazi Holocaust had happened, a question thinking people were asking all over the world. Why, in other words, had the moral collapse of Germany occurred in such a way that ordinary people were persuaded to do terrible things?

In the end, Milgram would arrive at the belief that it was fear of authority that caused it people to do evil things, although he denied that Germans were any different in that regard than anybody else. In the end it was a driving compulsion to investigate something he was personally obsessed by—the Nazi Holocaust and the capacity of humans to engage in radical evil—that gave Stanley Milgram the energy to carry through such an unusual and controversial psychological study, as well as his remarkable ability to rationalize the ethical issues involved.

3.

Stanley Milgram was born on August 15, 1933, in New York City, of immigrant Jewish parents from Eastern Europe. His mother's family came from Romania, his father was Hungarian; Samuel left Europe before the Nazis came to power. (The Hungarian government of the 1920s was both ultra right-wing and anti-Semitic, and many Hungarian Jews immigrated at that time.) His father was a hard-working baker, who was often assisted in the family bakery by Stanley's mother, Adele; both of Stanley's parents had a deep and abiding respect for education. Stanley was a brilliant child who loved science, enjoyed practical jokes, and quickly assimilated the moral implications of the world around him. After a child was killed by a speeding car on the street where Stanley lived, the neighborhood adults successfully petitioned politicians to rezone it as a one-way street; Milgram later said that this taught him much about the power of collective action. It was a secure and loving home, but the sensitive Milgram saw the world as a troubled place, and was himself likewise troubled; but he was surprisingly poised—and determined—in the way he expressed his discontents.

For example, he devoted his entire Bar Mitzvah speech, in 1946, to discussing the Holocaust and its effects on Jews everywhere. This seems a precocious choice of subject matter for a thirteen-year-old Bar Mitzvah boy, even a brilliant one; at that time the Nazi Holocaust was not something that people regularly discussed, especially not in a semi-public or celebratory venue. Partly this was because information about it was still coming out; but also because people were still uncertain how to integrate information about the Holocaust with what they had previously believed about human nature. The entire subject matter was especially overwhelming for Jews, and something the adults would typically discuss in whispers. It would be interesting to know why a thirteen-year-old boy would choose that for his Bar Mitzvah speech in 1946, what he said in his speech, and how the adults in the room reacted. It is impressive enough that he undertook to speak about it at all.

Milgram graduated from James Monroe High School (ironically, one of his classmates was Phil Zimbardo, another social psychologist whose work would attract great controversy) and attended classes at Queens College, graduating in 1954. McCarthyism was at its height during the 1950s; Milgram was reportedly impressed by those individuals who were called to testify at the Senate Internal Security Subcommittee hearings chaired by Senator Joseph McCarthy, people who refused to "name names," since giving names of political associates to the Subcommittee would have incriminated them. (Milgram would say later that he wished he had spoken out more effectively at that time in opposing the fear-mongering association with McCarthyism.) While a student at Harvard, Milgram met his future wife Alexandra "Sasha" Menkin, and they were married in 1962, ultimately raising two children, Michele and Marc. Stanley and Sasha had a good marriage, but Stanley had a weak heart, and worried Sasha with his at first occasional but increasing unwillingness to take care of his health. (She could not have been reassured by Stanley's frequent boast that he would die in his early 50s like his father.)

Although Stanley Milgram created what is without question the most controversial psychological study of the 20th century, much has been made about the fact that he never took a single psychology class as an undergraduate at Queens College—he was accepted into a PhD program at Harvard in 1954 only after taking six courses in psychology. He got his PhD there in 1960, and became an associate professor; but in the period after the obedience study, tenure for Stanley Milgram was apparently never a possibility at any of the Ivy League universities. According to his wife Sasha, this was because of the controversy surrounding his notorious study; but at least one colleague said on the record (and others said off the record) that Milgram had a tendency to berate and sometimes mock slower students. Eventually, however, he was accepted in 1967 at the Graduate Center of City University of New York as a full professor, and stayed there until his death of a heart attack seventeen years later.

Throughout his life Milgram was haunted by the Nazi Holocaust, a circumstance copiously documented by his biographer, Thomas Blass. Quite simply, Milgram felt a burning *personal* compulsion to come to terms with it, for his own reasons but also for the future of humankind. After all, his chosen academic field was the deconstruction of human behavior in society; but systemic evil wasn't a chess problem that one could solve with logic. Milgram said more than once that he identified very deeply, rightly or wrongly, with the Jews who died in Hitler's death camps. (In other words, he suffered from a kind of survivor guilt-by-proxy, since as an American coming of age in the 1950s and 1960s he was separated from the Holocaust by both time and distance.)

Milgram once wrote in a remarkable letter to a friend that his real spiritual home was central Europe, and that he should have been born a German-speaking Jew of Prague in 1922 (exactly the linguistic, religious and geographical milieu of Franz Kafka, who died in 1924). Carrying this morbid and somewhat pretentious fantasy further, Milgram confessed in this letter that by all rights he should also have perished in one of Hitler's gas chambers exactly twenty years later, in 1942. This was a personal fantasy, an attempt to accommodate himself emotionally to the most shocking event of the 20th century, but what are we to make of its morbid negativity? He was not identifying himself with one of the great intellectuals who opposed Hitler or even one who survived the Holocaust, but with an imagined *victim* of Hitler. Stanley Milgram would carry with him always the mute, accusing shadow of this phantasmagoric alter ego, emblematic both of a baseline pessimism regarding human nature and a concomitant tendency to introspection and self-absorption. Milgram's obedience study would be his sincere, if morally questionable and only partially successful, attempt to translate these thoughts and feelings about the Holocaust from a haunted and somewhat unhealthy obsession into something that could provide answers to the questions that people everywhere were now asking about radical and systemic evil.

If Stanley Milgram was obsessed by the Nazi Holocaust, he was not the only person who was. It was an obsession that was endemic among intellectuals—and not only Jewish and German intellectuals—beginning in the 1960s and continuing throughout the Cold War. If it was not often discussed in middlebrow culture at that time (because many people found it too depressing), it was a perennial obsession of high culture; and gradually images from the Nazi Holocaust crept into the popular media, and over time became instantly recognizable. The Holocaust haunted culture, politics and critical thought in the West, but at the same time had an uncanny power to corrupt those who would use it for personal or organizational gain. Milgram experienced his obsession in a way that was different from the way other people experienced it—rightly or wrongly, he saw it as a philosophical and psychological problem that he felt personally compelled to resolve. This problem was nothing less than the ancient question of good and evil, and the depths of evil in human societies—but presented in a new and terrifying circumstance, because of the technology of death that enabled the Nazis to create a machinery of evil that killed millions of Jews in only three years.

Milgram was almost surely attracted to social psychology at least partly because he sensed it could help him investigate the moral collapse that led to the horrors in Europe under Hitler. The philosophical problems posed by the horror of the Third Reich he would seek to unravel using the language of psychology—in his case, social psychology, since it dealt with group behavior. He would understand Auschwitz by understanding the individual moral bankruptcies that in the aggregate produced the mechanics of the Final Solution. But to do that, he would somehow have to experimentally create some core dynamic of the Third Reich in his laboratory—or at least that part of it that caused, on a person-to-person level, good people do evil things. He had once devised dangerous chemistry experiments as a child (including one that brought the fire department to rescue him and his family from the resulting explosion) but this one seemed even more perilous.

What was the problem posed by the Nazi Holocaust? If all the Germans who did terrible things acted on an evil morality, it was all quite comprehensible—they were all simply following the same evil moral code. But what about people who had *good* moral values— what caused *them* to participate in evil? What kind of invisible negative influence could cause good people to do bad things? As Stanley Milgram struggled with this, he was influenced by two important people in his life. One was Solomon Asch, his academic mentor at Harvard, a Gestalt psychologist who developed sophisticated studies that illuminated the nature of social conformity.

Asch showed convincingly that people could be persuaded to see things that didn't really exist, when under subtle pressure from other people—and the larger the group, the more likely subjects could be convinced to see things that weren't there. (His experiments, like Milgram's later obedience study, involved the use of confederates used to deceive subjects—in Asch's case, by insisting that one line was longer than another, when in reality it wasn't.) Another big influence on Milgram was Gordon Allport, also a popular professor in the Harvard psychology department. Allport thought Freudian psychoanalysts and therapists were wasting their time ransacking the past for half-forgotten clues to a patient's emotional development, believing that the critical and most malleable dimension of the personality is the part one experiences in the present moment. Similar ideas were taken up from a slightly different angle in the work of Walter Mischel, who believed unequivocally that the strongest determinant of behavior was not individual personality, but the situation in which a person finds himself.[46]

Milgram would take some of the best ideas and convictions of both Allport and Asch, and apply them to the design of his obedience study. Taken together, it seems in retrospect that all three psychologists—Allport, Asch and Mischel—were like men in a darkened room, feeling their way toward a new understanding of human nature. All three were almost surely to some extent touched by the horror of the Second World War; their interest in the importance of *situations* over *character* was probably influenced, consciously or unconsciously, by the crimes of the Third Reich. Ultimately Milgram's obedience study would find a strikingly original methodological framework for studying the tendency do evil things while "just following orders," allowing him to quantify human evil in what seemed like stark moral terms.

While a great many people were trying to figure out how the death camps had happened (often with a certain amount of pious hand-wringing), only Milgram had the sheer mind-boggling audacity to conceive of a psychological study that would, in effect, create a kind of greatly accelerated, time-lapse study of the moral collapse and degradation typical of German fascism. If he could not show *why* the death camps happened, he would show *how* they happened, by showing the sequential experiences of a single human being, apparently normal in every respect, systematically being induced to engage in a profound and utterly murderous form of evil while "just following orders." And that is exactly what Milgram preceded to do. Using the seemingly familiar props of a psychological laboratory, and the slightly odd premise of a "learning and memory" experiment, he set out to elicit in less than ninety minutes what had taken National Socialism two decades to produce in historical time.

Of course, nobody can reproduce in a laboratory the exact emotional, behavioral and political experience of a tragic historical epoch; but at first it appeared that Milgram had in fact managed to replicate in his laboratory a kind of evil that strongly suggested the robotic brutality of the Nazis—first, because it recalled the German respect for authoritarian leaders; and partly because Nazi war criminals at the Nuremberg Trials often used the excuse that they were "just following orders" as justification for their crimes. Milgram did not replicate Nazi evil; but he did find a way to elicit and quantify behavior that had more than a passing resemblance to what the world knew about the Nazi tendency to blindly follow the brutal and destructive commands of an authoritarian leader. But Milgram's study also demonstrated, to an extent that he probably never foresaw, that almost *anyone* could have done what the Nazis did, given the right circumstances.

He transformed ordinary people into moral zombies by subjecting them to an unusual and terrifying series of highly pressured events, put in place by deception and driven by a false consciousness of complicity in torture and homicide. The subjects in Milgram's study were technically free to get up and walk out of the laboratory, as Milgram liked to point out; but what was it in this "experiment" that made about two-thirds of them keep pulling down the switches until they were 'fully compliant,' even though they didn't want to comply? What was causing them to lose their moral and cognitive agency? Milgram always said he was surprised and horrified by this outcome, and that the outcome of his famous study was as much of a surprise to him as anyone else; but much of what he did prior to his famous experiment suggested that he was aware that it was at least *possible* to have such a shocking outcome to his obedience study, if not likely.

When previously doing studies involving 'naïve subjects' in Norway and France, Milgram went out of his way afterwards to ask the subjects their opinion about the ethics of the study they'd just experienced, an unusual procedure in experimental science at that time. This suggests that it was at least possible that Milgram was consciously or unconsciously preparing himself for a certain amount of controversy regarding his own experimental ethics. At Yale, before he began seeing subjects in the obedience study, Milgram went out of his way to elicit predictions of study outcomes by three different populations — psychiatrists, college students and ordinary middle-class adults — by asking them how they would themselves respond:

> In each case the respondents consist of an audience that has come to hear a lecture on the topic of obedience to authority... The audience is provided with a schematic diagram of the shock generator, showing verbal and voltage designations. Each respondent is asked to reflect on the experiment, then privately to record how he himself would perform in it.[47]

Perhaps not surprisingly, respondents from all three groups were sure that they would withdraw from the study as soon as cries of distress were heard. The psychiatrists, for example, predicted that they — and perhaps by implication most subjects — would not go beyond the 10th shock level (150 volts, when Mr. Wallace first begins to beg to be released) and that only four percent would go to the 20th level, with only one in a thousand reaching the highest level of 450 volts. *Every one* of the 110 respondents to Milgram's questionnaire was certain that he would break off the experiment at some point before hitting 450 volts, the highest level of voltage.

Milgram often responded to critics of his study by citing the questionnaires to the three groups mentioned above, pointing out that nobody had foreseen the extremely high level of subject compliance. But what respondent to a questionnaire would predict his performance as being sadistic in the extreme? The obedience study was set up precisely to elicit a brutal response, not a benign one; and indeed, a more benign reaction by subjects could have indicated a deficit in Milgram's design skills. Nonetheless, it was always easier for Milgram to elicit evil behavior than to explain it. That part remained a mystery, he said—he had designed a study that could call forth evil more proficiently than anyone could have predicted, but he could not easily describe why. Milgram describes somewhat ruefully what had transpired in his laboratory at Yale:

> This is, perhaps, the most fundamental lesson of our study: ordinary people, simply doing their jobs, and without any particular hostility on their part, can become agents in a terrible destructive process. Moreover, even when the destructive effects of their work become patently clear, and they are asked to carry out actions incompatible with fundamental standards of morality, relatively few people have the resources needed to resist authority.[48]

But *why* can't they resist authority? Was the problem something in individual human personalities, or was it something in the study that that Milgram wasn't seeing? In fact, the obedience study appeared at first to raise more questions than answered. The 'fully compliant' subjects (remember that "full compliance" was Milgram's euphemism for subjects who followed all commands of the Experimenter up to the maximum 450 volts) weren't necessarily bad people. These were people who were, for the most part, good people, and therefore knew it was wrong to torture an innocent man strapped to a chair, especially when he had been so kind as to mention that he had heart trouble, and was now screaming to be let out.

And as they later explained, they knew they were doing something wrong, yet they *couldn't stop when told to continue*. Like a robot controlled by a computer, as we would say today, they continued to torture a helpless man when the Experimenter told them to, even though they didn't want to. What the 'fully compliant' subjects were describing was a total physical, cognitive and moral loss of agency. The subjects were no longer in charge of their own minds and bodies. Even though they knew it to be wrong, when ordered by the Experimenter to continue, they did so.

Milgram developed two theories about why subjects followed the authority of the Experimenter. One was a theory of *conformity*. Just as emotionally and cognitively conflicted people will allow a group to make a decision for them, the subjects in the obedience study allow the Experimenter to take responsibility for making decisions. A second theory was the *agentic state theory*, in which subjects began to see themselves merely "as the instrument for carrying out another person's wishes, and they therefore no longer see themselves as responsible for their actions. Once this critical shift of viewpoint has occurred in the person, all of the essential features of obedience follow."[49] But *why* would people see themselves in this way?

These theories were extremely weak, consisting of little more than saying that people follow orders from people with more authority than themselves. But what constitutes authority? Why on earth would sane people follow the orders of a person they'd never met before, when the orders cause them to harm or kill a stranger? Milgram's ideas hardly worked as descriptions, much less compre-hensive theories. Some social scientists believed that obedience was an outgrowth—possibly biological—of gregariousness in humans, the same factors that can drive conformity in societies. There had been an enormous amount of political and social conformity in the US during the 1950s; and Milgram, with his interest in Central European history, had to be acutely aware of the tendency of the Germans to follow strong leaders.

He was also probably aware of an idea much discussed by the European existentialists (ultimately popularized by Erich Fromm) that people often prefer to give up their freedom rather than take responsibility for their own lives. But Milgram seemed deeply invested in the idea of authority as an unalterable force. Human beings, until they could learn how to refuse evil orders from authority figures, would be capable of unimaginable depths of evil; and the obedience study had, he thought, simply tapped into that.

But the very high levels of compliance in the obedience study indicated something much more robust than socially-conditioned conformity. These subjects were Americans, with their famous contrarian and even anarchistic tendencies; so why were they so fanatically obedient to a stranger in a grey lab coat? There was something in the circumstances of the study that was compelling people to follow the Experimenter's commands, even when they didn't want to. Why did subjects find it so hard to disengage from the study, once they'd passed a certain point? Was it obedience to authority, or was it something else in the study itself, perhaps something implicit in the interactions through which the study's authority was exercised?

4.

Everything we know about the Milgram obedience study indicates that it *traumatized* many of the unsuspecting subjects, which thoroughly disoriented them. The evidence also suggests that the subjects quickly became trauma-bonded to the actor playing the role of the Experimenter, and to the institutional aggression he represented. The subjects were traumatized by the screams of agony that arose from the adjacent room, before they could really assess—or even form a coherent opinion about—the completely unfamiliar situation they suddenly found themselves in. All attempts to get more information, to remonstrate about the cruel turn events had taken, or to protest what was happening, were met with scripted responses by the Experimenter. Unless the subject broke off the "experiment" early on, the trauma created by this situation would begin to create a bond to the Experimenter, as well as to the highly focused aggression inherent in his stern and authoritative commands.

The trauma began when the subjects found themselves torturing someone *before they realized what was happening*; and it was this, and their horror at what they were doing, plus the escalating cries of agony, which created the trauma bond. Like a hostage with 'Stockholm Syndrome,' the unsuspecting subjects quickly began to identify with the actor playing the Experimenter *as well as* his commands, obeying them even when they knew they were morally wrong. The critical element in the study was the deceit of the Experimenter. Had he not misrepresented the nature of the "experiment," the subjects would never have continued until they were traumatized by their sudden realization that they were doing something cruel and morally unacceptable.

The longer the subject stayed at the console of Milgram's 'Shock Generator,' the higher the voltage he was ordered to administer, and the more agonizing became the screams of Mr. Wallace. The sequentially escalating voltage, and the escalating level of Mr. Wallace's suffering, would inevitably create heightened levels of disorientation and emotional trauma as the "experiment" continued. This strengthened the subject's trauma bond to the Experimenter, after a certain point making it almost impossible to refuse his commands. Even Milgram himself often commented that once subjects passed a certain point, they were unable to stop obeying the Experimenter.

A common-sense interpretation typical of the early 1960s might suppose that the onset of the subject's disgust and strong objection to what he was doing would cause him to *reject* the authority of the Experimenter. But because of the clever bait-and-switch built into Milgram's deception, subjects were overwhelmed early on and (if they didn't quit early) quickly traumatized. One moment the subject was administering harmless shocks, as per the instructions of the Experimenter. Then, suddenly, Mr. Wallace is screaming piteously — and the subject responds by trying again, and then again, hoping each time that Mr. Wallace will get the word pairs right, so the subject won't have to shock him again. Mr. Wallace's response continues to get worse, until the subject realizes with horror that he is complicit in the torture of a helpless human being. What to do? The subject turns to the Experimenter for guidance.

But the Experimenter reassures him with a series of scripted responses. The subject is already trauma-bonded to the impassive Experimenter, making rebellion against his robotic instructions extremely difficult—in fact, almost impossible, once having passed a certain point. All other factors being operational (Yale prestige, the stern demeanor of the Experimenter, the desire to obey authority, a desire to "do a good job," a desire to get it over with), it is still trauma bonding that can best explain the obedience study's extremely high level of "full compliance."

The power of emotional trauma in the Milgram study was also enhanced by the fact that the subjects were experiencing *serial traumas*. The subject, in other words, had to administer 30 painful shocks to an unwilling victim to reach full compliance—and the escalating agony of the subjects was documented by Milgram and his assistant. This suggests that instead of causing the subject to break off the "experiment," the *sequential* and *escalating* nature of the shocks actually reinforced the naïve subject's original trauma. The effects of 'sequential traumatization' over a long period of time are well-known, partly because of the work done Dr. Hans Keilson, a Dutch/German psychoanalyst who worked with children of Holocaust victims after the Second World War. His findings, not surprisingly, were that subsequent emotional trauma greatly enhanced any trauma that had preceded it—but Keilson's work had to do with sequences of negative psychological experience over a period of years.

In the Milgram study, on the other hand, adult subjects were confronted by a series of extremely disturbing and increasingly traumatic choices in a very short amount of time—and the rapid sequencing seems important to the result, because it is clearly designed to overwhelm subjects before they can make sense of what is happening to them. Everything we know—starting with first-person accounts by Milgram himself, as well as later interviews with subjects—suggests that each new trauma intensified whatever emotional trauma the subject was already experiencing, and that such an enforced sequence of traumas added greatly to the likelihood of "full compliance".

Indeed, Milgram himself noticed that negative emotional effects on subjects were cumulative, and became increasingly powerful as the voltage level got higher. After a certain point the subject was helpless to challenge the commands of the Experimenter, adding to the subject's previous trauma the panicky realization that he could no longer control his behavior—that he had, in fact, lost his moral agency, and could no longer stop himself from doing everything the Experimenter required of him. Milgram himself referred to "binding factors" in his study that tended to lock subjects into doing things that contradicted their values and interests—but then quickly changed the subject by discussing relatively benign and unimportant factors, such as a desire to be polite.

Milgram became skilled at determining the moment when the subject first grasped the horrifying dilemma that he was in. (Remember Milgram was intimately aware of this because he was watching the "experiment" from behind a two-way mirror.) Subjects would typically respond by stammering, questioning, rubbing their faces, moaning, rocking, gibbering and giggling. At least one man experienced severe seizure activity, making a halt to the "experiment" necessary. Others pleaded with the Experimenter to stop. Some wept and shuddered; others sat impassively crying. (The most intriguing of the subjects' responses were by those who offered to give back their $4.50 to the Experimenter, raising an interesting question: was that done to convince the Experimenter to stop the "experiment," or to redeem their behavior?) Apparently it was mainly by way of getting the Experimenter to stop, and only secondarily to relieve them of whatever moral responsibility they felt for Mr. Wallace's pain.

But there were really only two ways for subjects to deal with the obedience study. One was to refuse to go on, by getting up and leaving, or by repeatedly arguing with the Experimenter (if a subject expressed reservations four times in a row without pulling down a switch, he was considered to be refusing further compliance); the only other way was to keep pulling down the switches on the 'Shock Generator,' to keep complying with the Experimenter until all the switches had been pulled down, 450 volts of electricity had been delivered, and Mr. Wallace was apparently dead or incapacitated. About one-third of the people who participated did in fact refuse to go on, and broke off the experiment—but we are still confronted with the fact that about two-thirds continued until they had achieved "full compliance." After the conclusion of the study, as we noted above, the subject would receive a full debriefing, during which they could discuss the study and their reactions to what had transpired.

One thing that remained constant in the different variations of the study was the very effective use of "prods" (Milgram's word) used by the actor playing the Experimenter. These 'prods' were carefully-scripted replies to subjects that were expressing doubts or objections about the pain experienced by Mr. Wallace; they were, in other words, replies to subjects who felt there was something wrong, and were scripted to be completely impersonal and completely consistent—and they sound very much like something a robot might say. They were invariably used in the sequence given below, increasing the robotic effect. There were four of these basic 'prods,' and were delivered in a completely neutral but still authoritative voice whenever a subject expressed doubts or disagreements with the progress of the "experiment":

"Please continue;" or "Please go on."
"The experiment requires that you continue."
"It is absolutely essential that you continue."
"You have no other choice, you *must* go on."

The second 'prod' is particularly clever, since it puts responsibility for Mr. Wallace's perilous and escalating discomfort on the "experiment" rather than any discoverable human agency. In addition to the four above there were two additional "prods" tailored to specific objections. When a subject became concerned that Mr. Wallace was dying in the adjacent room, and for that reason pleaded with the Experimenter to check on him, the response was: "Although the shocks may be painful, there is no permanent tissue damage—so please go on."[50] If the subject objected that the Learner in the next room was demanding to be released, the Experimenter would say: "Whether he likes it or not, you must go on until he has learned all the word pairs correctly. So please go on." Clearly this last "prod" is the most aggressive, its full malevolence summed up in the words "whether he likes it or not," since there had been no commitment whatsoever at the beginning by either the subject or Mr. Wallace to finish the "experiment."

Weirdest of all, when Mr. Wallace was apparently too incapacitated to respond to questions, the Experimenter would point out that his ominous silence constituted a "wrong answer"—and the subject was instructed to punish the dead or unconscious Wallace by shocking him again at a higher voltage! Even the last shock, at a lethal 450 volts, had to be administered *not once but three times*, long after the actor playing Mr. Wallace had stopped responding and was evidently unconscious or dead. If the subject refused to continue after four verbal "prods" by the Experimenter, or stood up to leave, the experiment was halted. Otherwise, it would not be stopped until after the subject had given the maximum 450-volt shock three times in a row, enough to kill most people. In almost all known variants of the study, as we've already noted, a full two-thirds of participants continued to administer shocks right up to the maximum, which means giving the unresponsive Mr. Wallace his full dosage of three lethal shocks (marked XXX on the 'Shock Generator') at 450 volts.

Again, *subjects were traumatized by tricking them into torturing an innocent man before they completely realized what they were doing*. The bait-and-switch insinuation of Mr. Wallace's gradually-escalating screams succeeded in making many subjects feel that they were already complicit in hurting someone before they really understood what was going on. When they suddenly comprehended the pain they had evidently caused Mr. Wallace, cognition was overwhelmed by emotion (including guilt and horror) and the emotional trauma of the subject escalated. Remember that there were some *thirty* different graduations of intensity on Milgram's 'Shock Generator,' so that most people found themselves administering a level of pain that they suddenly realized was grossly inappropriate before fully under-standing the situation they were in. Most subjects, in other words, didn't realize they were doing something wrong until after they had crossed the line. Once the Experimenter had taken them beyond that level, the emotional trauma they were experiencing would be likely to bond them to the Experimenter, making it very hard to break free of his authority—so difficult, in fact, that it is both amazing and heartening that fully a third, usually those who broke off the study early on, were able to reject the Experimenter's commands.

A fair number probably identified not only with the Experimenter but also with the power and aggression consistent with his role, enhanced greatly by his glib assurance that the subject would not be personally responsible for any consequences of the study. I think it quite possible that many people will act sadistically once they have been tricked into doing so, perhaps while engaging in the usual rationalizations available to them. But the stronger psychological mechanism involved in Milgram's obedience study was not merely to elicit the subject's inherent sadism, but also to create the bonding effects of emotional trauma. Once they felt complicit in an escalating sequence of torture and murder, many subjects who were bonded to the Experimenter and his aggression would find it extremely difficult, if not impossible, to break free of his commands.

Even Milgram commented on the cumulative effects of the process on subjects, as we've already noted. He remarked that if a subject continued to administer shocks up to 350 volts, he would almost surely continue to the ultimate 450; whereas if he resisted the commands of the Experimenter earlier, he had a much better chance of summoning up the strength to break off the experiment. In retrospect this makes perfect sense. The earlier the subject resisted, the weaker the bond would be; but the longer the subject put off making a decision, the stronger the bond would become. After 350 volts, independent decision-making and behavior by the subject would finally become almost impossible.

Blass, Milgram's biographer, was quite aware of the sequential nature of the pressure endured by the subjects, writing that "one of the distinctive features of the Milgram obedience paradigm is the sequential escalation of the delivery of the shocks. The learners' 'suffering' intensifies in a gradual, piecemeal fashion. Milgram considered this manner of giving shocks one of the factors 'that powerfully binds a subject to his role.'" Blass continues: "The importance of this unfolding process as a facilitator of destructive obedience in Milgram's laboratory has alerted us to the vital role played by the step-by-step, escalating process the Nazis used in the victimization of the Jews, as described by Hilberg... " (Blass' reference here is to Raul Hilberg's description of the step-by-step dehumanization of Jews in Nazi Germany in his classic historical work *The Destruction of the European Jews*.) Then Blass again quotes Milgram on sequencing: "'The laboratory hour is an unfolding process in which [one] action influences the next. The obedient act is perseverative.'" Blass further compares this to Hilberg's descriptions of Nazi injustice as one in which "a measure in a destructive process never stands alone... It always has consequences. Each step of the destruction process contains the seed of the next step."

But Milgram, for his part, never allowed himself to investigate further *why* obedience is "perseverative," and why sequencing levels of emotional pain would generate a "bind" that could cause such a significant loss of moral agency. If Milgram would have considered the possibility that his subjects were being traumatized, the pieces might have started to come together. But what experimental scientist wants to admit that he is traumatizing his subjects? Milgram could not consider that possibility, even though it would have been good science if he had. The truth was that many subjects might at first have been simply disoriented and overwhelmed; but as the screams of Mr. Wallace intensified, a great many without question were also overwhelmed and finally traumatized by the unfamiliar, violent and tragic situation that they found themselves in. It was this that caused their loss of moral and cognitive agency, and not necessarily anything inherently evil in their personalities. Exposed to the unique conditions of Milgram's study, "fully compliant" subjects jettisoned the moral training and values of a lifetime in little more than an hour.

5.

The first psychologist to use the word *trauma* when describing the effects of the Milgram study on its subjects was the child psychologist Diana Baumrind, whose paper criticizing the study—often described as "scathing"—appeared in the 1964 issue of *American Psychologist* ("Some Thoughts on Ethics of Research: After Reading Milgram's 'Behavioral Study of Obedience.'") Everything Milgram had himself written about the agony of his naïve subjects, she pointed out, suggested that his obedience study had traumatized them. She didn't comment on the ways that trauma might have increased compliance, because she was not concerned with the high level of compliance—she was concerned with the mental health of the subjects. But that Milgram's subjects were harmed, at the very least, and most likely traumatized, she was not in doubt. Diana Baumrind's nuanced but passionately critical paper became an overnight sensation.

Baumrind's paper was written with at least as much insight as Milgram's original paper "Behavioral Study of Obedience," which had appeared in the 1963 issue of *Journal of Abnormal and Social Psychology*. Baumrind's detailed ethical and psychological critique of the Milgram study ignited a firestorm of controversy that would change attitudes toward experimental science around the world; more importantly, it kicked off the most intensive debate about experimental ethics that had yet occurred in the history of psychology. In the US it would lead to the total reformulation of protocols for similar studies in the future, to be policed both by government and by Institutional Review Boards, or IRBs, which are in turn regulated by the Office for Human Research Protections (OHRP) within the Department of Health and Human Services. Because of these changes, and the intense debate that accompanied them, people who perceived the pivotal nature of the Milgram study could not, in the 1970s and 1980s, intelligently discuss the Milgram obedience study without taking into account Baumrind's critique.

There were, at that time, a number of psychologists who had come to the same conclusion as Baumrind; and they tended to be well-established professionals who were legitimately concerned about the future of experimental science. They believed that the ethical treatment of subjects trumped all other considerations, for a variety of very good reasons. Psychology was supposed to be a discipline that healed, not hurt; and its practitioners were supposed to inspire trust, not fear. In the back of everybody's minds was the horrific memory of the Nazi doctors and *their* brutal experiments — and articles in American media about the Nazi doctors were now appearing regularly. This would be a reoccurring irony in public debate of Milgram's findings: that his obedience study, which aimed at examining the exaggerated respect for authority and hierarchical rigidity that drove the Nazis, would itself often be accused of repli-cating Nazi cruelty toward human subjects in their many sadistic "scientific" experiments.

Therein also lay the dark irony of the Milgram/Baumrind debate. Baumrind, like Milgram, was Jewish, and had the same politically progressive ideas as Stanley Milgram and people in his circle. She, too, was concerned about the questions about human nature raised by the Nazis. They were both fascinated by the same moral problem—the use of systemic evil by the Nazis—that was agitating other intellectuals in the West. Milgram sought to resolve that problem by demonstrating that there is a Nazi in all people with his obedience study; but Baumrind, for her part, believed that Milgram *by his own testimony* had used a cruel and unacceptable methodology in eliciting and encouraging the Nazi in each of his 'fully compliant' subjects. Can a social psychologist quantify evil, no matter how important his discovery, by *using* evil to elicit it? Baumrind's answer was an emphatic "No," and she spoke for many others besides herself.

In short, Baumrind believed that ethical treatment of subjects trumped everything else in experimental science, no matter how brilliant, philosophically challenging or unique a study was, or how historically important its findings were likely to be; and this position became the majority consensus over the next few years, even among those who admired Milgram's daring and understood his concerns. Experimental science, Baumrind and her allies believed, had to go the way of strict ethical protocols, or it was already on the slippery slope that led to use of carefully rationalized brutality as a tool of institutional psychology—followed by an inevitable public revulsion, reoccurring exposés by media of brutal experimental methods, and ultimately a complete loss of legitimacy in the eyes both of science and the broader public. Then there would be little credibility for experimental science, and little funding to support it.

Milgram, in demonstrating the *potential* cruelty of obedience, had engaged in an undetermined amount of *real* cruelty to make his point. Mainstream psychology found it almost impossible to come to terms with this paradoxical moral dilemma at the heart of the Milgram study. The same problem is still with us, because it must inevitably come into play in any attempt to quantify human weakness. Would it be right to quantify the human capacity for adultery by luring married people into sexually compromising situations, using sex workers to quantify just how far each person will go, and then publishing the result? No, because it would be monstrous to destroy marriages in the name of science, and to moralize against adultery by encouraging it. You can attempt to quantify an *attitude about* wrong behavior, but actually tricking people into doing something that the persons designing the study (as well as the subjects themselves, and society at large) experience as immorality, simply because you have devised a sufficiently clever deception and a laboratory in which to carry it out, is not acceptable. You cannot elicit evil—or even significantly bad behavior—in order to denounce it.

That's the problem at the heart of the ethics issue presented by Milgram's obedience study. The problem can only be approached dialectically, by determining if the study had some demonstrable value *to the study's subjects* that outweighs the discomfort that they suffered. (Never mind trying to balance off the subjects' suffering against abstract value to science or to humanity—you can't use the ends to justify the means.) Baumrind and her allies suspected that many subjects did not wish to talk about their experiences because of shame, confusion and anxiety. Furthermore, in the early 1960s, at the time the Milgram study was first conducted, there was no way to guarantee future rehabilitation of subjects who might have been harmed. And that meant, to Baumrind and many others, that such suffering should never be imposed on subjects again in a psychological study, at least not until better and more ethical protocols were rewritten to prevent the possibility of harm.

For initiating the debate on experimental ethics in such a courageous way, Baumrind is justly famous. But she is also important for being the first psychologist to perceive that the obedience study's effect on naïve subjects was not just to disorient or disturb them, but specifically had the effect of traumatizing them. Baumrind quoted Milgram's own words: "Subjects were observed to sweat, tremble, stutter, bite their lips, groan, and dig their fingernails into their flesh. These were characteristic rather than exceptional responses to the experimenter. One sign of tension was the regular occurrence of nervous laughing fits. Fourteen of the 40 subjects showed definite signs of nervous laughter and smiling. The laughter seemed entirely out of place, even bizarre. Full-blown, uncontrollable seizures were observed for 3 subjects. On one occasion we observed a seizure so violently convulsive that it was necessary to call a halt to the experiment."

Baumrind responded: "It would be interesting to know what sort of procedures could dissipate the type of emotional disturbance just described. In view of the effects on subjects, *traumatic to a degree which Milgram himself considers nearly unprecedented in socio-psychological experiments*, his casual assurance that these tensions were dissipated before the subject left the laboratory is unconvincing." [Italics added] Indeed, Milgram's bland assurances that his subjects weren't harmed *were* quite unconvincing, partly because they had a pontificating, it's-true-because-I-say-so quality about them; but even more because they were so often contradicted by his own reported observations.

In the first paragraph of her paper criticizing the obedience study, Baumrind mentions that "the experimenter" (here she means Milgram, not the actor playing the role of the Experimenter in the study) must balance "his career and scientific interests" against the interests of his subjects. This was clearly a reference to an opportunistic streak in Milgram's character, and to the fact that Milgram was becoming a rock star of social psychology. (At the expense, one might add, of 'fully compliant' subjects, whom he was already publicly characterizing in interviews as behaving like proto-Nazis.) Nor did Baumrind flinch from deconstructing the self-serving 'end justifies the means' argument that Milgram and his supporters sometimes invoked. So his study had quantified the existence of evil—so what? What about the mental health of the subjects? Were they to be sacrificed to scientific knowledge—and, Baumrind hinted, to career and professional success?

Milgram hypothesized that his subjects—or at least some of them—possibly believed that shocking Mr. Wallace into unconsciousness was necessary for the good of science. ("*Thus they assume that the discomfort caused the victim is momentary, while the scientific gains resulting from the experiment are enduring.*") In other words, his subjects were making a considered decision that Mr. Wallace's pain—not to mention his apparent cardiac arrest—could be justified by long-term benefits to scientific research. But few people would consider themselves qualified to engage in such an off-the-cuff risk assessment, and in any case that kind of objectivity was not very likely to be encountered in subjects who were observed to "sweat, tremble, stutter, bite their lips, groan, and dig their fingernails into their flesh."

Baumrind understood this to be Milgram's own attitude projected onto the subjects: "Indeed such a rationale might suffice to justify the means used to achieve his end if that end were of inestimable value to humanity or were not itself transformed by the means by which it was attained." When a psychological study uses unethical techniques, she implied, the outcome of the study is contaminated. And psychologists are especially unqualified to decide if the ends justify the means, because the study of behavior is not as clear-cut as medical research: "Unlike the Sabin vaccine, for example, the concrete benefit to humanity of his particular piece of work, no matter how competently handled, cannot justify the risk that real harm will be done to the subject."

Milgram was not competent to judge his study's ultimate importance, Baumrind believed, and in any case that did not justify the suffering of his subjects. The means never justify the ends—the means *become* the ends. Baumrind describes the central interaction in the obedience study: "It is obvious from Milgram's own descriptions that most of his subjects were concerned about their victims and did trust the experimenter, and that their distressful conflict was generated in part by the consequences of these two disparate but appropriate attitudes. Their distress may have resulted from shock [sic] at what the experimenter was doing to them *as well as from what they thought they were doing to their victims.*" [My italics.]

Here Baumrind is describing what she has already identified as trauma, and what I would further describe as trauma bonding. The naïve subject is caught in a terrible dilemma. Mr. Wallace screams for him to stop, while the Experimenter demands that he continue. The resulting emotional trauma overwhelms the executive decision-making of the subject, leaving him unable to resist the commands of the Experimenter. Trauma-bonded to the Experimenter, the subject continues to torture the screaming Mr. Wallace whenever the Experimenter tells him to. The trauma bond gets stronger each time Mr. Wallace screams because each new scream is louder, and therefore more traumatizing; throughout this process the subject internalizes the aggression inherent in the "experiment," which is basically formatted as an experiment in electroshock torture.

Baumrind's insight that Milgram's subjects were traumatized is the key to understanding the obedience study. The subject's trauma bonds him to the Experimenter, who controls the systemic violence being meted out and whose intense aggression the subject begins to internalize. The Experimenter is the human representative of that aggression—that is, he controls and directs it—which explains his power over the compliant subject. Trauma overwhelms the ability of compliant subjects to make moral or even coherent choices, creating a trauma bond with the Experimenter so strong that two-thirds of them could not stop following his horrific commands *despite their own pain and horror at what they were doing and their knowledge that it was morally wrong.*

6.

In autumn of 1962, Milgram's application to the American Psychological Association was put on hold because of questions raised about the ethics of his obedience study. (Someone in the Yale psychology department apparently notified the APA of possible ethical objections; according to Robert Abelson, at that time a member of the department, the Psychology Department was "marinating" in gossip about Milgram's study.)[51] Furthermore, as soon as Milgram's first journal article was published, stories about it began to appear in the mainstream press. The *New York Times* ran a story under the headline "Sixty-Five Percent in Test Blindly Obey Order to Inflict Pain," which was picked up by *The Times* of London and—not surprisingly—*Der Spiegel* of Hamburg. The first overt criticism of Milgram's experimental ethics came a week later in the *St. Louis Post-Dispatch*, which carried an editorial boldly denouncing the study as "torture." The back story to this dramatic turn of events was that the *Post-Dispatch* had a long history of exposing fraudulent or dangerous medical experiments, and over the years that highly calibrated form of medical muckraking had became something of a house specialty.

The *Post-Dispatch* went to the heart of the matter, which was the suffering caused to the subjects, which it described in detail. It concluded that the study's central truth was "not one of blind obedience but of open-eyed torture, with an adverse score not of 65 per cent but of 100... It very much remains to be shown that there was anything in the performance worthy of a great university." Milgram was told about the editorial by a local psychologist named Robert Buckhout who happened to read it, which gave Milgram time to write a rebuttal; the *Post-Dispatch* carried it as an op-ed on its editorial page. Milgram took the approach that a higher good was to be served by the study: "The study started with a few questions that are of no small importance for humanity: What does a good man do when he is told by authority to perform acts that go against natural law?"[52]

But the concerns of the *Post-Dispatch* had not been about "natural law," whatever that meant, or even about the ultimate worth of the study's findings, but the unusual stress and emotional pain to which subjects had been exposed. Indeed, it is necessary to separate out the two concerns, because inflicting pain in the present moment can never be justified by the proposed scientific value of a study's findings in the future. It cannot be said too often: in experimental science, as in every other department of a democratic society, the ends cannot justify the means.

Throughout his career, Milgram was completely ambivalent, at least in public statements, about the emotional discomfort imposed upon subjects of his 'obedience study.' He had a tendency to exaggerate their pain when the authenticity of his study was questioned, but to downplay their discomfort when the questions were about his ethics. For example, Orne and Holland, two early critics of the obedience study, suggested that Milgram's naïve subjects actually saw through the attempted hoax, and suspected all along that the "experiment" was bogus—but continued because they didn't want to "ruin" it. When the verisimilitude of his study (and thus its historical importance) was questioned in this way, Milgram did not hesitate to acknowledge—indeed, to insist upon—his subjects' suffering: "Orne's suggestion that the subjects only *feigned* sweating, trembling, and stuttering to please the experimenter is pathetically detached from reality, equivalent to the statement that hemophiliacs bleed to keep their physicians busy."[53]

But when clinicians pointed out that Milgram's own descriptions of his subjects' behavior strongly suggested that they were traumatized, he reverted to classic damage control. To one such critic he actually compared his study to a movie: "Relatively few subjects experienced greater tension than a nail-biting patron at a good Hitchcock thriller."[54] So which was it, a good Hitchcock thriller or a deception so convincing that it caused subjects to behave like Nazis, and in the process "sweat, tremble, stutter, bite their lips, groan, and dig their fingernails into their flesh?" Milgram insisted that his subjects were ordinary people and not psychopaths, in order to make the point that ordinary people were capable of radical evil. But if they *were* ordinary people, wouldn't the 'fully compliant' subjects have to deal later—unlike the psychopath—with remorse about what they'd done? Surely they hadn't signed up for that when they agreed to participate in a "scientific study of memory and learning."

Milgram thought that the sadistic behavior of his subjects was caused by obedience to authority, but never dealt with the rather obvious objection that there are many different kinds of authority, ranging from the murmured suggestions of a loving parent to the homicidal commands of a fascist dictator. Most importantly, there is legitimate authority and illegitimate authority, not to mention the kind of authority that helps people and the kind that harms them. The extreme agitation of Milgram's subjects suggests that a particularly malevolent form of authority was being exercised, a form of authority particularly capable of getting people to do things they really didn't want to do. In short, Milgram never acknowledged the extent to which his obedience study might not have measured evil behavior but had, on the contrary, actually *created* it, by traumatizing subjects whom he had deceived about the nature of the "experiment."

The reality is that Milgram's obedience study was designed to *elicit* evil behavior, rather than provide an opportunity for considered moral choices. As we've seen, Stanley Milgram always insisted that the responsibility for refusing the Experimenter's commands was the subject's, because he had moral agency and could quit anytime he wanted to. But what if the obedience study employed techniques that were able to *destroy* moral agency? If the behavior elicited by the obedience study was uncharacteristic of the subject, what was the study really measuring? In retrospect, it now seems that the study may have been to a large extent quantifying its own effectiveness, rather than the baseline behavior of its human subjects.

Milgram had an interesting and self-serving blind spot in this area. The psychologists who had influenced Milgram most—Allport, Asch and Mischel—generally believed that the *situation* in which a person found himself was more important than *traits* or *character* in determining that person's behavior in the moment; and if that were true, it would have to be something peculiar to Milgram's study that was producing evil behavior, and not something inherent in his subjects. Milgram, of course, might have answered that it is precisely those kinds of peculiarities that people must learn to resist.

For his part, Milgram could never resist the tendency—at least in defending the obedience study—to hint that certain outcomes are so important, and have such transcendental or even meta-historical implications, that they might justify unusual stress or discomfort on the part of the subject. Milgram believed that his obedience study had profound historical importance, and in this he was correct, although his study became important for somewhat different reasons than he had originally imagined. He appeared on the *Today* show, *Donahue*, the *Dick Cavett Show* and made countless radio and TV appearances; the BBC did a special on the obedience study and a made-for-TV movie was made about him in the US; he was regularly interviewed throughout Europe and the United States. He also received awards and honors, although not as many as one might imagine. He was responsible for many unusual studies later on in his career, but it was the notoriety of his first and most famous study that fascinated the broader public, not only because of the frightening behavior of his subjects, but also the dark nature of Milgram's obedience study itself.

This whiff of the diabolical in Milgram's obedience study kept him from qualifying, at least in the public mind, as one of the great celebrity scientists of the time (one thinks of Jonas Salk, Albert Sabin, and the ubiquitous Linus Pauling) but to some extent suggested instead the criminal, the occult and the disreputable. Milgram's ability to conjure up evil in a laboratory reminded many people of the archetypal Mad Scientist, a category that included historical and literary bogeymen such as Doctor Faustus, Doctor Jekyll and Mr. Hyde, and Doctor Frankenstein, the most outrageous contemporary treatment of this archetype probably being Strangelove in the 1960s Kubrick film *Dr. Strangelove*.

The public was also queasily aware of the notorious Tuskegee "experiments" in which treatment for African-American men infected with syphilis was deliberately withheld so that doctors could study them while they died; and they also knew in a vague way about such scientists as J. Robert Oppenheimer and Wernher von Braun, brilliant but oddly detached men who received power and money for designing weapons of mass destruction, but who felt no inclination to justify or explain their motivations for creating these technological horrors, or assume any moral responsibility for the destruction they were capable of causing. There was a chilling disconnect in these men regarding the things they had invented, summed up brilliantly in the parodist Tom Lehrer's lyrics for his song about Wernher von Braun, inventor of the V1 and V2 rockets under Hitler and later a Cold War acquisition by the US. (*"Once the rockets go up, who cares where they come down? That's not my department,' says Wernher von Braun."*)

Some—most notably Alan C. Elms, a research assistant during the obedience study and later a psychologist—flatly maintained that the pessimism of Milgram's obedience study made people defensive and uneasy, and that these same people retaliated by criticizing the obedience study on ethical grounds. This is essentially an *ad hominem* attack, and quite untrue—there were many psychologists then and now who respected Milgram for his achievements, who nonetheless believed that his treatment of his subjects went too far, and who welcomed the subsequent reforms that protect human subjects in experimental science. What Milgram demonstrated in his obedience study, and the subsequent concerns about his ethics, are both important, and to a large extent can be analyzed as clinically separable issues. On the other hand, they are also connected, because human rights must be universal, or they are nothing. Our concern about radical evil—the concern that Milgram was desperate to arouse in all who read his study—must extend to human beings in psychological experiments designed by scientists such as himself, whether their ultimate motivation is ambition, idealism in the name of science, or (as it usually happens) both. Milgram's own ethical failures were a smaller but identifiable subsidiary part of the moral crisis he sought to illuminate.

Given Milgram's obsession with the Nazi Holocaust, it is interesting that the controversial Holocaust scholar Daniel Jonah

Goldhagen wrote that Milgram's most famous study had no relevance to the crimes of the Nazis. This was, he wrote, because Nazis *chose* evil. "In the real world, SS officers were killing during the day and going home to their families at night. In the real world, people have plenty of opportunities to alter their course of behavior. When they don't, it's not because they're scared of authority, but because they choose not to. The Milgram experiments illustrate nothing about this factor of choice."

Certainly most SS officers chose evil, as did Hitler and his criminal cohorts, but what about the ordinary people who followed them and made their evil possible? Goldhagen correctly objects to the pressured atmosphere of Milgram's obedience study, remarking that "subjects didn't have any time to reflect on what they were doing" — but that's precisely the way trauma bonding works, particularly the kind that leads to systemic evil. Trauma bonding as a component of systemic evil has a great deal more relevance to the Nazi tragedy than either Milgram or Goldhagen would be likely to acknowledge. Because people were traumatized by the overwhelming cruelty and might of the Nazis, they identified with their aggression and lost their capacity for making moral choices. Was not Milgram's study an example, on a greatly diminished level, of something quite similar? But if it illuminates how systemic evil works, it also exposes Milgram to criticism. In his desire to show how evil is elicited from Everyman, did not Milgram allow the Experimenter in his study to adopt the role of Goldhagen's SS Commandant?

Although Milgram created many innovative studies after 1963 (the best known of which is probably his Small-World study, often known as Six Degrees of Separation), it was with the obedience study that he attained celebrity status. And there were many, many variations on that study, most of them designed by Milgram himself. In one version, he added an extra person for added peer pressure on the naïve subject; and in another version, the subject was required to hold down the hand of the actor playing Mr. Wallace as he was shocked. In most of these variations there were few substantial changes in the outcome. A very high percentage of the subjects—invariably around two-thirds—followed the instructions received from the Experimenter and administered shocks right up to the lethal 450 volts, giving the last shock three times to a silent and presumably dead, dying or incapacitated Mr. Wallace.

Milgram and many other social psychologists conducted the study in different countries, with similar results. (In Munich, Germany, a whopping 85 percent of the subjects went all the way, applying the full lethal 450 volts to the screaming man in the next room as he pleaded to be released.) In one version of the study, women were chosen as subjects, and were slightly more willing than men to follow the stern prompts of the professor. The cruelest subjects of all turned out to be a group of nurses from Bridgeport, Connecticut, who overwhelmingly had little hesitation in taking the voltage straight up to 450, even at that point in the "experiment" when Mr. Wallace seemed unconscious or dead. Overall, however, the outcome of the study remained constant: two-thirds of the study's subjects continued to be fully compliant despite all the variations and the different venues.

Milgram originally thought he might find the key to obedience in personal characteristics of his subjects, but had to give that idea up. "I am certain that there is a complex personality basis to obedience and disobedience. But I know we have not found it."[55] At other times Milgram agreed that the key to the subjects' obedience lay in the interaction between the Experimenter and the subject. "You do not see yourself as acting on your own. And there's a real transformation, a real change of properties of the person."[56] But he never saw (or at least never acknowledged) what it was in his study that *caused* that "change of properties". As time passed after the obedience study, and Milgram published his book *Obedience to Authority: An Experimental View* in 1974, Milgram continued to portray the very high levels of compliance as the "unanswered question" of the obedience study.

Yet Milgram *did* admit on several occasions that his study had the power to deprive his subjects of normal decision-making: "[Subjects] even try to get out of it, but they are somehow engaged in something from which they cannot liberate themselves. They are locked into a structure, and they do not have the skills or inner resources to disengage themselves."[57] This "structure" could have lasting effects: "The same mechanisms that allow the subject to perform the act, obey rather than to defy the experimenter, transcend the moment of performance and continue to justify his behavior for him."[58] But Milgram never followed up these leads, probably because he sensed where they would take him: into an acknowledgment that many of his compliant subjects' were traumatized. For Milgram it was better not to go there, better not to look in that direction for answers, even if it could have helped him to explain the 'obedience to authority' he was supposedly trying to deconstruct. One of many ironies regarding the 'obedience study' was that Milgram himself was afraid to engage or systematically acknowledge the full implications of the study he had designed.

Subjects in Milgram's study did not always suffer what had happened to them lightly. One complained to the president of Yale; another consulted an attorney. (One wonders about the extent to which Milgram thought that the shame of admitting "full compliance" would keep subjects from 'going public' about the trauma they'd experienced in the obedience study.) Perhaps the strongest denunciation of the obedience study would eventually come from the celebrated psychologist Bruno Bettelheim, who compared Milgram's study to the medical experiments conducted by Nazis on living human beings.

Several people who experienced the Milgram study as naïve subjects have talked and written about the experiences they had, leaving little doubt about the nature of what the subjects experienced. One was a veteran named William Menold who had just been discharged from a Regimental Combat Team in the US army. He described how he felt when he was instructed to administer shocks of dangerously high levels of voltage to the man in the next room who was begging to be released. The following description appears in Milgram's biography, with his biographer Blass quoting the former subject Menold, while at certain points apparently paraphrasing what he said:

"It was hell in there," [Menold] said, describing the experiment. As the procedure progressed and the victim was getting the answers wrong, Menold "really started sweating bullets." When the learner kept on screaming, he felt so sorry for him that he offered to switch places with him. He thought he could learn the materials faster, "'cause I figured this guy's kind of dumb, you know, I mean he kind of looked... like he wasn't going to win any IQ tests..."

A fleeting thought occasionally crossed [Menold's] mind about whether the "thing was real or not... But it was so well done... I bought the whole thing." An especially difficult juncture in the procedure took place when the victim stopped responding: "I didn't know what the hell was going on. I think, you know, maybe I'm killing this guy." He told the experimenter that he was "not taking responsibility for going further. That's it." It was only after he was told that the responsibility wasn't his, that [the experimenters] were taking full responsibility, that he continued.

He ended up fully obedient: "I went the whole nine yards." During the experiment, he recalls "hysterically laughing, but it was not funny laughter... It was so bizarre. And I mean, I completely lost it, my reasoning power." He described himself as an "emotional wreck" and a "basket case" during the experiment and after he left the lab, realizing "that somebody could get me to do that stuff."[59]

There seems little doubt that the experience thus described, complete with involuntary laughter, involved emotional trauma.

Whether there was some benefit *to the subject* that could outweigh the trauma, we will deal with later. For the present it will suffice to say that the man who experienced what is described above was also apparently experiencing the paralyzing effects of a trauma bond, which is what made it so difficult for him to stop obeying the commands of the Experimenter. His military service had not prepared him for the swiftness with which this kind of moral and cognitive incapacitation could occur, and had perhaps even contributed to it.

Another account is given by Herbert Winer, an academic who "went public" with his experience in the obedience study at Yale in the early 1960s. Again I quote directly from the account given in Blass' biography of Milgram, *The Man Who Shocked the World*:

> To my dismay, [the learner] began to stumble very early in the game... It was quite clear that before we got very far, the level of shock was going to be increasing... this was the end of the fun part. It is very difficult to describe... the way my feelings changed, and the conflict and tension that arose. [Winer describes how the learner began to complain about his heart condition, and yet the experimenter insisted that he continue.] And I did so, for a couple of times, and finally my own heart condition went into an extremely tense and conflicted state... I turned to the chap in the gray coat and said, "I'm sorry, but I can't go on any further with this..."

Winer reacted strongly to finding out that the true nature of the "learning experiment":

> I stood there... I was angry at having been deceived. I resented the whole situation. I was a little embarrassed at not having stopped earlier, or seen what was going on earlier, and I was not totally unconcerned about my own heart rate. What if I had had a heart problem?"

"I went home in a cold fury... I called [Milgram] the following morning, as one assistant professor to another, and told him of my anger and skepticism, and the fact that we needed to sit down and talk about this. And he was somewhat upset, but agreed. And we had a series of meetings in 1961 and '62, which I found extraordinarily valuable, and which I thought to some extent he did too..."

"But at that time, he was fresh out of his own doctoral studies, and wasn't very much concerned with my somewhat inchoate but very strong talk about ethics, about deception, and about what struck me at the time, in view of what I felt to be my own physical reaction to this conflict, as imposing altogether unwarranted strain on people who had had no previous medical screening of any kind... And I was very upset... because I felt that *had* I had a heart condition, I could have been seriously inconvenienced."

"Stanley Milgram agreed, but... he said his proposal had been approved at the level of the president's office, and that a lot of people knew about it and they all felt that the *objective* justified whatever risks, which obviously he gave a much smaller value to than I did."[60]

This is particularly interesting, if Winer's memory is correct, because Milgram justified his study by first invoking a higher authority (his study "had been approved at the level of the president's office") and then the more predictable ends-justifies-the-means rationalization. It is interesting to note that Winer intuitively understood that talking to Milgram about what had happened could help him deconstruct the trauma he had experienced, partially unraveling its influence over him. Winer also notices the context in which the Milgram study took place ("he was fresh out of his own doctoral studies"), that context being the hyper-competitive world of ambitious post-doc academics seeking tenure. Would Milgram have been equally willing to talk to a laborer or a postal worker? Nobody will ever know; but such a person probably wouldn't have been in a position to complain about the study, so there may have been less incentive for Milgram to spend so much time talking with him.

7.

Milgram was acutely aware that his obedience study, which began in June, 1961, was running concurrently with the trial of Adolf Eichmann, which had begun a month earlier in Jerusalem. Milgram mentioned Eichmann more than once, both in correspondence and in conversation, in ways that made painfully clear his hope that his obedience study would shed light on people who did terrible things while "just following orders." When his first paper on the obedience study was published in 1963, Hannah Arendt's articles were just starting to come out in the *New Yorker*—and as British writer Ian Parker has pointed out, Milgram went out of his way to put Eichmann's name in the first paragraph of his first paper about the obedience study. But this was a time in which ordinary people around the world were deeply disturbed by revelations of Nazi atrocities; and one can easily understand Milgram's suspicion that "the banality of evil," Arendt's literary formulation of Eichmann's psychopathology, contained a difficult truth.

At the same time, there were other people around the world who were likewise struggling to come to terms with revelations of Stalinist brutalities, including many intellectuals who had once placed great hope in the Soviet revolution. Now that there was a Cold War arms race, a seemingly intractable stand-off had arisen between the US and the Soviets, and it clearly suggested the likelihood, ultimately, of a nuclear war. At bottom these concerns were all about the same thing, which was the sudden realization of humanity's seemingly endless capacity for evil. Milgram's obedience study became important to a great many people who sought to understand how the 20th century had gone so far wrong.

As it became clear that Milgram had ventured into an area that contained some provocative and unexplained material about human nature, interest in his study grew. His 1974 book, *Obedience to Authority: An Experimental View*, was a major contender for the

National Book Award of that year. For a variety of reasons, including innate writing ability and a very high level of cultural literacy (he was a gifted filmmaker, and was deeply interested in theater, literature and the arts), Milgram's book is a literary as well as a psychological tour de force. It is one of the few book-length psychological studies that can be read for pleasure, despite the unsettling nature of its subject matter. Indeed, Milgram's first published paper in 1963 ("Behavioral Study of Obedience") may be, from a strictly literary point of view, the most satisfying science paper ever published.

Milgram's 1974 book attempted to further explore the issues he'd raised in the earlier paper. Reading it today, one cannot help but wonder why people have not been more capable of deconstructing his obedience study as a systematic use of trauma, particularly after Baumrind's trenchant criticism in which she repeatedly identified its presence. Milgram's book is, in fact, a candid, detailed and ingenious demonstration of exactly how one would go about giving the subject of a psychological study a paralyzing emotional trauma in a laboratory. At the heart of the institutional aggression implicit in Milgram's charade of a "learning experiment" was a systematic and thoroughgoing use of deceit. The volunteers who participated in the study trusted Yale and its employees to tell the truth; they believed the Experimenter to be a trained clinician; and most importantly, they believed—since he had been entrusted with a laboratory—that he was qualified to understand the bounds of acceptable clinical behavior.

Milgram used that trust, however idealistic his reasons may have been, to trick his subjects in a way that resembled an elaborate and very painful con game. And his superb stage management didn't merely induce naïve subjects to believe something that wasn't there, to adopt a frivolous idea, or to create a false memory; Milgram and his graduate students were deceiving people *in order to make them believe they were torturing and murdering a human being in the next room,* which was a deception of an entirely different order of magnitude.

Some people might argue that it is precisely powerful, prestigious institutions like Yale that often engage in unethical or questionable behavior; and that the obedience study could be viewed as way of educating people to distrust the claims of such apparently benign social institutions. But trust and obedience are different things. Trust has a social dimension that obedience doesn't have—it is used by people to create social contracts that can be tested over a period of time, which makes it an extremely potent psychological and social instrument. Significantly, however, trust only works when it is in common currency, when people and institutions in a society are willing to appropriately engage in it, a least much of the time. Each time a person or an institution lies gratuitously, it corrodes and weakens the tenuous links of everyday honor that hold a society together. One can justify deception in *most* psychological experiments (I repeat, *most*), but this was an instance in which the subject was deceived into thinking that he was torturing someone, with all the horror and trauma such a realization would entail.

And it was this deceit that was used by Milgram in his obedience study to trick people into acting out their capacity for radical evil, traumatizing many of them in the process, and creating a trauma bond that destroyed their ability to make moral decisions. This leads us directly back to the central—and most disturbing—irony that is at the heart of the Milgram obedience study. While the actor playing Mr. Wallace received *simulated* aggression in the form of bogus electrical shocks, the naïve subjects were victims of *real* aggression, in the form of a complicated deception resembling a highly sadistic practical joke. The fact that unsuspecting subjects were subjected to institutional aggression and deceit is directly related to the outcome of the study. If the study was cruel, why are we surprised when the subjects acted cruelly?

Many viewed Milgram's study as a painful but necessary kind of cautionary drama, one that held a mirror up to the world and bade it look upon its own depravity. Milgram's obedience study may have used special circumstances to elicit the evil of his subjects, but how long, many people might justifiably ask, would it take for future psychopaths like Hitler and Stalin to figure out exactly how to use those very same special conditions politically? Science had no answers, and neither did religion, at least not in ways that were helpful to most people in daily life. Nor did psychology shed much light on the frightening human capacity for evil that seemed to have appeared in the 20th century. There was simply a sense that the welter of moral and cultural problems now facing humankind were too much, too difficult to resolve.

It was precisely this uncomfortable historical and cultural reality that Milgram brought into experimental psychology, in the form of a modern morality play, acted out by strangers in a basement laboratory at the university, with an audience of two clinicians (Milgram and his graduate assistant) watching behind a one-way mirror. If Hannah Arendt's *Eichmann in Jerusalem: A Report on the Banality of Evil* was a speculative and philosophical exploration of radical evil in Nazi Germany, the obedience study would be a practical and behavioral quantification of its universal reality. The underlying function of his morality play, as Milgram saw it, was not to aid any particular argument about different motives for murder-by-torture, but to create a uniform social situation that could cause ordinary people to *become* murderers, people who normally wouldn't hurt a fly, as they say.

It wouldn't show *why* evil happened, but *how*, a distinction that Milgram sometimes resisted. But Milgram hadn't begun by seeing himself in that role, as an 'illusionist' or magician *eliciting* the evil behavior of his subjects—the evil behavior came from *them*, he argued fiercely on more than one occasion, at least in the beginning, because they could have broken off the "experiment" at any time, refused to pull down the switches, and walked out of the laboratory. Milgram had convinced himself that they were free agents with a free moral agency, with the responsibility to make decisions; and he desperately wanted to believe that they operated—as he did himself—out of a presumption of free will.

Indeed, it was the very ordinariness of the subjects that was disturbing to all concerned, including Milgram. If the naïve subject was Everyman, Milgram's officious Experimenter in a gray lab coat was a secular Mephistopheles, a seductive figure capable of rendering three thousand years of moral and religious teachings irrelevant in about an hour and a half. But this terrifying evil, so quickly and effectively elicited by the thaumaturgy of Milgram's study, came not from Satan or mental illness or a fascist dictatorship, but seemingly from ordinary people who'd been paid a few bucks to engage in a memory and learning experiment. The evil appeared to be inside *us*, it wasn't a product of the Devil, nor did it arise from an accident of birth and social position; it was a democratically-distributed attribute that existed in more or less equal measure in *all* of us, right here, right now in the present moment, waiting to be triggered.

But how exactly *was* it triggered? "Good experiments, like good drama, embody verities," Milgram wrote—and with the use of the word "verities" he signaled the extent to which he hoped his obedience study would arrive at an ultimate truth. The obedience study was his big chance to do exactly that; and if he couldn't do it with that, he seemed to believe, he might not get another chance. To Milgram, the ultimate truth of the 20th century had to do with good and evil in society—which is also, this writer believes, the gut issue of social evolution, not to mention the foundational dilemma that most human culture is trying to work out. We are aggressive animals who have acquired reason and language, but why are we unable to control and direct aggression? Why does it cause us to do terrible things that we don't want to do, but can't stop doing?

At bottom, good and evil is about our failure to deal successfully with the aggression we inherited from the animal world—the lust to kill and eat flesh, to dominate territory, to force or manipulate people into sexual bondage, and establish hierarchies of power based on murder and torture. The crisis of humankind in our time is that we have reason, on the one hand, and a great deal of aggression, on the other; and there is a substantial and growing disconnection between the second and the first. That is to some extent because of latent aggression in all people, no doubt—*but* it is even more because of internalized aggression, acquired from violent experiences with other human beings, often reinforced and facilitated by technology.

For that reason aggression is firmly institutionalized in politics, in social relationships, and in human culture—not to mention every human heart. It tells people to kill and hurt and deceive each other, even in conflicts that could be easily resolved using a win-win strategy. Sadly, it causes us to engage in aggression that isn't necessary, to compete when we could cooperate, and to do harmful things we really don't want to do, things that we can't explain afterwards.

Milgram's study revealed a truth that everybody had sensed, but nobody had figured out a way to quantify. Humankind was clearly in profound moral crisis, to the point that in the 20th century everything people thought they knew about morality and human behavior had to be reexamined. Under normal circumstances, people could work collaboratively with others, and might well behave according to a cooperative ethic. But the most horrifying sadism could also be elicited *from those same people*, even when there seemed to be no physical coercion forcing them to behave in that manner. How could this be so? It was just a matter of time until powerful elites and leaders figured out how to become even more proficient at eliciting radical evil—they had already made a significant beginning in the 20th century. But the very proficiency with which Milgram was himself able to generate evil behavior among his subjects signaled a problem, beginning with some of Milgram's assumptions.

If systemic evil can be systematically elicited from people, Milgram was right to look at *how* it is elicited. But in so doing, we must accept that people are not completely free, and do not have moral agency in all situations—that their ability to make moral choices is different in different situations, and significantly less than people once thought. Where evil is concerned, the situation *is* more important than the individual—*if* the individual is not prepared for that particular situation. If that's true, what Milgram was really measuring in his obedience study was not an inherent individual capacity for evil in a subject, but an inherent capacity in the situation *that Milgram himself had created to elicit that evil.*

If people were traumatized in the Milgram study, it was mainly the trauma, and *not* the evil in the subject's personality, that the study was quantifying. Furthermore, Milgram himself was complicit in the very high percentage of 'fully compliant' subjects, because he designed the methodology that produced it. If he wished to know the main cause of his subjects' evil behavior in the obedience study, he had only to look in the mirror. That didn't make him a monster, as some of his critics said, but it did mean that he had been successful in eliciting evil because of special mechanisms he had designed. So what exactly was the connection between the Holocaust, which he had been so eager to examine as a behavioral problem reducible to the laboratory, and his study? As time went on, Stanley Milgram was increasingly less certain what the connection was, if any.

An undercurrent of despondency, of middling depression, had always been present in Milgram's personality; and in the 1970s and early 1980s this middle-level depression (the clinical name for which is dysthymia, or neurotic depression) gradually became more pronounced. Milgram went from one project to the next, taking up whatever interested him, but choosing strangely ephemeral under-takings, more often than not, and indulging in fanciful ideas that had little application to psychology, social or otherwise. (Some seemed strikingly unsound: his idea about Cyranoids, for example, people who spoke thoughts that originated with others, seemed more like a science fiction fantasy than the basis for an actual study or exper-iment.) He had four heart attacks in a row, one after the other, before the fifth and final one. Milgram had always been fatalistic about his own death, saying that he confidentially expected to die when his father did, in his early 50s. This fatalism was accompanied by a certain resignation regarding his career—yes, he'd created the most controversial social psychology study in the history of the science; yet for precisely that reason, there weren't that many higher peaks to scale.

Arguably, Milgram tended to see much in his everyday life as a kind of experiment (and many of his social interactions as a kind of theater), but unfortunately without always understanding the effects of his behavior on himself and the people around him. Although he had a good marriage and his family life was happy, Milgram's weird belief that he was fated to die in his early 50s, like his father, started out as a fear and then became something of an *idée fixe*, which morphed all too easily into something close to a self-fulfilling prophecy. Stanley Milgram had, in other words, an untrammeled self-destructive streak, which he sometimes repressed and sometimes gave in to. Or was it simply that once having gone *mano a mano* with the primary obsession of one's waking and dreaming life, it becomes a bit harder to come up with a thoroughly compelling reason to stick around?

Reaching one's life-goal—and engaging fully in its heights, paradoxes and limitations—can for many especially gifted or driven people lead to an unexpected but precipitous depression, a sense of hitting a plateau from which there will be no advancement. Stanley Milgram, even more than other intellectuals of his time, would always nurse a deep ache regarding the Nazi Holocaust; and felt the riddle of evil in a personal and sometime unhealthy way. Perhaps in his own experimental paradigm he saw something evil in himself, made visible because it was externalized. As a teacher, husband and friend he was an alert, well-adjusted and caring man; but there was also something of an emotional and intellectual disconnect, as though there was something in the world he could never quite forgive, despite the world's challenges and delights.

Milgram drank alcohol and took drugs—he is known to have taken peyote, mescaline, marijuana, amphetamines and cocaine, an activity his biographer Thomas Blass mentions more than once, but unfortunately does not discuss at length. It is known that he engaged in drug use, beginning with his first year at Harvard and continuing for the rest of his life, which suggests that this use went beyond simple experimentation. Blass' determination not to go into this material sometimes gives his book about Milgram the disappointing feeling of a classic 'authorized' biography, a sanitized version of a life that conceals as much as it is prepared to reveal. It would be interesting to know, for example, exactly how and to what extent Stanley Milgram's amphetamine use might have exacerbated his heart trouble during his last years, and why he was willing to incur such a risk.

Part of the depressive subtext of his later life surely had to do with his increasing doubts about whether he had really exposed the evil at the heart of the Nazi horror that had always haunted him. He had elicited evil in the laboratory; but was that the same evil that produced the Holocaust, or was it in some way different? There is evidence that over a period of time Milgram began to feel that his obedience study was too idiosyncratic to compare to Nazi evil. His study had produced evil, all right—but ultimately it wasn't the evil of the Holocaust, because the evil of Nazi Germany had arisen in a cultural and psychological and political vortex too complex and too culture-specific to capture in a laboratory. And the evil he had captured seemed, in retrospect, to be more the outcome of his cleverness than the gratuitous cruelty of Nazi violence. Furthermore, Milgram was aware that others in his profession had arrived at the same conclusion—that the obedience study was a good, probably great, study that showed humankind something we desperately needed to see; but that the evil committed by people like Adolph Eichmann was still as mysterious and maddeningly incomprehensible as before. No study could really help us understand it. This had to be depressing to Milgram, because so much of his life had been predicated on the idea that he could, in effect, defeat the Holocaust by capturing and then deconstructing its essence in a laboratory.

As early as 1964, Milgram responded to a letter from a young woman who had built a replica of Milgram's 'Shock Generator,' except that it had seven switches rather than 30. She had devised this contraption as an entry in a state fair. She reported to Milgram that 77 percent of the teenagers in her experiment pulled down all seven switches, which were supposedly giving painful shocks, and speculated that her subjects were comparable to Nazi youth who blindly followed Hitler's orders. Milgram replied that it was "quite a jump... from an experiment of this sort to general conclusions about the Nazi epoch, and I, myself, feel that I have sometimes gone too far in generalizing. Be cautious in generalizing."[61]

For many people, including a great many famous people with strong opinions on the matter, Milgram's study itself reminded them of the violent manipulations of the Nazi doctors. Dannie Abse, author of *The Dogs of Pavlov*, denounced Milgram's use of deception and the rapid, escalating introduction of agonizing emotional duress. He felt, he wrote, that some people "may feel that in order to demonstrate that subjects may behave like so many Eichmanns, the experimenter had to act the part, to some extent, of a Himmler." Milgram wrote a rebuttal that compared his study to what happens in a theater, suggesting that it was similar to the character of an old man who turns out to be a young actor after the greasepaint is removed. Of course, an illusion created by greasepaint is different from an illusion in which a subject believes he is complicit in torturing and killing an innocent person.

Bruno Bettelheim, the famous psychologist, author and concentration camp survivor, saw the study as "so vile that nothing these experiments show has any value... They are in line with the human experiments of the Nazis." Bettelheim was clearly overstating the case; he could be a difficult and hostile man, as subsequent writing about his life demonstrated. But Milgram's fiercest critics often touched on an irony mentioned earlier: that the obedience study elicited behavior typical of Nazis who did evil while "just following orders," but that the study itself seemed retrospectively to have used techniques that were themselves reminiscent of the Nazis.

Milgram surely saw the irony, but could hardly appreciate it, because it was one more sign that he had perhaps not really captured the ultimate insight into radical evil as he had once hoped to do—instead, he had himself been accused of using unethical techniques to produce dramatic results. By the early 1980s, Milgram must have been oppressively aware of the consensus among his peers that his obedience study should never be replicated, at least not in the same way he had originally done it. What did that say about Milgram's ethics?

According to his wife, Stanley Milgram's last day on earth included a complicated social interaction in which he felt ill during a student's defense of her PhD thesis, but hesitated to ask his assistant for a drink of water because she was a strong feminist, and Stanley feared that she might feel that he was treating her differently than a male colleague. (A set of circumstances that sounds like a sensational premise for an experiment, by the way.) But in retrospect one also has to wonder, how recently had Stanley Milgram used cocaine or amphetamines before his last and fatal heart attack? His biographer Blass doesn't know, or isn't prepared to say.

Milgram took the subway home on the day of his heart attack, accompanied by a worried friend. (Typically, men often deny they are having heart attacks, as Milgram, in his role as social psychologist, would have been the first to point out.) He was taken directly to the hospital by his wife, where he said to the attendant: "My name is Stanley Milgram, and I believe I'm having my fifth heart attack." Only then did he fall to his knees. The last thing the interns did in a desperate attempt to save his life was to put electrodes on his body and administer electric shocks; but by that time Milgram was unconscious, and therefore unable to enjoy this unexpected final irony. His last words were in the form of a joke to the surgeon that they try to secure a baboon heart. All deaths are untimely, none so much as that of Stanley Milgram, who was only fifty-one when he died. Yet if he was fated to die in his early fifties, as he believed he was, he could not have chosen a more fitting year. The year in which Stanley

Milgram died was, appropriately, 1984, the date that is also the title of George Orwell's last and most "Orwellian" novel.

8.

Stanley Milgram and Diana Baumrind are authentic culture heroes, whose greatness we may only now be able to comprehend. Both were trying to make the same point in different ways, although it was hard for people to see that in the 1960s. Milgram quantified with astonishing verisimilitude the cruelty that can be elicited under extreme emotional pressure in a laboratory study; Baumrind understood that Milgram's subjects were being traumatized, and correctly determined that her criticisms were a necessary moral corrective aimed at spurring the formalization of new protocols for experimental science. Furthermore, Baumrind's insight into the trauma of Milgram's subjects is the key to interpreting his data, because it helps us understand the extremely high rate of compliance in his study. There is no doubt whatsoever that Baumrind was right to demand higher standards for experimental ethics—nor can we justify Milgram's study solely on the basis of what it tells us about human evil under stress.

Baumrind, working at a time when there were few women in psychology, had to put up with the macho posturing of males who denounced her as a hypersensitive child psychologist who was herself childlike, and who sought to infantilize subjects of psychological studies. Ultimately the consensus came down on Baumrind's side, however; deception could continue to be a part of experimental science, but not when it was likely to traumatize human subjects. Baumrind's courageous insistence on the establishment of proper standards in experimental science was precisely the thoughtful noncompliance to authority that Milgram himself was forever calling for. By challenging the psychology establishment, Baumrind was raising the same issue that Milgram had, the difference being that Milgram saw the problem of human good and evil as a meta-drama exemplified by the Nazi Holocaust, whereas Baumrind saw an example of the problem in Milgram's own experimental attitudes and behavior. Both were real issues; both needed to be raised; and both needed to be thrashed out in an ongoing public debate, a discussion that is still underway.

Both Milgram and Baumrind had their supporters and detractors (some of whom changed sides as the debate over ethics intensified) but neither chose the easy way out; both permanently altered the course of psychology, of human thought, and history. The world could never be the same once they had acted out their personal dramas of discovery, resistance and moral imagination. After Milgram, it became increasingly hard to deny the existence of evil, as it became all too clear that people could be induced to do terrible things—and that was, arguably, Milgram's main objective, to quantify evil to the point at which it could no longer be denied.

The excruciating but Spartan clarity of Milgram's study, and the powerful effect it had on the study's subjects, also created the opportunity for Baumrind and others to articulate the case for needed reforms, and to raise consciousness regarding the role of an agreed-upon morality in behavioral science. Ultimately a consensus was achieved that an entirely new look at the rules regarding human subjects in psychological experiments would be necessary—and thankfully the psychology establishment set about creating the necessary reforms.

Diana Baumrind, by denouncing the ethics of the highly popular Milgram study, defied much powerful opinion within the psychology establishment, in the process demonstrating the very quality of rebellion against a perceived wrong that Milgram identified as being necessary to defeat radical evil. Milgram made us forever aware of the existence of evil; Baumrind gave us a similarly enduring example of how one can appropriately rebel against it, wherever it is encountered.

9.

Can the Milgram 'obedience study' be retroactively justified in 2012?

It certainly wasn't justifiable in 1961, because nobody knew what the effects of it would be on the subjects that participated in it, which was precisely Diana Baumrind's objection to it. But now we know a great deal more about the study's ultimate effects on the subjects that participated. Did Milgram's obedience study cause permanent damage to its subjects? Or—to put it another way—what was the attitude of subjects toward their participation in the study, and their assessment of how it had affected them? Milgram himself sent out a questionnaire asking subjects this question (whether they were glad they had participated in Milgram study) and the response was quite surprising.

A very high percentage of participants to whom this question-naire was sent filled them out and returned them. About these questionnaires Milgram wrote: "The replies to the questionnaire confirmed my impression that participants felt positively toward the experiment. In its quantitative aspect, 84 *percent of the subjects stated they were glad to have been in the experiment*; 15 percent indicated neutral feelings; and 1.3 percent negative feelings."[62] These are astonishing figures, and to this writer at first seemed improbable, or even impossible. But there is no evidence—repeat, no evidence whatsoever—that these results were anything but as Milgram reported them. But how could that be? How could 84 percent of the subjects have such positive feelings about the study, after the pain, discomfort and outright suffering they had gone through? The third of the subjects who had been defiant would have good reason to be satisfied with themselves, and therefore with the study. But what about the two-thirds, the ones that were 'fully compliant?' How could they come to terms with their own behavior in such a defin-itive manner as to actually feel good about the experience?

Is it possible that some subjects were still suffering the effects of trauma incurred during the 'obedience study'? One defiant subject was an engineer, an immigrant from Holland, who refused to continue cooperating with the study at 255 volts. Despite his refusal to continue the "experiment," he was very hard on himself for continuing as long as he had, accepting all responsibility personally and expressing chagrin and self-contempt. A few days later Milgram and his staff received a "long, careful" letter from him, informing them that he was contemplating a career change, because of a new-found conviction that "the social sciences and especially psychology are much more important in today's world." He then expressed a desire to come to work for Milgram as an assistant.[63] The expressed wish of the Dutch immigrant to change careers and to work with Milgram as his employee, so soon after participating in the obedience study, unmistakably suggests the presence of a trauma bond, despite the fact that he had broken off the "experiment" at 225 volts.

Was the very high percentage of subjects who were glad to have participated in the study likewise the result of trauma bonding? Were they still so bonded to the study's aggression that they felt obligated to speak positively about it? Some probably were, like the Dutch engineer described above; but that probably *wasn't* true of most subjects, because of the comprehensive aftercare procedures designed by Milgram himself. The aftercare procedures were precisely the kind one would design for people who had just experi-enced a traumatizing event, which was to talk about what had happened to them immediately after it occurred. While many of Milgram's subjects may have experienced traumata in the short term—or at the very least a great deal of stress and emotional disori-entation—his aftercare protocols seemed designed to counteract and to deconstruct the development of long-term traumatic symptoms. And in that, the aftercare protocols seem to have been mainly effective, at least according to the positive reaction of most subjects.

At first, long and sometimes informal discussions after the "experiment" was concluded were not merely allowed, but encouraged. Subjects who had just participated in the obedience study sat around the laboratory informally discussing the dramatic events in which they had just been a part, talking about it with Milgram personally, but also with the actors playing Mr. Wallace and the Experimenter. "Each subject had a friendly reconciliation with the unharmed victim [Mr. Wallace], and an extended discussion with the [E]xperimenter." Milgram mentions this several times, in both his original paper and in his 1974 book.

Although Milgram may not have understood its implications, the subject's "extended discussion" with the Experimenter almost certainly allowed the subject to begin unraveling, wholly or in part, the trauma bonding they had experienced relative to the Experimenter's aggressive commands, and the sadistic aggression the Experimenter had represented during the course of the 'obedience study' deception. As the subjects continued to talk informally at length with Milgram (as well as the two actors that played Mr. Wallace and the Experimenter) the power of the trauma bond would probably diminish, although many subjects surely felt some lingering influence of the aggression that the Experimenter represented. "In some additional instances," Milgram wrote, "additional detailed and lengthy discussions of the experiments were also carried out with individual subjects." Again, one wonders how Milgram himself construed this aftercare need for "lengthy discussions" of the study, discussion that would sometimes go on— according to Milgram's own report—for "several days or weeks." What was it about his study that made such lengthy discussions necessary? Almost surely it was because many of the subjects were traumatized, although Milgram would never acknowledge this.

By the time they received the questionnaire from Milgram, many of the former subjects had begun to understand the historic importance of the study, or at least its highly unusual nature. But there is probably another reason why 84 percent of Milgram's subjects were glad to have been part of the obedience study. They had been given the opportunity to experience something extraordinary and powerful and unique in themselves. They had been given the opportunity to experience *their own capacity for aggression and radical evil*, learning in the process that evil can be resisted successfully by ordinary people, if and when they learn the telltale signs of unacceptable aggression and refuse to become complicit before they get in too deep. That is, as this writer has tried to make clear, an extremely liberating thing, because by experiencing this difficult insight into one's own personality, one is brought face to face with 'the enemy,' so to speak, the worst thing this world has to offer. But by seeing it in the mirror and knowing that one is now able to recognize and thus defeat it, the nightmare loses its dark power and becomes just another harmless part of the deep background we all carry around within us.

It is oddly comforting to know that the destruction which threatens civilization is not an abstraction, but is actually in one's own personality, where one can grapple with and come to terms with it. Besides, emotional maturity is impossible without that kind of self-knowledge. The Milgram study made its subjects acutely aware that a particular combination of circumstances could compromise their ability to make moral choices. This, along with the liberating ethos of the 1960s, gave them permission to engage in some powerful introspection and self-criticism, resulting in new insight into their own personalities—insight they arguably could have gotten in no other way. The influence of American history at that time made people uniquely receptive to questioning established morality, and questioning their own values. It turns out that although Milgram's subjects were often traumatized by his controversial study, there was something in the historical ambience at that time that was uniquely helpful in assisting them in coming to terms with what they had experienced—and left them spiritually and emotionally stronger.

From the time of the first study in 1961–1962, until Milgram's book about the obedience study was published in 1974, huge and tumultuous changes in public attitudes were occurring. These changes began with the JFK assassination, which came as a huge shock to the American people and was never satisfactorily explained; then the escalation of the Vietnam War, the Civil Rights Movement and the assassinations of Bobby Kennedy and Martin Luther King. One must especially consider the special agony of the war in

Vietnam, in which it gradually became clear to many Americans that their government was lying to them, at a time when literally millions of young American citizens would have to make decisions about whether to defy state authority, or comply with it. Should one allow oneself to be drafted into the Vietnam War, or try to avoid service based on one's conscience? Should one fight on behalf of a government that habitually lies to its own people?

This generated a culture of introspection, on the one hand, and a systematic questioning of American institutions on the other; and the upshot of this powerful compound very often resulted in revolutionary changes in individual lives. As we will shortly see from direct testimony from former subjects, the unique 1960s *zeitgeist* played an unexpected but evidently important role in helping Milgram's subjects come to terms with—and make sense of—what they had learned about themselves in his laboratory. As many of the subjects integrated memories of the traumatic experiences in Milgram's laboratory into their memory, worldview and individual personalities, the process became for many a voyage of self-discovery, as certain subjects used the experience as a jumping-off point for important changes in their lives.

We can now see that Milgram's subjects were often going through a process of intense and systematic moral introspection regarding their participation in the obedience study. This process greatly resembled the forced stretching of America's moral imagination created by the Vietnam War, the Civil Rights Movement and the Women's Movement. In fact, a great many subjects were able to use what they'd experienced in Milgram's laboratory as a psychological touchstone for new emotional growth, their experience in the study having thrown into perspective the kind of person they wanted to be and the kind of life they wanted to live.

10.

In her challenging book *Opening Skinner's Box*, psychologist Lauren Slater interviewed people who had been subjects in the Milgram study. One was a crusty old World War Two vet who had been a defiant subject, but hadn't learned much from the experience, because he felt uncomfortable with self-examination. Interestingly, however, other subjects—many of whom had been 'fully compliant'—had seen their lives improve as a result of what they had learned.

One of them, whom Slater calls Jacob in her book, is a gay man who now lives in the Boston area. Jacob speaks about the Milgram study "as though it were yesterday," and tells Slater that his hands "still hurt" from what he did in the study. He was only twenty-three when he participated in the obedience study. He was going through a crisis at that time, struggling to accept that fact that he was a homosexual. Jacob's memory of his participation in the Milgram study is that although he realized how badly he was hurting the victim in the other room, he couldn't stop pulling down the electroshock levers. Here is Lauren Slater's account of her conversation with Jacob forty years later about his participation in the study, along with Slater's own comments:

"Well," says Jacob, "I just continued. I was so depressed I almost didn't care, and I was thinking, 'No permanent tissue damage,' he's got to be right, I pray he's right, I don't want any permanent tissue damage, do I have permanent tissue damage?" He describes a scene where the screams of the learner merged with his own self-loathing, a joint pain, and up he went, utterly without a center, having spurted it all out in secret shames.

"Afterwards," said Jacob, "when I was debriefed afterwards, explained what had happened, I was horrified. Really, really horrified. They kept saying, 'You didn't hurt anyone, don't worry, you didn't hurt anyone,' but it's too late for that. You can never," says Jacob, "really debrief a subject after an experiment like that. You've given shocks. You thought you were really giving shocks, and nothing can take away from you the knowledge of how you acted. There's no turning back."

I recall, while speaking with Jacob, the words of Boston College sociology professor David Karp, who said to me, "Just imagine what it must be like for those subjects, to have to live their whole lives knowing what they were capable of…"

"So," I said to Jacob, "I would guess you think the experiments were essentially unethical, that they caused you harm."

Jacob pauses. He strokes his dog. "No," he says, "Not at all. If anything, just the opposite."

I look at him.

"The experiments," he continues, "caused me to reevaluate my life. They caused me to confront my own compliance and really struggle with it. I began to see closeted homosexuality, which is just another form of compliance, as a moral issue. I came out. I saw how essential it was to develop a strong moral center. I felt my own moral weakness and I was appalled, so I went to the ethical gym, if you see what I mean."

I nod. I see what he means. "I came out," he says, "and that took a lot of strength and built a lot of strength, and I saw how pathetically vulnerable I was to authority, so I kept a strict eye on myself and learned to buck expectations. I went from being a goody-two-shoes golden boy with a deep secret headed straight for medical school, to a gay activist teaching inner-city kids. And I credit Milgram with galvanizing this."[64]

What Jacob is describing is a spiritual and moral transformation—a conversion experience, one might say. It sounds like the study came at just the right time for him, shaking up his neat expectations and establishing with unmistakable clarity how necessary it was for him to change his life. On the other hand, it sounds as though the experience was so powerful, so frightening, and so potentially mind-blowing that he almost *had* to do something positive to regain his self-esteem. Slater writes about other former subjects, many of whom also experienced life-changing experiences as a result of their participation in the Milgram obedience study. Here I again quote directly from Slater:

Harold Takooshian, a former student of Milgram's and a professor at Fordham University, recalls a binder of letters on Milgram's desk: "It was a big black binder filled with hundreds of letters from subjects, and many, many of the letters said how much the obedience experiments had taught them about life, and how to live it." Subjects claimed the experiment caused them to rethink their relationship to authority and responsibility; one young man even said that as a result of his participation in the Milgram experiments, he became a conscientious objector in the [Vietnam] war.

So this, perhaps, is what we're left with: an experiment that derives its significance not from its quantifiable findings, but from its pedagogical power. Milgram's obedience experiments had the ironic effect of making his subjects, at least some of them, less obedient. And that is pretty stunning—an experiment so potent it does not describe or demonstrate, so much as detonate, a kind of social psychology equivalent of the atom bomb, only this time in the service of creation, not destruction, for as Milgram himself said, "From these experiments comes awareness and that may be the first step towards change."[65]

The letters sent by former subjects to Milgram tend to suggest the aftereffects of trauma, but there are so many accounts of people who wrote to Milgram after being subjects in the obedience study that it cannot be solely ascribed to this cause. And of the people who wrote to Milgram afterwards, the vast majority expressed gratitude for having been in the study. None of them would have voluntarily chosen what Milgram forced them to go through—but once having experienced the obedience study, they could not resume their lives as though nothing had happened. To go on with their lives, they *had* to make sense of the study in which they'd participated. Their experience, and especially the experiences of the 'fully compliant' subjects, clearly suggests not only that they had confronted in a deeply personal way their own capacity for hurting another human being, but had also arrived at a point where they felt the necessity of changing their lives. The special ambiance of the 1960s would have encouraged that attitude toward personal transformation.

We, who know what the Milgram study revealed, find ourselves in somewhat the same position. However much we may disagree with the extent to which Milgram took risks with the mental health of his subjects, we also must live with what the Milgram study revealed; we cannot go on as though nothing has happened—we must face the reality of human evil, and if we do not like what we have learned, we must face the challenge of changing it. What the Milgram 'obedience study' showed us was that human civilization is fundamentally susceptible to aggression and evil, perhaps now more than ever. While in our personal relationships we may be kinder, better, and more insightful, in our social existence and institutions we are increasingly led by leaders committed to eliciting aggression, rather than leaders gifted in negotiating win-win solutions and making creative social contracts. Patriarchal leaders support war, torture and imperial aggression simply because the trauma inherent in those things reinforces their patriarchal worldview in society, and the aggressive emotional orientations that accompany them. And since those who choose aggression and deceit intuitively know how to manipulate everybody else, society is not getting *less* aggressive, but *more*.

The answer to the paradox of Stanley Milgram and his obedience study is finally a simple one. Milgram's subjects were traumatized, but were given the opportunity to deconstruct the trauma. They were taken 'backstage,' as it were, and shown how the machinery of deceit and trauma bonding work. They were shown a snapshot of systemic evil in society in which they were the unwilling protagonists. They saw how trauma causes a person to identify with aggression; and how control, deceit, victimology and their own wildly fluctuating guilt and horror enhanced that bond, so that even if they couldn't describe these components in words, they would be likely to recognize them if they encountered them in the future. Milgram's deception sucked them so deeply into an utterly diabolical process that after an hour and a half many of them were prepared to torture to death an innocent stranger. They saw how systemic evil took away their conscience, their internalized social norms and their religious and moral restraints—it took away, in other words, not only everything that made them civilized, but every good thing in their humanity. They could not deny that it happened, because it had happened to them.

That being irrefutably the case, they then realized that they had to do something to change their lives. For that reason, the study evidently turned out to be a turning-point of immense importance to many subjects. It was at that point that these subjects not only reexamined the moral code by which they had lived their lives, but also the circumstances in which they could be induced to commit evil acts. Having gone through this transformative self-examination, they could face the world with greater confidence. The main point about this transformation was not just that they underwent a *psychological* transformation, but also a *moral* one, in which a self-acceptance of one's own capacity for evil played a large part. A great many subjects apparently discovered one of the great truths of life: that happiness is impossible without a moral code to give it meaning, not to mention shape, limit and texture, depth and perspective; and one cannot really arrive at a powerful moral code without facing one's own capacity for evil.

As the former subjects found out more about the obedience study of which they had been a part, they could more easily understand Milgram's motivation for tricking them, because despite his personal ambition his motives, although obsessive, were understandable. Some subjects probably grasped that civilization is facing an unprecedented moral crisis, and had been brought to that realization in no small part by their own compliance in the Milgram study. Their understanding of this, combined with the historical moment that they inhabited, gave them a healing understanding of Milgram's reasons for using deception, stress and trauma to elicit unprecedented behavior. Because of these factors, many of them learned a critical lesson from their participation in the Milgram study, which for a great many—evidently most, according to their own report—ended up transforming their lives for the better.

How this happened is a complex and fascinating process, and tells us a great deal not just about trauma, trauma bonding and systemic evil, but how people deconstruct the effects of these overwhelming experiences. If they confront emotional trauma soon enough to stop the internalization of aggression, and if society—or a peer group somewhat like Milgram's aftercare services—will support their willingness to engage in self-examination, they are generally able to deconstruct the emotional bonds of trauma, although most will almost surely need help with it. In any case, in such a process Milgram's subjects were mainly able to transform themselves into stronger and better people.

The Milgram study is the only instance of which I am aware in which the deliberate elicitation of evil led to a generally good end. This happened, first, because Milgram himself designed good aftercare protocols, in which subjects were allowed to have extensive discussions with the actors who tricked them into doing something brutal and ugly. Secondly, many of the former subjects were able to figure out on their own various creative ways to improve their own lives—they made sense out of the Milgram study because they felt they had to. Third, the historical zeitgeist of the 1960s encouraged radical introspection and personal transformation, and the development of a personal moral code in opposition to the demands of the state. Finally, we cannot deny or leave out the enormity of the psychological truth revealed by the study—that all people are capable of radical evil—because the subjects themselves came to understand the importance of that truth.

The importance of this insight cannot be overemphasized. Underlying most science, art and culture generally is a quest to comprehend the problem of good and evil, to deconstruct the effects of eating from the Tree of Knowledge of Good and Evil; for in so doing is our only hope of defeating the death wish that Freud saw rising from the chaos of the First World War and the rise of Nazism, the "desire to return to inanimate matter." Indeed, the quest to understand the problem of good and evil is the central—not the only, but the central—dynamic of human culture, because arriving at some resolution of it, however partial, is the only hope of human survival.

Because we cannot understand ourselves without trying to understand evil, someone would have sooner or later designed something like Milgram's obedience study, because any species capable of both thought and aggression would need such an instrument by which to understand the contradiction inherent in their circumstances. We could not understand the gravity of the human predicament without the awareness that our moral agency can quickly be taken away from us by the right combination of aggression, deceit and trauma; and at this stage in history particularly, humanity is increasingly frightened and obsessed with the growing discontinuity between aggression and cognition. Milgram proved beyond a shadow of a doubt that sometimes we are unable to stop doing destructive things even though we want to stop. Indeed, had Stanley Milgram never lived, someone would have found it necessary to contemplate something like his obedience study. The Milgram study was one of the turning points of human consciousness, and therefore of human history.

But now that we know what it taught us, it can never be repeated. Milgram's subjects in the early 1960s were favorably transformed because it was a time of great idealism, rebellion toward authority and hope for a better world—but we can't be sure it would ever work that way again. Future subjects might well react to the same study with nihilism, using it as an excuse to engage in aggression or deception outside the laboratory. The Milgram obedience study was a 20th century experience of The Fall (or rather, it was quantifiable *evidence* of The Fall) as it existed in the laboratory where it was elicited. But once out of the Laboratory/Garden, and once having recognized the existence of evil, we can never go back; nor should we be allowed to replicate exactly the experiment that made us aware of our own knowledge of good and evil.

Any species that possesses both aggression and volition must find out, sooner or later, about its terrifying capacity for destruction and self-destruction. Milgram created not just a new way of understanding human behavior, but a new paradigm for understanding our desire to destroy ourselves. Once we thought cognition controlled aggression, but increasingly the opposite is true—there is, in other words, *a radical discontinuity between aggression and cognition, in which the former often controls the latter.* Something in the rapid changes brought on by the Industrial Revolution and the growth of a technology of death, but most of all the systematic use of aggression in ways that cause us to internalize and identify with it, has caused aggression to escape the confines of rational risk-assessment and decision-making and to become something that is close to being out of control.

Once we assimilate this profound paradigmatic change, we can never be the same again, nor can our world. The data is there, whether we like it or not; what is important is how we react to it. This book you are reading supplies, among other things, a workable theory to interpret that data, because Milgram unknowingly provided a quantifiable glimpse into how evil is elicited—in fact Milgram's study demonstrates exactly how trauma is used to bond people to aggression. In fact, Milgram's famous study also elicited in an amazingly short time all the major elements of systemic evil already discussed in this book. But Milgram's aftercare protocols also provide an example of how a trauma bond can be partially or wholly deconstructed, through frank discussion of the power relationship between the traumatized and the institution (Yale University) that traumatized them. Most of all, Milgram's subjects were able to deconstruct their trauma bond by talking about what had just happened to them.

Speaking of the many different versions of Milgram's obedience study, Lee Ross, a social psychologist at Stanford University, had this to say: "Perhaps more than any other empirical contributions in the history of social science, they have become part of our society's shared intellectual legacy—that small body of historical incidents, biblical parables, and classic literature that serious thinkers feel free to draw on when they debate about human nature or contemplate human history."[66] From Aeschylus to Freud, from the Prophet Isaiah to George Orwell, the reality is that there is a powerful undercurrent of pessimism about the ultimate fate of humankind. These truth-tellers tell us that there is something self-destructive in human nature that seeks to destroy us, that lead us into endless self-sabotage. But for those who take up the challenge, that's not necessarily pessimism. It's simply fair warning.

If humankind has something destructive in its nature, it must change its nature, starting with those individuals who are courageous enough to see the extent of the problem. Former subjects of the obedience study are good models for the kinds of changes each of us should consider making. The subjects involved in the Milgram study sought to make sense of their behavior, and ultimately the introspection they experienced helped many of them to make sense of their lives. The ultimate meaning of the truth revealed by the Milgram study is what we do toward changing ourselves today. The good of Milgram's study finally outweighed the pain it caused—and we know that not because of abstract calculation about ultimate worth, but because so many of Milgram's subjects personally testified to its worth in their lives.

In experimental science, the well-being of the subject must of necessity trump everything else; and the fact that Milgram's subjects were able to use their painful experience to become better people trumps every other retroactive justification for Milgram we could possibly imagine. Furthermore, these subjects point to the kind of world we should try to build. If we are sufficiently humble, we will put ourselves in the shoes of Milgram's subjects, and face the world as they faced it: that is, we should commit ourselves to the personal transformation that begins with acknowledging our own capacity for evil. The best effect of Milgram's magic theater may have been to act out a cautionary drama that demands a response not just from former subjects, but from humanity. If the 'Milgram paradigm' warns us of the omnipresence of trickery and aggression, it also means that all men and women should be encouraged to change their lives, and to arrive at a personal combination of psychological defenses that can help them recognize and defeat evil, both personal and systemic.

II.

So what is the 'Milgram paradigm'? If it means anything, it means accepting that good people can be tricked to do extremely evil things by people that have more power than they do. We don't have to apply the 'Milgram paradigm' to the real world, as much as to acknowledge that it *came* from the real world. Long before it was anybody's paradigm, there were trickery, exploitation and psychological aggression used by the strong to enslave the weak, in order to create and exercise power. Milgram merely imitated and acted out these psychological, political and social realities in a laboratory, replicating a powerful kind of short-term psychological enslavement. But Milgram also designed aftercare protocols, let us remember, for overcoming its worst effects; and that makes him different from the demagogues who would use such techniques solely for personal power and gain.

In the modern world, powerful people tend to lie to less powerful people when they want them to do something; they use aggression to enforce their norms and bond people to their goals. There are, thankfully, honorable exceptions to this grim rule, but they are mainly notable as exceptions. Therefore, avoiding trauma bonding and systemic evil will depend to a great extent on recognizing that powerful elites will seek, through deception and aggression, to psychologically, socially and economically enslave those who are less powerful than they are, despite whatever pretty or seductive names they may give their experiments in domination. Milgram's subjects were enslaved for less than two hours, but in that short amount of time the 'fully compliant' ones found themselves doing terrifying things.

Then, afterwards, they were encouraged to go backstage and see how deception contributed to their loss of moral agency. After subjects had experienced the full range of pressures in Milgram's magic theater, they were allowed to discuss what had happened with the principle actors in the theater's performance. They were able to discuss how the actor playing the Experimenter felt about his role, as well as the actor playing the dutiful Mr. Wallace; and listen to Milgram himself explain how he had scripted the obedience study — and probably hear directly from Milgram regarding some of his concerns about the Nazi Holocaust, and the kind of evil that is done by people who are "just following orders." After being able to talk the experience over with those most intimately involved in it, the unraveling of the trauma would begin.

Later, as we've seen, subjects continued to struggle with what had happened to them, but a great many were able to use their experiences in the Milgram obedience study for purposes of emotional growth. Finally, a substantial majority were able to arrive at a place where they were grateful for being part of the study, despite the suffering they had experienced. It had ultimately been a life-changing experience — because so many of them decided to use it in that way, aided by the historic ambience of the 1960s which emphasized personal transformation above all. Milgram had discovered in the design of his famous study almost exactly the right combination or constellation of forces necessary to elicit evil behavior in a very short time. Having been subjected to the study, and living in a society in which the basic attitudes of many people were being challenged, Milgram's subjects were challenged to find through introspection the right personal constellation of forces necessary to defeat systemic evil if and when they encountered it later, in the world outside the laboratory.

Milgram himself sought not to rule a society or reap its profits, but simply to make a reasonably successful career in social psychology. Ultimately, however, he achieved notoriety rather than fame, and a middling success in New York rather than the tenure at Harvard that he would have preferred. But he tried valiantly to realize his dream of defeating the Holocaust by discovering and exposing for all time its toxic heart of evil; if in the end he failed, the purity of his passion and the reality of his near-success must have given him some satisfaction.

What Milgram did in his laboratory was to create a form of evil, which was, in its purest form, institutional aggression plus deceit. As Baumrind saw, trauma was present—in such a manner, this writer would say, that a trauma bond was created, which explains the extremely high rate of "full compliance." Interestingly, the obedience study also demonstrated how *quickly* a clever form of systemic evil can be put in place. Expressed in this way, the 'Milgram paradigm' may strike many people as nothing more than a kind of harrowing secular Calvinism without any concomitant salvation, since we may be certain that variations of it will be used forever by demagogues and dictators with fewer scruples than Stanley Milgram. Is evil fated to prevail, then? Not for those worthy of its challenges. The harsh truths of the Milgram paradigm tells us unequivocally that evil exists and can be quickly elicited, but provides some important information necessary to defeat the deceit and aggression that drive it, not to mention the trauma that binds people to it. That will not be easy, of course; but there is little evidence that the survival of the human species is fated to be an easy exercise.

Chapter 6

America and the Trauma Bond

"You inherit the sins.
You inherit the flames."
Bruce Springsteen
Adam Raised a Cain

I.

The bombing of Pearl Harbor horrified millions. But the horror of 9/11 was even worse, because many millions of Americans watched it in real time on TV *while the Twin Towers came down.* This writer was one of those Americans. I watched it happen on TV after working all night at a mental health facility in California, sitting next to a desperate colleague who was calling her mother in New York to see if she was out of danger. (My colleague's voice became a horrified wail as we watched the first tower come down on TV, then a wracking sob as the reality of mass death hit us.) If you were watching it, you simply couldn't accept that so many people were inside those structures dying, although you knew it was happening. It was very much like a bad dream, compounded with a very bad science fiction film from the 1950s, especially the enveloping, evil black cloud of dust that raced across downtown Manhattan with people running in terror before it.

But I was in California and there was nothing I could do about it, so I drove home in a deep funk and tried to sleep; but like a lot of people, I couldn't pull myself away from the television and the excited voices of the broadcasters. The images haunted my dreams and waking fantasies for months. Others were similarly affected. Of course, it was people who were in New York at that time (and most of all, those who lost family members or friends in the terrorist atrocity) who were most deeply affected.

For them, the trauma—and the way they found to deal with it—

would deeply alter their lives, and its effects would last a lifetime. They would have to arrive at the best way to live with an experience that had changed (and those who lost loved ones, defined) their lives forever. It is part of this book's premise, of course, that such an experience will inevitably change people's attitudes and behavior. Many did a great job, ultimately translating the aggression of the 9/11 atrocity into humanitarian work or advocacy for peace. Some became advocates for interfaith understanding that profoundly benefited the living; others became obsessed with revenge, which always creates the danger of more innocent deaths. Others came down somewhere in between the two extremes. The big question was not just about how it affected you, but what you did about it. That question became a lifetime assignment for all who lost loved ones, and to a lesser extent that became the task for other Americans too, even those who were not affected nearly as deeply.

The emotional trauma associated with 9/11 was so powerful that the political class of America responded by internalizing—then emotionally identifying with—the aggression of the lunatic fanatics who attacked America, as well as the attackers' goals and values. That may sound like a startling accusation, but consider the facts. The Bush presidency began to dismantle the US Constitution and the Bill of Rights, while engaging in various forms of state terrorism, including torture (often of innocent people). At first, of course, the US military response was appropriate—since Al Qaeda (the terrorist group that attacked us) was based in Afghanistan, military action against both the terrorists and their Taliban hosts in Afghanistan was not only justified but necessary.

But the Bush administration did not concentrate on tracking down the top leadership of Al Qaeda—Osama bin Laden would not be taken out until 2011, as a result of the hard work of the Obama administration. Nor did the US concentrate on dismantling the Taliban in Afghanistan, and use its treasure to rebuild that country in such a way that the Taliban could never come back. Instead the US political class, under the leadership of the Bush administration, started a completely unnecessary and unrelated war by invading and occupying the country of Iraq in 2003, which quickly led to a deadly insurgency, which in turn led to a costly counter-insurgency campaign. This incredible and unnecessary invasion of a sovereign country that had never attacked us was justified by the assertion that Iraq possessed "weapons of mass destruction," an accusation that was quickly proven false.

Sadly, nobody was allowed to question the government propaganda that prepared the American people for this unnecessary war because America's media enthusiastically agreed to go along with—and even to enforce—the dissemination of Bush administration falsehoods. The effect of 9/11 on American leaders (and on many of the American people themselves) became a horrific example of mass trauma bonding, in which a government, a political class and a strong plurality of the people identified with the aggression—not to mention the fanatical values—of the terrorist aggressor. And many Americans, under the sway of that same bond, supported the new aggression with the inchoate fury of the traumatized. The unpleasant truth is that the US invasion of Iraq caused more death in the world than Osama bin Laden could ever have imagined.

When President George Bush attacked Iraq on March 19th, 2003, subduing its corrupt government and beginning the long and violent US occupation, he was attacking a country that had nothing to do with the mass atrocities of 9/11. But that didn't make any difference—the US had been attacked, and President Bush and his administration wanted to attack some country or entity in the Middle East, and it didn't really matter who the victims were. Few qualifications for death were needed, except that they had to be Muslim and that they speak some form of Arabic. To the shock and surprise of the US military brass, the Iraqis responded with a robust insurgency, an entirely predictable outcome of the US occupation. At least a hundred thousand Iraqis were killed, perhaps as many as a million—but let's say just a hundred thousand, since everybody agrees on that as the lowest possible estimate, with about four thousand unnecessary American deaths along with them. (Remember also that sixty thousand American military personnel came home maimed or wounded.) And all this gratuitous slaughter drove America deep into debt, and all the people who supported it knew this, regardless of what they said later about the country's deficit.

That's what the most conservative section of the US political class wanted, that part of it dominated by neo-conservatives, and most Americans went numbly along with it. The horror of 9/11 made it all possible. And indeed, George Bush's invasion of Iraq was at first easy from a military point of view because America had been cooperating with Saddam Hussein's intelligence services to help him kill Iranians during the eight years of the Iraq/Iran war, so American military planners knew the main players. Whether Iranians or Iraqis, it made no difference to them anyway: after 9/11, all the American political class and its traumatized supporters wanted was a body count. Anyone who doubts that Americans were deeply traumatized by 9/11 needs only consider the shock and outrage directed toward the few dissenters brave enough to speak prophetically about the aggression that people were feeling, and who spoke prophetically and honestly about its irrationality—especially the irrationality of attacking Iraq as a response to 9/11.

2.

Chris Hedges, a Pulitzer Prize-winning war reporter from the *New York Times*, was asked to give a commencement address at Rockford College, a liberal seat of higher learning in Illinois. The administration apparently wanted the usual 'go out and make your mark' inspirational nonsense, with perhaps a few youth-oriented jokes thrown in; but it so happened that Chris Hedges had been in war zones as a war correspondent for the better part of fifteen years, and he had a few things to say about the US invasion of Iraq. His opening words put his audience on notice that they wouldn't be receiving the usual inspirational boilerplate: "I want to speak to you today about war and empire." It quickly became apparent that this was an antiwar speech, a speech *opposing* President Bush's recent invasion of Iraq. When he mentioned "the Christian Evangelical groups who are being allowed to follow on the heels of our occupying troops to try and teach Muslims about Jesus," his microphone was turned off for the first time. Some people had already started yelling so they wouldn't have to hear his words. People screamed, blew fog horns, and turned their backs on him; some rushed the stage in a desperate attempt to make him stop.

One of the things that really outraged the people listening to Christ Hedges was when he talked about the emotions aroused by 9/11. "Think back on the days after the attacks on 9/11. Suddenly we no longer felt alone; we connected with strangers, even with people we did not like. We felt we belonged, that we were somehow wrapped in the embrace of the nation, the community; in short, we no longer felt alienated."

Hedges was accurately describing, this writer would say, the trauma bonding that victims of aggression experience as they internalize the aggression they've experienced; and indeed, many Americans had experienced exactly such feelings. Hedges spoke of the illusion inherent in that process: "The danger of an external threat that comes when we have an enemy does not create friendship; in creates comradeship. And those in wartime are deceived about what they are undergoing. And this is why once the threat is over, once war ends, comrades again become strangers to us. That is why after war we fall into despair."

That describes with admirable exactitude what often happens when the addiction of aggression can't be fed—the victim often experiences precipitous depression, which can only be assuaged by more aggression. I think that's what was happening to people after 9/11—all that emotional trauma, and all the anger and aggression that followed, but no way to express it. But now, now there was a new enemy to fight in Iraq! That feeling of relief, of having a new target for all that built-up anger, aggression and frustration, was something that had already swept across America—which is mainly why, after all, the dominant group in the US political class had wanted a war. That was what Chris Hedges was talking about in that all-too-insightful graduation speech; but as it will often happen when a prophetic truth-teller tells too much truth, his listeners responded as a mob driven by inchoate fury.

The president of the college intervened, pleading that Hedges be allowed to finish his address—but the yelling and catcalling continued, as people tried every way imaginable to make noise. Each time Hedges started speaking, the microphone would be turned off again. (In a detail this writer finds especially revealing, some people actually *covered their ears with their hands*.) Obviously the crowd was not going to allow Chris Hedges to finish his speech. The looming threat of violence was too great, validating his words about the aggression that people were feeling—because that same aggression that had been visited upon New York on 9/11 was there at Rockford College that day, present in the screams and menacing behavior of the crowd.

Like a bad but somehow predictable movie, the campus police arrived. They dutifully took Chris Hedges, the erstwhile commencement speaker, into custody. They escorted him to the edge of the campus, dropped him off and *told him not to come back*. It was the only time in American history this writer is aware of that the police arrested somebody for a commencement address. It was all very much like those pre-Civil Rights Southern sheriffs who escorted vagrants and suspected troublemakers to their county lines, leaving them standing on the road and advising them not to come back. All this scene needed in the way of verisimilitude was some stentorian old white guy in a string tie saying, "Boy, don't let the sun set on you on *this* campus."

The mob at that college graduation might have beaten Chris Hedges to death, or at least out of all recognition, if he hadn't been taken away by the campus gendarmerie. The mob didn't stop him from talking for any good reason, because reason had nothing to do with it—they were being driven by emotions that bypassed reason, emotions that had to do with the blind rage of internalized aggression. They wanted their military establishment to kill Muslims in a far-off land, and they really didn't care which Muslims, and they didn't want anyone to point out the evil that killing innocent people would constitute. *Somebody* had to pay for the suffering of 9/11, and they didn't want some two-bit commencement speaker telling them they were killing the wrong Muslims.

When people internalize enough aggression, there *is* no wrong victim. There are only more victims, until the traumatized people get tired of killing them. It wasn't an *alternative* to 9/11; it wasn't an *answer* to 9/11, it wasn't even *revenge* for 9/11. The hundred thousand dead Iraqis was a *continuation* of 9/11, a continuation by other means, of the same hate and murder that took close to 3,000 lives in Manhattan and Washington DC and Pennsylvania on 9/11.

3.

How much worse would it be, then, if Americans were traumatized on a *permanent, continuing* basis by unresolved social problems peculiar to their own society? Wouldn't that affect peoples' attitudes and behavior in momentous ways? Yes, it would—and it has. In America there have been three historical sources of ongoing stress, conflict and trauma that arose from established social phenomena. *First,* was slavery, and the racial segregation in the South that followed it; *secondly,* the Indian wars; and *third,* the uprooting and replanting experience of mass immigration and the intense experiences of each immigrant generation. Each was intertwined in some fundamental manner with the nation-building experiences of the American people; each had a fundamental effect on our individual emotional orientations and our collective national character.

Slavery and the Indian wars were driven by systemic evil of an exceptionally malignant nature; and even immigration, usually thought of as more or less benign, was hugely disruptive and to a large extent based on deception, especially self-deception. These three phenomena did not traumatize all people all the time, nor was all traumata solely or even mainly from physical violence, even though slavery, and white America's Indian policy, were both driven by institutional violence. When the physical violence wasn't present, the psychological effects of violence were, because you cannot use or threaten *institutionalized* violence without that implied and threatened violence also changing everybody involved in the social equation.

The intensity of racial segregation was brought home to me as a teenager living in New Orleans in the late 1950s, especially in my interactions with African-Americans. (Or Negroes, which is how I thought of them at that time.) New Orleans was a pretty liberal town compared to Mississippi, next door; and even in some rural parts of Louisiana there were the remnants of a populist tradition going back to the governorship of Huey P. Long. Political corruption and violence was unbelievably rampant, but also there was a great deal of tolerance of unusual or eccentric behavior. I was living in the French Quarter, and those whom we would today call gay people seemed fairly open about who and what they were.

But most of the Black people I met in New Orleans, especially those that came from other parts of the South, were at that time pretty jumpy—these were very unsettled times. Black people were both frightened and thrilled by the success of Martin Luther King's bus boycott in Montgomery; but it was hard to tell which way the wind was blowing. Would things get worse, or get better? If you committed to the Civil Rights Movement, you had to be all in—you couldn't be half in, at least emotionally speaking. Black people longed for some kind of change that involved taking down segregation, but one had the feeling that many Blacks were terrified of their own longing, and were as a consequence incredibly conflicted. Lynching happened, and Black men got shot under suspicious circumstances by the police; everybody knew stories about it. Every Black male had experienced some kind of run-in with white men in which violence was in the air, or had even become an overt—if usually indirect—threat.

As a result, many Black men had extreme difficulty talking to white men. I encountered Black men who had such difficulties talking to white men—even a mildly-deranged and completely inconsequential teenager such as myself—that they stuttered terribly. Certain words or topics seemed to bring the stuttering on. Black men's eyes would suddenly widen as they feared a topic beginning to veer off in the wrong direction, especially if there were adult white men in the conversation; and the stuttering and the sudden ejaculations of laughter set in, sometimes becoming convulsive. The stuttering was the most pronounced I have ever witnessed. I was extremely immature, but even so, I could not avoid seeing that something was in the air, and that it had to do with life and death.

I determined to smile and keep eye contact when talking to Black men, but would deliberately break eye contact and look off into a middle distance if the stuttering got too bad, all the time smiling and pretending that the stuttering wasn't happening. (That ability to ignore unpleasant realities was a peculiarly Southern skill, but I didn't spend enough time in the South to really master it.) But sometimes the stuttering became so paralyzing, that when a Black man began to whoop or exclaim or laugh in a strange way I pretended to be laughing along with him, but not at him. You could feel the trauma of centuries in such a conversational interaction. I dreaded the stuttering that almost always set in at some point. When Black men had difficulty talking to whites, there was no way to pretend that there wasn't something very tense going on, and you knew at times it must feel potentially lethal to them; there was no way, in other words, to pretend that the stuttering man wasn't experiencing fear, pain and a certain amount of emotional paralysis.

Some Black men, especially the older ones, dealt with their fear with an exaggerated and obsequious courtesy toward white males, including a certain kind of shuffling obeisance. These Black men often addressed white men by putting the word "Mister" in front of their first name; so if his name was John Smith, the Black man might call him "Mister John," usually articulated as "Mistah *John?*," with an implied question mark at the end. This was often accompanied by a grotesque grinning smile, so exaggerated that anyone could have seen the anger in it—if they had wanted to. After the required obsequies were out of the way, furthermore, the Black men who engaged in this kind of obeisance often seemed to completely block the white males out of their consciousness, as though they had completely disappeared. (Uncle Tomming the hell out of a white man seemed, in certain situations, to be the price one paid to completely ignore him afterwards.) I posed a special problem for Black men, however, because while I was white, I was such an immature and completely off-the-wall white youth that any Black man desiring social intercourse with me would have to decide whether I was worth the effort of doing a shuffle or not. Usually they settled for talking as straight as they could if they were alone with me; but if they needed to talk with me and there was an adult white male somewhere around, they would get in a shuffle or two just to be on the safe side.

Why did these Black men go so far out of their way to be obsequious, and why did so many Black men have such difficulty speaking to whites without stuttering? The answer is *fear*, because the entire social system in the American South was based on a loosely organized regional form of state terrorism, centered in law enforcement and in municipal, county and state governments. The actual acts of terrorism were performed by sadistic white men who could easily be recruited for such work, and by the occasional mobs that engaged (or threatened to engage) in lynching, beating or intimidation. A sociologist might make the point that the actual acts of violence were few and far between—but the memory of those acts had a way of permeating the minds and hearts of everybody involved. It was that fearful consciousness that kept the whole social system between whites and African-Americans in place.

The pay-off, to a remarkable extent, was an economic one; Blacks had since Reconstruction in the South received much less money for the same work performed by whites, and in many parts of the South the plantation system still existed. The fear used to maintain slavery was somewhat different from the fear used to maintain segregation of the races, but only in degree. Its objectives were the same—to keep a money-making system in place, and to give white people with no skills, little curiosity and no cultural literacy someone to look down on.

4.

To understand slavery, and the peculiar notions that caused men to identify deeply with the fortunes of the Slave Power, one begins with certain American attitudes toward wealth. The New World was for a long time seen as the land of El Dorado, the City of Gold; and going there to seek enormous, overnight wealth was a recurring European preoccupation. In other words, the get-rich-quick schemes I receive daily in e-mails from various excited sources are not the outcome of some recent phenomenon—it was a huge European fantasy for centuries, and to some extent it existed in the minds of almost all who came here, even if only as a pleasant or humorous conceit. The Puritans also sought money, but they deeply influenced everybody else because they had a unique and essentially *religious* attitude toward money.

In the beginning American Puritans saw themselves as a Chosen People and America as the Promised Land. God favored them, they thought, because of their virtue and piety. Like the extreme Calvinists they were, they believed God would 'make visible' those saints who were of 'the Elect,' those saints chosen by God at the beginning of time to live with Jesus in eternity. So to make them visible, New England Puritans believed that God rewarded those he loved with wealth, so therefore wealth had to be a sign of God's grace. But Puritan thinkers began to rethink this simplistic formula, since they could not explain why so many bad people became *rich*, and so many good people stayed *poor*. So the main Puritan thinkers in New England gradually, over a period of three generations, put aside the idea of wealth-as-grace, since it was clearly bogus. But although the Puritan divines jettisoned the idea of God rewarding virtue with gold, the masses of people in American never did. The heresy quickly proliferated through the colonies, and became a part of a larger American success-ethic, surfacing in good and times and bad ever since. Today it flourishes among evangelicals as "the Prosperity Gospel," which is promulgated by such tiresome preachers as Oral Roberts, Benny Hinn and Joel Osteen. But it was also absorbed by the great mass of secular people as well as a fundamental American truth.

It generally takes the form of an unabashed worship of wealth and power as an acceptable form of idolatry—but with a redemptive dimension. It you did something exploitive to get your wealth, the money you gained would redeem your behavior retroactively, in rather the same way that Jesus' blood sacrifice redeems sin retroactively. Something similar applied to violence used against slaves and the Indians. If you ended up making money from your depredations, whether against slaves or against the tribal people, the money and power created by violence retroactively redeemed every bad thing done to get it. Some even believe that God will help Christians become wealthy because he wants them to take over society and set up a Christian dictatorship.

In a relatively short time American wealth became synonymous with salvation, a righteous foretaste of the heavenly delights that waited in the New Jerusalem. Of course, the Puritans in Britain had been from the beginning acutely aware that wealth was also quite dangerous, because it could lead the believer into sin and sensuality. But that did not stop the British Puritans in the New World from feeling that wealth and God could be, and often were, the same thing. If God had chosen them to be the first people to experience money as spiritual capital, that was because He thought them able to enjoy it without slipping into an inappropriate love of luxury or personal ornamentation—the trust in which God held them was but one more indication that they were the Chosen People. Later, as I've already pointed out, Puritan thinkers denounced the easy connection between riches and salvation; but by that time, it had proliferated to all corners of the American imagination, and had become a profound emotional orientation, usually an unconscious one, rather than a theological doctrine.

It is, despite the Puritan embellishments, a rather old story. Nations and tribes begin by thinking that they're being rewarded by the gods, a goddess, or by fate—and end up worshipping the reward itself. But in times of empire, nations also become bonded to the worship of wealth by the traumatic impact of the violence necessary to *get* the wealth. (Remember Will Rogers' story about Pilgrims holding guns to make sure they got what they were praying for?) For all the reasons already examined in this book, at the same time these early immigrants to the New World worshipped the Christian God, they also worshipped the violence and aggression necessary to obtain the money and power that made them 'visible saints' of 'the Elect.' Not surprisingly, aggression was quickly incorporated into American religion, enhancing the violent Calvinist imagery already at the heart of New England Puritanism. Their spiritual power gradually became conflated, to both their tribal interlocutors and the Puritans themselves, with the power of their guns, which were much more powerful than any weapons available to the tribal warriors.

Slavery added another wrinkle to the American worship of wealth, power and aggression. The British had an old idea that it took a full three generations to make a true gentleman—he must have the right ancestral digs, the right public schools, the right social skills and (above all) an effortless confidence, based on his ability to quickly and in good humor accommodate the paradoxes of political and cultural power. It was the educated British gentleman that men of pre-Revolutionary British America unconsciously looked up to as the highest achievement of human civilization. (And this continued through the Revolution, as the Founders persisted in thinking of themselves as enlightened British gentlemen who just happened to be engaged in making a new country that would be culturally British, except better.)

It was the special conceit of the American South that rapid wealth through slavery could underwrite the creation of a gentleman not in the traditional three generations but *in one generation*. It could do this because of the price of cotton, and the fact that the man who owned a plantation could, if he had luck on his side, become fabulously wealthy in very little time. He would then spend his money at his leisure in assimilating all the special habits and attitudes of the true gentleman. Those men in the throes of this corrupt dream also worshipped money, not for its ability to reward 'the Elect,' but for its supposed ability to propel the transformation of the bumpkin into a scintillating conversationalist, a thoughtful aphorist capable of quoting Bolingbroke and Shaftesbury, and a completely fashionable man of many talents—that is, an American version of the landed (and educated) British gentleman.

There were a couple of things terribly wrong with this fantasy. There was no way one could *buy* gentleman status, and the idea that such a thing could be possible was a peculiarly self-serving American fantasy. Gentlemen status would have to be laboriously built up over generations of shared experiences and would consist of a highly nuanced understanding of one's situation, and a detailed comprehension of social skills and byways that could be laboriously learned only from the elites of a particular time and place. Furthermore, the landed British classes educated at Oxford or Cambridge had since the Glorious Revolution been primarily Whigs, which meant they were almost invariably opposed to slavery, and were sometimes skeptics in religion. In any case, the landed gentleman of Britain of that time was usually not a particularly democratic individual, nor was he representative of a wildly attractive social ideal either then or now. (Anybody tempted to idealize the aristocrat as a social type is well-advised to consider how Mozart was treated by the aristocracy of Salzburg and Vienna.)

The value of the gentlemen as an idealized type aside, the point must be made that it was simply not possible to learn all the attributes associated with such an estate in one generation. Furthermore, there was always a hint of public service connected to the British landed classes, however little it was acted upon; whereas the slave-holder of the New World generally possessed no concept of public service whatsoever, the single exception being active military service in times of conflict.

The most egregious mistake in the fantasy of the one-generation gentleman, however, has to do with the nature of slavery itself. Slavery was a stupefyingly brutal and sadistic institution that required compartmentalization of thought and feeling, and a certain inborn capacity for denial. Furthermore, the slave system required a debilitating set of folk beliefs that asserted that it was something that it clearly wasn't. It took an enormous amount of focused brutality and indirect threats of violence to keep it going; but also there was the high degree of self-deception involved in not comprehending the brutality of it. Finally there was no way to avoid the sheer sexualized corruption of the institution. There was an enormous temptation for white men to take advantage of the asymmetry of power between the slave-owner and his Black slave women—and to rationalize it in many ways, perhaps; but there could be no rationalization, not really, for such behavior. Then there was the requisite need of white women to studiously ignore the things their white men were doing with Black women.

The slaves were human beings, however degraded their circumstances in human bondage made them; and there was never a time when even the dullest person did not comprehend the fact that slavery caused enormous suffering to the slaves themselves. At the time of the great slave rebellions, in the early 1830s, it must have been obvious to all that slaves rebelled against slavery, assuming in the process such uneven odds, only because they were completely miserable in their enslaved status—to the point that they saw death as a preferable alternative. Regardless of what they said, in their heart of hearts the whites understood the cruelty of slavery, which is precisely why they were so terrified of further slave revolts—those who identified with slavery did so while to some extent aware of the horror they were perpetuating.

The reality is that white planters who owned slaves ended up identifying deeply and completely with slavery's institutional aggression. The internalization of enormous amounts of aggression was therefore inevitable, to the detriment of every other emotional orientation. The overwhelming weight of this aggression, and paranoia and fear that went with it, made the acculturation and training of real gentlemen impossible. The one-generation aristocrat was a self-congratulatory fantasy of the American Slave Power, arising only because of the self-delusion inherent in the criminality of slavery itself.

The brutality inherent in the institution of slavery generated ongoing trauma to the human beings who suffered that brutality; and those whites that were complicit in it were invariably bonded to aggression as the central organizing principle of southern life, however much they tried to deny and ignore it. If your consciousness is affected (or perhaps even defined) by an awareness of the aggression necessary to your social system, the growth of curiosity and moral imagination will be greatly inhibited, and finally extinguished. A refined and civilized lifestyle could be realized only in such a highly compartmentalized way as to approach total insanity—the overarching emotional reality of slavery was a deep and inalienable awareness of its aggression, social as well as personal, by those whose daily lives were lived in the system itself. So the more aggressive the slave owners became, the more they thought about what could happen in a slave revolt, and the more aggression was internalized by all parties who had any involvement in the South's 'peculiar institution.' This is finally what made representatives of the slave-holding states unable to discuss slavery rationally.

Thus the caning of Charles Sumner by Preston Brooks on the floor of the Senate in 1856 was ultimately not surprising, since

Southerners by that time had decided that the whole subject was to them so sensitive (I would say guilt-ridden and fearful) that it could not be publicly discussed. Southerners of the slave states did not like to discuss it because that might imply that there were two sides to the issue—and Southerners much preferred to live with the fiction that slavery was in no way controversial, but simply a fact of life that all Americans needed to accept, even if grudgingly. Furthermore, when attempting to discuss it most Southerners in the Senate generally became too agitated to speak well.

That was not true of Charles Sumner. In his last speech before his caning, Sumner had inserted powerful and skillfully-conceived sexual language into his speech, by comparing the intent of the Slave Power as similar to a rapist intent on ravishing a virgin—which was heard by slave owners (and was almost surely intended to be heard) as an indirect but painfully obvious reference to the sexual bondage of Black slave women. Southerners said that abolitionists regularly introduced inappropriate sexual language into their anti-slavery speeches because the Northerners were obsessed with sexuality to the point of madness, that the sexual exploitation associated with slavery was nowhere near what the Northerners said it was. In that they were right—sexual exploitation of slave women was far *worse* than any people of that time (whether Southern or Northern) were willing or able to talk about. It existed everywhere that slavery existed, which we know today because of the very high level of European DNA in the African-American population.

Brooks could have replied to Sumner with a speech of his own, of course, but he was not a particularly clever man; and he, like most of the Southern Senators, was simply not as capable as Sumner as a speaker. Nor was there much that he could point out that was attractive about slavery, since the North now knew a great deal more about it than it had fifty years previously. Brooks could have challenged Sumner to a duel, which is what most so-called gentlemen from the South would have done, if unable to reply to a powerful speech with an equally powerful speech of their own.

Brooks instead revealed the true vulgarity—one might say the barbarity—to which slavery had taken the white men of the South, by beating Sumner with a cane as though Sumner was himself a slave. Thereafter the ongoing Southern demand was that slavery no longer be discussed in Congress. Thus did the American people learn that as long as human bondage existed on American soil, there could be no free speech in representative government about this most important and controversial institution in American life.

5.

From the outbreak of the Revolutionary War, it had become painfully clear to many thoughtful people that slavery contradicted the Enlightenment ideals on which the great arguments of the American Revolution were being made. And it would be for exactly these same ideals that slavery had been, or soon would be, abolished in all the Northern states. During the Revolutionary War, anti-slavery language found its way into the Declaration of Independence and the US Constitution, but were stricken out by constitutional delegates desirous of compromising with the slave-holding Southern states; even more harmful, because more personal, was the fact that scores of these 18th century idealists, perhaps most of all those who disapproved of slavery, personally compromised with it by *owning slaves themselves.*

In so doing, they personally defined a major American contra-diction: the ability to comprehend those things in life that are both noble and psychologically acute, while embodying a behavioral lifestyle that is vulgar and addictively brutal. This prefigured the uncomfortable position in which the American people would find themselves after the American Revolution: they would, in the next two centuries, discover themselves to be a money-worshipping and backward people in many important respects, but a people nonetheless ruled by highly nuanced, unabashedly civilized and astonishingly enlightened foundational documents, specifically the US Constitution and the Bill of Rights. But until the Civil War it neither mentioned nor prohibited human bondage.

Many enlightened Southern men thought they were stronger than the Slave Power with which they compromised—that they had a personal code of honor that was somehow stronger than slavery's brutality. But the evil too often swallowed them whole, as countless men became addicted to its power, and to its brutal sexual opportunities. That in turn continued the suffering of countless Black women in slavery, as they bore children of the slavers yet could not protect them even as they were sold off as profitable chattel. Everybody knew of this, but nobody talked about it. The Southern states increasingly made of slavery a kind of doom-laden, guilt-ridden sacrament of daily life, the details of which nobody was permitted to examine too deeply, but around which all of the most important activities of life in the South nonetheless revolved. If Americans were the Chosen People and the New World was the Promised Land, slavery was clearly the Original Sin: indeed, the way in which slavery became sexualized perfectly fulfilled the American need to arrive at a worldview that saw sexuality as violent, dangerous and base. The American Southerner could never quite figure out whether he was living East of Eden or in the fleshpots of his own imagined Babylon, as the psychological weight of his system seemed to indicate.

Sex was sinful, as slavery was increasingly seen as sinful by many; but the nature of slavery's sin was not the secret sexual liaisons at the center of it, but the asymmetry of power between the white man and the Black woman, which made everything having to do with these powerful and sometimes unconscious attractions potentially a source of enormous personal agony, most of all for the Black women who ultimately bore the children. They were the most vulnerable; to them fell the most victimization.

Thomas Jefferson, a man of certain ideas that over time had the most to do with the conception of America, was deeply involved in such a relationship, because he had a slave mistress, Sarah—or Sally—Hemings, who bore him six children, four of whom survived into adulthood. We will never know all that went on in their relationship, but we are oppressively aware that he was free, and she was not. Nor did he make her free during their relationship—Sally was eventually freed by Jefferson's daughter, Martha. For the widowed Jefferson to free Sally during his lifetime would have tended to confirm the existence of a sexual relationship—and would also have given the older Sally a choice about where to live, and what she wanted to say publicly, and to whom.

Of course, when Thomas was in France as Ambassador in the 1780s, Sally, who had accompanied him, could technically have appealed to the French courts for her freedom; but she was too young to take on such a debilitating legal struggle. Thomas and Sally had evidently begun a sexual relationship at that time, so the emotional connection of the teenage Sally to Jefferson would have been too strong for her to contemplate such a move. Jefferson's daughter Martha may have finally freed Sally as the result of some agreement, either tacit or verbalized, with her father Thomas. But the secrecy with which the relationships were acted out, not to mention their excruciatingly personal nature, tell us a great deal about the profound national contradiction in which they were all enmeshed. The most startling aspect of the love between Thomas and his slave Sally was that she was the half-sister of his wife, as we will presently make clear.

For a long time many Southern historians were flagrantly scandalized by the fact that Jefferson had a long-time sexual affair with Sally Hemings, his slave and a servant in his house. But these honorable gentlemen were not scandalized, it turned out, because of the asymmetrical power relationship between a slave and a man who was simultaneously her lover and her owner. Southern historians, it seemed, were barking mad because their beloved Virginian, Thomas Jefferson, *had been sexually attracted to a Black woman*. But being attracted to an African-American woman is no scandal, then or now; it is simply a preference, and an attraction. The world is full of such attractions. But having sex with a woman who is powerless and enslaved was evil for a far more reprehensible and immediate reason: he was free, and yet held in his arms a woman who was not, whom he *could* have freed but didn't.

If Thomas Jefferson loved something good or powerful in their relationship, should he not have found a way to free Sally before, if not soon after, the first embrace, the first kiss? Would he have not at least found some written legal instrument by which to formalize her eventual freedom, and protect their children? At the very least, would he not have *promised* her freedom some day, so she could live with the children they had brought into the world? Truly, we will never know what went on between them. Perhaps somehow, in some way unknown to us, they found a method to normalize or enlighten what was a common, yet profoundly difficult and inevitably demeaning relationship. But I doubt it.

The sin was not in the pleasure of the sexuality, or in any other part of the sexuality. The sin was in the asymmetry of power between Jefferson and Sally—*the fact that he owned her*. That by itself causes one to wonder whether or not Jefferson's attraction was based on sadism, or solely on the fact of her availability (after all, she was his property) rather than exceptional sexual desire. One must acknowledge that, no matter how the lovers sought to construe or alter it, considering the laws under which their sexuality was acted out it was entirely a kind of rape; it was part of the property relations of two human beings, the owner and the owned, expressed as a thing of desire and convenience to two people—but to only *one* party could we be completely sure that it was altogether a choice, whereas the other party was always and inevitably subject to coercion, whether covert or overt, conscious or unconscious. Sally could have appealed to Jefferson's daughters, but shame would have prevented that, most likely; and in any case, such an expedient might only have resulted ultimately in dismissal from the house to the field. Always there was the unspoken trauma of coercion, in the short term—and even more powerfully and hurtfully, over the long run.

By not articulating the moral issue in that way, or by not even *seeing* it, many American historians, especially the Southerners, reveal an astonishing inability (or more likely, unwillingness) to imagine or understand the systemic evil of slavery. It was not that Jefferson had sex with Sally that made him corrupt and a sinner; it was that he had sex with a woman he *owned*, and to whom he therefore denied, or refused to make himself the legal guarantor of, the freedom that a passionate love always deserves. Without it love cannot grow, for only within love's full range of opportunities can any real intimate choices be consensual. And if Thomas expected his daughters to pretend that they didn't know about any of this, as most plantation owners of that time did, the daughters were likewise taken hostage by the secrecy and denial that human bondage engenders. If Sally was not free, and if Thomas' daughters were likewise not free to speak about who she was to her father, how free were any of them?

This does not in any way change the immensity of Jefferson's contribution to the American Revolution, and the subversive beauty of the Declaration of Independence. Nor does it change for one moment the mysterious and sensational reality that it was precisely Jefferson's ideas that would eventually destroy slavery; and would a century after the Civil War bring down racial segregation and denial of the vote based on race. The same Jefferson who brought six children into the world with a slave also provided the ideological basis for the freedom of millions—that is who he is to America. But we are considering only Jefferson's own *domestic* situation now, as it began in Paris after Jefferson was widowed, and as it continued later at Monticello. The fact will always remain that at the moment of the most fervent connection with Sally, the woman in his arms was protected by nothing he ever wrote or thought. All she had was *him*, but in a connection that had already been compromised to a place beyond right and wrong. Trauma and aggression and danger were present in anything they did, because it existed for every slave, at the heart of slavery itself.

One suspects that at some point Thomas may have extracted—or tried to extract—some kind of highly indirect permission from his daughter Martha, in the way that powerful men often do. (Because it was the daughter who eventually freed Sally after her father's death.) The depth of conflicted emotion in this family system would have been almost unfathomable. The neighboring plantation owner John Wayles was Sally's father, since he had taken Sally's mother as a slave mistress, with whom he had many children; but it also happened that John Wayles was the father of Thomas Jefferson's wife Martha Wayles Skelton. What kind of dysphoric fate made the father of Thomas Jefferson's wife the father of the young lover he would someday embrace? What this meant was that Sally was not only the half-sister of Jefferson's late wife, but the aunt of his daughter Martha. Did Thomas sometimes see his wife when he looked at Sally? Did Martha sometimes see her mother? How could they not have done?

Perhaps the relationships were much easier than we can imagine—some people have a way of making compromises and never looking back. One really can't know for sure. All one can know for sure is that it is much, much harder for the enslaved than for the free, because their lives depend not only on what they know, but what they pretend to know. And we also know that Sally greatly resembled Thomas' deceased wife, whose half-sister she was. What did Sally believe about Thomas' feelings for her, and the role she played in his life? If she was his wife's half-sister, did she share some of the same personal characteristics? What could Thomas allow Sally to know, and how much could she let Thomas know about her own thoughts regarding this situation?

Imagine the trauma that must have beset the young Sally to live in constant knowledge that her children did not belong to her, but to the slave system to which Thomas Jefferson belonged and of which he was the local representative. Jefferson did better by Sally than most men in his situation, of course; all of Sally's four surviving children—Beverly, Harriet, Madison and Eston—were ultimately freed. (Three of them identified as white, as have almost all of their descendents, and Beverly and Harriet went to Washington DC, where they were said to have made good marriages.) All six of Sally Hemings' siblings were house servants; and—as Southern historians like to point out—were also 'trained artisans,' whatever that may have meant or is intended to mean. (It seems intended to mean they were house servants, and not field slaves.) It was a better fate than that of most who labored in the fields, to be sure. But they lived always with their secret relationships with the white males who owned them, Sally with Thomas Jefferson and her mother with John Wayles, the white planter who was father both to Thomas Jefferson's wife and to Sally.

Yet they could never publicly acknowledge this web of relationships, which added emotional baggage to legal bondage. Now multiply that by hundreds of thousands. This went on for as long as there was slavery; and continued in a greatly diminished form right up to the 1960s, when the plantation system in the South received its death blow. No human mind can calculate the psychic and physical violence involved in this aspect of human bondage, traumatizing especially to women, but also to Black men who watched it happen and could do nothing to protect their mothers, sisters and daughters.

And yes, it was traumatizing also to whites, although to a lesser extent, because of the fear, rage and unacknowledged guilt it engendered. Think of the mad jealousy (made worse by the fact that they were bonded to silence) of white women who knew very well what their men did when they went to the slave quarters at night, or met their slave lovers at hidden sites on the plantation. Imagine, also, the manner in which the suppressed guilt of the husband regarding his sexual philandering must have contributed to his gnawing fear of a slave revolt. Fear is by far the most toxic of the negative emotions, outstripping anger and even guilt in its ability to corrode the soul; and after the Nat Turner rebellion, fear of a catastrophic slave uprising crept into the waking and sleeping dreams of the white South, along with the bloody memory of the women and children

Turner murdered, enhanced in their turn by suppressed memories of slaves brutalized and raped.

Turner was a man besotted with violent psychotic visions, a man driven insane by slavery, and perhaps also by something violent in his own personality; and the white slave-owners soon followed him, psychologically speaking, in his descent into madness. Instead of easing the situation by giving more rights to free Blacks and better conditions to the slaves themselves, the white Slave Power identified completely with the terror of the Turner revolt, and the terrorism of slavery itself. They passed laws depriving free Blacks of their rights, tightened the screws on the slaves they held, made it illegal to teach a slave to read, and were hyper-vigilant about anything even slightly critical of their system; American slavery gradually tended to become more a form of public torment based on free-floating hysteria than the basis of a viable agricultural system. As the price of cotton fluctuated, furthermore, slaves gradually became the most valuable product of the slave-owner; so instead of a means to wealth they became—irony of ironies!—the wealth itself. Plantation after plantation was destitute except for the slaves, the breeding of which remained the slaveholder's most valuable commodity. Plantations became factories producing Black human beings for sale, with their labor during harvest only a secondary and greatly diminished source of profit.

Slavery became crueler; slave-owners become more hysterical and defensive; and everybody became more violent, as the country half-consciously prepared for civil war. Interestingly, the early advocates of manumission, and even the most outspoken abolitionists later on (denounced as extremists by the majority of American historians until recently), were in reality infinitely more rational than the slave-holders, whose position tended to be expressed in shrill threats of war against everybody who did not agree with them. Calhoun's famous speech on slavery, for example, was based entirely on a belief that the crisis facing the US was caused by the North. He did not understand the moral crisis of the South, because he could not allow himself to contemplate even the possibility that slavery was immoral.

Indeed, after the 1830s the entire subject became so "sensitive" — which is what people in the grip of a trauma bond often say when others insist on discussing their obsessions objectively — that by 1835 it became a criminal offense in most parts of the South to even *discuss* slavery, much less oppose it in print. Finally the slaveholders began to demand that it not even be discussed in the Senate or House of Representatives in Washington, where elected politicians from all parts of the nation met. This Northern Senators and Representatives were unwilling to do, correctly seeing the Southerners' demand as an attack on their freedom of speech. The insane attempt by the Southern states to stop the elected representatives in Washington from talking about slavery was the final example of the self-destruction inherent in slavery itself. At that point, it was just a matter of time until the Civil War began, despite Lincoln's frequent reassurances that he did not want to abolish slavery.

Evil, as we know, is unacceptable aggression plus deceit — it is aggression that its perpetrators seek to conceal, dissemble or rationalize. Systemic evil is when this rationalized aggression becomes a society-wide psychological and social reality. People involved in acting out systemic evil suffer, as we know, from chronic unhappiness, depression and low self-esteem. At some point they have been victims of, or witnesses to, or heard about violence that deeply affects them, at which point they are likely to internalize various amounts of aggression. At times they may understand that they are in the grip of negative emotions that overrule their ability to make rational decisions; but they lash out at those who would help them escape from it, because being already traumatized — perhaps repeatedly — causes them to identify deeply with the aggression that enslaves all parties to the system.

As the great plantations of Virginia and South Carolina began to make more money by producing slaves than from harvesting cotton, the entire South became addicted to slavery, entering willy-nilly into the Faustian bargain typical of addictions—a short-term payoff in wealth, followed by long-term lack of productivity, punishment in the form of fear, guilt, anger and the chronic unhappiness those negative emotions produce, in this case leading finally to the debacle of civil war. All the negative emotion involved in slavery invariably compromised judgment, until finally the Southern states engaged in an all-out civil war they had no hope of winning. When one has swallowed whole a corrupt and unproductive system, and one's behavior is defined totally by it, all that is really left is the ability to die in some dramatic and 'honorable' way. That was the 'way out' provided by the peculiarly-entitled patriarchy of the Slave Power.

After the Civil War, the self-esteem of white Southerners sank even lower. All that was left to them was the memory of the Confederacy's military exploits, which post-Civil War whites in the South managed to weave into a fantastic legend of a hopeless chivalry too wonderful to survive; this became a fantasy that the North, rapidly tiring of the South and its various excitements, was too fatigued to denounce. But underlying everything in the South was a powerful current of self-contempt. It was necessary to sacrifice virtually everything for whites to rebuild the plantation system in a new form, which in the 1890s was finally codified in laws institution-alizing segregation of schools and public facilities based on race. As in slavery times, it was held in place by an indigenous terrorist network supported and concealed by local law enforcement, the arrangement resting entirely on the fact that Blacks were prevented by force from voting, which kept them powerless. The plantation system once again thrived on subsistence labor not much different than slavery.

Then that second system of racial oppression was overthrown by the Civil Rights Act of 1964 and the Voting Rights Act of 1965, which taken together constituted the Second American Revolution, which desegregated the South and established voting rights for Southern African-Americans. For a long time progressive-minded people in the North—and some Southerners—had believed that once segregation was dismantled, Southern white people would turn toward self-advancement, education and a better way of life. To achieve that, they would join coalitions with Blacks, liberals, the labor movement and other progressive constituencies to address their own poverty. But the effects of trauma bonding do not go away just because the social forces that originally caused them are dismantled.

Today, some fifty years later, a great many Southern whites without inherited land or wealth still wallow in self-hatred and ignorance, not to mention resentment of anybody more intelligent, more affluent or more educated than themselves, watching Fox News and voting for the Republicans they once hated, because the aggression that was systematically directed at Black people for so long has now turned inward. The South is backward—culturally, intellectually, socially and politically—because too many people there, particularly white males, believe that they *ought* to be backward. One might say that they are *facing* backwards, because the psychic toll of slavery caused them to believe that the only identity worth having is to dominate others. Slavery and racial segregation provided for millions of painfully mediocre men a single population they could look down on, the African-Americans of the South; and once that ability to look down on somebody was taken away from them, they could only look down on themselves.

There is one exception to this dreary picture. The one thing that white Southern men excel in doing is military service. Southern men have a special (I would say intuitive) grasp of the needs of modern American empire, which is why so many volunteers for the US military are from the South or the Border States. And there is the additional incentive of controlling, punishing and killing people—in Iraq and Afghanistan, for instance—who are not 'Christian,' and who do not enjoy the special outlook of American evangelical or Pentecostal Christianity, and who are, above all, not white. For many young Southerners it must be heaven itself to lord it over some pathetic gaggle of poor people with guns in hand. The fact that the skins of the locals are not white, in those places where they are so often sent, is icing on the cake.

A cautionary tale I have heard more than once, which I offer in evidence of my thesis: There was a particular Southern state with a relatively progressive governor (a Republican, interestingly) who was tired of seeing his state's schools and hospitals rated last in the US. He created a bill that would tax the corporations a little more in his state in order to improve the schools and health services. Citizens of his state, including the poorest and least educated, overwhelmingly voted it down. While I agree that those voters had the right to vote as they did, I think that the outcome mentioned above can only be explained by understanding that a pivotal percentage of Southern whites are pathologically self-hating. It isn't that they voted against their own interests, because in a democracy people can decide what their interests are. My point is simply that their interests happen to be pathological ones, and the pathologies involved are a direct result of a traumatizing, brutal system that lasted hundreds of years.

The self-disgust of the angry Southern white men, or even rural white men in the Midwest and Border States, is often expressed as an obsession with real or imagined enemies. But this usually translates into enemies that are not in a position to fight back, usually Muslims and immigrants. This hate is expressed ritually by the one hundred and fifty to two hundred or so talk show 'hosts' across the nation associated with AM Hate Radio, whose main job has been the creation of a populist form of American neo-fascism in the base of the Republican party; they do this by giving permission to undereducated males to discharge their self-disgust by hating people who don't look like them. (Gays are no longer the target of choice, since gays have organized themselves well enough to have a fair amount of clout in the media—and as we know, hate-mongers prefer targets that can't fight back, since they are also cowards.)

This self-hatred is endemic among undereducated, underemployed white males in all parts of the country; and may be partly responsible for the rapid spread of Southernisms in language among working-class whites outside the South. In some regions of Appalachia, the greatest scandal imaginable is to rise above one's poverty—to make, through a good education, hard work and application of one's talents, a relative success of oneself. In this respect the Southern male most resembles a certain minority of young Black men in the Northern ghettos of the US who have chosen a criminal lifestyle, not to mention a similarly-inclined minority of Latino youth in the *barrios*. To complete the irony, the middle-class African-Americans who have returned to the American South often tend to be quite educated, highly motivated and focused on bettering themselves and their children, something that Southern whites might well learn from.

This, then, is the legacy of slavery for the Southern white man—"the chivalry," as the white South once melodramatically referred to itself in antebellum novels. Sadly, white southerners still carry the trauma of slavery and racial oppression with them in their individual and collective cultural DNA, selected by the inexorable national computer of American history. But it is a trauma that is now multigenerational, and is therefore often experienced as something vague and amorphous. The ultraconservative Southern white male usually does not wholly understand what drives his profound aggression expressed as self-defeat, or his gnawing self-hatred expressed as cultural belligerence.

William Faulkner wrote about being taken by his grandfather to an African-American graveyard and hearing the old man say, "See all these graves here? We *owned* these people once. They were ours, they *belonged* to us." One can only imagine how hard this would be for a sensitive child already uncomfortably aware of the guns and violence around him, and probably fearing them, trying to figure out what these words and symbols meant. The unspoken message of the grandfather would probably come across something like this: "You can't escape from this past, this slavery. But if you internalize it and make it part of you, it won't be quite so scary." But if you internalize it, you end up identifying with its aggression.

As much as its aggression invaded and became a major influence in the waking and dreaming lives of white Southerners, it was not the whites who suffered most, day in and day out, from segregation and the plantation system. It was Blacks who suffered most, and who were finally forced to take the experience into their personalities until the aggression they identified with became, for many Black men, the main part of their identity. Thus the organized aggression that drove the plantation system and the system of racial segregation in the South, right to the 1960s, also entered the personalities of a great many African-American men. There were also a fair number of them who saw through the trauma they were feeling, who saw that it was part of a system with its roots in American history, which meant it could probably be unraveled and deconstructed at some point, freeing not just themselves but everybody else too. Certain insightful and resilient Black people became the teachers and prophets of America. (Douglas, Du Bois, Bayard Rustin, Dr. King, and many others—Bayard Rustin even refused to be apologetic for his homosexuality, at a time when there was no support system for gay Black men, making him a double prophet.) Slavery and the plantation system of the South, and then the nihilism of the Northern ghettos, constituted—when taken together—the American holocaust of the Black family; and its members carried inside of them that terrible personal holocaust, some of them identifying with its aggression, waiting to act out that aggression in a desperate if mistaken attempt to recover at least a fraction of the authenticity that had been taken away from them.

The most murderous and horrifying acting-out of this anger happened among the young Black men who were part of the great migration north, among the minority who decided to engage in the crime life in the big cities (and who accepted the idealization of the thug life that defines extreme emotional or economic poverty). So let us think for a moment about the young Black man who has made that bad choice, whose purse does this the young ghetto street criminal steal? He will steal the purse belonging to some older Black woman in the community. And where, and against whom, did he and others like him vent these tidal waves of aggression they had internalized? Why, against themselves, naturally, in the form of heroin, crack cocaine and alcohol; but also and even more frighteningly against people—other young Black men—who are mirror images of themselves.

In the great migration North, African-Americans escaped the South, but they took the trauma of the South with them; and the emotional identification with violence and aggression, the gun and knife, upon which the entire Southern ethos rested. But the migrating Black families found the North no more of a Promised Land than had the immigrating Pilgrims in the New World. Once they had got Up North, what did they have? Far too many discovered that they were stuck with the internalized aggression they had carried Up North with them. Once they got to the big cities they found that they had brought themselves with them, and now they had to face what was happening to them. Then the Black family began to unravel, and there were no fathers to show the young men how to deal with the fury they had internalized, as the would-be fathers left their children because they could find no jobs; and some of the younger Black men began to act out their aggression against each other.

Many times this aggression did not even require the formalization of a gang culture, like the one developed by Latinos in their barrios, whose gangs were often prison-based and organized as extended families. The young Black street criminal acted out his aggression on the streets against anybody who happened to get in his way, maybe with one or two buddies; but mainly he acted it out against other young Black men who looked like him.

And so the evil culture of segregation—the fear of the rope, the rifle and the mob—was internalized by Black Americans in the South, to be acted out subsequently in the North, with the razor, the Saturday (Night) Special, and the drive-by. In the sprawling inner-city hood that stretched across America, aimless, fatherless, nihilistic young Black men acted out the aggression they had internalized, and with which they now identified; and in the process loss contact with everything that had been strong and resilient and liberating and spiritual in the Negritude that had suffered yet somehow resisted in the South. And they began methodically to replace it with a popular culture based on rage and misogyny, thug violence, power-worship and a get-rich-quick drug ethos, the whole package so primitive that it was little more than a ticket to the morgue and the state prison. Even the insane irritability of the Southern white man, his tendency to worship knives and guns, his paranoid conviction that others must be disrespecting him, was acted out daily in the Black ghettos of America, and is still acted out. It is said that one-third of all young Black men are in prison, on parole or on probation. And who are their victims?

Yes, reader — other young Black men.

That is where the intergenerational trauma of slavery, segregation and the plantation system has taken us. It was internalized in both white and Black, and the accompanying self-hatred is now acted out in living color, Blacks against each other in ghettos, poor whites in a funk of self-congratulatory, low-rent ignorance, achieving excellence only in the US military, a place which for many poor and working class men has become the only proving ground of manhood. The aftermath of the plantation system is a study in self-hatred and stunted emotional growth in Black and white, with neither the white Southerner nor the ghetto youth possessing the slightest idea how to cope with the malignant emotional orientations that are pulling them downward toward ritualized violence. An addiction to drug profits holds a death grip on a some urban Blacks (because of crack cocaine), not to mention Northwestern, Southern and Border State rural whites (methamphetamine labs); a high percentage of the dealers and users of this dream-candy ending up dead or in prison, and many innocent people, often children, are killed in turf battles.

Likewise the long-suffering Mexican people have been taken pell-mell down through the trapdoor of get-rich-quick into the death worship of the *narcotrafficantes*. But remember who consumes those illegal drugs, my North American readers. Sixty to seventy percent of the world's illegal substances are consumed by North Americans; and *all* the drugs in Mexico are headed north, to the Almighty Dollar of *El Norte*. If we North Americans were not buying the drugs, there would be no drug problem in Mexico.

Neither poor whites nor poor Blacks have recovered from the plantation system that began in 1619 and mainly ended in the 1960s, although some African-Americans have made great progress. We have come a long way—and we have a long way to go. Both poor Blacks and poor whites are stuck in the same internalized self-hatred and the same emotional identification with aggression that arose from the trauma of human bondage based on race. Racism is real, race counts, and when somebody's car is pulled over by the police it could be a vastly different experience for a Black male than a white woman. But is it not immensely tragic, and is it not revealing—above all, is it not beyond irony—that the most debili-tating circumstance of the young African-American male who chooses a criminal lifestyle, that he has all too often internalized into himself the same aggression that made the white plantation owner rich, up in his house on the hill?

6.

The Indian wars were the second great trauma of the American nation-building experience. I remember my grandmother talking about the Indians who had lived in the Missouri county where her ancestors—*my* ancestors—had settled in 1831. Even after the tribal people (the Sac, the Fox and others) were driven out, there was still the occasional sighting of a brave or two, mainly in the caves down in the Sac and Little Sac Rivers. These rare glimpses were especially frightening in an especially incongruent way, like seeing a ghost in a new house. Even when white people didn't see Indians personally, they often talked about seeing traces of them—pottery shards and arrowheads, mainly, buried in the rocky Ozark soil the farmers struggled to cultivate. And those who didn't see them in the caves heard other people talking about seeing them down there, until the vision of a ghostly presence became the unconscious property of almost everybody.

And there was the occasional missing sheet or garment from the clothesline—was it a hobo or kettle-mender from Springfield or Arkansas City, or was it one of the furtive (and perhaps insane or drunken) Indian braves who were supposed to live in the river caverns, still lurking around the neighborhood that they once called home? One never knew for sure; but there was that uneasy feeling about the Indians, who in some way seemed to represent the dangerous unpredictability of the Ozark foothills. Stories of Indian sightings no doubt conjured up a great deal of unacknowledged guilt amongst the farmers, who knew about the Indian wars and had guilty knowledge, through the stories and folklore of the region, of the way the whites had reportedly 'cleaned out' the last settlement of local tribal people. The very presence of the arrowheads and pottery shards seemed calculated to prevent the white farmers from forgetting that they were building their new civilization in the tribal haunts of an older one. And in the gritty, rocky soil these emblematic remnants became one more impediment in a difficult life.

Frontier families were more conscious of Indians even after they were 'gone'—that is, after a tribe had been mainly killed or driven out—because of the way trauma and guilt worked together to create a heightened consciousness of an aggression nobody wanted to talk about. That happened because in almost every new territory there would at some point be a massacre of an Indian tribe, including women and children. In almost every new territory, the same process could be observed. Tribes went on the warpath when white settlers encroached on their hunting grounds; there would be skirmishes, settlers would be killed, including women and children (although women and children were sometimes kidnapped); and a period of open warfare would ensue. A militia would be organized, and the Indian warriors would be pushed back into the interior of the territory they had previously controlled. And then, at some point, there would be a bloody massacre of a main tribal group, including men, women and children. The survivors would flee, be taken prisoner, or go into hiding.

This traumatic process began with the Pequot War in 1637, and ended about two hundred and fifty years later in the far west. In 1637, the Pequot tribe was a dominant group in southeastern Connecticut who had allied themselves with the trading interests of the Dutch. The British Puritans were offended when the Pequot refused to pay them for the deaths of two white men they had killed (one of whom had been surprised while kidnapping women and children to sell as slaves in Virginia) and hostilities broke out. On May 26, 1637, Puritan leader John Mason led a force of about 400, many of whom were Narragansett and Mohegan allies. He attacked the village of Sassacus, the redoubt of the main Sachem, or tribal chief, but Sassacus was gone with his warriors. John Mason, the Puritan leader, set afire the Pequot palisade, burning to death between 600 and 700 Pequot women and children, also hacking them to death as they attempted to flee into the woods.

The Narragansett and Mohegan braves were horrified, and immediately left to consider what they had witnessed, and to process the emotions that arose from it. The Eastern tribes valued the warrior above all; but war had a symbolic significance to them in a way that wasn't true of the white settlers—it was something practiced by men against men, and had a certain ritualized quality about it. This kind of scorched-earth war that was practiced by the Europeans was mainly unknown to the Eastern tribes; and to say that it traumatized them would be an understatement. But they quickly learned to identify with the aggression of the British (not to mention their economic interests as opposed to the Dutch), and soon the Mohegan, Narragansett and Metoac were taking the Pequot as slaves. The Mohawk of New York obligingly killed Sassacus, the chief of the Pequot, and sent his scalp to the Puritans; the Puritans themselves took Pequot Indians as slaves and sold them in Bermuda or the West Indies.

Colonial Puritan officials declared the Pequot extinct and made the speaking of their language a crime, while actively encouraging the hunting down and murdering of surviving Pequot by whites and tribal people alike. The Puritans had no trouble using Christian arguments to justify their actions, since Indians were assumed by them to be demons—the white settlers even used a kind of pietistic 'just war' argument to seize Pequot lands. About the massacre itself, John Mason wrote that it was all an act of God who "laughed his Enemies and the Enemies of his People to scorn making [the Pequot] as a fiery Oven... Thus did the Lord Judge among the Heathen, filling [Mystic] with dead bodies..." Since God clearly wanted those dead Indian bodies, there must have been no sin in killing them.

In Mason's view, he was simply acting out God's will, which was inevitable and could not be questioned, thereby absolving Mason of any responsibility for the things he did. This same attitude, and roughly these same events, would occur in the same sequence for the next two hundred and fifty years: escalating tensions between settlers and Indians; isolated atrocities on both sides; then the outbreak of open warfare by both sides. The whites would always dominate because there were so many more of them. The Indian war would usually wind up with white soldiers making their way to the main camp of the tribe, where the whites would conduct a massacre of a big part of the tribe, including women and children, leaving survivors scattered and in hiding. This might or might not be followed by the signing of a treaty, which would quickly be broken whenever is suited the white settlers to do so.

One of the last venues where this sequence of events was acted out was in California. In 1911, a disoriented Indian in Oroville was taken into custody by a sheriff, who arrested him for his own protection. (The prevailing ethos among many cattlemen in the area was that Indians should be killed on sight, since they were universally regarded as cattle rustlers.) Eventually this particular Oroville Indian, who appeared to be in early middle age, was taken to the

Museum of Anthropology at the University of California at Berkeley, California, where he was befriended and given a home by the anthropologist Alfred L. Kroeber. He talked at length to Kroeber in his own language about his life, and his language was recorded and studied by linguists. He was called Ishi, a word for 'man,' since in his language it was taboo to speak one's name out loud.

Ishi told Kroeber that he was born into the Yahi, the last surviving group of the Yana people of California. He had lived most of his life completely outside white European influences. He and the Yani lived a nomadic but extremely marginal existence in the foothills around Lassen Peak, at one time numbering as many as 3,000. They probably stole from settlers, and it is known that settlers pursued and killed them. Hostilities grew until the inevitable massacre occurred. In 1865, in what is called the Three Knolls Massacre, the main group of the Yani were killed, with Ishi surviving with a small group of about 40. They went into hiding; but over the years they succumbed to disease and old age (and the occasional murder by whites) until Ishi was the only Yahi left. In 1911 he grew weary of living along, and came down out of the hills.

Later Theodora Kroeber, the wife of Alfred Kroeber, wrote a book about him called *Ishi in Two Worlds*. The story of Ishi's life is important for many reasons, the most obvious of which is as a compelling story of physical and psychological survival against great odds. But he is important for another reason: his saga suggests that his association with Kroeber become a means to deconstruct the constant fear of death that had previously defined his life. Ishi escaped from the grinding loneliness of hiding alone in the hills, and from the emotional trauma associated with the constant fear of death, by becoming a dedicated and somewhat bemused student of the white society that had displaced his people. What began as something close to a pure trauma bond based on fear of the threatening white world gradually became something far more shaded. As he worked through the trauma, Ishi came to a realization of his common humanity with the white usurper; and over time the

Kroebers began to have similar feelings about him. Ishi especially exhibited a profound interest in the machines, conveniences and conventions of white civilization; and it is safe to say that he learned as much about whites as the professional anthropologists learned about him.

One of my favorite stories about Ishi is his confrontation with the modern typewriter. He greatly enjoyed watching white people type, and watched not with awe but with something like respect—it was, after all, a great preoccupation of his hosts to sit before a typing machine and make words appear in black ink on white paper. He would often watch the typist at his work, and would then sometimes go off by himself to process what he'd seen. Later, it was said by those that witnessed it that he often laughed to himself after watching white people use the typewriter, as though privately enjoying a complex but rewarding joke.

What did he find so amusing about the typewriter?

We will probably never know, because the white understanding of the Yani language, and his mastery of English, did not provide enough nuance and depth to communicate this very personal feeling. It may have resembled something in one of the Yani legends or stories. Maybe there was something deliciously amusing about the look on the typist's face. Or maybe it was the operation of the typewriter itself, the rapid motion of the keys in response to the typist's fingers. It was something completely new to him, that much we can know.

Ishi and the Kroebers found a way to deconstruct Ishi's trauma by facing it head-on. The Kroebers studied whatever was recognizably human in Ishi, in the sense that Alfred Kroeber studied the world of Ishi at the same time that Ishi was studying the life of Kroeber. (Remember that Ishi came down from the hills and voluntarily joined white society because he didn't want to live alone anymore.) This was done on both sides not just out of respect, but with genuine affection and a certain amusement. (One could call this trust-building, which is quite important when working with traumatized people, since their ability to trust others has been compromised.) The many-faceted friendship grew up between Ishi and the Kroebers, which for Ishi had the added advantage of learning a completely new way to experience life. This was probably a great relief from the loneliness of his years hiding in the mountains, especially considering Ishi's age.

Both Ishi and Alfred Kroeber—and the other white friends Ishi made in Berkeley—made great progress in dissolving the toxicity of the violent Indian wars as it had touched their own lives, even though the whites had heard of it mainly through hand-me-down stories. Of course it could never bring back the many people with whom Ishi had lived out most of his life, the people who had given him his world and taught him how to live in it. Yet despite his loss Ishi was more than happy to share these things with the Kroebers, as they became more fluent in the Yani language. Having lost his family and his tribe, Ishi accepted the Kroebers as his adoptive family.

7.

It is this process—isolated atrocities, escalating hostilities, culminating in a massacre of tribal men, women and children—that we mainly refer to when we refer to the Indian wars. Of course there were variations, the most frequent being the signing of peace treaties. Sometimes the peace accord would be signed before the biggest wave of settlers arrived, who promptly ignored the stipulations of the treaty, and another and more bitter Indian war would break out. Surviving tribal people responded to these catastrophic, successive defeats by internalizing the aggression that had been used against them. In the years since the defeat of the plains tribes, alcoholism has been rampant among tribal people, as was spousal and child abuse and various other forms of social self-destruction. The number of tribal people who die from alcoholism even today, or in automobile accidents related to alcohol consumption, is staggering to contemplate.

Nobody but the Quakers made any attempt to really negotiate a long-term arrangement with any of the tribal groups, because they were the only whites who imagined that Indians had self-interests which they were able to articulate. In Pennsylvania, the Quakers negotiated with the local tribes, whereas everybody else was too much in a hurry to carve out their place, consisting of productive farmland, to even bother about Indians, or to contemplate for a moment what tribal people wanted from those same lands. (In a great many cases, the land that the settlers wanted to clear and use as farmland the tribes experienced as hunting grounds or as sacred territory.) Penn personally negotiated with the Delaware (Lenni Lenape) Indians at Shackamaxon, arriving at an arrangement that seemed likely to work for all. But it did not last, because the frontier was constantly in flux.

The Scotch-Irish settlers who arrived later had little sympathy for Quaker goals, and the Quakers themselves, because they were strict Christian pacifists, could not physically stop the Scots-Irish from attacking the Indians. The most honorable attempt to negotiate with tribal people *as though they were people* was Penn's, but it did not last long; yet we must count it an honorable attempt, and a model for future efforts. In the Indian wars that inevitably followed, the Delaware and other tribes went out of their way to spare the Quakers, easily identifiable because of their homespun garments.

There is in the collective imagination of both tribal people and white Americans the vestigial memory of unspeakable savagery in the Indian wars. In whites, this meant memories of innocent people being murdered, often white women being mistreated in unspeakable ways—raped, or being tortured in sexualized ways. (There is a brief reference to this in *The Searchers*, in which John Wayne knocks a man unconscious to prevent him from seeing the remains of a tortured woman.) For Indians, the vestigial memories are of genocide. Massacres of entire tribes were traumatic in the way that deliberate massacres of innocent civilians are always traumatic; but there was more to it than just the killing.

Tribalism means that each tribe was *a world*—each had its own language, its own religion, its own byways and laws and customs. For centuries each of these worlds had suffered from a steadily diminishing population caused by diseases brought by the Europeans. Therefore each massacre threatened to finally and completely wipe out the small world that constituted each tribe, along with its collective memory, language, myths, rituals and worldview. Killing all members of a tribe was almost worse than genocide; it killed not merely all tribal members, but also the cultural and linguistic and imaginative world that they inhabited. (A process later institutionalized in reservation schools, where for years Indian children were not allowed to speak their own languages.) A white man might lose his family in the Indian wars, but he still had his world. When the Indian lost his tribe, he lost his world. Therefore the massacres had the same traumatic effect on surviving Indians that the Holocaust had on many surviving Jews—it traumatized them in such a way that emotionally they came to feel that the universe was not just evil but hostile to them personally.

That total state of trauma caused American Indians to identify to an astonishing degree with the aggression that white civilization that visited upon them, and once the aggression was internalized some Indians practiced forms of self-destruction of an almost unimaginable ferocity. Like some Blacks after the horror of slavery and segregation, some of the tribal men proceeded to destroy themselves and everything good in their world with alcoholism, spousal battery and child abuse. It is for that reason that now, after a hundred-plus years, some young people of the plains tribes have decided not to drink socially, not to even touch alcohol, because they have learned that because they lack the European enzyme that would break down alcohol, their drinking is likely to become violently alcoholic from the first drink.[67]

All of these things happened to Indians not only because they were defeated, but because of an unconscious process generated by that defeat. It must have been a horrible feeling to know that there was nothing in their world that they could use as a weapon to stop the destruction of their tribal world. Their bravery meant nothing when outnumbered ten to one; their medicine men were helpless against the European diseases that killed millions from the 16th century onwards; their magical ghost dances were impotent against the Gatling gun. Everything in their psychological and cultural arsenal was completely useless in stopping the white intruders who were destroying their world, simply because there were so many more whites than Indians. Everything about the Indian wars was traumatic to tribal people.

So they did what the traumatized always do—they internalized the organized aggression that was wiping them out, because they were helpless against it. The internalized aggression became the fulcrum around which many tribal people—men especially—laboriously built new personalities. Some went into the military and performed heroically, as long as there was an enemy to fight and kill. But many tribal men acted out their aggressive emotional orientations in self-destruction and spousal abuse. Many destroyed themselves in a particularly public way, so that the whites could see them, by getting drunk and staying drunk in public places, particularly in Southwest towns.

For tribal people, especially men, moving past self-hatred typically requires that they look it full in the face and acknowledge that it's there, even if nobody can completely understand how the self-hatred was internalized. Tribal history in North America has two parts. First came the countless millennia of tribal life that ended with the mass murder by European diseases and warfare that began in the 1500s and ended in the 19th century; and the second part is the self-destructive savagery of the 20th century, during which many tribal people destroyed themselves, sometimes taking their families down with them.

This is hard to acknowledge—it would be hard enough for most people to admit that they were defeated, and almost impossible to admit that they were defeated twice, the second time by themselves.

But on the other side of that psychological Golgotha, on the other side of that deconstructed trauma bond, lies the possible reconstruction of the tribal worlds, created lovingly from a synthesis of past, present and future. That can be accomplished by the recovery of all that is left of the tribal languages, rituals and beliefs, and by the conscious decision of modern tribal people (and some whites, too) to internalize the most useful and liberating of those things; and the decision to combine those powerful values with those forms of knowledge—the white man's law, for example—that can help with the resurrection and protection of the tribes in the modern world. (The most rampant exploitation of traditional Indian lands by business interests stopped when young tribal men and women started getting scholarships to law schools.)

Above all they must learn to love themselves. They have every right to do so; they are the unacknowledged heroes of the Western Hemisphere. They have many things to teach white people. But first, however, they must take care of themselves, especially through a recovery from alcoholism. *It is not their fault that they cannot drink alcohol with safety.* But it *is* their responsibility to face that fact and disavow alcohol forever. For many tribal people, that recovery must begin when they are born, and will necessarily also be a recovery from the worst effects of white European civilization.

8.

As the Indian wars began to accelerate, white America suddenly discovered the rationale for what they were doing. It was as if they had suddenly discovered—or rediscovered—an enduring truth about themselves, even as they acted it out in the world. At the height of the Indian wars, whites engaged in what could fairly be called systemic evil, and when they killed innocent people the tribal people engaged in the same kind of systemic evil. But the whites did not call what they did evil. They called it by more pleasant-sounding names, including the sonorous and rather spacious-sounding (and suspiciously newspaper-friendly) moniker of Manifest Destiny.

With their intense religiosity, the Puritans had to find a religious reason for everything they did, even if religion had little to do with their real motivation. Since the Puritans enjoyed God's favor and the Pequot did not, it was obvious and inevitable in 1637 that God would cause the Pequot women and children to perish in an exceedingly violent fashion at the hands of triumphant whites. But religious rationalizations became less important as the frontier pushed deeper into the tribal lands of the plains Indians. As successive waves of white settlers raced to the frontier and beyond, a new philosophy arose to justify the dispossession and killing of Indians.

This philosophy, which by the 1840s became known as Manifest Destiny, was in reality little more than a reiteration of a fundamental American idea from the 17th century. This idea, which had previously been expressed in religious language, would now be expressed in nationalistic language. *If one has the power to dominate someone, you should do it simply because the power exists.* That is the fantasy world of the American male adolescent and the American comic book, with its superheroes who must act out their powers simply because they possess them. (The idea that great power requires discretion and restraint had no place in this popular American imperative.) Manifest Destiny suddenly became obvious—that is, it 'manifested' itself—to those white Americans, and especially those whites headed west, who suddenly realized that there were many, many more of them than the Indians. And the pull of cheap or free land to the West was so strong, and the waves of humanity heading there had become such an unstoppable current, that they would be able to seize the rest of the Indian lands simply because they had the sheer numbers to overwhelm the tribes who lived there. They would take the land where the tribal people lived *because they wanted it*, and they would kill the tribes or drive them out.

When 19th-century white settlers acted out this form of aggression, they saw their actions as 'inevitable,' much as their Puritan ancestors had rationalized their aggression as being God's predestined will. The movement of settlers to the western territories was the direct result of many millions of individual decisions, culminating in an intoxicating acquisitive ethos that affected everybody. People saw that they had a chance to get something for themselves and their families, a chance that many of them had never had before, and might not have again. Besides, they reasoned, everybody else was doing it, so why not themselves? Perhaps, in this situation, might *did* make right. Ultimately whites were going to take away the Indian lands anyway. So why, the pioneer frontiersmen and frontierswomen asked themselves, should they be so pristine as not to join in the rush for land? Were they not willing to risk their lives to get their share?

Thus Manifest Destiny was not so much an argument as a way of thought and behavior about something that seemed inevitable, and therefore felt predestined. But the language in which this ecstatic insight was expressed was no longer religious, but nationalist. A new American nationalism would be the emotional motivation that not only drove American civilization westward, but was the new force that transformed white civilization by giving it a bold new self-awareness of its own vitality. (Very similar thoughts and feelings were extant in Europe as various forms of nationalism, and had already become quite profitable in the form of European colonialism in the developing world.) Nationalism was a new secular religion—but it could also function well as a rationale for exploiting people whose skins weren't white; and that was important because violence-equals-wealth-equals-salvation had been an equation at the center of the American experience since the Puritan settlement, and now it had a secular expression. Together this combination of violent nationalism and worship of the market-place began—slowly at first and more quickly later on—to enter the heart of organized American Christianity, in many instances surpassing or eclipsing most other elements of belief and behavior.

Of course, religion was formally distinct from government, and distinct forms of new Christianity continued to spring up in America. Many of the new religious denominations expressed the longing for the New Earth promised in the Book of Revelation. The Mormons, the Seventh-day Adventists and Jehovah's Witnesses all claimed to act out on American soil, in one way or another, a search for the New Jerusalem promised in Revelation and sought by the Puritans. Mary Baker Eddy of Christian Science saw it hiding in the health theories, remedies and fads of the American middle class; and so did the manufacturers of patent medicines, many of which put out compounds heavy in addictive opiates, cocaine and even mercury. But a violent form of American nationalism was now at the exact center of that American experience; and after the Civil War, the Christian churches meekly adjusted themselves to the unspoken demands of the political class, not to mention the rising strength of the military and corporate elites.

The worship of money became the centralizing force of American religion, along with something else that had long obsessed the Puritans, and which now became an obsession of the growing American middle class: the worship of *respectability*, with its elevation of propriety over charity and salvation. (But propriety required a certain class status, a certain income, to be sustained.) In foreign policy, and in government policy toward tribal people, middle-class support for the state became a way for letting the dirty work of empire be done by others. Since evangelical religion was especially vulnerable to the idolatry of nationalism, the idea that the American state was acting out God's will also began to get traction among evangelicals. But the impulse that it expressed, however differently nuanced, was still fundamentally the same as the impulse that resulted in the destruction of the Pequot women and children in 1637.

Thus did a fundamental flaw in the American character, one that had been there since the founding of the Puritan colonies, find a new expression: the idea that America could dominate or destroy anybody or anything it had the strength to conquer, no matter how much suffering it caused, as long as it resulted in more money and power for Americans. That became the thinking of American corporate, military, and political elites, and still is. (Remember Thomas Friedman, the New York columnist and neo-con, who argued that we ought to invade Iraq, *because we could?*) This ethos, both adolescent and nihilistic, unfortunately entered every department of American life.

But the important thing to remember is that it didn't just enter American life as a series of ideas that somebody woke up with one day. It entered American life as an after-the-fact rationalization of ongoing tragedy and aggression, generating trauma that involved millions of people. It came from many acts of war and violence; and the atmosphere it engendered flowed in a wholesale form into the collective American unconscious, and into the unconscious minds of all that participated in it, bonding our ancestors together to make us children of violence. That's one reason for the almost sexual feelings that men in the South, Border States and the West (not to mention rural areas in all parts of the US) have for their guns—their guns are not just a remnant, but the most important symbol and appurtenance, of the ongoing trauma bond formed by the violence that was so often at the heart of American nation-building.

"In American mythogenesis the founding fathers were not those 18th-century gentlemen who proposed a nation at Philadelphia," wrote historian Richard Slotkin. Rather they were those people who, he said, "tore violently a nation from the implacable and opulent wilderness—the rogues, adventurers, and land-boomers; the Indian fighters, traders, missionaries, explorers, and hunters who killed and were killed until they has mastered the wilderness; the settlers who came after, suffering hardship and Indian warfare for the sake of a sacred mission or a simple desire for land; and the Indians themselves, both as they were and as they appeared to the settlers, for whom they were the special demonic personification of the American wilderness. Their concerns, their hopes, their terrors, their violence, and their justifications of themselves, as expressed in literature, are the foundation stones of the mythology that informs our history."[68]

And that mythology was always a mythology of violence. But it was acted out in a country whose governance derived from the opposite kind of impulse, the impulse for fairness in human affairs, the intensely civilized desire to rationally balance competing interests in a free society, not least of which are the rights of the individual as opposed to the state. That impulse, which expressed itself in the Declaration of Independence and the US Constitution and the Bill of Rights, was the height of civilized late 18th-century thought. On the other hand, the world that Slotkin describes above was not a civilized one; yet it was real enough, and still is. There are vast expanses of American territory in the Midwest and South and Border States ("flyover America," as it is called by some people on the Coasts) where a great many human beings—not quite a majority, perhaps, but a vociferous and turbulent plurality—are driven by the violent worldview described above. To the men among them, the gun is precious and sacred, an instrument savored and valued by many of them who (while not abusive or necessarily bad husbands) nonetheless love their guns inestimably more than their wives. To men ensconced in the world's most volatile gun culture, the gun is transcendent in ways they cannot even begin to explain.

In other words, the internalization of aggression that drives American thought and behavior occurs in a country whose governing documents contain some of the most delicate and complex ideas ever designed by the mind of humankind. And yet great masses of the people governed by those same exquisite documents are enmeshed deeply in belief systems and behavioral patterns approaching pure barbarism, who worship guns and embrace religious beliefs that are little more than the rankest kind of super-stition. That is the real mystery and drama of America, as I have tried to suggest: that Americans are part of an experience that includes the very heights of progressive human thought (in its 18th foundational documents), intertwined with emotional orientations that are intrin-sically barbaric (in much of its everyday behavior). This is a story of enormous moral refinement, on the one hand, and the most unrepentant and childlike kind of savagery on the other, with both in constant tension with each other. Will the tension remain a steadying and complementary force, will these two emotional and social worlds remain in relative harmony, or will they fly off careening away from each other? Nobody can predict how this story ends, because its narrative elements are too insanely disparate.

We see this clearly in the life of Thomas Jefferson. Here was a man of surpassing intelligence and insight, from whose beautiful mind sprang, in large part, an entire country's governance. Yet he owned slaves; he held in his arms the half-sister of his wife, conceiving one secret child after another with her, without acknowledging as his own the children that he conceived. Imagine that uncanny drama of luxurious deceit called Monticello; imagine *if you can* the deception and self-deception necessary to daily life in that beautiful Italianate residence; and you will begin to understand the unearthly contradictions of America that have haunted it from its inception.

Can one doubt that the hypocrisy that defined Sally's life was not a form of violence; and that this violence, when concealed and kept secret, was not a flagrant form of evil? Thomas Jefferson imagined freedom for humankind, but in Monticello he lived out the bondage of one race by another; and in so doing, he defined himself by a private evil that civic virtue could not erase. He brought into existence a secret family, not with his mind but with his body's implacable desires (in passionate concourse with a very young lover who faithfully gave him six children), producing a ghost family that lived and died and loved and worked in the very interstices of Thomas' life; but who were, nonetheless, never allowed to acknowledge his name as theirs. *That* was a betrayal, I say to the reader, not just of liberty, but of love.

9.

We have already alluded to the importance of guns in slavery times and the Indians wars. To those who doubt the importance of guns in the nation-building of America, I suggest the following: simply consider, in all its irrational and violent manifestations, the ecstatic gun culture that prevails *today* in the US, a near-worship of guns as symbols of freedom and self-reliance, not to mention of patriarchal protection of one's family. The most powerful organization representing these insanely romanticized but deeply-felt and internalized emotional values is the National Rifle Association, one of the two or three most powerful lobbies in the country. In reality, however, the NRA is simply an advertising representative of businesses that manufacture guns, and therefore a consortium of individuals who wish to generate even more of the considerable profits from the sale of weapons than they do at present. To accomplish this they operate as bundlers of vast amounts of money which they give to politicians as a kind of legal bribery. Since the NRA makes political endorsements of enormous importance to the Southern males in the Republican base, it is therefore a major political, social and cultural force.

While the NRA promotes gun ownership as an investment in the safety of one's family, simply owning a gun is itself incredibly dangerous. But gun owners already know that—the danger is part of the excitement. Most gun owners like to say that they would kill someone only to protect themselves or their family, but being perennially prepared to kill someone is a peculiarly American state of mind. Men in other cultures would, presumably, be just as willing to take a life to defend *their* families, but they do not anticipate or brood upon the possibility that such a violent act might occur with the same degree of excitement as American men do. And men in other industrialized democracies are far less likely to be put in such a position, since the rate of violent crime—murder, for example—is generally far, far less in those countries than in the United States. Gun-owning men in America typically anticipate situations in which they will be required to kill people in order to protect all that is dear to them. As a result, they end up killing far more people than they would if they didn't think about the challenges of life in such barbarous and juvenile terms. Most of the most important turning-points of life on this planet depend not on pulling a trigger, but on one's social skills, moral code and sense of humor.

The volatile emotions surrounding the ownership and use of guns in America did not arrive yesterday. They arose over a period of many generations during the 250 years when the American frontier dominated the consciousness of the people. Men in the South, the Middle West and the Far West—in fact, men in every rural area of this country—tend to regard guns as a basic accoutrement of male identity, so self-evident that it would not even occur to them to justify it. And it isn't just the rural areas where guns are prized as the highest totem of manhood: they are also similarly regarded in ghettos and *barrios* throughout the land, where the idolization of handguns and automatic weapons is supported by hip-hop artists, movies, MTV and radio, not to mention an entire idealized folk culture based on death worship by young males. (All exceptions happily granted, of course: when hip-hop or rap artists are good, they tend to be good precisely to the extent that they can ditch the death worship and misogyny of their peers.)

Not too long ago, I had occasion to call a staffer working for an elected Republican official from a Border State. The staffer courteously gave me the information I wanted; we exchanged some pleasantries, and he hung up. About a month later, I got a telephone call from a complete stranger. This caller rather bombastically asked, "How do you feel about the United Nations' plan to take away your guns?"

The United Nations? Taking away people's guns?

Then I figured out what had happened: the Republican staffer had taken my name and telephone number, and added them to a list compiled for 'push-poll' calls. The so-called 'push-poll' refers to a covert method of disseminating disinformation and raising money while pretending to ask a question. (The classic colloquial example being, "When did you stop beating your wife?") Of course, there is no UN plan to take away anybody's guns, not in the US, at least; but

Republicans, including so-called libertarians like Ron and Rand Paul, like to make political points by encouraging a completely fictitious conspiracy theory that any day the UN will swoop down and start confiscating guns.

The really interesting focus of the disinformation is the heart-pounding *panic* that men in certain parts of the US feel when they consider life without guns. Even the most tenuous reference to 'gun control' reminds them of how desperately they really *need* their guns; and such a reference also allows them to talk about it, by forcing them to think about what life would be without them. Many who joined the so-called militia or patriot movement in the 1990s were similarly convinced that somewhere, somehow, some agency or person was likewise plotting to take away *their* guns, although there was never the slightest shred of evidence that such a thing might happen.

The implication of my 'push-poll' caller seemed to be that if I wasn't outraged by the very *thought* of losing my gun, I probably wasn't much of a man—and indeed, the caller wasn't disturbed by my observation that there wasn't really any UN plan to take away his guns. My caller waxed prophetic about the kind of world it *might* be without guns; and I began to realize that for this gentleman the important thing was to *talk* about guns, and how terrible the thought of a world without them would be. The whole idea of the UN taking away guns was simply a kind of metaphor of the conservative imagination used to start a conversation about the caller's favorite subject, which was his frantic and unalloyed gun-love.

It turned out that the caller was calling to raise money for a Republican political candidate, who apparently could imagine no more attractive message than his willingness to protect American men from unnamed foreigners who are plotting to emasculate them. And the emasculation is always imagined in the same way—that *somebody*, some unnamed and perhaps imaginary people, are plotting to take away their guns.

That American men have an enormous attraction to guns

shouldn't surprise us, because guns were needed to win the Indian wars, used to enforce slavery, and were needed in the Old West to protect oneself; and they became *very* important during the Civil War, not least in the Border States where death and destruction were dealt out not by regiments of disciplined soldiers but by rifles and revolvers in the hands of hundreds of psychopathic bushwhackers, almost all of whom had their own scores to settle. Furthermore, it was clear even at the time of the Civil War that Americans made the best handguns and rifles; Americans invented the revolver, which became a staple of the American way of life and death, the revolver being more important historically only in the single instance of the Irish Republicans, who used it in their war of liberation in 1918–1922 against Britain.

Several of my ancestors were maestros of the six-shooter in Missouri, Kansas and Arkansas, one of them learning the art as a 13-year-old mule-skinner during the border wars in Missouri (or so he claimed) then using it to help himself to some Yankee payroll; another carried one as a captain in the Union cavalry. It was just something they did. One of these gents, a champion fiddler who was one of my great-grandfathers, claimed to have ridden with Jesse and Frank James, but it would probably be a mistake to attach much historical verisimilitude to this, since just about every man of his generation who could mount a horse made the same claim. But he told stories of Jesse and Frank firing their revolvers while riding pell-mell into a skirmish, holding the reins of their horses in their teeth. (Which gave you twelve shots instead of six, according to the storytellers.) The six-shooter lent itself to mythology, and the stories that the ancestors told had an emotional logic all their own, because the gun was somehow the central instrument of the mythology.

Everybody had guns, probably more in some areas than others, but everything having to do with them was potentially violent; and when trauma arrived in the form of instant and irreparable death, it was internalized whole by the men involved in it. A very, very strong trauma bond was created between American men and their instruments of death; and as befits a country founded by extremely violent Puritans, it had a sexual flavor to it, as well as an aura of dread, shame and demonic evil. These were guns manufactured in the US and intended for use by American men, totems simultaneously of liberty, patriarchal protection of the home, and death to all who challenged one's manhood. For a brief period after the Civil War the cowboy, and then the intrepid and murderous gunslinger, became the big culture hero in the US—arguably more in the East than in the Western states, where people were more or less aware that many of the most celebrated gunmen were mentally unbalanced.

But the gunman and his weapon of choice—the handgun—had arrived in the center of the collective imagination of the Americans; and it has never departed, although today the gunman is more likely to be a policeman, a detective or a private investigator. Indeed, it was said that the studio executives began to realize what a hot property Humphrey Bogart was when they saw that he was one of the few actors in Hollywood who looked right holding a gun.

Film critic William Bayer has pointed out that Americans instantly recognize the conventions—that is, the important parts of the back story—of western movies. "We are at home in any frontier town. The main street, the cemetery (often called 'boot hill'), the saloon, the general store, the stable, the bank, the railway terminal, and the sheriff's office enclosing a jail are all immediately recognizable places. We also know the people who inhabit these towns: the sheriff, the doctor, the prostitute, the telegrapher, the saloon keeper, and the quiet, mysterious stranger who wanders in and may be the fastest gun alive."

Bayer believes that *Shane* and *The Wild Ones* are both great films because the first film aestheticizes the mythology of the American West, whereas the second explodes it. But both films are capable of achieving such effects only because the western story *is* an American myth, one that we all understand instantly because it has entered the collective unconscious of the Americans. "When we hear that Jean-

Paul Sartre considers himself a connoisseur of westerns," Bayer writes, "we must smile slightly at his presumption. [Americans] knew more about them when we were sixteen than he can ever hope to comprehend."[69]

To this day millions of American men have a deeply sexualized (not love exactly, but sexualized) feeling toward their guns, characterized also to some extent by dread and excitement in equal parts. The hunting done by American sportsmen seems based on two opposing emotional motivations: the first is to control and punish nature, because the wilderness is unpredictable and therefore evil; the second, paradoxically, is to enjoy the exciting, 'uncivilized' world of the forest primeval with one's male buddies, which can be exciting precisely because it *is* uncontrolled. (And when hunters get to drinking, as they often do, the gunplay can become pretty dodgy.) The American hunter permits himself to be enticed by that same untrammeled nature mentioned above, and greatly enjoys its freedom in the short run; but he must bond himself to it by killing animals and eating them, because only in that way can he demonstrate his control of nature while enjoying its dark pleasures. Two of my ancestors—Michael and John Swaim—claimed to have gone on "the Long Hunt" with Daniel Boone, which was a seasonal thing that was partly exploratory of new hunting territory, but also aimed at killing enough deer in the winter to supply venison for a small community. The whole shebang had the feeling of a hunting ritual going back to prehistoric times. The American version of the hunt is unusual because of the passion with which it was pursued, and because of the great importance placed on the gun, not as a means to an end but as a totem of male power in the wilderness.

These powerful rituals—men alone in the wilderness, killing animals (and often each other, because of the hard liquor consumed)—reinforced an emotional identification with controlled aggression as the standard for authentic manhood. That this can contain fantastic elements of homophobia, homoeroticism and ritualized rape is thoroughly explored in the novel *Deliverance* by

James Dickey, and also the film version. (In Dickey's tale the weapon used is a bow and arrow, but it has the same resonance as a gun, and has the advantage of covertly suggesting the favorite weapon of tribal people.) But however ritualized and 'rationalized' by the imposition of annual hunting seasons, the bonding with weapons first arose in the thick of the relentless drama of the frontier. Guns were there, and there were *always* guns, because of the dangers associated with the Indian wars, slavery, the Civil War and the essential lawlessness of frontier life; not to mention Reconstruction and the re-imposition and maintenance of the plantation system in the 1890s until the dismantling of legal segregation in 1964–65.

The trauma bonding involved in the evolution of the gun into an American totem of patriarchal power also created—and continues to create—low self-worth, depression and a hyper-competitiveness that makes it difficult for American men to trust each other, to cooperate, and to enjoy the blessings of everyday life. Of course, physical courage and certain kinds of ritualized high-risk behavior are intrinsic to patriarchy everywhere, and are not limited to it. My point here is that American patriarchy is far more aggressive and obsessed with guns that most others, generating violence that appears to be random but is actually systemic, because of the centuries-old traumas that are encoded in gun lore.

Other nations had wars, civil disturbances and cruel institutions based on race, but few had such things nonstop for 300 years; and few had them enmeshed so deeply into the fabric of everyday life. Furthermore, those that did were generally not blessed with an instrument of governance as relatively sophisticated as the US Constitution and Bill of Rights. The American is governed by arguably the most sophisticated constitutional instrument ever invented, but it governs men so barbaric that they define the loss of their guns as synonymous with a loss of personal integrity, reproductive powers and death. ("You won't get my gun until you pry it from my dead, cold fingers.") I say again, the dilemma of America is the staggering contradiction between the sophistication of its foundational documents, and the vacuity, depravity and patriarchy of its people, particular its men. Even the Japanese samurai and the Prussian military man did not identify so strongly with weapons as *personal* devices of male honor and identity.

10.

The third and last trauma of the American saga came from immigration, the voluntary relocation of millions from their homes of origin, mainly in Europe, to the United States. Immigration had been consistent from the time of British America in the early 1600s, but from the Civil War until the early 1920s the Catholic and Jewish immigrant groups arrived. They came in huge numbers, these waves of Irish and the Italian and Polish and Greek and Slovak Catholics, along with the German and Polish and Russian Jews. The Catholics went to the mines and mill towns and stockyards and factories of Chicago, and to the large cities of the East Coast; so did the various Jewish immigrant groups, settling into the garment trades and small businesses, with some Jews also going directly into the mills and factories. Second-generation Jews worked their way into public education and social work, the garment industry and the nascent movie business; and through the fanatical Jewish obsession with education, they also fought their way into medicine and law and accountancy in large numbers, fighting the quotas every inch of the way to get into the universities. Both Catholics and Jews were consistently—one might say ritually—exploited, and almost invariably regarded with contempt. Everything in the literature of immigration indicates that immigrants to the US faced discrimination, often from hustlers and parvenus within their own group.

The immigrants arrived in Ellis Island because each person had, at some point, experienced a moment—not necessarily a mental epiphany, but a moment of decision—when they decided for sure they were going to immigrate to the New World. For those people there simply came a moment when they decided they'd rather be an American than continue to be whatever they'd always been before—

in effect, they became Americans at the moment that they decided to immigrate from their mother country. Except for many African-Americans, every American is *descended exclusively from people who have made such a decision.* (Incidentally, more African-Americans than one might imagine descend not from slave ships of the middle passage, but from African or Caribbean immigrants who came to Ellis Island in the US just like all the other immigrants.)

Immigration was, in fact, a vast self-selection process by which millions of people, through *individual* decisions to immigrate, *collectively* created the national character of America, in the process reinventing themselves personally through the multitude of social and cultural conflicts facing a newly-arrived immigrant. As products of those untold millions of decisions to reinvent oneself—in the process inventing America—we have inherited both a certain gambling spirit, and the disappointment that comes from gambling and losing. And that can be devastating when all you have to gamble is yourself. But my main point here is that immigration constituted a mighty self-selection process that, immigrant by immigrant, determined the true national character of the United States of America.

Part of the problem facing the new arrivals was that the great employers, the new captains of industry, very often lied to the immigrants about what they would find in America, much like the modern recruiters of farm laborers lie to the people in Michoacán and Guanajuato and other poor states of rural Mexico, to lure them to *El Norte* to work in US agribusiness. But certain kinds of poor people, especially those who are being pushed from the middle classes back into peasantry, also have a pronounced tendency to deceive themselves, because once having left poverty they can do almost anything but tolerate the idea of returning to it.

The dreams of those who immigrated to the United States were often grandiose, even when the dreamers were not entirely conscious of their own grandiosity. America was seen variously as a new Garden of Eden (where the living was easy), a righteous New Jerusalem (tasked with redeeming the world), the venue of

Coronado's luxuriant City of God (where one got rich overnight), or the enchanted country of Ponce de Leon's fountain of youth (where you could reinvent yourself while becoming young again). Sometimes—too often—these eager new Americans were bitterly disappointed with the mundane but inescapable reality, which was that American society was waiting to exploit them economically. So those extravagant hopes and dreams were deferred, and the hopes were transferred to their children.

One cannot blame European immigrants for fantasizing about a better life. Immigrants often had no idea what the future held for them in America; and when people cannot see into the future, the imagination rushes in to supply a narrative. Europe had been rife for centuries with wild and fantastic stories of America as a magical place where there were no rules, the laws of physics were suspended, and cities of gold awaited the courageous and the resolute. Maybe this happened because Europeans had become queasily aware that they were increasingly unable to feed their growing population, and they enjoyed fantasizing about an Edenic place where all the good things of life were plentiful.

Or maybe it happened because the dreamers were often people who had once enjoyed a modest affluence but were now being pushed back into poverty. People who have had a whiff of money and respectability, who are suddenly threatened with poverty again, are likely to become quite desperate, and their dreams can be equally desperate. In any case, the rude shock of the real America, as opposed to the imaginary one they carried in their heads and hearts, was traumatic; and it was the immigrant family—the immigrant ancestor, the second generation, and finally the third generation—who lived out the intergenerational experience in different ways.

The immigrants' trauma was shared by the second and third generations because many of the immigrant generation (which historians and genealogists call the *first* generation) made a conscious decision to live for their children (the *second* generation).

The three-generation paradigm of the immigrant family was most comprehensively explored by the great scholar Marcus Lee Hansen, and his findings became a cultural reference point that Americans still recognize instinctively.[70] What Hansen was really describing was often a kind of intergenerational trauma, created by a culture of grandiose expectations and greater disappointments that has directly influenced American politics, culture and society. For example, there are few immigrant families that don't have (at least within the first three generations) some version of what we might call the 'Streets of Gold' narrative, regarding at least one of their immigrant ancestors. In one common version of this narrative, an immigrant arrives in America expecting to find the streets paved with gold; but upon leaning down to inspect the curb, is disappointed to find that they are merely made of mud, asphalt, concrete or paving stones. This tale of a magical land far to the West (and often an Edenic place with trees heavy with ripe fruit for the taking), followed by the inevitable disappointment (the grinding poverty of New England, the dangers of the Gold Rush and the silver mining towns that rose and then disappeared, the boom and bust of the American economy) would be spun again and again over several hundred years.

This old-new story, of the dream that becomes a nightmare, radically changed the national character of the Americans, just as had the plantation system and the Indian wars. It often directly resulted, because of the trauma involved, in millions of immigrants and their descendants identifying with the most competitive, exploitative and aggressive aspects of the America in which they found themselves. The manic attempt of the second generation to become 'good Americans' was often simply an addiction to the worst vices associated with the American success ethos, which is almost invariably defined as money and power, rather than a considered attempt to balance off the good against the bad in the American experience. Those kinds of thoughtful choices would very often have to wait until the third generation, who were distant enough from the original immigration-trauma to make decisions relatively free of its influence.

II.

This theme of intense hope and then disappointment—what we might call 'Trauma in the Promised Land'—runs through virtually all treatments of the immigrant experience to the New World, including oral histories, first-person narratives, family histories, and the considerable scholarship that focuses on the impact of immigration on American civilization. Persons who immigrated to the United States, it would seem, either didn't find what they were looking for, or—if they did—discovered that it couldn't give them the happiness or the success or the excitement they anticipated after all. The theme of anticipation and disappointment, dream and violent disillusionment, became the controlling metaphor of the greatest works of immigrant literature.

Nowhere is this more notable than in the immigrant novel. Arguably the first great example of this genre is *The Rise of David Levinsky*, published in 1917, which takes place in the Lower East Side when that neighborhood was the cultural and economic center of American Jewish life, roughly from 1885 to 1915. *Levinsky* tells the story of a Russian Jew who immigrates to the United States, fleeing the pogroms that were increasingly occurring in the early 1880s. Born in 1865 in Russia, his father dies when he is two, and his mother nurtures a desperate dream that he will be a great scholar of the Talmud. She is tragically killed by a mob when she tries to retaliate for the beating of her son by Christian bullies; and young David becomes obsessed with redeeming his mother's death by immigrating to America. He is given money for his passage by an idealistic young woman, after he promises to use it for his religious education. (This plot element is a touch of genius that informs everything else in the novel.)

Levinsky compares his arrival in America to being born again. As his ship passes Sandy Hook, Levinsky opens his prayer book to

Psalm 104, praying to God in Hebrew as he stands rooted in awe, helplessness and ecstasy. His goal in the New World is nothing less than to redeem his mother's death by becoming the Talmudic scholar she dreamt of; but once in New York, he engages nonstop in the accumulation of wealth—and that, in turn, causes the only two women whom he could ever love to reject him, because they are deeply involved in social justice issues associated with the rise of Progressivism.

So what happens to his quest to redeem his mother's death? Levinsky finds the garment industry too profitable to resist. Carefully strategizing ways in which to undercut and outsell the German Jews who had heretofore dominated the *schmatta* trade in New York, Levinsky invents ingenious ways to evade the growing power of the garment workers' union, sometimes stealing designs from other garment designers, including his former partner. Had Levinsky found a way to use some of his wealth to promote social justice—or at the very least some form of philanthropy—he could have at least partially redeemed his mother, who was murdered by the ultimate social injustice of that time and place, which was anti-Semitism. But to maintain his wealth, he must think about business all the time; and he loses his faith, both in God and in the power of America to transform his life. The novel ends with his complaint that his life is meaningless.

Another novel that portrays a similar process in a Catholic immigrant group is Mary Doyle Curran's *The Parish and the Hill*. It is about the second generation of Irish-Americans, but is told by a young female narrator who belongs to the third generation. Mame, one of 17 children born to an immigrant Irish couple, marries James, a good worker and provider, but a man who hates all things Irish, although he himself is Irish. So crippling is his self-hatred that he will associate only with Yankees, and ultimately moves his family to the poorest street on Money Hole Hill, a memorably-named Yankee (that is, Protestant) neighborhood.

He dreams of becoming "lace curtain Irish"—that is, respectable enough to associate with Protestants—rather than "shanty Irish," working class and unrespectable. Not surprisingly, each of his seven sons drinks alcoholically. One kills himself, one dies of alcoholism, and another becomes a political fixer and wife-beater; all live out their lives in desperate alcoholic binges, often jobless and alienated from their family. The father, unable to face the role of his own violence in demoralizing his sons, denounces them as "dumb beasts" that "fight for the love of fighting," hating them for the same reason he hates himself: for being a drunken, rowdy, unrespectable shanty Irish.

Mame, the long-suffering mother of the family, offers an alternative. She personifies the best of the poor Irish in the Parish—a sense of community, a willingness to help, a deeply religious temperament without any need to impose dogma. She fearlessly denounces the nativism of the Yankees, the snobbery of the lace-curtain Irish, and the toxic racism of her sons. When her husband refuses to join a union, she takes his place on a picket line. Mame's method for survival-with-honor is to combine the best aspect of the old communal peasant culture of Ireland with the best and most cooperative aspects of the new industrial culture arising in America. Sadly, however, her sons and husband do not follow her example, destroying themselves in orgies of self-hatred.

But perhaps the most compelling stories of immigration can be found in the novels of Ole Edvart Rölvaag, the chronicler of Norwegian-American immigrants in the late 19th century. Rölvaag often wrote about Norwegians who came to America and went directly to the frontier. Thus Rölvaag became not only the great bard of Scandinavian immigration, but also—to a great extent—of the frontier as well. Rölvaag saw the impulse to immigrate as a delusion that ultimately destroys the dreamer, because the immigrant is unable to see clearly the psychological mechanisms that are driving him to escape the past, often into an impossible fantasy. And that was invariably tragic, because the destructive nature of immigration in the 19th century contained a hidden, unspoken Faustian covenant.

The immigrant to America (and likewise the emigrant to the frontier) seeks to exchange an old identity, partially or wholly, for a new one. The pilgrim-immigrant always assumes that he'll end up with a better identity than before—but in reality he tends to end up with less. He is short-changed by the hidden gods of rampant American commercialism, or by his own magical thinking, ending up with an identity that is composed of the worst of both past and present.

Giants in the Earth, Rölvaag's greatest novel, tells the story of a Norwegian couple, Per Hansa and his wife Beret, who settle Dakota Territory in what is now South Dakota. Per Hansa is thrilled with the chance to own his own land in the prairie, and thinks of it as the founding of a kingdom, and himself as the protagonist in a cosmic drama or fairy tale. His wife Beret, on the other hand, finds the prairie and its lack of humanity a source of evil, and loathes the life they are sharing there. The novel, then, is about two opposing moral visions.

Beret longs for the boundaries she knew in Norway—not just environmental and geographical ones, but social boundaries, a sense of human rooted-ness that one can rebel against, if one must, but which at least provides a human context. To her, there is something not only dangerous about the American prairie, but also sinful, in the sense that the taming of it seems to require a pride that can only be destructive. But her husband Per is thrilled by their new challenge. Building his sod house, searching for his lost cows, meeting the local Indians, fighting off Irish squatters—in the midst of all these tasks, Per experiences an excitement unlike anything he has ever known. Seized by a "divine restlessness," Per imagines that he is building a castle, that he is in fact invulnerable.

Like the Puritan immigrants before her, Beret associates her situation with unredeemed sins. She remembers the way in which her attraction to Per had blinded her to the spiritual danger into which he was to lead her. Per is acting out the accumulated desire of the powerless for untold generations, now loosed upon the New World as a kind of unquenchable lust for a new and better and more powerful identity, masquerading as a quest. As if to drive home this point, Per asks Beret to adopt American family names—which she does, while feeling even more sinful and untrue to herself for doing so.

Per sees Dakota, as the Puritans had once seen New England, as a New Canaan. But the horror of an invasion of locusts, flying in huge swarms, pushes Beret over the edge into insanity, even though Per succeeds in driving them away. Beret hides, crouching, in her immigrant chest with her smallest children, waiting for death. (Rölvaag pictures the prairie, still seductively beautiful but now also dangerous, chuckling softly to itself.)

Per at last arrives at an awareness of the deep injustice he has done Beret—and the narcissism that lies behind his wish to immigrate, because he dreamt of a fairy tale world of instant wealth and prestige. But his new insight is not enough for Beret. To regain her sanity, she has adopted a Puritanical new religious faith, one that is lacking in love and humility, which drives her to retaliate against her husband. Beret has regained her sanity, but a new and calculating hardness has entered her personality. Now what motivates Beret is the need to act out the aggression she has internalized, and get revenge against her husband.

Hans Olsa, their only friend, lays on his deathbed. Taking care of him, Beret sadistically threatens him with visions of eternal doom. When Per arrives, Beret insists that he go to fetch the minister, so that Hans can be converted on his deathbed, and thereby saved from hellfire. Per insists that no pastor is necessary; besides, there's a snowstorm raging outside. Hans, however, has been thoroughly terrorized by Beret's talk of Satan and an eternity in hell, and begs Per to go—and Beret ruthlessly makes fun of Per's manhood. This taunt by his wife is the last straw: Per sets off in the snow. His body is not found until next spring. Beret has gotten her revenge.

At its heart, *Giants in the Earth* deals with the loss experienced by immigrants, who depart for a New World but end up with their old demons in a new setting. And when they do manage to leave behind their old-world demons, they find an identity in the New World that feels essentially false. There can be excitement in such a pilgrimage, despite the dangers, because adventure is a basic instinct of the young. Yet the self-delusion that haunts the traveler to a New World is always there, with all its potential to compromise judgment and morality. As in most immigrant narratives, Beret feels that she has traded in her identity for a new self, but somehow losing her humanity in the process.

The Danish critic Jørgen Bukdahl put it best in his 1929 review of *Giants* in the magazine *Politiken*. "Rölvaag's book is a tragedy, because people do not with impunity break out of a cultural context that has been built by the struggle and strife of generations." There was also another reason why the story was a tragedy: "These people wanted to escape from all the problems that pained and blocked them at home. But the problems *were awaiting them on the prairie*, and no one saw that except Beret, because they were so filled by the adventure and the challenge." [My italics.]

Here Bukdahl puts his finger on a recurring delusion at the heart of immigration. The immigrant can and often does imagine that he or she will leave behind certain problems by leaving one place and going to another (a process some psychotherapists call "the geographic cure"); but people who immigrate to a New World take their old problems along with them, which reappear when they arrive in the new place, often in some frightening and unexpected new form. And the problems are compounded by the trauma resulting from the disappointment of arriving in a place that is not a Garden of Eden, a New Jerusalem, a City of Gold or a Land of Eternal Youth, but a hyper-competitive country and a hellish, hardscrabble life in which predatory capitalists await to liquidate their dreams and turn them into profits for the corporate elite.

In Europe, the people who did not immigrate confronted the inequalities of industrialization by organizing the great socialist, social democratic and labor parties, creating an alternative to both Marxist-Leninists and to unregulated capitalism. But the immigrant to America is a bird of a completely different feather. He believes he will accomplish earth-shaking things simply by coming to America and insinuating himself into the miracle of the American experience. The result is disorientation, loss of identity, self-hatred and trauma. We should not be surprised by this—the entire unspoken nature of the immigrant experience is of few winners and many losers; and the winners are often empowered to just the extent that the losers are defeated.

The historian Richard Hofstadter has written about the way that the self-selection process of mass immigration shaped the national character of American. The historian, he wrote, would be advised to "consider the effects of selective migration—not merely in the sense that dukes and bishops did not emigrate, and that the American population drew mainly upon the middle and lower orders of Europe, but also in the less demonstrable sense that, since millions more suffered from one form or another of malaise and oppression than actually removed themselves, there may have been some selection by psychological as well as social type, with America receiving more than its share of the exceptionally restless, the exceptionally bold, the cranky and the intractable."[71]

The psychological type described above would, I suggest, be sitting ducks for those who wish to exploit them. They would tend to be exploitive themselves, or potentially so, because the very excitement of starting out anew in a new world could blind them to the political and cultural realities around them; and as a result blind them to the psychic costs of their actions on everybody else. The key to this deficit is the moral blindness of those who seek more than the world can give them. In one's imagination, this is not dangerous— all first-rate art is based on it. But in real life, such strivings are acted out only through Faustian bargains, and such bargains tend to end in tragedy. Immigration is one of the purest examples of such a bargain.

In *Giants in the Earth* the frontier, especially the prairie, is an empty stage waiting for actors. Per suffers from the unmistakable grandiosity of narcissism, evidently generated by his brutal experiences with youthful poverty. First it drives his wife insane; she then taunts him to his death. It would not have happened if he had faced this aspect of himself before leaving Norway. But he had to act it out, before he could know it—and to do that, he had to come to the New World, because America was one of the very few 19th century stages on which such fateful (if pathological) dramas of self-knowledge were being acted out. The result was a tragedy that he could not foresee.

12.

The second generation struggles to turn the negative power of the immigrant parents' disappointment into a positive. Very often they do this by adopting all things 'American,' and develop an intense dislike for anything reminiscent of the Old Country. They change their names to make them sound more American. They are ashamed of their parents' accents, and may not introduce their friends to them because of it. They admire American hustle, identify with the American success ethos (power and money), and defend its foreign policy even when they suspect it is wrong. They strive to be 'good Americans,' and cannot imagine themselves living anywhere else.

The gung-ho identification of the second generation with all things American often feels like an outcome of unacknowledged shame and psychic failure, in the same way that narcissists create a flawless, heroic persona in response to low self-esteem. It is understandable that the children of immigrants should want to carve out their own niche in America; but their frenzied attempt to adopt what they see as the American way of life leads us to believe that something else is driving them: they have inherited something of their parents' shame for being 'foreign,' but in the process have lost something real in exchange for something that feels contrived.

What is this process? It is in a great many cases unmistakably a form of intergenerational emotional trauma, the second generation bonding with the aggression that has, to a greater or lesser extent, exploited their parents and against which their parents struggled. Of course, the second generation can deal more directly and in a more savvy way with the challenges that often baffled their parents; but it is precisely the second generation that so often internalizes the same hyper-competitiveness that wounded their parents—even while experiencing that wound as the emotional ticket to becoming American. Most Americans experience competitiveness and cooperation as opposite sides of their social beings, struggling to keep the two in balance. But hyper-competitiveness represents a permanent loss of that previous balance, and as a result becomes a cause of depression, alienation and the need to act out more aggression, because it reduces everything to winners and losers in a marketplace that is shorn of human values. The takeaway point is this: the hyper-competitiveness that the second generation often embraces, and then internalizes, is exactly the same as the concealed aggression that waited at dockside to exploit their parents in the immigrant generation. In fact, the second generation may unconsciously identify with it precisely because of the intergenerational trauma the second generation feels compelled to redeem.

Of course, not all children of immigrants respond to the trauma of their parents' immigrant experience in that way. For some in the first generation, immigration was no trauma at all, and they found a new language, new customs and new laws relatively easy to negotiate. Even among the majority of immigrant families that found life in the New World very difficult at first, there were those who were able to deconstruct the resulting trauma and break free of its intergenerational effects. As we have seen, even people who suffer emotional trauma are sometimes able to deconstruct and overcome its effects on their own personalities; and it is these people that become the teachers, visionaries and positive leaders of a time and place, both within populations at risk and in society at large. It is the others, those that cannot overcome the harsh memories of the past and who cannot unravel the aggression they have internalized, who end up identifying with all that is most aggressive in American society, institutions and culture.

13.

These three institutionalized social phenomena—slavery and segregation, centuries of Indian wars and the self-selection process of immigration that defined America—reached critical mass in the 19th century; and in so doing they created the dark side of the American national character. If the best thing about the American people is their foundational documents (the Declaration and the US Constitution and the Bill of Rights), we might say that the demons of the American experience arose over the generations from the roiling exploitation of slavery and segregation, tribal genocide and rank exploitation of immigrants. Manifest Destiny, with its idea of the transcendental nature of irregular warfare, took hold in the American psyche; and while no longer referred to as such, it is just as strong today as it ever was, although to some extent it is acted out in highly-militarized video games rather than society. At its heart is the deeply-felt American belief to which we have previously alluded: *if you want something and are strong enough to take it, you are wrong not to do so*. Implicit is the idea that if the American male does not take what he needs, he runs the risk of damnation—that is, of losing his soul (and perhaps his identity).

Of course, Manifest Destiny is nothing less than the enjoyment of endless greed and boundless plunder. That completely contradicts the spirit of the US Constitution, which is about negotiating rights outside of physical force, and navigating the claims of different interests through a separation of political powers; the Constitution is a legal instrument that aims not to enshrine a single power, but to create the daily experience of relative fairness between contending powers. That is a powerful idea, and one that is directly and completely opposed to the main operating thesis of patriarchy, which is that a small group of strong men deserve to dominate everybody else—not to mention nationalism, which is for one's own country to oppress another. But then, the most intense American realities always have to do with the tension between the 18th-century idealism of the Constitution, on the one hand, and the way Americans actually behave, on the other.

Think of Thomas Jefferson. When you think of Jefferson, think of the delicious, sonorous language of the Declaration of Independence, part barbaric yawp and part grandiloquent formulations of freedom written in Shakespearian English and the sweet phraseology of the King James Bible, as applied by a self-conscious gaggle of highly-educated revolutionaries to the society and politics of the new country they were creating. But when you think of that Declaration and of its author Jefferson, think also of Sally Hemings: think of the children she and Jefferson brought into the world (children Jefferson refused to openly acknowledge); and think of Sally's brother, drinking himself to death as he was forced to witness every nuance of his sister's predicament. Jefferson wasn't just a cad, he was a monster of patriarchal sexual exploitation—but he was also able to put into words the 18th century dream of the rights of man that still determine our best laws and legal decisions today, a dream that would someday make the Emancipation Declaration possible, as well as the Civil Rights Act of 1964 and the Voting Rights Act of 1965, the two statutes that define for all time the Second American Revolution.

I, for one, am glad that Jefferson could imagine such ideas, and could conjure the words to express those ideas. He was both the presiding genius of the American experience and a monster of domestic abuse. How can a person be both? Slavery made him both, not just because of the attraction he felt toward his lover Sally, but because he took advantage of an asymmetrical and essentially coercive power relationship that he must have known to be wrong—a wrong only capable of redemption with the freedom of Sally and her children. Sexual passion could not for long block out the true guilt of the Slave Power, even when it seemed to, because the worst parts of our world always comes rushing back.

What made slavery, the Indian wars and immigration important was that they deeply traumatized Americans in ways that Americans barely understood, then or now. Manifest Destiny first captured the imagination of white Americans in the 1840s because it was a catchphrase that justified and gave transcendent value to their greed, a seemingly ennobling context to their ambition, and most importantly, historical importance to the violence and dread of the Indian wars that were already embedded in their unconscious minds. Likewise the trauma of slavery was to a great extent enhanced by the staggering loss of life in the Civil War, which Americans came to understand as their own Greek tragedy with Puritan overtones. Likewise immigration—with its huge effect on the American family—became such a profound experience because of the emotional dislocation it generated, a dislocation that cast its long shadow for three generations in every immigrant family.

Those three crucial American traumas created aggressive emotional orientations that had the power to overwhelm cognition, and usually did. The unconscious identification with force created by these phenomena influenced everything, resulting in the American definition of success as being heavily weighted toward an authoritarian kind of power, and an almost completely selfish approach to the responsibilities inherent in wealth. Yet Americans insisted on seeing these things as redemptive. The idea was not simply that that power and money could help a person get what they wanted, but that the entire process could transform and redeem. And this became a part of the American mind at a time—not coincidentally, I believe—when nationalism burst onto the scene as a new secular religion. Violence against dark-skinned Indians, long a function of the older Puritan religion, was now perceived as being close to the heart of American nationalism. Thus did the essential aggression in American nationalism (not to mention westward expansion) reinforce the idea that war and violence could lead to moral transformation.

As the 19th century drew to a close, the violence of America's nation-building experience no longer belonged solely to individual actors. Now every battle, every lynching, every gunfight at the OK Corral, was shared with everybody who could read, and many who couldn't. (The habit of reading newspapers aloud extended well into the twentieth century.) And because those who read newspapers cannot change the events they read about, or alleviate the suffering they cause, the result was to create an irrational sense that one is complicit in the suffering of those events. Once one feels complicit in something, one is on the road to internalizing the aggression inevitably present in the social dilemmas that caused the suffering.

Nationalism, Manifest Destiny, and the institutionalization of violence in society—they came together to create the emotional orientations of a new America. At its core, emotionally speaking, were various forms of a new American nationalism. Its faith was in the American nation as an exciting, violent and transformative emotional experience; its presence was signaled by the redemption supposedly inherent in money and power; and it was most purely and intensely experienced in the holy ecstasy of war and conflict.

Money, like the Puritans had first imagined, really *could* function as a form of grace; but its redemptive power arose from the fact that it was usually earned through some exploitation of one's fellow man. To be a member of the Elect one had also to worship competition as the highest good, especially and particularly in the marketplace. It was only one step further, then, to understand fully what Manifest Destiny had been sent to teach—that the highest truth was aggression in the service of the American nation, and that the highest good was to obtain, facilitate or encourage individual wealth.

Again: Americans are best understood as a conservative, money-worshipping people governed by progressive documents. Of course, there are Americans that live out the spirit of the Constitution and internalize it emotionally, because they see that the worship of power and money leads to depression, self-hatred and nihilism—so there are those vigorous and valiant people seek a new way. But those who worship power and money will often win the battle, and lose the war—that is, they will not discover until later the secret emotional deficits of winning. In the long run, America will probably take its place with all the other empires that have failed because of greed and hubris.

But the ideas in the US Constitution and the Bill of Rights will live forever, to be applied in other venues with changes according to each situation by other peoples and nations. The US Constitution and the Bill of Rights reduced to writing certain unalienable precepts regarding self-government, not just for one time, but for all time. It was perhaps simply a matter of fate that somehow these imperishable ideas came roaring into the forefront of the collective human imagination in the 18th century; but their importance could not be denied either then or now—there will never again be a truly democratic society, for example, that will not employ in some form a separation of political powers.

Until we can really understand and internalize the US Constitution in such a way as to live out its precepts, it is the responsibility of good people to wrestle the demons that haunt the American mind, and to deconstruct the trauma bonds that generate those demons and give them such disproportionate power in daily life. But that task is not, as the Puritans imagined it, a World Mission to ferret out evil among the unwashed heathen—rather we must task ourselves with understanding the evil in ourselves, in an America both washed or unwashed. It is always possible that we may lose this battle in the end, but that is no reason for not waging it in the present, because the present is where we live; and in moral terms, as James Baldwin famously wrote, the time is always now. If America has a world mission to destroy evil, we will find that evil mainly by looking in the mirror. Once having seen it we should try, even if in a very small way, to do something about it.

It is not that the Americans are more evil than the rest of humanity, but that they are more powerful, and that they are more obsessed with power itself than with using it well. For reasons not wholly of its own making, America is the world's only remaining superpower—in terms of sheer destructive power, then, the president of the United States is inevitably the CEO of planet earth. Think of that—then think of the passionate love that American men feel for their guns. Think also of the fact that America now has many more nuclear weapons than any other country in the world—and the largest military establishment the world has ever seen. It is precisely the power of these weapons of mass destruction that makes Americans so dangerous to themselves and to the world—that is to say, what is dangerous about the weapons is not the killing power, but the moral blindness in those Americans that worship that kind of power as an end in itself. Men who love their guns suffer from a kind of moral autism that causes them to live deep in the emotional slough of an endless and ultimately shallow patriarchal drama, and sadly, one that they are forced to endlessly repeat, even if only in their imaginations. In a sense they live to kill, which is a dark fate indeed.

D.H. Lawrence said that at heart, the American is a killer. That's not fair, of course, because there are so many different kinds of Americans—many more kinds, in fact, than Lawrence or others of his generation could possibly imagine, given that the American people are not a race but a people made up of every race and religion in the world. Lawrence was right only to the extent that anonymous evil is so influential down the generations, and that American nation-building was historically so violent, and its aggression so well hidden and so often rationalized. It is all too often, he saw, that it is spoiled adolescents in adult bodies take things because they have the power to do so, and they are the Americans (people like George Bush, for example) who are the ones that permanently shape the American mind and society. And because their weapons have become so destructive, because their worship of power and profit does not recognize the civilized virtue of restraint, the American political class may seek the destruction of all that is best in the 21st century. Truly as Shakespeare said, it is the evil that men do that lives on after them, and it is affecting generations untold.

But even as systemic evil looms larger than any one person among us, and even as we grapple with the traumas that have generated many forms of systemic evil over the generations, we must look to the brave individual people who opposed those evils (however they may have failed in their own time); we must remember those who played David to the Goliath of systemic evil, who did lonely battle *against* the injustices of racial oppression, the massacres of tribal people, and the exploitation of immigrants — it is they that we must remember with awe and fondness. It is they, the prophetic minority in all times and places, that we must study and learn from. Even as we sometimes stagger under the past's accumulated evils, we contemplate with joy the brave and beautiful souls that found a way to throw off the weight of institutional aggression.

If they could do it, so can we. That's their message that comes down to us.

This is the best epitaph for many abolitionists, including some of this writer's ancestors: today when we still struggle with the historical aftereffects of slavery, it is the names of those that opposed it that we must remember, because they give proof that humankind might survive its own destructiveness. American first denounced as mad those who opposed slavery and other injustices; but the value of those early activists is that they discovered something in themselves that they overcame, in the process learning how to articulate the case against that same evil to others in their American world. We can never forget or properly thank enough those precious women and men who found a way to personally overcome, and then publicly challenge, those forms of systemic evil that grew up in this New World — as they showed us also how to survive the aggression both inside and outside the informed heart. There is no sweeter justice East of Eden, east of the Garden from which we were driven long ago, than the remembrances of those that first confessed aggression in their own hearts, then struggled against it in a strange land's wilderness.

Chapter 7

War and the Trauma Bond

I.

According to several sources, Karl Rove, President Bush's political advisor, strongly advised him in late 2002 to invade Iraq. Various interest groups had been calling for 'regime change' in Iraq for some time, of course, including the neo-conservatives, the Israel Lobby, the Religious Right, and major British, American and Dutch oil corporations. By December 2001, the combined military might of the US had toppled the Taliban government in Afghanistan—and rightly so, since the Taliban had provided a base for the terrorists that attacked our people. But attacking the sovereign nation of Iraq, a country that had not attacked us, would be an unprecedented form of aggression, likely to isolate America internationally while creating an extraordinarily dangerous precedent. But Karl Rove was a political advisor, not a foreign policy advisor, and he wasn't advising an invasion of Iraq for reasons of national security. He was advocating it because of President Bush's presidential candidacy in 2004.

Rove was perfectly well aware that the government of Iraq, while one of the most brutal in the world, had nothing to do with 9/11— that in fact there was no moral, legal or military justification for an armed invasion of that country. But Rove was also aware that if the US was involved in a war *President Bush would have a better chance of winning the 2004 election.* It was this domestic political calculation that probably tipped the scales; as a result, untold thousands of innocent people would die, and the American economy would be driven deep into debt. For this and other reasons having to do with systemic evil it is important that we understand the emotional dynamics that underlay President Bush's highly calculated use of aggression. The unpleasant reality is that aggressive, patriarchal leaders very often start unnecessary wars for no other reason than their own selfish political advancement.

Why would starting a war help President Bush win the 2004 election? Because voters don't like to vote against a war leader. But *why* don't voters like to vote against a war President? The answer is hard for people to comprehend (and to accept), partly because of what it says about human nature and partly because of the ability of aggression to trump logic and emotion. War generates an enormous amount of emotional distress, victimizing not merely the families of those killed or wounded, but even those people who are personally untouched by the war; this happens because of the constant exposure to images, film footage and media reports of the ongoing death and destruction.

But it also has an exciting, oddly compelling attraction arising from the explicit nature of its aggression. Civilians in wartime may not be traumatized by a single image or report, but from the inexorable, cumulative impact of many such images on a daily basis. The cumulative impact is even worse when the war is an unnecessary one, for reasons we will examine later on. Political elites, for reasons of their own, often use the aggression, pain and trauma of war *to bond people to their aggression and their aggressive policies*. How they do this will become clear as we deconstruct the process—and since it's important for readers to understand this, we'll go slow, with a fair amount of emphasis on the takeaway parts.

2.

Governing elites also use the trauma created by war to silence opposition. Patriarchal leaders know intuitively how to do this, because patriarchy sees war as the most important activity of civilization and the warrior as the central culture hero; and they know how to use the emotions aroused by war, because they see these emotional orientations as the most important people can feel. They start out by encouraging the public to identity with troops in the field—but also, in an even more powerful and uncanny way, they encourage the people to identify with those who have died in the war. Typically, they will then represent dissenters who oppose the war as undermining the troops, but also as *disrespecting and harming the dead*. (Yes, that's irrational, but aggression is irrational, and it causes us to behave in irrational ways.) Portraying one's political adversaries as disrespecting the honored dead has long been a favorite demagogic device of the powerful, the classic example of this hoary patriarchal tactic being the funerary oration of Mark Antony in Shakespeare's *Julius Caesar*.

As the bloody, mauled corpse of Caesar lies before him, in full view of the Roman crowd, Marc Antony goads the mob into a slow burn of anger and frustration; and then, with repeated references to the "honorable men" who had conspired to murder Caesar, he pushes them over the edge into mob violence. The speech starts out as a defense of Brutus and ends—as Antony knows it would—with a public riot. In a ghastly detail typical of Shakespeare's genius, an innocent poet is murdered by the mob in the resulting melee, because the poet had the same name as one of Caesar's murderers.

To build support for his 2003 invasion of Iraq, President Bush asked the wider public to identify with the war dead of Afghanistan and to internalize the aggression represented by their untimely death; and having done that, he simply encouraged the public to redirect their resulting aggression onto anybody courageous enough to oppose his fraudulent invasion of Iraq. (Remember what happened to the war correspondent Chris Hedges, when he tried to publicly criticize the Iraq invasion at Rockford University?) Bush's attack on antiwar opponents was a further source of anxiety and disaffection among the American people, which arose, for many, from the sheer frustration of not being able to speak the truth and be heard. Dissenters—patriotic Americans who saw what a moral disaster the Iraq war would become—were represented by the Bush administration as diabolical interlopers seeking America's destruction.

Getting people to identify with the war dead is the premier method for opening up the unconscious mind to aggressive emotional orientations, which can then be manipulated by the state into attacks on anybody or any group critical of the war. It is from these two major sources, *violent public images of war*, first, and secondly, *widespread public identification with the war dead*, that trauma is most likely to be generated by patriarchal men and governments, so that the aggression inherent in their appeals can be internalized by supporters in the public. You will notice, then, that almost from the beginning of Bush's disastrous invasion of Iraq he kept referring to the beautiful young people (always Americans, of course) that had "made the ultimate sacrifice" for their country—that is, those whose lives had been wasted in his unnecessary war.

There were the predictable positive responses from the base of the Republican Party—that is, from ultraconservative white males and self-righteous right-wing evangelicals in the South and Border States—who were already inclined to be cheerleaders for *any* type of war. Remember that patriarchal men don't have to agree with the objective of a war to approve of it: if people are being killed in a war, that's enough for them. Patriarchal men intuitively understand that war is an instrument for inculcating patriarchal values, mainly through trauma, the resulting internalization of aggression, and identification with aggression as a worldview. So a great many white men in rural American, the American South and the Border States will support *any* kind of war, even an unnecessary invasion, because it could not help but strengthen the values of their true secular religion, the fanatical identification with the aggression that drives American patriarchy.

3.

The Iraqi insurgency depended heavily on improvised explosive devices, or IEDs, which tended to create horrific (and often undiagnosed) head trauma, which when added to the frequent incidence of undiagnosed PTSD created a huge problem amongst US military personnel. The American occupation of Iraq, it turned out, was as close to hell on earth as such an occupation could be. American troops did almost daily patrols in unfamiliar and extremely dangerous neighborhoods; troops continued to be deployed long after they should have been rotated back home. At the same time millions of middle-class refugees left Iraq, and most of them still haven't come back, caught in the limbo caused by the personal ambition and imperial hubris of an American President a world away. Meanwhile, images of the horrors in Iraq were broadcast into American homes on a daily basis, so that everybody was to some extent aware of the carnage. In time, those images had their effect.

The tidal wave of daily images deeply affected the American people, as I've already mentioned, but I think it probable that most weren't entirely aware of *how* it was affecting them. When it became clear that the original reason for the invasion (the existence of weapons of mass destruction) was and always had been false, the trauma was amplified. President Bush responded very much like a sociopath: it never occurred to him to apologize for starting a war under false (or at least mistaken) pretenses, and in fact he didn't seem to care much one way or the other. But it was now clear to the American people that the invasion of Iraq was completely and totally *unnecessary*; and it was this fact that ultimately made the Iraq occupation so distressing.

Paradoxically, however, this was not a bad thing from the perspective of the Bush administration, because each new falsehood and betrayal demoralized the most decent elements in American society, which had the effect of driving them deeper into an unwilling submission, which demoralized and further isolated them. The patriarchal men who supported the war were ascendant in the public sphere. It was for just this reason that Karl Rove had advised Bush to invade Iraq—once the invasion got underway, the political implications of invading another country without good reason were going to go Teflon. When anybody criticized Bush's war, he would simply point at images of the young American soldiers fighting in Iraq, or those that had already been killed, and say, "Why aren't you supporting our troops in Iraq? *Don't you care about them?"* Bush would reap the political gain from this despite the fact that it was his lies that made the slaughter possible.

But *why* was this gambit so effective—and why is starting wars *always* so effective—in silencing dissent? Because, first of all, it confronts us with the phenomenon of death, which humans experience as the most overwhelming paradox of life, since we know death occurs but can never consciously accept it. (Because the conscious mind cannot accept its own obliteration.) Secondly, by repeatedly making us conscious of the war dead, and keeping it in the forefront of the public mind, patriarchal politicians make us unconsciously feel complicit in the tragedy of their death. This bonds us to the process by which they are murdered—again unconsciously, but very powerfully—that causes us to identify with the war in question. This is aimed at making us support the war aims of the political leaders, in order to give 'meaning' to their sacrifice—but in reality, it is aimed at making us support the war so that more young people can die unnecessarily, for the greater glory of the patriarchal old men who have started the war for their own political advancement.

When unscrupulous leaders arouse unconscious feelings of complicity with war, it ultimately traumatizes people who value life and who are tying to live with respect for it. What the patriarchal leaders are trying to do is to get people who *consciously oppose* unnecessary wars to *unconsciously identify* with the dead created by them. The sense of complicity in the death of the young on the battlefield, which the unscrupulous politicians seeks to create, bonds us to war in the same way that the sacrifice of Christ bonds an evangelical Christian to the cross. But this bonding process is pathological, because it is filled with aggression, and causes the believer to identify with violent solutions to human problems. The patriarchal leaders piously ask us to love and feel reference for the war dead, but *in creating a sense of complicity with their death they actually seek to bond us to the war that killed them*. This is very hard for many people to understand and accept. This insight asks us to accept the harsh reality that sometimes modern leaders, to the extent that they are patriarchal, fundamentally seek destruction of life, and gain both status and political power from manipulating the deaths of innocent people.

Bush used the deaths of young Americans to silence and overwhelm the American people, and also to bond them to torture, war, political repression and the so-called "unitary executive," a jargon phrase used by Bush Republicans for soft fascism. The unnecessary Iraq war would now be used to justify the Bush administration's efforts to dismantle the rule of law. Throughout the long years of the Iraq occupation Bush repeatedly instructed the American people to identify with the dead, the most extreme form of identification with Bush's own aggression: *"Think about those who have given their lives.* Do you want it to all go for nothing, after all that they've done for you?" Once a political leader mentions the honored dead, it is usually a sign he is about to descend into the next level of criminality, because such rhetorical gambits exist precisely to prepare people for the descent, rung by rung, into systemic evil. The invocation of the dead stirs up the most fundamental kinds of aggression, automatically casting all war dissenters in the role of traitors who are complicit in the death of American soldiers.

Writer and commentator Chris Hayes (of MSNBC) found out just how insanely protective American patriarchy is of language idealizing the war dead on May 27, 2012, on Memorial Day Weekend. Hayes made comments on his show regarding the common use of the word *hero* as applied to American service members killed in action. "I feel uncomfortable about the word because it seems to me that it is so rhetorically proximate to justifications for more war. Um, and, I don't want to obviously desecrate or disrespect memory of anyone that's fallen, and obviously there are individual circumstances in which there is genuine, tremendous heroism, you know, hail of gunfire, rescuing fellow soldiers, and things like that. But it seems to me that we marshal this word in a way that is problematic."

"But maybe I'm wrong about that," he added.

Needless to say, there was a tremendous uproar over Chris' thoughtful words—when you attack the patriarchal idealization of the war dead, you are attacking the staple tactic of the political right. You are also conducting a frontal assault on patriarchy in its purest form—remember, reader, that patriarchy idealizes war (*any* war) because its death-dealing violence is important for instilling aggression, which for the patriarch constitutes the highest good. To the right-wing propagandists the great value of the war dead is precisely that they're dead, and can therefore be used as emotional blackmail to compel compliance in the next war, without asking permission from those who were actually killed. Chris Hayes eventually apologized for his remarks—which in this writer's opinion was not necessary, because he did nothing wrong—but his nervous corporate bosses might have thought it necessary.

Chris' point was a good one, although on a cable news program it is a very difficult point to make. Probably the best way to open up such a discussion in a popular venue is simply to neutralize the reaction from the patriarchal right by partially agreeing with it, then counter-punching and ending with an antiwar argument.

One might say something like this: "Of course, we think of all fallen servicemen and servicewomen as heroes on Memorial Day, because of the enormity of the sacrifice they made. We grieve for them because of the awful heartache that war brings to so many families. But even as we grieve, is it not also appropriate to ask if we are doing everything we can to keep the next war from happening? Perhaps we can best honor those who made the ultimate sacrifice by continuing the search for peace. One way we can honor our war dead is to think twice before we start the next war."

Reading an antiwar letter written by someone in the military who was killed in action is also an effective way to challenge the right-wing patriarchy's ecstatic celebration of death-in-war; also something by an antiwar poet such as Wilfred Owens, a superb British poet killed in the last weeks of the First World War. These things honor the war dead by reading the words of some who died, but their antiwar message short-circuits the efforts of patriarchy to use the war dead to glorify war, and thus to prepare us for more unnecessary wars in the future.

Almost any public recognition of those who have died in war will be interpreted by some as an articulation of patriarchal values, no matter what words you use. It is probably for this reason that Abraham Lincoln kept his 'Gettysburg Address' short and used language that deliberately ignored popular rhetorical conventions. Lincoln insisted repeatedly in his amazing speech that *nothing* the living could do would ever honor the war dead at Gettysburg. Luckily for him and for us today, brevity in that instance served the cause of literary excellence. It was the rarest of funerary orations: it was rational, it was short, and it respected the dead without using them. Instead of portraying them as heroes, it referred to them simply as "brave men" whose great achievement was to consecrate the earth simply by being buried in it.

4.

Of course, it was President Bush himself who was directly responsible for the deaths of so many young Americans in Iraq, by starting an unnecessary war under false pretenses; but once the American populace felt the overwhelming weight of war-trauma invoked by the state, few could see or comprehend that simple truth. It was simply too horrifying to accept. One of the tragic effects of emotional trauma caused by big, overwhelming historical events is that people begin to see the man-made disasters hurtling at them as fundamentally impersonal, like a hurricane or a flood, rather than the handiwork of particular elites and identifiable strategies. And because the American people were silent in 2003, and did not rise up against the usurping of international law and common decency, the sacrifices of the individual soldiers, airmen and seamen of the US military actually *did* go for nothing, except to remind the people of the world of the awesomely destructive nature of American arms, and the mendacity of its leadership. But the world already knew that; and it was disgusted beyond measure by the American murder and maiming of tens of thousands of innocent people, because they had the bad luck to be Muslims, to speak Arabic and to live in the wrong country at the wrong time.

Bonded to a silence that encouraged the further internalization of their government's aggression, a majority of the American people obediently (and rather numbly) reelected President George Bush to another term. As previously mentioned, undemocratic and tyrannical rulers have used this process for millennia, and gotten away with it because people do not understand the psychological dynamics of trauma bonding. Whenever he feels himself in political trouble—for political incompetence, abuse of office, or any of a thousand other reasons—what does the corrupt and ambitious leader do? He unleashes a violent campaign of persecution against some unlucky minority, or starts a war. In the ensuing violence, enough aggression is usually internalized to create a strong bond with the government. (In this instance, only the Iraq invasion was needed—Bush did not demonize Muslims. Discrimination against American Muslims would come later.)

Again, the emotional content of this gambit plays out like this: the demagogic leader starts an unnecessary war and then implores the public to identify with the war dead; an emotionally battered people feel the full horror of the war's trauma, and internalizes its aggression; the leaders encourage them to direct their internalized aggression against dissenters—who are then characterized as domestic subversives intent on helping whatever enemy the military or political establishment happens to be fighting. Then the population is hounded to direct its aggression toward 'the enemy,' which has been selected by the all-knowing state. If you were one of the brave few that had publicly opposed Bush's war, the charge (sometimes unspoken, but often spoken) would likely be that *you* were complicit in the death of young soldiers, for after all the dead soldiers *were fighting to protect your freedom*. So being complicit in that manner, you should shut up and support the war.

To which this writer says, let's be real for a moment. This is painful, but it needs to be faced. If American soldiers in an unnecessary war die for anything, it is so that their own government can more easily *take away* the citizenry's freedom. (This is, I might add, a good argument for not being in the military unless the political leadership is reasonably good, and leaving it if the leadership is bad.) Unnecessary war brings repression, not freedom, and a general restriction of civil liberties. Guilt over the death of brave young soldiers makes people more vulnerable to trauma, and thereupon more vulnerable to the internalization of aggression. The ache of loss for the young people killed in such a war also transforms the impersonal catastrophe of war into a personal and emblematic pain that can be intimately experienced by the individual citizen. This is especially true when images from the war appear on the evening news *each night* for many years—and it was probably for this reason, however unconsciously the decision was made, that news organizations were allowed to embed their reporters alongside America's fighting men and women: the more images of carnage that they could get on TV, the more the people would internalize the government's aggression, and turn that aggression against 'the enemy,' as well as anyone who might criticize the war.

The more images the American people saw of the Iraq war in the print and electronic media—and they saw them on a daily basis, sometimes many times a day—the more the aggression of the war crept into the collective unconscious of the people. The more disturbing the pictures and reports (especially those about ethnic cleansing by the sectarian Iraqi militias) the more they were likely to numb and traumatize people who watched them. The only exception to this was the photos or film footage of the American dead in body bags or flag-draped coffins—*that* sight (an instantly recognizable one) usually tended to inspire as much introspection about the war as internalization of aggression—so the Bush administration quickly banned photos of American dead. And it is also true that some people 'burn out' on images of suffering, and struggle to detach from what is going on. But even those who stopped watching the evening news because they wanted to avoid the images of carnage, even those Americans who despised the war, invariably internalized its aggression—in fact, those who found it repulsive tended to internalize its aggression more quickly than most, because internalizing it was the only way they could live with it. They accepted it first as only an unfortunate 'reality,' but as the counterinsurgency wore on, the approved liberal position gradually became that the Iraq war did not deserve support because *it could not be won.*

Progressives went from a moral to a pragmatic argument against the war, pointing out the 'un-winnable' nature of the Iraq counterinsurgency, since that seemed to be the only realistic approach to criticizing the Iraq war; and no doubt that was true, it *was* un-winnable. But that's exactly how trauma bonding works—a large country invades a small one, the invasion becomes an occupation, and the public is exposed to endless images of the resulting insurgency. Because of the public's internalization of all those images of aggression, they make an emotional adjustment to it, and become less critical of the invasion from the point of view of morality, or even international law. They make an *emotional adjustment to the immorality of the war,* in other words.

And since mass trauma bonding is unconscious, people are mainly unaware of how images of violence are changing their deepest values, which they believe to be inviolable. While this process has some of the characteristics of cognitive dissonance, it is emotions more than perceptions or ideas that are being affected; the proximate cause of the shift is the constant exposure to aggression— the images, speculations and conversations about the war. Decent people begin to accept the war as inevitable, because they can't imagine any alternative to the terrible reality forced upon them.

As Bush knew it would, the overwhelming and traumatic nature of the Iraqi counterinsurgency robbed elected American leaders—

especially the leadership of the Democratic Party—of their ability to denounce the war as immoral. That is why neo-cons place such importance on "creating facts on the ground"—they know that once a particular war is started, or once torture or targeted killings are done on a regular basis (that is, once systemic evil is institutionalized), people tend unconsciously to make an adjustment to its immorality. In so doing, they internalize the aggression involved. As Karl Rove had foreseen, President Bush was able to denounce critics of his war (and by implication the leaders of the Democratic Party) as being complicit in the crimes of insurgents killing American soldiers. People who opposed the state terrorism of the Bush administration were themselves denounced as complicit in terrorism.

This last gambit, borrowed from the fascists of the 1930s, has become one of the most popular moves in the neo-conservative playbook. Progressives and older paleoconservatives often fail to grasp the psychological mechanisms used, but the younger, aggression-worshipping neo-cons intuitively comprehend its negative power. It *works*, at least in the beginning. That's why the Likud government of Israel uses it in its relationships with the Palestinians and in its public relations with the rest of the world—first the Likudniks kill, then they pour on the *hasbara* [propaganda], endlessly enumerating all the reasons why it had to happen, while repeatedly stressing the victim status of the Israeli state. Meanwhile the basic facts about the mechanics of Israeli oppression are obscured. That is the fundamental equation of the patriarchal oppressor.

5.

When Germany was on the brink of war in August of 1914, the major political parties competed with each other to vote for it. That included the Social Democrats, a large socialist party that had until that moment taught its membership that war was a trick of the capitalists, good only for turning workers against each other. The Social Democrats were, in other words, a totally antiwar party. They also represented the interests of the workers in the legislative branch of German government, and those interests were almost exclusively economic interests, at least in peacetime. But guess what—when war came, the workers were as crazed with enthusiasm for it as everybody else. They didn't share for one moment the pacifistic ideas of their enlightened leaders.

"If we didn't vote for war," said one Social Democratic leader, "the workers would have smashed our brains out against the Brandenburg Gate."

So much for working-class solidarity. German workers couldn't wait to start killing French workers.

This brings us face-to-face with another big problem in any thoughtful discussion of war. One very painful reality about unnecessary wars is that although they may be started for reasons that benefit only a few; and although wars often bankrupt governments, destroy brave young lives for nothing, and bring out the very worst in human nature, people can't seem to resist its lure. Once the bitch of war is loosed, to paraphrase Brecht, everybody is infected with the same insane thoughts and feelings, as though an entire country had gone into heat at the same time. But it doesn't go into heat for purposes of procreation, but for reasons more urgent and compelling than procreation, which is organized mass murder—in short, when the war fever progresses from a rumor to the actual thing itself, people have a way of simply dropping everything and rushing to support it. In fact, those least likely to benefit materially from war are often the most anxious to engage in it—an astonishing proof, if ever one was needed, of the *essential* aggressiveness of the human species.

Because liberals, socialists and social democrats did not understand the emotional appeal of patriarchy, nationalism and militarism (and still don't), they were helpless to stop it. In fact people on the Left, by minimizing the enormous appeal of war to workers, practiced an extraordinary form of self-delusion at a time when radical honesty was required. The biggest problem in 1912 in

Germany was not reformism versus militant socialism, as Rosa Luxemburg thought, but coming to terms with Pan-German militarism and the ancient warrior culture that underlay it. But such honesty about the working class would have quickly revealed that workers were no more capable of producing a truly just society than anybody else. Psychologically, workers were (and still are) vulnerable to the same trauma bonding—and the same aggressive behavior—as everybody else. Thus they are incapable, either strategically or psychologically, of creating a new and better society, at least not alone. The inability of the Left in Europe to understand the tremendous appeal of militarism and nationalism led directly to the success of fascism.

This is also true of whatever is left of organized labor in America, not to mention American liberals and minorities. The good news about the Democratic Party is that its potent coalition of liberals, labor and minorities—first put together by President Roosevelt in the 1930s—is capable of creating some important social democratic initiatives domestically, the latest being the Affordable Health Care Act of 2010. The bad news, however, is that the majority in each of these three constituencies are likely to become bonded to the mesmerizing influences of the war dance, although some recover from it faster than others. In wartime the great masses of the people are vulnerable to manipulation by the government, which encourages them to scapegoat intellectuals questioning the war, whereas the intellectuals themselves tend to become systematically demoralized.

Thus one sure way for conservatives to derail the Rooseveltian coalition of liberals, labor and minorities is to start a war. Nationalism and war trumps everything, *everything*—which is why this writer believes that the neo-cons promoting religious war between Iran and the West are currently the most toxic political force in America. They have a long history of selling an increasingly unattractive Israeli government to the American people, and know all the right buttons to push regarding various forms of guiltmongering and emotional blackmail. Above all, they know that starting a war is the quickest and shortest way to power, and once they get the religious war going, they'll never let it stop. And the weird thing is, Americans don't seem to mind being fooled by them. (Maybe it's the historic American respect for a good patent-medicine sales pitch.)

One sees an overwhelming sentimentality (and dishonesty) in modern discussions of war, implicit in the argument that whole populations are 'tricked' into accepting war by evil leaders. Well, they may be tricked into it in the beginning; but it is not long before the free-floating trauma of war, the images and slogans and twisted thinking, are picked up and parroted by people of all castes and classes, further traumatizing and overwhelming the populace. The poor, the working poor, the middle class and the upper middle class: they *all* fall under war's emotional influence and become bonded to the aggression it represents; they, too, clamor for war and 'patri-otism,' which in wartime morphs into the most violent and bigoted kind of nationalism. If national leaders are careful not to overplay their hand, ordinary people will become just as addicted to war as the military and business elites, and often more so. Military leaders may support war for reasons of professional advancement; the military-industrial complex supports war to make money; ordinary people have little to gain from it. Yet ordinary people clamor for it, and they always will—until they can see through and deconstruct the way elites use the trauma of mass violence as an addictive super-drug.

The liberal and progressive intellectuals of Europe, who should have been able to stand up to the pressures of the war fever in 1914, were similarly helpless before it—indeed, they often became especially vehement spokesmen for it, once the violence began and they fell under its spell. The few intellectuals in Germany, France and Britain who saw its dangers quickly discovered that they were strangers in a strange land, surrounded by people speaking a language they could no longer understand—people who, while completely normal human beings only a few weeks before, now perceived anyone who spoke for peace as leprous traitors.

Yet as George Orwell wrote much later in "Notes on Nationalism," antiwar intellectuals often have their own forms of vicarious warlike nationalism. The pro-Soviet leftist thinking of Orwell's time was often a sublimated celebration of Russian nationalism; and British Catholics such as G.K. Chesterton often romanticized French militarism because of its identification with Catholicism. Well before the establishment of the state of Israel, Zionism was already driven by a violent kind of religious nationalism, one that provided pleasure to the British or American supporter, without forcing him to look closely at the cruelty to Palestinians necessary to achieve a Jewish-majority country.

The human dilemma, as this book tries to make clear, is that humans are a species who are *essentially* aggressive—but who have also, through the laborious processes of social and biological evolution, somehow developed the power of reasoning. Reason allows us to imagine rational alternatives to violence and war; yet once the war drums start, the aggressive animal in all of us keeps us from following rational alternatives. (Something similar happens during an ugly divorce; both parties start out trying to be "civilized," but end up acting on pure aggression. And very often loving it—detaching from someone emotionally is a lot easier when you're furious at them.) It is this debilitating and seemingly endless conflict between reason and aggression, a conflict that aggression is increasingly winning, that civilization and culture are trying to resolve.

Of course, some aggression is latent in the human personality— but this book argues that violent past experiences, whether experienced momentarily or cumulatively, whether experienced individually or on a mass basis, whether experienced personally or through generational or cultural osmosis, is the proximate and most important interaction in the transmission and internalization of aggression. That in turn causes us to identify with aggression wherever we encounter it—we become bonded to aggression as the premiere way to solve human problems. When we learn to deconstruct and weaken that process, we will begin the long-sought breakout from the cycle of aggression in which we find ourselves.

That'll be hard, because trauma bonding is unconscious—aggression is not something we internalize willingly or consciously. Human aggression overwhelms the conscious, rational mind, and the unconscious internalizes aggression when we least expect it; these acquired aggressive orientations create enormous pressure for us to act on them, especially when combined with the latent aggression already in the personality. The mass internalization of aggression affects society in profound ways, usually in exalting patriarchy in novel but seemingly never-ending ways, especially when war is in the air. Men become more aggressive in their private lives, and are likely to identify powerfully with the more patriarchal, aggressive and exploitive social institutions and movements. Women who internalize aggression, on the other hand, tend to become depressed and self-destructive, turning their aggression inward on themselves. A great many people become both. Internalized aggression does not care where or how it is expressed: it simply seeks maximum destruction.

This battle between reason and aggression goes on inside all of us all the time, but reaches a state of acute excitement in time of war, because it is a time in which we cannot help but be deeply affected by the images, sounds and scenes of organized conflict. When the war is necessary, people tend to pull together and approach war as an unpleasant job that nonetheless needs to be done. When the war is unnecessary, however, after the first rush of traumatic images and arguments the society becomes demoralized, and individual personalities are especially conflicted. (Except for those under the influence of patriarchy, of course—they're ecstatic.) We all know that there are alternatives to an unnecessary war, we know there are win-win solutions that could easily be negotiated, yet we cannot force the powerful elites running society to listen to us; and sometimes we are even afraid to articulate such ideas because we are likely to be despised and pilloried by people under their influence—then we feel guilty for *not* speaking out, which makes us vulnerable to further demoralization. We are especially likely to feel hopeless about the situation when we do not understand what is driving the aggression, or our reactions to it.

This is the hidden struggle that drives the problem of good and evil, but it boils over during wartime. It is also the reason for our vulnerability to nationalism and patriarchy: it triggers, among other things, a sudden release of the tension generated by the struggle between aggression and reason in normal life. War is the smiling Mephistopheles who murmurs, "Oh, *stop* trying to be such a pretentious idealist. There's nothing you can do about this war, there's nothing anybody can do about it. Go *ahead*, you pathetic wannabe saint, go ahead and *enjoy* all the nationalist fervor, at least for awhile." Of course, if you *do* enjoy it, it becomes a part of you and you of it. Yet you cannot put your head in the sand and pretend it isn't happening.

War gives release to the accumulated resentments that arises from the day-to-day struggles between workmates, spouses, lovers and friends. It allows the immediate loosening of our half-conscious daily grievances into a focused national frenzy directed against a hated enemy. (That is, a frenzy directed by the state at the enemy it chooses.) Leering gargoyle faces of the 'Other' begin to appear in newspaper cartoons, as the deepest hurts and fears of Everyman and Everywoman emerge to form a composite image of a hated figure that needs to be punished, hurt and killed. The process of 'Othering,' in which we start to project everything bad we have ever experienced upon an imagined enemy, is inevitable in war.

Although we can imagine social justice, the political class knows there is something inside us that wants annihilation: it is easier and more direct, it offers relief from the pain of life's problems, and it rescues people from the vexation of making moral choices. Consequently corrupt elites in the political class will use threats and juvenile fibs (such as Bush's easily-disproved whopper about weapons of mass destruction) to bulldoze the country into an unnecessary war even when it knows better; in Iraq, sadly, that resulted in at least a hundred thousand deaths, and probably more. The state violence, corruption and torture going on today in Iraq are just as bad, or worse, than it was in Saddam's time. Furthermore, the Arabic-speaking world is now in the throes of the Arab Spring, but Iraq has been robbed for all time of its opportunity to arrive at its own kind of freedom. Too many of its best people have already been killed or driven into exile, for it to overthrow the new crooks and torturers put in place by the US.

6.

If there are ongoing injustices in society, they provide the emotional fuel upon which the conflagration of war feeds, while temporarily distracting people from the original cause of the injustices. Chris Hedges deals in part with this in his book *War Is a Force That Gives Us Meaning*, specifically in the parts where he writes of Argentina during the Falkland Islands war, which he covered as a journalist. Hedges, you will remember, was the war correspondent that the administration of Rockford College asked to give a commencement address in 2003, in response to which Rockford's gendarmes ended up escorting Hedges off the campus. In his reports from Argentina, Hedges provides good examples of the manner in which corrupt political elites use war to distract people from issues of social justice.

"The military junta that ruled Argentina, and was responsible for killing 20,000 of its own citizens during the 'Dirty War', in 1982 invaded the Falkland Islands, which the Argentines called the Malvinas. The junta, which had been on the verge of collapse and beset by violent street demonstrations and nationwide strikes in the weeks before the war, instantly became the saviors of the country."

"The invasion transformed the country. Reality was replaced with a wild and self-serving fiction, a legitimization of the worst prejudices of the masses and paranoia of the outside world. The secret interior world arrayed against Argentina became one of strange cabals, worldwide Jewry trotted out again to be beaten like an old horse, vast subterranean webs that had as their focus the destruction of the Argentine people.[72] All that was noble and good was embodied, like some unique gene, in the Argentine people. Stories of the heroism of the Argentine military—whose singular recent accomplishment was the savage repression of its own people—filled the airwaves."

"Friends of mine, who a few days earlier had excoriated the dictatorship, now bragged about the prowess of Argentine commanders," Hedges writes. "One general, during a dispute with Chile, flew his helicopter over the Chilean border in order to piss on Chilean soil. This story was repeated with evident pride. Cars raced the through the city streets honking horns and waving the blue and white Argentine flag, Argentines burst into the national anthem and ecstatic cheering at sporting events. The large Anglo-Argentine community sent delegations to Britain to lobby for the junta."

"I had spent nights with Argentine friends talking of a new Argentina, one that would respect human rights, allow basic freedoms, and perhaps put on trial the generals responsible for the Dirty War. Now such talk was an anathema, even treasonous. On the street any dissent, especially from a foreigner, could mean physical violence. Any suggestion that the invasion was not just and correct and glorious was unpalatable. One never referred to the islands by their English name. Overweening pride and a sense of national solidarity swept through the city like an electric current. It was as if I had woken up, like one of Kafka's characters, and found myself transformed into a large bug." Hedges added: "I would come to feel this way in every nation at war, including in the United States after the attacks of September 11."

"This was my first taste of nationalist triumphalism in wartime. There was almost no one I could speak with. A populace that had agitated for change now outdid itself to lionize uniformed killers. All bowed before the state. It taught me a crucial lesson that I would carry into every other conflict. Lurking beneath the surface of every society, including ours, is the passionate yearning for a nationalist cause that exalts us, the kind that war alone is able to deliver. It reduces and at times erases the anxiety of individual consciousness. We abandon individual responsibility for a shared, unquestioned communal enterprise, however morally dubious."[73]

7.

War is trauma; it bonds people to organized aggression through an unconscious identification with the violence it unleashes. But as Chris Hedges saw, it does so in a manner that temporarily resolves a basic human predicament. Humans are hugely aggressive animals that have, somewhere in their social and biological evolution, assimilated the ability to reason; and these two powerful human forces— reason and aggression—are at this historical moment clearly in a state of radical discontinuity. Aggression and reason are in such wildly different (and mutually exclusive) worlds that they are for all intents and purposes in eternal and perpetual conflict with each other. *Yet they must coexist in the human personality*, and ultimately the cognitive, reasoning mind should be in charge of the individual person's behavior. Cognition uses logic to engage in risk assessment and crisis planning, combining the function of memory with an ability to imagine and shape the future. But the frightening aspect of this historical moment is that the conscious mind *is often not in control of aggression*; indeed, the situation is often the other way around. The rational mind would like to regain control of the shadowy ghosts in the killing fields of aggression, but doesn't know how.

Aggression seeks only destruction, including the destruction of the person driven by it. Humankind is caught in a life-and-death wrestling match not with angels, nor with gods, but with itself. Behavior after trauma often changes in ways that we don't understand; this is because aggression enters the unconscious mind in ways we haven't been remotely aware of before. Behavior changes after traumatizing experiences in ways neither the victim nor his closest family members understand. That is the basis for the often-voiced complaint of the families of combat veterans with PTSD that the family member who went to war is not the same one that returned. When you add severe traumatic brain injury to PTSD, the picture gets even more complicated. Family members of people with brain damage typically relate that they have to go through a fresh socialization process to get to know the new person—the old person, the person they knew before, is dead and apparently gone forever. The process of socializing the person suffering from PTSD, while subtler than head trauma recovery, is in the beginning really not all that different in kind.[74] There was one person before and a different person today, although the person with PTSD probably has the best chance of recovering his most characteristic personal qualities than the head injury patient.

The conflict between reason and aggression goes on inside all of us, and there are things about it that we may *never* know, because aggression operates, we must remember, out of a part of the personality that is mainly hidden from us. Once it has been internalized, the most important things we know about aggression come from what we observe about human behavior under its influence. At the same time, we are constantly reacting to other instincts that we likewise do not completely understand, because the impulses that drive them are similarly unconscious. Humans are highly sexualized (oversexed, I would say), they have complicated aesthetic instincts, they adore their children, and they are gregarious by nature; and as a result of this last trait they enjoy helping each other in various ways. This gregariousness can lead to a stultifying conformity, of course, but it is also life-enhancing, since it is often expressed as cooperation with other people—and that encourages trust, problem-solving, and a capacity for kindness.

War offers total, short-term relief from the tension between reason and aggression. All that is required is to 'do your duty' and fight the enemy, and suddenly you have all the intimacy, shared emotions and gregarious feelings that you could ever want. War is a communal project in which the people of a nation work together in ecstatic harmony, but only in order to inflict maximum harm on people in another nation—which is, after all, simply a collection of human beings engaged in doing fundamentally the same things as ourselves. Inevitably, suppressed doubt and guilt become part of the problems experienced both by civilian and combat soldier, precisely because of the identification with civilians and soldiers on the other side. So the ecstasy of war is modified by negative feelings that have to be suppressed, especially unacknowledged guilt—but people often seek out more violence precisely in order to suppress the unacknowledged guilt that is threatening to surface. If that sounds like a vicious cycle, be assured that's exactly what it is.

The shared emotional trauma of modern war, and the way it powerfully bonds all who respond to its shared aggression, is a big part of the reason for its immense and often misunderstood attraction. It's hard to overstate the experience of solidarity that people feel in wartime, which can arouse profound short-term feelings of love and transcendence. Many male soldiers say that the bond of brotherhood in war is the most uplifting thing they've ever experienced. *The evil genius of war is that it uses humanity's gregarious instincts to heighten aggressive behavior, often by allowing for expressions of solidarity with one's countrymen that are normally devalued in peacetime.* For many males who have lived an entire lifetime without experiencing emotional intimacy, the intimacy that the soldier feels toward his brother soldiers is extremely powerful. But after the war those feelings wear off, as Chris Hedges has pointed out, and are very often replaced by depression, anxiety and desperation.

Of course, sometimes war is necessary, such as the war against Hitler and Imperial Japan. But the wars that the US has engaged in since Korea have been mainly unnecessary. The invasion of Afghanistan was necessary—and I would argue that killing bin Laden was healthy both for the US and, I would insist, for the Muslim-majority countries, where bin Laden did most of his killing. But an unnecessary war has a different and very toxic effect on people in the long run. The ecstasy of destruction is soon compromised by guilt, fear and anger while hostilities are still ongoing; sometimes a precipitous depression descends without warning after hostilities are concluded. Once the excitement is over, former soldiers are stuck with the same problems they had before; and those that came back from Iraq with PTSD or severe head trauma (or both) found those problems much harder to resolve.

Like the ecstasy provided by psychedelic drugs, sooner or later the abnormal excitement of war dissipates, and the individual is left with himself and his perennial dilemmas. Soldiers go back to their civilian lives, often suffering from the delayed stress of experiences that might have formerly seemed transcendent. There is usually less freedom after a war; but a fair number of modern Americans, especially men that fear the loss of patriarchy, despise freedom to begin with. And that is—surprise, surprise!—exactly the reason they are attracted to militarism and war in the first place. In war they do not have to experience anything as right or wrong, because the state tells them what to believe, and what they are supposed to feel. "We abandon individual responsibility for a shared, unquestioned communal enterprise, however morally dubious," Chris Hedges writes. There are more people than one might imagine in the US who would prefer such a trade-off as a *permanent* arrangement. What are the Constitution and the Bill of Rights when compared to a "shared, unquestioned communal enterprise" that relieves the individual of the responsibility of making moral choices?

8.

Almost all Americans know about basic training in the US armed services. A few nervous young recruits arrive at an isolated military depot, and are almost immediately bullied and abused by a screaming Drill Instructor. Their hair is cut off and they are given clothes that don't fit them. Thereupon follow days, weeks and months of verbal, physical and situational torment by the Drill Instructor. The recruits are awakened before the sun comes up, drilled incessantly on muddy parade grounds, and forced to perform strenuous physical feats during long days of training. They are fed substandard food high in starches and carbohydrates, are constantly threatened and verbally attacked, and are never allowed to get enough sleep. The Drill Instructor makes obscene jokes about each recruit's name, his appearance, and his mother. There is absolutely nothing the recruit can do that is not directly under the gaze of the drill instructor, who endlessly seeks to humiliate him in front of his peers.

This is basic training, and usually lasts approximately four months. Even those who have never personally been through it know about it because it is centrally featured in classic American war films of the late 1940s and 1950s. It almost always involves an officer screaming obscenities directly into the face of young recruits, forcing them to do a variety of seemingly impossible things while tired, hungry and under great pressure, and ritually humiliating them in front of as many people as possible. The idea is that such pressures will enable to them fight and kill when ordered to do so by superior officers, and when necessary to die themselves.

Ask any American—particularly a male American—about the purpose of basic training; most will tell you that it is intended to 'toughen up' a recruit so that he can function during the rigors of combat. Exactly what psychological mechanisms are involved in this, and how long their effects are likely to last, are never discussed—nor is the morality of conditioning young people to follow orders from leaders who lie, and whose lies might cause them to die for nothing. One quickly surmises, then, that questions related to military training are not that different than the fundamental questions we should ask of war itself. Is a particular war necessary? If not why are young people asked to die in it?

Repeatedly—on a daily, hourly, and minute-by-minute basis—the noncommissioned officer engages in verbal abuse of the recruit. The Drill Instructor intuitively understands the important of insulting not only the young person repeatedly, but also his family members, especially his mother. (He does this to expunge any memory of parental kindness, the better to replace it with his own aggression.) Recruits are sometimes awakened in the middle of the night to do meaningless things, and are forced to run and exert themselves for many hours every day. Anything that will destroy cognition and the decision-making capability of the young person is employed. He is repeatedly called a worm, a maggot, a douchebag, and other things calculated to demoralize and traumatize him, especially since he can neither get away from the Drill Instructor nor fight back. Whatever elements of a personal identity he has managed to build up in his life are systematically attacked.

Why does this happen? It is part of a strategy, about which the military is fairly explicit. The drill sergeant—and other officers—work very hard to *tear down and destroy the personality of the young person*, so that it can be replaced with a set of automatic reflexes to be used by the officer corps for the duration of his military service. Everything the child has laboriously learned from its parents, every loyalty to family and community, every value or belief, must be dismantled and replaced by a mechanical need to reflexively, immediately and unquestionably obey every order of a superior officer. And driving these reflexes are aggressive emotional orientations caused by the recruit's internalization of the violence, threats and verbal attacks of the Drill Instructor. The DI strives daily to tear down and destroy everything the parents have taught their child, and replace the original personality of the young person with his own aggression—causing the recruit to instantly and without question act on the aggression of his superior officers by obeying their orders.

Why do young people—especially young men—put up with this, and why do parents allow it to happen? Much of it has to do with economic class, with the fact that many youngsters feel intimidated by college, or can only attend college with the financial help given by the military. Sometimes signing up for the military may seem to such people like the only way to get out of their parents' house, acquire some self-discipline, and see the world. But the young man or woman undergoing basic training is not taught about the world, nor do they become better persons, internalize new social skills, or learn an occupational skill that they can feel good about. Basic training is an education in death. It conditions young people to kill when ordered to do so, and to sacrifice their lives if ordered to do so. The abuse, the repetition, the long hours, the coercion to perform strenuous physical acts when tired and hungry, all make it much more than simply a form of conditioning. Although some will be offended by the comparison, basic training is really not that different from Jim Jones of People's Temple rehearsing his followers every day to drink the Kool-Aid, preparing them for the day when they, too, were expected to do whatever Jones, the cult leader, told them to do.

But since basic training involves a great deal of shouting, physical intimidation, and psychological violence, it is hugely cinematic. Depiction of basic training is common in American war films, and because the anger seems contained by the ritualized nature of the interactions, it seems safe. It is not uncommon for there to be a fair amount of good-natured laughter from audiences, especially from men, during those scenes in which a Drill Instructor ritually humiliates and insults a trainee. Male-on-male verbal abuse is instinctively understood by many men as an essential part of a patriarchal system that involves positive emotional identification with the abuser's aggression. To men who have been abused as children—and even some who weren't—verbal abuse is very often experienced as affection; such an instant emotional accommodation to abuse greatly speeds up the process of trauma bonding.

Many men believe that such abuse is 'necessary' to help the recruit survive combat. Therefore they tend to accept without question the reality of an older man systematically humiliating, tormenting and traumatizing a young person, usually seeing it as a kind of humorous—if stressful and slightly perverse—activity between consenting adults. But such emotional trauma may also mean the inculcation of a worldview consisting of the identification with aggression as the highest good. (The youngster who has been physically abused may be intensely grateful for such a validation, because he may have gone through a childhood as chaotic and as violent as the basic training itself.) Other young persons may not be entirely aware of the manner in which their personalities are being changed, partly because the physical challenges they are undergoing are demanding and sometimes gratifying. But even as the recruit's physical health is improved by exercise, his mental ability to make good choices is being stripped away to prepare the recruit to unhesitatingly follow orders.

Once basic training is over, many young people seem to bounce back quickly, driven to some extent by the animal energies of youth. But do they really recover? Probably not as completely as we would like to believe. For one thing, their very perception of themselves— that part of the brain used in self-reflection—has probably been physiologically altered. There is no System Restore button that can magically bring those young people back and transform them into the people they were before basic training. Recruits often spontaneously remark that they are unable to compare themselves, after four months of basic training, with the persons they were before. They may have noticed the changes as they were happening, some subtle and some very powerful; but since these changes occur at the most basic levels of their personalities they have, so to speak, *already* internalized them, and will likely be unable to completely verbalize them. If they can, they may proceed to rationalize them in any way they can. (Society is only too willing to provide them with such rationalizations.)

The experience of basic training is essentially humiliating, essentially dehumanizing, and essentially productive of a deep-seated identification with cruelty. The depth of the aggression internalized through basic training, and the extent to which the ego then identifies with extreme aggression as natural and inevitable, may actually help the soldier survive a war. Indeed, that is the purpose of basic training—to create an internal identification with war precisely so the soldier can survive it. But it also creates an emotional orientation that causes the recruit to feel that war is the highest—or at least the most important—human activity; and that the good soldier is sometimes the lucky recipient of a transcendent emotional state. It creates people who see things in military terms, who will look at conflict not as an opportunity to negotiate win-win solutions but who reflexively seek to impose win-lose solutions by force. That is the fundamental ethos of both militarism and fascism, and that is what is created in the crucible of cruelty that is basic training.

Basic training, then, is a fascinating example of how patriarchal aggression replicates itself in the world. With the use of multiple traumas, inflicted on a moment-to-moment basis for four months, under conditions of consistent sleep and protein deprivation, the recruit's personality is stripped clean and replaced with a reflexive, machine-like compulsion to obey orders. Above all, he is emotionally traumatized so many times that he reflexively identifies with the aggression of his Drill Instructor, and internalizes huge amounts of it. Thus transformed, he is better able to survive a war, but not to live in a world at peace. He is trained to think *automatically* in terms of war—to believe without hesitation that violence is the way humans should solve their disputes. Basic training prepares the soldier for war, but it increases the likelihood of more wars, because it conditions large numbers of people to automatically accept the emotional premises of war as the way that countries ought to resolve their disagreements. Of course, there are many people who have the character and stability to bounce back from the rigors of basic training without much personal damage, but many internalize its aggression without realizing how much it has changed them.

And they can change very quickly, because the innate aggression of human beings is one of the strongest—I would say *the* strongest— components of the personality of young males. Without careful mentoring, young males can quickly become hoodlums, serial rapists and murderers. Diplomacy, negotiation, and the ability to arrive at win-win solutions are learned activities, as is courtship,

which is itself an extremely comprehensive form of social negotiation. But these things require different emotional styles because
they aim to create a different world, and therefore take more than
four months to internalize. Perhaps the best lifelong training for
win-win outcomes is that unique dance of aggression and
tenderness, erotic love and friendship, that we call courtship and
marriage. Blessed are young people who have had good models in
their parents! But how can someone who has internalized the ethos
of militarism *fundamentally* value a relationship based on talking
about—or talking out—conflicts, rather than imposing a winning
strategy through force?

9.

In 1944, in the September issue of *Politics*, the American political
writer Dwight Macdonald wrote about a training manual for
commandos. During one phase of the training, recruits participated
in an exercise that required them to make their way through a
darkened house while stabbing dummies, as part of a scenario
obviously designed to simulate house-to-house fighting. "But there
is one rather interesting problem in operating the course. Although
the writer never states so directly, it would seem that there is danger
that the student's inhibitions will be broken down so thoroughly
that he will shoot or stab the coach who accompanies him... The
coach is advised to keep himself in a position to grab the student's
gun 'at any instant,' and after the three dummies along the course
have been stabbed, 'the knife is taken away from the student to
prevent accidents.' The reader was also advised that there was "no
place on the course where total darkness prevails while [the]
instructor is near the student."

George Orwell, who in 1944 was writing a weekly column for the
socialist newspaper *Tribune* in Britain, quoted from this section of
Macdonald's piece in one of his columns. Both Orwell and
Macdonald saw that once aggressive orientations were in place it
might be hard to control them, at least in the short run. But as this

book attempts to demonstrate, such orientations are also hard to control in the long run. Once the trauma of the training described above has stimulated aggressive emotional orientations, they may be present, in one form or another, for a lifetime. This creates problems not just for the individual person but also for society.

Orwell commented on ancient Japanese techniques for similarly traumatizing young males in order to bond them to a patriarchal/aggressive ethos: "The Japanese, incidentally, have been experts at this kind of thing for hundreds of years. In the old days the sons of aristocrats used to be taken at a very early age to witness executions, and if any boy showed the slightest sign of nausea he was promptly made to swallow large quantities of rice stained the color of blood."

10.

One great American film that focuses extensively on basic training in the military is the astonishing Stanley Kubrick classic *Full Metal Jacket*, which may also be the best movie treatment of the Vietnam War. We've already touched briefly on this film in the first chapter, but it's worth visiting it again. *Full Metal Jacket*, besides being a first-rate movie, demonstrates how basic training not only manipulates trauma, but in a larger sense fits into what is really a *culture* of male war trauma. Instead of telling the story of Vietnam from a historical point of view (which many Americans would never accept anyway, because it would involve political realities that many of them deny), the film instead focuses on the basic training of a small group of Marines preparing for combat in Vietnam. They turn out to be a compact, flesh-and-blood representation of everything that is wrong with the patriarchal, military mindset that got us into the Vietnam War in the first place. Most interesting of all, Kubrick's film narrative displays an intuitive grasp of the way trauma bonding works in basic training. This is, to be sure, the familiar movie world of verbal and physical violence used by a Drill Instructor to relentlessly terrorize a group of impressionable young men, some of which is funny and some of which is appalling. But what *Full Metal Jacket* does best is to illustrate what happens when one recruit internalizes the brutality of his Drill Instructor too well, and becomes dangerous in a way that nobody could predict, much less control.

A group of young Marines are receiving training from Gunnery Sergeant Hartman, the Drill Instructor assigned to turn them into soldiers. The first half of the film is entirely taken up with depicting the brutality dealt out on a daily basis to the recruits by Hartman, who particularly focuses on a recruit that he contemptuously nicknames Gomer Pyle. Hartman brutalizes Pyle repeatedly, making him into a platoon scapegoat for the other recruits, who by now have totally assimilated Hartman's aggression. Harman even appoints another recruit named Joker to be Pyle's personal squad leader; and Joker obligingly does his best to whip the clumsy Pyle into shape. Unfortunately, however, during an inspection Hartman finds a jelly doughnut inside Pyle's locker. Harman now unleashes one of patriarchy's most successful techniques for mass trauma bonding of young males: he announces that every time Pyle makes a mistake, everybody in the platoon will be punished.

That night the platoon beats up Pyle as he lies pinned under a blanket in his bunk.

After the beating, Pyle is sullen and isolative, and begins to disassociate from reality. He is good on the rifle range, which pleases Hartman, but Joker notices uneasily that Pyle is now carrying on animated conversations with his weapon. When basic training is completed, everyone in the platoon prepares to be shipped out to Vietnam. On the last night, Joker is on guard duty, but discovers Pyle in the latrine loading his rifle with live ammunition. Joker tries to calm Pyle down, because it is clear that he is in a delusional state. Instead Pyle begins to shout out drill commands and proceeds to execute the commands in the style of his drill instructor. Meanwhile Hartman, who has been sleeping in the next room, is awakened by the commotion and runs in the latrine. He orders Pyle to put down his rifle, but Pyle shoots him dead—and then proceeds to shoot himself while sitting on a toilet, as Joker watches.

This concludes the first part of the film, with the second part occurring in various combat situations in Vietnam. But the first half is arguably more about Vietnam than any combat film could ever be. It is in basic training that young men internalize the psychic and emotional reflexes that make them killers. Those who succeed go overseas and kill strangers, in wars that may not be necessary. Some of those who fail, such as Pyle, kill themselves and other innocent people. (The footage of Pyle shouting out Hartman's drill commands and then actually killing the Drill Instructor who taught them to him is one of the best psychological deconstructions of war ever seen in a popular film.)

The Vietnam War was fought by people like Pyle and Joker, young men from no-name towns who wanted to do something good for their country, but ended up doing brutal things for an American-style imperialism that benefited nobody, not even the political elites that supported it. (It certainly didn't stop Communism in Vietnam, not to mention Laos, and it kicked off the Khmer Rouge genocide in Cambodia.) The process begins with the methodical brutality of basic training, the ultimate trauma bonding instrument of the patriarchal mind, an emotional and mental ethos that one finds everywhere in the American military. Is it not significant that the second half of *Full Metal Jacket* shows Marines dying in less than heroic ways, more often because of stupid decisions rather than courageous ones? The last scenes have Joker shooting a teenage Vietnamese girl, a Viet Cong sniper; he finishes her off as she lies dying, and afterward marches off into the sunset with his platoon singing the theme song of the *Mickey Mouse Club*, the ultimate antiheroic put-down of the Vietnam War.

Kubrick's pitch-perfect understanding of basic training as both fulcrum and metaphor for patriarchal militarism makes *Full Metal Jacket* a cinema classic. To survive basic training, one *must* internalize the brutality of the Drill Instructor. In the same way, the combat soldier in war must likewise internalize the aggression going on all around him, but to an even greater degree, since his survival depends on it. He must allow the war to penetrate his personality, and he must identify with it completely, so that he can kill the enemy soldier before he kills him. He must adopt a psychological stance of hyper-vigilance, which for all intents and purposes means that he must *become* the war, if he is to survive it.

This is the most extreme form of trauma bonding, one that involves a complete identification with war on all levels of the soldier's personality, especially the unconscious level. His hyper-vigilance causes him to trust no one. In this extreme emotional state, everything in the mind and emotions of the soldier must be oriented toward killing and if necessary dying. When one *becomes* war, the war seems more comprehensible, however hideous it may be, because the reality of it feels like an extension of oneself. This total emotional identification with the aggression of war, while temporary, is the strongest emotional state known to men and women except for strong drugs, the heights of sexual gratification, and the ecstasy of a mystical religious experience. And it doesn't just affect soldiers. It also affects others who find themselves in the vicinity of war, or who are regularly exposed to it.

II.

"I began covering insurgencies in El Salvador," writes the journalist Chris Hedges, "where I spent five years, then went on to Guatemala and Nicaragua and Colombia, through the first *intifada* in the West Bank and Gaza, the civil war in the Sudan and Yemen, the uprising in Algeria and the Punjab, the fall of the Romanian dictator Nicolae Ceausescu, the Gulf War, the Kurdish rebellion in southeast Turkey and northern Iraq, the war in Bosnia, and finally to Kosovo."

Hedges' life was often in danger. "I have been in ambushes on desolate stretches of Central American roads, shot at in the marshes of southern Iraq, imprisoned in the Sudan, beaten by Saudi military police, deported from Libya and Iran, captured and held for a week by the Iraqi Republican Guard during the Shiite rebellion following the Gulf War, strafed by Russian Mig-21s in Bosnia, fired upon by Serb snipers, and shelled for days in Sarajevo with deafening rounds of heavy artillery that threw out thousands of deadly bits of iron fragments. I have seen too much of violent death. I have tasted too much of my own fear. I have painful memories that lie buried and untouched most of the time. It is never easy when they surface."

In his book *War Is a Force That Gives Us Meaning,* Hedges writes not just of the trauma personally experienced during his time as a war correspondent, but of the addictive nature of that trauma. "I learned early that war forms its own culture. The rush of battle is a potent and often lethal addiction, for war is a drug, one I ingested for many years." Despite all he knew objectively about its horrors, he found it nonetheless exerted an astounding emotional attraction because of its "excitement, exoticism, power, chances to rise about our small stations in life, and a bizarre and fantastic universe that has a grotesque and dark beauty."

It changes everything. "It dominates culture, distorts memory, corrupts language, and infects everything around it, even humor, which becomes preoccupied with the grim perversities of smut and death." Once traumatized in war, you identify nonstop with aggression in that war, especially the aggression of the enemy. Hedges explains this using the language of recovery from addiction: "When we ingest the anodyne of war we feel what those we strive to destroy feel, including the Islamic fundamentalists who are painted as alien, barbaric, and uncivilized. It is the same narcotic. I partook of it for many years. And like every recovering addict there is a part of me that remains nostalgic for war's simplicity and high, even as I cope with the scars it has left behind, mourn the deaths of those I worked with, and struggle with the bestiality I would have been better off not witnessing."

There is a place in the land between life and death that is so intense that it may feel like eternity. Adolescents know that feeling, religious ascetics sometimes know it, and so do men in combat.

"Even with its destruction and carnage it can give us what we long for in life. It can give us purpose, meaning, a reason for living. Only when we are in the midst of conflict does the shallowness and vapidness of much of our lives become apparent. Trivia dominates our conversations and increasingly our airwaves. And war is an enticing elixir. It gives us resolve, a cause."

And because that moment when everything is at risk feels timeless, we simultaneously embrace death and feel ourselves invulnerable to it. "There is a part of me—maybe it is a part of many of us—that decided at certain moments that I would rather die like this than go back to the routine of life. The chance to exist for an intense and overpowering moment, even if it meant certain oblivion, seemed worth it in the midst of war—and very stupid once the war ended." The Irish poet W.B. Yeats captured this transcendent, dangerous moment in his poem "An Irish Airman Foresees His Death."

> I know that I shall meet my fate
> Somewhere among the clouds above;
> Those that I fight I do not hate,
> Those that I guard I do not love;
> My country is Kiltartan Cross,
> My countrymen Kiltartan's poor,
> No likely end could bring them loss
> Or leave them happier than before.
> Nor law, nor duty bade me fight,
> Nor public men, nor cheering crowds,
> A lonely impulse of delight
> Drove to this tumult in the clouds;
> I balanced all, brought all to mind,
> The years to come seemed waste of breath,
> A waste of breath the years behind
> In balance with this life, this death.

This is unmistakably a death wish, however temporary it may be, because it assumes that no other experience could be as powerful as this one. This death wish is often a central aspect of trauma bonding, for it creates a mental universe in which time stops and reason does not work. (Notice the intense lyricism in the poet's expression of the moment, which assumes a luminous transcendence that 'normal' life could never match.) For many people, the staggering power of such a moment never quite leaves the memory, forever threatening to draw one's personality back into the dark intoxication of war and internalized aggression.

Hedges writes explicitly about the connection between wars and his own self-destructive emotional orientation: "I covered the war in El Salvador from 1985 to 1988. By the end I had a nervous twitch in my face. I was evacuated three times by the US embassy because of tips that the death squads planned to kill me. Yet each time I came back. I accepted with a grim fatalism that I would be killed in El Salvador. I could not articulate why I should accept my own destruction and cannot now."

Yet that self-destructive aggression is always ready to flip, to become aggression aimed at others. "When I finally did leave, my last act was, in a frenzy of rage and anguish, to leap over the KLM counter in the airport in Costa Rica because of a perceived slight by a hapless airline clerk. I beat him to the floor as his bewildered colleagues locked themselves in the room behind the counter. Blood streamed down his face and mine. I refused to wipe the dried stains off my cheeks on the flight to Madrid, and I carry a scar on my face where he thrust his pen into my cheek. War's sickness had become mine."

War's sickness had become mine. That is the way trauma bonding operates in war. The aggression is so overpowering and so ongoing that one can function only by allowing war to invade the personality completely, to identify completely with the war, to let one's personality *become* the war. One can wage war most effectively when one's entire personality is subsumed wholly in war. The intense, multiple traumas of war must be internalized whole and complete, because they happen so fast and are so overwhelming. The soldier must think of himself only as a function of war, and his identity must not venture further than that—otherwise the idealized memory of life in 'the world' could paralyze him. Those who live in war must *become* the war of which they are a part. Only by identifying with it completely can one achieve something like control, because the war and the self becomes the same thing.

Some people, of course, may choose the warrior life because they believe in some larger cause. There are also those who are ready to die because, for whatever reason, they want to die. (An emotional state Chris Hedges acknowledges having from time to time.) Some who get tangled up in war may be benefactors of humanity who wish to serve those who are wounded by war; and some are criminals who long for the freedom of war to act out some particular form of sadism. Some may be believers in the patriarchal mythos of the heroism of war, and believe war to be the highest good; or they may believe that war (this is very common) is a necessary passage to manhood. Or they may be a reporter like Chris Hedges whose determination to experience the emotional realities of war and write honestly about them—including his self-destructive addiction to it—makes him a prophetic voice in the modern world.

But many of the people described above will, sooner or later, be forced to identify with the war to keep from going mad—to *become* the war in order to continue functioning emotionally. (Consider, for example, all the soldiers who signed up for second and third tours in Vietnam, long after most of them knew that the war was not only lost, but wrong. One of the symptoms of trauma bonding is, in fact, an overwhelming urge to 'get back in the shit'.) When warriors identify completely with war it relieves them of the power of critical thought, it takes away their insight into their own hearts and minds, and it relieves them of an awareness of how they are being changed. Yet in the short term there is often no other way, short of a fanatical belief system or access to a strong drug, to survive emotionally in a war except to become part of it. And it is not until much later that the difficulty of coming back from such an emotional journey becomes apparent.

12.

This process of becoming war in order to survive it emotionally is played out in fascinating detail in the German film *Die Fälschung* (*Circle of Deceit*). A film by the German director Volker Schlöndorff, it is set in Beirut during the outbreak of the Lebanese civil war. A German journalist Georg (Bruno Ganz) and his nihilistic photographer Hoffmann (Jerzy Skolimowski) conduct interviews in the midst of the war, constantly confronted by death and danger. Georg witnesses a massacre of Palestinians by Christian Phalanghists, and later sees another massacre by a Palestinian commander; they exchange or sell photos of dead families as though they were baseball cards.

The various commanders vie with each other to have heroic pictures taken, while both photographer and combatants wonder whether those same pictures will later be used against them at a UN war-crimes trial. Georg loves the heart-pounding intoxication of the danger inherent to a war zone; but the trauma of gratuitous death is starting to make him feel that he is on the verge of an emotional collapse. The intensity of the killing is too much, and too many of the victims are helpless civilians; most frustrating of all, he is only an observer. He internalizes the violence around him, and longs to act it out, but he cannot recycle this internalized aggression against a victim of his own because as a noncombatant there is nobody he can kill. He is building up to either an explosion or a breakdown.

To escape from the organized mayhem around him, he engages in a love affair with a German widow living in Beirut. But he cannot commit emotionally to her any more than he could commit emotionally to his wife at home in Germany. He has found the ultimate emotional high in war, but is queasily becoming aware that he has lost the ability to make a commitment to another human being. (The film hints that perhaps he never had that ability, and chose war consciously as an alternative to love—but if so, war has simply made things worse.)

War excites him more than anything in the world; but having internalized war he now feels pressures in his personality that he cannot sustain. Finally, alone in a bomb shelter with a stranger during a bombardment, he gives in to the aggression raging inside himself, and kills the stranger. In so doing, he abandons observer status—by killing a total stranger who has never hurt him, he has *become* the war. He feels relief, but suspects the relief is only temporary: now in addition to his internalized aggression he must carry the burden of guilt for having murdered an innocent person.

13.

When one's personality is completely subsumed into war, it enables one to shrug off the deaths of others, but it can also lead to one's own death. It can go either way. As we have seen, the bizarre and surrealistic forms of excitement generated by war already contain a fair amount of classic death wish. When war truly becomes an addiction, a dangerous syndrome goes into effect. Like any untreated addict, the combatant or journalist who identifies totally with war always needs more of his drug. Just as the untreated addict often longs for oblivion, the person who has *become war* likewise longs for the next step, which is to *become death*. Finally comes the day when war no longer satisfies, but instead generates a deadly ennui. The individual feels a piercing, unspeakable, unbearable emotional pain (similar to that of major depression), and starts looking for a way to extinguish himself.

Chris Hedges writes of such a person, a war correspondent like himself.

"During the war in El Salvador I worked with a photographer who had a slew of close calls, then called it quits. He moved to Miami. He took pictures of tepid domestic stories for one of the newsweeklies. But life in Florida was flat, dull, uninteresting. He could not adjust and soon came back. From the moment he stepped off the plane it was clear he had returned to die. Just as there are some soldiers or war correspondents who seem to us immortal and whose loss comes as a sobering reminder that death has no favorites, there are also those in war who are locked in a grim embrace with death from which they cannot escape. He was frightening to behold, a walking corpse. He was shot a few months later through the back in a firefight. It took him less than a moment to die."

14.

When one *becomes* war one thinks with the mind of war, as witness perhaps the most unforgettable line from the Vietnam War. These words were uttered during a press conference in 1968 in Rach Kien, Long An Province, 20 miles from Saigon. It happened during the Tet Offensive. The 3/39 Infantry Battalion of the 9th Infantry Division, based next to Rach Kien, had taken an extremely high number of casualties trying to get back into Bến Tre, which had been overrun by Viet Cong. The army brass called in air strikes, which killed not only enemy soldiers but also incinerated all the men, women, children and animals living in the village.

That is to say, according to most accounts, it wiped out the entire town.

"Why," the reporters wanted to know, "was so much deadly force used against the entire village, when there were so many civilians present?"

"We had to destroy the village to save it," a frustrated officer snapped.

A more experienced officer quickly stepped up and took over the press conference, but the previous statement became the most famous quote of the war.

What made the officer say this? Here's one explanation: Americans who feel that their government is always right are likely to kill anybody who gets in its way. But there's another and more likely explanation. During counterinsurgency campaigns, soldiers are traumatized by a sense that the aggression of war is everywhere, all around them. The people of Bến Tre had reportedly become Viet Cong, and that was not acceptable. US soldiers had to internalize this aggression or be paralyzed by fear. *The safest way to fight such a war is to become that war.*

The frazzled officer at the Rach Kien press conference probably identified with war so strongly that it had taken the place of any previous identity he might have had; and he was so crazy he was ready to fight to keep his new identity. When he answered the question about the destruction of Bến Tre, he inadvertently revealed his deepest psychological disposition. In the violent emotional world he was in, it was not only possible but necessary to destroy villages to save them. Since war was what he had become, the irritated officer at Rach Kien therefore had no doubt that destruction for Bến Tre really *was* salvation, because at last its people had achieved the highest, the most honorable and most exalted status of war, which was to be clinically and unequivocally dead.

15.

For every soldier in war, there comes a moment when a certain existential truth hits him. It goes something like this: "I really could get killed by this shit. This is really happening. If I don't kill the other guy first, he's going to kill me." What has been an idea of death before now becomes an acute, overwhelming sensation of fear that he will die. This emotional orientation comes entirely out of the soldier's powerful identification with the enemy's aggression, since that enemy is similarly motivated to kill *him*. This trauma alone is enough to bond the soldier to aggression; but so is seeing someone get killed, or killing an enemy. The most immediate kinds of wartime trauma bonding have to do with one or more of these experiences.

The effect of seeing a friend killed is powerfully conveyed in *A Long Way Gone*, Ishmael Beah's first-person narrative of fighting as a child soldier in Africa. Beah was kidnapped by one of the rogue armies fighting for power in Sierra Leone, and at the age of 13, he sees two friends killed before his eyes by a commander who wants to use him as a soldier. At that point Beah realizes that he *has* to kill people, because it's the only way he can live with himself. There follows a dreamlike period in which Beah functions as an effective killing machine, helped along by massive amounts of drugs given to the boy soldiers by the commander of his unit. Later, he would look back on soldiering as an addiction from which he had to recover. At a rehabilitation center for child soldiers, he does recover, and ends up going to college in the US.

There has been a fair amount of controversy surrounding Beah's book. His passage from a chaotic civil war into the less violent but still ruthless world of American publishing featured an increasingly familiar modern scenario: an ambitious editor, agent and writing teacher, the latter of which advises an inexperienced author to make a non-fiction account out of something he originally intended as a work of fiction. (The non-fiction account will sell better because it is more believable. There is a good market for such books: there is now in print a first-person account of a *girl* soldier in Africa.) I do not believe that the timeline for the events Beah writes about is accurate, not least because his extremely precise and detailed memories may be an indication of false memories—real memories are usually not so detailed. And the powerful drugs that the author was given as an adolescent soldier, and the disorienting environment in which he was given them, would similarly make memory suspect.

But I have no doubt that Beah participated in armed conflict in Sierra Leone as a very young teenager, and that he gets it right when he describes the moment when he saw his friends killed—and at that moment *knew* he would have to kill people to live with that experience. In fact that, and fantasizing about how he would kill other people when he got the chance, was probably the only way he could keep going emotionally. That's the essence of trauma bonding—the mind absorbs the aggression that it is witnessing, precisely so that it can survive; and no trauma bonding is as powerful as witnessing an atrocity against a helpless victim or victims. I recently encountered an example of precisely this phenomenon this while researching the life of a wealthy man who was a soldier in the American Revolutionary War in North Carolina.

16.

John Pyle was a colonel of a loyalist militia in Chatham County, North Carolina, during the Revolutionary War. His story is of interest to me partially because I am directly descended from him. (Interestingly, John Swaim, who lived in the adjoining county, and from whom I am also descended, enthusiastically supported the Revolution.) But Pyle was a dyed-in-the-wool, wealthy, monarchy-supporting, atheist-hating Tory; and in 1781, he undertook to lead some 400 of his fellow loyalists, all of whom were armed and mounted, to join forces with the British Colonel Banastre Tarleton, who was operating in the neighborhood. As many historians have pointed out, the American Revolution was as much civil war as insurgency against a colonial power, and it is revealing that even at this late date there were Americans willing to take up arms in defense of the barking madman King George III, and against the continental dream of an independent country contemplated by the revolutionists. But Pyle's story also reveals exactly how Quixotic and criminally stupid many of these back-country Tories could be.

John Pyle was no doubt influenced by the fact that King George had just appointed him the *esquire* of Chatham County, the rank of esquire being the very lowest in the ranks of the landed British aristocracy. No doubt Pyle saw grander things in store for himself, maybe a knighthood or better, after the war was over and the King's influence was restored in the land. Perhaps he envisioned moving himself and his family from his own plantation into Governor Tryon's grand castle, the first proper castle in the New World. Anyway, once they joined forces with Tarleton, they would indeed be a formidable fighting force, at least in the mind of John Pyle.

To fortify himself for this joyous eventuality, Pyle stopped at every farm and plantation in his neighborhood, partly to call his fellow loyalists to arms, but also to drink a toast to King George. (The drinking of such a toast was by way of swearing an oath, at least for the purposes of the militia's imminent active service.) But that was a very stupid idea, for drink after drink of strong brandy did nothing to enhance anybody's clarity of thought, with tragic consequences. After a few hours of brandy-driven meandering from plantation to plantation, Pyle and his would-be loyalists were thoroughly soused. In this drunken and pathetic state, late in the day of February 24, Pyle and his loyalists happened upon what appeared to be the green-clad mounted troop of Tarleton's British Legion.

At the head of the columns rode two British officers. Relieved that he had found Tarleton, Pyle dutifully prepared to present his troops.

Unthinkable tragedy awaited him. It was not Tarleton's troops he had stumbled upon, but those of Henry (Light-Horse Harry) Lee, a shrewd and resourceful Virginian who was a general on the revolutionary—or continental American—side. Lee was a scion of the Lees of Virginian, a good friend of General Washington, and an opportunistic and clever tactician. The two British officers that John Pyle saw were actually prisoners Lee had captured earlier in the day; Lee had ordered them to ride at the head of the column, precisely to fool any loyalists whose attention he happened to attract. Lee was also quite aware that the green uniforms he and his men were wearing resembled Tarleton's; and as Pyle got closer, Lee doubtless noticed that Pyle and his erstwhile troops were to a very great extent indisposed—that is, roaring drunk—from all the brandy they had been so eagerly consuming.

Lee saw his chance. Pretending to be Tarleton, the British commander, Lee grandly reined his horse aside and invited Pyle to present his troops. Poor Pyle, too addled with alcoholic beverages to suspect the lethal trap into which he rode, proceeded to do so. One of Lee's men at the end of the line grew suspicious and asked Pyle's man whom he served; that soldier cheerily replied that he, too, was one of the King's men. Once the cat was out of the bag, the slaughter began. Lee and his men attacked with musket and sabers, mainly sabers, killing a great many of Pyle's 400 men, who went to their deaths shouting "God save the King!"

It was a sickening slaughter, although technically a military victory for Light-Horse Harry Lee and the American Revolution. Since they were completely befuddled by the deception, not to mention their own drunkenness, Pyle's men did not—at least at first—resist. For this reason little honor accrued to anyone or anything concerning the events of that day, although it was pivotal in dampening loyalist feelings in the area. (In that part of North Carolina, Pyle's disastrous defeat became known gruesomely as "Pyle's Hacking Match" or "Pyle's Massacre.") In his published memoirs, Lee was notably defensive about the entire event, which came across as more of a massacre than a battle. Lee always said later that he would much prefer to have simply taken Pyle's men captive, rather than slaughter them as the result of a deception. Ultimately, however, few can blame him for taking advantage of Pyle's stupidity, to capture him if possible, to fight him if he must. Had John Pyle and his men not spent so much time drinking toasts to the King, and arrived at their meeting with Tarleton in a timely manner, they would never have encountered Lee; and even had they done so, they would at the very least have joined the gruesome fight as sober men, and therefore been better able to defend themselves.[75]

After the main encounter was over, and most of Pyle's troops had either been killed or taken prisoner, there was a second incident, this one even more shocking. That evening a few of Lee's mounted troops, still influenced by the trauma of killing some 400 fellow Americans who had thought them to be friends, suddenly fell upon surviving members of Pyle's party, proceeding to hack them to death with swords. There were about twelve or fifteen victims, and they were unarmed prisoners; and since this was long after the original battle was over, it constituted an authentic and very serious atrocity of war. An American soldier in Lee's command, a young man named

Moses Hall, witnessed this atrocity and was sickened by it. How he processed his resulting trauma is quite instructive, for what it tells us about the way trauma bonding works in wartime, particularly concerning a soldier's witnessing of such an over-the-top war atrocity.

Hall wrote about the killing of the prisoners in 1781 much later, in an application for a pension that he wrote in 1835. "At first I bore the scene without any emotion, but upon a moment's reflection, I felt such horror as I never did before nor have since, and returning to my quarters and throwing myself upon my blanket, I contemplated the cruelties of war until overcome and unmanned by a distressing gloom." This continued until the next day, until something happened to relieve his depression. "I came to Tarleton's camp, which he had just abandoned leaving lively rail fires. Being on the left of the road as we marched along, I discovered lying upon the ground something with the appearance of a man. Upon approaching him, he proved to be a youth about sixteen who, having come out to view the British through curiosity, for fear he might give information to our troops, they had run him through with a bayonet and left him for dead. Though able to speak, he was morally wounded."

"The sight of that unoffending boy, butchered rather than be encumbered... on the march, I assume, relieved me of my distressful feelings for the slaughter of the Tories, and I desired nothing so much as the opportunity of participating in their destruction."

It is not too hard to surmise what happened here. Hall had been thoroughly traumatized by seeing unarmed prisoners hacked to death with sabers. Throughout the night he struggled with the horrifying aggression he had seen and internalized. But after seeing the second atrocity the next day he quickly embraced the aggression roiling inside him, deciding he could come to terms with it if he was prepared to commit similar atrocities. Indeed, a 20th-century commentator on this pension application, John C. Dann, remarked that young Moses Hall had used the occasion of his pension application to record "his own radicalization," as "the horror of senseless bloodshed" transformed him "into a hardened soldier, anxious to commit brutal acts himself." That's exactly what seems to have happened.

Not surprisingly, the young soldier found the murder of helpless and unarmed prisoners too traumatic to assimilate in the short run. (That he goes into such detail in a pension statement tells us something about how deeply it affected him.) Clearly it threatened his ability to function, because depression and psychological paralysis is what happens to soldiers who cannot quickly internalize the aggression of such an atrocity. But the second trauma—the curious boy bayoneted by Tarleton's men and left to die by the roadside—enabled Hall to integrate the internalized aggression of both acts, and identify with it as appropriate to his task as a soldier. Indeed, the *second* atrocity apparently triggered Moses' ability to integrate and identify with the aggression he had internalized while watching the *first* atrocity.

He was now prepared to commit similar violent acts himself. He probably experienced great relief, as most of us would at that age, because it was the only way he could accept what he'd seen emotionally. It is instructive to note the way that young Hall was empowered by the death agonies of the patriot boy, to come to terms with the aggression he had internalized during the slaughtering of Tory prisoners the previous evening. Something in the aggression of the second atrocity allowed Moses Hall to integrate the aggression of the first atrocity, and to identify with the combined aggression of both. Since the second victim was unambiguously a local boy, it would have been easier to identify with his pain—but to just that extent more necessary, if he was to survive emotionally, to act out the aggression of the British soldier who killed the lad, as well as his internalized aggression of those who killed the prisoners the night before.[76]

17.

Some books testify most effectively to the power of the trauma bond by their systematic misunderstanding of its effects. During the 1960s and 1970s a book about what we would today call asymmetrical warfare, written by the Algerian psychiatrist Frantz Fanon, aroused enormous interest in the West. This book was *Les Damnés de la Terre*, which in English is rendered as *The Wretched of the Earth*. First published in 1961, it was written during (and about) the Algerian war of liberation against the French. The thesis of the book was that oppressed Black people had a kind of moral imperative to free themselves by violent revolution against white governments and their white proxies. Furthermore, Fanon believed, violence against white governments and white people generally was the *only* way Blacks and other Third World people could free themselves psychologically from the malignant and addictive nature of European cultural influences.

On one level, it was easy to see this book as another fantastic example of the tendency of intellectuals in the West to be fascinated by—and identify with—violence, especially when it involves dark-skinned people far away, exudes exotic circumstances, and conjures up no discernable dangers to the immediate interests of the white reader. But it also aroused interest because this particular book advocated a psychological process that was already in place, but that nobody had been previously willing to discuss, much less defend, as psychologically liberating. Fanon believed that black, brown and yellow people in the developing world could fully detach themselves from the colonialism of white Europeans only by being prepared to kill its white representatives. He was noncommittal about terrorism *as a tactic*, apparently believing that Third World people might have to kill innocent white people simply because a national liberation struggle would always create collateral damage—and besides, innocent civilians in Algeria were being killed by French soldiers, and who cared about them?

What made this interesting was Fanon's idea that killing white people was necessary not just for national liberation but for *personal liberation* as well. (The "Introduction" to Fanon's book by Jean-Paul

Sartre, which appeared in the French edition, predictably focused on this aspect of Fanon's thesis.) Black, brown and yellow people had to expel white European civilization not only from their countries, but from their own souls. National liberation wasn't just a political strategy, but a *psychological* strategy for creating mental health in the developing world by killing white oppressors or their proxies. The false values and pernicious practices of white European civilization was a psychological addiction that the Third World needed to violently terminate—a view that is perhaps understandable, if not acceptable, if we remember that Fanon saw the complexities of European civilization only (or mainly) in the context of colonialism in Algeria.

The only sure deliverance from the infrastructure of colonialism, and especially the psychological tyranny that was an integral part of it, was for Third World people to engage in violence against their oppressors. An armed national liberation struggle provided the necessary catharsis for the oppressed masses to break the pathological bonds of fear and dependence that linked Third World people to white Europeans. (Fanon provided several examples from his own psychiatric practice of Algerians who felt enormously revitalized after engaging in violence against whites, usually—but not invariably—against representatives of French colonialism.)

The very process of killing in a national liberation struggle became a sacrificial (or sacramental) ritual that would cleanse and redeem the black, brown and yellow people of the world. Violence against the white colonial enemy, in the context of national liberation, might be the only way the oppressed could free themselves from the mental illness of European culture. Traumatized by the white conqueror and occupier, they could break the bonds of this trauma only by killing the white representatives of colonialism and eradicating their culture. The result would be the recovery of emotional well-being for the oppressed, and the development of productive societies in the developing world.

What is amazing about this thesis is the way it described, with enormous exactitude, the process of trauma bonding. The bond was real, but Fanon's mistake was in misunderstanding—or perhaps mischaracterizing—the nature of the bond. The oppressed were indeed traumatized by the racism and injustice of colonialism; and to survive, they internalized the very kind of aggression that the white colonialists had been practicing for centuries against Asians, Africans and Latin Americans. Ultimately, once having internalized the violence of their white masters, the colonial subjects were supposed to direct that aggression against representatives of the European system that exploited them. But there was a huge but unforeseeable problem associated with this. By acting out the violence they had internalized, people in the national liberation movements did not discharge the aggression but internalized it even more deeply—indeed, they normalized it among those engaging in national liberation. This guaranteed that their countries would continue to suffer under exactly the same kind of exploitation for a very long time, except that this time the tyranny would come not from white European colonialists but from their own people. In Algeria it was the Algerian National Liberation Front (FLN) commanders who had most thoroughly internalized the violence of the French colonial project, as well as the violence of their own national liberation struggle.

To just the extent that the European colonialists had been vicious, exploitive and sadistic to the people of the developing world, so did the military elites of those same oppressed people act out that aggression against their own people, once they wielded enough power to form governments. The best example of this comes from Algeria itself, the country in which Frantz Fanon wrote his book. No sooner had the French been kicked out of Algeria in the early 1960s than the Algerian military elite, who because of their leadership in the armed national liberation struggle had become the most powerful institution in Algerian society, began plotting to institutionalize dictatorial powers. They flung the brilliant and progressive Ben Bella, Prime Minister of Algeria, into the nearest prison cell in

1965, and seized power for themselves. Women were reduced to pariah status, business initiative was siphoned off to the various cronies of the new dictatorship, and social justice became a matter of whom one could bribe. This continued unaltered for decades.

An emergent Islamist movement tried to participate in civil society by running candidates in a national election declared in 1991. But the military quickly canceled the second round of elections when it became clear they were losing badly. This led to an unimaginably brutal civil war throughout the 1990s in which at least a hundred thousand people died, despite the efforts of all opposition parties agreeing to a 1995 program for ending the war and restoring democracy. (Evidently the government preferred to continue the civil war rather than restore democracy.) Thereafter some of the Islamist groups took up flagrantly extremist tactics, including a long and protracted series of gruesome massacres; while the security forces of the government increasingly seemed more interested in destroying all chance for future democracy than winning the war.

Algerian society has been stuck ever since in the rigidity of institutionalized violence, greed and corruption, comparable only to Guatemala after 1954. Its government has frequently seemed little better than a gang of thugs; there are few new ideas from any sector, and no freedom that would allow anyone to express such new ideas. An election was declared in 2012, but there was a marked lack of public interest, the people seemingly unable to marshal up any enthusiasm for democracy as long as it had anything to do with the government. The violence, paranoia and sadism of the European imperialists, internalized by the Algerian military leaders and others active in the struggle of the 1950s, was acted out faithfully in the succeeding Algerian governments and can still be felt in every action and interaction of Algerian society today. Fighting violent colonialism with violent national liberation did not expunge the psychological effects of tyranny, but made them worse, and drove them deeper into the personalities of the new indigenous Arabic-speaking tyrants.

The Algerians defeated the French in their successful national liberation struggle, but today their situation is worse than it was fifty years ago. Why? Because they internalized the furious aggression of the white colonialists, to begin with; and they unfortunately used the same kind of organized violence to 'liberate' themselves and build a new country. But copying the violent methodology of the French was a tragic and monumental mistake, because the Algerian government has consistently been one of the most brutal and oppressive in the developing world. If you internalize the brutality of your oppressors, and identify with that brutality as a tool to make yourself free, you will do nothing but replicate the same tyranny in a different form.

Fanon was wrong. Violent opposition did not delivery Third World people from the oppression of the Europeans, but rather created the psychological basis for that same aggression to be acted out by a new Algerian military government. The faces were brown, the faith Muslim, and there were different fingers were on the triggers; but the atrocities, the violence, and the institutionalized aggression were all too similar. Aggression does not create liberty, but more aggression.

I do not argue that the Algerians should have suffered quietly the horrors of European colonialism. They had every right to rebel. And it is somewhat unfair to criticize people like Fanon for their mistakes, given that they were in uncharted territory as they sought a way to extricate themselves from a particularly rabid form of French colonialism. But we must also conclude that armed struggle tends to lead to more institutionalized aggression in the long run, not because of any transcendent meta-historical reason but simply because that is what happens when people pick up the gun. Far from freeing armed fighters for national liberation from the bonds of colonialism, it creates a new bond based on the trauma of daily killing and fear of being killed. The systemic evil of the oppressor is internalized in its entirety, and a new repressive regime sets up shop soon after liberation.

Today we can say that a much better way to create democracy is with campaigns of underground agitation, strategic use of strikes, mass dissemination of democratic ideas, various kinds of civil disobedience, and appeals to the international community. There are exceptions, of course: the ensconced rulers of Syria can perhaps be dislodged only through civil war. But whenever possible, general resistance in the form of ceaseless, dedicated nonviolent agitation is not only more effective, but also safer, because less likely to lead to new oppressors.

Fanon's idea that violence could be liberating was spot-on wrong. Violence is never liberating except to sociopaths—normal people are invariably corrupted by it, and end up internalizing it. In the short term, Fanon simply observed what was going on around him. He saw that when people crushed by oppression fought back, they did so with a special ferocity. He also understood that in the short term such people—many of whom he encountered in his psychiatric practice—experienced a short-term sense of liberation. But he could not comprehend what the long-term effects of the national liberation struggle would become because he died young, and was not able to observe the deterioration of Algerian society. He did not foresee, as perhaps no one could, that once colonial oppression becomes institutionalized the trauma of violent national liberation creates a profound new psychological bond to inter-nalized aggression among the formerly oppressed. Violence against violent oppressors is understandable; but it ensures that a similar violence will be ensconced in the new society that replaces the old, and soon acted out against new victims. Everyone who participates in armed struggle is bonded to violence as rigidly as the addict is bonded to his comfort drug of choice. There are some apparent exceptions to that rule—George Washington and the American revolutionaries come to mind, and the modern revolutionaries of El Salvador, who negotiated an honorable end to their war in the 1990s under commendably liberal terms—but even in those enlightened instances, there was violent fallout: George Washington had to deal with the armed insurgents of the Whiskey Rebellion, and Salvador ended up with the worst crime in Central America.

Fanon was important for his intuitive grasp of the connection between institutionalized aggression and the aggression of those who suffer under it. His own anger was palpable, giving his book much of its power—but literary violence does not kill or maim, whereas actual violence does. He concluded that the Algerians who engaged in armed struggle for national liberation could win psychological liberation only if they used violence to defeat the oppressor. But this revolutionary violence was merely an internalized form of the oppressor's own aggression.

What Fanon saw as a potential for psychological liberation was actually a process of psychological enslavement—those who internalized the systemic aggression of the oppressor eventually ended up oppressing their own people just as brutally as the French had ever done. The tragedy of Fanon is that he sought to celebrate as the highest good, and to apotheosize as psychologically liberating, the very aggression the French had visited upon the Algerians. And it was they, the Algerians who had internalized that same French aggression, who would continue to oppress the Algerian people for many decades after the French had left.

18.

The images of war most modern people carry in their minds probably derive more from Goya than any other artist. War had traditionally been something sublime, as in the *Iliad*, or a violent explication of the concealed will of an angry Jehovah; or at the very least the expression of the unknowable nature of fate. Terrible, yes, war had always been terrible, but in the primitive sense of something awe-inspiring, inspiring fear but also wonder. It was horrifying, but fascinating—in fact Goya was himself fascinated by war, and he had the insane, over-the-top talent to draw and paint war in fascinating ways. But he also portrayed the raving madness of it: he was the first artist in history to understand that in addition to everything else, war was also disgusting. Goya expressed for the first time in the history of art the utter *wrongness* of war. Yet what Goya expressed was also compelling.

His vision was a shocking moral statement expressed in light and pigment, and it was both prophetic and stunning. What was subversive about it was that the viewer could continue to see, if he chose to do so, the traditional view of war—a terrifying event involving the clash of men, civilizations and beliefs about the world; but encoded into that traditional pictorial representation was a new vision, one that could creep up on the viewer without much warning. It was a vision of war as something so horrible that any sane and healthy person would feel compelled to avoid it. It was also a vision that comprehended that war was often used for no more noble purpose than to exploit other human beings—to keep them in slavery to some illegitimate power. In his faces of combatants in the midst of war he shows a kind of horror, the growing realization that they are participating in an irredeemable madness. Goya's depictions of war were intended to traumatize ("So many butcher's chops!" says a worker as he drags the bodies left by war) but it was often a kind of stealth trauma, as one only gradually becomes aware of how Goya's images are able to alter one's thoughts and aesthetic responses.

This was not the grand storm of war, with its religious overtones of the apocalyptic, of which *Iliad* and Torah had long been both literary and scriptural incarnation. That meaning was arguably there, but Goya saw beyond that. Goya was the first to see—and to make us see—the horror and disgust that overwhelm the senses in war (that is to say, he makes us see what is traumatizing about war), particularly in wars by tyrants against the popular movements of the people. What the rich and powerful were doing was not an abstraction, Goya saw, but very concrete, in that it stimulated the cycle of death and destruction on which patriarchy depends, and through which patriarchy and tyranny enforce their aggression.

One cannot underestimate the importance of images in war. When William Randolph Hearst decided to start a war with Spain in

1898, he commissioned photographs. "You send the photographs, I'll supply the war!" he telegraphed famously to one of his employees in Cuba. That loyal employee did indeed send the required photos, and Hearst whipped up the war fever he wanted. But he did it with *images* of war, which were accompanied by nationalist-patriotic rhetoric which instructed the viewer how to make historical sense out of the emotions aroused by the photos. But the images were what did the trick. It was an early example of creating support for a war in a place most people didn't know much about. It was an unnecessary war, and a tragic one, as a direct result of which America ended up making the Philippine Islands a colony, sparking a national-liberation struggle in which hundreds of thousands of Filipinos perished fighting American troops.

The Spanish-American War was the first time the press was able to produce a war in the same way that a theatre puts on a theatrical production. And did Hearst do this with factual arguments for the necessity of war? No, he produced it with *images* of war—logic could not be used, because the war he contemplated was unnecessary, and was therefore not amenable to reasonable argument. The intent was always to overwhelm the entire nation with photos of ongoing violence, apparently unending and unstoppable, and then, and only then, to supply the cutlines for the photos (and the copy for the newspaper stories) to explain how it was all happening, and *what everybody was supposed to be feeling*. (They were supposed to experience an extreme nationalist fervor, and a great many people did.)

But the photos came first. *Images* of war are crucial—they are used to overwhelm, and to create aggression that is then internalized. In the fullness of time the images of war can be used to demoralize, and ultimately to trivialize the war they started. In any case, dramatic photos send a subtle message that they are to be taken more seriously than the newspaper copy that accompanies them, because more action is encoded into them than in words—thus they are more "real" than a mere verbal account. The actual newspaper copy supplies deep background and handy quotes of the main characters, along with the main storyline: who the enemy is, and why the reader should feel aggression toward him; but it is the images that kick off the aggressive emotional orientations of war that eventually are capable of overwhelming the viewer.

Picasso saw how wars were created. So did Unamuno, the Spanish philosopher of the "Generation of '98" who had, like so many other Spanish intellectuals, been traumatized by the Spanish-American war and the loss of Spain's remaining empire. His understanding of the undercurrents of insanity that were besetting Spain made him one of the few sane voices even as fascism took over Europe, personified in Spain by Franco. As Civil War in Spain threatened and the Fascist rector of the University of Barcelona cried *"Viva la Muerte!* Long live death!" Unamuno courageously and publicly denounced the nihilism of Spanish fascism in front of thousands of students and academics. But Spain was already descending into Civil War. Not long afterwards Unamuno left Spain.

It was up to Picasso to grasp the searing vision that Goya had first translated onto canvas, and that Unamuno likewise embodied as he defied fascist supporters in Barcelona, a fierce reaction to the same aggression that had been hijacked and ultimate trivialized by the idiot jingoism of a rich, narcissistic American newspaper publisher in 1898. For in the Spanish Civil War of the 1930s, Picasso saw more than Spain's demoralizing defeat by the US in 1898, and something very close to hell on earth; and portrayed it in one of the most famous paintings in the history of art, and of civilization itself. Hell was on earth in Guernica, a quiet but fair-sized Basque city in Spain that was destroyed in a day by Nazi Germany, as it consummated the fascist vision of violent death as the highest good. On April 26, 1937, the German bombers of the German Luftwaffe's "Conder Legion," coordinating with Franco and intent on practicing their saturation bombing on living civilians, destroyed the town and several hundred civilians as they went about their business. It was an early example of the use of terror bombing, aimed specifically to kill civilians, which would be used extensively by the Germans during World War Two. (And then finally by the American and British in the 'saturation bombing' of Tokyo and the main German cities.) Picasso's painting *Guernica* is a big, violently cubist canvas that represents the agony of several Basque civilians in Guernica at the instant that they are being burned to death by Nazi bombs.

Guernica challenges and disorients the viewer, now more than ever. It forces us to see the pure, death-dealing *injustice* of any kind of war against civilians at the moment the multiple bombs explode. The story of the painting is simple: *It is evil to burn civilians alive as they innocently pursue their daily lives.* But since it was wrong in Guernica, it was also wrong in Dresden, when that highly ornamented city was firebombed; wrong also when Hiroshima and Nagasaki incinerated civilians by the hundreds of thousands. And also wrong when the Palestinians destroy a bus or the Israelis drop white phosphorus on schools in Gaza. That is what Picasso is telling us. Such a universal way of looking at systemic evil is inevitable and unavoidable today, but at that time they were very new ideas. *Nunca Más, Nie Weider*, Never Again: that was the fiery whole of Picasso's message, because to him war against innocent civilians was no longer acceptable. He sought to make it a form of unacceptable aggression forever; and in *Guernica* it will never be acceptable, as that single explosive visual idea constitutes the entire painting.

To look at *Guernica* is itself excruciating; and if we look at it too much it quickly becomes traumatizing. But that is exactly what Picasso wanted. His great mural uses horror and trauma to bond us to a representation of gratuitous violence, and to pull us halfway into death, where aggression in the process of *creating death* is the standard for everything else. *Guernica* weaves a dangerous spell. It pulls us halfway into violent death, yet still allows us to escape; but to get out we must resist diligently, because if we give in, we become part of the living dead who are bonded forever in the phosphorus glow of gratuitous mass murder.

As a species we stand at the threshold of *Guernica's* horror. We are still in the borderland between the love of life, expressed most directly in the love of our children, and our clamoring adulation of violent power; and we are deciding whether to pass over into the kingdom of aggression, or doggedly pull back and try to find a better way. That is what looking at Picasso's *Guernica* does to us, and that is what it is supposed to do to us. It forces us to accept what Picasso sees, and to fight our way out of it. *It forces us to make a conscious decision.* Multiply that decision by billions of individual personalities, and you have the answer to whether humankind will survive or destroy itself. There is no other painting of the 20th century about which one could say something like that.

19.

Is *all* war therefore uniformly evil?

Even Chris Hedges, perhaps the most articulate antiwar voice in modern America, acknowledges that sometimes military action in necessary. "I, like most reporters in Sarajevo and Kosovo, desperately hoped for armed intervention. The poison that is war does not free us from the ethics of responsibility. There are times when we must take this poison—just as a person with cancer accepts chemotherapy to live. We can not succumb to despair. Force is and I suspect always will be part of the human condition."

Let us be honest. It is hard to imagine how Hitler and Imperial Japan could have been stopped without war. They worshiped war as the highest of all human activities. Both Prussian officers and the Samurai warrior class were steeped in war's emotional ethos; both were bonded to a way of life that culminated in armed conflict; and in fact the central actors in both traditions went to enormous lengths to start worldwide conflicts that killed untold tens of millions of people. The vast majority of people who supported the Allies against the Axis could not see any alternative but to fight back against them, at least until their ability to wage war had been destroyed. It is equally hard to imagine, also, how the genocide of those who preached a Greater Serbia could have been stopped except by force of NATO arms.

Finally, it is extremely hard to imagine how slavery in the United States could have been extinguished without civil war. I don't believe the US could have remained even nominally a democracy if slavery had continued. Evidence for that can be found in the extraordinary demands made by the slave-owners on the Northern states in the late 1850s. The Slave Power of the South did not wish merely to keep slavery in the states where it already existed, but were demanding that slave territories be extended. They also demanded that elected representatives in Washington agree to not even *talk* about slavery on the floor of the Senate or House of Representatives. (Note the guilt underlying this totally unrealistic demand.) Thoughtful Americans, including many in the North who were trying to avoid civil war, realized that the Southern leadership could no longer think rationally, and that civil war was inevitable. The moment of truth had arrived.

My great-grandfather James Quinn was a Quaker who hated war as only a Quaker can. He thought war a hideous sin. But he came to feel that slavery was an even more monstrous sin. Once the Civil War was upon the nation, James had to make a choice. It was a hard choice, but he took off his Quaker gray and put on the blue uniform of the Union Army. Because he was an excellent horseman, a good leader and a year or two older than most recruits, he was first made a sergeant; and soon afterwards offered a commission as a Captain in the Union Calvary, which he accepted. On my wall I have a likeness of him in his uniform on the day in 1863 when he received his commission. He looks angry, thoughtful, and very, very determined.

Can we blame those who fought in the Civil War to rid America of the evil of slavery? I don't see how we can. It had to be done.

20.

"At the beginning war looks and feels like love," Chris Hedges writes. "But unlike love it gives nothing in return but an ever-deepening dependence, like all narcotics on the road to self-destruction. It does not affirm but places upon us greater and greater demands. It destroys the outside world until it is hard to live outside war's grip. It takes a higher and higher dose to achieve any thrill. Finally, one ingests war only to remain numb. The world outside war becomes, as Freud wrote, 'uncanny.' The familiar becomes strangely unfamiliar—many who have been in war find this when they return home. The world we once understood and longed to return to stands before us as alien, strange, and beyond our grasp."[77]

Very often people who experience multiple traumas, who are bombed hard enough and shot at long enough, simply burn out. In that case the trauma bond is likely to simply unravel, especially when the cause of the trauma is neutralized. When Hitler had the power to kill people and send them to death camps, people wept with joy when he appeared in public—that is to say, they identified with his power, however unconsciously, and however loathsome that power really was. But there was no mourning for him when he was gone. Observers of post-Second World War Germany in the late 1940s invariably report a dazed and demoralized people, often unwilling or unable to make eye contact, striding disconsolately through the rubble while keeping their thoughts to themselves. Hitler was so far from being a hero in Germany after the Second World War that most Germans would go to great lengths to avoid talking about him.

Like their cities, the Germans were burnt out. That is what happens when people are bonded to aggression for too long—there comes a time when the mind can no longer maintain such a feverish pitch of excitement, and the entire social psychology of systemic evil breaks down. It was the same story in Italy, where the former fascist leader Mussolini was so discredited in the collective unconscious of the Italian public that within a very short time he seemed merely a half-remembered bogeyman, a passing embarrassment whose rumored sins were to some extent canceled out by the fact that he was killed by his own people. In the ruins of Imperial Japan, the Emperor was reduced to the status of a mere human by a simple radio broadcast, in which he acknowledged that he was not divine. Many Japanese wept when they heard this; but once the truth was out, there was no going back to the way they'd felt about the emperor before.

Indeed, corrupt leaders that start unnecessary wars often underestimate the dangers to themselves, and to perceptions in their political base. Those who play with the fire of war often get burnt, because they do not understand that aggression seeks to destroy all players in the game: once manipulative and violent leaders ante up, they had better be prepared to win every time. They will not be nicer people for winning an immoral war, but losing is likely to cause their political demise. George W. Bush may be ignorant, a liar or a murderer—he is probably all three—because he initiated a completely unnecessary war; but ultimately the American people ended up despising him simply because he could not win, in an uncomplicated and forthright way, the war that he started.

The Christian West has a huge emotional and cultural investment in war. Militarism, which is almost pure patriarchy, is still the model for heroism and 'service' for most people in the United States. (What about all the other kinds of service we should be encouraging our young people to participate in? Why is military service the most important?) One thing is sure: war is increasingly unnecessary for the US, in the sense that the normal diplomatic alternatives usually suffice in our relationships with other countries, as does a more intelligent and thoughtful cooperation with other governments in the UN and elsewhere; at the very most, irregular operations (such as the mission that killed Osama bin Laden) may sometimes be necessary and desirable. But there are powerful people in the political and corporate upper classes that will try to initiate unnecessary wars, especially if they think they can get away with it; and they will spend millions trying to convince everybody else that *their* war is absolutely necessary, because war is the perfect—and traditional—method for inculcating patriarchal values in the maximum number of young people. There are also the neo-cons, who unambiguously seek a worldwide religious war between Islam and the West, because they mistakenly believe it would help the Likud Party of Israel, and enhance their own power in the US.

People who see war as the highest and most exalted human activity are quite the most dangerous type of humans known—so how do we protect ourselves? The best way to start is to make ourselves less vulnerable *personally* to the way trauma is used to bond people to mass aggression. (This is a personal reckoning that different people will address in different ways.) Political and cultural progressives need *as a group* to be careful of leaders who like to talk about big, impersonal, violent events—such as the Holocaust, the Second Coming of Christ or the fear of something horrible that Iran *might* do—to justify another war in the Middle East. Ultimately, we must learn to participate meaningfully (that is, without fear or apology) in a public debate in America about what kind of war is necessary, and what isn't.

Above all, good people must come to a firm understanding of the supreme importance of resisting a 21st century religious war. War against Iran is one the US can neither win nor afford. But there are people in our country who want it—and in fact many of these same people want an ongoing religious war of the West against Islam. These extremists are Christians, Jews, ambitious politicians and religious bigots—but above all, they are without exception dangerous fanatics. Religious wars are horrible exercises in brutality and sadism in which mainly women and children suffer, and which nobody wins. They are something good and responsible people everywhere must strive to avoid. Yet there are the fanatical few who seek this religious war, using Israel/Palestine as a detonator. Deconstructing and ending their power is a big assignment for enlightened Americans of our generation, who would save our country from the horrors of a long, agonizing and completely unnec-essary worldwide religious conflict.

Many who are still in the grip of past traumas of the 20th century are unconsciously seeking to incite a Final Battle that will resolve all the aggression, disorientation and rage they feel—they long, in other words, for the destruction of themselves, and of the world. But as the third and last book of this trilogy will make clear, such apocalyptic scenarios need not occur—those who break free from the emotional trauma of the past, and who deconstruct their internalized aggression inherited from that haunted past, can live the good life and enjoy its beneficial effects in the freedom of the present. We begin by acknowledging our own internalized aggression, and whatever evil of which we may be personally capable. Once acknowledged, those orientations will never have the same power over us again. Our weapons are words, our struggle is justice, and our dream is a safe place for our children and grandchildren—and for all the world's children.

Afterword

How do we break free of unacceptable or inappropriate aggression in our lives? How do we deconstruct and put into proper perspective the effects of past trauma and internalized aggression? How can we become committed moral beings in the present moment, whether as individuals or as members of a victimized group, without acting out the aggressions of the past? How do we go from being enslaved by victim status, to being a survivor, and finally acting as a protagonist for good in the present moment?

In my next book—the third and last book in the **Genesis Trilogy**—we will together find answers to these important questions. We'll investigate the ways in which people break the bonds of past trauma, whether from violence experienced personally or from systemic evil. Whether internalized aggression comes from intergenerational trauma, or from past trauma artificially stimulated by the state, the individual can make the decision to break free of its influence. *We must become the protagonists of our own life-stories;* because our lives work best—and we are most happy—with a robust moral code informed by reason, along with an emotional commitment to ideals and social initiatives that lead to a better and more just world. But to make that work, we must free ourselves from those emotional orientations that make us slaves to the past.

This third book of the **Genesis Trilogy** will deal *specifically* with recovery from past trauma on the part of people who have decided to deconstruct the aggression that haunts them, and step out of the cycle of violence and exploitation in which humanity is caught. It will examine individual recovery from the trauma of the Nazi Holocaust, and how people have found liberation from its ongoing effects. The stories of the children of Holocaust survivors are examined—one celebrated individual in particular—and how this person came to terms with intergenerational trauma through a quest for truth and by working for universal human rights.

This book will take what we know about recovery from the trauma bond, and apply it to the conflict in Israel/Palestine. The book also examines reconciliation in South Africa, Bosnia and Rwanda, closely studying how people break free of the ongoing influence of past events. One story tells of a man who overcame his obsession with the army officer who tortured him; another tells of the reconciliation of Tutsis with Hutus that killed their family members. While different people do these things differently, they often do so for the same reason—they become conscious that they were beginning to act out negative behavior arising from an emotional orientation based on the internalizing of past aggression. They reject the tyranny of past violence, and decide to live in the present moment in order to help create—and to enjoy—a better and more loving world.

The title of this third book in the **Genesis Trilogy** will be revealed at the time of its publication.

Lawrence Swaim
Napa Valley
2012

Notes/References

Chapter One

1. Donald G. Dutton and Susan L. Painter, 1981, "Traumatic Bonding: The Development of Emotional Attachments in Battered Women and Other Relationships of Intermittent Abuse." *Victimology: An International Journal* 6 (1–4). Dutton and Painter did a follow up paper in 1993, in which they refined key elements of their theory as "The Battered Woman Syndrome," afterwards widely cited in various legal cases and often referenced by the media. Dutton and Painter put great emphasis on the intermittency of good and bad behavior. I have difficulty defining *any* behavior as "good" in a context of violent control, although I acknowledge that a battered woman might interpret it that way. The evil of racial segregation in the US South arose not from intermittently kind behavior by white Southerners, but from the violence that kept the whole system in place. The intermittent kindness of white Southerners (that is, white paternalism) was *part* of the systemic evil, whether Southerners were consciously aware of it or not.

2. Anna Freud, *The Ego and the Mechanisms of Defense* (New York: International Universities Press, Inc., 1966), pp. 109–113

3. Ibid., p. 113

4. Jacques Derrida, "Foreword," Nicolas Abraham and Maria Torok, *The Wolf Man's Magic Word* (University of Minnesota Press, 1986), p. xxi and p. xvii

5. Gavin de Becker, *The Gift of Fear* (New York: Dell Publishing, 1997), p. 4

6. The police psychiatrists that examined Hettinger quickly saw that guilt over the death of his partner was a major component of his depression and aberrant behavior, but Hettinger always denied this. It appears that Hettinger and his psychiatrists were talking at cross purposes. Hettinger had concluded that he'd made no procedural mistakes the night of the murder, so he

denied guilt. But not making a procedural error in one's police work is a totally different thing than *feelings* of guilt, which are essentially irrational—it is quite possible that one could have performed perfectly, yet had terrible feelings of guilt nonetheless. Hettinger probably started out denying guilt because he didn't want to face departmental charges (or judgment by peers), but got so stuck emotionally in demonstrating his competence as a police officer that he could never explore the irrational guilt that was eating him alive. This also probably served to keep his trauma alive, as he went back repeatedly in his memory to Campbell's murder, to prove to himself again and again that he hadn't made any mistakes.

7. Joseph Wambaugh, blog posting, The Daily Mirror, *LA Times*, January 27, 2010. Wambaugh's posting is in response to another posting by retired LAPD Lt. Max Hurlbut, C1.

8. This subject matter is distressing, but we need to accept that systemic evil affects women disproportionately. During the Bosnian genocide in particular, rape was used as a conscious and deliberate weapon to induce psychic suffering and disorientation. Stevan M. Weine, one of the best authors dealing with psychological effects of ethnic cleansing, has suggested three books in particular about the systematic use of sexual abuse against Muslim women in Bosnia. Alexandra Stiglmayer, *Mass Rape: The War Against Women in Bosnia-Herzegovina* (University of Nebraska Press, 1994); Beverly Allen, *Rape Warfare* (University of Minnesota Press, 1996) and Seada Vranić (*Breaking the Wall of Silence: The Voices of Raped Bosnia* (Zagreb: Antibarbarus, 1996).

9. Stevan M. Weine, *When History is a Nightmare* (New Brunswick, New Jersey, and London: Rutgers University Press), pp. 34–60. The narrative voices of survivors appear in slightly different ways throughout this section of Weine's book. The story of H is actually interspersed with questions or comments by Weine, since the testimony came as part of a psychiatric interview—as

a part of the victim's treatment, in other words. Here H's story is likewise represented as a narrative told by H, interrupted only by occasional comments by this writer.

10. Robert Jay Lifton, *The Nazi Doctors* (New York: Basic Books, Inc., Publishers, 1986), p. 344

11. Ibid., p. 380

12. Harry Kessler, *Berlin in Lights: The Diaries of Count Harry Kessler (1918–1937)* (New York: Grove Press: 1961 in Germany, 1971 in Great Britain), translated and edited by Charles Kessler, p. 72

13. Adolph Hitler, "Speech at Königsberg, 1933" in *The Great Quotations*, compiled and edited by George Seldes, (Secaucus, New Jersey: The Citadel Press, 1983), p. 319

14. Avraham Burg, *The Holocaust is Over; We Must Rise From Its Ashes* (New York: St. Martin's Press, 2008), pp. 52, 54, 57, 62, 63, 64, 65, 66 and 67

Chapter Two

15. "Hobbes' Moral and Political Philosophy," *Stanford Encyclopedia of Philosophy* (SEP), Chapter 14, paragraph 5

16. Even in his mugshot he is smiling sweetly, creating for the camera the very epitome of a benign and beaming countenance. But he had been practicing the benign smile his entire life. He looked so innocent and wholesome that the local police almost apologized for arresting him, one of the officers saying that he "wished more than anything that he wasn't the murderer." But he definite *was* the murderer, one of the most malignant that California every produced.

17. Jared Diamond, "The Worst Mistake in the History of the Human Race," *Discover* magazine, May 1987, pp. 64–66

18. Elif Batuman, "The Sanctuary," *New Yorker*, December 19, 2011, pp. 40–49

19. As I've tried to make clear elsewhere, victimology has traditionally meant the scientific study of victimization, including the relationship between victims and offenders, as well as the

interactions between victims and the criminal justice system (police, courts, social workers and prisons). I use the word in a completely different way. I use the word to denote the use of emotional blackmail associated with alleged victim status, to compel people to do certain things and to adopt certain policies. I use it also to mean the use of alleged victim status by powerful forces to get what they want by manipulating people. At its worst, it is the use of past crimes to justify committing new crimes in the future. The situation is further complicated by the fact that past trauma is deliberately kept alive in order to bond people to new violence. It is my contention that right-wing politicians and demagogues know intuitively how to do this, very often because of trauma in their personal lives.

20. George Lakoff, *Moral Politics: How Conservatives and Liberals Think* (Chicago: University of Chicago Press, 2001). The first edition of this book in 1996 was suggestively named *Moral Politics: What Conservatives Know that Liberals Don't.*

21. George Orwell, *The Collected Essays, Journalism and Letters of George Orwell (Volume 2: My Country Right or Left, 1940–1943),* Sonia Orwell and Ian Angus (eds.) (New York: Harcourt Brace Jovanovich, Inc.), pp. 12–14

22. Gavin de Becker, *The Gift of Fear: and Other Survival Signals that Protect Us from Violence* (New York: Random House, 1997), pp. 292–315

23. Avraham Burg, *The Holocaust is Over; We Must Rise From Its Ashes* (New York: St. Martin's Press, 2008), pp. 72–79, 81, 83

24. Patricia S. Churchland, *Braintrust: What Neuroscience Tells Us about Morality* (Princeton, New Jersey: Princeton University Press), p. 9

25. Ibid., p. 14

26. Ibid., p. 145

27. Edward O. Wilson and David Sloan Wilson, "Rethinking the Theoretical Foundation of Sociobiology," *Quarterly Review of Biology,* November 28, 2007

28. Jonah Lehrer, "Kin and Kind," the *New Yorker*, March 5, 2012, p. 36

Chapter Three

29. http://www.nydailynews.com/news/crime/lady-kidnappers-article-1.396520

30 "Abduction victim of 1933 kills self." The *Montreal Gazette*, January 22, 1940, p. 6. Web. April 16, 2010

31. Frank M. Ochberg, "The Ties That Bind Captive to Captor," *Los Angeles Times*, April 8, 2005, Cl

Chapter Four

32. Punishing dissenters means *silencing* them, by preventing news outlets in the South from publishing antislavery commentary or articles. In the single period of 1830–36, almost all the newspaper editors in the South that were known to be opposed to slavery were silenced, either by killing them, causing them to leave the South, or intimidating them into no longer carrying antislavery stories or opinions in their newspapers. One of this writer's collateral ancestors, William Swaim, an antislavery editor who founded the *Greensborough Patriot* in North Carolina, died of a wound received under mysterious circumstances in 1835. Another member of the Swaim family took over the editorship of the paper, but no more antislavery stories or opinions appeared in it from that time on.

33. George Seldes, editor, *The Great Quotations* (Secaucus, New Jersey: The Citadel Press, 1983), p. 319

34. Ibid., p. 317

35. Ibid., p. 317

36. Ibid., p. 317

37. Ibid., p. 317

38. Dr. Haris Silajdžić, as head of the Bosnia and Herzegovina Delegation to the United Nations, 63rd Session of the General Assembly, said in a statement September 23, 2008, on the

occasion of the General Debate: "According to the ICRC (International Committee of the Red Cross) data, 200,000 people were killed, 12,000 of them children, up to 50,000 women were raped, and 2.2 million were forced to flee their homes." It is generally conceded that between 8,000–9,000 were killed in the Srebrenica massacre alone.

39. Scott Higham and Joe Stephens, "New details of Prison Abuse Emerge," *Washington Post*, May 21, 2004

40. Written in early 2008, before the election of Barack Obama as President. Banished for a time from power, the neo-cons have once again come to the fore. Furthermore, the goal is still the same: to manipulate Americans into war against Iran, which could easily result in a worldwide war against the Muslim and Arabic-speaking worlds. Just before the 2012 election PM Netanyahu of Israel succeeded in grossly overplaying his hand, causing several people usually supportive of him to suggest that he butt out of American politics.

41. Machiavelli, Niccolo, Angelo M. Codevilla (ed.) *The Prince* (New Haven: Yale University Press, 1997), p. 54

42. Ibid., pp. 32–33

43. Ibid., p. 112

Chapter Five

44. Stanley Milgram, *Obedience to Authority: An Experimental View* (New York: Harper and Row, 1974), p. 16

45. Thomas Blass, PhD, *The Man Who Shocked the World* (New York: Basic Books, 2004), p. 77

46. Thomas Blass, PhD, *The Man Who Shocked the World* (New York: Basic Books, 2004), Mischel and "situationists", p. 101; Asch's influence on Milgram, pp. 26–29, 60, 282; Allport's influence on Milgram, pp. 15–18, 23, 131, 190

47. Stanley Milgram, *Obedience to Authority: An Experimental View* (New York: Harper & Row, 1974), p. 27

48. Ibid., p. 6

49. Ibid., p. 216

50. The Bush administration rationalized the issue of torture used in interrogations in somewhat the same way, by insisting that if an interrogation technique didn't cause "major organ failure," it wasn't torture. But the entire intent of torture is to cause unbearable pain while not leaving any evidence. That's why American police who at one time commonly used so-called "third-degree" tactics typically beat suspects with rubber hoses, because they didn't leave marks or break bones. That in no way lessoned the emotional trauma involved, as the victim was typically seated with light shining in his eyes, so he never knew exactly when the next blow would come or the identity of those questioning him. The same is true for electroshock techniques used by torturers around the world. But electroshock torture, like other forms of torture, does create internal physical changes, it turns out; most torture has discernable effects on the brain, and in the case of electroshock torture, produces shrinking of the brain, something that can reportedly be quantified.

51. Thomas Blass, PhD, *The Man Who Shocked the World* (New York: Basic Books, 2004), p. 111

52. Ibid., pp. 122–123

53. M.I. Orne and C.C. Holland, in A.G. Miller (eds.) *The Social Psychology of Psychological Research* (New York: The Free Press, 1972)

54. This remark occurred during Milgram's 1963 defense of his experiment to the critical editorial in the *St. Louis Post-Dispatch* that referred to the obedience study as torture.

55. Stanley Milgram, *Obedience to Authority: An Experimental View* (New York: Harper and Row, 1974), p. 196

56. Philip Meyer, "If Hitler Asked You to Electrocute a Stranger, Would You?" *Esquire*, February 1970, p. 79

57. Ibid., p. 81

58. Stanley Milgram, *Obedience to Authority: An Experimental View*

(San Francisco: Harper and Row, 1974), p. 195

59. Thomas Blass, PhD, *The Man Who Shocked the World* (New York: Basic Books, 2004), p. 197

60. Ibid., p. 241

61. Ibid., p. 279

62. Stanley Milgram, *Obedience to Authority: An Experimental View* (San Francisco: Harper and Row, 1974), pp. 194, 195

63. Ibid., p. 52

64. Lauren Slater, *Opening Skinner's Box* (New York: W.W. Norton, 2004), p. 59

65. Ibid., p. 62

66. Thomas Blass, PhD, *The Man Who Shocked the World* (New York: Basic Books, 2004), p. 283

Chapter Six

67. American tribal people are particularly susceptible to alcoholism for physiological reasons—they apparently lack an enzyme that helps break down alcohol, an enzyme that most Europeans have. My point is that many Indians, and particularly males, continued to drink long after they were aware that something made them more susceptible to alcoholism than most white people. In other words, they drank not in *spite* of this physiological abnormality, but *because* of it. Pathological self-hatred, and a consequent desire to hurt and punish oneself, must be reasonably inferred as part of the reason this happened. Of course, that self-hatred was systematically instilled by the aggression of the white Americans—but nobody can engage in the recovery of tribal people but the tribal people themselves.

68. Richard Slotkin, *Regeneration Through Violence* (NY: HarperCollins, 1973), p. 4

69. William Bayer, *The Great Movies* (New York: Grosset & Dunlap, Inc.), p. 26

70. Arthur M. Schlesinger, "Introduction", Marcus Lee Hansen, *The Atlantic Migration, 1607–1860: A History of the Continuing*

Settlement of the United States, Harvard University Press, Cambridge, 1940, p. vi

71. Richard Hofstadter, *The Progressive Historians* (New York: Knopf, 1968), p. 161

Chapter Seven

72. This might have been one of the very last modern uses of anti-Semitism in wartime by a dictatorship. But any war between Iran and the US will give the Islamophobes in America an opportunity to use Islamophobia exactly the same way as the right-wing Argentinians used anti-Semitism, to portray Muslims as "an enemy within" that seeks to subvert the war effort.

73. Chris Hedges, *War Is a Force That Gives Us Meaning* (Perseus Books, Cambridge, MA 02142), pp. 43–44.

74. Veterans with combat-related brain trauma may also have some PTSD. And it is at least possible that in some people PTSD might be partly a psychological expression of the cluster of physiological symptoms associated with brain trauma.

75. Pyle and his son were ultimately taken prisoner, and since both were doctors, they were given the chance to join up with the soon-to-be-victorious Continentals, and even given commissions in the rank of Captain. Several descendants have gained admittance to the Sons and Daughters of the American Revolution based on John Pyle's brief service to the American cause, perhaps unaware that through most of the war the violent Tory activist did his best to defeat the American Revolution.

76. Carole Watterson Troxler, *Pyle's Defeat: Deception at the Racepath* (Alamance County Historical Society, Graham, North Carolina), p. 66

77. Chris Hedges, *War Is a Force That Gives Us Meaning* (Perseus Books, Cambridge, MA 02142, p. 162

Books by Lawrence Swaim

Novels
Waiting for the Earthquake
The Killing

Non-Fiction
(Genesis Trilogy)
The Death of Judeo-Christianity: Religious Aggression and Systemic Evil in the Modern World
Trauma Bond: An Inquiry into the Nature of Evil

**PSYCHE
BOOKS**

The study of the mind: interactions, behaviours, functions. Developing and learning our understanding of self. Psyche Books cover all aspects of psychology and matters relating to the head.